OUTDOOR RECREATION CHECKLISTS

OUTDOOR RECREATION CHECKLISTS

BY DON AND SHARRON BRUNDIGE

DRIVE-IN & BOAT-IN CAMPING HIKING & BACKPACKING
GLACIER/WINTER CLIMBING & ROCK CLIMBING
BICYCLE TOURING & MOUNTAIN BIKING NORDIC & ALPINE SKIING
SNOWSHOEING SNOWMOBILING CANOEING & KAYAKING
SAILING/POWER BOATING WATER SPORTS INLAND & SEA FISHING
Plus FIRST AID KIT & MEAL SELECTION INFORMATION

DISCLAIMER

Safety is a concern in all outdoor activities. General suggestions for safe outdoor conduct have been offered herein. However, no book can alert you to every hazard or anticipate the technical, physical or medical limitations of every reader. Therefore, descriptions of equipment and its uses in this book are not representations that a particular gear item will be safe for you or your party. Nor do we claim that we have covered every safety issue that the reader may encounter. Whenever you participate in the activities described in this book, you assume responsibility for your own safety. There is no substitute for seeking active, informed instruction and following through with proper training, thorough preparation, keeping informed on current conditions, and exercising common sense once in the outdoors.

Printed by Moore Graphics Services, Van Nuys, California
Photo Work by A-1 Photo, San Pedro, California

Published by B-D Enterprises
122 Mirabeau Ave.
San Pedro, California 90732-3117
(e-mail: bnyduk@aol.com)

Photography by Don and Sharron Brundige (unless otherwise noted)

Library of Congress Catalogue Card Number 96-095421
ISBN 0-9619151-9-6

Published in the United States of America

WE WANT TO HEAR FROM YOU!

Corrections and updates will make this a better book and are gratefully appreciated. Publisher will reply to all such letters or e-mail. Where substantive changes are made in future updates, submitter will be acknowledged in subsequent printing and given a free copy of the current or subsequent printing (as specified by submitter).

Front and Back Covers: Artistry of Sam Nunez

TABLE OF CONTENTS

DEDICATION

To Margaret Thelma Davis
....Who is not here to share the joy of our book
and
To Momma and Poppa "B"
....Who are

as well as
To Sally Bond
....Who we wish a quick and full recovery

ABOUT THE CONTRIBUTORS

There are no world-famous names in our contributor's list -- just a crusty group of outdoors people who have learned from the ground floor up and have an impressive amount of experience. Better yet, these are folks who have a perspective that can be appreciated and communicated to novices and more advanced outdoor spirits alike.

Don and Sharron Brundige. Don and Sharron are the authors of eight Southern California on-road and off-road bicycle touring guides. Both have extensively camped across the "Lower 48" for nearly 25 years and have hiked or backpacked many of the mountain ranges on the West Coast. As outdoor lovers, they have participated, to varying degrees, in almost every other outdoor activity listed in the book. Both have been known to whip up exotic dishes in the outdoors, whether out of a drive-to campground or a remote site. As the co-authors of the book and co-owners of B-D Enterprises, they take full responsibility for the entire contents of this book.

Doug Holker. Doug has been hiking and backpacking for 25 years and has led group tours out of nearly every trailhead in the southern Sierra Nevada Mountains. He has hiked and backpacked in British Columbia, Scotland, Switzerland and Norway. Doug has canoed in California and British Columbia, as well as the inland waterways of Virginia, New Jersey and Maine. He has extensive alpine skiing experience across the U.S. and in Europe. His Nordic skiing exploits include tours in the Rocky, Wasatch and Sawtooth Mountains. Sea kayaking, light glacier/winter climbing and fishing round out Doug's other outdoor interests. Doug is our outdoor recreation "ombudsman."

Kees Kolff. Kees and his wife Helen have backpacked extensively in the Pacific Northwest. They have also done extensive Nordic ski touring and kayaking. They recently returned from two years of volunteer work with The Mountain Institute in the Peruvian Andes where they published Peru's first field guide, *Wild Flowers of the Cordillera Blanca*. Kees, who is a physician, taught for two years in the mountain rescue course for the Peruvian Mountain Guides Association and plans to publish a bilingual booklet for them on mountaineering first aid. He has climbed with his son Adam in Alaska and Washington, and most recently in the spectacular glaciers and icy peaks of the Peruvian Andes. Kees is actively involved with the Jefferson Land Trust, a non-profit organization focused on the conservation of natural resources.

Anders Ljungwe. Anders has hiked and biked throughout the western and mid-western United States, Europe, New Zealand, Australia and China. His specialty is long-distance bicycle touring, including both self-guided and planned group tours. He has cycled on over 50 tours of 100 miles or more, including several U.S. trans-state rides and has several dual-centuries under his belt. Anders also has competed in numerous marathons and triathlons, collecting many trophies and awards in his age group. He is the consummate minimalist -- "less gear is always better."

Susan Cohen. Susan has been a downhill skier for approximately 25 years and has skied slopes throughout the Sierra Nevadas and Rockies. Though primarily a pleasure skier, she has also competed in club NASTAR slalom races, winning several silver and bronze medals. Susan is also a big watersports fan. She is an accomplished water skier and enjoys snorkeling, jetskiing, and rafting. Some of her other interests include bicycle touring, mountain biking and hiking.

B.R.H. B.R.H has been snowmobiling in the Eastern and Central Idaho area for 28 years, including forays into the Sawtooth and Bitterroot Mountains. He has ridden machines ranging from the M.S. 18-634 Moto Ski and SkiDoo Everest to his current high-horsepower Arctic Cat Wildcat 700. B.R.H is one of a small group of riders who have homecrafted technical modifications into his machines that have been subsequently incorporated by many commercial snowmobile manufacturers. His other outdoor interests include camping and alpine skiing.

Walt and Sally Bond. Walt and Sally have camped throughout the United States, taking time to hike, mountain bike and kayak at every available opportunity. Their varied kayaking activities over the last 11 years include paddling in the Chesapeake Bay, numerous rivers and lakes throughout the Western United States, and many points along the Pacific Coast, including the Channel Islands. The couple have raced their custom-designed ultralight sloop in the Southern California area, collecting numerous trophies. Sally has skippered boats up to 50 feet in length; the couple has sailed much of the Southern California and Mexican coast, with several ventures in the Caribbean. Sally is a former medal winner in her class in the Ironman Triathlon. Both are alpine skiers and snowmobilers who have tested the slopes all over the Western U.S. and Canada; Sally holds many NASTAR slalom ski racing medals. The couple are also bonified river rats and all-around watersports enthusiasts. Walt is the group's primo banjo player.

Jill Morales. Jill and her family have been waterskiing for 25 years and have organized trips throughout California, Arizona and Nevada. Her daughter and son are also accomplished waterskiers, with her son also being highly skilled at ski boat maintenance. Jill and her friends have amassed a wide array of water towing toys, which are the center of their many outstanding camping and waterski vacations. She is a supreme outdoor cook. Jill also enjoys downhill skiing (four operations later), snorkeling, rafting, bicycle touring, mountain biking and a hearty sip of good wine.

Jim Cradduck. Jim has fly-fished, spin-fished and bait-fished throughout the western U.S. for nearly forty years. He has fished both ocean and freshwater from Baja California to Alaska, including most of the western states (Nevada, Idaho, Wyoming, Montana, Utah, Arizona, Colorado and New Mexico). Jim has also fished in Arkansas, Texas and Missouri, as well overseas in England, Scotland and Germany. His self-guided and commercially-guided ventures include drive-to, hike-to, backpack-to, boat-to and fly-into access to fishing sites. In addition to being a fishing fanatic, Jim has also done a considerable amount of camping and backpacking throughout the western U.S.

Bob Hardy. Bob has been fishing since the age of five when he would spend his summer trout fishing at June Lake in the Sierra Nevada Mountains. In his teen years, he fished off the piers and shores of the South Bay coastal area near Los Angeles. He has fished for halibut and salmon in British Columbia and Alaska. Now in his retirement years, Bob enjoys tournament bass fishing in California and Arizona, with periodic stops to other vacation locales throughout the U.S. Among Bob's tournament awards are a seventh place finish in the 1994 Las Vegas Open.

Sam Nunez. Sam has a great appreciation for the things out of doors and the sky that enfolds them. Sunsets... ahh... he's still looking for the green flash! Hiking... so many more places to go. Cycling, he'll do them over again. Downhill skiing, still lots of room for improvement... let's go! Snorkeling, okay; but let's go somewhere warm... where's his floaties? Fishing, it's okay; but he'll leave it for the pelicans... now, that's cool. Rafting, one of these days...(Authors' notes: Sam is our unparalleled, all-around artist-athlete. A master of understatement, Sam has logged over 100,00 bicycling miles in addition to numerous other proud accomplishments in the outdoors.)

Additional Contributors. We also wish to thank Norm Bennett, Harry Yoshikawa, Don Stromberg, Troy Campbell, Marvin Mackey, David Kiel and Betty Ketter for their varied and important contributions to this book. They include reviewing particularly difficult sections of the book, providing advice about book layout and scope, supplying great photography and/or providing sometimes needed encouragement.

FOREWORD

Almost anyone who has spent time in the great outdoors will suggest that some of their greatest life experiences and favorite fireside stories are entwined with those adventures. For most, the outdoors leaves its indelible mark, regardless of activity. The fabulous pine grove, the sunrise from a panoramic vista point, the alluring campsite after a long cycling day, the challenging ski run, the coral reef and its beautiful fish, the brilliant sky and calm seas after a storm, the scenic river running with fish -- these are but a few of the unparalleled pleasures offered in the outdoors.

Ask experienced nature lovers what have been there fondest memories. They may be as simple as hearing only the sound of the wind on a hike, tasting pristine, glacier-fed mountain water, observing a shy fox or, perhaps, a pod of whales, or lazily paddling a quiet lake while watching the clouds go by. Alternately, they may be as complex as attaining the summit of a formidable peak, running a demanding set of river rapids, Nordic skiing to a remote winter cabin, making a deep dive to a shipwreck or transiting stormy seas to reach a protected anchorage.

The treasures of the outdoors are there for both novice and expert, young and old. What it takes to safely explore the great outdoors, however, is a respect for Mother Nature, a certain amount of know-how, adequate training and the right equipment. In this book, we have attempted to focus on the last item.

We started thinking about this endeavor over eight years ago, when, on a bicycling-by-day/motel-by-night tour, we managed to leave our luggage at home. (We spent two days in our cycling clothes, buying a few of the most critical hygienic necessities and going to "drive-throughs" for dinner.) This was not the only time that we left important gear behind. Though we had informal checklists for several different activities, we did not use them religiously, nor did we spend enough time updating them. That changed immediately!

Two years ago, we searched for a reference on the market that would provide equipment checklists for a broad array of outdoor activities. Not finding anything other than numerous single-activity-specific lists, we decided to start a project of our own. We also decided to enhance the checklists with a brief description of each included gear item.

Based on our own experience, the expertise of the folks who were kind enough to review and edit our manuscript, the many excellent sources of material listed in the Reference section and the help of many recreation shop employees who we peppered with questions, this book is the product. **To our knowledge (at the time of printing) the breadth of activities treated herein, at even this limited level of depth, cannot be found in any other currently available single source.** We hope that it becomes invaluable to your future outdoor activity planning!

Don and Sharron

Don and Sharron Brundige

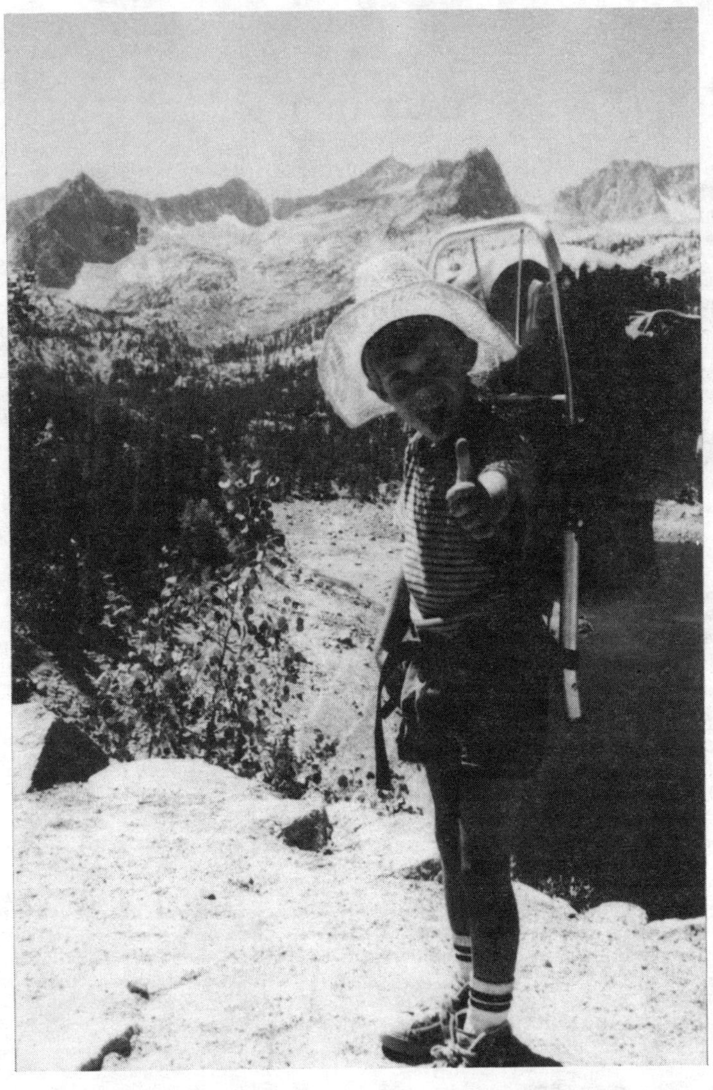

South Lake, Sierra Nevadas, California Courtesy of Doug Holker

INTRODUCTION

What is the purpose and scope of this book? This publication is intended to be a general guideline for equipment needs for a **wide set of popular outdoor recreation activities**. We do not tout this as an everything-you-need-to-know-about-equipment manual, but rather an entry- and intermediate-level book which identifies key features of outdoor equipment that you should consider before proceeding on your adventure or before purchasing. Some advanced gear is discussed for those thinking to move beyond the intermediate level. For more detailed information, we would steer you to the reference books listed near the end of this book and to the many excellent outdoor recreation shops which sell individual activity gear. The **equipment lists and top-level equipment tradeoffs** were compiled by a group of individuals with expertise across the activities. The detailed equipment lists are necessarily broad in order to **cover the four seasons as well as regional differences**. They include door-to-outdoor item considerations, i.e. from auto anti-freeze to recreation gear for cold-weather activities.

As a fallout, this book might serve to identify alternate activity uses for gear you already own. It may also assist you in selecting gear which will best serve multiple activities, given that you don't have the pocketbook to buy the optimum gear for each activity.

The intent is not for the reader to take every listed item to the great outdoors, but rather to tailor his or her needs from a large list of items, picking and choosing between necessities and conveniences, subject to packing space and weight limits. In many cases, outdoor gear can be carried in by one member for use by the group. The lists are laid out for convenient multiple-activity use, e.g., where a camping trip is planned with mountain biking and/or water sports conducted out of the base camp. There obviously will be gear that is overlooked because it is not part of our group's repertoire. Since each user may also have unique needs that are not listed, space is provided to add to the base checklists. The book focuses on equipment, however there are limited discussions on how best to live with Mother Nature scattered throughout.

How is the book organized? A short description of the best method for use of this book is provided initially. In the **SAMPLE CHECKLIST** section which follows, the checklist organization is discussed and a filled-in example is provided for camping (VEHICLE-ACCESSIBLE CAMPING activity) combined with mountain biking (MOUNTAIN BIKING-Daytime activity). Next, the **GENERAL CONSIDERATIONS** section discusses the responsibilities of people in the outdoors to themselves, to others and to the environment. The book's core is in the **EQUIPMENT SELECTION** section; this starts by describing the specific need for and characteristics of each item in the VEHICLE-ACCESSIBLE CAMPING activity, since these tend to be items which are common to many of the subsequent activities. Beyond are the checklists and item discussions for hiking (HIKING, BACKPACKING), climbing (GLACIER/WINTER CLIMBING, ROCK CLIMBING), biking (BICYCLE TOURING, MOUNTAIN BIKING), winter sports (ALPINE SKIING, NORDIC SKIING/SNOWSHOEING, SNOWMOBILING), boating (CANOEING, KAYAKING, SAILING, POWERBOATING), water sports (WATER SPORTS) and fishing (INLAND FISHING, SEA FISHING) in that order. FIRST AID and MEALS, which are common to all activities, are provided with their own checklists. A LIST of PRIORITY GEAR follows, identifying key equipment that is common to many activities. Next is the **REFERENCE** section containing a few selected sources that provide additional detail in the individual activity areas. (Some are reference standards. Others are lesser-known, but highly informative sources. View this as a "starter-kit" list.) Finally, the **INDEX** is key to finding descriptive information for specific equipment items, since items common to many activities may be discussed in only one place.

HOW TO USE THIS BOOK

1. Select the activity (e.g., VEHICLE-ACCESSIBLE CAMPING) or activities (e.g., VEHICLE-ACCESSIBLE CAMPING with MOUNTAIN BIKING out of the campsite) of interest for your next trip. The latter will be used as an example in the discussion that follows.

2. Refer to the relevant checklist(s) and make a photocopy of each (VEHICLE-ACCESSIBLE CAMPING and MOUNTAIN BIKING). Set the photocopier for 135% enlargement to get standard 8-1/2 inch by 11 inch copies. These copies can be used for the next five trips, since there are five checklist columns on each page. Make a copy for each member of your party. (Note also that there are blank checklist forms in the back of the book.)

3. Scan those checklists for related needs, e.g., MEALS and FIRST AID. Make photocopies of those lists also.

4. Review the checklists and decide what items you want to bring. Note that the items that are *italicized* are considered optional or for special-purpose use. Read the item descriptions and tradeoffs in the relevant activity section if you need an explanation of an item. If the item description is not in the section you are reading, consult the **INDEX**. In many cases the description is common to many activities and appears in another (most commonly, earlier) section. For example, many camping item descriptions are found in the VEHICLE-ACCESSIBLE CAMPING section.

4. Check the items that you plan to bring. An example of a method for using the checklists is found in the **SAMPLE CHECKLIST** section which follows.

5. Head out on your trip and enjoy Mother Nature!

SAMPLE CHECKLIST

The example provided is for two days of mountain camping (VEHICLE-ACCESSIBLE CAMPING activity) combined with mountain biking (MOUNTAIN BIKING-Daytime activity) in the early spring. The camping area has pit toilets, no shower facilities, and each site is equipped with a grated fire ring. The VEHICLE-ACCESSIBLE activity list is provided first, followed by the other lists which apply to this trip. Since we don't have to carry all items on our backs, we tend to err on the side of bringing extra goodies. The example provides our bookkeeping scheme, however do whatever works best for you.

For the main activity (VEHICLE-ACCESSIBLE CAMPING, pages 3-6), candidate items to be considered are noted under the first column. Items that are considered optional (niceties or special purpose) are *italicized*. The second through sixth columns provide the space for noting what you want to bring along, each column representing one trip. Thus, each checklist page is usable for five trips. (The uppermost entry of the column is for logging the trip date.) Spaces are left for you to enter items not included on our list, for instance, gear specifically for children, prosthetic devices, etc. In addition, blank checklist pages are included at the end of this book.)

How do we actually use the checklists? A numeral indicates how many of each item we plan to bring and a zero notes that we will leave it at home. (We like a zero as opposed to a blank entry to cue us that we have not simply overlooked the item.) An "X" in the entry means that the gear item has been accounted for in one of the other checklists for this trip. When we have actually loaded the item in the car, we put a cross-line through the item entry (not shown in example). The "First Aid Kit" entry under the "Safety" sub-category and "Meals" under its own sub-category are pointers to the separate checklists found in the FIRST AID and MEALS sections of the book, respectively. Filled-out examples of these checklists are included on pages 7-10 and 11-12 respectively. The same marking process as for the main activity is used. Note that we do not go through the FIRST AID checklist each trip unless it is to be a markedly different adventure. Nominally, we simply replace out-of-date or used items after we return from each outing.

For the secondary activity (MOUNTAIN BIKING-Daytime, pages 13-14), the biking items to be taken or left at home are also noted under the first column. The same bookkeeping process as for VEHICLE-ACCESSIBLE CAMPING is used.

If we are sharing an activity with a group, we photocopy a full set of relevant checklists for each participant. We get together and decide which member is responsible for bringing each shared gear item (e.g., cooking stove and fuel). That person's initials are noted on each member's checklist. If we are sharing food, the group agrees on the menu, then determines who will bring which food items or which full meal(s). Again, the responsible party's initials are noted. Recommendation: bring all gear to a central location before departing. Pack all gear into its final state, checking off each item as it is stowed. This process is particularly critical for some of the more challenging activities where the group is depending on the gear for safety or survival purposes.

We suggest that you save these lists and, after the trip, note what items were not used and what items you wished that you had brought along. This makes for a great future reference.

Activity

VEHICLE-ACCESSIBLE CAMPING
(Overnight)

Select items based on trip needs, weather conditions and degree of luxury desired.

ITEM	DATE				
	4/3/98				
Camping Gear (Shelter/Comfort)					
Auto Gear Rack/Locks	X				
Tent & Rainfly	1 1				
Stakes & Poles	1				
Seam Sealer	0				
Ground Cloth	1				
Tarp(s)	1				
Tent Broom & Sponge	1 1				
Sleeping Bags & *Blankets**	2 1				
Sleeping Pads	2				
Air Pump (miscellaneous use)	0				
Camp Pillows	2				
Hammock(s)	0				
Camp Chairs	2				
Lantern & Mantel(s)#	1 1				
Lantern Fuel#	1				
Fuel Funnel/Strainer	1				
Oil (pump lantern & stove)	1				
Gas Heater & Fuel*	1 1				
Waterproof Matches & Lighter	1				
Stuff Sacks (for tent, pads, etc.)	4				
Camping Permit	CONFIRM				
Camping Gear (Cooking)					
Stove & *Wind Break*/Stove Fuel	1 0				
Wood & *Charcoal*	1 0				
Newspaper/*Fire Starter*	1 0				
Camp Grill (self-standing)	0				
Hand-held Grill (for fish etc.)	0				
Coffee Pot	1				
Skillet/Frypan	1 1				
Cooking Pots	2				
Non-stick Cooking Lubricant	1				
Pot Holders/Pot Grippers	1				
Dishware (plates, bowls etc.)	2 sets				
Paper Plates	1 pack				
Cups (plastic, paper)	2				
Cooking Utensils (spatula etc.)	1				
Can & Bottle Openers	1 0				
Eating Utensils	2 sets				
Sponge & Scrubber	1 1				
Dish Tub/Dish Towel	1 1				
Paper Towels/Napkins	1 roll 1 pack				
Biodegradable Dish Soap	1				
Water Jugs/Bottles	1 0				
Portable Ice Chest(s)	1				
Ice & "Blue Ice"	1 bag 4				
Insulated Bottle	0				

this trip

next trip

select needed items from overall list

gear items

bring pemit or confirm reservation

sub-category

optional item

bring one

bring one of each

VEHICLE-ACCESSIBLE CAMPING
(Overnight)

ITEM	DATE				
	4/3/98				
Trash Bags	1				
Resealable Plastic Food Bags	5				
Camp Table	0				
Tablecloth & Hold-down Clips	0 0				
Dining Canopy & Mesh Screen	0 0				
Personal Gear					
Heavy Jacket/Parka	2 parka				
Long-Sleeve Shirt	2				
Sweater /Turtleneck	0 0				
Long Pants	2				
Hiking/Camp Shorts	2 camp				
Hat (pullover* & wide brim)	2 of each				
Underwear	2 sets each				
Thermal Underwear*	0				
Gloves/Mittens*	2 0				
Windbreaker	2				
Raingear	2				
Hiking Boots/Socks	0 0				
Camp Shoes/Socks	2 4				
*Gaiters**	0				
Bandanna/Sweatband	X				
*Hand/Foot Warmers**	0				
Head netting	0				
Stuff Sacks (parka, raingear etc.)	4				
Hygiene					
Towel	2				
Wash Cloth	2				
Biodegradable Soap	1				
Biodegradable Shampoo	1				
Personal Toiletries/Ditty Bag	1				
Toilet Paper & Towelettes	1 roll 0				
Toilet Trowel	0				
Sun Shower	1				
Clothespins	0				
Laundry Bag	1				
Portable Toilet & Liners	0				

cold weather use

accounted for in linked activity (mountain biking)

VEHICLE-ACCESSIBLE CAMPING
(Overnight)

ITEM	DATE				
	4/3/98				
Safety		see FIRST AID checklists which follow			
First Aid Kit (see FIRST AID)	1				
Water Filter/Tablets	0				
Sunglasses & Lanyard	2 2				
Reading Glasses & Repair Kit	2 1				
Nylon Cord	50 feet				
Pocket Knife	2				
Sunscreen	1				
Lip Balm	1				
Insect Repellent	1				
Whistle	2				
Flashlight#	2				
Extra Batteries & Bulb#	2 2	for night use			
Fire Starter/Heat Tabs	X				
Emergency Blanket	X				
Timepiece	2				
Thermometer	1				
Phone Change	1				
Pen & Notepad	1				
Accessories					
Camera & Extra Film & Battery	1 2 1	bring all three items			
Camera Bag, Lens Cleaning Kit	1 1				
Binoculars	1				
Wood Saw	1				
Ax	1				
Shovel	1				
Swim Suit *& Life Preserver*	0				
Portable Radio (weather info.)	0				
Brochures, Articles, Books	2 read. bks.				
Indoor & Outdoor Games	cards				
Daypack/Rucksack/Fanny Pack	X				
Frame Pack	0				
Toboggan/Sled & Plastic Sheet	0				
Auto Tire Chains & Anti-freeze	0				
Auto Tool Kit	1				
Spare Keys/Credit Card/$	1 1 1				
Tool Kit	1	see text in VEHICLE-ACCESSIBLE CAMPING activity for detailed list			
Tools					
Repair Gear					
Replacement Gear					
		see MEALS checklist which follows			
Meals (see MEALS section)	1				

Italicized items are optional (niceties or special purpose). *items for cold weather #items for night use

↑ symbol descriptions

VEHICLE-ACCESSIBLE CAMPING activity

FIRST AID

select items from list to suit *your* needs

Tailor for your activity based on trip type & duration, potential dangers, & your individual constitution

Item	Activity						
	VAC	Hkg	BkPk	GW/d[1]	GW/e[1]	RkCl[2]	BkT/d
First Aid Manual	x	x	x	x	x	x	x
Equipment							
Cotton Swabs	x	x	x	x	x	x	x
Scissors	x	x	x	x	x	x	x
Razor Blade	x	x	x	x	x	x	x
Safety Pins	x	x	x	x	x	x	x
Needles	x	x	x	x	x	x	x
Tweezers	x	x	x	x	x	x	x
Oral Thermometer	x	o	x	x	x		
Snakebite Kit	o	x	x			o	
Pen Light	o		o		o		
Tourniquet	o	x	x	x	x	o	
Splints		o	x	x	x	o	
Latex Gloves	x	x	x	x	x		
Resealable Plstc. Bags	o	o	x	x	x		
Bio-Hazard Waste Bag	x	x	x	x	x		
Eye Dressing Kit	o		o		o		
Dental Repair Kit	o		o		o		
Bandages/Dressings							
Band-Aids	x	x	x	x	x	x	x
Gauze Pads	x	x	x	x	x	x	x
Gauze Roller Bandage	x	x	x	x	x	x	
Adhesive Compress	x	o	x	o	x	o	
Triangular Bandages	x	o	x	x	x	o	
Battle Dressing	x	o	x	x	x	x	
Ace Bandage	x	x	x	x	x	x	o
Moleskin	o	x	x	x	x	o	
Butterfly Closures	x	x	x	x	x	x	
Adhesive Tape	x	x	x	x	x	x	x
Sports Tape						o	
Ointments/Topicals							
Soap/Cleaning Cloth	x		x		x		
Antiseptic Towelettes	x	x	x	x	x	x	x
Antiseptic Meds.	x	x	x	x	x	x	o

items are most often essential

items may be useful

item probably not needed

VEHICLE-ACCESSIBLE CAMPING activity

FIRST AID

Item	Activity						
	VAC	Hkg	BkPk	GW/d[1]	GW/e[1]	RkCl[2]	BkT/d
Tincture of Benzoin	o		x		x		
Burn Ointment/Spray	x		o		o		
Pain-Relief Meds.	x	x	x	o	o	o	
Itch Relief Meds.	x	x	x	o	o	o	
Eye Drops	x	x	x	x	x	x	o
Baking Soda	x		x		o		
Instant-Cold Pack	o	x	x			x	o
Heating Balm	x		x	o	x	o	
Ammonia Inhalant	x	o	x	x	x	x	
Internal Medication							
Headache/Fever/Pain	x	x	x	x	x	x	x
Dehydration (salt tab	x	x	x	x	x	x	x
Stomach Upset	x	o	x	o	x		
Constipation	x		x		x		
Diarrhea	x		x		x		
Cough	x		x		x		
Sinus Congestion	x	o	x	o	x		
Dental Pain	x		o		o		
Seasickness							
Ingested Poison	o		o		o		
Prescription Meds.							
Personal Need	x	x	x	x	x	x	x
Contingency			o		o		

[1]assumes snow approach to climb [2]gear carried by climber; see "Hkg" column for other items

MOUNTAIN BIKING (Daytime) activity

FIRST AID

Tailor for your activity based on trip type & duration, potential dangers, & your individual constitution

Item	Activity						
	BkT/o[3]	MtBk/d	MtBk/o	ASkSn[4]	NSS/d	NSS/o	Snomo
First Aid Manual	x	x	x	x	x	x	x
Equipment							
Cotton Swabs	x	x	x		x	x	x
Scissors	x	x	x		x	x	x
Razor Blade	x	x	x		x	x	x
Safety Pins	x	x	x	o	x	x	x
Needles	x	x	x		x	x	x
Tweezers	x	x	x		x	x	x
Oral Thermometer	x	o	x		o	x	x
Snakebite Kit	o	o	x				
Pen Light	o		o			o	o
Tourniquet	x	x	x		o	x	x
Splints	x	o	x		o	x	x
Latex Gloves	x	x	x		x	x	x
Resealable Plstc. Bags	x	o	o	o	x	x	x
Bio-Hazard Waste Bag	x	x	x		x	x	x
Eye Dressing Kit			o			o	o
Dental Repair Kit			o			o	
Bandages/Dressings							
Band-Aids	x	x	x	o	x	x	x
Gauze Pads	x	x	x		x	x	x
Gauze Roller Bandage	x	x	x		x	x	x
Adhesive Compress	x	o	x		o	x	x
Triangular Bandages	x	x	x		o	x	x
Battle Dressing	x	x	x		o	x	x
Ace Bandage	x	x	x		x	x	x
Moleskin	x	o	x		o	x	
Butterfly Closures	x	x	x		x	x	x
Adhesive Tape	x	x	x		x	x	x
Sports Tape			o			o	
Ointments/Topicals							
Soap/Cleaning Cloth	x		x			x	x
Antiseptic Towelettes	x	x	x	o	x	x	x
Antiseptic Meds.	x	x	x		x	x	x

MOUNTAIN BIKING (Daytime) activity

FIRST AID

Item	Activity						
	BkT/o[3]	MtBk/d	MtBk/o	ASkSn[4]	NSS/d	NSS/o	Snomo
Tincture of Benzoin	x		x				o
Burn Ointment/Spray	o		o			o	x
Pain-Relief Meds.	x	x	x		o	o	o
Itch Relief Meds.	x	x	x		o	o	o
Eye Drops	x	x	x	o	o	o	o
Baking Soda	o		o		o	o	o
Instant-Cold Pack	x	x	x				
Heating Balm	x		x		o	x	o
Ammonia Inhalant	x	o	x		o	x	x
Internal Medication							
Headache/Fever/Pain	x	x	x	x	x	x	x
Dehydration	x	x	x		x	x	
Stomach Upset	x	o	x		o	x	o
Constipation	x		x		x		
Diarrhea	x		x		x		
Cough	x		x			x	o
Sinus Congestion	x	o	x		o	x	o
Dental Pain	o		o			o	
Seasickness	o		o			o	
Ingested Poison							
Prescription Meds.							
Personal Need	x	x	x	x	x	x	x
Contingency	o		o			o	

NOTE: First Aid kit for mountain biking is a separately packaged unit from that used for camping.

[3]Assumes overnight camping [4]Assumes skiing inside the ropes

MEALS

this trip

Select items based on activity type, weather conditions, trip duration and personal preferences.

ITEM	DATE				
	4/3/98				
Entrees					
Eggs, bacon/sausage	1 1 ← *bring one of each item*				
Soups (dehydrated, canned)	0				
Stews (dehydrated, canned)	0				
Canned hash, chili, Spam	0 1 0				
Canned tuna, salmon, sardines	0				
Canned baked beans, macaroni	1 0				
Canned roast beef, ham	0				
Fresh or frozen meats					
- poultry	hot dogs				
- fish	0				
- beef	0				
Deli meats	0				
Beans	0				
Cheese	0 ← *item not brought*				
Pre-prepared dishes	0				
Freeze-dried meals	0				
Fruits & vegetables					
Fruit: (fresh, frozen, canned)					
- mixed fruit	0				
- apples, oranges, grapes, etc.	apples				
- melons	0				
Freeze-dried fruits	0				
Vegetables: (fresh, frozen, can)					
- mixed vegetables	0				
- carrots, celery, potatoes, etc.	0				
- lettuce, cabbage	1 0				
Freeze-dried vegetables	0				
Bread & Grain Items					
Cereals, breakfast rolls	1 0				
Biscuit & pancake mixes	0				
Bread, rolls, biscuits, buns	hot dog bun				
Crackers	1				
Chips	1				
Flour, meal, rice	0 0 1				

MEALS

this trip →

ITEM	DATE				
	4/3/98				
Spices/Sauces/Spreads					
Sugar, salt, pepper	0 1 1				
Other spices	0				
Margarine or butter	1 0				
Salad dressing(s)	1				
Syrup	0				
Basting/barbecue sauce	0				
Meat tenderizer	0				
Dips (pre-prepared, packaged)	1				
Spreads	0				
Mayonnaise, mustard, catsup	1 1 1				
Pickles, olives, peppers	0 1 0				
Peanut butter, jam, jelly	0				
Dessert Items					
Cookies	0				
Marshmallows	1				
Candy	0				
Puddings, gelatin desserts	0				
Pre-prepared dishes	pie				
Freeze-dried desserts	0				
Cooking Aids					
Cooking oil, grease	0				
Pan sprays	1				
Drinks					
Milk (liquid, powdered)/cream	0 / 1				
Fruit juices (frozen, canned)	froz. orange				
Coffee, cocoa, tea, cream	1 0 1				
Soft drinks	6-pack				
Canned, powdered electrolytes*	1 can				
Alcoholic beverages, mixes	brandy				
Snacks*					
High energy bars	1				
Trail mix/granola	0				
Fresh fruit/dried fruit	0 / 1				
Beef jerky	0				
Nuts	1				

*Dual-purpose use in-camp and for out-of-camp activity

MOUNTAIN BIKING

secondary or linked activity

(Daytime)

this trip

Select items based on trip needs and weather conditions.

ITEM	DATE				
	4/3/98				
Bicycle Gear					
Auto Gear Rack	1				
Bicycle(s)	2				
Rear Bike Rack	2				
Handlebar Bag/Rack Trunk	0 2				
Bungee Cord(s)/Strap(s)	2 0				
Tire Pump	2				
Lock & Cable	0				
Clip-on/Clipless Pedals	0				
Water Bottles/Cages	4				
Timepiece/Odometer/*Altimeter*	2 2 0				
Front Light#	0				
Battery Pack#	0				
Permit	Not Rq'd.				
Personal Gear					
Cycling Shorts/Pants (padded)	2 shorts				
Cycling Jersey	2				
Cycling Jacket/Sweater	2 0				
Windbreaker	2				
Underwear/Thermal U-wear*	X				
Socks/Oversocks/*Footwarmer**	4 0 0				
Cycling Shoes	2				
Helmet	2				
Pullover Hat (fit under helmet)*	X				
*Over Booties (contingency)**	0				
Raingear (contingency)	0				
Cycling Gloves (padded)	2				
Bandanna/Sweatband	2				
Toilet Paper	X				
Toilet Trowel	X				
Safety					
First Aid Kit (see FIRST AID)	1				
Water Filter/Tablets	0				
Sunglasses & Lanyard	X				
Sunscreen	X				
Insect Repellent	X				
Lip Balm	X				
Whistle/Signal Mirror	X 0				
Waterproof Matches & Lighter	X				
Fire Starter/Heat Tabs	X				
Emergency Blanket	X				
Map(s)	1				
Compass	1				
GPS Receiver	0				

item for night use

item for cold weather use

item brought as part of main activity (camping)

optional item

MOUNTAIN BIKING
(Daytime)

this trip →

ITEM	DATE				
	4/3/98				
Pocket Knife	X				
Flashlight#	X				
Extra batteries & Bulb#	X				
Reading Glasses/*Repair Kit*	X				
Thermometer	X				
Phone Change	X				
Pen & Notepad	X				
Accessories					
Camera, Extra Film *& Battery*	X X X				
Camera Bag, Lens Cleaning Kit	X X				
Binoculars	X				
Nylon Cord	X				
Daypack/Fanny Pack	0				
Swim Suit	0				
Trash Bag (small litter bag)	X				
Auto Tool Kit	X				
Spare Keys/Credit Card/$	X				
Tool Kit					
Tools:					
Tire Levers (2-3)	1 set				
Allen Wrench Set	1				
Crescent Wrench	1				
Screwdrivers (Phillips & flat)	1				
Vice Grips	1				
Valve Stem Remover	1				
Socket Wrench Set	0				
Chain Rivet Tool	0				
Spoke Wrench	0				
Repair Gear					
Patch kit (+ talcum powder)	1				
Chain Lube/Oil Rag	1				
Replacement Gear					
Spare Tube	1				
Valve Caps	2				
Snacks	X				
High Energy Bars					
Trail Mix/Granola					
Fresh Fruit/Dried Fruit					
Beef Jerky					
Nuts					
Electrolyte (for water bottle)					

Italicized items are optional (niceties or special purpose). *items for cold weather #night-riding items

GENERAL CONSIDERATIONS

TRIP PLANNING/PREPARATION

We are absolute believers in advance planning. You minimize nasty surprises and have the joy of two trips for one (the anticipated trip and the physical trip itself). *Familiarize yourself with the trip ahead of time* -- start by reading recent tour guides and talking to people who have been there before. *For remote adventures, we do not recommend going alone.* For some activities such as GLACIER/WINTER CLIMBING, ROCK CLIMBING, backcountry SKIING/SNOWBOARDING, SNOWSHOEING, SNOWMOBILING, and sea KAYAKING, even when limited to day tours, always go with a partner or group.

Plan outdoor activities that are within your group's physical and technical abilities. Start with less-demanding trips and work your way up the difficulty ladder. Work on physical fitness and technical skills between trips to maintain or improve your abilities. Take courses with professional leaders and/or learn the necessary skills with an accomplished veteran in that activity area. As part of the training, learn first-aid techniques and use of the kit as appropriate for your activity.

For inland trips, look over the topographic maps and get a feel for the key areas of elevation change and locate the key trail junctions. Don't place total confidence in the topos with respect to trails and roads -- these maps are out of date to varying degrees as noted by the date in the lower right-hand corner. Get USFS maps (or equivalents in other countries) or other area maps to complement the topos. Mark key junctions, landmarks and points of interest. Check that the trails or waterways are open and available for public travel by making advance inquiries. Identify contingency routes if there is any doubt as to your ability to follow the nominal plan or if adverse weather, trail or waterway conditions could require trip alteration.

For sea trips, study navigation and tidal charts. Ensure that the latest charts are in hand. Identify potential obstacles, key lights and other navigation aids and landmarks along the route. Select a route that suits your abilities. Mark major course change points and dependable navigational markers. Identify safe land let-in points or anchorages for the nominal trip and for contingencies of adverse weather, equipment or medical problems and the like.

Once you have identified your outdoor adventure, *assess your gear needs* for the trip. Work with your group to define individual responsibilities for group gear items. Ensure that you know how to use each piece of activity gear before departure. Maintain your gear, particularly that most critical to safety, and perform a pre-trip check that gear is in design-operable condition.

If your gear needs include securing a permit, act well ahead of time if you are going into access-limited areas. Ensure that you understand all conditions of your permit, whether it be allowed length of stay or fish-catching limits. Bring along any necessary personal identification and registration information. If you will be abroad, don't forget your passport.

SAFETY

Always let somebody know your trip plans, your rough schedule and when and who to call should you not show up at critical points. Assure that all essential gear is in your transportation vehicle before departing from home. Perform the same check when you load your gear onto your back or stow it into your transportation source before leaving the trip start point. These latter two considerations, together with the trip planning, are the genesis of this book.

Check the weather report for anticipated temperatures, wind, sea state and any signs of incoming inclement weather. Check before you start your trip and, if possible, each morning while underway. If you have any reservations about total trip time, *start in the early morning* for day trips. For many outdoor activities this has its own advantages as far as temperature and shade. For longer tours, allow a pad for arrival at each intermediate destination and identify alternate stop points.

OUTDOOR RECREATION CHECKLISTS

For inland trips, bring a compass and learn how to use it in conjunction with a topo. Other smart options to minimize the chances of getting lost are to keep a sharp eye on the odometer (bikers) and clock (all) to check against known points on the map. Compare the terrain and elevation against expectations and look back frequently in the direction you came should you have to retrace your incoming route. You will do fine on most trips without all this effort; however, it's that time when you drop steeply in elevation, or paddle a couple miles downstream and realize that your incorrect choice of route means you get to retrace your steps. Or try the feeling of running out of water with night coming on and not being sure if you've got two miles of "bad road," creek crossings and more elevation gain ahead, or a simple flat outlet. (These examples are based on real-life experiences, of course!).

For sea trips, ensure a proficiency in using a compass for position estimation within sight of land and other devices (dead reckoning, sextant, GPS receiver, etc.) when at sea. Bring or mount a permanent timepiece with the accuracy needed consistent with navigation equipment on board. Also bring at least one backup timepiece for emergency use (not necessarily of the same quality). If land activities are planned, one timepiece per individual "marauding" group makes sense. Ensure that all other navigation, communication and other safety-related equipment is operational and members on board know how to use it.

Keep an eye on the weather and add or subtract layers of clothing as appropriate. If weather threatens or if you find yourself well beyond your abilities, don't be ashamed to turn back, to take a well-researched shortcut (life is miserable when a shortcut becomes a "shortcut") or to seek intermediate shelter. *Bring contingency equipment* for the event that the trip goes "sour;" this is discussed in the TEN ESSENTIALS in the **EQUIPMENT SELECTION** section and in individual activities that have their own specific gear needs.

COURTESY

Frequently, you will share outdoor space with other adventurers. Use of *common courtesy and common sense* will cover most bases relative your mutual enjoyment.

Keep your speed down to the point that you can react quickly and safely when you encounter others. Always slow in the company of others. Let others know clearly what are your intentions. This particularly applies to higher-speed activities such as biking, skiing, boating and some water sports or any activity where space is shared with others such as hiking or mountain biking. Give equestrians and packers with animals the right of way. Whatever the activity, understand and apply the applicable "rules of the road."

When fishing, honor the other person's angling space. Take heed of private property and other boat "keepout" zones when underway or seeking an anchorage. When anchoring a boat, assure that you have allowed enough space to account for changes in current and wind direction to prevent intrusion into another boat's anchorage. This includes dropping anchor without fouling another's anchor rode.

Keep your noise down to a level that is acceptable to other parties sharing the outdoor space and within local regulations. Obviously, the noise level for a backpacking site will be different than that at a weekend water sports area.

RESPECT FOR THE TERRITORY

Minimize your impact on the environment. Pack or boat out what you take in. Take out other's trash if feasible. (We almost cried while passing through one of the most remote areas in the San Gabriel Mountains in Southern California and finding an amazing amount of hiker's litter.) Avoid outdoor recreation during weather or seasonal periods where you may cause permanent environmental damage, e.g., mountain biking on wet/damp roads or trails. Stay on marked trails or waterways where passage is legally restricted. Avoid routes which are tenuous or potentially damaging to the environment, particularly shortcuts.

Minimize your general impact when camping. Pick established campsites or, if not available, select a location to minimize environmental damage. Do not dig water runoff channels around the tent. Select toilet, dish washing and bathing sites well removed from natural water sources and bury human waste when in the outback. Use biodegradable soaps and shampoos. If legal and if you must have a fire at a hike-in site, build small fires in existing rings using downed wood. (Many outdoor activists discourage fires in all but cases of emergency or at vehicle-accessible campsites where wood is supplied by camp authorities or brought in by the camper himself.) Whenever you leave your campsite or bed down for the night, fully extinguish your campfire. This means dousing the embers with water, turning them over and rewetting, then covering them with a layer of soil.

Few activities have more potential to create a long-term environmental impact than snowmobiling. Stay out of areas specifically marked as taboo to mechanized travel, most of all Wilderness areas. Use bonified access roads and trails to get to areas that are open to snowmobile usage. Finally, use common outdoor sense and common courtesy when transiting areas that are not clearly marked relative to usage.

When boating, use consideration and care when using established anchoring and docking facilities and equipment. This includes employing accepted docking procedures and using hookups and personal facilities as recommended by the dock owner/operator. When ashore in undeveloped terrain, honor the rules established for hikers, backpackers and bicyclists, as applicable.

There are many outstanding *reference sources* dealing with minimizing environmental impact. One of those is the National Outdoor Leadership School (NOLS) "Leave No Traces: Outdoor Skills and Ethics," which is cited in the **REFERENCE** section. The series of publications covers different geographical areas and climes, focusing at the regional, national or global level, depending on the volume. The series also includes backcountry horse use. The multi-volume set is endorsed by the following U.S. agencies: National Park Service, Forest Service, Department of the Interior and Fish and Wildlife Service.

BUGS N' BIGGER THINGS

Learn to recognize *poison ivy, poison oak, stinging nettles* and other nasty plants that abound in true outdoors. Watch where you bike, walk and even where you lay down your bike as the offending oily substance adheres to almost any surface. Wear long pants and long-sleeve shirts if you travel in poison-oak or tick-infested overgrown trails. Check for *ticks*, particularly around cinched areas such as cuffs, waistbands and socks. Remove ticks before they burrow into your skin. Take them off gently with tweezers -- the key is to ensure that you get the head of the insect out, otherwise it will fester. *Mosquitoes* can also be a problem, particularly if you are in areas with standing water. Bring mosquito repellent if you have any doubts.

Rattlesnakes and are found throughout many areas covered by this book and are most prevalent in the spring when they lie out in the sun for warmth. In summer, they tend to hide in shady places. They are usually at lower elevations and near water. Rattlers generally give ample warning if bothered and will retreat if given a chance. There are many other vipers in deserts, mountains and jungles worldwide that give no such notice. Venomous waterborne varieties inhabit some of the southern U.S. waterways and warm tropical waters.

There are still some larger animals of prey in the mountain regions of the continental U.S. such as *bobcats* and *coyotes* and a lesser number of *mountain lions and bears*. These animals or their brethren are far more common in Alaska and some of the more remote regions of the world. In the U.S., posted signs will most often let you know if there have been any problems with these species, ever-more threatened and sometimes reacting to man's encroachment.

Sharks can be a problem for boaters and swimmers in some U.S. coastal areas, although the frequency of encounters is low. This is not the case in many tropical oceans. The issue is mainly one for expedition kayakers in remote areas and is treated in the SEA KAYAKING section. *Seals*, *sea lions*, *dolphins* and *orcas* are frequent visitors to sea kayakers, although none are overly aggressive (playful, but certainly not dangerous).

For many land activities, you will have to *protect your food* against anything from small to large, generally furry, critters. The methods of food storage are activity oriented. Refer to the "food storage" entry in the **INDEX** for advice.

Finally, get the recommended *immunizations* if you are heading for areas with significant disease problems. In your planning, allow lead time for those immunizations that require a minimum waiting period to become fully effective.

LOGISTICS/COMMUNICATION

Many land activities are one-way trips requiring a car shuttle. So here are a few suggestions applicable to *car shuttle trips* in general and loop trips in some cases. Visit the outlet point so that both you and your shuttle can clearly identify a meeting place. (This is a natural occurrence if you are leaving a car at both entry and outlet.) Agree on an outlet arrival time and a "get concerned" time, i.e., a time to notify the proper authorities that there may be a serious problem. Identify those phone numbers ahead of time. Get a telephone message recorder which allows you to play your messages from remote locations or identify family or friends' phone numbers who can act as go-betweens. This is particularly useful if you return to civilization at an unplanned location (due to navigation errors or physical inability to complete the trip) -- you call and let your car shuttle know where he/she can find you. The trick is to have your shuttle start checking the message machine or go-betweens after some agreed-on time.

We have recently followed the news of lost hikers in Southern California and winter climbers on Mt. Rainier being rescued as a result of cell-phone communication. The increasing frequency of this type of occurrence is causing all of us "old-timers" to rethink the issue concerning *carrying communication gear*. If your load is on your back or bicycle, there is a question as to whether you want to carry a walkie-talkie, cell-phone, CB transmitter/receiver or other communication device. Weight and bulk are not as major issues for kayakers and canoeists, thus suggesting that carrying communication equipment is, at least, practical. It seems inevitable that more and more outdoorsmen will follow this direction in the future.

Note that, if your trip is in remote territory or you are traveling through deep canyons, none of these devices may be of use. However, with global communication via cell-phone (through satellite linkage) on the horizon, there may be a neat future solution to the problem of communication accessibility.

For boaters, there is a generally available option is to leave a float plan (essentially an itinerary, your boat characteristics and call letters) with the harbormaster. Near-coastal seagoers frequently carry along a cell phone, while most blue-water sailors view ship-to-shore (marine) radios as standard equipment. Additional detail about land and sea communications is provided in the individual activity discussions which follow.

PARKING

Park legally and pay all self-registration day-use fees. Park well off the road, ensuring not to block other motorists, residents or emergency vehicles access to equipment or roadways. We have watched illegally-parked cars towed away from trailheads and cited at vehicle-accessible campsites. Don't make a lot of noise at the trip start or end point; do not litter and do not bug the locals for water or telephone use unless it is an emergency.

For boaters, both long-term and short-term parking are available at most marinas. Common sense dictates checking the parking time limits and parking only in areas authorized for your vehicle or vehicle and trailer. If you are a marina member, you will more than likely have access to special set-aside parking -- this may include space to park a recreational vehicle exclusive of, or in addition to, your boat trailer. As an aside: If you have a slip at your home marina, you can exercise your "reciprocal rights" agreement to arrange for a slip at your destination -- this includes having transportation left behind for you at your destination.

EQUIPMENT SELECTION

GENERAL COMMENTS

For most items listed, we have suggested a few simple tradeoffs and, in some cases, noted our preferences. This is not intended to be an exhaustive reference. What you choose should be based on your needs, abilities and "comfort zones." We suggest that you go to the applicable outdoor recreation shops and discuss these tradeoffs. Review documents like those listed in the **REFERENCE** section to get additional detail. Also talk to equipment owners about the advantages and defects of their gear prior to buying. In addition, much of the equipment listed can be rented, providing the user with a hands-on opportunity for evaluation prior to final selection.

ORGANIZATION

The highlight discussion of equipment properties and gear selection starts with the classic TEN ESSENTIALS, a group of necessary contingency survival items applicable to varying degrees across most outdoor activities.

The outdoor activities covered are summarized, in order, in the **TABLE OF CONTENTS.** Each activity has its own complete, tailored checklist and an accompanying discussion of equipment items. The initial activity discussed is VEHICLE-ACCESSIBLE CAMPING (i.e., camping accessible from either land or water), because the gear used in camping is common to many of the outdoor activities which follow. (It also should be more than adequate for picnicking.)

In subsequent activity sections, a simple guideline is used: if the equipment item has not been discussed in a prior activity section or its attributes are different than those previously described, the discussion of the item appears in that activity. This eliminates the need to keep repeating the same information throughout the book. Refer to the **INDEX** to locate the discussion of the equipment item of interest in any given activity checklist.

The individual activity checklists are further broken out into sub-categories as follows: 1) "Activity Gear" (e.g., "Bicycle Gear," "Hiking Gear," "Boat Gear") - this is the equipment specifically associated with this activity. Water supply and gear storage are included; 2) "Personal Gear" - focuses on wearing apparel and apparel packaging; 3) "Camping Gear" or "Underway Living Gear" for shelter, comfort and cooking both on land or underway, respectively; 4) "Hygiene" - items needed for personal hygiene; 5) "Safety" - catch-all category includes the "First-Aid Kit" (broken out separately in the FIRST AID section) and any items that directly or indirectly affect personal safety or health; 6) "Accessories" - contains items that may enhance the outdoorperson's pleasure, ease the accomplishment of tasks, or maximize the smooth flow of the activity; 7) "Tool Kit" - tools or other items specific to the activity that may be necessary for maintenance, repair or replacement of gear; 8) "Snacks" - specific goodies to maintain energy level required for daytime activities; and 9) "Meals" - a pointer to the generic MEALS section, for overnight activities.

In the checklists, some items in the sub-categories may apply to more than one sub-category. An attempt has been made to log these items consistently throughout all activities, although ambiguities do occur. For instance, is a "helmet" listed under "Rock Climbing Gear" or is it "Personal Gear?" Finally, note that all sub-categories do not apply to all activities.

CHECKLIST ITEM DESCRIPTIONS

The checklists and discussion of equipment items are covered in the activity sections which follow. It is not intended that you take all the items in the list, rather that you tailor the equipment needs to your particular trip. In the checklists, items that are considered optional or special purpose are *italicized*. For most lists, symbols are used to indicate that items serve specific needs, e.g., cold weather use, night use, etc. The meaning of each symbol used is noted at the bottom of the last checklist page for each activity.

TEN ESSENTIALS

1) Maps. Carry a map or maps (charts for sea-going activities) which cover the entire area to be traveled with some additional extra-area coverage to assist in landmark recognition and for usage should an emergency outlet route be needed. The map scale should be commensurate with providing the necessary level of detail. *Multiple map types* (e.g., U.S. Geological Survey [USGS] topographic maps in conjunction with the latest U.S. Forest Service [USFS] plan maps for HIKING, MOUNTAIN BIKING, outback NORDIC SKIING/SNOWSHOEING, CANOEING, etc.) may be useful for resolving ambiguities or providing varied types of travel information whether on land or traversing inland waterways. They may also find use for in-shore SAILING and POWERBOATING.

Maps should be carried in a water-tight container if they are likely to be exposed directly to moisture (e.g., BACKPACKING or MOUNTAIN BIKING). Maps and charts should be protected by, or even sealed into, a waterproof cover if direct exposure is likely (e.g., KAYAKING, SAILING and POWERBOATING). Selected waterproofed maps and charts can be bought off-the-shelf or you can apply a light waterproofing spray yourself.

For ocean-going activities such as KAYAKING, SAILING and POWERBOATING, there are frequently few or no identifiable landmarks. For kayakers and small-craft sailors, course plotting on the chart is often accomplished using compass heading and estimated speed in conjunction with wind speed/direction information. The latter is obtained from the weather band on a marine radio.

In some instances, you also may want to take along a published trip guide. Well-written guides have saved many an outdoorsperson from taking the wrong fork at a trail or creek junction or missing a markerless turn point on a mountaineering climb.

2) Compass. A compass is used in conjunction with maps to take bearings on known landmarks in order to triangulate back and estimate current location. Compass quality needed varies as to whether one is hiking (a simple model suspended on a lanyard around-the-neck suffices) or navigating tight shoals (a reference-mounted, high quality compass is needed). *The hiking compass* should have a transparent base plate with straight sides, a rotating central dial, also with transparent base, graduated clockwise in one- or two-degree increments. The central dial enclosing the pivoting magnetic needle must be liquid filled to dampen oscillations and permit fast, accurate results. This same type of compass is useful for most other activities (including when driving to or from the trip start point) except as noted below.

Some compasses include a *clinometer* feature for measuring vertical angles and, thus, elevations or slope steepness. This is a valuable tool when in avalanche country, where slope steepness may give one clue as to avalanche likelihood. Upper-end cross-country backpackers and mountain climbers may also improve their estimate of slope, relative to that estimated by interpreting a topo map, which could be valuable to route selection.

A good quality *boating compass* is professionally installed. Once mounted, it is custom-calibrated to remove errors which may be induced by the boat structure itself. Refer to the SAILING activity for more information.

3) Flashlight with Batteries and Bulb. The flashlight is basically an emergency tool. For remote land travel, the rule is to *always have eight hours of light* in order to allow for an emergency all-night trek out to safety. A plastic flashlight with "C" alkaline batteries and a PR-4 bulb or two sets of smaller flashlights with "AA" alkaline batteries and PR-4 bulbs should suffice for all but extreme or specialized activities. (There are two series of standard flashlight bulbs: those identified by a number preceded by "PR" have smooth, flanged bases; those identified by a plain number have screw bases.) These are spot-focused lights (non-adjustable, preset beam width) that weigh a few ounces and fit into the palm of your hand. Add more spare batteries if the intent is for significant alternate use such as for in-camp lighting. Reverse one battery when not in use to avoid an inadvertent turn-on while the flashlight is in a carry pack.

Brighter *spot* and *adjustable-focus flashlights* are available if needed. Light intensity improvement of factors of 5-10 or greater are available. These lights normally use two to three "D" batteries or four "AA" batteries, the former providing about 15 hours of light at 70 degrees Fahrenheit (70°F), the latter about three hours. At 0°F these useful lifetimes are reduced by about 1/2 to 2/3. Fully-loaded weights are of the order of 1 to 1-1/2 pounds and six ounces with sizes about 12 inches (length) x 2-1/2 inches (diameter) and 6 inches x 1-1/2 inches, respectively.

An interesting innovation was developed for the Russian army in 1956 and is still a military staple. The flashlight requires no batteries, as it is powered by a *hand-squeeze-operated generator* to supply power to the bulb. The pistol-gripped light has an adjustable focus and can fit into a large (hiking) pant's pocket.

There is a reasonable likelihood of dropping your flashlight or encountering wet conditions for waterborne activities such as CANOEING, KAYAKING, SAILING, POWERBOATING and some WATERSPORTS (e.g., jet skiing). Don't think a second time about springing for a quality waterproof flashlight.

Head lamps keep the hands free and are useful for many activities. Activities such as GLACIER/WINTER CLIMBING and scuba diving (WATERSPORTS) require the brighter lights, head lamps with the toughest/waterproof cases and perhaps special batteries. (Alkaline cells do not function well below 20°F; lithium batteries, though expensive, excel in extreme cold.) Both adjustable and spot-focusing models are available. Most use 2-4 "AA" batteries , while some models use 1-2 "D" batteries or several "C" batteries. The standard fare is a vacuum bulb while the brightest models gas-filled bulbs (e.g., halogen, krypton, xenon). Battery life is similar to that for the flashlights discussed above. Three- to five-inch light diameter is typical and total weight (with batteries) ranges from about 4-14 ounces.

Some general comments: A practical lighting device should be simple to dismantle for replacing battery(s) and bulb (particularly in low- or no-light situations), have simple, sturdy construction, and use standard-design bulbs. Accessory features to look for include fittings for wrist cords, bulb storage within the device case and a luminous external strip for assisting in finding the device when misplaced. Note that some lighting devices may not handle lithium batteries or accept other than vacuum (as opposed to the brighter gas-filled) bulbs.

There are additional discussions of flashlights and other lighting needs which have been reserved for individual activities. In those cases, the focus is on needs which are unique to that activity.

4) Extra Food and Water. "Extra" means just that, rations up and above those for the nominally planned trip. Store the *extra, high-food-value items* such as canned tuna, Spam (items that you are not likely to "raid" unnecessarily) or high-energy bars in a special container away from your normal food supply. Extra water means carrying at least an additional 50% above that planned for the nominal day's excursion (e.g., HIKING) or to the next reliable water source (e.g. SAILING).

5) Extra Clothing. The type of extra clothing needed depends on trip duration and weather conditions. For daytime activities, sufficient clothing should generally be carried to allow you to stay out on an emergency overnight. For extended-period activities, the extra gear should see you through unexpected foul-weather conditions. The *key is to dress in layers and to carry clothing that maintains warmth when wet,*

Regardless of activity, preparation for weather rests on the *layered clothing concept*. The idea is to have multiple layers of clothing which can be added or removed dependent on weather conditions and level of exertion. The inner or *underwear layer* serves to move moisture away from the skin. This layer should be snug, but comfortable. The middle or *insulating layer* provides warmth by holding in body-generated heat. Insulating gear should include ventilation adjustments such as zippers and buttons. The *shell layer* protects your body against wind, rain and snow. This layer should allow room for insulating layers underneath, but be snug enough, through use of cinches, belts, snaps and other adjusters, to minimize heat loss. It should also have vents and closures, such as cuffs, hoods and zippers, that seal tightly and still open freely. The makeup of each layer depends on activity, weather conditions and personal preference. The combinations of items used for each layer in any given activity are very large in number. Some items may serve as a dual layer, such as a nylon-coated down parka, which will retain body heat under cold, mildly-windy conditions (part of the insulating layer plus shell layer).

Extra clothing may involve any of the three layers mentioned above. Examples are an additional heavy shirt, sweater, a tucked-away set of thermal underwear, long pants, parka, raingear or windbreaker or some combination of these items. This could also include an additional pair of gloves, spare socks or warm piece of headgear and a Mylar "space blanket."

Almost anything goes for VEHICLE-ACCESSIBLE CAMPING and other activities where you can bring nearly an unlimited amount of gear. Clothes get wet and you replace them. The temperature drops and you dig through the pile of goodies to find an extra sweater or jacket. In spite of this, you will see few entries in this guide calling for such as urban sweatshirts, tee-shirts and blue jeans for outdoor recreation activity use. Why? Most citywear has little or no insulating ability when wet, thus its use for other than light activities, fair-weather campsite use or going into town is not recommended. Besides, bringing a set of versatile, all-weather clothing simply minimizes the amount of stuff you have to tug along. In addition, much of this all-weather gear can be used for other outdoor activities. The types of *insulate-when-wet materials* for each clothing layer are discussed in the activity sections which follow. They include both natural-fiber (like wool) and synthetic fiber (like polyester) materials.

6) Sunglasses. Sunglasses are not so much for looks as for protecting your eyes. Consider buying more than one set or a set that has interchangeable lens or filters -- tailor their use for the planned activity. Regardless of activity, buy quality glasses that have the *transmission* properties to block a very high percentage of ultraviolet (UV) light and are shatterproof. Sunglasses are generally categorized as follows: 1) "Cosmetic" - blocks 70% of UVB rays, 20% of UVA, and up to 60% of visible light; 2) "General Purpose" - 95% of UVB, 60% of UVA, and up to 90% of visible light; 3) "Special Purpose" - 99% of UVB rays, 60% of UVA, and up to 97% of visible light; and "Special Purpose" whose tags read "absorbs UV up to 400 nanometers" - nearly complete absorption of UVA and UVB rays. The latter two groups are the standards used in backcountry snow activities.

Lens materials such as glass have the highest level of optical clarity and scratch resistance. Borosilicate and mineral glass are ultra-durable forms of glass. Polycarbonate is less optically pure and scratch resistant, but is lighter, virtually shatterproof and less expensive. Acrylic is least expensive, but has lower optical clarity and durability. *Tints* of gray, green and brown tend to render colors most true, making them most pleasing for most outdoor use or driving. Rose, gold and amber tints enhance contrast, making them most useful in low-light conditions. This would be a good choice for fast-paced activities (e.g., MOUNTAIN BIKING, ALPINE SKIING/SNOWBOARDING, NORDIC SKIING and SNOWMOBILING) on cloudy or overcast days.

Polarized lenses block flat, reflected light which comes off snow, water or glass, thus reducing glare. This is a useful property for GLACIER/WINTER CLIMBING, CANOEING, KAYAKING, SAILING, POWERBOATING, WATERSPORTS, LAND and SEA FISHING or automobile driving. These lens reduce contrast, however, making them less attractive to some active pursuits like ALPINE SKIING/SNOWBOARDING or SNOWMOBILING, where reading the terrain is important.

For general use, around 15-25% light transmission is standard. *Photochromic lens* vary transmission depending on scene brightness. They are becoming increasingly popular with drivers and for less dynamic outdoor activities as HIKING, sea KAYAKING, SAILING, POWERBOATING, etc., but have not yet gained wide acceptance where sportsmen may experience rapid scene brightness changes, e.g., MOUNTAIN BIKING and ALPINE SKIING/SNOWBOARDING. Activities at high altitude and/or in snow call for glasses with no more then 10% transmission. Prolonged exposure to sun at high altitude without low-transmission specs can result in sore eyeballs, snow blindness, or, in the worst case, permanent eye damage.

Frame materials include metal, nylon and acetate. Metal frames and nylon with a flexible wire core are adjustable to your face. However, pure nylon frames are more durable and less expensive, followed by acetate. High-quality frames tend to have durable nickel-silver hinges, while the hinges are molded into lower-priced frames. Sunglasses should fit snugly (i.e., not tightly cinched or sliding down the nose) on the nose and ears with the weight evenly distributed. Metal frames allow a certain amount of bending to allow custom fitting the nose.

Sport Glasses. Sport glasses are designed for all-around use and are suitable for most activities. Most have a two-lens body and come in gray, emerald, brown, amber, rose and gold tints.

Wraps. This type of eyeglass wraps around the face offering extended protection for fast-moving activities such as ALPINE SKIING/SNOWBOARDING. The most common tints are brown and gray, followed by rose, gold and amber. A few models have interchangeable lenses, typically brown, gold and clear. Light transmissions of 10-20% are most prevalent.

Shields. For cycling or other high-speed activities, shields feature a single lens which wraps around the face, offering maximum sun and wind protection. Most models come with gray tints with optional lens' available including clear and gold. Typical light transmissions are 10-20%.

Glacier Glasses. These models are designed for use on snow or at altitude, where light and UV conditions are most extreme. Light transmission is typical in the range of 5-10% and most common tints are gray, amber and green. Glasses should have side protection (usually leather side blocks) and bottom protection (designed into the shape), as well as adequate ventilation to prevent fogging. Many climbers carry two sets of sunglasses, one for average conditions and one for the intense glare of snow and high altitude glacier travel. Glacier glasses should come equipped with cable temples, which are metal or wire-core extensions which bend behind the ears. This feature holds the glasses in place during exertion. Purchase sunglasses with adjustable cable temples -- they provide a more comfortable fit and keep the shades in place under even the most contorting activities. Prescription snow/glacier glasses are available, but expensive. Some climbers and skiers use regular prescription glasses with goggles.

Get a strap or lanyard which keeps the glasses from falling free during strenuous activities -- many a person has lost a much-needed set of sunglasses while rock climbing, skiing or performing other outdoor activities and had to endure the uncomfortable consequences.

7) Pocket Knife. The pocketknife is a multi-purpose tool for food preparation, first aid, emergency fire building, etc.; the choices here are limited only by what the outdoorsperson is willing to spend. A *"comfort" model* might have a couple of standard blades, can opener, bottle opener, finger nail file, screw drivers, leather punch, tweezers and a toothpick. Other available features are corkscrew, scissors, hook, wire stripper, wood saw, magnifying glass, pliers with wire cutter and fish scaler. Get a steel model with a key ring. Many outdoorsmen run a cord through the ring, pass the cord around the belt or through a belt loop, and tuck the knife in the pocket. This prevents easy knife loss while still keeping it readily accessible.

Many sailors look for a knife known as a *rigger's knife*, which is a basic knife and marlinespike combination. As with any other multi-use knife, there are models that also have other blades. The next most useful blade is specifically designed for releasing shackles on the boat deck.

8) Waterproof Matches. Buy *waterproof matches* at a sporting goods store or make your own by dipping large kitchen matches into heated paraffin (not wax) or by coating them with clear fingernail lacquer or airplane dope. The ultimate new commercial matches are advertised to light when wet and be able to sustain a flame in the rain. Put the matches with a small strip of sandpaper. *Add a throw-away butane lighter* as an alternate source. Store both in an absolutely waterproof container.

9) Candle, Fuel Tabs or Other Long-Burning Fire Starters. These are for *starting a fire with damp kindling*. The candle or chemical fuel should sustain a flame for about ten minutes, sufficient to dry kindling and then ignite it. Bring an extra starter or two for more remote trips or trips conducted under extreme conditions such as GLACIER/WINTER CLIMBING. If you are carrying a stove that requires primer fuel, the primer can be used; for liquid, non-primered-fuel models, the fuel itself may suffice. (Both are contingency options.)

10) First Aid Kit. Though one of the least used items in general outdoor activities, this is not an area to shave weight or bulk. Build a custom kit or buy a pre-packaged unit. A kit should be carried, as a minimum, by each separate unit of a group. A separate unit is any sub-group or individual separating from the main group for a planned side or separate activity. The conservative approach is for each individual to carry a minimum kit -- this allows for most contingencies, including unplanned group separations. One person should carry a more substantial kit. Each person's kit should be in a *separate sturdy container*. Develop a *working knowledge* of everything in the kit prior to outdoor recreation departure -- it is very difficult in pressure situations to read and follow even simple instructions. A separate, comprehensive checklist and limited equipment discussion is provided in the FIRST AID section.

Eleventh Essential? There are many amongst our crusty group that insist that there is an eleventh essential! It is a twenty-dollar bill for buying snacks and liquid refreshment at the completion of an exhilarating outdoor activity.

Using the "Eighth Essential" Courtesy of Doug Holker

VEHICLE-ACCESSIBLE CAMPING

(Accessibility from Land or Water)

See INDEX for checklist items not discussed below.

VEHICLE-ACCESSIBLE CAMPING implies either ground or waterborne access to a camp. Many equipment items listed under this section are common to many other activities, although there may be some activity-related variations in item needs. In order to preserve discussion continuity, the specifications for some equipment items for other activities may be included in this section. The relevant activity(s) is clearly cited. In the checklist, items that are considered optional (niceties or special purpose) are *italicized*. Gear items for cold weather are noted with an asterisk(*) and those for nighttime used indicated by a pound sign(#).

Safety Considerations: 1)review the **GENERAL CONSIDERATIONS** and TEN ESSENTIALS discussions; 2) learn to use camping gear properly, particularly those items with greatest potential to cause personal injury -- ax, stove, heater, wood saw, etc.; 3) take the necessary precautions when lighting and using a campfire; and 4) keep your eye on small children in camp and don't let them wander too far from the campsite. If you are combining secondary activities out of your campsite (e.g., hiking, fishing), consult the relevant section for more safety information.

Camping Gear (Shelter/Comfort)

Auto Gear Rack/Locks. Spring for an automobile overhead rack (or sports utility rack) that can haul various kinds of gear. Most passenger-car assemblies consist of four towers that clamp to your car's roof (with model designs for many different roof styles) and a set of crossbars. One crossbar attaches to the forward set, the other to the rear set of towers. Numerous assemblies can be temporarily, but securely, attached to the crossbars. They include hold-downs for bicycles, skis, snowboards, canoes, kayaks and gear storage units. A rack equipped with a gear storage unit provides more room and comfort for campers inside the car. These plastic or metal removable storage units are usually either open storage trays with gear secured using a bungie-corded stretch net or quick-latching, enclosed (watertight) shells. For one of the most popular manufacturers, shells have volumes of roughly 10-15 cubic feet, weigh approximately 40-45 pounds and have typical gear-carrying weight capacities in the 100- to 150-pound range. The most convenient-to-use models have gas-filled struts for easy opening and loading.

These gear storage units are also useful for many of the other activities discussed in the book. They are naturals for HIKING, BACKPACKING, GLACIER/WINTER CLIMBING, ROCK CLIMBING, SNOWBOARDING, SNOWSHOEING, SAILING, POWERBOATING, WATERSPORTS, and LAND FISHING and SEA FISHING where segmented rods are used. The largest units can accommodate gear needed for ALPINE SKIING/SNOWBOARDING and NORDIC SKIING and most non-segmented rods used for LAND FISHING and SEA FISHING. Specialized assemblies are needed for the other activities. Note that with a wide enough set of crossbars (if they fit your automobile), you may be able to carry a small gear storage unit together with bicycles or skis.

Unfortunately, people steal utility racks and the equipment mounted to them, making it prudent to invest in one or two sets of *locks*. One set of locks will hold the towers to your car and another (usually a cable lock) will hold the shell to the rack, plus prevent shell access. If the shell has its own locks and its mounting mechanisms are inaccessible when it is locked, there is no need for the second set. Most commercial racks are designed to accept slip-in locks which fasten the towers to the car. The cable lock, which secures the shell to the rack (if needed), is a separately-purchased item.

Tents and Tarps. For VEHICLE-ACCESSIBLE CAMPING, SAILING, POWERBOATING and to a lesser extent, CANOEING, there is little concern for weight or bulk. The key considerations are number of people, comfort level desired, maximum campsite size, season and worst-case conditions of inclement weather.

OUTDOOR RECREATION CHECKLISTS

There are many roomy 2-man, 4-man, 6-man and larger *tents* with high ceilings that fit the bill. Typical sizes are 8 feet x 10 feet and 10 feet x 12 feet which handle 2-4 people and 4-6 people respectively. Larger models with partitioned sleeping areas are also on the market. If outdoor stays of several days are planned, get a tent that you can stand up or nearly stand up within. Days are long when you are trapped indoors by hard rains! Cheeriest colors are sky blue, red, orange and yellow -- the latter three are easiest to spot when returning to camp from a hike or other activity. A three-season tent will generally be fine, as you can make up for cold with additional insulating gear or heat sources. Confirm that the tent is reasonably easy to construct and sturdy enough to withstand a strong wind.

San Bernardino National Forest, California

Many camping tents are single-layered. The single-layer models most often have multi-coated waterproof, rip-stop nylon walls, waterproof polyester roofs and waterproof polyethylene, reinforced floors. With this non-breathable waterproof exterior, ventilation is provided through mesh openings that have waterproof, protective overflaps. If the ventilation is cut off for a lengthy period (in driving rain or severe cold), body moisture will collect on the tent walls and run down to the tent floor (bummer!).

Most experienced campers favor two-layer tents with a breathable basic tent and a waterproof rainfly (over-cover), which have a large mesh entry door in the basic tent (additional mesh windows are a bonus). Look for a two-tier tent that has a waterproof floor and sidewalls to exclude rain that blows under the rainfly. The sidewalls should extend no more than a few inches off the ground. Otherwise there will be a large interior surface area to collect moisture for eventual deposit on the tent floor. Never, never leave the rainfly at home!

Of course, nothing prevents you from putting your backpacking or bicycle-touring tent to double use if you are willing to give up the luxury of the Taj Mahal models above. See the BACKPACKING section for information on lighter-weight, higher-portability tents.

For other than where a tent is a necessity, i.e., in severe weather, a light-weight *tarpaulin* is a viable (but seldom used) VEHICLE-ACCESSIBLE CAMPING option. Most tarp use for this activity is as a secondary cover. That is, tarps might serve to shade eating or sit-down recreation areas. Our northwest brethren have introduced us to using tarps as a rain cover for the campfire area. Nothing beats sitting dry around a campfire, cooking or playing games outdoors in a steady rain.

Tarps of polyethylene (lightest, but shortest life), coated nylon, or waterproof canvas (heaviest, but most durable) are candidates. The latter two tarps mainly come with reinforced grommets sewn into the sides and corners for easy rigging. Tarps lacking grommets can be rigged by tying off each corner around a small pebble, rubber ball or any small, dull-edged object. Typical sizes are 9 feet x 12 feet and 11 feet x 14 feet. Tarps can be shaped into a flat-shed roof, tent or any one of many options, only limited by one's imagination. They can be attached to trees, tied to rocks or boulders, motor vehicles, boats or surly campers forced to serve as a permanent stays. (Just a thought.) Individual tarps can also be connected together, increasing the size, shape and versatility options. Bring plenty of strong nylon cord.

Stakes & Poles. Tent stakes come in a multitude of sizes, shapes and materials. Unless you will always be camping on soft surfaces, toss the plastic stakes that you get with many tents and replace them with the necessary number of metal stakes, including a couple of spares. Where weight is not a consideration, buy railroad tie spikes. There are also numerous lighter-weight metal stakes. Note that in combination with a plentiful supply of strong nylon cord, any tent can be stood up in any territory, even with the lighter stakes.

For snow camping in soft snow conditions, use line to tie to any heavy, stable object that is near the tent site. Better yet, invest in a separate set of higher-surface-area stakes or deadman anchors. Use them as "dead men" by burying them in a trench in a horizontal position and perpendicular to the tent guy wire. Guy lines can be secured using a stuff sack filled with rocks or even snow. Just bury the sack, stamp down the snow above, and connect the guy line to the sack's cord or sling.

Most all vehicle-accessible and remote camping tents sold today use shock-corded tent poles. Most often, these are light-aluminum, hollow-core poles with an elastic cord running through the center section. Not only lightweight, but also strong and flexible, each pole can be folded into sections and the full set compressed to fit into a small storage sack. For the more remote activities, many campers bring a replacement sleeve that can be fitted over a broken pole. A four-inch piece of PVC, copper tubing or aluminum (supplied by the manufacturer) with a diameter slightly larger than the pole, will do the trick.

For folks who use tents with fiberglass poles, the sleeve concept will work for near-breaks. However, the best hollow fiberglass wands are now spun such that short damaged sections can be nurtured back to use with duct tape or fiberglass strapping tape.

Seam Sealer. Tents will leak at the seams over time. A modest supply of *seam sealer* often comes with the tent. Otherwise buy the proper seam sealer for your tent with the help of outdoor recreation shop personnel. Do this task prior to departure. Some tents come with *patch kits* for tears or holes in the tent shell. Most nylon, rip-stop tents can only be repaired by a qualified seamstress -- take exceptional care of these type of tents both when you use them and store them. If possible, buy a seam sealer that doubles for use on wearing apparel such as raingear.

Ground Cloth. Coating on waterproof tent floors becomes non-waterproof with normal use. *Polyethylene sheeting* below the tent floor will minimize ground wear and limit leakage from outside. The same sheeting can be used in the tent interior, cut to fit such that the edges lay flat on the floor or just overlap the tent sidewalls. Another option for the interior floor is to use the *emergency space blanket* that you carry in your pack. For this double duty, you need the heavier-duty refoldable model, not the one-time use, compressed (golf-ball size) space blanket.

Tent Broom and Sponge. To prolong the life of your tent bottom, shake the tent out after use (sponge the floor if it is really cruddy). For larger tents, use a *whisk broom* or other small hand broom to clear out the debris before sponging. A common practice to minimize tracking debris into the tent is to place a piece of old carpet or other *foot-wiping material* at the tent entry.

Sleeping Bags. The preferred outdoor recreation sleeping device, the warmth of the bag depends on the type and amount of insulating fill, the thickness (loft) of the fill and the bag's size, style and method of construction. Sleeping bags are typically categorized as *summer, three-season or four-season* types. Manufacturers supply comfort ratings, indicating the lowest temperature at which the bag will be comfortably warm. Rating methods vary from manufacturer to manufacturer, thus this is not a strict comparative guideline. Very rough guidelines (our own) are that summer bags might be rated in the 40-50 degree Fahrenheight (°F) range, three-season bags about 20-40 °F and four-season bags roughly -5 to 20 °F. Mountaineering expedition bags may be rated down to -20 °F or lower. You can put a thin overbag around the sleeping bag in cold weather to improve its performance. Another option, used in below-freezing conditions, is to use a vapor-barrier liner inside the bag. This improves bag performance by 10-15 °F but also traps body moisture inside the liner.

The most common *styles* are mummy bags or rectangular bags. Mummy bags are the warmest and lightest, but are most restrictive in terms of allowing sleeper movement. Rectangular bags can frequently be zipped together for snuggling, but have a broad, breezy opening. If you go this route, ensure that you buy one bag with a right-side zipper and the second with a left-hand zipper. Rectangular bags are most popular for summer use or for three- to four-season VEHICLE-ACCESSIBLE CAMPING, where other warming layers such as blankets are available.

A good mummy bag should have a form-fitting hood or a semi-circular piece with drawstring to maintain head warmth and prevent heat loss. The better four-season bags have an insulated shoulder yoke to provide extra warmth around the shoulders and provide extra insulation in critical areas, such as chest and feet. Most bags have ripstop nylon outer shells. Some three- to four-season models have vapor-wicking liners which, in conjunction with a breathable outer shell, minimize the amount of moisture trapped within the bag. Some bags are offered in both standard and extended sizes for persons up to six feet and about six feet, six inches tall, respectively. Bags with the largest zippers are easiest to enter and exit and to adjust ventilation, but are most susceptible to heat loss. This is generally not a major issue, provided the zipper is well-backed up with a tube of insulating material.

The warmth, weight, bulk and cost of bags are chiefly driven by the kind and quality of *insulation*. Wool and kapok bags are inexpensive, but relatively heavy and bulky. They retain a significant amount of their insulation properties when wet. Dacron is also inexpensive, but weighs somewhere between wool and down and is very bulky. These bags are best used for three-season VEHICLE-ACCESSIBLE CAMPING or for snoozing while underway (e.g., SAILING and POWERBOATING) in moderate weather. Goose down remains the most efficient insulation per unit weight. Down bags are warm, highly compressible, retain their loft well over time and are long lasting when well cared for. The "downside" is that it is expensive and loses its insulating properties when wet. In reasonably good weather, a soaked bag can take a full day to dry. This makes down a questionable choice in wet weather, unless great care is taken to keep it dry (packing within a watertight enclosure, seam-sealing the tent, etc.). Synthetic insulation (frequently polyester-based) is resistant to moisture, maintains much of its insulating properties when wet, and dries relatively quickly. These bags are less expensive than down for a given comfort temperature. However, synthetics are slightly heavier than down bags, do not compress quite as easily, and do not last as long because they lose much of their loft with use.

Three primary *methods of construction* are used in keeping the down uniformly distributed: sewn-through, slant tube and overlapping tube. Sewn-through is the least expensive, but one which allows substantial heat loss at the seams. Slant tube construction is more expensive, but provides improved insulation properties. The most efficient and expensive designs have overlapping tube construction. In addition, many designs use channel blocks, which are baffles to prevent down from shifting. The two most common construction styles for synthetic bags are single and multiple offset quilting. Both are effective although the quilting method is more complex, requiring two to three carefully-offset layers to avoid cold spots.

One final note: Best bag performance is achieved by proper use of dual-use wearing apparel. In winter, at altitude, it is not unusual for our crew to wear heavy long johns, heavy wool socks inside of down booties, and a heavy wool cap. It is not unknown to throw in a down parka if the going really gets rough!

Sleeping Pads. The proper insulation below the sleeping bag serves a dual purpose, one to limit loss of body heat and the other to provide a soft sleeping surface. For VEHICLE-ACCESSIBLE CAMPING, SAILING and POWERBOATING where weight and bulk are not key considerations, we have seen outdoorspeople use large air mattresses, carpet under cushions, bed mattresses, grabbing Z's on the boat deck or in the sail locker -- whatever works!

Twin Lakes, Colorado

For other activities, a myriad of alternatives also exists, including sleeping on clothing, backpack and other gear. However, most active outdoorspeople invest in an *air or foam mattress*. An air mattress provides the softest bed for its weight and bulk and is the choice for other than snow, cold ground or general cold surfaces. For cold surfaces a relatively thin (3/8-inch) pad of closed-cell foam (ensolite) will do the job nicely. There are also blow-up mattresses with a closed-cell interior, the top of the line for sleeping pads. A four-foot long (typically at least 20 inches wide) pad is adequate, using other equipment to prop up legs and feet. However, we prefer as close to a full body length pad as is available.

Some inflating pads can be made into light-use camp chairs. A slipover cover, purchased separately, is fitted over a partial length of the pad. The pad is folded and straps are used to attach the folded section (the backrest) to the unfolded section (the seat).

Air Pump. Bring a standup bicycle-tire pump (with a pressure gauge) for inflating air mattresses, inner tubes, rafts, toys, sports equipment such as a volleyball or bicycle tires, and even inflatable tents. The gauge will be useful for achieving recommended pressure, rather than having to do it by feel. Also available are higher-volume inflation gear such as foot pumps and motorized pumps. Use the latter with care unless you are one of those people who enjoy watching things explode! Note that some motorized models have connectors for automobile cigarette lighters, automobile and boat batteries, and/or standard electrical outlets.

On a smaller scale, there is the Pocket Pump. The long-stemmed pump is single-hand, squeeze operated and is meant for inflating volleyballs, basketballs, footballs and the like. It is tiny enough to fit into a sports bag or even a big pocket.

Camp Pillows. For VEHICLE-ACCESSIBLE CAMPING, SAILING and POWERBOATING, standard pillows are the norm. Small, *compact down- and synthetic-filled pillows* are available for other activities, although most outdoor people use clothing items tucked inside a stuff sack. There is even a stuff sack which, when turned inside out, has a soft-fleece covering. Whichever pillow you choose, stay away from the laundry bag!

Hammock(s). Few camping pleasures rival lying in a hammock and watching the world go by. Styles range from the one- or two- person garden-variety designs to "jungle" models with attachable rainflys and built-in, fully-surrounding, zippered mosquito netting, Hammock floors made of heavy-duty nylon, cotton and polyester are popular, the latter most commonly associated with woven, as opposed to solid, floors. The classic style has heavy wood stretchers. The lines from the stretcher at both head and foot are nominally fed through heavy (frequently) steel rings. A few styles thread directly from floor to ring, which tends to bunch up near the head and feet, a great two-person style if you seek "coziness." Hanging lines are typically made up of several strands of 1/4-inch twisted nylon or polyester.

Camp Chairs. *Fold up chairs* are the norm for camping since they are easiest to pack, whether into an automobile, a boat or onto a frame pack. Backyard chairs work for VEHICLE-ACCESSIBLE CAMPING, SAILING/POWERBOATING (land or at-anchor use) and WATERSPORTS (land or "shoreline immersion mode" use). Several models of more-compact, lighter-weight chairs are also available. They include beach chairs, collapsible stools, and small, foldable wooden or aluminum loungers. The option of carrying a chair with a backrest is worth the cost and penalty of additional bulk if your back suffers.

Lantern and Mantel(s). For outdoor trips where traveling light is a must, flashlights, candles and/or campfires will probably be the primary light sources. Otherwise, the best outdoor light source is a long-burning lantern. The most popular lanterns use liquid (corrosion and rust inhibiting) *lantern fuel or propane*. Most older models require direct flame against the mantels to start, while newer, more convenient versions have a built-in spark initiator -- the difference is that you must partially dissemble the older lanterns to light them. Old mantels can disintegrate without warning, particularly when the lantern suffers a physical shock from being dropped or banged against a hard object. Learn how to mount and prime mantels beforehand and test that the lantern works before nightfall.

Fuel Funnel/Strainer. Our kerosene stove refused to sustain a flame on a backpacking trip. When we returned home, we discovered that long-term fuel corrosion had resulted in flaking within the fuel reservoir and was clogging the fuel line. We have never gone without a fuel strainer since or at least strained all fuel that we expect to use on an upcoming trip.

Oil (pump lantern and stove). The pump mechanisms on older outdoor appliances, particularly lanterns and stoves, require that the pump piston cap be moist. A few drops of *machine oil or motor oil* will do.

Heater & Fuel. For outdoor activities where weight and bulk are not issues, heaters are a nicety in cold weather, particularly in a tent when you are changing into night wear. For safety and ease of use, most veterans have never considered any option other than a liquefied gas heater, typically propane. Fuel comes in a simple screw-in canister. Keep the business end of the heater away from the tent sides and other combustible objects within the tent.

Waterproof Matches and Lighter. Refer to the TEN ESSENTIALS section.

Stuff Sacks. You can never have enough of these articles for outdoor activities. They are great for organizing and protecting your gear. *Stuff sacks* are available in varied sizes, styles and purposes. On VEHICLE-ACCESSIBLE CAMPING, SAILING and

POWERBOATING trips, use stuff sacks or duffel bags for tent, poles, sleeping bags, down parkas, clothing in general, and any other group of items that you want to keep together. This same philosophy is used for more remote adventures, BACKPACKING, GLACIER/WINTER CLIMBING, BICYCLE TOURING, MOUNTAIN BIKING, NORDIC SKIING/SNOWSHOEING, CANOEING and KAYAKING. The difference, for the more remote activities, is that there is a particular premium to keeping cold-weather clothing and sleeping gear dry. Stuff sacks can also prevent this type of gear from being torn or punctured. A common practice for waterproofing is to pack those key items in *3-mil thickness laundry* or *trash bags* (double or triple layers for whitewater canoeing or kayaking). The bags are then compressed to force out excess air, tied off, and placed within the stuff sack. Waterproof containers (dry packs) specifically tailored for CANOEING and KAYAKING use, are discussed in the CANOEING activity.

Camping Permit. It used to be that you could pack up your gear and plop down at almost any camping area without advance notice, for at least three seasons of the year. In today's world, check to see if reservations and/or a camping permit are required and attempt to get them well in advance. Bring the paperwork with you!

Camping Gear (Cooking)

A few words about food storage. Rather than leave your food out at night (or daytime, should you leave the campsite) or tuck it into your tent, store it in a location inaccessible to campsite critters. Your automobile or enclosed boat will do. Some campsites offer boxes for this purpose, but are generally limited in space. If none of these options is available, store your food as is done for more remote activities -- see the BACKPACKING activity for a detailed description.

Before turning in or heading off-site, haul your trash and garbage to the containers provided. Another option is to burn these items in your campfire, then place any non-burnable items (such as metal cans) in the trash at a convenient later time. You haven't lived until you've popped out of your tent and put your flashlight on a bear who is feasting on your "left-behinds." The first question you ask yourself is "what will it go after next?"

Jalama Beach, California

A digression: We had such an event early in our camping careers. We were tent-camping in Northern California when a bear decided to check out a Styrofoam cooler that we had jammed under a nearby picnic table bench. We abandoned the tent and wound up huddled in a nearby couple's camper, listening to their soothing explanation that the bears had not recently hurt anybody. (Easy for them to say while they were enclosed in their metal "fortress.") Though we have had many bears in the proximity of our campsite since, we have not been bothered by them. Everything of any potential interest to these magnificent creatures now gets stored in the auto before we retire for the night.

Stove & Windbreak/Stove Fuel. For VEHICLE-ACCESSIBLE CAMPING, assuming built-in stoves (such as those in some recreational vehicles or boats) are not available, a variety of single or multi-burner stoves are on the market. Weight and size generally are not key issues. Liquefied gas (typically propane) is the preferred fuel for camping because of its ease of use. There are also stoves that operate with fuels such as gasoline, white gas and kerosene and some that burn multiple fuel types. Key features are compactness (weight and bulk), ease of operation and stove/pot stability. For multi-burner stoves, minimum distance between burners should be the greatest pot width that is planned for use (typically, at least 10 inches). If you will be cooking in the wind, look for stoves with sturdy, built-in windscreens.

Liquefied gas fuel is sold in its own high-pressure bottle. Non-pressurized liquid fuel should be stored in *well-marked, leak-proof containers*. This can be the original container. Alternately, where weight and space are key considerations, fuel can be transferred into a tightly-closed, marked container such as an aluminum bottle with a screw top, backed up with a rubber gasket. These aluminum bottles come in roughly 1/2 pint to quart sizes. There is a similarly-constructed screw top with an attached spout. This temporarily replaces the screw-on closure when you need to fill a stove (or lantern) fuel tank.

Grizzly Creek Redwoods State Park, California

Fire Starter. For VEHICLE-ACCESSIBLE CAMPING, check to see if fire wood is available. If not, bring your own wood, including larger pieces from which to make kindling. Another option is to bring long-burning, pressed-composite fireplace logs. Most campers generally bring newspaper for use as an initial source of flame. For cooking fires, where warmth is not an issue, consider using charcoal -- it is most easily controlled and provides the most uniform fire. Bring along a small additional supply of treated instant-light coals and liquid fire starter. Also consider mesquite, oak or other chips which provide outdoor barbecue flavor enhancement. In the outback, use the fire-related material discussed under the TEN ESSENTIALS.

Camp Grill. *Self-standing*, single- or multiple-pot camp *grills* are handy for use over an open fire. Where weight and bulk are issues, a small *legless grill* may be useful for cooking items that do not readily fit into a pack-in set of cookware, e.g., fish. A good intermediate weight and bulk alternate is a grill with extended handles (use gloves) that opens into two identical sections. It has a lock ring which slides over the handles to put a pressure fit on the barbecued item -- this keeps the item in place. The method for legless and *hand-held grills* is to build a small fire in an existing ring, placing a few rocks or other suitable items to properly elevate the grill. A perforated aluminum foil cover placed directly on the grill or wrapped around the hand-held model will help distribute the heat more evenly and still allow excess juices and fat to spill out.

Coffee Pot. This might more generally be considered a pot for boiling water. For coffee lovers, where electricity is available, bring the *house brewer* or a compact *travel unit*. Otherwise, there are numerous *outdoor pots* that make excellent coffee over an outdoor fire -- use pre-packaged coffee packets as opposed to loose grounds for convenience. Where all supplies will be in your pack or where packing space is limited, think hard about carrying a small aluminum *"teapot"* together with instant coffee, tea or chocolate.

Pots, Pans N' Other Stuff. For VEHICLE-ACCESSIBLE CAMPING, SAILING and POWERBOATING, the sky's the limit on what gear to bring. Save your old pots and pans, utensils, and dinnerware for camping and select what is needed based on the planned menu. To minimize cleanup, use paper plates placed on top of dishes for support. For CANOEING, a full set of gear might include an old skillet or fry pan, a couple of cooking pots with covers, a set of hard-plastic dishes and bowls, a limited set of silverware and utensils and plastic or insulated cups. You will probably have to slim down this set for KAYAKING because of the more-limited storage capacity available. Whatever the activity, an insulated cup with a top having drinking and pressure-relief openings will serve you well. At minimal added weight and bulk, you can keep your soup or drink hot in cold weather.

For other activities where all gear is on your back, take only lightweight-aluminum, nested cooking gear. This includes two small surface-lined (e.g., Teflon) pots and lids and a frying pan, a small teapot, plastic bowls, large cups and eating utensils. This cooking group can support up to six people. For two people, the largest pot is 1-1/2 quart size, while for six, it is six quarts. A 1-1/2 quart teapot is adequate. The bare bones minimum, which might best apply to BICYCLE TOURING and MOUNTAIN BIKING, is to drop the inner pot, fry pan, bowls and retain only spoons (add forks if the menu requires them) as eating utensils. Your cutting tool is the pocket knife. For cookware which does not have an insulated handle, use an insulated *pot holder* or *glove*. *Pot grippers* clamp onto pots and handleless pans, making them useful for older/broken and some light-weighted, remote-camping cookware.

Dish Washing. There is little that is mystical about *cleaning cookware* where plenty of hot water, soap, dishpan, an array of cleaning accessories and a safe disposal site are available. Where this doesn't apply, the tried-and-true cleaning method is to use *non-stick cooking lubricant* in pans; soak all relevant gear as soon as emptied or clean immediately; use paper towels to clean off initial layers of goo, followed by cleaning with a *lightly abrasive pad*; dispose of resultant waste well away from sources of water and the campsite. Use biodegradable detergents cautiously, if at all. If used, ensure that the cookware is thoroughly rinsed and dispose of soapy water away from sources of water. Another clever option is to store *precooked food* in heavy plastic bags and heat in a pan of hot water. No mess!

Water Jugs/Bottles. No matter what the activity, it is wise to overindulge on this precious commodity. Conservatism should lead you to carry all the water needed, including a pad, until the next <u>guaranteed</u> water source is available. For VEHICLE-ACCESSIBLE CAMPING, CANOEING, KAYAKING, SAILING and POWERBOATING, check for availability of potable water ahead of time. Even if sources are plentiful, pack in a couple of gallons of water for the first three activities and considerable water to the potable water tanks for the latter. No matter what the activity, authorities recommend an average daily intake of two quarts of water during active exertion and four quarts in hot weather. We have knocked off five quarts individually just during the course of a single, long day's very strenuous mountain-biking adventure. Additional water is required for cooking, dish washing, showering and other uses. In our garage are one-, two-, and a set of *five-gallon water containers* (filled for earthquake purposes in our Southern California area) -- we select what we need based on trip expectations. For activities where these large containers are brought along, also pack some smaller intermediate containers for more convenient use. Bring cups, glasses or water bottles to pour off water from the larger containers.

For other activities requiring packing in supplies via the back muscles, carry anywhere from two to six quarts of water per person depending on the trip difficulty and availability of water. *Wide-mouth polyurethane quart bottles* are the norm. They are much more convenient than narrow-mouthed bottles for scooping up water or snow and for catching water trickles. (Cold weather activities may call for insulated bottles or use of insulating bottle sleeves. See the "Insulated Bottle" entry below.) Also consider carrying in a 1/2- or one-gallon *collapsible water bag* (per twosome). These collapsible single- or double-thickness polyurethane containers are brought in empty and filled for use at the campsite. This minimizes the number trips from the camp to the water source. The more expensive versions, with longer use lifetimes, have a protective nylon fabric outer shell.

Steel and aluminum containers, typically *canteens*, are heavier and sometimes impart a metallic taste to water. One major advantage, however, is that frozen contents can be thawed by holding the canteen directly over flame. Consider this benefit when you are planning a trip at below-freezing temperatures. (A digression: If there will be sub-freezing temperatures at night, consider storing as many water bottles as needed next morning inside the sleeping bags.)

"Desperation" Campsite Near Dixie National Forest, Utah

Frequently, *juices or electrolytes* (e.g., Gatorade) are substituted for some of the water for both variety and for help in replenishing salt, sugar, calories and minerals. Salt lost by sweating must be replaced and it is recommended that two grams of salt per quart of water be drunk. This can be accomplished by drinking these types of electrolytes or using salt tablets. (For the latter option, which is rapidly falling out of favor, spread out tablet intake to coincide with water consumption as opposed to taking multiple tablets at once. Check with your personal physician for advice in this area.)

Portable Ice Chests. Confined to activities other than pack-ins, choose an ice chest(s) which fit into the confines of available space. There are many space-age chests with high insulation properties ranging from all-Styrofoam coolers with form-fit, free tops to those longer-life models with plastic and plastic-metal combination external surfaces and hinged tops. They can be bought with a open interior or with such features as moveable shelves and bottle holders. Models with an open/close drain near the bottom of the cooler storage bottom are easiest to drain as ice melts.

Longest cooling life is achieved with block ice as opposed to ice cubes, however, packing capacity is sacrificed. A combination of small *ice* blocks made by storing water in selected size containers in the home freezer in combination with ice cubes is a handy mix. *Refreezeable ice containers* such as "Blue Ice" are also useful. Dry ice is a favorite with many, although it is not as easy to find in retail outlets.

Insulated Bottle. A portable container for hot or cold liquids, soups etc. is a handy add-on for activities where weight and bulk are not issues. Wide-mouth bottles are more versatile for item storage, while narrow-mouth models tend to be preferred if only liquid is stored. Pick a type(s) which is hardy (all-metal bottles and bottles which fit into cushioned, insulated sleeves are options) and has the capacity to suit your expected needs.

Bottle *insulating sleeves* are important for GLACIER/WINTER CLIMBING, NORDIC SKIING/SNOWSHOEING AND SNOWMOBILING. They keep your water or other liquid from becoming uncomfortably cold to drink or from freezing. The sleeves come in various sizes and thicknesses. The thicker insulators can keep a drink hot for hours in freezing temperatures.

An insulated (e.g., Thermos) bottle is a must for long SAILING and POWERBOATING trips. Having hot coffee or tea at your fingertips when standing watches in the middle of the night or in cold weather is a lifesaver.

Trash Bags. No matter what the activity, carry several 2-3 mil bags in which to store and carry trash. At drive-to camping sites, the trash bins are not always conveniently located. Using these bags minimizes the number of trips to the bin. (In areas with appreciable scavenger-animal population, make at least one trip before nightfall!) For pack-in and remote boat-in activities, a small *litter bag* is needed to carry out the trash that is generated on the trip. Passing through one of the most remote hike-in sites of the East Fork of the San Gabriel River in Los Angeles County, we were surprised and appalled at the amount of litter strewn about. It is hard to comprehend that hikers who had the background and skills to reach this site didn't have the mentality to haul out their trash. For SAILING and POWERBOATING, *trash bags* provide a convenient haul-out method as opposed to carrying trash containers.

Resealable Plastic Food Bags. These containers are of similar universal value for smaller outdoor activity items as stuff sacks are to larger items. Whatever the activity, these sealable (not sandwich) bags are useful for grouping items separately and serve the additional purpose of providing waterproofing. Various size bags are available with *pressure locks, zip locks and twist ties.* Bag TEN ESSENTIALS items such as flashlight/spare batteries and bulb together and do the same for waterproof matches/fuel tabs for all activities. Hygiene items are bagged together. Food items can be bagged together by type or by meal. This is particularly useful for pack-in trips where bulky packaging can be discarded at home and the basic food items protectively stored in easy-to-find groups. You get the idea.

Camp Table. We have never used this item, however we've been at many vehicle-accessible campsites where there are no camping tables. If this is an important consideration for you, find a light-weight, fold-up *table* which fits into the storage that you have available on the road or underway. Wind-blown *tablecloths* have been known to create messy disasters -- find a set of hold-down clips (four, minimum) which fit your tabletop width if your intention is to set a fancy table. The other, old-fashioned option is to weigh down the tablecloth corners with suitably-heavy camp gear or rocks. Plastic tablecloths are robust and easiest to clean. Of course, if you have a recreational vehicle, you may just choose to eat inside.

Dining Canopy and Mesh Screen. Nothing is more irritating outdoors than to be surrounded by flying pests on a regular basis. For activities where weight and bulk are not an issue, think about building an enclosed mesh (mosquito netting) outdoor area. With a tarp, sufficient mesh to cover the desired area, and plenty of nylon cord, a combination sun canopy and mesh sidewall structure can be constructed with a little bit of ingenuity. The upper mesh corners can be suspended and lower corners secured as described for “Tarpaulins” earlier in this section. An alternative is to build a pure mesh structure. The simplest method is to hang the center from a tree (reinforce the mesh at the hanging point) and simply secure several points at ground level.

Upper Santa Ynez River, California

Personal Gear.

As discussed in the TEN ESSENTIALS section, the base principal is to dress in layers and lean towards clothing items that maintain insulation properties when wet. The phrase "lean towards" applies to VEHICLE-ACCESSIBLE CAMPING, but becomes "ensure selection of" for more remote adventuring such as BACKPACKING, GLACIER/WINTER CLIMBING, NORDIC SKIING/SNOWSHOEING, etc. Most *underwear layer* items on the market are polyester, polyester/Spandex and polypropelene, with a smattering of wool-blend models. For the *insulating* layer, wool, wool-blends, polypropylene, acrylic, polyester fleece and pile, polyester fleece/spandex, and other synthetic blends are most common. The synthetics mentioned for underwear and insulating layers are lightweight, relatively non-absorbent and quick drying. Wool and wool blends, the historic and well-tested standards, are more absorbent, heavier and slower to dry. They are still very good insulators when wet *Shell layer* candidates are dominated by waterproof nylon and breathable liner/nylon (shells), and goose down/nylon shell (insulating, dry-weather shells). Note that classic wool outdoors gear (particularly pants and heavy shirts) can be bought cheaply at thrift, war surplus and army-navy stores. Better fit, better looking and “low itch” wool-blend and synthetic outfits can be found at most outdoor recreation stores at increased expense.

Heavy Jacket/Parka. Well-insulated jackets of various materials and down parkas are necessary as the outer insulating layer in cold weather. In inclement weather, they can be worn under waterproof rain gear.

Because of weight and bulk limits on pack-in trips, *goose-down parkas* (down liner with ripstop nylon shell) are the reigning standard with tremendous insulation per weight when dry. They lose all insulating value when wet and take an appreciable time to dry. Down parkas come in sleeved (with either a light or heavy hood for the head) and sleeveless versions. For outdoor activities at freezing temperatures or warmer, a quality-sewn, roughly 18-ounce long-sleeved down parka (about 10-12 ounces for the vest version) will generally suffice. For colder activities, one might consider a down parka in the 24-30 ounce range and 36 ounces or above for high altitude mountain expeditions. Though seldom worn when performing high-exertion activities, down parkas are unexcelled for cold hours in camp, bivouacs and emergencies.

The parka selected should drop well below the waist and be roomy enough to accommodate the clothing layers below. There is a strong preference for parkas which have a waist cinch belt, a full-length zipper with protective overflap, a deep set of pockets for the hands, and Velcro pocket closures. The parka hood should be roomy enough to allow wearing a pullover hat and have a drawstring for securing the hood snugly around the face

Another option is a heavy *polyester pile jacket*. Most backcountry pile garments are made of polyester, which is a better insulator than its nearest competitor, nylon. However, nylon does hold its shape better and offers less wearing friction. The term "pile" is generally used for several fabrics made from the same base material, which is napped by machine to give its terry-cloth-like texture. Garments napped on the outside are referred to as "fleece" and on both sides as "bunting." True pile is fleece that has been put through an additional process to enhance its bulk. Because of their open texture, most piles provide little protection from wind, unlike the shell-covered down parkas. In high-wind settings, they are typically worn with a windbreaker.

Jackets are very popular in cool weather or as an outer insulating layer in very cold weather under conditions of exertion. (Yes, you do get to take breaks. Simply don an additional warming layer when you start getting cool.) When combined with other heavy insulating layers, pile jackets can also serve well in very cold temperatures in camp. They are available in both vest and long-sleeve, high-neck and hooded, and in zippered or pullover styles. These jackets are slightly heavier and bulkier for a given comfort temperature than down, but they insulate when wet and dry quickly.

Long-Sleeve Shirt. Buy a shirt which has lengthy tails sufficient to tuck into pants and a collar and sleeves that can be buttoned or cinched. The latter features make shirts great ventilators. Adjustments to temperature and level of exertion are made simply by buttoning and unbuttoning. Wool-blend shirts of varying weights are very popular as are a variety of synthetics such as polyester and polypropylene. In milder weather, whether for purposes of warmth or to keep the sun off of your torso, look into lighter, breathable shirts (e.g., two-ply, treated ripstop nylon with a mesh lining or lighter-weight versions of the first-mentioned shirts above).

Sweater/Turtleneck. An outstanding combination for the inner insulating layer in cold weather is a sweater over a shirt or a turtleneck under a shirt (our personal preference). The *sweater or turtleneck* weight and style selection varies with the weather conditions under which you plan to use them. Garment weights exist which support the range of activities from high-altitude mountaineering to protecting the camp chair on a cool evening. Pure pullover styles minimize heat loss but do not allow for ventilating. Full- or partial-zippered models make up for that shortfall at some expense in warmth. A quality turtleneck can provide in the range of 5-10 °F in comfort temperature and fully shelters the neck. Wool, wool-blend and polyester fleece are typical of the preferred materials.

For lighter activities and warmer conditions, there are also lightweight turtlenecks that we refer to as *turtleneck "T"-shirts*. They are made in a multitude of materials, including cotton blends. However, stick to the excellent outdoor materials such as polyester and polypropylene which readily wick moisture away from the body, dry quickly and retain body heat even when wet.

Long Pants. Buy a little extra in length if you will be wearing these over hiking boots or foul-weather boots, loose enough in the waist to allow tucking in heavy shirts and baggy enough to be comfortable sitting, standing, bending or during exertion. Deep pockets (front, side and rear) for storage and buttonable/cinchable overflaps on front and rear pockets to protect from loss of gear are preferred by many outdoorspeople.

Lava Lake, Oregon

Pants with zippered sections near the ankles have the advantage that they can be pulled on directly over boots. This is a particularly nice feature when shifting from shorts to long pants or adding a layer of long pants over full-length thermal underwear. (Yes, folks, an ever-growing popular method of stomping around at high altitude in the middle of the day is to wear long johns with a pair of overshorts.) See GLACIER/WINTER CLIMBING for the option to wear knickers.

Some of the most popular materials are wool, wool blends and synthetic pile. Note that you can get some real bargains in army surplus stores on long pants. Other wool items such as shirts, scarves and pullover hats are available, but appear to be less in stock over the recent years.

Hiking/Camp Shorts. When weather permits, nothing beats shorts. Most shorts' materials are comfortable cotton twill or more rugged cotton canvas. Outdoor favorites are cargo shorts with deep pockets and the additional bonus of a set of covered pockets in front. Our preference is Velcro versus buttons, snaps or zippers for covered pockets. These items are equally handy underway on the water.

Hat (pullover and wide brim). Hats serve to protect the head from heat, cold, wind and wet. An unprotected head can account for one-third to one-half of the body's heat loss, thus it needs to be cooled during body overheating and insulated when the body is chilled. A *rain hat with brim* can double as sun protection. A *battered-wool felt hat* serves well in cold and rain. Brimmed hats should have a tie so that they do not fly away in a wind gust. A warm, insulating *pull-over* cap of wool, polyester or pile to fit under the parka hood is necessary in cold weather. They generally cover the head and ears. A *balaclava* or wool stocking hat with limited facial exposure covers both head and neck. Some carry a *wool scarf* for the neck in addition to the pull-over cap or balaclava. In the sun, many use a sweat band or handkerchief/bandanna knotted at the corners and dampened periodically with water. Others use a brimmed hat with attached handkerchief to protect the neck and sometimes the face.

Underwear. For light activities in mild-to-hot weather, the options are simple. *Fishnet briefs or boxer shorts* and *fishnet long- or short-sleeved tops* (loose or tight weave) of polyester or polypropylene allow the body to breathe and wick away moisture to the outer garments. These same underwear are available in solid, paneled designs in the same materials. Follow the synthetics' washing instructions carefully -- for example, some polypropylene products can become abrasive if machine dried. (Ouch!)

For more challenging endeavors, the under layer of a multi-layered active person's outdoor outfit plays an important role for overall warmth. In addition to basic insulation, it should transport (wick) perspiration away from the skin, providing a dry, comfortable environment. This inevitably leads to considering *thermal underwear*. The most effective wicking/insulating underwear currently on the market are mostly 100% polyester or predominantly polyester with small amounts of material such as Spandex for cuffs, neck and waistbands. Desirable properties are high warmth per weight; odor, mildew and stain resistance; and machine washability. Wicking ability is an inherent fabric property, although there are excellent designs which use special treatments in fabrics that do not wash or wear out. Single-faced, bi-faced (e.g., inner face of soft, high-profile pile against the skin and a flat-pile outer face to wick moisture) and double-faced underwear for extreme cold activities are available.

Thermal underwear *weight* selection should be governed by the type of activity planned, with consideration for whether it is solely for daytime or must double for overnight use. Typical total (top plus bottom) outfit weights are 10-16 ounces. *Lightweight underwear* are for mild weather or highly aerobic activities in cool conditions, typically including HIKING, BACKPACKING, BICYCLE TOURING, MOUNTAIN BIKING, NORDIC SKIING, SNOWSHOEING, trail running, CANOEING and KAYAKING. *Middleweight underwear* are best suited for stop-and-go activities in cold weather, particularly VEHICLE-ACCESSIBLE CAMPING in winter, BACKPACKING, ALPINE SKIING/SNOWBOARDING, NORDIC SKIING/SNOWSHOEING CANOEING and KAYAKING. They also are suitable for lower-exertion activities in cold/windy conditions such as SNOWMOBILING, SAILING, POWERBOATING and both INLAND and SEA FISHING. *Expedition weight underwear* are for outdoor activities in extreme cold, particularly GLACIER/WINTER CLIMBING, but also VEHICLE-ACCESSIBLE CAMPING in winter, BACKPACKING, NORDIC SKIING and SNOWSHOEING. Lightweight gear generally comes in crew neck-style tops, while middleweight and expedition weight items offer both crew neck and turtleneck options. Lightweight- and medium-weight bottoms may be full length, briefs or men's boxer shorts. Expedition-weight bottoms are mainly full length or one can purchase an integral top-bottom set of "long johns," reminiscent of Wallace Beery in the old flicks.

Gloves/Mittens. For VEHICLE-ACCESSIBLE CAMPING in winter, HIKING, BACKPACKING, ALPINE SKIING/SNOWBOARDING, NORDIC SKIING/SNOWSHOEING and GLACIER/ WINTER CLIMBING activities, *mittens* are better than *gloves* for warmth since your fingers are snuggled together. For additional warmth, a heavy mitten can be worn over the glove. Best fit is a snug glove and looser mitten with inner mitt and outer mitt length sufficient to cover the wrist and lap under or over the parka sleeve. Preferred materials are wool, polyester or pile. Synthetic pile can be wrung out when wet and maintains most of its insulating loft. Though an excellent insulator when wet, wool is not quite as effective as pile.

For CANOEING, KAYAKING and SAILING, gloves are a must. They spare the hands when paddling or when tending lines. Particularly for the first two activities, use of gloves will also reduce the risk of getting Carpal Tunnel Syndrome. Detailed glove characteristics and tradeoffs for these waterborne activities are found in subsequent sections. Refer to the INDEX for the location of those descriptions.

Windbreaker. The primary function of the windbreaker is to cut down wind chill. In cold weather, it fits over your clothing, providing critical outer-shell insulation. These are typically *unlined nylon wind shirts with a hood* and either cinches or drawstrings at the waist and head and cinch bands at the wrists. The most robust designs have hoods that are roomy enough for a hat, fit well up over the chin and have a face tunnel as opposed to a bare opening. The skirt extends almost to the knees. Pullover designs have no zippers (with their incumbent problems of binding up or freezing shut), providing greatest warmth. Zippered designs may lose slightly more heat, but can be opened or closed depending on ambient conditions. Large tooth nylon zippers are best. Large slash pockets on the front with buttons or zippers are useful for warming hands or storing gear. They are light and compact enough to stuff into a pocket, but have very little resistance to rain. The windbreaker should be tightly woven. Quality can be determined by trying to blow through the material and observing resistance.

There are also *water-resistant shells* which serve to break the wind as well as shed water in light rain or moisture. They are made of specially-coated nylon (moderately breathable) or lightweight fibers/microfibers with superfine weaves (highly breathable). These garments will become soaked in a heavy rain. They are lightweight, highly compressible/stowable and cost significantly less than waterproof/breathable shells. The nylon-coated shell is most useful for HIKING, BICYCLE TOURING, MOUNTAIN BIKING and ALPINE SKIING/SNOWBOARDING activities at limited exertion levels, while the superfine-weave shell is geared for those activities at higher exertion levels, as well as trail running and NORDIC SKIING.

Raingear. The perfect or near-perfect rainwear is yet to be designed. Regardless of activity, a discussion of rainwear will get all participants in an emotional state. One option is a full-length *poncho*. This is effectively a rain proof blanket with a hood. A coated nylon poncho can double as a tarpaulin and weighs about 3/4 pound. It sheds rain and allows significant air circulation. Its problems are that it is cumbersome, mainly restricted to use in camps and on open hiking trails. It flies around in gusting wind and becomes a hazard if one goes into the water (e.g., white-water canoeing or slipping into a fast-running creek). Another drawback is that the makeshift sleeves serve as a perfect sluiceway for rain with each canoe paddle stroke when the elbow is raised above the shoulder.

South Fork, American River, California

A *cagoule* is a roomy knee-length pullover parka in conjunction with rain-proof chaps used below the knees. It provides good air circulation and the coated (nominally polyurethane) rip-stop nylon fabric makes it lightweight and compact.

The minimum coating density considered desirable is one ounce per square yard. This fabric is somewhat vulnerable to rips and tears and loses its water-proof properties with heavy use. It is also a hazard (though less so than a poncho) if one goes into the water.

A *rain suit* is a combination pair of rain-proof pants in combination with a parka for the upper extremities. Uppers may be full zip-front or pullover (partial-zipper) designs. Most rain suits have terrific water-repellent characteristics and are form fitting, thus easy to move in and not a hazard in water dunkings. They are also great for sitting glissades on snowy mountain slopes. However, the less-expensive rip-stop nylon models have the same fabric liabilities as cagoules. Further, under exertion, the wearer is effectively enclosed in a "steambath." They are great for pure CAMPING, where even moderate-exertion activities are minimal.

Foul-weather gear for SAILING and POWERBOATING is somewhat specialized. Some of this gear is too heavy and bulky for any of the pack-in activities. The details of this gear are discussed under "Foul-Weather Suit" in the SAILING activity.

A much improved, but very expensive option for many activities, is to buy a *breathable rain suit*. One option is the *water-resistant shell* discussed under the "Windbreaker" item above. The next step up in performance, versatility and cost is a *waterproof/breathable shell* . These shells are truly waterproof, yet are designed to let the body breathe during high-exertion phases of HIKING, BACKPACKING, GLACIER/WINTER CLIMBING, BICYCLE TOURING, MOUNTAIN BIKING and NORDIC SKIING. There are many designs, so the Goretex construction is used as an example. The core of these garments is a special membrane that restricts the entry of larger-size raindrops, but allows the transport of smaller-size body moisture droplets outward. In their two-layer shell model, the membrane is bonded to a durable nylon fabric -- a separate liner is then added to protect the membrane. In the three-layer design, a liner fabric is bonded directly to the inside of the membrane. The three-layer option is most lightweight, breathable and durable. Ensure that you follow the care instructions if you purchase any of the breathable designs on the market.

A well-constructed rain suit of any type will have a roomy hood to allow wearing a hat underneath, will have a taut over cover for any zippered areas, pockets in both pants and oversuit, quality cinch bands at the waist, wrists and near the ankles. Ensure that the suit is loose fitting and has rain-protected "breathing" outlets at the underarms and on the back, the latter located under a protective flap. The most efficient venting systems generally use a mesh insert sewn into the upper back and shoulder areas. Top-of-the-line models most often have Velcro snaps or zippers at these locations so that the wearer can loosen up or tighten down for comfort and/or air flow. Finally, zippered areas near the ankles allow slipping the pants over any type of boots or shoes.

Waterborne adventurers, particularly those involved with CANOEING and KAYAKING have gravitated towards foul-weather gear that has its own unique properties. This equipment is covered for those activities in subsequent sections

Hiking Boots/Shoes. Working foot gear may have as much or more to do with the positive or negative outcome of an outdoor activity than most other gear. This is one of the most important areas not to hedge on expense. Do a lot of research and carefully test the boots and learn how to prepare and maintain (e.g., waterproofing, cleaning) them. Put the boots through a careful and lengthy break-in prior to taking the "big" trip.

For VEHICLE-ACCESSIBLE CAMPING, *general-purpose athletic shoes* should be suitable. Think about upgrading to (or adding) a set of lightweight (lowtop or hightop) hiking boots if your plans include active exploration around the camping area. Low tops are great for hiking on roads or quality trails. Think hard about high tops if your itinerary includes hiking on poorly-maintained trails or rocky surfaces in general. For rain or snow camping, consider bringing boots more of the type described in the HIKING or CANOEING activities or the apres-ski boots discussed in the ALPINE SKIING/SNOWBOARDING activity.

Socks. While camping in mild weather and performing light recreation activities such as short hikes on quality trails or guarding your favorite camp chair, streetwear cotton socks will usually serve the purpose. This is also true for that easygoing power-boat trip. Even for these lighter activities, however, consider more comfortable and durable outdoor *casual socks* of cotton/nylon. Another option is to get light *athletic socks* which offer thin, dense padding underfoot and are made of numerous blends such as wool/nylon, acrylic/stretch nylon or polyester/stretch nylon. Seek out socks which have the wicking properties to keep feet dry. Some are double-layered to prevent blisters. Consider athletic socks for such activities as VEHICLE-ACCESSIBLE CAMPING, light HIKING, BICYCLE TOURING, MOUNTAIN BIKING, light CANOEING or KAYAKING, SAILING, POWERBOATING AND FISHING under mild weather conditions.

Siskiyou National Forest, Oregon

For use in inclement weather, emphasize selection of athletic socks which maintain insulating qualities when wet and which can readily wick moisture away from the feet. (Most blends noted above will suffice, provided that the blend is heavily weighted toward the wool, acrylic and polyester components.) See the HIKING section for more robust options.

Boot insoles or *inserts* added to the boot interior provide insulation and cushioning. They will add to your comfort for casual hiking and, for more serious hiking endeavors, are considered essential gear by many. If you intend to use them, bring the insoles when trying on new boots. Insoles of felt, leather and lambskin absorb moisture and must be removed when drying boots. Opt for synthetic insoles, which are non-absorbent, do not become matted when damp, and have a loose structure that aids foot ventilation.

Camp Shoes/Land Shoes. Provided the activity allows the additional weight and bulk, nothing beats getting out of a pair of hiking boots, rain boots or the like into a pair of light comfortable shoes. With proper choice, some activities like MOUNTAIN BIKING may be amenable to comfortable *dual shoe use* (the biking shoe is used for camping, not the opposite). By far, the general activity favorite is a pair of *broken-in athletic shoes*, low top or high top as preferred by the user. Some have a special pair that are devoted to the ravages of wet ground, rocks, mud or other natural challenges that beat up or dirty up everyday "dress" athletic shoes. These shoes should still be in good physical shape, including having good tread. For pack trips in snow or cold, a few have paid the additional price for a pair of *rubber-soled down booties*. The booties should have a drawstring near the ankles to maintain the shoes on the foot when walking around the campsite. These niceties can be worn in the sleeping bag to keep feet toasty warm.

In warm weather, some choose to wear *sandals*. The most common (and lowest price) models have a heavy, treaded sole, thick leather upper straps and quality stitching. Manufacturers such as Teva tout their sandals as active sportswear on land or in water. The upper end of the line features models claiming topsoles that allow cooling airflow and water drainage from underfoot, a form-fitting, easy-to-adjust strap system that hugs your feet and durable neoprene pads that cushion the feet from straps and posts. All sandals can trap sand and gravel under the straps, which can prove to be very uncomfortable over time -- they should be cleared out before you cast off from the beach. The latter shoe-types are proving to be extremely popular for warm-weather CANOEING, KAYAKING and WATERSPORTS.

Gaiters. Gaiters may be useful for stomping around the camp area or doing hikes out of the campsite in snow. Campers hiking in areas of loose rock or gravel will also appreciate these simple marvels. See the HIKING activity for more detail.

Bandanna/Sweatband. These items keep that wet, salty stuff from attacking your eyeballs when you are pushing it on hot days. Either can be peppered with mosquito repellent to help drive these insidious creatures away from the face. The bandanna is the more versatile of the two. It can be worn at the neck, on the brow or stuffed under a hat and used as a Foreign Legion-type of neck protector.

Hand/Foot Warmers. Most *battery-operated warmers* are held in the pockets and hands. (There are some gloves and mittens specifically designed to incorporate hand warmers.) They typically have operating lives of hours to a day at a nearly constant temperature of 140-150 °F. One-time-use *chemical warmers* are carried in a similar fashion, however there are also specially-designed toe warmers. Once activated, these foot warmers are placed on the outside bottom of your socks using the integral adhesive strips provided. For all chemically-driven designs, simply removing the outer package and exposing the inner packet to air activates the warmer. A nominal brand will provide an average 130-140 °F source for 6-7 hours. Highest temperature is at activation, dropping to near body temperature at end of life.

Head Netting. Many activities are not amenable to having the mesh canopy previously described. The best backup may be to bring sufficient *mosquito netting* to fit over a brimmed hat (this keeps the netting from laying directly on the face) with room to tuck the netting around the neck. During the day this also serves as a face and neck sunscreen, providing limited ultraviolet light exposure reduction. With clever selection (or some cutting and shaping), the netting can serve campsite double duty in and out of the tent. There are specialty models for hiking which fit over the head or a small-brimmed hat. They have a lightweight ring that holds the netting out away from the face. The netting lower edge is at the shoulders.

Hygiene.

Towel & Wash Cloth. Bring along your favorites if gear weight and bulk are not issues. Otherwise limit yourself to one of each and plan to wash them out at every opportunity. Ultimate lightweighters have been known to bring along a wash cloth and extra paper towels.

Biodegradable Soap and Shampoo. Few outdoor recreation areas (other than some larger, vehicle-accessible campsites) and limited watercraft are equipped with a shower; consider it a bonus. For those circumstances, enjoy an experience that is like eating food outdoors -- it is twice as good as at home! Most outdoor recreation enthusiasts will settle for clean hands and face for a couple of days and a dip in the water whenever it is available and not too cold.

If you bathe in the outdoors, stick to biodegradable products and use them with care. First, ensure that you *know the rules for 'dipping'* in the outdoors -- in some areas, it is illegal. Do not ever bathe directly in creeks, streams, rivers or lakes if you are using any type of soap; it pollutes and encourages growth of non-indigenous algae that tend to eventually stagnate the water source. For soap bathes, take a sponge bath out of a container or get a sun shower -- in any case, bathe well away from any sources of water.

On many smaller watercraft at sea, fresh water is at a premium. One option is to hop in and take a periodic saltwater wash-cloth-only bath. For extended trips, or if this solution seems too barbaric, consider purchasing one of several liquid soaps on the market that produce suds in saltwater.

Personal Toiletries and Ditty Bag. Like most everything else, convenience dictates a separate storage site for personal toiletries. Where space and weight are key, most can fit their needs into a large zip-lock or pressure-lock bag. Typical items: toothbrush, toothpaste, dental floss, tooth picks, soap, shampoo, toilet paper, hair brush, nail clippers, cotton swabs, mini sewing kit, sanitary napkins, plastic shaver/razor (if you must) and mirror (a metal signaling mirror serves a dual use).

If your activities permit taking additional items, consider what you take when on a non-outdoor vacation and start eliminating until you get to a satisfactory set.

Toilet Paper and Towelettes. Leaves are OK. Avoid bark. The best bet is to bring a suitably-sized partial roll of your favorite TP. Store it in a large zip-lock or pressure-lock plastic food bag. Some also carry chemically-treated towelettes as a follow-up cleaner. This is a serious consideration if you may go for an extended period without bathing.

Toilet Trowel. In many outdoor areas, you may be encouraged to bury your waste. The trowel assists this action and can also serve as an aid to extinguishing campfires with dirt and can provide other ingenious uses (that you will think up when on your own adventure).

Angeles National Forest, California

Sun Shower. A sun shower is effectively a plastic bag that is filled with water and left to heat in the sun. The user simply hangs the bag in some suitable location, stands underneath, and allows the shower head to spray warm water. The lightest option is a one-ounce shower assembly, essentially plastic tubes and a small showerhead, used with a collapsible water bag. Specialized water showers (not for carrying potable water) with up to 2-1/2 gallon capacities weigh in at about the 12-ounce range. The most practical models have a sturdy carrying/hanging handle.

Clothespins. We submit that this is primarily a favorite of folks on extended trips which do not require "carrying the trip on one's back." In the backcountry, such items as safety pins and small electrical alligator clips can be substituted. (We solicit differences of opinion on this one.) Bring some nylon cord as a clothesline.

Laundry Bag. Use a cloth, wide-mesh bag of a size to fit your needs. This keeps "dirty wear" in a breathable area but separate from your other gear. Some outdoor gear comes with a breathable mesh outer pocket(s) (e.g., panniers, backpacks), which can be used for the same purpose.

Portable Toilet and Liners. Some outdoor adventures such as canoeing portions of the Green River in Utah require that outdoorsmen pack out their human waste. Most common is a 3-5 pound fold-up unit which stands on four legs when deployed. It has a contoured seat and is equipped with plastic disposal bags. For camping and those boating activities with plenty of carry room, lugable plastic, bucket-style chemical toilets with hinged seats are the norm. Typical dimensions are 14-inch diameter and comparable height. The lower-capacity models weigh in the 6-10 pound area when empty.

Safety

First Aid Kit. See the discussion under TEN ESSENTIALS and the separate, comprehensive checklist and limited equipment discussion in the FIRST AID section.

Water Filter/Tablets. Sadly, the quality of water below timberline in many mountain areas and in most near-urban waterways is suspect. Humans, cattle and industrial waste have all contributed. *Water filters* remove protozoa (e.g., giardia and cryptospordia) and bacteria (e.g., cholera and salmonella), the most common waterborne pests in North America. For added protection or extended travels in regions where viruses (e.g., hepatitis A and B) are a concern, consider getting a *water purifier* which also incorporates iodine treatment. Viruses, small and difficult to simply filter, are least common in industrialized countries. Most common pint-container-sized water filters and purifiers can provide drinkable water at rates of about 1/2 to 1-1/2 liters per minute and weight from 8-24 ounces. For large groups, candidate options are to carry high-volume pumps, gravity-fed models or to bring multiple water filters.

The control filter unit will eventually need cleaning or replacement, although some units advertise ability to provide 1000's of gallons of clean water first. Some can be cleaned in the field, others not. For extended trips, bring the necessary cleaning gear, replacement filters and parts or carry alternate water treatment sources. Boiling water is 100% effective against all pests, but requires hauling along extra fuel.

Chemicals are light, inexpensive and a good backup if the filter or purifier becomes inoperable. *Iodine* is effective against both bacteria and viruses, as well as protozoa in clear, warm to cool water. It does impart its own odor and taste (removable by strainers or filter cores that use carbon). It requires a longer contact time and elevated dosages in cold or murky water; however, even then it is rated as only 85% effective by the Environmental Protection Agency (EPA). *Halazone*, a form of chlorine, works well when used within its shelf life, but only under near-ideal conditions. It's performance with cold, murky water, however, is in question. It is being stocked less and less in outdoor recreation outlets.

If you use iodine (it comes in tablet and crystalline form), bring it in its original tightly sealed container. Note that you can mask the chemical taste that it imparts by mixing the water with a fruit drink or by adding Vitamin C tablets.

Another option, the oldest and safest, is to *boil your water*. This will cost you stove fuel and time and "flatten" the natural water taste. Though the recommended boiling time to kill human pathogens has classically been 5-10 minutes, there are studies underway that may eventually recommend that simply bringing the water to a hard boil will be sufficient. Until this recommendation is officially tendered, however, we recommend that you stick to the classic boiling cycle.

Where relatively safe sources of water are available (e.g., springs, virgin snow fields), some folks bring *coffee filters* to strain out soil and other natural debris. This use is more a matter of producing aesthetically-pleasing water than of protecting your health.

Sunglasses and Lanyard. See the discussion under TEN ESSENTIALS.

Reading Glasses & Repair Kit. If needed, *glasses* are particularly important for activities requiring map and compass reading. Consider prescription sunglasses where bright sun and glare could be a problem. Strap the glasses on with a lanyard which goes around the neck. Place in a standard and convenient location when not in use. Consider bringing a small eyeglass *repair kit*, which contains a mini-screwdriver, eyeglass screws and a small plastic magnifying glass.

If you require prescription glasses for normal daily activity, it is hard to envision that you wouldn't bring them along. Thus, a separate checklist entry is not provided for this item. Strongly consider bringing an extra pair, however.

Nylon Cord. No matter what the activity, bring along some strong, light nylon cord. The amount and width of cord varies with the activity; as a rough guide, we generally take 50 feet of 1/8-inch diameter cord on remote tours and 100 feet for drive-in and boat-in camping activities. Some potential uses are tent guy-line extension, general tarpaulin use, dining canopy/mesh screen construction, hanging clotheslines, hanging food sacks on bear lines or trees, transferring day packs/ rucksacks/backpacks across creeks or down cliff faces, bundling collected downed firewood, tying down equipment in boats, portaging mountain bikes up or down steep slopes, tying canoes together, etc.

Pocket Knife. Refer to the TEN ESSENTIALS section.

Sunscreen. Sun protection is a necessity for most outdoor adventures. This is true for both clear and cloudy days. For VEHICLE-ACCESSIBLE CAMPING, a *high SPF sunscreen* (15, or up to 45 for sensitive skin) will be more than adequate; this will protect you from the burning ultraviolet rays.

Activities in the snow, at high altitude and on water are the chief offending environments, the former because of intense sunlight and the latter because of sunlight combined with a frequent lack of external (clothing) cover. By far the best protection is clothing, even though covering up may sometimes be uncomfortable. For GLACIER/WINTER CLIMBING, ALPINE SKIING/SNOWBOARDING and NORDIC SKIING/SNOWSHOEING, sea KAYAKING and SAILING, the best bet is actor's *grease paint* or *zink oxide paste*. They give virtually complete protection and do not wash off with perspiration. One application per day is sufficient except where the paste is worn off with activity. People with a susceptibility to fever blisters should use a total *sun-blocking cream* or zink oxide on the lips continuously.

For lengthy water-related activities, consider zink oxide for sensitive spots such as noses or lips. A high SPF sunscreen can be used elsewhere. Manufacturers' claims for some lotions is that a generous application will provide rub-proof and water-proof protection for eight hours. A conservative approach is to apply every few hours or whenever those little "voices" say you need more.

Sunscreen, lip balm and insect repellents cause a skin reaction for some. Test these products at home or on short tours before you commit to their use on a lengthy outdoor venture.

Lip Balm. For less solar intense activities, any commercial lip balm applied frequently will keep lips from becoming dry and cracking over periods of long exposure. For higher sun-exposure conditions, specifically get lip balms containing p-amino benzoic acid (PABA) or zink oxide. This will also keep your smoochability factor high.

Insect Repellent. Other than being low on water, being too cold or too hot or having feet that are killing you, few things can spoil an outing like a steady insect swarm. Complete coverage by clothing and fine netting is the best defense, but rarely practical. *Colors* have an effect on repelling insects, with orange found to work best, followed in order by yellow, green and white. Intense or bright colors, as opposed to drab, are best. Consider wearing long sleeve, button-collar shirts or turtlenecks, sewing shirt cuffs shut, wearing cinches around trouser bottoms or tucking trousers into high sox, or using netting.

Beyond this, insect repellents may be necessary. For general purpose use N, N-diethyl-metatoluamide (*diethyl toluamide or DEET*), has been judged most effective by military and leading commercial vendors. One generous application (over all exposed areas) of one of the stronger concentrations generally lasts a few hours in camp but may be reduced significantly during periods of high exertion. (Sweating and evaporation are the key culprits of repellent loss.) Neckerchiefs, headbands and head netting peppered with repellent are also useful. DEET is marketed in concentrations up to about 75% active ingredients and manufacturer's claim it is effective against mosquitoes, flies, no-see-ums, chiggers and ticks.

Sparks Lake, Oregon

There are many of us that question DEET's effectiveness against biting flies. Consider using *ethyl-hexanediol* or *dimethyl phthalate* against black flies and deer flies. (Unfortunately, these chemicals don't do much to ward off mosquitoes.) Repellent forms are cream, lotion stick, aerosol spray and foam.

There is a small camp that suggests that thiamine (a B Vitamin) in your blood tends to repel mosquitoes. Though we have not tried it, there are slow-release thiamine tablets made expressly for this purpose. A new (and again, untested by us) natural product on the market is Bite Blocker, containing a mixture of soybean oil, geranium oil and coconut oil. Its manufacturer claims that it is 97% effective for more than three hours after application. We have tried to binge on garlic several days before a trip, but we remain unconvinced that it made us any less of "mosquito bait." If you decide to try the latter route, there are odorless tablets that you can take that will keep you from smelling like an Italian pasta dish.

Whistle. A whistle is useful for VEHICLE ACCESSIBLE CAMPING for position communication when wandering around the camp area. One camper, left unnamed, relates to losing his way back to the campsite at dusk after dropping off dinner scraps to a bear-proof trash container. (Well, it was a large well-forested campground!?) A set of whistles divided between participants would have been helpful.

For more remote land adventures, whistles also serve for position communication and as a means for gaining attention, particularly when one is lost or in trouble. It can also be used as a noisemaker to scare off unfriendly animals. Some outdoorspeople develop a simple message communication system for periods when they are intentionally or accidentally separated.

We are not aware of a quality hierarchy of whistles for general outdoor use, so buy a *plain old cheap model*. A metal or hard-plastic is preferred since sportsmen in camp are known to sit and step on anything breakable. (An exception: For sub-zero weather usage, look for a whistle with materials that won't freeze to your lips.) Tie a small cord loop to the whistle to allow wearing around the neck or keep it in an easily accessible spot.

In waterborne activities, it is standard practice to have a whistle which is attached to your PFD. The key purpose is to signal distress or to warn other boaters or jet-skiers of your presence. Special Coast Guard-sanctioned whistles and those for cold-water usage are discussed in the KAYAKING section.

Flashlight, Extra Batteries and Bulb. Refer to the TEN ESSENTIALS section .

Fire Starter/Heat Tabs. Refer to the TEN ESSENTIALS section.

Emergency Blanket. These lightweight, compact, space-age blankets have been lifesavers, used as body-heat-saving devices in wind, rain and snow. A contingency item, these Mylar blankets are about the size of an average-size soap bar when packaged. They weigh on the order of two ounces and fold out into a typical 4-1/2 feet x 7 feet life shield. (They have also served as great "snuggle-up" devices around the campfire.) Once unpackaged, they will never come close to fitting into the original container.

There are also heavier-duty, more-durable versions of this blanket. Though not as light and small as the above design, they are refoldable and some come with a storage pouch. They also are warmer and can be used in camp for other purposes, e.g., as a ground cloth under the tent or in the tent interior or, with a little engineering, as a hanging sunshade. These heavy-duty models fold out to about the dimensions above and weigh about 10 ounces. Some have grommets on each corner to aid in rigging them to suit the occasion.

Timepiece. For many activities, a timepiece is invaluable for trip planning. It is important to determine when to turn around on an up-and-back trip, when to set up camp or push on to the next camping area, or when to seek help for an overdue outdoor partner. A timepiece is also useful as a complimentary means of estimating your location on remote trips. It also can be used to measure heart rate if needed. Best bet is to set aside an *inexpensive wrist watch* for this use. (Other than for activities where a chronometer is required for navigational accuracy.) Wear the watch below protective clothing in inclement weather. Under extreme conditions (e.g., whitewater canoeing/kayaking), bag the watch in a watertight resealable plastic bag and tuck in a pocket or where easily accessible. A more expensive option is to get a *water resistant watch*. Good watches with water resistance to 100-200 feet depth are available at a nominal additional outlay. Consider leaning toward watches advertised as "sports" watches as they tend to have improved shock resistance.

Thermometer. In many cases, a thermometer is simply a device that confirms why you are too hot or too cold. It is useful for storytelling, when you tell your soulmate or Aunt Mary that you were winter climbing or snowmobiling in -20 °F weather or dunking in the river while the surrounding desert environs were roasting at 120 °F. Outdoorsmen, when subjected to periods of non-activity, have found innumerable other uses, ranging from the clever to the inane. The serious use of this device is to warn you when it is time to shut down an activity and make camp or return to the shelter of home base. This is particularly true if you record temperature changes that foretell the arrival of inclement weather. Note that the thermometer only measures the ambient temperature. You will need an estimate of the wind speed and a set of conversion tables to account accurately for the effect of wind chill.

For highly-active land-based activities, one good bet is a small thermometer with appropriate metal or plastic guarding over the exposed bulb to limit the likelihood of breakage. The most convenient and accessible models have a small latch that allows using it as a key chain or attaching it to anything with a buttonhole, zipper or latch. They are normally worn on the outer clothing layer and can be read "on the run." Many of these models have wind-chill conversion tables on their backs. For less rigorous activities, there are thermometers that come in a sealed plastic case which is equipped with a pocket clip. There are special underwater diving models, including some which are built into dive computers.

Twin Lakes, Colorado

Phone Change. Pack a couple of quarters for an emergency phone call, whether for car problems or to contact emergency assistance. Sound stupid for remote adventurers? We have some friends who saved a severe heart-attack victim on a Sierra Nevada Mountains hike. One backpacker high-tailed it out and got to a phone (at a "booked up" trailhead which they had been required to pass up on the ride in) a precious hour before he would have reached their original parking area. The lucky victim was helicoptered out and survived! Many recreational area roads now have emergency telephone boxes scattered along their length.

Pen and Notepad. It may be necessary to leave a note for one of your party members, rangers, or simply to record your thoughts. Bring some extra paper for games. Or you could bring this checklist and note gear additions/deletions for your next trip.

Accessories

Camera and Camera Supplies. A camera is a permanent way to capture memories of outdoor activities, both good and "bad." When we thought back about it, we have taken photos at times when things have gone very wrong (e.g., cross-country hiking when a planned trail junction was missed, portaging bicycles when it was found that the trail had caved in, reaching a dead-end inlet on a planned river shortcut or diversion, snow skiing in a worsening whiteout). These wound up being some of our most memorable and prized photos.

Key consideration for choosing a camera are weight, bulk, adaptability to environment and cost. Quality small or *miniature cameras* are available in abundance, weighing as little as several ounces and as small as a package of cards. Many carry reusable cameras although *throw-away cameras* (one-time use) are becoming more popular. Good scenic picture quality is available, but close-up portrait shots (less than a couple of feet) are inferior. Whereas *reusable cameras* are generally equipped with change-out lenses, you can buy standard format, wide-angle or panorama throw aways.

Another more-versatile option is the variable-format camera, with standard, wide-angle and panoramic modes that can be selected with little effort. (However, our experience is that the quality of these photos is not up to that obtained with a single-mode 35-millimeter camera of comparable optical aperture.) Finally, some 35-millimeter photographers may bring a 3:1 to 5:1 zoom lens, bulky, but very quick and flexible for picture formatting.

Both reusable and *throwaway underwater cameras* are available. Depth of operation for the lower-priced models is about ten feet. Higher-quality reusable underwater cameras with depth of use of 100 feet and below are also on the market. A middle option is to get one of the clear PVC cases on the market. It is designed to hold compact cameras and allows you to photograph down to about 60 feet. Check your diving or sporting goods shop for more detail on these options.

Many prefer aim-and-shoot cameras as opposed to focus cameras because some of the best outdoor recreation shots are spontaneous and short duration. Outdoor activists have been known to break camera lenses. If your lens is worth protecting, put a haze filer or other filter in front of the lens. Filters are relatively cheap to replace. Bring some extra film and a replacement battery(s), since a variation of Murphy's Law says that what can go wrong, will ... and at the worst possible time.

Camera packaging is a key consideration for many activities. The protective package should be large enough to hold camera and related gear (particularly a spare battery and bulb and a small cleaning kit with lens airbrush, cleaning fluid, and lens-cleaning paper). Some hikers, bicycle tourers, sailors, boaters and alpine skiers carry cameras in a fanny pack or in a small padded carry case strapped to the waist by passing a belt through the case loops. For mountain bikers, many pack the camera in a well-insulated shell inside a pannier, top-rack-mounted bag or handlebar bag. Storage location should be high on the bike if the trip involves water crossings. For activities in rough water, consider a water-proof camera or a water-proof storage container. The container should have a positive pressure, rubber seal -- test the container ahead of time for watertight integrity.

Bring a *tripod* for best quality photos or if you want to ensure that the entire gang is in the picture. A lightweight 1/2-inch diameter, six-inch length, plastic model with a Velcro-tipped canvas strip for tying the unit and camera to a tree or other vertical structure is the low end. There are many high quality tripods, at the expense of bulk, weight and cost, depending on your needs.

Binoculars. This item is useful for enhancing activity enjoyment, identifying distant landmarks or otherwise assisting in route finding (whether in the mountains, at sea or scouting out the next set of rapids). Binoculars are identified by two numbers. The first number is the magnification - a larger number indicating higher magnifying power. Magnifying powers greater then 10 make steady hand-viewing difficult, an added hindrance when under exertion. Consider higher magnifying powers for activities such as HIKING (combined with bird-watching or other nature-watching activities), SAILING, POWERBOATING and SEA FISHING (in calm weather) where binocular/telescope support is more likely available and gear weight and bulk are not issues. The second number is the size of the objective lens - the one furthest from the eyes. Dividing this number by the magnification yields the size of the exit pupil in millimeters (mm). The larger the exit pupil, the easier it is to maintain a clear image in spite of hand motion. Also, a larger exit pupil collects more light, allowing better viewing under low light conditions. Exit pupils in the 2.25 to 3.0 mm range should suffice for most uses, while 4.0 mm range or more is needed for viewing near dawn and dusk. Typical *formats* are 8x20, 8x25 and 10x25. Binocular *field of view* is the width of the area viewed in a single glance at 1000 yards. Fields of view of 250-500 yards are typical for most outdoor activities.

Center-controlled focusing is most convenient. Since the vision in each eye may vary, consider models which also have a secondary focus on one eye piece. Adjustable roll-down rubber collars enable use while wearing prescription glasses and sunglasses. The collars also protect the eye-glass lenses from scratches. The binoculars should have lens caps for storage.

Binoculars typically weight 5-10 ounces with *heavily-armored models* running out to 16 ounces and above. Glasses with high impact plastic, rubber armor, aluminum casing or other protective shock-resistant features are recommended for all strident outdoor activities. Strongly consider waterproof binoculars for waterborne activities such as CANOEING, KAYAKING, SAILING, POWERBOATING, WATERSPORTS, INLAND FISHING and SEA FISHING. Saltwater leakage into the interior casing, particularly, can cause damage to the internal hardware in a matter of days.

Kennedy Meadow, Dome Land, California

At the lower extreme is a *monocular*, about the size of a standard bar of soap, with typical formats of 4x15 or 6x20, which weigh as little as several ounces. They are meant for adventures where light-weighting is critical and provide you with modestly-improved views of distant landscapes, flora and fauna. At the upper end are heavy and bulky *telescopes*, usually on stabilizing platforms with lens magnifying powers of 100-200 or greater. They are geared for outings where setup time and resultant loss of some mobility are not an issue. For detail observation, such as identifying distinct features of varying bird types, the capability of the larger scopes is unparalleled.

There are also infrared binoculars and monoculars for *night viewing*. Both passive models and active designs with low-intensity illuminators are available in a limited array of formats. They are handy for checking out wildlife under low-light or dark conditions, whether within or outside the camping area. Note, however, that it is probably hard to justify the extra weight associated with these glasses for pack-in activities, since the practical gains are limited.

Wood Saw. With few exceptions, never head to the outdoors with the expectation of cooking or having a warming campfire using wood collected from the ecosystem. These exceptions are where it is necessary for survival or warmth under extreme circumstances, or where it is posted as acceptable. A *wood saw* is a contingency item for remote trips and a staple when used to cut up the chunks of wood that you bought from the camp overseers (e.g., USFS, national or state park rangers or commercial camp proprietors who oversee the area). Best saws for this use have widely separated and jagged teeth. Small folding saws of about a foot in length (the sharp teeth fold into a channeled handle) are most appropriate if you are packing in your gear. A two foot or larger length Swedish bow saw is ideal if you have space availability. Most saws of the latter type have a sleeve which can be placed over the blade; this is recommended to prevent the inadvertent tearing of stuff sacks and the like in transit.

Ax. The same rules that apply to the wood saw apply to the *wood ax*. These are a necessity if you are at a drive-to camping area that provides or sells wood rings (roughly 6-12 inch deep cross sections from trees over a foot in diameter). A typical wood ax has a 2-1/2- to 3-pound head and 28- to 30-inch handle. Handles are most commonly made of wood or metal. Wood absorbs the shock of the striking blow better, while metal has a longer life. Best bet is to get an ax with one cutting blade and a opposed flathead surface (in contrast to a two-bladed model). The flathead surface serves as a sledge for driving tent stakes and performing other neat campsite duties. Hand axes and hatchets serve primarily to split smaller pieces of wood, to create shavings, or to be used as a tent-stake driver (more conveniently than a bulky, full-size ax).

Shovel. For trips without weight and bulk limits, bring a shovel from home that allows covering embers from campfires after use (also douse thoroughly with water). Military pack shovels, found at army-navy type surplus stores, are smaller and lighter. They have a fold-up handle for convenient storage. Toilet trowels also serve the purpose, albeit with much smaller dirt volume per scoop.

Swim Suit and Life Preserver. While camping in the great outdoors we are partial to swim suits that are comfortable (maybe not so flashy) and dry quickly. For instance, nylon shorts and tops with the necessary mesh innards suit us fine. A handy extra feature is a suit with roomy, self-draining mesh pockets. Some women swear by the light, comfortable, single-piece Speedo suits for outdoor wear.

If swimming is in your plans, bring life preservers (more commonly called personal flotation devices or PFD's in the outdoor community), especially for all small children and any person who can't swim. There won't be lifeguards around for many outside-camp dips in lakes or streams! The PFD should have adjustable straps or other mechanisms to keep the device snug and secure against the body and sufficient buoyancy to keep the user's head above water without the need for paddling. PFD types are discussed in depth in the CANOEING section.

Portable Radio. Provided your radio can bring in a station or stations in your location, a radio might be useful for checking on *weather* conditions or tracking the status of potential emergency situations such as a local forest fire. This is probably not worth the weight for remote pack-in trips, but may be very useful for many other activities. Outdoor models on the market typically run on batteries, although some can be bought with adapters if a source of power is available. There is also a five-pound AM/FM/short-wave windup radio that provides up to an hour of playing time after a 30-second winding. Consider purchasing a model that can pick up a weak signal if you will be camping far from transmitting stations or in signal-blocking terrain.

People in remote camping areas who play their portable or car radios loudly for entertainment should consider staying home! We were unfortunate enough to camp in the serene San Jacinto Mountains of Southern California, only to have a group arrive in a van. Their first action in setting up their site was to pull two giant speakers out of their van and proceed to blast out the camping area. Between the camp ranger's and several other camper's visits over several hours, they finally decided to move on. Unfortunately, this discourteous camping style appears to be more prevalent than in the past.

San Bernardino National Forest, California

Brochures, Articles, Books. Bring along the information that describes how to get to the trailhead, provides general road maps of the area being visited, identifies key natural/man-made landmarks, gives information on flora or fauna, describes nearby rural/urban activities of interest, etc. Best bet is to keep the material together in a single container. Take along some pure pleasure reading that has nothing to do with anything, if you've got the space. (No job-related stuff allowed!)

Indoor and Outdoor Games. Cards and commercial board games are good general fun and a great way to pass the time when inclement weather drives you under protective cover. In good weather, outdoor games might include darts, horseshoes (provided the pits exist), badminton, catch (baseball, football, Frisbee etc.) -- the possibilities are endless.

Daypack/Rucksack/Fanny Pack. These articles are useful in carrying gear for hikes out of the campsite or for storage of odds and ends that you want to keep together while camping. Definitions vary, but day pack/rucksack/fanny pack refers to a range of small contoured packs just large enough to carry snacks and the TEN ESSENTIALS (fanny pack) to that for hauling the gear needed for a one-day summit climb (daypack/rucksack). The *fanny pack* straps around your waist. It is generally unobtrusive and designed to carry gear needed for modest hiking or exploring. Most likely, at this level, you can find a double duty for the model that you use for such activities as longer-distance jogging or alpine skiing. There are higher-powered versions with greater capacity and most often built with side pockets for a couple of water bottles and a couple of other exterior zippered recesses for quick accessibility to other must-have-access-to items. These are for fast-moving, motivated hikers and climbers with aggressive daytime objectives in friendly weather. See the HIKING activity for more information.

Frame Pack. Frame packs can serve secondary functions for many non-remote activities, e.g., as an additional storage unit or as a means to transport gear from car to camp (VEHICLE-ACCESSIBLE CAMPING) or boat (SAILING and POWERBOATING). However, it's primary purpose is to carry gear for activities such as BACKPACKING,

GLACIER/WINTER CLIMBING, NORDIC SKIING/SNOWSHOEING and CANOEING. See the BACKPACKING section for additional detail.

Toboggan/Sled and Plastic Sheet. Provided the terrain and snow conditions exist, a great winter activity is tobogganing or sledding. The poor man's option is to substitute heavy plastic sheeting (e.g., a polyethylene tarpaulin) which is large enough to support at least one person (four-foot square minimum) or a four-foot by seven-foot swath for more exotic multiple person or "mummy" (body-wrapped) sliding. For sledding and sliding, build a compressed snow runway first and then let her rip!

Auto Tire Chains and Antifreeze. Buy a set of chains or snow tires if there is the faintest hint that you will wander onto snow-laden roadways. One "slip-slide-rotate" adventure on an icy road will fully convince you! The best bet is to learn how to install tire chains well before wallowing under a car in the wet snow and cold with frozen mitts. (One trick to make chain installation easier is to lay out each chain, then place a small block of wood, which has been cut to size, between two adjacent cross-links -- do this for each tire. When you roll the car up on the two-by-four blocks, there is clearance between the chain and tire, allowing you greater freedom of chain adjustment.) Also put the antifreeze in the radiator before starting into potentially freezing weather. Use a variable weight motor oil (10-30 or 10-40 weight) which will provide the right oil viscosity in both hot and cold weather.

Additional items to consider for cold-weather: small broom to remove snow from the roof, hood and headlights; plastic trash bag or tarpaulin to lie on when applying tire chains; traction mats to provide additional tire traction; and snow shovel to remove snow from under the tires. It is assumed that all gear described in the TEN ESSENTIALS section is already packed into your automobile, regardless of season.

Automobile Tool Kit. Keep your vehicle operating instructions in the car. Bring a kit for basic common repairs which may be needed on the way to or from the activity. A simple kit: high-power flashlight or lantern, spare tire/tire-changing gear, large and small crescent wrenches, flat-head and Phillips-head screw drivers, socket wrench set, hose boot material/duct tape/spare hose clamps, extra motor oil and radiator coolant, battery jumper cables and road flares.

Spare Set of Keys/Credit Card/$. Minimize the number of keys that are taken on an activity and leave unneeded keys in the vehicle. As a backup, consider hiding an ignition and trunk key on the underside of the car chassis. Many products exist including magnetic boxes. Since magnetic devices have been known to sometimes fall off (violent bumps, dirty contact surfaces, gremlins, etc.), there may be a better option. First, find a fixed tubular structure (e.g., fixed strut, gas tank hose) under the car, ideally within easy access. Attach a hose clamp to the structure, slip the key(s) under the clamp and tighten it. The clamp can be loosened with a dime, a pocket knife blade or other readily available flat, thin object.

Bring a credit card (and personal identification) to cover large, unplanned expenses such as automobile repairs. There are many small, out-of-the-way stores and markets that don't accept "plastic," so bring some greenbacks. Note that few people accept personal I.O.U.'s in this day and age. Store away a package of quarters for phone calls -- collect calls may not be accepted.

Tool Kit

Tools. Bring any special tools which might be needed to repair camping gear, whether it is cooking equipment, a lantern, a heater or the classic wiggly camp chair. Many needed tools should already be in your automobile tool kit, or should be.

Repair Gear. Cloth tape for the tarpaulin and ripstop tape for parkas, bags and tent are useful items. A patch kit for inner tubes, bike tires or other inflatable items might come in handy. The key is to go through your gear item list and tailor the repair items to your needs.

If you are on an extended tour, add a sewing kit for repair of wearing apparel, tent, sleeping bag, etc. The kit might include safety pins, thread, needles, yarn, string, buttons. If you are into serious repair work, bring a heavy sewing needle or awl and coarse thread for permanent sewing repair of such items as tarpaulins and tent floors.

Replacement Gear. If your pump lantern is not holding pressure like it used to, bring a pump replacement kit. Though just an example, revisit your gear list and ask yourself what items are most suspect that could have the greatest impact on your having a good time.

Big Bear Lake, California

Secondary Activities

Activities that might be conducted out of a vehicle-accessible campsite include HIKING, BACKPACKING, GLACIER/WINTER CLIMBING, ROCK CLIMBING, BICYCLE TOURING, MOUNTAIN BIKING, ALPINE SKIING/SNOWBOARDING, NORDIC SKIING/ SNOWSHOEING, SNOWMOBILING, CANOEING, KAYAKING, SAILING, POWERBOATING, WATERSPORTS, LAND FISHING and SEA FISHING.

VEHICLE-ACCESSIBLE CAMPING
(Overnight)

Select items based on trip needs, worst-case weather conditions and degree of luxury desired.

ITEM	DATE				
Camping Gear (Shelter/Comfort)					
Auto Gear Rack/Locks					
Tent & Rainfly					
Stakes & Poles					
Seam Sealer					
Ground Cloth					
Tarp(s)					
Tent Broom & Sponge					
Sleeping Bags & *Blankets**					
Sleeping Pads					
Air Pump (miscellaneous use)					
Camp Pillows					
Hammock(s)					
Camp Chairs					
Lantern & Mantel(s)#					
Lantern Fuel#					
Fuel Funnel/Strainer					
Oil (pump lantern & stove)					
Gas Heater & Fuel*					
Waterproof Matches & Lighter					
Stuff Sacks (for tent, pads, etc.)					
Camping Permit					
Camping Gear (Cooking)					
Stove & *Wind Break*/Stove Fuel					
Wood & *Charcoal*					
Newspaper/*Fire Starter*					
Camp Grill (self-standing)					
Hand-held Grill (for fish etc.)					
Coffee Pot					
Skillet/Frypan					
Cooking Pots					
Non-stick Cooking Lubricant					
Pot Holders/Pot Grippers					
Dishware (plates, bowls etc.)					
Paper Plates					
Cups (plastic, paper)					
Cooking Utensils (spatula etc.)					
Can & Bottle Openers					
Eating Utensils					
Sponge & Scrubber					
Dish Tub/Dish Towel					
Paper Towels/Napkins					
Biodegradable Dish Soap					
Water Jugs/Bottles					
Portable Ice Chest(s)					
Ice & "Blue Ice"					
Insulated Bottle					

VEHICLE-ACCESSIBLE CAMPING
(Overnight)

ITEM	DATE				
Trash Bags					
Resealable Plastic Food Bags					
Camp Table					
Tablecloth & Hold-down Clips					
Dining Canopy & Mesh Screen					
Personal Gear					
Heavy Jacket/Parka*					
Long-Sleeve Shirt					
Sweater/Turtleneck					
Long Pants					
Hiking/Camp Shorts					
Hat (pullover* & wide brim)					
Underwear					
Thermal Underwear*					
Gloves/Mittens*					
Windbreaker					
Raingear					
Hiking Boots/Socks					
Camp Shoes/Socks					
Gaiters*					
Bandanna/Sweatband					
Hand/Foot Warmers*					
Head netting					
Stuff Sacks (parka, raingear etc.)					
Hygiene					
Towel					
Wash Cloth					
Biodegradable Soap					
Biodegradable Shampoo					
Personal Toiletries/Ditty Bag					
Toilet Paper & Towelettes					
Toilet Trowel					
Sun Shower					
Clothespins					
Laundry Bag					
Portable Toilet & Liners					

VEHICLE-ACCESSIBLE CAMPING
(Overnight)

ITEM	DATE				
Safety					
First Aid Kit (see FIRST AID)					
Water Filter/Tablets					
Sunglasses & Lanyard					
Reading Glasses & Repair Kit					
Nylon Cord					
Pocket Knife					
Sunscreen					
Lip Balm					
Insect Repellent					
Whistle					
Flashlight#					
Extra Batteries & Bulb#					
Fire Starter/Heat Tabs					
Emergency Blanket					
Timepiece					
Thermometer					
Phone Change					
Pen & Notepad					
Accessories					
Camera & Extra Film & Battery					
Camera Bag, Lens Cleaning Kit					
Binoculars					
Wood Saw					
Ax					
Shovel					
Swim Suit *& Life Preserver*					
Portable Radio (weather info.)					
Brochures, Articles, Books					
Indoor & Outdoor Games					
Daypack/Rucksack/Fanny Pack					
Frame Pack					
Toboggan/Sled & Plastic Sheet					
Auto Tire Chains & Anti-freeze					
Auto Tool Kit					
Spare Keys/Credit Card/$					
Tool Kit					
Tools					
Repair Gear					
Replacement Gear					
Meals (see MEALS section)					

Italicized items are optional (niceties or special purpose). •items for cold weather #items for night use

HIKING (Daytime)

See INDEX for checklist items not discussed below.

Single-day hiking could range from a short hike in fair weather to full-day bouldering or winter hiking in snow. The HIKING activity, as used here, does not require the use of technical climbing gear (see GLACIER/WINTER CLIMBING), or special gear for traveling in deep snow, such as skis or snowshoes (see NORDIC SKIING/SNOWSHOEING).

A popular form of hiking in Europe is to travel by day from hostel to hostel. Depending on the hostel offerings, this most often forgoes the need to carry camping gear, a tool kit, and possibly some of the contingency gear that you would bring along on a classic backpacking trip. You may be able to get by on a daypack/rucksack. There are also tours that arrange to carry your full luggage from stop to stop, which further eliminates the need to carry your eveningwear and most of your hygiene-oriented gear -- and a backpack.

Safety Considerations: 1) review the **GENERAL CONSIDERATIONS** and TEN ESSENTIALS sections; 2) plan your hike with an eye for elevation gain and loss and technical difficulty of the route; 3) turn back if the route exceeds your capability or inclement weather threatens; and 4) know your route well enough to minimize the chances of getting lost, but bring contingency gear in case you should be forced to stay out overnight.

In the checklist, items that are considered optional (niceties or special purpose) are *italicized*. Items noted with an asterisk(*) are those needed for hiking in very cold weather and snow or ice. Pound sign(#) entries are contingency gear for nighttime travel.

Hiking Gear

Daypack/Rucksack/Fanny Pack. Definitions vary, but day pack/rucksack/ fanny pack refers to a range of small contoured packs just large enough to carry snacks and the "Ten Essentials" (fanny pack) to that for hauling the gear needed for a one-day summit climb (daypack/rucksack). The *fanny pack* straps around your waist. It is designed to carry gear needed for modest hiking or exploring and should be unobtrusive in fit. Most likely, at this level of use, you can find double duty for the model that you use for such activities as longer-distance jogging or alpine skiing. There are higher-powered versions with greater capacity and most often built with side pockets for a couple of water bottles and other exterior zippered recesses for quick accessibility to other must-have-access-to items. These are for fast-moving, more-motivated hikers and climbers with aggressive daytime objectives in non-threatening weather.

The distinction between *rucksacks and day packs* is slowly getting lost. (At one time rucksacks were differentiated from day packs in that they had a frame, either internal or external.) Both are used for single-day activities and will be treated as one. They are carried on the back and have greater gear capacity than fanny packs. They are limited to carry weights of about 30 pounds. Applications vary from fair-weather hiking to single-day bouldering, backcountry skiing or mountain climbs in snow.

The pack should fit comfortably and have the necessary capacity, be designed to carry the load high and close to the pack through the use of adjustable shoulder straps, and have an adjustable waist band for load stability. Most are top loading with a drawstring or zipper(s) to close off the storage area(s) and snap down, tie-down or clip-down overclosures to protect against the elements. For *light day trips*, a simple nylon pack cloth bag with two side pockets for water bottles will cut it. These packs normally have drawstring closures, a simple latching overclosure and lightly-padded shoulder and waist straps.

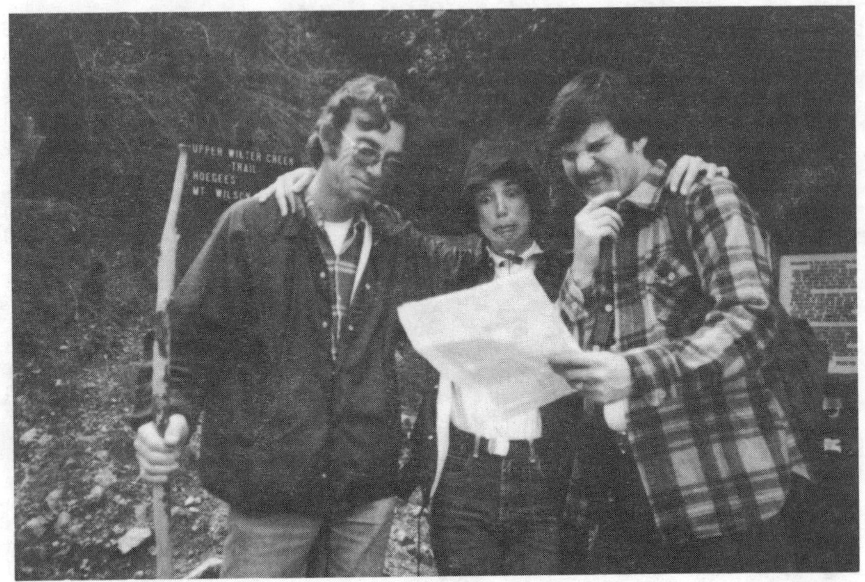

"Navigation Experts"

For *more rugged activities*, additional desirable attributes are: expanded carrying capacity (of the order of 2000 cubic inches); a more robust exterior material such as reinforced ripstop nylon; a double bottom of nylon or leather; a more secure closure/overclosure system; wide and heavily-padded shoulder and waist straps; and inclusion of haul straps and ice ax strap/carrier. Some of the higher capacity models (2500 cubic inch capacity and above) have a comfortable supporting backpad or back panel; the most robust models add back frames with aluminum stays to help ensure pack stability while in motion. Other accessories on the pack exterior, such as sealed or mesh side pockets, flap pocket, straps for attaching rope, crampons or skies, are matters of personnel preference and anticipated use. Note that there are day packs/rucksacks that can be attached to frame packs of the same make and model.

Hiking Permit. Wilderness areas and some of the more popular hiking trails require a permit for entry. Check ahead to ensure that you don't drive a long distance to find that you get to be a spectator.

Personal Gear

Gloves & Mittens. For VEHICLE-ACCESSIBLE CAMPING in winter, HIKING, BACKPACKING, ALPINE SKIING/SNOWBOARDING, NORDIC SKIING/SNOWSHOEING and GLACIER/WINTER CLIMBING activities, *mittens* are better than *gloves* for warmth since the fingers are snuggled together. For additional warmth, a heavy mitten can be worn over the glove. Best fit is a snug glove and looser mitten with inner mitt and outer mitt length sufficient to cover the wrist and lap under or over the parka sleeve. Preferred materials are wool, polyester or pile. Consider bringing a spare set of *leather gloves* if you suspect that the hike will take you through tangled or thorny brush.

Hiking Boots. For hiking activities such as intensive HIKING, BACKPACKING, GLACIER/WINTER CLIMBING and SNOWSHOEING, a quality *hiking boot* is an essential. (Those comfortable around-the-house work boots won't cut it, as one of the authors found out on one of his early hikes.) Boots should be a combination of tough, solid, flexible and comfortable for the planned activity. While lighter and more flexible three-season boots are effective for common hiking trails, a heavier, more rigid boot is required for four-season hiking and backpacking over rocky zones or for mountain and glacier exploration. With little exception, most experienced hikers use a boot with an upper that is high enough to protect the ankles, even for pure trail hiking. High-topped boots are available, although six-to-eight inch high boots are most often used.

The boots should have a thick, Vibram-type sole of fairly hard rubber. The upper lacing should be through hooks or pulleys rather than eyelets. The top should open wide so that, when the boot is wet or frozen, it can be put on with minimum struggle and pain. Boots should have a tongue gusseted to the top and have a minimum number of seams; a properly waterproofed boot with this construction will allow slopping through water and wet snow (provided none enters over the boot top), for extended periods without the feet getting wet.

A boot with a soft-leather or leather/nylon upper and flexible *sole* is most comfortable for trail walking and easy off-trail terrain. The uppers are normally glued to the sole as opposed to being sewn together as in the heartier boots with a welt. A stiffer double upper, heavier sole and hard toe are more desirable for scree (small gravel or fine particles frequently found on slopes in glaciated areas) and snow and moderate climbing. These are typically leather boots with a half-length nylon, steel or fiberglass shank. This shank provides additional rigidity above the lightweight boots, but maintains significantly more boot flexibility compared to serious climbing models. A very stiff (fully-shanked) upper with reinforced sole is preferred for high-angle rock and ice. Double-and triple-insulated boots are for cold weather and expeditionary climbing. (See GLACIER/WINTER CLIMBING for more detail on the latter options.)

Mt. Islip, San Gabriel Mountains, California

Boots should have sufficient room to allow wiggling of toes, yet not be so loose that the foot can slip around inside when the tie-downs are tightly drawn. On the trail, the toes should not touch the boot on the downhill and, on the uphill climb, the heel and ankles should not slip within the boot. Try the boots on with the number and types of socks (and inserts or wetsuit bootie, if applicable) that you will actually use.

Waterproofing is best applied a day or more before the next hike or climb to allow the preservative to soak in. The type of preservative used depends on how the leather was tanned (ensure you find out when buying). Use silicone-base wax for chrome-tanned leather and wax or grease for vegetable-tanned leather. Special care should be taken on waterproofing seams, the most subtle and demonic area of seepage into the boot. Some hikers use epoxy coating to protect the toe and seams.

Bring an extra set of *shoelaces*. Many a trip has been compromised by a jury-rigged shoe-holding system. Also bring some *moleskin* to prevent blisters or ease the pain after onset -- boots may seem to fit perfectly on a short break-in hike, but may provide unpleasant surprises on more lengthy tours. (Refer to the FIRST-AID section for more information.)

Parka/Jacket. If this is a modest day hike in moderate weather, leave the parka or heavy jacket behind. For longer tours in cooler weather, what you bring depends on your expectations for evening weather, or nighttime weather if you are planning an aggressive hike and are allowing for contingencies. We can't think of anything that we'd rather have had when an all-day, cross-country hike in the San Bernardino Mountains turned into a cold night foray -- and this was in early fall!

Socks. For light hiking, get light *athletic socks* which offer thin, dense padding underfoot and are made of numerous blends such as wool/nylon, acrylic/stretch nylon polyester/stretch nylon. These socks are described in the VEHICLE-ACCESSIBLE CAMPING section.

For the more foot-strenuous activities in a variety of weather extremes, heavier *hiking socks* with similar fabrics noted above are the choice. Outer socks are designed to offer varying degrees of insulation and cushioning. Thicker socks offer maximum warmth and cushioning. Thinner socks are cooler, lighter and give a better "feel" for the trail. Typical outer socks have dense padding at the heels and balls of feet, lighter-density padding on insteps to distribute pressure of boot laces, and Spandex or stretch nylon rib-knit tops to help keep socks in place. For thermal insulation, natural fibers such as wool and synthetic insulators using hollow-core polyester fibers are ideal. They are frequently blended with acrylic and polypropylene to take advantage of the wicking properties of these materials.

Outer socks can be worn alone or with *liner socks* which wick moisture away from feet to the outer sock. Liner socks keep feet warmer in winter and cooler in summer and also prevent chafing and blisters. Strongly consider using liners (typically of polypropylene or polyester blends) for long treks, strenuous outings or any outings in cold weather. This might include HIKING, BACKPACKING, ALPINE and NORDIC SKIING, SNOWBOARDING, SNOWSHOEING, SNOWMOBILING, CANOEING and KAYAKING.

Horsehead Lake , Sierra Nevada Mtns., California Courtesy of Doug Holker

Another interesting option, particularly suited for activities in wet, or wet/cold conditions is a *waterproof, breathable over sock*. Considerably more expensive than the standard outdoor activity socks, these little dandies fit over your athletic or hiking socks and are of roughly equivalent height. They keep your feet dry and comfortable while fording creeks, portaging canoes through ooze or paddling your canoe or kayak. (Let's face it, water is insidious in finding its way into the cockpit bottom.) When your boot interior is soaked, your feet are still dry, yet, like the wool's and synthetics discussed above, these over-socks will steadily wick the moisture out of the boot.

Boot socks are a serious consideration for off-trail (cross-country) HIKING, BACKPACKING and GLACIER/WINTER CLIMBING. Though commonly associated with the "ground-pounder" domain, other uses are for NORDIC SKIING/SNOWSHOEING. They might even double for SNOWMOBILING use. Most are heavy wool or wool blends for maximum insulation and offer extra padding. Specialized socks for mountaineering boots offer high-density padding at the heels and balls of the feet, medium density at the shins, and wool toes for warmth. They are worn in conjunction with a second layer (liner or second sock) and, in extreme cold, sometimes with a third sock layer.

Gaiters. Gaiters serve the purpose of keeping such nuisances as snow, rocks and gravel out of the boots. They cover the area from trousers to boots. A full-length zipper or lacing allows them to be put on without removing boots. They typically have an elastic top and bottom and fit snugly over pants and boot tops. A strap under the instep holds the gaiter down to the boot. Neoprene straps work well in snow, but wear out quickly on rock. Heavy cord holds up well on rock but sometimes balls up with snow.

Winter gaiters are frequently made of nylon packcloth. The portion of the gaiter covering the boot should be treated (waterproof) nylon while the upper is most often uncoated (water resistant, breathable) nylon. Uncoated nylon allows your legs to breathe, but will lose its water resistance with continued snow contact. This could be a real issue if there are plans to travel through deep snow in boots. Breathable, waterproof gaiters such as Goretex models cost more than nylon, but solve this uncoated-nylon limitation. Gaiters nominally fit above the calf.

Side lacing is favored by many for winter and high-altitude climbs as wet zippers can freeze overnight and become difficult to work. If your preference is the zippered style, look for heavy-duty zippers with large teeth. A flap that closes with snaps or Velcro protects the zipper from damage; in the event of zipper failure, this design can keep the gaiter closed and reasonably functional. Pure Velcro closures are convenient but can become clogged with snow.

Short, five-to-six inch gaiters of tough cotton or uncoated nylon are mostly used in the *warmer seasons*, when wearing short pants. Their purpose is to keep gravel, scree and corn snow out of boots. Cotton may be the low-cost preference in summer or shallow snow since nylon does not breathe as well and feet can get hot and sweaty underneath.

Consider shaping a piece of one-inch wide *webbing* over the undersole strap to keep it from wearing through from friction on hard rocks, ice or gravel. This is especially important if you have straps that are sewn onto the gaiter, as they cannot be fixed without halting and putting in a spartan repair effort. For non-sewn models, you can bring a spare strap for replacement due to normal wear. However, if one of your original (and in-good-condition) straps gets chewed up and you foresee no letup in the terrain, you can almost count on a simple replacement being inadequate.

Safety

Whistle/Signal Mirror. A signal mirror is particularly useful in open country for attracting attention of other hikers or outdoorsmen or an overhead aircraft in emergencies. There are pocket-sized models that have a sighting guide to help you set the mirror angle to reflect light accurately to the intended recipient.

Map(s). The *USGS topographic maps* depict topography by showing contour lines that represent constant elevations above sea-level. These maps identify major landmarks through the use of symbols and coloring to depict vegetated versus nonvegetated areas, roads and trails, as well as lakes and streams. These maps are useful for any hiking trip and are essential for off-trail (cross-country) travel. These maps come in a 7.5-minute series (roughly 2.6 inches per mile, covering an area of about 7 by 9 miles at 34 degrees latitude) and a 15-minute series (about 1.3 inch per mile, covering about 14 by 18 miles at 34 degrees latitude). The maps can be obtained through sporting goods stores and other commercial outdoor-recreation outlets or by contacting the USGS directly.

Land management and recreation maps which show only the horizontal relationships of natural and man-made features are useful for trip planning. (Many USFS sites offer these types of maps.) They are updated frequently, thus providing current details on roads, trails, ranger stations and other marks of man. Many hikers transfer this information to the sometimes out-of-date USGS maps. Most are obtained at the site or by contacting the specific site management agency.

Relief maps attempt to show terrain in three dimensions by use of color shadings, terrain sketching or raised surfaces. They are helpful for visualizing the ups and downs of hiking routes when doing initial planning. These maps are available for some areas, but not others. Sources are USGS, land management and recreation sources, as well as guide books.

Mt. Baden-Powell, California

Aerial photography serves the same type of function as relief maps, but tends to provide higher resolution for identification of smaller features. They have the unique characteristic of allowing identification of local vegetation, e.g., shrub versus tree forrestation. In addition, they are unexcelled in providing fodder for after-trip story-telling. Excellent photography is available from the Department of the Interior, U.S. Geological Survey and Earth Resources Observation Systems (EROS) Data Center. Most imagery supports maps with the same scaling as the 7.5-minute, USGS topographic series. The National Aerial Photography Programs (NAPP) provides complete coverage of the contiguous U.S. and is updated about every five years. Image resolution is sufficient to identify hiking trails and ground features which are of the order of 1-3 feet in diameter.

Altimeter. The altimeter is a useful aid for hikers and backpackers for pinpointing location. In conjunction with a topographic (topo) map showing your route, a compass bearing and resultant intersection with the route, combined with an altimeter measurement, will establish your location with little ambiguity. In dense forest, where bearings to landmarks are unobtainable, the intersection of the appropriate altitude contour with your route will, at worst, identify multiple locations on an up-and-down route. Further observations, common sense and intuition will narrow this ambiguity considerably. For cross-country hiking, multiple compass bearings will generally establish your location with reasonable certainty. If a quality set of landmarks (2-3 non-ambiguous markers at well-separated bearing angles) is not available, a series of compass directional and altimeter measurements, in conjunction with some thoughtful topo investigation, should help establish an approximate location.

For *mountaineers*, every climbing party should have an altimeter. Many turning junctions are in broad snow fields or other areas with few local, easily identifiable landmarks. These junctions are frequently identified in trip guides by altitude. Altimeters are also critical for establishing rate of climb -- these estimates are invaluable for estimating the time required to reach key objectives (or a signal that it is time to turn back and try again another day).

An altimeter is essentially a calibrated barometer which operates based on the uniform change of pressure with altitude. The elevations determined by the altimeter are only approximate because this instrument is strongly affected by changes in weather and temperature. To maintain an absolute calibration, the altimeter should be reset, if needed, at points of known elevation. Typical mountaineering instruments, when properly calibrated, are accurate to plus or minus 20-30 feet.

Complimentary equipment to compass, map and altimeter is a *Global Positioning Satellite* (GPS) *receiver*. Why do we say "complimentary," since it gives location to about 10 meters, accurate altitude, and some models even store routes and maps? Read the warning label on these receivers. Manufacturers realize that there is a finite probability of failure and certainly encourage users to have a reliable backup (like maybe a compass and altimeter?). These receivers are the size of a small television remote channel selector and weigh about 1-2 pounds with batteries (4 AA's are typical). Some come with a connector and battery recharging unit. Key features to look for in outdoor use are wraparound rubber armoring, waterproof construction, a scratchproof illuminated display and a covered carrying case.

Ice Ax. The ice ax is a multi-purpose tool that finds many uses for HIKING, BACKPACKING, NORDIC SKIING/SNOWSHOEING and GLACIER/WINTER CLIMBING. For the first two activities, it can be used as a makeshift walking stick, a heavy-duty cane on step uphill, a "third leg" for stream fording, or a touch-and-go balance point for hopping across talus (a sloping mass of rocky fragments). It can also serve as a step-by-step brake on a steep downhill or as a self-arresting device for spills on steep snow or dirt slopes. (Sounds like a dirt ax?) The ax is equally supportive for skiing and snowshoeing. It is also one of the most dangerous tools in the hands of those untrained in its use. Leather or rubber guards are available that fit on the sharp points and edges when the ax is not in use. (Refer to the GLACIER/WINTER CLIMBING activity for more detail.)

Crampons. If your route may involve crossing an occasional snow field or patches of ice and snow in precarious spots along the route, consider bringing a set of *instep crampons*. These are mini-crampons with four or six points (not intended for mountaineering use). (See the GLACIER/WINTER CLIMBING section for more information about crampon characteristics.)

Climbing Rope. As with crampons, this is a contingency item. Its primary purpose is to rope hikers together when crossing occasional snow fields or snow/ice patches. (See GLACIER/WINTER CLIMBING for further description.)

Communication Device. More and more, outdoorspeople are bringing along portable communication devices. They are potentially valuable for emergency situations. For example: A climber on Mt. Rainier in the Spring of 1998 used a cellular phone to notify park authorities about two other climbing parties caught in an avalanche at 11,400 feet at Disappointment Cleaver. Though one life was lost, his timely warning was credited with saving others. However, there is also some future concern of facing a bevy of recreationalists who bring just the thing to the outdoors that many naturalists seek to leave behind -- convenient ties to the outside world! For other than climbing activities, where ready access may be critical, those who carry them frequently relegate the equipment to the least accessible part of their gear pack(s).

Horsehead Lake, Sierra Nevada Mtns., California Courtesy of Doug Holker

Examples range from limited-range walkie-talkies for intergroup coordination to cellular telephones for outside communication near developed areas to longer-range carrier-band (CB) transmitter-receiver units. Regardless, all are useless when the terrain prevents unit-to-unit or unit-to-repeater access (e.g., when in a deep canyon trying to communicate with a person not within line-of-site). Whether good or bad, the near-future holds the high likelihood of cellular telephones with direct satellite access worldwide, The decision to bring or leave behind this gear is, and will continue to be, a personal one.

Accessories

Walking Staff. This time-honored hiking aid is particularly useful for support on steep upgrades and for braking on the downgrade. It may also prove useful for making water crossings. A well-selected tree branch (from home) works for some. There are also high-quality models of aluminum and various wood types that have high-pizzazz finishes and elegantly-carved stocks. Some of the metal models disassemble into two or three sections.

The staff can also be used for BACKPACKING as an assist for hanging food or as an ad hoc tent pole. Colin Fletcher, in the "Complete Walker" (see the **REFERENCE** section), suggests other uses including: as a backrest prop, fishing rod and as a camera monopod or part of a camera tripod.

Litter Bag. Carry a small bag just for packing out your own refuse and/or that which you may find along the way. This should be a standard practice for any outdoor activity in which you participate.

Tool Kit.

It is unlikely that you will need any tools other than your trusty pocket knife. Still, bring a few alternate-size safety pins to temporarily repair broken zippers or replace missing buttons. Also, don't forget that extra pair of shoelaces.

Secondary Activities

Typical of activities that are linked to HIKING are swimming (WATERSPORTS activity), ROCK CLIMBING, and LAND FISHING. See the relevant activity for the associated additional gear needs.

HIKING
(Daytime)

Select items based on trip needs and worst-case weather conditions.

ITEM	DATE				
Hiking Gear					
Auto Gear Rack/Locks					
Daypack/Rucksack/Fanny Pack					
Water Bottle(s)					
Hiking Permit					
Personal Gear					
Hiking Shorts					
Long Pants					
Underwear					
Thermal Underwear*					
Long-Sleeve Shirt					
Turtleneck Sweater/T-shirt					
Parka/Jacket*					
Windbreaker					
Socks					
Gloves & Mittens*					
Hiking Boots/Spare Shoelaces					
Pullover Hat* & Brimmed Hat					
Raingear					
Gaiters*					
Bandanna/Sweat Band					
Toilet Paper					
Toilet Trowel					
Swim Suit					
Safety					
First Aid Kit (see FIRST AID)					
Water Filter/Tablets					
Sunglasses & Lanyard					
Sunscreen					
Insect Repellent					
Lip Balm					
Whistle/*Signal Mirror*					
Waterproof Matches & Lighter					
Fire Starter/Heat Tabs					
Emergency Blanket					
Map(s)					
Compass					
Altimeter/GPS Receiver					
Timepiece					

HIKING
(Daytime)

ITEM	DATE				
Thermometer					
Pocket Knife					
Flashlight#					
Extra Batteries & Bulb#					
Reading Glasses & Repair Kit					
Nylon Cord					
Ice Ax•					
Crampons•					
Climbing Rope					
Phone Change					
Communication Device					
Pen & Notepad					
Accessories					
Camera, Extra Film & Battery					
Camera Bag, Lens Cleaning Kit					
Brochures, Articles, Books					
Walking Staff					
Sitting Pad					
Binoculars					
Litter Bag					
Auto Tool Kit					
Spare Keys/Credit Card/$					
Tool Kit					
Safety Pins					
Spare Shoelaces					
Snacks (see MEALS section)					
High Energy Bars					
Trail Mix/Granola					
Fresh Fruit/Dried Fruit					
Beef Jerky					
Nuts					
Electrolyte (for water bottle)					

Italicized items-optional/special purpose. •items for cold weather #nighttime travel contingency gear

BACKPACKING (Overnight)

See INDEX for checklist items not discussed below.

Backpacking could range from an overnight outing in fair weather to a multi-day mountain journey in inclement weather or patchy snow. The BACKPACKING activity, as used here, does not require the use of technical climbing gear (see GLACIER/WINTER CLIMBING), or special gear for traveling in deep snow, such as skis or snowshoes (see NORDIC SKIING/SNOWSHOEING). Gear items such as tent, cooking gear and water filter can be shared by the group. Note that backpacking on most Government land will require a permit.

In the U.S in some mountain ranges, a variant of this style is to backpack between warming huts. These huts are, most often, simple shelters or cabins. If warranted for your planned trip, this option might allow you to leave behind your tent (or substitute a less robust option like a "bivy" sack) and to lighten up on some of your contingency gear. Note that, in inclement weather, it may be wise to bring your full gear contingent and simply view your warming hut stops as a perquisite or "perk".

Also, there is an option to hire a trail outfitter who will haul in the bulk of your gear on pack animals. The outfitter drops your gear at a pre-arranged location and returns on a preset date to pick your gear back up, rain or shine (known as a "spot trip"). A drop-off with no pickup is also available ("one-way trip"). These are excellent options for families with children or groups with members who may not be up to the task of carrying a pack over distance at high altitude. Once the hard work of getting the gear to the remote site is accomplished, the opportunities to day hike out of the drop-off site or move the campsite short distances are limitless.

Safety Considerations: 1) review the **GENERAL CONSIDERATIONS** and TEN ESSENTIALS sections; 2) review the "Safety Considerations" noted for the HIKING activity, as applicable; 3) bring a healthy contingency of food and stove fuel, since you may be stuck in your tent for significant periods in severe weather or be forced to alter your trip plans; and 4) develop contingency plans in the event that you face unforeseen obstacles such as high water, ice, trail wipeout, etc.

In the checklist, items that are considered optional (niceties or special purpose) are *italicized*. Items noted with an asterisk(*) are those needed for backpacking in very cold weather and/or snow and ice. Pound sign(#) entries are gear for planned or contingent nighttime travel.

Backpacking Gear

Proper *weight distribution* is one of the keys to hauling a pack comfortably. Place heavy gear as near your back as possible and high in the main compartment -- this compartment's lower edge will be at or near waist level. Regrettably, most tents won't fit into the main compartment of an external frame pack and must be carried externally and near or below the waist. Depending on your packing technique, your sleeping pad and sleeping bag may also wind up on external mounts. (Try to get the bag stowed internally, if possible, or place it in a rugged stuff sack that can handle the abuse of tree branches and other sharp outdoor objects.) Though most packs have air space (external frame pack) or some padding (internal frame pack) between the pack and your back, ensure that you don't store sharp-edged objects near your back. If there is no other choice, use clothing or other softer items as makeshift padding.

Frame Pack and Cover/Liner. A *frame pack* is preferred over a day pack/rucksack if the load exceeds about 30 pounds. Both external- and internal-frame models are available. The *external-frame pack* is generally preferred for trail use and for long, easy mountain-climb approaches where the daypack/rucksack is used for the summit climb. The pack should be designed with sufficient capacity and features to carry camping gear, alternate activity gear and supplies for a week or more. The external pack is essentially a large carry bag lashed onto a long rigid frame, held away from direct back contact by taut nylon or mesh back bands or a network of strings or webbing. Because there is no direct back contact, this pack will keep you cooler than its internal cousin. It is designed to carry the load high on the back and uses adjusting straps to share the load amongst shoulders, back and hips. Shoulder and hip straps should be wide, padded and easily adjustable.

Internal-frame packs are the common choice for climbers and ski mountaineers. These bags are meant to carry the gear needed for the approach, climb and bivouacs over several days to a week. They allow weight to be carried lower and do a better job of hugging the back. These are essential features that minimize pack movement on a key move, where 40-60 pounds of weight shift may cause a person to lose balance. The clean, narrow profile of the internal design also allows them to be hauled up steeper rock pitches.

Sixty Lakes Basin, Sierra Nevada Mtns., California Courtesy of Doug Holker

The most common pack materials are nylon/nylon blends or nylon/packcloth. Pack styles include a large variety of combinations of pockets, compartments and closure arrangements. Most prefer packs with one large central well, particularly because it allows more gear-packing flexibility. A highly adjustable system (pack-to-frame, hip and shoulder straps) and a wide, well-padded set of hip and shoulder straps maximizes the likelihood of personal comfort. For internal frame packs, a well-padded chimney of padding between the back and frame will limit frame-induced discomfort. Easy-access waterproof and mesh pockets help compartmentalize frequently-used on-trail gear, limiting search time. They may also limit the number of times that you must drop and reopen your pack.

Extension collars are a positive feature. These collars are at the top of the pack and allow for storing the added gear for a lengthy trip. When not needed, they are compressed through cinches or tighten-down straps to minimize the pack profile. Additional positive pack attributes are ice ax strap/carrier and straps for attaching rope, crampons or other gear. Packs that utilize zippers for load-carrying structure or crucial closures should be viewed with caution since failure of a zipper could disable all or part of the pack.

Choices are matters of personal preference and anticipated use. Try different pack styles with assistance from qualified recreation outlet personnel and rent or borrow gear before locking into a final decision. Bags with capacities of about 3500-4500 cubic inches might serve for easy-going, short duration trips, while 4500-5500 cubic inches will cut it for all but multi-day mountaineering expeditions. In the latter case, consider packs with 5500-6500 cubic-inch capacities. Save the long, remote trips until settling on a frame pack. Don't be embarrassed to load up the pack in the store, make the available adjustments, and check whether this model is comfortable for your body frame. (A book author we know wore off a couple of layers of hip skin on his first Trans-Sierra Nevada journey because of inadequate pack fit and cheap hip pads.)

Pack covers are used to shield the pack from heavy rain or just from overnight moisture. The packs themselves, which should be at least water resistant, were not built to repel extended periods of heavy moisture (i.e., they are not generally waterproof). Even if advertised as waterproof, there can be seepage through zippers, pockets, the top opening, or places where the coating has worn off. The cover should be effective while on the move or while in camp.

Some bags come with a water-repellent add-on pack cover, mainly nylon. Some packers make their own cloth cover, while many others simply use a 3-mil thickness laundry or trash bag. The cut-to-fit bag is placed over the pack and tucked into the webbing to keep it from blowing off in high winds. Wet clothing is stored in its own bag and stored in the pack interior.

Pack liners are the more sensible choice for mountaineering. (They can be a nuisance when rummaging through your pack interior, but they do serve a noble cause.) The same plastic laundry or trash bag noted above is used as a interior liner for the main gear compartment. Wet clothing is simply stowed between the liner and the sides of the pack.

Straps. Consider bringing a couple of extra backpack straps. They are useful for strapping on gear items that you may want to easily access or to simply dry out items that would normally go in your pack. In conjunction with the tape and wire in your tool kit, they might also be a good addition for making temporary backpack repairs.

Daypack/Rucksack. Unless you have a frame pack with a removable, framed rucksack, you will probably want to tote a daypack. This nifty little item is what you use for peak-bagging off the nominal backpacking trip. When stored in your frame pack, it can be used to store groups of items that you want to keep separate from the rest of your equipment.

Camping Gear

First a word about critters and food. Rodents will attack your food by day (birds will go after your munchies if left out in the open), while bears and other of the larger creatures are the prime culprit in the night hours. Even small rodents can gnaw through plastic bags, tents and even backpacks.

Develop a good system for protecting your food, which generally means learning how to hang it from a tree. Bring at least 50 feet of nylon cord specifically for this purpose. A thumbrule: When completed, the counterbalanced food stuff sacks should be at least eight feet off the ground (12-15 feet is preferred) and four feet (5-6 feet is preferred) from the tree trunk. (Watch out for mice that can walk a tight line and drop down to your sacks. If concerned, rig a small rat-guard-type of shield for each sack, a miniature version of what you've seen on ship's mooring lines when docked.) At some camping sites, there is a pre-hung bear line for campers to hang counterbalanced food sacks. They might be strung between trees, built over a ravine, or otherwise placed as the terrain permits.

Other advice: Best bet is to use a downed tree branch, walking staff or other long, rigid article to push the second (counterbalancing) bag up to the required height and to retrieve the bags. Some use a climber's carabiner as part of the tie-up to facilitate the process. Keep the cooking area and food storage well away from where you sleep. Package food in containers with tight lids or in sealed bags to conceal the smell. If there are no suitable trees, innovation is required, such as placing food items under a carefully-constructed rock pile.

Tent. For BACKPACKING, GLACIER/WINTER CLIMBING, BICYCLE TOURING, MOUNTAIN BIKING, NORDIC SKIING/SNOWSHOEING and KAYAKING, there is a premium on minimizing weight and bulk. Selection for these activities favors lightweight tents or lightweight tarps. Though kayaking activities are less restrictive on weight, the tent or tarp must fit into the boat hatches.

Lake Peak Area, San Bernardino Mtns., California

A *tent* is a necessity above timberline, for glacier/winter camps, in strong winds and in mosquito country. For three-season, non-glacier or non-winter camping, the simplest options are a loose waterproof sleeping bag cover, tube tent or one-man tent. The latter is a 1-2 pound "mummy" breathable tent with waterproof rainfly or the newer single-layer breathable, waterproof bivouak ("bivy") sack. The first two options are particularly good for fair-weather BICYCLE TOURING and MOUNTAIN BIKING, where weight and bulk are most critical. Amongst these lightest-weight options, the one-man tent excels in inclement weather.

Lightweight multi-person tent materials can provide housing for 2-4 pounds per person, including poles and hardware. The choice between two-man or four-man versions depends on the use intended, comfort desired (four-man typically has a higher roof), campsite size and ease of dividing gear amongst participants. Our preference is to stick to two-man versions for GLACIER/WINTER CLIMBING, BICYCLE TOURING and MOUNTAIN BIKING. (We also opt for the two-man over the one-man version, the tradeoff being getting a better night's sleep in less-confining space versus the ease of transporting the smaller one-man package.) Rip-stop nylon tent/rainfly combination tents with a large mesh entry door and waterproof tent floor and low sidewalls are the standard.

Tent shapes such as A-frames and domes are available. Interior poles intrude into the living space, but are generally simpler and lighter; external poles provide tent sidewalls with less wind flap, but are more complex to rig and require more hardware. The free-standing dome needs no guy lines and can be picked up and moved as a unit. (It still must be staked down to keep it from blowing away.) Four-season tents are more expensive then three-season tents. Err on the side of the year-round model if you have any doubts.

Various designs offer zip doors, tunnels, interior pockets for storage and cooking/gear storage alcoves. Cooking inside, protected from the wind, considerably reduces fuel consumption and may be necessary in storms. Two-man tents often have a cooking alcove since the living space is too small, unlike four-man tents. (Ensure you clearly understand the dangers/safe operating conditions for using open-flame gear in your tent before departing on your venture.)

Choose cheery colors such as yellow, red or orange, for the times that weather forces you inside the tent. These colors also tend to contrast with most outdoor backgrounds, making them easier to spot when you return to the camping area vicinity after hiking, fishing, etc.

For other than where a tent is a necessity, as noted earlier, a light-weight *tarpaulin* is a viable option. Tarpaulins or tarps are adequate shelter in all but extreme weather. The campsite area must also have features allowing the tarp to be anchored (trees, boulders, logs, etc.) or some very clever engineering is required. Tarps of polyethylene (lightest, but shortest life), coated nylon, or waterproof canvas (heaviest, but most durable) are candidates. The latter two tarps mainly come with reinforced grommets sewn into the sides and corners for easy rigging. Tarps lacking grommets can be rigged by tying off each corner around a small pebble, rubber ball or any small, dull-edged object.

Typical sizes are 9 feet x 12 feet (2-4 people) and 11 feet x 14 feet (four people in comfort). Tarps can be shaped into a tent, flat shed roof, or three- and V-shaped (closed end into the wind) structures. Additional shaping can be achieved using tent poles, walking staffs, ice axes or other items, only limited by one's imagination. Individual tarps can also be connected together, increasing the size, shape and versatility of options. Bring plenty of strong nylon cord.

Franklin Lakes, Sierra Nevada Mtns., California — Courtesy of Doug Holker

Stakes. For BACKPACKING, GLACIER/WINTER CLIMBING AND NORDIC SKIING/ SNOWSHOEING in soft snow conditions, choose higher-surface-area stakes. Use them as "dead men" by burying them in a trench in a horizontal position and perpendicular to the tent guy wire. Other options are to buy dead-man anchors specifically for these snow conditions. Guy lines can be secured using a stuff sack filled with rocks or even snow. Just bury the sack, stamp down the snow above, and connect the guy line to the cord or sling.

East Fork, San Gabriel River, California

Tent Broom & Sponge. In the outback, keeping the tent floor free of debris and water is more than just good housekeeping. Floor punctures caused by grinding in debris can allow moisture seepage from the ground, which could soak into sleeping bags and other important gear in the tent. Moisture runoff from the tent walls and water or snow brought into the tent will contribute to the same problem. As a minimum, clean and air out your tent daily or at each repacking, whichever comes first.

Sitting Pad. A small sitting pad or "sitzpad" (small square of closed cell foam) is the standard. It is useful for many outdoor activities because it allows you to plop down anywhere without worrying about the nature of the surface. It is a must for snow trips to keep your bottom dry during rest periods. Sitting on a wet or cold surface can also sap heat quickly if you need to rest or are injured. Typical sitzpads are 12-inches x 18-inches in size.

If in-camp comfort is worth the weight addition, think hard about adding a *travel chair* onto your pack. One option that fits into most packs is a closed-cell foam, 1-1/2 pound chair where seat tilt is adjusted with side straps. It is still best used when propped up against a rock, tree or other convenient backstop as the pressure on the sewn seams may cause stretch and tearing with extended, unsupported use.

Other packable chairs with back support include 3- to 4-pound models with lightweight, dissassembleable tubing typically with nylon or canvas seat material -- they are higher cost. We have toted in aluminum-framed, canvas-topped beach chairs on short trips. One of our contributors, who shall remain nameless, has been known to haul in a full-size aluminum-frame model on remote Sierra Nevada Mountains trips. In the latter two cases, the chairs must be strapped to the pack exterior. This can be a problem if the trip will take you through dense brush or low-hanging tree cover.

Stove & Windbreak/Stove Fuel. For most weight-limited activities, light, compact single-burner stoves are the standard. Most use white (unleaded) gasoline, burning kerosene or liquefied gas fuels. A typical small *gasoline* stove weighs about one pound empty, burns for about one hour on 1/2 pint of fuel and boils a quart of water in less than ten minutes. These stoves generally do not have pumps; initial pressure is built up by burning a small amount of fuel in a priming cup on the top of the tank. Once ignited, pressure is maintained by heat from the burner. White gasoline, specially prepared for pressurized stoves, is mandatory; its properties are that it is least likely to clog fuel jets, operates at required pressure and does not emit toxic fumes.

The Minarets, California Courtesy of Doug Holker

Kerosene produces roughly the same heat per unit weight as gasoline, but is less volatile. These stoves are pressurized with a pump and require priming with alcohol, gasoline or a flammable tube paste, again using a priming cup. These stoves are slightly heavier than gasoline or liquefied fuel, but are most impervious to the cold.

Liquefied fuel stoves are comparable to gasoline and kerosene stoves in terms of weight and heat capacity. They are the easiest to light and operate and use disposable cartridges as opposed to requiring refueling from a bottle. Low ambient temperature can reduce efficiency to the point of non-functioning unless the fuel is warmed. The stove will not function below 32 degrees Fahrenheit (°F) at sea level, 22 °F at 5000 feet and 4 °F at 10,000 feet.

Minimum fuel is used if the flame is shielded from wind, the flame is regulated below the point of licking up the sides of the pot, and pot lids are used. With pump stoves the internal pressure can be regulated. Non-pump stoves are governed by internal fuel pressure and must not be allowed to get cold. Keep these stoves off the snow by placing them on a 5-6 inch square *ensolite or masonite pad.*

You will use significantly more fuel while cooking in a direct wind than in a still- or wind-blocked environment. Some backpacking/remote camping stoves come with a small portable *wind screen*. Manufactered aluminum screens are available, but plain, old aluminum foil can be also be used -- it produces a lighter-weight, though less-stable screen. One austere option is to wash out your freeze-dried food packages. You can cut and shape the foil packages to suit your needs. In the absence of a working screen, place the stove in a *sheltered nook*, e.g., behind a barrier of rocks, snow or outdoor gear such as a backpack.

Candle Lantern. After you've spent a few nights out trying to cook and housekeep with your limited-beamwidth flashlight, you'll give serious consideration to this device. There are many model variations, but the design crux of this wide-area illumination device is a slow-burning stearene candle enclosed in a Pyrex sleeve, mounted on a metal holder. The holder has an attached metal bail for hanging the unit. Variants in design include full 360-degree to partially-blocked illumination fields, fixed-shelf and spring-mounted shelf designs (the latter maintain the candle flame's vertical position in the middle of the sleeve), and fixed-cylindrical to folddown-rectangular shapes.

The better-quality designs operate outdoors in low-wind, have at least a four-inch bail to keep the flame off of any additional tying apparatus such as nylon cord, have a base that will collect all tallow that might dribble down, and can be easily and robustly packed. Since the candles are not a breeze to replace, consider buying a model that provides long candle life (2-9 hours is the typical range) The lanterns can be used in tents and can provide warmth in addition to light. A qualifier: Learn the tenets of safe use of your particular lantern. Many a tent has been scorched or burned by improper candle lantern use.

Tool Kit

Tools. A small set of pliers is the most likely tool of use for backpack repair, as well as for all-around kitchen and camp use. Tailor any extra tools for your specific backpacking gear items, for instance, those for disassembly of stoves and water filters.

Repair Gear. The sewing and patching kit might include safety pins, thread, sewing needles, yarn, string, buttons, wire, heavy tape and patch material (for wearing apparel, sleeping bag, backpack, clothing and tent). For extended trips, consider bringing a heavy sewing needle or awl and coarse thread for permanent sewing repair of such items as tarpaulins and tent floors.

Replacement Gear. Take along a spare set of bootlaces. If there are critical bolts, clevis pins, closure rings or other pack (or other item) hardware, bring spares. Include pole splices or a spare tent pole or have a well-rehearsed plan for "jury-rigging" a fix.

Secondary Acivities

Typical of some related activities are swimming (WATERSPORTS), ROCK CLIMBING, peak bagging (HIKING, daytime GLACIER/WINTER CLIMBING) and LAND FISHING. If you plan to link up one of these secondary activities with your trip, refer to the additional gear needs associated with that activity.

BACKPACKING
(Overnight)

Select items based on trip needs and worst-case weather conditions.

ITEM	DATE				
Backpacking Gear					
Auto Gear Rack/Locks					
Frame Pack & Cover/Liner					
Spare Straps					
Daypack/Rucksack					
Water Bottles/Water					
Collapsible Water Bag					
Wilderness/Camping Permit					
Personal Gear					
Hiking Shorts					
Long Pants					
Long-Sleeve Shirt					
Turtleneck Sweater/T-shirt					
Underwear					
Thermal Underwear*					
Parka (w/p stuff sack)/Jacket					
Windbreaker					
Socks					
Gloves & Mittens*					
Hiking Boots/Spare Shoelaces					
Brimmed Hat & Pullover Hat*					
Raingear					
Head Netting					
*Gaiters**					
Bandanna/Sweat Band					
Camp Shoes					
Swim Suit					
Camping gear					
Tent & Rainfly					
Stakes & Poles					
Seam Sealer					
Ground Cloth					
Tent Broom & Sponge					
Sleeping Bag (w/p stuff sack)					
Sleeping Pad					
Stove & Windbreak/Primer					
Fuel Bottle					
Fuel Funnel/Strainer					

BACKPACKING
(Overnight)

ITEM	DATE				
Cooking Pot					
Skillet/Frypan					
Teapot (hot water)					
Non-Stick Cooking Lubricant					
Scouring Pad					
Pot Holder/*Pot Gripper*					
Plate & Cup					
Cooking Utensils					
Aluminum Foil					
Can Opener					
Eating Utensils					
Sponge					
Biodegradable Dish Soap					
Paper Towels					
Spare Stuff Sacks					
Reusable Plastic Food Bags					
Candle Lantern					
Litter Bag					
Hygiene					
Towel					
Wash Cloth					
Biodegradable Soap					
Biodegradable Shampoo					
Personal Toiletries/Ditty Bag					
Toilet Paper & Towelettes					
Toilet Trowel					
Sun Shower					
Laundry Bag					
Safety					
First Aid Kit (see FIRST AID)					
Water Filter/Tablets					
Sunglasses & Lanyard					
Sunscreen					
Insect Repellent					
Lip Balm					
Whistle/*Signal Mirror*					
Waterproof Matches & Lighter					
Fire Starter/Heat Tabs					
Emergency Blanket					

BACKPACKING
(Overnight)

ITEM	DATE				
Map(s)					
Compass					
Altimeter/GPS Receiver					
Timepiece					
Thermometer					
Pocket Knife					
Flashlight#					
Extra Batteries & Bulb#					
Reading Glasses & Repair Kit					
Nylon Cord					
Ice Ax*					
Crampons*					
Climbing Rope					
Phone Change					
Communication Device					
Pen and Notepad					
Accessories					
Camera, Extra Film & Battery					
Camera Bag, Lens Cleaning Kit					
Brochures, Articles, Books					
Binoculars					
Walking Staff					
Sitting Pad/_Camp Chair_					
Sewing Kit (see **Tool Kit**)					
Indoor Games					
Auto Tool Kit					
Spare Keys/Credit Card/$					
Tool Kit					
Tools					
Repair Gear					
Replacement Gear					
Meals (see MEALS section)					

Italicized items are optional/special purpose *items for cold weather/snow/ice #nighttime travel gear

GLACIER/WINTER CLIMBING (Daytime)

See INDEX for checklist items not discussed below.

Single-day climbing infers making a daytime approach and peak climb. In contrast to the HIKING activity, the climb requires use of technical climbing gear. The approach also may require special gear for traveling in deep snow, such as skis or snowshoes. The properties of this special equipment is described in the NORDIC SKIING/SNOWSHOEING activity. Technical rock-climbing gear may also be used for GLACIER/WINTER CLIMBING. That equipment is discussed in the ROCK CLIMBING activity.

Most gear unit properties in this section are defined in international metric units. To convert, use the following: 1 millimeter = 0.0394 inch; 1 meter = 39.4 inches or 3.28 feet; 1 gram = 0.0352 ounces; 1 kilogram = 2.20 pounds. Some stores advertise the force that gear can handle in terms of kilonewtons. One kilonewton is the force applied by 223 pounds (a heavy climber) accelerated by Earth's gravity (falling).

Safety Considerations: 1) review the **GENERAL CONSIDERATIONS** and TEN ESSENTIALS sections; 2) review the "Safety Considerations" noted for the HIKING activity, as applicable; 3) study the climb and descent beforehand, establishing a route and alternatives that are within your group's physical and technical capabilities; 4) master the reading of both weather and snow/ice (including potential avalanche) conditions; 5) practice your self-arrest techniques; 6) practice belay, rappel and rescue techniques with your group before attempting the next-level climb; 7) ensure that there is a group leader with experience in higher-difficulty climbs than the one you are attempting; 8) develop plans for contacting rescue units in an emergency; 9) practice techniques needed to extricate an injured climber from the climbing area; 10) replace all worn or suspect climbing gear; 11) bring severe-weather contingency gear in the event that you are forced out overnight; 12) wear a hard hat if the climb warrants its use; and 13) turn back at the first indication of severe weather onset.

In the checklist, items that are considered optional (niceties or special purpose) are *italicized*. Pound sign(#) items are those used for contingency nighttime travel.

<u>Hiking/Climbing Gear</u>

Auto Gear Rack. Purchase a vehicle overhead rack that can haul various kinds of gear. A rack equipped with a gear storage unit provides more room and comfort for climbers inside the car. Also, though we have hauled skis inside a car, it isn't a very accommodating environment. Add some rack hardware for hauling skis and you've got both the storage unit and skis on the car roof.

Ice Ax. The ice ax is a multi-purpose tool that is used for HIKING, BACKPACKING, NORDIC SKIING/SNOWSHOEING and GLACIER/WINTER CLIMBING. The use of an ice ax for other than GLACIER/WINTER CLIMBING is discussed in the HIKING activity.

The key ax components are the head, pick, adze, shaft and spike. The *head*, usually made of steel, has both the pick and adze mounted to it. The head has a center hole (carabiner hole) which is primarily used to attach a wrist leash. The purpose of the leash is to secure the ax to your wrist or harness -- this is important when on long steep slopes or crevassed glaciers. The loss of this valuable tool could put an you in danger for any of the activities noted, either from the standpoint of pure equipment loss or from the danger to climbers below.

The leash also provides flexibility to make needed moves on the occasional rock encountered during a snow climb. Both short and long leashes are available. Short leashes are standard for basic snow and glacier travel because they offer more positive control. Longer leashes are preferred when climbing steep snow or ice slopes due to the versatility added with the increased single-hand radius of ice ax use.

The *pick* is normally curved or drooped and has a row of teeth on its underside -- this is the business end used for self-arrest. The curved design has a modest curvature and is most commonly used for the lighter land and snow activities. Hooked designs dig in faster (causing a more violent arrest) and are the more common mountaineering choice. Standard mountaineering designs have a moderate hooking angle of 65-70 degrees from the shaft. A sharper angle of 55-60 degrees is more characteristic for technical ice climbing. Pick end clearances can be positive, neutral or negative. The positive clearance design has the greatest "grabbing" power, making it the preferred choice for self-arrests on ice, but more likely to subject the user to violent arrests in hard snow.

Mount Baker, Washington Courtesy of Don Stromberg

The *adze* is used for step-chopping in hard snow or ice. Adze design choices are flat versus curved, straight-edge versus scalloped, and straight-out or drooped. The flat, straight-edged, non-drooped option is probably the best all-around tool for step-chopping.

The *shaft* is most commonly made of metal (aluminum or titanium) or a composite (fiberglass, Kevlar or carbon filament). Shafts may be plain or have a section of rubber-type material to increase gripping power. The penalty of having the grip is that the gripping material can keep the ax from penetrating as easily into the snow -- this is an important consideration when the ice ax is frequently used for probing, boot-ax belay or self-belay. As a result, it is not recommended that ice ax use for basic mountaineering have this feature.

Shaft lengths of 70 centimeters (about 27 inches) or longer are most common for HIKING, BACKPACKING and NORDIC SKIING/SNOWSHOEING, where they are mainly used as mobility aids. The longer lengths are also very useful for crevasse and cornice probing and as snow anchors in GLACIER/WINTER CLIMBING. For these general activities and for glissading, the longer the length you are comfortable with, the better. Lengths of 60-70 centimeters are generally used for mountaineering activities on moderately-steep snow slopes in an alpine environment for self-belay and self-arrest. Axes less than 60 centimeters are typically used as ice-climbing tools. They are built for placements on steep slopes at the sacrifice of some self-arresting capability.

The *spike* is the sharp metal tip, which is used to drive the ice ax into ice and snow. If used for other activities such as hiking on hard, dry surfaces, ensure that you resharpen the point afterwards. Note that the spike is not intended for hole poking, trash spearing, fire-stoking or spear-fishing -- it can cause great harm if misused on a climb, as well as misused elsewhere!

Keep *rubber or leather guards* on the pick, adze and spike when use is not planned over an extended period. These can be purchased or innovated by cutting up materials such as an old garden hose.

Nevado Huascaran, Peruvian Andes Courtesy of Kees Kolff

Crampons. Today's standard is 12-point crampons, most commonly made of chrome-molybdenum (chrome-moly) steel. There are 10 down-pointing "teeth" and two forward-pointing teeth in the design. There are also 10-point models with no forward-facing teeth, although they are disappearing from production, since they are inadequate for very steep ice.

From there, crampon selection involves a tradeoff between what works better for technical ice climbing versus general alpine climbing. This is dictated by the configuration of the first two rows of points. For *highly-technical use*, the first row (front points) is drooped and the second row is angled forward toward the first row. This configuration allows lowering of the boot heel (thus reducing calf strain) while still maintaining a good bite. Straight points are a better choice for flat-footing and *general alpine use*.

Both *hinged and rigid crampon body* configurations are used. The hinged version can be attached to any mountaineering boot, full shank or not, and to plastic boots. It performs better in mixed terrain and is typically lighter (the full range of options weighs from about 2-3 pounds). Attached to full-shank or plastic boots, hinged crampons are nearly equal in ice-climbing performance to rigid crampons. Rigid models require full-shank or plastic boots -- they are at their best for front-pointing up technical ice.

Crampons are secured with traditional strapping methods or with step-in/clamp-on bindings. Both are amenable to use with either rigid or hinged crampons. *Strapping methods* most commonly used are four independent straps, two independent straps and the Scottish system. All use the attachment posts on the crampon together with buckle straps. The Scottish system has a strap with an integral ring in the middle, which is connected to the front two posts; the rear strap is the same as in the two-strap system.

The *step-in/clamp-on design* attaches to the boot with a wire toe bale and a snap-up bale on the rear. Each crampon has a safety strap to prevent loss should the crampon comes off the boot. These models are fast and easier to put on, but require a closer fit to the boot. The boot must have a pronounced welt at both the heel and toe, making this design a natural for plastic boots.

A large proportion of leather climbing boots are bought with a welt that is more flush with the boot upper: a narrow-welt boot, when worn without crampons, is superior to wide-welt models on small footholds. Thus, leather boots tend to be paired with the strapping method.

A few *purchasing tips*. Try on crampons with the boot(s) that you plan to wear. Many crampons are adjustable, to a limited degree, allowing use for more than one boot. Fit the crampons while wearing any other gear that may interfere, such as super gaiters or the sole-shaped flat piece of foam that some stick between the boot and crampon for insulation purposes. Examine the front crampon point protrusion beyond the boot toe (3/4 to 1 inch is about right). Check that the attachment posts of the strap-on crampon hug the boots snugly without significantly bending to fit. To check snugness, place each boot in its crampon, turn upside down, holding onto the crampon. The post should hold the boot without straps. The heel wire on some strap-on crampons has a particular advantage. It keeps some boots from slipping through the rear post set, particularly the plastic models. For step-in/clamp-on bindings, the boot welt is particularly important. Preferred welts are Norwegian-style, double stitched welts on leather boots and indented toe and heel on plastic boots.

When not being used, stow the crampons with *rubber protectors* over the points and/or stow in a special *heavy-walled pouch*. Failure to do so may give your pack sides or interior gear more character than is considered cool. Bring some *duct tape* to place under the bottom face of the crampon in soft, sticky snow or purchase anti-stick snow plates. This prevents the snow from congealing under the crampon and potentially compromising footing.

Ice Tools. These items are purely and simply scaling and descending tools that find little use on the approach. Most ice tools have shorter shafts than ice axes, typically 50-60 centimeters in length. Tools with a hammer in place of the adze may be as short as 35 centimeters. For alpine ice climbing, most use a combination of ice ax in combination with the shorter hand tool. On more technical routes, many climbers go with an ice tool in each hand. Bring a spare pick if your tool has a replaceable pick feature. For long and demanding ascents, a third tool may be carried as a backup in case of loss or damage. The spare may also serve as an anchor at belay points or as a protection placement.

There is a varied set of ice tool designs in terms of pick, adze, shaft and spikes (in contrast, in terms of design, "hammers is hammers"). Holding and releasing characteristics of the *pick* are determined by its weight, shape and teeth. Heavy-headed tools will penetrate more easily, but also be more difficult to extract. (Some models have removable weights that allow for some tailoring.) The steeper the droop of a pick, the sharper, deeper and more frequent the teeth, the better the pick will hold. Also, the smoother the pick, the easier it is to remove. Thin, sharp edges penetrate and hold best, but are most subject to damage when they strike rock or are being twisted during extraction. Thick-bladed picks are more likely to dislodge plates of ice during removal.

The most common *adze* is straight, extending perpendicular to the shaft or drooping slightly downward. The straight adze is excellent for cutting steps with sharp corners. Some adzes have a downward curvature more characteristic of ice picks. The shape and curvature of the adze end surface is highly varied and some even have a slightly inward bend. Many ice tools accept interchangeable adzes; some allow interchange of an adze with a hammer.

Most *shafts* are straight although curved designs are available. The curved design intent is to keep your knuckles from banging against the ice during placement. This should not only save some grief on knuckles, but also assist in achieving better placements. Assure the design is tailored to suit your natural swing.

Spikes are solid or tubular. Solid designs have a flat plate or cone-shaped tip. Most spikes have carabiner holes on or near the tip. This allows clipping to the ice tool as a temporary anchor when setting up a belay anchor.

A *wrist leash* secures a dropped tool, helps add control and force in swinging the tool, and lets you rest your grip by hanging your weight from it. The leash is attached through the carabiner hole in the head. It should be just long enough to allow you to grasp the shaft near the end of the spike. Make allowance in length to place a knot in the leash to create a hand loop. Many climbers secure the leash to the shaft just above the leash knot.

Carabiners. Though most commonly associated with rock climbing, this item is integral with most roped climbing and rescue operations on mountaineering trips. Carabiners (or 'biners) for climbing are mostly aluminum alloy; there are also heavier-duty steel models for rescues. They are subject to the rigid standards of the Union International Des Associations d' Alpinisme (UIAA), the internationally-recognized authority on the subject. These standards set minimum breaking strength along the unit's long axis and short axis with gate closed and along the long axis when the gate is open. (Current minimum criteria are 2000 kilograms, 400 kilograms and 600 kilograms, respectively.) Carabiners come in a variety of shapes, sizes, and styles. (Heard that one before?) To ensure minimal chance of accidental gate opening while in use, the gate of any carabiner that you purchase should have a pronounced sharp (i.e. non-rounded) notch at the latch point.

Mount Independence, California

The most common *shape* is the classic oval, the symmetry making it a good all-purpose item. All-purpose "D" carabiners are stronger than the classic oval because more of the load is transferred to the long axis and away from the gate. Offset-D models have the advantage of the standard Ds, but have a wider, more-accessible gate. Bent-gate carabiners are most commonly used on difficult approaches where the eyes cannot comfortably be diverted from the hold; fast clipping and unclipping by pure physical feel is required. They should always be used with a runner so that they are free to rotate.

Locking carabiners have a sleeve that screws over one end of the gate; it is designed to prevent accidental opening. This provides an additional margin of safety when belaying, clipping into anchors and climbing ropes or repelling. The locking model takes the place of two standard carabiners for many actions which are highly dependent on a single placement. An even more safety-conscious version of the locking carabiner is a spring-loaded design that automatically positions the sleeve whenever the gate is closed. There are other carabiners optimized for specific maneuvers, belaying techniques and general styles.

Sizes are generally identified by gate-open clearances which range from about 15-30 millimeters. Weights range from about 15 grams for light ovals and Ds to 300 grams for the steel locking Ds used for rescue.

Climbing Rope. Yesteryear's twisted nylon climbing ropes have been replaced by synthetic kernmantle ropes, designed specifically for climbing. This rope is composed of a core of braided or parallel nylon filaments encased in a smooth, woven sheath of nylon. They are the single rope approved by the UIAA. The UIAA *conducts strength and impact force* tests to simulate severe, real-life climbing falls.

Certification for single ropes (9.8-12 millimeters in diameter) requires that they survive five falls with an 80 kilogram weight. The test uses a 2.8-meter rope attached to a fixed drop point of attachment. The weight is raised vertically and dropped, resulting in a total free fall of five meters. UIAA criteria are that the impact force not exceed 1200 kilograms. Certification for double ropes (each between 8-9 millimeters in diameter) is performed with a weight of 55 kilograms and impact force cannot exceed 800 kilograms. Static tension tests are performed to test stretch using an 80-kilogram weight (for both types of rope) and a one-meter rope section. For acceptance, the wider rope cannot elongate more than 8%. The narrower rope used for two-rope applications cannot stretch more than 10%.

Nevado Huantsan, Peruvian Andes — Courtesy of Adam Kolff

Water-repellent ropes have the advantage that they do not absorb water and thus cannot increase weight or freeze. Wet rope can lose up to 30% of its normal strength -- another case for investing in the water-repellent option. Sheathes and cores of these "dry" ropes are most often treated with either a silicon-based or Teflon-based coating. An additional advantage of the higher-cost water repellent ropes is that they are more abrasion resistant and create less friction when used in conjunction with gear such as carabiners.

Make a note of the date of purchase of your ropes. Perform an *inspection* of the rope for punctures or signs of sheath tattering after each trip. Damage to the rope's ends may simply require cutting off a small section, while damage near the center may call for its retirement. Ropes sustaining a severe fall, constant hard usage over short periods of time or moderate use over several seasons should be considered candidates for replacement.

Rope can be carried in coils or in a *rope throw bag*. These bags protect the rope, keep it cleaner and drier, and reduce the chance of tangling. Standard 10-11 millimeter climbing ropes are the most commonly used for snow and ice climbing, although this depends on the type of climb and the climber's preferences. The length standard is 50 meters, although some use extended lengths to permit longer pitches. For glacier travel, some parties carry an additional 8-9 millimeter, 100-foot rope as an emergency rescue line.

Web Runners. *Webbing* is used for making your own runners and etriers, among other uses. Standard widths are 9/16 to 1 inch. *Sewn runners* and etriers are also available. *Homemade* or *tied runners* are cut to size, ends melted and then tied with the appropriate knot. Their advantages are that they are less expensive and more versatile. You can cut them to any length. They can be easily untied and retied around anchors for use as a rappel sling and the sling length can be enlarged by tying together multiple runners. All tied webbing must be melted at its ends to ensure that it doesn't unravel.

The tie-off knots used vary with application, but water knots are most common. After tightening the knot under full body weight, the tail lengths should be at least two inches. Standard webbing lengths needed for tied runners are 5-1/2 feet, 9-1/2 feet and 14 feet for single, double and triple runners, respectively. Purchase different color webbing for these different lengths to help you easily identify them while on the climb. Strength ratings for 9/16-inch webbing are of the order of 5-10 kilonewtons. Typical weights are 0.2-0.4 ounces per foot.

Sewn seams are stronger than ties. *Sewn runners* are lighter and less bulky. Sewn runners can be cut, if needed, but this neutralizes the reasons for their purchase. Some materials in sewn runners are too slippery to hold a knot well; consult your dealer to ensure that you are aware of any such limitations. Sewn runners come in many lengths. Some of the most common are 2-inch and 4-inch "quick draws," 12-inch "half-lengths," 24-inch "full lengths" and 48-inch "double lengths." Strength ratings for 9/16-inch webbing are of the order of 20-30 kilonewtons.

Always write the date of purchase of web runners with an indelible marker on the runners themselves. Perform an *inspection* for damage after every trip. They should be retired after heavy use or several seasons of aging, primarily the result of ultraviolet (UV) light exposure.

Cord Runners. Cord runners are frequently tied as opposed to sewn. *Accessory cord* has a wide range of uses, from making prusik slings to slinging chocks. It comes in 4-millimeter to 9-millimeter widths, with 8-9 millimeter perlon cord most common for upper-end climbing use. Spectra Cord and Spectra A-Cord in 5.5-millimeter widths have the equivalent strength for about half the weight, but is also about twice the price. Special care is required in melting the ends (both cord and sheath) of these materials. Consult with the store of purchase. The tie-off knots used vary with application, but double or triple fisherman's knots are most common. After tightening the knot under full body weight, the tail lengths should be at least two inches. The 8 millimeter (40 grams per meter) and Spectra cords (20 grams per meter) are rated in the 15-20 kilonewton range. For contrast, 5-millimeter perlon cord (20 grams per meter) is rated at about 5 kilonewtons.

Utility cords in the 2-3 millimeter are not rated by the UIAA as are the webbing and cord runners. They serve well for special (non-primary load-bearing) use when climbing or for general use in camp.

Full Body Harness. The only commercial harnesses approved by the UIAA are *full body harnesses*. Incorporating both chest and seat harness, they have a higher tie-in point, reducing the chances of flipping over in a fall. Because the integral, full-body design distributes the force of a fall throughout the trunk of the body, it reduces the likelihood of lower-back injury. In spite of the safety features, it is not embraced by many climbers. Full-body harnesses are costlier and more restrictive, making it more difficult to add or remove clothing. Rather, many climbers prefer a seat harness, used with an improvised chest harness when the situation calls for both to be used. To evaluate full-body harness characteristics and test its fit, see the individual harness discussions below.

Mount Baker, Washington Courtesy of Don Stromberg

Seat Harness. *Commercial seat harnesses* are design-optimized for several different applications. *Alpine harnesses* are typically lightweight and have droppable leg loops that allow you to answer calls of nature while remaining tied in. They incorporate non-water-absorbent materials and are highly adjustable (to allow changing layers as the day progresses). Some models come with harness-integral gear-racking loops.

Big-wall harnesses generally have lots of padding at all key pressure points to accommodate long hangs as well as on-harness racking to take some of the weight off of your shoulder gear slings. Additional features are an integral belay/rappel loop and full-length haul loop for attaching a haul rope.

Sport/cragging harnesses are probably the best all-around harness, mixing the features of the alpine and big-wall rigs. They are equipped with padded leg loops and waist belt, integral belay/rappel loop, droppable leg loops and gear-racking loops.

A simple *homemade seat harness* can be made from about 22 feet of 1-inch width tubular webbing. This homemade rig might serve for light climbing or as an emergency backup for a broken or lost harness.

Commercial *swami belts* in conjunction with leg loops serve the same functions as a seat harness. The belts are wide enough to provide support around the middle of the waist and lower back and to distribute the weight of a fall. However, to ensure a fuller body distribution and to keep the belt from creeping up and constricting your breathing in a fall, the leg loops are needed. These belts are secured to the waist with a buckle or water knot. The climbing rope is tied through the belt/leg loop upper with a rewoven figure-8 or rewoven bowline. Going this route is a great way to optimize fit, since you can size each item separately. Avoid mixing brand-names when buying both items, as they may not work well together. Also, don't wear the swami and leg loops separately -- it would be terribly uncomfortable and could be very unsafe should you take a fall!

Fit and ease of use are especially important parameters for full-body and seat harnesses. When trying them on, wear the type of clothing that you will be climbing in. The waist belt should be snug (but not uncomfortable) and should ride just above your hip bones. You should not be able to even aggressively pull the harness over your hips. The leg loops should be snug but not binding. Adjustable leg loops are highly desirable. Having the waist buckle located toward one side helps avoid conflict with the locking carabiner that is clipped to the front of the harness.

You can add two *holsters* or a double-sized holster to your seat harness for carrying ice tools. Try out the tools in the holster before using it. Ensure that the tools are accessible and easily removable.

Chest Harness. Chest harnesses can be readily improvised using standard tubular webbing. Carabiner and baudrier harnesses are two of the most common examples. The carabiner harness requires use of a double-length runner and the baudrier harness a somewhat longer length runner.

Gear Rack. A gear rack (not the one on the auto) is the collection of organized climbing gear (carabiners, chocks, chock picks, cams) placed onto a *gear sling* that is carried over the shoulder. The sling can be purchased or crafted using 2-inch flat webbing which is sewn into a loop. About half of the webbing is rolled and sewn up to emulate a rope-like shape. The wide strip goes over the shoulder, while the rolled strip handles the gear. Climbing packs designed with easily accessible gear-holding rings are another option.

Belay/Rappel Devices. Most devices sold today are dual purpose, i.e., for belaying and repelling, although some climbers are more comfortable with separate gear. Repelling devices for rescue are predominantly single-purpose.

Belay devices amplify the function of the braking hand by passing the rope through an opening and wrapping it around a post. The post of all belay devices is a locking carabiner or part of the device itself. Currently, the most popular belay method is to clip the belay device into a locking carabiner on your seat or body harness rather than directly to an anchor. Aperture devices provide a passage for rope through a metal plate with slots (such as the Sticht plate) or a cone-shaped tube.

The figure-8 device was originally designed for repelling, but many models now serve double duty. The smaller hole in the figure-8, if it is the size of a typical aperture device hole, can be used like a slot or tube. The figure-8 can also be used in the standard repel configuration for belaying. The Bachli device, a streamed-lined figure-8 in appearance, is another belay option.

Among devices, slots and tubes produce the least friction in routine rope handling, which allows you to take up rope faster on easy ground. The Bachli configuration has less friction when holding a fall than slots and tubes. This is a desirable feature for ice and snow where belaying stances and anchors are generally weaker than in rock and would benefit from a lower force. Also, the consequences of a longer fall are often not as important. Slot devices require the least force to hold the climber's weight, but are also least smooth in lowering the climber. Slots and tubes can be tethered to keep them from sliding out of reach. Some of these devices include a hole for tether attachment.

The Bachli and figure-8 devices are the smoothest for *repelling*. However, both put a twist on the rope, potentially producing snarls in the coils later. Slot devices produce a jerky ride that put unnecessarily high loads on the anchor. Tube devices lie between the two groups in terms of smoothness of use.

Most belay/repel devices are designed to handle 8.5-9 millimeter double rope and 10-11 millimeter single rope (typically weighing 50-125 grams). Rescue figure-8 repelling devices are designed to handle a range of rope widths, some up to 19 millimeters width for single rope and 16 millimeter for double rope (typically weighing 220-290 grams).

Snow Anchors. Snow anchors are normally deadman anchors, that is, objects buried in the snow as an attachment for the rope. The most common is the *snow fluke*, a specially shaped aluminum plate with a metal cable attached. Its holding ability increases with size, or more specifically, the surface area that pulls against the snow when it is put under load. Flukes are available with bent faces, flanged sides or fixed cables -- features intended to maintain the correct orientation or to make them self-correct if deflected.

Ice axes, ice tools and pickets can also serve as deadman anchors. A *picket* is a stake (normally aluminum) driven into the snow as an anchor. Lengths are typically 18-36 inches. They come in many shapes, including angled or "T"-section stakes and round and oval tubes.

Mount Rainier, Washington Courtesy of Don Stromberg

Pickets work well when the snow is too firm for flukes, but too soft for ice screws. They can be driven in with a rock or side of an ice ax, although the most reliable method is to pound them in with the hammer on an ice tool. (Suitable rocks may not be available and an ice ax may be damaged if used for this purpose.)

A *bollard* is a man-constructed mound of snow that serves as an anchor when webbing or, less desirably, rope is positioned around it. Properly constructed, snow bollards provide highly reliable anchors for belaying or repelling in soft snow. They are possibly the most reliable in all snow conditions. The rub is that it takes time to build a bollard. Safety may require that it be up to 10 feet wide, surrounded by a 1-1/2 foot deep trench, in soft snow. (Think hard about bringing a snow shovel if there is a reasonable chance that you may be required to become a "bollard engineer.")

Ice Anchors. The counterpart to snow anchors, the most common ice-anchor gear are ice screws and ice bollards. *Ice screws* are sold in both solid and tubular designs, with the latter considered the strongest and most reliable. Typical designs work well in both summer and winter temperatures. As a minimum, the screw should have an integral metal fixture near its top that accepts another ice screw or ice tool for leverage. Some screws provide a kind of built-in racheting capability, simplifying screwing them in.

The hollow design minimizes fracturing of the ice by allowing displaced ice to work its way out of the core of the screw. The ice inside the core must be cleaned out immediately after screw removed. Otherwise it may freeze and render the screw temporarily useless. The interior of some designs is conical, making ice removal easier. A tubular screw holds a greater load than a solid one of the same length. Similarly, a large-diameter screw supports more weight than a smaller-diameter screw of the same length.

Hammer-in, screw-out designs are also available, both in solid and tubular versions. Their advantage is quicker placement. The solid versions can offer good protection in water ice at below-freezing temperatures. They are less effective in other forms of ice and at higher temperatures. Melt-out is sometimes rapid because the ice in the drive hole is compressed rather than displaced; this can lead to their shearing through ice when under load. The hollow-core versions are less prone to the melt-out problem. Like its solid counterpart, the hollow-core ice screws work best in hard ice, but can be unreliable in above-freezing temperatures.

Ice bollards are the colder-weather versions of snow bollards. They can be used for rappelling or belaying. The strength of the bollard is proportional to its size, trench depth and hardness of ice. In hard ice, typical bollard diameters are 12-18 inches at the widest point and depth is at least six inches. All features are cut out using pick and adze. To prevent the belay/rappel rope from slipping over the top of the bollard, the sides and top half of the bollard are undercut to create a holding channel.

Rescue Pulley. There are brute force methods for rescuing a fallen climber. Small groups without enough muscle to execute these tactics should consider bringing a rescue pulley. A *"C-pulley" provides* close to a 2:1 mechanical advantage for the lifting task. To use it requires a fallen climber who is conscious, since he or she must clip into the pulley. The pulley is attached to the unused end of the accident rope or a separate rope entirely, of sufficient length to be lowered to within the climber's reach. (Where the accident rope is jammed or otherwise not usable, this makes a case for having the spare rope.) The *"Z-pulley"* is actually a two-pulley system that offers a 3:1 advantage. It can be operated with no help from the fallen climber and uses the accident rope. "C"s, "Z"s and piggybacked systems that provide even higher mechanical advantages are also available

The lightest pull-ups (50-250 grams) have strength in the 3500 to 5000 pound range. They typically have aluminum side sheaves. The heaviest-duty models have steel side plates, steel or aluminum sheaves and weigh in the 400-800 gram arena. Their strength ratings are in the 10,000-15000 pound range. The smaller pull-ups generally will fit rope sizes up to 12.7 millimeters, while the heavy-duty models will handle up to 15.9 millimeter ropes.

Mechanical Ascender. Along with extra line, runners and carabiners for rappelling, rescue pulley(s), and a snow picket or ice screw, the mechanical ascender is a very handy rescue device. It is also used for solo climbing. When attached to a sling, it can be used to replace friction knots (such as the prusik) for self-rescue and for anchoring an accident victim. Ascenders attach to the rope more easily than with the friction knots, work better on icy ropes, and can be operated more readily with gloved hands. On the negative side, this gear is heavy and expensive. As mechanical devices, they are more prone to failure than knots. (Well-tied knots are not prone to come off the rope.)

All ascenders are designed for one-person static loads. They should not be used to catch a dynamic load in a belay situation. Ascenders are usually used in pairs, and some models come in a right- or left-handed version. Most ascenders are made for use with rope sizes out to 13 millimeters. From the least to the most robust, ascenders weigh roughly in the 150- to 600-gram range.

Hard Hat. Hard hats protect your noggin from falling rock and equipment dropped by partners higher on the "climbing chain." Falls have the bad habit of slamming climber's heads against rocks. Need further rationale for wearing a climbing helmet? The equipment should be lightweight (about 1/2 pound), well ventilated and comfortable, but with allowance for a snug pullover hat. The hard hat should also meet UIAA specifications for shock and energy absorption, conical impact and retention strap security. For climbing where the greatest concerns are rockfalls, refer to the discussion under "Hard Hat" in the ROCK CLIMBING activity.

Avalanche Beacon. Used to locate buried victims, this small electronic device can be switched between either a transmit or receive mode. The world standard frequency is 457 kilohertz; the U.S. switched from 2275 hertz to this standard in 1995. The beacon electronics are packaged in a crush-proof case inside a pouch that is normally worn around the neck and under the exterior clothing layer. Tiny earphones are connected to the electronics case. All climbers in a group set their beacons to the transmit mode in normal conditions, switching to the receive mode if a group member(s) is suspected of needing rescue.

A standard method of search for a buried member's beacon is conducted by homing in on beacon transmission, through signal strength monitoring. Once the buried victim's location is pinpointed, the next steps are to dig and reestimate the beacon location every couple of feet. Since digging with the hands or other makeshift tools available is slow, this process makes a strong case for carrying a snow shovel.

Two important cautions: First, if some party members have dual-frequency devices, ensure that everybody is tuned to a common frequency. Second, don't get lulled into thinking that a dangerous slope is safe because your group has beacons. They may only help you locate a victim; however, there is still an issue of timely extraction.

Mount Hood, Oregon Courtesy of Don Stromberg

Snow Shovel. Even for daytime trip use, a *small, collapsible snow shovel* may be handy to have. Emergency conditions may require that you dig an emergency shelter or dig out an avalanche victim. (Though not a high-volume snow-removal tool, the small shovel is certainly more efficient than hand-and-arm digging.) Most shovels are lightweight aluminum with a fold-down and/or removable scoop or a scoop that fits onto the end of an ice ax, all designed to simplify storage. A few models have longer shafts that can be broken down. The small unit is also useful for campsite preparation for overnight climbers.

Overnight parties should think hard about adding a heavier, bulkier *grain scoop*. It is a wide-faced shovel, often with a "T"-shaped handle for leverage. Most designs can be broken down to scoop, shaft and handle pieces. It is ideal for moving large amounts of snow quickly and, together with a snow saw, a valuable piece of gear for building igloos or performing other snow construction (e.g., building a protective wall to inhibit snow from drifting into the campsite confines). The shovel length should be consistent with providing good leverage, but short enough for use in a confined area (e.g., an under-construction snow cave).

Wands. Wands are used to mark snow and glacier routes to make the return easier, faster and safer. They are very useful in clear conditions, but also have potential crisis-avoidance use in poor visibility.

You can purchase these units or easily make your own. To self-manufacture, buy green-stained bamboo poles sold at garden supply stores as plant supports. The favored method is to slit the first couple of inches at one end, insert a strip of bright, durable waterproof tape into the slit, leaving a large enough end piece to tie it off with the main tape piece. Next, use a waterproof adhesive tape at the pole's end to close the slit above the bright marker tape.

Wands are normally from 2-1/2 to 4 feet in length. Smaller lengths may not be high enough to be easily seen when driven to the proper depth in the snow, while larger lengths become unwieldy to carry.

Skis/Snowshoes. Skis and snowshoes can minimize the pain in making an approach through deep snow fields of appreciable length. Skis also can offer a safety bonus for crevasse crossings since they distribute your weight over a wider area. They can also support rescue work when converted into a makeshift stretcher or sled. The downside for both skis and snowshoes is that they add weight and bulk. With a heavy pack, skiing can be difficult on all but modestly-sloped terrain. Strapped-on skis also will make traveling over steep or rocky terrain more awkward.

Nordic skis require a special boot which may not be compatible with your mountaineering needs. Nordic skiers also need the special skill of telemark turning for going downhill. Ski mountaineering employs a wider, heavier ski (sometimes referred to as the *randonee ski*) that is more like a traditional alpine ski. It has a dual-use binding that allows freeing the heel for uphill mobility (like a Nordic ski) and locking in the heel for downhill control (like an alpine ski).

To provide uphill traction, mountaineering skis are often fitted with removable climbing skins. You chose the width of the skins for the steepness of the trip. The narrower the skin, the less the traction, but the better the forward glide. The skins are effectively an assembly of skin surface and connected holdown hardware. The ends of the assembly clip over the ski tips and backs and frequently have an additional holddown nearer the center. (The skin is textured material known as nylon plush.) (Refer to the NORDIC SKIING/SNOWSHOEING (Daytime) section for more information on the use of skins on Nordic skis.)

Snow shoes are a traditional aid to snow travel. They are lighter than skis and allow travel over a broader variety of terrain. Snow shoes are cumbersome for step-kicking uphill and you may find yourself back to "post-holing" with boots on very steep, snowy slopes. Although slower than skis on flatter terrain, snow shoes have the additional advantage that they do not require special boots. Said differently, if you can winter backpack or winter climb in your boots, you can also snowshoe in them! (See the NORDIC SKIING/SNOWSHOEING section for additional detail about skis and snowshoes.)

Ski Poles. Ski poles aren't restricted to use with just skis or snowshoes. A wise investment up front may provide you with a tool that has equal use for winter and glacier climbing. They are superior to an ice ax for balance when you are hauling a heavy pack over level or low-angle snow, slippery ground or scree, or when your objective is a stream or boulder field crossing. They outperform ice axes fitted with snow collars in soft snow.

There are special features which make the poles even more valuable for dual use. A pole that telescopes provides adjustability on various angles of slope; these same designs fold up into a compact package when not in use. Models with removable baskets are ideally suited as probes for crevasses or avalanche victims. Some poles have interchangeable sections which allow fastening multiple pole parts together to fashion a deeper probe. Finally, some models have built-in springs on the shaft which absorb shock and prevent sore arms on extended trips. (Refer to the NORDIC SKIING/SNOWSHOEING section for additional detail about ski poles.)

Alarm Timepiece. You get caught up in the climbing and completely forget that there is a critical time to turn back or start seeking a bivouac site. Beep-beep-beep!! Your watch or other suitable timepiece breaks the euphoria with an alarm. You get the idea. A waterproof watch or a hearty sports watch (with alarm) tucked under your sleeve are good bets. Bring a spare power source if your timepiece is battery-operated.

Nevado Huascaran, Peruvian Andes Courtesy of Kees Kolff

Head Lamp and Batteries. Climbs frequently begin before dawn and often end after dark. A quality hand-held flashlight is perfectly adequate if the hands are free at all times. However, the head lamp has obvious advantages on climbs where rope, ice ax and other gear place frequent demands on the hands. Alternately, an emergency night exit over rough terrain might make the head lamp a life saver.

The nominal design is a lamp cartridge containing batteries and secured by a wide head strap. Another design used has the lamp, only, secured to the head and is wired to a power supply that is carried in the daypack/rucksack or frame pack. Armored, watertight models are worth the added expense, since they will function reliably with rough use and in all weather.

Choice of size and type of batteries and bulbs depends on purpose and planned duration of usage. A PR2 *bulb* connected to a three-volt power source is bright enough to illuminate a cross country route, while a 1.5-volt source with a PR4 bulb is just adequate for following a trail. For climbing ventures, the tendency is to go with a brighter source than for trail hiking, because the route is typically more unforgiving. Gas-filled bulbs are commonly used to achieve enhanced illumination, although they draw more current (amperage) and shorten battery life. Some climbers carry bulbs of different amperage, using the low-current bulbs around camp and the higher-current bulbs when a brighter beam is needed.

The common choices for *batteries* are alkaline, nickel-cadmium (Ni-cad) and lithium. Alkaline batteries are the best general-purpose batteries commonly available at mass-merchandisers. However, their voltage (and resultant light brightness) drops significantly as they discharge and their life is drastically shortened by cold temperatures (they operate at only 10 to 20% efficiency at 0 degrees Fahrenheit or 0°F).

Ni-cads are rechargeable, maintain brightness throughout most of their discharge, and are about 70% efficient at 0°F. Their shortfall is that they don't store as much energy as alkalines. A single lithium battery has about twice the energy storage capacity of two alkalines, maintains a steady brightness as it discharges and its efficiency at 0°F is about equal to that at room temperature. It's main drawback is that it is expensive. Because one lithium battery has twice the voltage of regular batteries, you'll need to rewire your light to run off of half the number of batteries or purchase a light that accomodates these modern-day marvels.

Personal Gear

Long Hiking Pants/Knickers. For GLACIER/WINTER CLIMBING and NORDIC SKIING/SNOWSHOEING, many forgo long pants, favoring knickers placed over long sox. (Knickers haven't made the style list for most winter backpackers or Alpine skiers, which amazes us.) Gaiters are generally required since the boot or shoe top is directly exposed to snow. Knickers allow fuller knee movement. When the lower legs get wet (which they often do in deep snow in spite of gaiters), it is easier to change sox instead of pants. Knicker fasteners at the knees can be opened for ventilation when needed. Both belt-high and high-waisted, bib-style knickers are available. The latter provide additional warmth and snow exclusion protection when glissading or crashing into snow banks and the like. The most popular materials are wool, wool/polyester blends, and synthetic pile (the least wind-resistant of the group), all of which maintain their insulating qualities when wet.

Socks. On mountaineering expeditions in cold weather, a *vapor-barrier liner* may be worn between two sock layers. These liners keep moisture next to your feet and prevent wetting your thick, outer socks. They also keep your feet warmer by preventing the evaporation of sweat. Their purpose is to reduce the danger of frostbite in sub-freezing weather. (The penalty of extended exposure to trapped perspiration is trench foot, a serious malady. If you use these liners, thoroughly dry your feet daily.) (See the HIKING section for more detail on less-extreme sock options.)

Gloves/Mittens. For VEHICLE-ACCESSIBLE CAMPING in winter, HIKING, BACKPACKING, ALPINE SKIING/SNOWBOARDING, NORDIC SKIING/SNOWSHOEING, non-technical GLACIER/WINTER CLIMBING and SNOWMOBILING activities, *mittens* are better than *gloves* for warmth since the fingers are snuggled together. For additional warmth, a heavy mitten can be worn over the glove. Best fit is a snug glove and looser mitten with inner mitt and outer mitt length sufficient to cover the wrist and lap under or over the parka sleeve. Preferred materials are synthetic pile and heavy wool.

For technical GLACIER/WINTER CLIMBING, an inner/outer mitten set with a *water-repellent outer mitten* is a better choice. An outer-mitt option is a waterproof mitt with waterproof/breathable nylon on the backside. For improved tool control while climbing, consider an over-mitt with a non-slip coating on the palm -- the backhand side of the mitt should breathe, so choose a waterproof/breathable fabric. (Some climbers double up, using these gloves together with tools that have a low-slip covering on the shaft.) The overmitt should overlap the outerlayer (e.g., shirt, sweater or jacket) sleeve some 4-6 inches and have elastic or Velcro closures to cinch the mitt to the forearm. Look for mitts and over-mitts which are equipped with a security cord (which prevent their loss when taken off the hands), or sew on your own.

Nuevo Rurec, Peruvian Andes Courtesy of Kees Kolff

Thin *leather gloves* are important for safety when rappelling or managing some belays (e.g., hip belay); they prevent rope burns that might hamper subsequent climbing efforts or cause you to release the rope. These gloves are also useful on the approach in thorny brush. Because they are difficult to waterproof and also to dry, don't count on them as a warming layer.

In performing climbing chores that require high manual dexterity, many climbers opt for polypropylene *glove liners* or a pair of *fingerless gloves* inside their mitts. Below about 0°F, exposed fingers freeze to metal; the liners are a safer choice under these conditions. You can buy fingerless gloves or make your own by cutting the fingers off a pair of army-surplus wool gloves.

Heavy Hiking/Climbing Boots. Refer to **Crampons** and **Skis/Snowshoes** above. Some use thick (1/8 inch or above) felt inserts to keep the bottom of their feet warm in sub-zero climbing conditions. The inserts are washable. If you plan to use inserts, ensure that you include them when trying on boots for size.

Nordic Ski/Snowshoe Boots. Refer to **Skis/Snowshoes** above.

Gaiters. The short-length and full-length gaiters discussed in the HIKING activity are more than adequate for many climbing efforts. The high-end option is super gaiters, which cover the boot from the welt up. The boot lug soles remain exposed for traction. The gaiter is held to the boot by a strong, wide band of elastic material. Super gaiters are insulated throughout their interior, including the full upper boot section. They are designed to minimize snow access to the boot and, thus, reduce the chance of frostbite during cold-weather climbs.

Goggles and Extra Set/Filters. Goggles provide additional protection (relative to sunglasses) against ice chunks that go flying when you are using your ice tools, as well as against falling ice and other debris. They are invaluable in conditions of blowing snow. Some models are designed to accomodate filter interchange, a boon if you plan to use them on the approach and in all stages of the climb.

The goggles must provide the necessary sun protection (see "special purpose" glasses under the TEN ESSENTIALS), have adequate ventilation to prevent fogging, fit over prescription glasses (if relevant), and fit under the helmet, if one is used. Additionally, the lenses should be shatter- and scratch-resistant. The goggles should have padding next to the face (normally foam) and a robust, adjustable head strap. Since they are so critical to the climbing effort, many mountaineers bring an extra set for the event of loss or breakage.

Some *fog-preventative measures* are in the design, e.g., use of double or triple lenses or application of an anti-fog coating on the interior lens. Additional measures available are to wipe the lenses with a chemically-treated cloth or fog-retardant paste.

<u>**Tool Kit**</u>

Tools. A starter set of useful tools includes a standard-head and Phillips-head screwdrivers, Allen wrench set (if applicable to your gear), small pliers and a small wire cutter/shear.

Repair Gear. Duct, filament and ripstop tape and mini-sewing kit (assorted needles and thread, assorted buttons, and fabric), extra wire and cord, and a crampon repair kit (extra screw, connecting bars, flat webbing) are typical of repair items to bring along.

Replacement Gear. The emphasis in this area should be gear items which, if lost or broken, would have greatest impact on safety or full-trip completion. Examples are spare bootlaces, sunglasses or goggles, ice ax/ski pole basket, ice pick (if replaceable on your ice tool) and ice tool.

<u>**Secondary Activities**</u>

Every now and then, you will find a snow or glaciated area with hot springs -- swim suits are optional. Some backcountry skiers/snowboarders perform winter climbs solely for the purpose of an exhilarating "make-fresh-tracks" downhill ride. Others, particularly snowboarders, truck the boards up mountains in order to make a quick, efficient return from a summit climb. We refer you to the NORDIC SKIING/SNOWSHOEING and ALPINE SKIING/SNOWBOARDING sections (specifically for information about skis/boards, bindings and poles) if you have these kind of aspirations.

GLACIER/WINTER CLIMBING
(Daytime)

Select items based on trip needs and worst-case weather conditions.

ITEM	DATE				
Hiking/Climbing Gear					
Auto Gear Rack/Locks					
Ice Ax					
Crampons					
Ice Tools					
Carabiners					
Climbing Rope					
Web Runners					
Cord Runners					
Full Body Harness					
Seat Harness					
Chest Harness					
Gear Rack					
Belay/Rappel Device					
Snow Anchors					
Ice Anchors					
Rescue Pulley					
Prusiks/*Mechanical Ascender*					
Hard Hat					
Avalanche Beacon					
Snow Shovel					
Wands#					
Nordic Skis/Skins; Snowshoes					
Ski Poles					
Alarm Timepiece					
Head Lamp & Batteries#					
Water Bottles/Water					
Bottle Insulating Sleeve					
Daypack/Rucksack					
Hiking/Wilderness Permit					
Personal Gear					
Long Pants/Knickers					
Long-sleeve, Heavy Shirt					
Turtleneck/Heavy Sweater					
Underwear					
Thermal Underwear					
Parka (w/p stuff sack) or Jacket					
Windbreaker					
Socks					
Gloves/Mittens					
Heavy Hiking/Climbing Boots					
Spare Shoelaces					
Nordic Ski/Snowshoe Boots					
Balaclava					
Brimmed Hat					
Raingear					
Gaiters					
Bandanna/Sweatband					
Turtleneck Dickie or Neck Scarf					
Goggles & Extra Set/Filters					

GLACIER/WINTER CLIMBING
(Daytime)

ITEM	DATE				
Toilet Paper & Towelettes					
Safety					
First Aid Kit (see FIRST AID)					
Water Filter/Tablets					
Sunglasses & Lanyard					
Heavy-Duty Sunscreen					
Lip Balm					
Whistle/Signal Mirror					
Waterproof Matches & Lighter					
Fire Starter/Heat Tabs, Spares					
Emergency Blanket					
Map(s)					
Compass/*Clinometer*					
Altimeter/*GPS Receiver*					
Pocket Knife					
Flashlight#					
Extra Batteries & Bulb#					
Reading Glasses & Repair Kit					
Thermometer					
Phone Change					
Communication Device					
Pen & Notepad					
Accessories					
Camera, Extra Film & Battery					
Camera Bag, Lens Cleaning Kit					
Monocular/Small Binoculars					
Sitting Pad					
Litter Bag					
Reusable Plastic Food Bags					
Spare Stuff Sacks					
Swim Suit (hot springs)					
Auto Tire Chains & Anti-Freeze					
Auto Tool Kit					
Spare Auto Keys/Credit Card/$					
Tool Kit					
Tools					
Repair Gear					
Replacement Gear					
Snacks (see MEALS section)					

Italicized items are optional (niceties or special purpose). #contingency nighttime travel gear

GLACIER/WINTER CLIMBING (Expedition)

See INDEX for checklist items not discussed below.

GLACIER/WINTER CLIMBING could range from an approach and overnight outing in fair weather to a multi-day mountain journey in inclement weather. It involves bivouacs in the classic mountaineering sense. The activity, as defined here, requires the use of technical climbing gear. Additional gear for traveling in deep snow, such as skis or snowshoes, may be required. Note that gear items such as tent, cooking stove and water filter can be shared by the group.

We do not pretend to treat world-class expeditions, requiring immense amounts of support personnel or specialized gear such as oxygen equipment. However, included in our group are folks who have climbed to nearly 23,000 feet in terrain demanding exceptional conditioning and mountaineering skills. See the **REFERENCE** section for sample sources that treat higher-difficulty levels of activity.

Safety Considerations: 1) review the **GENERAL CONSIDERATIONS** and TEN ESSENTIALS sections; 2) review the "Safety Considerations" noted for the HIKING, BACKPACKING and GLACIER/WINTER CLIMBING (Daytime) activities, as applicable; and 3) bring a healthy contingency of food and stove fuel, as you may be stuck in your tent for significant periods in severe weather.

In the checklist, items that are considered optional (niceties or special purpose) are *italicized*. Pound sign(#) items are those used for planned or contingency nighttime travel.

<u>**Hiking/Climbing Gear**</u>

Snow Shovel. A snow shovel serves for digging out avalanche victims or building snow caves in contingency situations. A winter camp in severe weather requires preparation that may include building snow walls around the tent area to prevent drifting snow from engulfing it. In addition a shovel is often used to support the construction of trenches and even build traditional igloos. All uses call for a trusty grain-scoop shovel. (Refer to the GLACIER/WINTER CLIMBING [Daytime] for additional information.)

Sled. These are a staple for emergency rescue units in snow. Also, some climbers pull sleds or tobaggans to carry gear on long, relatively-flat glacier trips, particularly when traveling on skis. Even a plastic child's sled can work and towing harnesses can be rigged to attach to a climbing harness or pack.

<u>**Personal Gear**</u>

A few additional comments on the tradeoffs employed in the layered clothing concept. Though the down parka is a staple for in-camp, insulation-layer wear in a large number of activities, many expedition mountaineers opt to go with a heavy jacket and additional clothing layers instead. On an exerting climb, the parka serves little use except during long rest periods.The concept is to go with the versatility of adding and subtracting clothing layers, whether actively climbing or in a bivouac.

<u>**Camping Gear**</u>

Nowhere else in this book is there a stronger need for quality camping gear. It will be needed to provide warmth in extreme cold, stand up to high winds and to have the capacity and design for storing hiking and climbing gear.

Four-Season Tent. A wind-stable, strong (able to handle a limited snow mantel without collapsing) tent/rainfly combination is a must for winter climbing. Select the light, highest-quality tent that meets your requirements for the number of occupants, head room, floor space and gear storage. The most popular shapes are those that make maximum use of space and minimize the number of stakes and guy lines needed. These are free-standing dome tents, two- or three-hoop tunnel tents and the traditional A-frame.

Entrance designs offer zip doors, tunnels, alcoves, vestibules, hoods and a few offer dual points of entry. Other useful features are gear pockets inside the tent for organizing small items and interior web or cord loops for hanging clothes or a candle lantern. The best designs should keep out the maximum amount of rain or snow as you enter and exit. Vestibules are a particularly nice feature -- they shelter the sleeping area entrance and provide additional room for gear, dressing and cooking.

Nuevo Huantsan, Peruvian Andes — Courtesy of Kees Kolff

Mosquito netting at the sleeping-area entry allows the flexibility to circulate air in the tent in warm weather, in addition to keeping out flies and mosquitoes. The netting must be part of a two-panel system that includes an exterior weather panel if netting is integral with the rainfly. This dual-panel feature is desirable if there is netting in the tent door itself; it allows you to set the level of airflow to maximize comfort year-round.

Single-walled tents of rainproof, breathable fabric have recently come onto the market. They are lighter than dual-walled models, but have a greater tendency to ice up on the inside wall. Though not as heat-retentive as the dual-walled designs, the higher-quality models have proved to be very well suited for high-altitude climbs in severe weather.

Most four-season tents come with shock-corded aluminum *tent poles* which are usually stronger than their fiberglass counterparts. High-tech poles of such materials as Kevlar and carbon fiber are now appearing in outdoor recreation outlets. They provide more strength per unit weight than aluminum, at additional cost.

Seam Sealer. Trying to seal your gear in the wet and snow shows little class, besides limiting the chance of success in closing off those demonic leak sites. Do a careful job before leaving; if you have any doubts, give your tent (and raingear for that matter) a backyard rain shower with the hose. (Be careful to simulate the dynamics of a rain shower and not a flash flood!)

Snow Saw. Nothing beats a grain scoop shovel in tandem with a snow saw for igloo building. The saw is almost a necessity for cutting form-fitting snow blocks out of compacted snow. A saw-toothed blade with length of about 20 inches and about two-inch width is needed, Aluminum is preferred for its high strength/weight ratio and low cost. The saw can be purchased or made at home. The latter option is straightforward. Buy the blade, sandwich the blade handle between two cut-to-size wood handle pieces, and run screws or bolts through the handle assembly. The saw should be fit to a sheath when in the pack to avoid chewing up your gear. Heavy cardboard, light, pliable plastic sheeting or other such materials càn be formed to fit over the teeth.

Hygiene

Pee Bottle. We just didn't know which sub-category to put this item into ("Safety" or "Tool Kit" or ....). Anyway, when the weather conditions outside the tent are severe, this sealable bottle is for relieving yourself in relative comfort. There are form-fitting devices that also make this conveniently usable for women.

Tool Kit

Tools. A starter set of useful tools includes a standard-head and Phillips-head screwdrivers, Allen wrench set (if applicable to your gear), small pliers and a small wire cutter/shear.
Repair Gear. Tent repair kit (pole splices, spare pole), stove repair kit, tape (duct, filament, ripstop-nylon tape) mini-sewing kit (assorted needles and thread, safety pins, assorted buttons, snaps, buckles, "D" rings, Velcro, Cordura and ripstop nylon fabric patches), extra wire and cord, and a crampon repair kit (extra screw, connecting bars, flat webbing) are typical of repair items to bring along.
Replacement Gear. The emphasis in this area should be gear items which, if lost or broken, would have greatest impact on safety or full-trip completion. Samples of spares are bootlaces, sunglasses or goggles, ice ax/ski pole basket, ice pick (if replaceable on your ice tool) and ice tool.

Secondary Activities

Refer to the GLACIER/WINTER CLIMBING (Daytime) activity.

Mount Baker, Washington Courtesy of Don Stromberg

GLACIER/WINTER CLIMBING
(Expedition)

Select gear based on trip needs and worst-case weather conditions.

ITEM	DATE				
Hiking/Climbing Gear					
Auto Gear Rack/Locks					
Ice Ax					
Crampons					
Ice Tools					
Carabiners					
Climbing Rope					
Web Runners					
Cord Runners					
Full Body Harness					
Seat Harness					
Chest Harness					
Gear Rack					
Belay/Rappel Devices					
Snow Anchors					
Ice Anchors					
Rescue Pulley					
Prusiks/*Mechanical Ascender*					
Hard Hat					
Avalanche Beacon					
Snow Shovel					
Wands#					
Nordic Skis/Skins; Snowshoes					
Ski Poles/Avalanche Probe					
Alarm Timepiece					
Head Lamp & Batteries#					
Water Bottles/Water					
Bottle Insulating Sleeve					
Collapsible Water Bag					
Daypack/Rucksack					
Frame Pack & Cover/Liner					
Sled					
Hiking/Wilderness Permit					
Personal Gear					
Long Pants/Knickers					
Long-Sleeve, Heavy Shirt					
Turtleneck/Heavy Sweater					
Underwear					
Thermal Underwear					
Parka (w/p stuff sack) or Jacket					
Windbreaker					
Socks					
Gloves/Mittens					
Heavy Hiking/Climbing Boots					
Nordic Ski/Snowshoe Boots					
Balaclava					
Brimmed Hat					

GLACIER/WINTER CLIMBING
(Expedition)

ITEM	DATE				
Raingear					
Gaiters					
Bandanna/Sweatband					
Turtleneck Dickie or Neck Scarf					
Goggles & Extra Set/Filters					
Camping Gear					
4-Season Tent					
Stakes & Poles					
Seam Sealer					
Ground Cloth					
Tent Broom & Sponge					
Snow Saw					
4-Season Sleeping Bag (w/p s/s)					
Sleeping Pad					
Bivouac Sack					
Stove & Windbreak, Primer					
Fuel Bottle					
Fuel Funnel/Strainer					
Cooking Pot					
Teapot (hot water)					
Non-Stick Cooking Lubricant					
Scouring Pad					
Cup & *Plate*					
Eating Utensil(s)					
Candle Lantern					
Paper Towels					
Reusable Plastic Food Bags					
Spare Stuff Sacks					
Litter Bag					
Hygiene					
Towel & Washcloth					
Personal Toiletries/Ditty Bag					
Toilet Paper & Towelettes					
Toilet Trowel					
Pee Bottle					
Laundry Bag					
Safety					
First Aid kit (see FIRST AID)					

GLACIER/WINTER CLIMBING
(Expedition)

ITEM	DATE				
Water Filter/Tablets					
Sunglasses & Lanyard					
Heavy-Duty Sunscreen					
Lip Balm					
Whistle/Signal Mirror					
Fire Starter/Heat Tabs, Spares					
Waterproof Matches & Lighter					
Emergency Blanket					
Map(s)					
Compass/*Clinometer*					
Altimeter/*GPS Receiver*					
Pocket Knife					
Flashlight#					
Extra Batteries & Bulb#					
Reading Glasses & Repair Kit					
Thermometer					
Phone Change					
Communication Device					
Pen & Note Pad					
Accessories					
Camera, Extra Film & Battery					
Camera Bag, Lens Cleaning Kit					
Monocular/Small Binoculars					
Sitting Pad					
Swim Suit (hot springs)					
Auto Tire Chains & Anti-Freeze					
Auto Tool Kit					
Spare Keys/Credit Card/$					
Tool Kit					
Tools					
Repair Gear					
Replacement Gear					
Meals (see MEALS section)					

Italicized items are optional (niceties or special purpose). #nighttime travel gear

ROCK CLIMBING (Daytime)

See INDEX for checklist items not discussed below.

Single-day rock climbing infers making a daytime approach via a hike-in or from a base camp. Gear needed for a hike-in is described in the HIKING activity and from a base camp in the BACKPACKING section. We have not attempted to cover multi-day, big-wall climbing. See the **REFERENCE** section for sample sources that treat higher-difficulty levels of activity.

The rock climbing needs described are broken out as to whether the activity is free climbing or aid climbing. Free climbing, as used here, assumes the use of protective hardware for safety; however the ultimate goal of the free climber is to make the climb without putting weight on the rope or the protection. Aid climbing is associated with the technique of using gear to support your weight as you climb. Clean aid climbing involves leaving the route as you found it. This means not defacing the rock with pitons or bolts and removing of all non-permanent climbing hardware after use. Pitons and bolts, in today's standard of climbing ethics, are reserved for first ascents of major walls, unprotected, dangerous sub-routes that have not been climbed or have deteriorated, and emergencies.

Safety Considerations: 1) review the **GENERAL CONSIDERATIONS** and TEN ESSENTIALS sections; 2) review the "Safety Considerations" noted for the relevant activity that describes your approach to the rock climb site; 3) master the reading of both weather and snow/ice conditions -- if there are doubts, put off the rock climb for another day; 4) practice your free-climbing or aid-climbing techniques; 5) practice belay, rappel and rescue techniques with your group before attempting the next-level climb; 6) ensure that there is a group leader with experience in higher-difficulty climbs than the one you are attempting; 7) develop plans for contacting rescue units in an emergency; 8) practice techniques needed to extricate an injured climber from the climbing area; 9) replace all worn or suspect climbing gear; 10) bring contingency gear if there is any reasonable possibility of getting stuck on the rocks overnight; 11) wear a hard hat if the climb warrants its use; 12) turn back at the first indication of severe weather onset or if you feel the climb is above your skill level.

In the checklists, the gear items nominally reserved for aid climbing are noted with a "plus" sign(+). Items that are considered optional (niceties or special purpose) are *italicized*. Items noted with an asterisk(*) are those needed for climbing in cold weather. Pound sign(#) entries are contingency gear for nighttime travel. Note that all gear items noted in the checklist are not necessarily carried on the climb. Rather, some gear may be left at the base for post-climb usage.

<u>**Rock Climbing Gear**</u>

Athletic Tape. Athletic tape on the hands protects against rock abrasions, especially when working jam cracks. When applied, the tape must stay securely in place and not unravel during the climb. The most common method is to tape the knuckles and the back of the hand, leaving most of the palms free and flexible. Tape can also be used to provide support and/or protection for the finger joints that can be overstressed in difficult rock climbing.

Chalk Bag. Many climbers use gymnastic chalk to improve their grip, particularly in hot, sweaty weather. The bag should be easily accessible at all times. Most often the chalk bag is carried on the back of the harness or attached to a separate runner tied around the waist.

Climbing Rope. The kernmantel rope described in the GLACIER/WINTER CLIMBING section is also the standard for rock climbing. Single-rope climbing is normally performed with 10-11 millimeter rope and double-rope climbing with color-coded 9-millimeter rope. Rope length for unaided climbing is highly dependent on the nature of the climb. For aided climbing, 165-foot, 11-12 millimeter rope is most common. A haul line is used when you must shed your pack to make a difficult pitch, climb a narrow chimney, or the like. It is typically an 11-millimeter or 9-millimeter line which doubles as a backup rope and a second rope for long rappels.

Stoney Point, California Courtesy of Vernon Reid

Wedges. Artificial chocks (as opposed to natural chocks such as chockstones and boulders) are either wedges or cams. Chocks are designed for use in rock features. Larger chocks are generally heavier and stronger than smaller chocks. Some smaller chocks aren't even meant to hold a fall, but are strong enough to support a climber's weight when aid climbing. *Passive wedging chocks* are tapered down from top to bottom. They come with straight sides, slightly curved sides and combinations of the two. Some hexagonal passive cams (hexes) are tapered such that they can double as wedges. Wedges can also be used in combinations (chock stacks). Any single wedging device works only within a specific range of crack sizes, making it necessary to bring an array of devices.

Spring-loaded wedging devices feature two pieces in opposition, a variation of the chock-stack principle of operation. Primary use is in tiny finger cracks. The most common designs use a sliding piece (wedge-, ball- or curve-shaped surface) which moves up against a fixed surface to create a minimum profile when the trigger is pulled. When the device is fully inserted into the crack and the trigger is released, the sliding piece reverses direction to maximize the two-piece profile. The movement ceases when the combination profile of the two pieces jams the crack wall. These devices can be operated with a single hand and used in both vertical and horizontal cracks.

Cams. Traditional *passive camming chocks* have a balanced hexagonal shape. Alternative shapes, where each pair of sides is a different distance apart, are more flexible in use. There are also cams with irregular shapes that include combinations of flat, rounded and pointed surfaces on a single cam. These devices tend to work in a wider range of cracks than the hexs and asymmetrical hexes. However, like wedges, an array of devices is needed to cover a wide range of crack sizes.

Spring-loaded camming devices use 3-4 single-action cams on a single stem. The operation sequence using the trigger mechanism is similar to that for a spring-loaded wedging device. With the device, protection can be placed with one hand for a wide range of crack sizes. The stem must be oriented to the direction of pull for safest use; it would follow that its greatest use is in vertical cracks. Some newer designs have flexible stems, which allow for safer use in non-vertical cracks. In a fall, all cams try to rotate and expand further, gripping the crack even more securely.

Large cracks present a special problem because large spring-loaded camming devices are extremely heavy. One alternative is to use a *spring-loaded tube chock*. The tube chock has a spring-loaded inner sleeve. Release the spring and the sleeve pops out far enough for the tube to bridge the crack. A locking collar keeps the tube extended. After setting the chock, the climber clips into a sling attached to the other end. With a load on that end resulting in an upward force on the sleeve end, the device acts like a passive camming chock.

Chock Slings. Chock slings are normally made from accessory cord, tubular webbing or wire cable. Smaller chocks usually come with a wire cable sling, which is stronger than cord or webbing of comparable size. The cable ends are swaged together. Larger chocks generally come pre-drilled with holes for accessory cord. Some chocks come pre-slung with tubular webbing.

There is an advantage to using wire cable with passive wedges -- the wire's relative stiffness makes the wedges easier to place. However, with passive camming chocks, it's generally better to use accessory cord, provided it's strong enough. The cord allows the device to rotate and cam freely, as it is meant to do. Most modern hexes are drilled to accept 5.5-millimeter cord.

Owens River Gorge, CA Courtesy of Troy Campbell

The classic slings have been made of 6-millimeter nylon cord and nylon webbing. An alternate fiber called Kevlar is becoming more popular since it is smaller, lighter and stronger than nylon. This cord is weakened by repeated bending, thus the manufacturer recommends it only for tying chock slings. (These slings are tied just once and, if properly used, not subjected to repetitive bending.) A new fiber, Spectra, is even lighter, stronger and more abrasion resistant than Kevlar. For use as chock slings, the Spectra fiber is used in 5.5-millimeter cord or 9/16-inch webbing. Some materials in sewn runners are too slippery to hold a knot well, thus they should not be cut and retied. Check with a qualified salesperson or veteran climber to ensure that you are buying the proper webbing.

Some additional tips. When purchasing, ensure that holes drilled in the chock have rounded edges and are burr-free. When in use, tie off cord ends with a double fisherman's knot. Common sling lengths are 8 to 14 inches, adequate for flexible use without hanging down far enough to interfere with footwork when climbing.

Chock Picks. Sometimes, chocks are more difficult to remove than to put in. An aid to removal is the *chock pick*. The thin metal tool is used to pry and poke and tap and tug the reluctant chock. All picks have a hand grip at one end and a pick at the other, though from there, the similarity ends. Styles include shelf bracket, piton type, Leeper, skewer type (or tent stake) and Friend of a Friend. Picks should be sturdy, because you'll often have to hammer on it to tap out lodged chocks.

Gear Rack. Some climbers opt for a double gear rack. It has gear slings on both sides of the body, which distributes hardware weight. This improves balance and comfort and reduces neck strain caused by a single rack. With proper design, it can also serve as a chest harness for jugging up on a mechanical ascender (for aid climbing or for emergencies). The features needed include wide, padded shoulder straps, a wide chest band, solid strap-cinching hardware and an overall robust sewn-webbing body.

Hard Hat. Rock climbing helmets have a small brim (if any), have head bands and chin straps connected to the helmet at four points for fore and aft stability, and include interior padding and suspension. The lightest and most comfortable ("light-duty") helmets are for light alpine climbing and any climbing area with limited rockfall. The "medium-duty" model is a good compromise between weight, comfort and protection. The "heavy-duty" hard hat is for high-rockfall climbs, having the most weight and foam padding, the latter resulting in the least ventilation. Some models extend down far enough to cover the ears.

Fanny Pack/Daypack/Haul Bag. On short climbing efforts with little chance of getting caught out in the elements, it's easy to make the argument to leave the weight and bulk of this gear behind. A *fanny pack* that holds your water, some snacks and the "success-oriented" version of the TEN ESSENTIALS will probably cut in fair weather.

If in doubt, carry a *daypack* with a more conservative approach to satisfying the TEN ESSENTIALS (particularly in the "extra clothing" area) as well as including contingency repair gear. Packs with streamlined, non-obtrusive exteriors are preferred. They should snug up to the body and carry weight in a position that is comfortable to your balance. Ideally, they will only be large enough to accommodate the gear that you need or are segmented or cinched/draw-stringed in a fashion to keep your gear from shifting within the pack. A hauling loop and rugged pack design to allow hauling up and bouncing off of rocks is a given. An extra benefit is a pack with gear loops for backup climbing hardware, an ice ax or any other nifty gear that you may need access to in a pinch.

It is unlikely that a *haul bag* would be needed for a day climb. These are rugged construction bags with heavy haul straps normally reserved for hanging and hauling big-wall gear for multi-day climbs. Haul bags typically have capacities in the 3000-8000 cubic-inch range and weigh from about 5-10 pounds.

Knee Pads. Knee pads are more typically used for tight chimneys, ascending a fixed rope and by big wall climbers in general. Basic rock climbing is done using hands and feet, although there may be a lot of knee contact with rock. If purchased, they should have ample padding with robust base material and seams. Pads should be comfortable and allow good circulation.

Belay/Rappel Device. Though not part of a free climbers forte, consider bringing along this device for an emergency. It also may be useful when the weather, your wristwatch or a reluctant climber suggests making a quicker and/or safer exit.

Bolts. A bolt is a permanent piece of protection driven into a hole drilled in rock. It supports a bolt hanger that is used for carabiner attachment. A threaded nut is sometimes used to attach the hanger to the bolt. Steel hangers tend to be stronger than aluminum. Also the latter become brittle with use. Why the long-term interest? More than likely, you will be using in-place protection much more often than providing it. If, however, you are driving first-time protection, it seems fair to provide the sturdiest option. In some climbing areas, bolt hangers are customarily removed by climbers after use. Thus, it might be prudent to carry along a few hangers and nuts in the 1/4-inch to 3/8-inch range. (As with pitons, first-time placements are discouraged, unless necessary for safety.)

South Platte, Colorado Courtesy of Troy Campbell

Hangers. These devices are used with bolts. *Wire hangers* are wire loops commonly 1/8-inch or 3/32-inch in diameter with a slider to cinch the wire tight over both studs and rivets (basically, bolts with a wide head). *Regular hangers* and *keyhole hangers* serve a similar function as wire hangers, but are shaped pieces of metal rather than wire loops. They are especially useful at belay anchors and for in-place bolts that have no anchors. The regular anchor has a unique bolt hole at the upper surface for direct placement on the bolt. Keyhole hangers have the metal between the bolt hole and carabiner hole filed out to allow slide-in placement over rivets and buttonhead bolts.

Pitons. Modern-day pitons (also referred to as pins) are made of chrome-moly steel. Unlike the malleable devices of yesteryear, they mold a crack to their form, forever altering the landscape. As a result, their use is universally discouraged unless deemed absolutely necessary for safety. For instance, they are still one of the few usable options for climbing overhanging rocks and working with thin cracks. For winter mountaineering, when cracks are filled with ice, they may be the only viable means of protection. The piton body has a forward-pointing shaft with edges -- the business end, and a rear portion for driving the piton which has a hole (eye) or holes as attachment points Pitons vary greatly in shape, size and ultimate use. They are discussed in the order from smaller to larger sizes below.

The Realized Ultimate Reality Piton (RURP) is a postage-stamp-sized, hatchet-shaped pin used in incipient cracks. It will usually support body weight. The pin derives its limited strength by minimizing the leverage between the piton and the 'biner supporting your etriers. Some models have offset sides for use in corners.

Knife blades are long, thin pitons that have two eyes -- one directly at the rear end of the shaft or blade and a second at the offset portion of the pin. They come in variable blade lengths and thicknesses ranging from 1/8 inch to 3/16 inch. They are commonly used to fit many cracks that are too thin for small nuts.

Lost Arrows are similar to knife blades, but have a single eye that is centered at the offset portion of the pin. These too are commonly used pitons that come in different lengths and thicknesses (5/32 to 3/8 inch). Their primary use is in horizontal cracks.

Angles are pitons formed into a "V." The V varies in height from about 1/4 inch to 1-1/2 inches. Both large-angle and small-angle shafts are available. Their strength lies in the metal's resistance to bending and spreading. *Sawed-off versions of the angle pins* are sometimes used in shallow placements. Nominally available in 3/4-inch to 1-inch lengths, their added value is that they leave shallow pin scars.

Leeper Z pitons obtain their thickness through their "Z"-shaped shaft profile as opposed to the "V"-shape of an angle pin. These pitons are very solid and work well for stacking. This feature, combined with short lengths, makes them very useful for bottoming cracks.

Bongs are the "battleship" of pitons, angles varying from 2-6 inches in width, and meant for big cracks. They can double as large chocks. Bongs generally have multiple eyes of different widths scattered over both sides of the V. Large camming devices, which tend not to leave scars and are removable, have largely replaced bongs.

Malleable hardware is designed to hold weight where the crack surfaces are highly irregular. The method is to pound the malleable portion of the device into the crack, thus melding the soft head of the placement with the rock. The devices range from simple hangers with a malleable copperhead or aluma-head (aluminum) at one end and a loop at the other, to circular (circle head) hangers with the malleable portion(s) integral to the loop.

Copperheads are more durable than aluma-heads, but are less malleable. Because of these properties, aluma-heads tend to be used for the larger sizes and copperheads for the smaller. The main body of most of these devices (also known as "mashies") is wire cable. The security of these mashies varies greatly with rock composition, depth of placement, and other factors which make it hard to gauge placement strength. These devices should be thought of as last-resort equipment.

Piton Hammer. Preferred piton hammers have a flat driving surface for cleaning and driving pitons, and a blunt pick for prying out protection, cleaning dirty cracks, and placing mashies. In addition to a sling-attachment hole at the shaft's lower end, some hammer shafts come with a shock-absorbing grip section. Shafts should be long enough to forcefully drive pins and short enough to fit comfortably into a belt holster. A carabiner hole in the head is useful for cleaning pins and malleable pieces. One end of the attachment sling ties into the shaft hole. The other end is looped over one shoulder -- its length should be adequate to allow full upward arm extension when using the hammer.

Etrier(s). Etriers are ladder-like slings that allow climbers to step up (rather than climb) from one placement to the next when they are clipped to a chock, piton or another aid device. As with runners, etriers can be bought or self-constructed. For alpine climbing, a single 9/16-inch to 11/16-inch webbing is most commonly used. For most aid climbing, one or two etriers with one-inch webbing is more suitable. The choice of one or two pairs depends upon the nature of the route and personal preferences. These devices commonly have four to six steps and are about five feet in length.

Tying your own etriers lets you tailor their length to your application. Overhand knots are used at each step and a frost knot to create the loop for carabiner attachment. The knots need to be checked periodically for slippage, unlike the pre-sewn gear. *Commercially-made* or *home-sewn etriers* are preferred over the tied versions for routes requiring extensive aid; this is because the etrier loops remain open for foot placement when weighted. *Metal-ring etriers* have the same advantage, but are less likely to blow in the wind. They are heavier and can cause pain if they swing into you or your partner.

Daisy Chain. This gear item consists of tied or sewn slings with a loop formed every 3-6 inches. The nominal daisy-chain length is one that, when attached to your harness, reaches as far as your raised hand. Most often, a carabiner is attached to every loop or every other loop in the chain so that you can quickly clip into an aid placement and rest on your harness. Some carry a second daisy, without carabiners in each loop, for other purposes. Examples are attaching to ascenders while jugging or for preventing loss of etriers if a hook placement fails.

Small Nuts. Aid racks customarily include small specialty nuts, beyond those included on free-climbing racks. These tapered nuts are often used in place of thin pitons, but they have less strength. They are designed to hold body weight, so they may fail if fallen upon. There are two most commonly-used styles. One is a smaller version of a common tapered Stopper. The other has both horizontal and vertical taper and is more secure in flaring cracks and old piton scars.

The heads of small nuts are made from aluminum, brass or stainless steel. Aluminum and brass bite into the rock and hold better in marginal placements. However, steel nuts are less likely to deform and fail if you take a fall on them.

Fifi Hook. These gizmos function somewhat like daisy chains, but are attached to your harness with a smaller sling, usually 2-6 inches in length. You can quickly clip the hook into an aid piece, allowing time to rest on your harness. Aid climbers usually carry one Fifi hook for use on bolt ladders and fixed pitches. The hook's working surface is in the rough shape of a half-carabiner; however, there is no latch. Thus users must be careful not to relax the tension or change the angle in a fashion to cause it to become unhooked from the protection.

New River Gorge, West Virginia Courtesy of Troy Campbell

Hero Loops. These are very short tie-off slings, normally about 4-6 inches in length, that are threaded through fixed protection in place of a 'biner. Most often, climbers tie their own out of 1/2-inch webbing. Hero loops find most frequent use along routes with many in-place bolts and pitons. They are used to tie off partially driven pins and to prevent the loss of stacked pieces such as chocks. Additional uses are for establishing anchors and extending placements to reduce rope drag.

Hooks. General hooks come in many shapes and forms and are most commonly used to grip ledges or small holes. The standard hook is constructed of chrome-moly steel for strength. The non-hook end should be wider and curved to provide the necessary stability. *Sky Hooks* (yes, there really is such a beast) are shaped like wide-body fish hooks and are useful for small flakes and ledges. Greater stability is achieved on some routes (i.e., dependent on the geology) if the tip of the hook is fixed to a point. This allows setting the hook into small holes drilled at the back of tiny ledges. *Fish hooks* or *ring clamps* are large sky hooks and are used to grip larger flakes or ledges. *Logan hooks* are L-shaped. The wide, flat style is particularly suited to (most stable for) tiny ledges and flakes, and the narrow style can be used in narrow pockets. *Bat hooks* are basically a narrow style Logan hook with a pointed blade. These are used in shallow 1/4 inch holes which have been drilled for their use.

Drill Kit. Drill holders for setting bolts or creating holding surfaces for hooks are either hand- or battery-powered. The *hand-powered kit* consists of the holder, a chisel or pointed-end drill bit and an internal driving pin. The climber literally hammers the holder to drive in the bit. The kit is relatively light, however it requires about 15-20 minutes of effort to drive a hole in hard rock.

The *battery-powered version* weighs 7-10 pounds, consisting of the holder with a grip handle, an Allen key and drill bits. It typically uses carbide-tipped, pointed end bits, and can drill a hole in about a minute. Typical battery life is sufficient to drill about 6-12 holes in hard rock. The bits themselves come in 1/4-inch, 1/2-inch and 5/16-inch sizes for both kit types. Some battery-powered devices can also handle a 3/8-inch bit.

Personal Gear

Climbing Outfit. Choice of clothing should be based on considerations of weather and route. Baggy pants or shorts that allow maximum freedom of movement are preferred by most. However, some climbers, with an eye to minimize interference of clothes with rock features, choose to climb in body-hugging tights made of materials such as Lycra. Some climbers find that knickers provide the needed freedom of movement and all-around utility in an alpine environment. Upper bodywear is governed by similar considerations. Common options are shirts and sweaters that allow ventilating while on the climb. Loose-fitting (to prevent chafing) polyester/Spandex or polypropylene underwear, with their superior wicking and warmth-when-wet characteristics are commonly used. Protective layer gear selection is governed by the same qualities discussed in the VEHICLE-ACCESSIBLE CAMPING activity with one proviso. The gear should not limit freedom of movement to the point where it severely restricts climbing ability.

Climbing Shoes/Boots. *Mountaineering boots* are commonly used on alpine climbs of modest difficulty or where weather or conditions (such as presence of snow or ice) favor their use. Narrow-welt boots generally hold well on larger edges, but are less useful than climbing shoes on small edges and for "smearing" on holds. The strength provided by a full- or 3/4-shank boot, that is so valuable for front-pointing on ice and snow, can become a drawback where shoe flexibility is called for.

A pair of *approach/boulder shoes, cross-training shoes or light hiking boots* will probably suffice on simple rock scrambles or short non-technical climbs. For more difficult climbs, *rock climbing shoes* are made specifically for the task. Key features of the climbing shoes are its shape and construction. The "model foot" around which the shoe is built (its shape) most commonly comes in traditional semi-flexed-last and cambered-last designs. The traditional, semi-flexed last replicates the natural anatomical shape of the foot and therefore provides more comfort. It can be used for all-day, free-climbing activities. The cambered last uses compression to limit your foot's flex, forcing your toes to crimp downward. This provides the stiffness essential for secure edging. This design normally comes with thin midsoles which accentuate sensitivity for the rock. Cambered-last shoes are specifically designed for ultra-steep routes and sports climbs of limited duration. For either last shape, a tapered, low-profile toe will let you make the most of jams in finger cracks.

Most climbing shoes are equipped with special "sticky" rubber-compound rands and soles that increase the friction between rock and sole. Slip-lasted and board-lasted construction are the two most common options. Slip-lasted construction incorporates thinner insoles and midsoles which make these shoes very flexible and sensitive. This enhances your ability to grab holds with your toes, to take advantage of smaller dips, and to smear on steeper angles. Board-lasted construction uses stiffer insoles and midsoles making these shoes more supportive. This construction is superior for working on tiny edges and on multi-pitch edging and crack climbs. Stiffer midsoles will keep your feet from overflexing during strenuous heal-and-toe jams. Board-lasted shoes can be resoled.

Motherlode, Kentucky Courtesy of Troy Campbell

All-purpose shoes are designed to handle it all -- thin cracks, wide cracks, friction and edging. They are ideally suited to multi-pitch climbs. All-purpose shoes are usually high cut for ankle protection, feature board-lasted construction and have a traditional, semi-flexed last.

High-performance shoes are for competition or difficult sport climbs where edging/fast-climbing technique is paramount. These shoes are low cut for flexibility and generally have slip-lasted construction. Most have a cambered last, but some have a traditional, semi-flexed last shape.

Slippers are ideal for training, thin cracks, bouldering and competitions. Because of their lack of edging power, they require enhanced foot strength or, alternately, are very useful for increasing foot strength in training. Slippers are low cut, of slip-lasted construction and usually have a traditional, semi-flexed last shape.

Proper shoe fit is paramount. Try fitting shoes later in the day when your feet are most expansive and also wear the socks that you intend to climb in (if at all). Climbing shoes should be snug, but not painful. Correct fit through the toe-box area is crucial. Go tighter for shorter, high-difficulty climbing and less so for all-day routes. Shoes will stretch a quarter or half a size -- mostly in width, not much in length. Linings will minimize stretch.

Socks. Opinions vary on use of socks with climbing shoes. Socks, in general, will provide additional comfort at some cost for feel of the rock. Slippers and cambered sports shoes are most often worn without socks. All-purpose shoes are more comfortable with thin liner socks, especially if you plan to spend all day climbing in them.

Gloves. For cold weather ROCK CLIMBING, *fingerless wool gloves* are useful when you don't want a layer of fabric between your fingers and the rock. You can buy them or make them on your own by cutting the fingers off of a pair of army-surplus gloves. The amount of finger exposure depends on your intended climbing use, the weather conditions under which you intend to use them, and your individual comfort zone.

For aid climbing, *leather belay/rappel gloves* are important when rappelling or managing some belays (e.g., hip belay). They prevent rope burns that might cause you to release the rope and, as a result, cause BIG heartburn for the belayed party.

Tool Kit

Whether the gear discussed below is carried on the climb or left at the base is dependent upon the nature and duration of the climb.

Tools. Bring the tools that are specific to any critical gear that you may carry. (e.g., wire and a set of clippers for daypack repair).

Repair Gear. Duct tape may find use for temporary repairs on clothing items, a pack or, possibly climbing gear. You may want to bring along some of the sewing equipment discussed in the BACKPACKING activity for repair of apparel between climbs.

Replacement Gear. The wise climber brings replacements/spares for critical gear items such as shoelaces, carabiners, chocks and climbing rope. If the climb dynamics allow a shoe change, consider bringing an alternate set of climbing shoes for long climbs with a variety of pitches (e.g., add a high-performance shoe for highly technical sections of an all-day climb).

Secondary Activities

The most likely related activities are those that involve the approach to the climbing site. Refer to HIKING and BACKPACKING sections for gear needs related to the approach.

ROCK CLIMBING
(Daytime)

Select items based on trip needs and worst-case weather conditions. Some gear not carried on climb.

ITEM	DATE				
Rock Climbing Gear					
Auto Gear Rack/Locks					
Athletic Tape					
Chalk Bag					
Carabiners					
Climbing Rope					
Web Runners					
Cord Runners					
Wedges					
Cams					
Chock Slings					
Chock Picks					
Seat Harness					
Shoulder Harness					
Gear Rack					
Hard Hat					
Fanny Pack/Daypack/*Haul Bag*					
Water bottle(s)/Water					
Belay/Rappel Device					
Knee Pads					
Ice Ax+					
Bolts+					
Hangers+					
Pitons+					
Piton Hammer+					
Etrier(s)+					
Daisy Chain+					
Mechanical Ascender+					
Small Nuts+					
Fifi Hook+					
Hero Loops+					
Hooks+					
Drill Kit+					
Personal Gear					
Climbing Shorts					
Climbing Pants					
Long-Sleeve Shirt					
Sweater/Jacket*					
Underwear					
Thermal Underwear*					
Windbreaker					
Climbing Shoes/Boots					
Socks					
Gloves					
Sun Hat & Pullover Hat					
Bandanna/Sweatband					
Toilet Paper					

ROCK CLIMBING
(Daytime)

ITEM	DATE				
Safety					
First Aid Kit (see FIRST AID)					
Sunglasses & Lanyard					
Sunscreen					
Insect Repellent					
Lip Balm					
Whistle					
Waterproof Matches & Lighter					
Fire Starter/Heat Tabs					
Emergency Blanket					
Map(s)					
Compass					
Altimeter/GPS Receiver					
Timepiece					
Thermometer					
Pocket Knife					
Flashlight#					
Extra Batteries & Bulb#					
Reading Glasses & Repair Kit					
Phone Change					
Pen & Note Pad					
Accessories					
Camera, Extra Film & Battery					
Camera Bag, Lens Cleaning Kit					
Sitting Pad					
Monocular/Small binoculars					
Litter Bag					
Auto Tool Kit					
Spare Keys/Credit Card/$					
Tool Kit					
Tools					
Replacement Gear					
Repair Gear					
Snacks (see MEALS section)					

Italicized items are optional. +aid-climbing gear *cold-weather items #night travel contingency gear

BICYCLE TOURING (Daytime/Nighttime)

See INDEX for checklist items not discussed below.

This section describes on-road neighborhood cruises to all-day tours. Included is night riding, whether it be for pure recreation, commuting to or from work, or the result of unforeseen delays in a day ride. Bear in mind that special night-riding gear is essential -- our experience is that we have had at least one potentially-dangerous encounter with an automobile on every night ride within the city limits of large urban areas.

Safety Considerations: 1) review the **GENERAL CONSIDERATIONS** and TEN ESSENTIALS sections; 2) learn to bike in quiet residential areas and on Class I routes (off-highway bike paths or bike trails) before venturing out into heavily-trafficked roadways, Work up to Class II (on-highway, separated) bike lanes, Class III (on-highway, signed, but not separated) bike lanes, and open road as you improve your skills; 3) learn traffic laws as they apply to cyclists; 4) particularly where autos are concerned, bike defensively; 5) wear a helmet; 6) err on the side of being a "Christmas tree" at night -- invest in high-illumination equipment; 7) maintain your bike in top mechanical shape; 8) know how to use your repair and first-aid kits; and 9) bring biking apparel and contingencies appropriate to the weather.

In the checklist, items that are considered optional (niceties or special purpose) are *italicized*. Essential night-riding gear are noted with a pound sign(#). Carry these as contingency items if there is a reasonable chance that your day ride could spill over to dusk and beyond. Items for cold-weather biking are noted with an asterisk(*).

Bicycle Gear

Auto Gear Rack. If you are a multi-sport outdoorsperson, get a roof-mounted rack that has accessories to handle your favorite equipment. Rack accessories can accommodate bicycles, skis, canoes, kayaks, watersports equipment and luggage There are also rack-mounted, sealed storage containers for holding a multitude of sports-related or travel gear. Our preference is for racks that have built-in security locks. For bicycles, both fork style and upright mounts are available. The former requires removing and locking down the front tire separate from the rest of the bike and is most aerodynamic. The latter is more convenient, but also has a higher overhead. This is an issue for many parking areas, in parking structures and hotels. (Just imagine the sound of a bike carrier and bike being mashed at an old-fashioned, low-overhead gas station, as we once experienced!)

There are also special top-mount racks for tandem bicycles, racks for pickup truck beds, and rear-mounted racks for motor vehicles with and without hatchback windows, swing-out doors and rear-mounted tires. Note that for the rear-mounted racks, the bicycles are placed side by side. This may mean accidentally stuffing pedals into spokes upon mounting or having the bikes bumping together as a result of wind buffeting. When using the side-by-side models, well-secured padding placed on key bike components will minimize chances of damage.

Bicycle. For light touring, the possibilities are endless. Just check out the standard road bikes (including both uprights and recumbent, singles and tandems, production or custom models), hybrids, mountain bikes, beach cruisers, bicycle motorcross (BMX) bikes, three wheelers and even unicycles on the pavement.

If the love of your life is daytime touring, stick with a standard, skinny-tire road bike. If you are a long-distance touring fanatic, think hard about a touring bike. If you also mountain bike, consider buying a second bike. Note, however, there is a growing trend toward using mountain bikes fitted with road tires for touring. The attraction is added stability because there is more rubber on the road. (The penalty is added weight and increased road friction.) If you are less than a dedicated "roadie" and want the most versatile choice, get a hybrid bike. Hybrids are a current favorite for light road touring and dirt-road biking (not to be confused with serious mountain biking).

Take your candidate bike on a road test before making the big leap into the wallet. Ensure that the seat and handlebar height are suitably adjusted. (Most dealers are more than willing to offer this opportunity.) The discussion below is focused on standard road bikes.

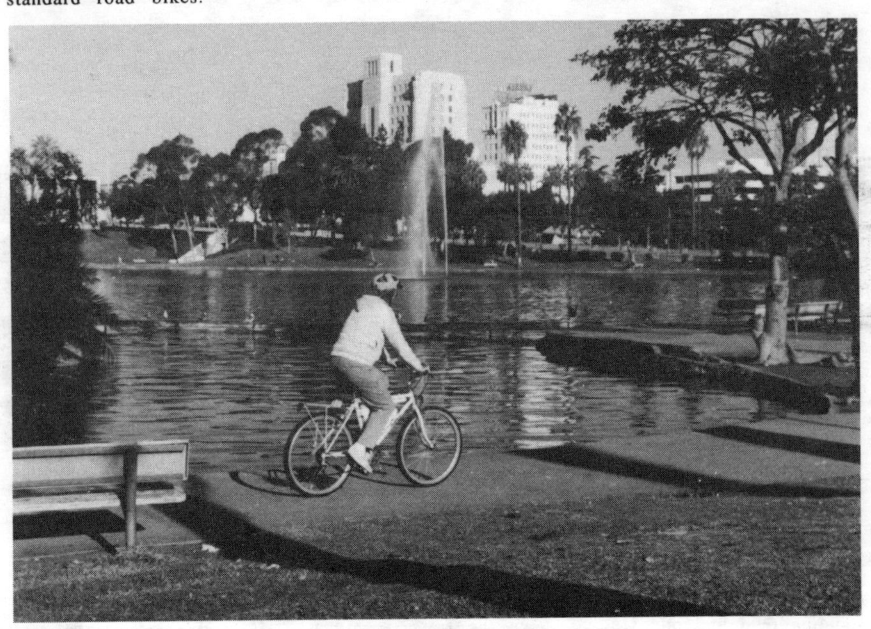

City of Los Angeles, California

• *Bicycle Structure* is a prime consideration and will have the most impact on riding comfort, cycling speed and endurance .... and price. Key structure parameters to consider are frame material, frame size/type and overall body fit after adjustments to frame-attached components have been made ("fine tuning").

Frame Material. Key factors which drive frame price are weight, high strength-to-weight ratio, and quality of frame fastening (i.e., quality of fitting tubes together). Use of lower-quality steel combined with assembly-line framing requires that a significant amount of steel be used to provide the necessary minimum strength. Though not a consensus, most experts contend that high-quality steel, aluminum, titanium, magnesium and carbon-fiber composites all have similar ultimate strength-to-weight ratios. Similarly, high quality workmanship renders lugged, welded or brayed frames equal. Bottom line is that mass-produced, heavier bicycles will cost less than independently-built, lighter models and that many materials are equally suitable for the upper end of the spectrum.

Steel is a common frame material. *Low- or plain-carbon steel* is typically used for bicycles that are very heavy and relatively sluggish in terms of responsiveness, but are lowest cost. *Low-alloy steel* provides strength with lightness and provides a frame that will better absorb road shock and feels lively and responsive, but is significantly more expensive. *Very-high strength steel* is the top of the line, usually reserved for specialty bikes (e.g., racing machines), and is very expensive.

Composites such as *carbon-fiber* and frames of *titanium* and *magnesium* are in the same category. Various *aluminum alloy* frames are available with a range of strength-to-weight ratio options available similar to steel. *Combination-material* frames are also on the market. They include aluminum/alloy-steel tubing and a combination of thin-walled, high strength steel tube with a carbon and Kevlar fiber-reinforced epoxy composite tube inside the steel tube. These models are in the mid-price and very expensive price ranges, respectively.

Frame Size/Type. Bicycles come in a variety of frame sizes measured by the distance from the top of the seat tube to the center of the bottom bracket spindle. Most shops have a starting guideline relating height to frame size (different for road bikes and mountain bikes). Next, straddle the bicycle. There should be at least 1 to 1-1/2 inches of clearance between your crotch and the top tube. Ignore "ladies" frames which have no top tube unless your activities are purely local and/or include biking in a skirt. They are less efficient in transmitting pedaling energy into the frame and are slightly more difficult to brake and shift gears due to the extended cable routing needed. Note that there are a limited number of off-the-shelf standard-frame (i.e., with a top tube) bikes made just for women.

Quick-release wheels are almost a standard. Without them, fixing flats on the road is a real chore. On quality models, the tires are reinstalled by simply placing the axle into the fork channels and snuggling it up against set screws -- thus, no side-to-side tire alignment is required.

Fine Tuning. A road test really determines whether the frame and the total bike are right for you. This might involve adjusting saddle height and tilt, handlebar stem height and, possibly, location of brake and shift levers. Perform this checkout before making the big leap into the wallet.

• *Shifting Mechanisms and Gearing* are the next biggest cost drivers. Most road bikes have friction shifters located on the down tube. Up or down movement of one shifter controls the chainwheel sprocket (front), the other, the freewheel cog (rear) selection. Some road bikes and most mountain bikes have index shifters generally located on both sides of the handlebars. One shifter controls the chain-wheel sprocket selection. It has a big lever that moves the chain to a larger sprocket and an alternate lever for movement to smaller sprockets. A similar shifter on the opposite side of the handlebars performs the same functions for freewheel cog selection. There is also a combination brake and shift lever unit for road bikes -- be aware that the unit is of sufficient complexity to require professional disassembly.

Most cyclists treasure a wide gear range, with specific needs being highly individual. Most road bikes have 18-21 gear combinations or speeds, usually with three chainwheel sprockets (front) and 6-7 free-wheel cogs (rear). Some higher-end bikes have eight free-wheel cogs. Gear ratios relate the number of teeth on the chain-wheel to that on the free-wheel that you are engaging. Typical factory road bikes have lowest ratios (for hill climbing) on the order of 0.85 to 1.0 and highest ratios (for speed) of about 3.6 to 4.2. (Or in the industry terms, 22-26 gear-inches and 94-110 gear-inches, respectively, for bikes with 26-inch diameter rear tires.)

Other off-the-shelf choices are available. Custom installment is another option although it is important to ensure that derailleur capacity is consistent with the planned upgrade. As of this writing, the biggest rear cog has 34 teeth and the smallest compatible chainwheel sprocket has 24 teeth -- resulting in a "wall-climbing" ratio of 0.63.

More expensive road bikes tend to have a wider gear-ratio range and components which provide smoother, more accurate shifting. In addition, their components will tend to provide considerably more refurbishment- and repair-free miles.

• *Handlebars* come in many styles. By far, most road bikes have drop down handlebars with brake levers extended from the most forward-reaching part of the bar. For racing in the tucked position or just to relax arms and elbows on a long ride, consider installing aerobars with attached shifters and arm rests. Since the head is tucked, a clever option to maintain normal vision of the road ahead is to add a forward-looking mirror. To reduce hand soreness on a long ride, try one of the soft, cushion add-ons or replacement grips (bar grips) available. They are used in addition to your padded gloves.

• *Tire and tube* selection is another important consideration. Road bike tire options are numerous, with choices of treads for such as general purpose riding, plying wet roads or navigating bumpy or glass-filled streets. Most require tubes which can vary in weight, materials and valve stem type. To minimize road punctures, many cyclists use a plastic liner seated between the tire and tube. Other options, particularly for city commuters, are to install solid or semipneumatic tires. Though not quite as comfortable as pneumatic tires with tubes, these models will not go flat, blow out or pop off the rim.

Tire size is dictated by your riding style and itinerary. Narrow tires provide low rolling resistance and a faster ride on hard surfaces. Wide tires offer more traction and stability, especially on wet or soft surfaces. With respect to the tire weight, choose the lightest model that suits your needs, especially if your plans include long-distance touring or racing. For greater durability, select heavier tires; consider tires with high-tech, tough reinforced belts.

Tire treads include file, siping and slick designs. File treads are thin parallel ribs running down the tube center, while siping treads are short, parallel groves that run at an angle to the tire center. Both provide enhanced road adhesion in wet weather. File treads are mainly ascribed to add most to the durability, while siping treads provide better traction on soft surfaces. Slick tires are completely smooth, providing lowest rolling resistance though they sacrifice some traction on wet surfaces. File and siping treads are most common for all-around use, while slick tires are most often selected for higher performance/racing.

Foxen Canyon Road, Santa Barabara County, California

• *Brakes* are most often of mechanical design with cantilever, center-pull or side-pull options. All have a lengthy proof-of-design track record, although many consider the side-pull design best for emergency power braking. Hydraulic brakes are just appearing on the market. The price and difficulty of replacement varies with the model. Positive attributes are smoother and improved graduated braking control and much greater stopping power. There are no rods or cables that stretch and break. Once adjusted, hydraulic brakes need no further adjustment.

• *Seats* are one of the most replaced items on bicycles. The proverbial "pain in the backside" is what you'll experience if it's not right for you. Unfortunately, you won't know for sure whether it's the right one until you've logged in lots of miles. Important initial impressions about shape, firmness and ease of adjustability are important. For competition bikes, seats are exceptionally firm and light-weighted; typical is a plastic seat with titanium frame. For the rest of us, best candidates are firm, but pliable, leather or gel-filled seat pads. A low cost upgrade option is a gel-filled pad that is tied down or otherwise secured atop the existing seat. A few bikers lean to seats with underside coil springs or seat/seat post combinations with hydraulic suspension. There are a few seats specifically designed for women, touted as being particularly beneficial on long rides.

Most road bikes require a wrench for seat post height adjustment, although a few can be adjusted using a quick release lever similar to that for wheel tightening or removal. This is a necessary feature for mountain bikes where constant adjustment for terrain and conditions is the norm. It is more of a ride enhancer for road bikes. There is hardware on the market to convert a tool-adjusted seat to one with a quick-release seat height adjustment.

Horn/Bell. Some consider a "polite" sounding *horn or bell* a necessity when biking on crowded bikeways to forewarn bikers and pedestrians or even friendly animals. These noisemakers certainly save the voice. A light-weight, frame-mounted *air horn* is better suited for auto drivers and threatening animals. (The same beast, you say?) Most can be recharged with any bicycle pump. Look for a model on the market with volume control -- set it loud for automobiles and worrisome animals and at the "tweak" level for others.

Rearview Mirror. These gizmos are quite useful when changing lanes for a left turn, when crossing high-speed traffic exits and entrances, for spotting an on-charging RV whose side view mirror is going to cream you, and for other potentially treacherous situations. *Helmet-mounted* or *handlebar-mounted* (on the bar or extended out of the handlebar tube) are the most common options.

Rear Bike Rack. Key features are strength, low profile (you want to keep the load as low to the ground as possible) and adjustability. If the bike does not have frame-mounted and threaded fittings for a rear rack, ensure that the rack is compatible with your bike structure, as is, or with the addition of simple, easily-tightenable hardware. Large-gauge, solid rod rack construction is generally the strongest, and is most commonly used for extended bicycle touring. Narrower gauge, hollow-tube structures will cut it for day rides where loads are typically light.

Underseat Bag. If you carry only one bag, it will probably be an underseat bag. In its smallest form, it carries a tire repair kit. Larger versions may be used to store such items as a tire-repair kit, general repair tools, sunscreen, lip balm, a multiple use knife, mini first-aid kit, phone change and a power bar to boot! An expandable model may even handle a light shell or other clothing layer.

Handlebar Bag/Rack Trunk. Cyclists frequently carry more than one bag, however, key features of each are similar. *Carrying capacity* is paramount. Base single or multiple bag selection on the amount of gear you expect to carry. For added flexibility, consider bags with expandable compartments, extending collars and/or compression straps. This allows tailoring your gear-carrying capacity to the trip. *Convenient access* is a boon. Models with numerous pockets and dividers, wide openings and easy-to-use closures are favored. Quick-release mounting is more convenient than strap-down designs. Look for special features that fit your planned needs such as padding, waterproof fabric, mesh pockets for wet gear, mud flaps or custom-fit rain covers. Finally, consider versatility features such as a removable fanny pack, dual-use rack trunk/fanny pack or models that may double as hiking day packs (see further discussion in the "Accessories" sub-category below).

Handlebar Bag. Out of the way, yet easy to access, these bags are excellent for carrying lighter, frequently-accessed gear such as maps, gloves, small camera, lip balm, sunscreen, and a light shell or other clothing layer. Some have a plastic sleeve on top so you can view your map as you ride or, at least, have ready access. Larger bags are available but, heavily weighted, they will begin to interfere with steering. These bags are available for both drop-style or straight handlebars, with some models fitting both. The bag's popularity rests on its ease of mounting and use, plus it doesn't require a bike rack for mounting.

Poway Lake, San Diego County, California

Rack Trunks. For extra storage space with little added wind resistance, consider this sleek bag which mounts on a bike rack. A wide variety of sizes is available with various models having many of the following: several compartments, expandable features, outside pockets, quick-release mounting, waterproofing and padding. This handy-dandy, store-all device can handle additional clothing layers (or a change of clothes), camera and/or binoculars, picnic items, etc. (Largest sizes will not help in transporting large household items, however.) Tailor the bag properties to your expected needs.

Panniers (or saddlebags or bags) are an overkill for most day trips, unless you are commuting to work, planning a picnic or some activity along the way that requires significant extra gear. On the other hand, if you have panniers for longer trips, certainly use them versus buying extra gear. Best bet is to mount them on the rear rack for these shorter trips. (See BICYCLE TOURING [Overnight] for more information).

Rain Cover(s). Some bags, trunks and panniers come with integral or add-on rain covers. If not, consider bagging the gear contained within the storage unit. Alternate solutions are to sew rain proof materials to make custom-fitted models or to use the old classic garbage bag and bungee cord (or rubber band) solution. The covers should not only protect from rainfall, but also from water kicked up by the wheels. The most versatile sewn covers have drawstrings that help you tailor the cover fit to the amount of bag fill or, if applicable, to bag size. Some covers zip into their own self-contained pouch for easy storage. Bright colors which show up well in rain (e.g., yellow or red) are preferred.

Bungee Cords/Straps. These gizmos are handy in tying down a limited amount of gear to a rear rack in lieu of buying the more expensive trunk rack or panniers.

Tire Pump. Tires have Schraeder or Presta valves. Most pumps fit only one valve, although dual-valve models are available, as well as a value adapter unit that converts a Shraeder valve pump to work on Presta valves. Pumps come in different lengths to fit specific frames and there are several variations in mounting hardware. There are also mini pumps which can fit into a pannier.

Lock and Cable. Disappointingly, bike locks are a necessity in most places. The favorite choices are lock and cable and integral "U"-locks. Buy a lock that will make a thief work hard to heist your bicycle. (No lock in existence will keep a determined thief from getting your bike, given the proper opportunity.) Lock and cable are most versatile, since the cycle can be cabled to posts, trees, bike racks, etc. They can be stored by winding around the seat post. Integral models tend to be stronger (i.e., harder to cut) and can be flush-mounted to the frame using simple hardware. They are the definite favorite in high-theft areas. (Some manufacturers provide a free, fixed-limit, anti-theft insurance policy to show their confidence in the most-robust U-locks.)

Clip-on/Clipless Pedals (& Shoes). Much depends on trip duration and the tourist's interest in efficiency and speed. For short daytime trips, many cyclists suffice with a pair of *general-purpose athletic shoes* on plain bicycle pedals or with pedal-attached, *step-in or strap-in toe clips* (clip-ons). The toe clips improve cyclist efficiency by allowing application of pedal power on both the push- and lift-pedal strokes. The step-in design is generally easier to enter and exit and is the preference of many beginning riders. The strap-in design is more efficient. The next level of shoe improvement might be to acquire a low-cut, well-ventilated shoe with stiff, extra sturdy soles (double up on use of your mountain biking shoes, for instance).

For longer trips or speed cycling, quality *cycling shoes* are a necessity. Cycling shoes are light, but highly rigid, allowing transmission of a great fraction of the push- and lift-power applied to the pedals. Shoe type depends on whether clip-on or *clipless* pedals are used. Clip-on shoes have a cleatless bottom or a recessed cleat (should you want to exercise both options). The clipless style maximizes pedaling efficiency by locking the shoe, via a shoe cleat, to the attachment hardware on the pedal: the cyclist merely twists her shoe to release it from the pedal when coming to a stop. Clipless pedals are the standard for competition cyclists and cyclists wanting to push their own personal envelopes. Most clipless-pedal designs are "single purpose," that is, only one side of the pedal is effectively usable and it is very inefficient when used with a non-cleated shoe. A few designs are "multi-purpose," with a cleated pedal on one side and a standard pedal surface on the other.

If you go with clip-ons, test shoe fit; the step-in design should be snug, but not pinch your toes. The (adjustable) strap-in design should provide snugness, but also allow smooth entry and exit. Confirm that the toe-basket leading edges (either design) do not interfere with front-wheel turning movement. For clipless pedals, ensure that shoes, shoe cleats and pedals are compatible; note particularly that different equipment makes may not match. The clipless pedal should have an adjustment for shoe retention force. For both shoes types, seek a snug, but comfortable, basic design fit. Secondary fit adjustment is accomplished with Velcro tightening straps, shoe laces, or a combination of the two. Velcro straps are convenient for quick adjustment, while laces allow better tailoring of the secondary shoe fit to the foot. Most cycling shoes have a combination leather or synthetic/mesh upper to combine strength with breathability.

Note that it is exceedingly difficult to walk any distance in most cleated cycling shoes. (The exception is a small number of cycling/trekking shoes with soft, rubberized tread and recessed cleats.) Some shoe models can be fitted with cleat covers. This protects the cleats but does little to ease the discomfort of walking. If you may be off your bike for extended time periods, or if you are a contingency planner (preparing for the case that your bike cannot be repaired on the road), bring along a set of walking shoes.

Front and Rear Lights. Many cyclists think that lights are necessary only if the plan is to ride at night. However, darkness has a way of sneaking up on ambitious riders. Even at midday, a sudden storm or fog bank can make it difficult for motorists to see you. Relying on reflectors alone will not cut it. Key features to consider when shopping for lights are weight, durability, water resistance, brightness, battery life and ease of mounting. (Of course, price is no object, as usual.)

Front Lights provide enough light to get you home at dusk or to ride at night in well-lit areas. For commuting or serious night traveling, a high-powered system is needed. Front lights with Xenon and halogen bulbs are the most common since they provide much brighter battery-powered illumination than other bulb types. Typically they use four "AA," four "C" or four "AA" nickel-cadmium (rechargeable) batteries. For non-rechargeable batteries, alkaline are preferred for their longer life (still only 2-4 hours). Most models run from 2-4 pounds and are handlebar mounted.

If you ride a lot at night, consider a modern, high-performance, *generator-powered light*. There is no battery to die and leave you fumbling around for replacements and no recharging regimen. The unit is frame-mounted in a sturdy cage and works off a friction roller that rides on the tire rim. It adds a modest, almost unnoticeable additional friction to the pedal cycle. A single flick of a lever engages or disengages the roller.

Higher-power front lights with a separate battery pack are being sold in ever larger numbers. They provide an additional margin of safety on-road and are almost a necessity for any mountain-biking activity in poor visibility or at night. They generally mount on your handlebars, although some models can be helmet mounted.

One or two halogen bulbs are the standard. Some have both high and low beam selection. Nickel-cadmium (Ni-cad) batteries are most common, with a few sealed-lead models available -- all are rechargeable. Sealed-lead designs provide power in roughly the 10-20 watt range, weigh about 2-3 pounds (total package), and have operating lives in the 1-1/2 to 3-hour range (fixed-beam or high-beam modes, as applicable). Low beam operation roughly doubles useful life. Ni-cad batteries dominate the upper end of the power spectrum, with designs providing anywhere from 10-45 watts. Package weights are similar to those for sealed lead, as are the operating lifetimes for the lower-power models. Higher-powered Ni-cads have about an hour of high-beam life and 2-6 times that in low-beam operation, depending on model type. All have charge times of about 10-15 hours.

Battery packs have been designed to fit inside a water bottle, nest on your frame or seat post, or ride comfortably around your waist. In most cases, quick-release mounting hardware is included so you can take your light when you leave your bike. Some of the models swivel (particularly the double-mounted designs) so that you can examine features out of the line-of-sight while stationary or biking.

Rear Lights provide added visibility to help motorists see you while riding at night. Most use light-emitting diodes (LED's), provide about 1/4 mile visibility, use "AA" or "AAA" batteries and are very light weight (several ounces). Many models have duel-mode operation with battery life of 15 to 70 hours in steady mode and about 100-300 hours in the flash mode. Most are belt or seat-post mounted, although armband and helmet-mounted options also exist. For the justifiably paranoiac, consider a one-mile visibility seat-post mounted strobe with a Xenon bulb which operates about 15 hours in the flash mode on two "AA" batteries.

Reflectors. Front, rear and spoke-mounted reflectors are standard equipment on new bikes and are a recommended minimum set.

Reflective Gear/Tape. Reflective materials, which announce your presence to motorists, are invaluable at night and also useful in daytime. A reflective windbreaker or over-vest, cycling pants with reflective prints and reflective helmet covers are but a few of the gear options available. Outer bike gear peppered with self-adhesive reflective tape is another option. The spot application method might include adhesive dots/strips on your bike frame, helmet, clothes, water bottles and bike packs.

Water Bottles/Cages. Most bikers carry a couple of quart-size *bottle* cages on their bike frames. Other options: 1) a cage mounted behind the seat; 2) half-quart bottles tucked into bike jersey pockets (definitely the lightest option); and 3) quart bottles suspended on stomach belts with or without drinking tubes. Finally, there are lightweight, multi-activity, *liquid-reservoir* devices (one or two quart options) that strap on the back and are equipped with a water delivery tube. A more recent version is a similar-capacity pack worn on the hips, similar to a fanny pack. The advantages are that the water load is nearer to your center of gravity and it doesn't give you a case of "sweaty back." Not having tested it, we do not know the extent (if any) to which it might interfere with pedaling motion.

Mount Haleakala, Maui, Hawaii — Compliments of Maui Downhill

Specialized water bottles are also available. One model is self closing. Another has a screw top which allows you to put in the largest ice cubes, then screw the section down and use it as a standard water bottle. Insulated water bottles keep your liquid cool longer. Another option is a bottle with built-in filter which eliminates giardia, cryptosporidium and other water nasties (good up to several hundred refills). Capacities of these specialized models are typically 20-32 ounces, all with the standard bottle width for snug fit within the standard cages..

Most *cages* are designed for screw-in attachment onto existing braze-on mounts. Where braze-ons are not available, most designs can be mounted using simple adaptive hardware. The heaviest-duty (and heaviest) cages, generally designed to hold even the highest-capacity bottles firmly, are the favorites of most mountain bikers.

Timepiece/Odometer/Altimeter. The general group of bicycle-mounted trip measuring devices are known as cyclometers. All these articles are useful to trip monitoring with the timepiece and odometer being important to trips of any length, group rides with preselected meeting locations or simply for determining whether it's time to up the pace to get off the road before dark. For bicycle touring, an altimeter serves to mark workout altitude gain or, for extended tours, confirm route and establish location. Most cyclometers monitor *elapsed trip distance*, *total distance* since the computer was mounted, *time of day*, *trip elapsed time* and *current speed*.

Other special features are available for advanced/competitive cyclists. *Freeze-frame memory* allows for freezing all display data at a peak moment, e.g., crossing the finish line. *Auto on/off timer* operates only when the wheels are turning, giving the option to measure time in motion exclusive of time spent at stoplights or other delays. *Speed comparator* notifies the rider that current speed is above or below a preprogrammed average speed band, a useful feature for maintaining a consistent and efficient training speed. *Altimeters* typically display current altitude, total trip vertical feet/meters and total cumulative vertical feet/meters since the altimeter was mounted. Ensure that the cyclometer measurement ranges and resolution are consistent with your expected needs and that it is water resistant.

Ventura Harbor Area, California

Other features to consider are the *display type* and *mounting method*. The display should be easy to read (e.g., large distinct numerals, good numeral /background contrast possibly incorporating a back-lighting feature) and mode-switching devices should be convenient to use. Both wired and wireless mountings are available, but there is a strong case for wireless models if there is a reasonable chance of snagging the cable in your travels. Strongly consider wireless models for any activity involving bike portaging or for off-road use in general. The cyclometer body should be conveniently removable /reinstallable from the hold-down device and batteries reasonably easy to install or replace.

Child Seat/Trailer. So you want to haul the future road champions around? One option is a sturdy *child seat* attached to the back (usually the rear rack) of the bike. The seat should have sturdy, well-anchored restraining straps to hold the child safely and side guards to keep those little feet from dueling with the spokes.

For longer trips, a *trailer* is more comfortable for both rider and child and much safer. The trailer can double as a bike trailer for carrying extended tour gear. (In fact, some designs can be rewickered, when detached from the bicycle, for use by runners.) Designs vary, however most hitch to the seat post, have solid aluminum tubing construction, see-through window panels, and well-designed child harnesses. Some models have netting to keep the interior both cool and insect free and a nylon canopy for rainy-day cover. Others have optional drum brakes that, when hooked up, are automatically activated when the bike brakes are applied. Consider designs that use the same tire size as your bicycle -- this feature will certainly minimize the number of spares that you might carry along.

<u>Personal Gear</u>

Cycling Shorts/Pants (padded). The choice of *shorts or pants* is a clear function of weather. Shorts are the outfit of choice for some in moderate weather, however, pants keep the muscles warm and promote greater comfort and higher efficiency in cold conditions. Strongly consider owning both if you are a four-season, all-weather cyclist. Bibs and full suits offer additional fit advantages and resultant wind-resistance benefits for on-road ("road") enthusiasts/competitive cyclists. Road bottomside gear are designed to offer excellent moisture transfer properties, slick styling for wind resistance (and cool looks), and comfort in the tucked cycling position (or upright sitting position for that matter).

Key properties of pants or shorts are fit, construction, fabric type and padding (for other than short, leisurely spins, padding is a blessing). The categories for and properties of *biking pants* are similar to those discussed for shorts below. *Competition shorts* highlight a streamlined fit for aerodynamic, lower wind-resistance cycling. Their construction is commonly 6-8 panels cut for high form-fitting design and most popular fabric is nylon/Spandex followed by polyester/Spandex. Typical of the designs at all cycling levels, these synthetic fabrics offer good moisture transfer, abrasion resistance and ease of care. Padding in the crotch minimizes chafing and limits pressure on sensitive areas, important features whether racing or working up a good sweat on your favorite route. The best (and highest price) padding does not have a center seam, and, as is princibly the case at all price levels, incorporates a synthetic chamois. These synthetics provide the soft, padded chamois feel, but are easier to care for and are commonly layered with a moisture-wicking fabric.

Athletic shorts have a less-streamlined fit than their competition counterparts and are cut to allow more freedom of movement. They most commonly incorporate a six-panel design, but are generally of the same fabrics (exterior and padding) as for competition designs. Cyclists frequently find dual use of these designs for mountain biking.

Relaxed shorts have an oversized silhouette for recreational cyclists seeking maximum wearing comfort, yet enough technical features to support a lengthy and/or rough ride. They are mainly four-panel designs and are frequently made of cotton, cotton jersey knit, cotton canvas or nylon. Relaxed wear with quality padding can double for off-road use.

In inclement weather, you can wear the classic nylon/Lycra long pants under raingear for rain protection or warmth. Barring extreme cold, there is an option to get nylon/Lycra pants laminated with a waterproof, breathable membrane. They will serve as an outer layer that will keep you dry while under exertion, even in the rain. Naturally, this upgrade comes with an added price.

Cool mornings and warm afternoons make the decisions on cycling pants versus shorts and jersey length tough ones. One option is to combine cycling shorts and a short-sleeve jerseys with arm, leg and/or knee warmers. These typically Lycra/nylon/polyester-mix tubes fit snugly over the limbs when needed. The warmers can be tucked into a jersey pocket when not in use.

Cycling Jersey. Key jersey *wearing properties* are that they fit comfortably under normal biking conditions and have sufficient flexibility not to pull and/or bind when you are performing exerting activities. Short- and long-sleeve versions are available. Almost all jerseys are tight fitting for aerodynamic shaping, have elastic arm/wristbands and waistband, together with a zippered crew neck. They should have added length on the back panel to eliminate gaping when you are bent over the bars. Their design should include a two- or three-section pocket across the lower back for storing things you might need while riding (quick snacks, alternate sunglasses, maps -- or recording device and altimeter if you are a bicycling book author).

Important *fabric* characteristics are that they wick perspiration away from the skin, have toughness and durability, wash easily and dry rapidly without shrinking, fading or retaining odors. Excellent lightweight fabrics for moderate-to-hot weather (or as an underlayer in colder weather) are nylon, polyester and acrylic, frequently with Spandex for the cinch bands. In addition, these fabrics are often dyed in vivid, fade-resistant colors. Cyclists who are allergic to synthetics might opt for cotton or silk which are soft and smooth to the touch. However, neither fabric has much wicking capability and, under constant exertion on hot days, will provide you with a soggy jersey.

In cold weather, look to heavier jerseys, including the traditional wool and wool blends, treated polyester, polyester/microfleece or options like treated nylon/

Spandex blends (the treatments enhance moisture transport). Not generally made in the striking designs as are the synthetics (they are mostly single color), these heavier, long-sleeve jerseys will trap body heat better and provide warmth when wet. They are also a great choice as an outer layer on cold days for high-exertion rides. Some jerseys come with an additional sewn-in panel to provide additional torso protection.

Cycling Jacket/Sweater. A layered upper-torso set in cool weather might consist of thermal underwear, a heavy cycling jersey, and a raingear top/windbreaker. In extreme cold, an additional warmth layer may be needed. For cycling, this is the "grab-bag" layer, since few gear items are manufactured specifically for this purpose. Depending on your style, or gear availability, this may be a warm, wicking heavy (synthetic pile, wool or wool-blend) jacket or pullover sweater. Both are typically equipped with chest and side pockets. Preferred models have zippered or buttoned closures to allow you to adjust ventilation and high necklines that minimize heat loss and neck exposure.

Palm Springs Airport, California

Windbreaker. In addition to the windbreakers discussed in VEHICLE-ACCESSIBLE CAMPING, consider a special model that converts to a self-contained fanny pack. You simply reverse the stomach-level storage pouch, pull out the belt loops, then stuff the windbreaker into its own pouch.

Underwear. Cycling underwear should be snug fitting to avoid chafing. They should also have seams located such that they do not dig into tender places -- center seams, particularly, can become a nuisance. Cotton underwear may be adequate on short trips in mild weather. However, consider undergarments such as wool-blend or synthetics (e.g., polypropylene) if a lengthy, high exertion trip is planned. A fishnet top of either material is ideal for warm days, providing both ventilation and sweat-wicking capability under your cycling jersey. Wool, wool-blend or synthetic thermal underwear may be a necessity in cold weather (see VEHICLE-ACCESSIBLE CAMPING). Synthetic/Lycra/Spandex tights that fit over the legs are becoming popular with many cyclists. They are thin enough to fit under most cycling pants, provide excellent wicking ability, and maintain warmth in wind and cold. Note that these underwear come in many styles, including briefs, for some models.

Socks. Cotton athletic sox that you wear everyday around the house should be adequate for light tours. We have also worn them to cycle a Century in mild weather. Our preference is to use over-ankle types since the ankle bone frequently seems to be attracted to hard metal things. If you have any doubt that your feet will be a problem, get athletic or *special biking socks* with flat toe seams, extra cushioning on top for protection on the upstroke and added padding for heals. Some designs have dual layers to limit direct sock-foot rubbing and resultant blisters. Good wicking qualities are desirable. Polypropylene, polypropylene/wool blends, polyester and cotton/ nylon blends are the most common materials used.

In very cold weather, wear shoes a size larger than normal and wear *heavy wool socks or wool blends* or even the old hiker classic, a thin silk underlayer with a wool outer layer. Other options are waterproof, breathable and windproof oversocks (e.g., Gore-Tex models); preferred are mid-calf lengths which cover the lower (sometimes-zippered) portions of cycling pants. For rides in weather below freezing (Yes, Martha, we know a few bikers like this!), one solution to resisting the pain of cold feet is to use *electrically-heated shoe inserts*. These inserts are thin, light and connect by a thin metallic strap to a rechargeable battery pack.

Cycling Shoes. See **Baskets/Clipless Pedals (& Shoes)** above.

Helmet. We do not get on our bikes without a helmet, whether on-road or mountain riding. Most fatal bike accidents involve head injuries. Studies have also shown that fatal head injuries of cyclists involved in an accident are at least 60% more likely to occur to the helmetless rider. Quality helmets which meet the *Snell or A.N.S.I.Z90.4 standards* (preferably both), as noted on a label inside the helmet, can be bought for a nominal fee. Pricier helmets are generally more aerodynamic, stylish, colorful or attention getting, but offer little additional head protection.

Two of our contributors, Anders Ljungwe and Sally Bond, have recently taken "headers" over the handlebars. Anders was road biking, while Sally was mountain biking. Both sustained serious injuries; both also attested that, without a proper and properly-worn helmet, the accidents could have been fatal!

Helmet fit is crucial. The helmet front should rest about an inch above the eyebrows when it is sitting flat on your head. Higher means it is too small and lower (almost covering your eyes) is too large. Our preference is for helmets that fit naturally and snugly when the tension strap is cinched, as opposed to helmets that use little Velcro-attached pads to tailor the helmet interior to your head.

Some helmets have *visors* that are secured with Velcro (preferred for adjustability) or snaps. The visor's purpose is to keep the sun out of your eyes. When shopping, estimate whether the visor will interfere with your road vision in the normal helmet position. The visor can be removed and you can switch to sunglasses, or you can simply buy a visorless model.

Pullover Hat. In cold weather, the issue is more keeping the head warm than getting air ventilation. Get a wool, wool-blend or orlon *pullover hat* which rolls down to the upper forehead. In extreme cold, consider a *balaclava*. This is a wool stocking cap with a restricted opening for the eyes that fits down to the neckline. Other options are helmet liners with attached *ear muffs* and ear protectors that Velcro-fasten to the interior helmet shell.

In rainy weather, there are one-size-fits-all *helmet covers* with elastic cord to secure the cover. The choice of covers is between watertight (typically treated nylon) models or highly-water-resistant, breathable designs. The latter are slightly more expensive, but will not have your head feeling like it's in a steambath after extended periods of exertion.

Raingear. Most common raingear options for cycling are *ponchos* and rain suits. Both have been discussed in the VEHICLE-ACCESSIBLE CAMPING section. For cycling applications, make sure that the *poncho* you select has elastic thumb loops to prevent fly-ups. A large contoured hood, big enough to fit over a helmet, is needed. The hood should also have a drawstring for adjustable closure to ensure a close fit; otherwise it will block your visor.

If your choice is a *rainsuit,* select a model that has the inherent room or stretch/pleated panels at the knees to accommodate normal cycling motion. A breathable rainsuit is highly desirable for all-day, all-weather tour or any ride under exertion in wet weather.

To keep your feet dry, consider getting *booties* which can be pulled over or zippered onto your cycling shoes. Neoprene booties, which are durable, block wind, and maintain foot warmth when wet are a natural choice. These overshoes are also useful in cold weather conditions.

Cycling Gloves (padded). To protect hands from the long-term effects of handlebar gripping and road shock, relatively thick pads at the palms are needed. Foam padding is the norm, while gel-filled and gel-filled with neoprene gloves represent the upper comfort end. Avoid models with bulky seams on the palm. Gloves should have finger openings (stopping well below the knuckles) which fit snugly, but do not bind. Velcro straps used to snug up the gloves at the wrist are the standard. Our personal preference is for brands that have ventilation holes or mesh in the top of the glove in addition to the classic open port next to the Velcro strap.

For cold weather biking, a workable option is to slip a pair of *wool or synthetic gloves* (not mittens) over the standard glove set. A better option, which minimizes hand slippage, is to get wool or synthetic dot gloves which have little gripper dots on the palms and fingers. Winter gloves typically come in four-finger and two-finger models (five-finger and three-finger if you insist on counting the thumb).

Bandanna/Sweatband. In warm or hot weather, keep sweat out of the eyes by wrapping a bandanna or sweatband around the head or keep the bandanna handy for mop up.

Safety

Map(s). Special cycling maps exist in tour guides for local, regional and national touring. The Adventure Cycling Association provides some excellent regional maps which can be laid side-by-side to present a national collage. The waterproof, three- and four-color contour maps note (by town) the availability of such features as campgrounds, bike shops, gas stations, hostels, grocery stores and post offices. In addition, elevation profiles in mountainous regions, general local climate, large-scale detail sub-maps of urban areas, and even some local history are included.

Cascade Highway Loop, Central Oregon

Bikers have long used *map stays* mounted on their handlebars to hold down bike-tiks or to store full maps for easy access. New on the market is a flat map surface that is clipped to the handlebar and stem with nylon straps. Side stays allow the map to be held firmly in place The surface is close to parallel to the airstream, thus cutting down flutter and potential "liftoff." When fully open, it displays a full 8-1/2 x 11 inch map and a 4 x 5 inch map when folded.

Flashlight. Bring a flashlight for any tour that has the remotest possibility of extending past nightfall. Ever tried to make minor repairs or fix a flat in low-light conditions?

Animal Repellent. We are animal lovers. However, several lengthy chases from fired-up farm dogs and their unleashed city brethren have shaken our confidence. (In all cases we were on flat land and could outdistance these 15-mile per hour, stay-in-their-territory terrors). If you can't outrun them there are old-fashioned negotiation solutions (most are untested by us): 1) don't challenge the animal -- try facing it and speaking in a low, friendly manner -- and don't bear you teeth; 2) if the dog wants to sniff you, let it do so; 3) if you are convinced that this animal is out for blood (yours), use your bike to shield yourself from it and try to summon help; and 4) in the worst case scenario, grab your tire pump or best available bludgeon and prepare to protect yourself. An alternate solution is repellent. Liquid spray repellents are illegal in some jurisdictions -- so check with the police in your own locale. These include knockout pepper spray (carried by postal carriers) and Liquid Bullet spray (like Mace, but fortified with pepper and a much stronger deterrent). An alternate is an ultrasonic dog deterrent such as Dog Dazer which is painful to a dog's ears, but does it no physical harm.

Accessories

Fanny Pack/Daypack. *Fanny packs*, which are cinched around the waist, are popular for short tours, where limited gear is needed. They effectively replace the rear pockets which are customary to most cycling jerseys. Most have sufficient room for snacks, maps and safety essentials such as sunscreen, lip balm, a medical kit etc., while a few add water bottle pockets.

Some cyclists let their hiking *daypacks* double as a gear carrier, particularly for extended touring trips. Various-size models that have a storage compartment(s), large hydration compartment(s) with attached drinking tubes, zippered side pockets, mesh pocket, mesh back panel and stabilizing hip belt, or some combination thereof, are being sold in bike stores and mail catalogues. Though roomy and compartmented, the drawbacks are that it gets unwieldy when heavily loaded (it is high above the biker's center of gravity) and is prone to cause a case of "sweaty back" on hot days or under exertion.

Tool Kit

The philosophies dealing with the breadth of the on-road tool-kit varies amongst cyclists. A few day tourers bring a bike lock and sufficient money to take the bus home in the event of breakdown. Some kind-hearted, grizzled veterans bring sufficient tooling to counter almost any problem -- theirs or the strangers they meet. We tend to take the middle road, where we will take enough tools for the highest-likelihood problems. Beyond that point, it's time to do "push-a-bike" and find the nearest bike shop or phone. This philosophy also applies to our mountain biking excursions, where the penalty for "failure" may mean a long walk out!

Different bikes require different tools. Invest in a set of tools that fit into your underseat bag, separate from your other home tools. Ensure that the tools fit your bike through hands-on test. Separate tools can be purchased although there are many excellent multi-use mini-tools and prepackaged tool kits on the market. Lightweight tools with basic features are adequate for short trips on easy terrain, while a more heavy-duty and complete set is called for on long-duration or remote tours or rides on demanding terrain.

Tools:

Tire Levers. Our lean is toward wide, round-edged levers to minimize tire pinch on tire removal or replacement. The opposite end of the lever should be notched or curved such that you can latch that end to the spoke. This feature keeps the lever in place while you apply the other lever(s).

Allen Wrench Set. These are a necessity for most of today's' bikes to adjust such hardware as brake pads, handlebars and saddle. The most commonly used sizes are 4, 5 and 6 millimeters.

Crescent Wrench. An adjustable wrench saves the weight and space of carrying an individual wrench set. Select the smallest wrench which has the range consistent with your bike design and still provides adequate leverage.

Screwdrivers. Carry both flat-head (standard-head) and Phillips-head screwdrivers. Head widths should be consistent with screw slots. The design should have sufficient shaft width or (multi-tool) grip size for needed hand leverage, yet allow access to screws without blockage.

Vice Grips. A small set of vice grips or pliers is useful for handling bike cable or serving the purposes which one miraculously discovers on the road.

Valve Stem Remover. Valve stems leak and sometimes fail. This handy gadget beats all the other makeshift tools that we tried on one fateful trip. Oh yes, bring a spare valve stem also.

Socket Wrench Set. These are usually required for brake adjustments (8, 9, 10 millimeter standard) and crank bolt adjustments (14, 15 millimeter) although all bicycles do not require them.

Chain Rivet Tool. Its primary use is for chain removal, cleaning and lubrication at home. However, some chain problems can mean the end of the ride without one, and a resultant long walk home.

Spoke Wrench. Normally for truing wheels at home, this tool serves to straighten them out after hard bumps or a crash on the road. Sizes 14g and 15g will fit most spokes.

Repair Gear:

Patch Kit. The kit should be carried on any trip, whether for your use or to help some poor unprepared soul who's far from homebase. In addition to the patches and adhesive, bring a dusting powder to prevent accidental bonding of the tube to the tire from excess adhesive around the patch.

Chain Lube/Oil Rag. The rag lets you clean your hands no matter what the repair. The chain lube is a contingency item where effects of wet weather or long-term negligence requires that you relube. Low-resistance lubes which "shed" or "repel" dirt and water (advertising language) will keep friction to a minimum and maximize time between cleanings/relubes.

Replacement Gear:

Spare Tube. Stuff a spare tube into your underseat bag. This allows you to replace, rather than attempt to repair, a badly damaged tube. Besides, attempting to find pin-hole punctures on the road (without having a water bath handy like at home) will make you crazy.

Valve Caps. Get a leaky stem that you can't tighten or replace? Put a cap on it! We feel its just good general practice to use valve caps.

Snacks

Light, compact, high-energy snacks are preferred by most roadies. Also think about bringing a little electrolyte (available in liquid or powder form) to supplement your water supply. We typically split our drinking supplies between electrolyte mixes and pure water on hot days.

Secondary Activities

On-road cycling can take you to fishing and watersports sites, amongst others. See the relevant linked-activity description for its own unique gear needs.

BICYCLE TOURING
(Daytime/Nighttime)

Select items based on trip needs and worst-case weather conditions.

ITEM	DATE				
Bicycle Gear					
Auto Gear Rack					
Bicycle(s)					
Horn/Bell					
Rearview Mirror (bike/helmet)					
Rear Bike Rack					
Handlebar Bag/Rack Trunk					
Rain Cover(s)					
Bungee Cord(s)/Strap(s)					
Tire Pump					
Lock & Cable					
Clip-on/Clipless Pedals					
Front & Rear Lights#					
Reflectors					
Reflective Gear/Tape#					
Water Bottles/Cages					
Timepiece/Odometer/*Altimeter*					
Child Seat/Trailer					
Personal Gear					
Cycling Shorts/Pants (padded)					
Cycling Jersey					
Cycling Jacket/Sweater*					
Windbreaker					
Underwear/Thermal U-wear*					
Socks/Oversocks*/Footwarmer*					
Cycling Shoes					
Helmet					
*Pullover Hat (under helmet)**					
Raingear					
*Over Booties**					
Cycling Gloves (padded)					
Outer Gloves/Mittens*					
Bandanna/Sweatband					
Toilet Paper					
Safety					
First Aid Kit (see FIRST AID)					
Sunglasses & Lanyard					
Sunscreen					
Insect Repellent					
Lip Balm					
Map(s)					
Compass					
Reading Glasses & *Repair Kit*					

BICYCLE TOURING
(Daytime/Nighttime)

ITEM	DATE				
Pocket Knife					
Flashlight#					
Spare Batteries & Bulb#					
Whistle					
Phone Change					
Waterproof Matches, Lighter					
Fire Starter/Heat Tabs					
Animal Repellent					
Thermometer					
Pen & Notepad					
Accessories					
Camera, Extra Film & Battery					
Camera Bag, Lens Cleaning Kit					
Fanny Pack/Daypack					
Litter Bag					
Auto Tool Kit					
Spare Keys/Credit Card/$					
Tool Kit					
Tools:					
Tire Levers (2-3)					
Allen Wrench Set					
Crescent Wrench					
Screwdrivers (Phillips & flat)					
Vice Grips					
Valve Stem Remover					
Socket Wrench Set					
Chain Rivet Tool					
Spoke Wrench					
Repair Gear					
Patch kit (+ talcum powder)					
Chain Lube/Oil Rag					
Replacement Gear					
Spare Tube					
Valve Caps					
Snacks (see MEALS section)					
High Energy Bars					
Trail Mix/Granola					
Fresh Fruit/Dried Fruit					
Beef Jerky					
Nuts					
Electrolyte (for water bottle)					

Italicized items are optional (niceties or special purpose). *items for cold weather #night-riding items

BICYCLE TOURING (Overnight)

(includes long-distance, extended touring)

See INDEX for checklist items not discussed below.

Overnight bicycle touring covers single-overnighters to long-distance days-to-week tours. For extended touring, this writeup is geared for a "bike in rain or shine" mentality. This puts emphasis on bringing equipment that will keep you warm and dry, regardless of weather. It also places an increased emphasis on: 1) purchasing panniers and other storage items that will keep your "vulnerable" gear dry; 2) separately rain-packaging this "vulnerable" gear, within storage units, if necessary; and 3) independently packaging bulky, non-storable items (e.g., sleeping bag) to prevent exposure to the elements. Night riding is assumed, whether it be as a contingency or as part of the nominal trip plan. The checklist covers trips that rely on overnight camping; simply tailor them down if your plan is to stay at motels, hotels or residences.

For group touring, cyclists should share gear. This is particularly important for trips that include camping. Careful planning can result in a dramatic reduction in gear weight, whether it involves sharing locks and cables, tents, cooking gear, the "master" first aid kit, binoculars or the more "exotic" tools. One caution, however, is that the sharing of some critical items (e.g., master first aid kit) places a stronger need for the group to stay in reasonable proximity. Ever trusted the "spare brake cables" to the free-wheeler who has left the group behind?

Safety Considerations: 1) review the **GENERAL CONSIDERATIONS** and TEN ESSENTIALS sections; 2) review the "Safety Considerations" noted for the BICYCLE TOURING (Daytime/Nighttime) activity, as applicable; 3) load your bike properly, particularly as it affects stability of steering and braking; 4) bring a well-thought-through set of tools, as well as repair and replacement gear; and 5) think twice about biking in dangerous weather conditions such as in lightning storms or on icy roads. It might be a good day to stay in camp or motel and wait it out.

In the checklist, items that are considered optional (niceties or special purpose) are *italicized*. Essential night-riding gear are noted with a pound sign(#). Items for cold-weather biking are noted with a asterisk(*).

<u>Bicycle Gear</u>

A thorough study on the preferred *gear weight distribution* of on-road bicycles for performance and safety is reported in Reference 1 for the BICYCLE TOURING activity. The study did not attempt to account for gear placement on top of the rear rack, but rather concentrated on pannier loading in conjunction with a light handlebar bag. Four panniers and a handlebar bag with a total of 80 pounds of sand were used in various placements, for different size bags, and for different bag locations (high or low, forward and backward). The extreme weight was considered an absolute maximum for test purposes only. Characteristics considered were high-speed stability, standing and hill-climbing stability, cornering ability, and how well the bike tracked.

Their basic conclusion: medium-size panniers mounted as far forward as possible and at standard height on the rear carrier and medium-size bags mounted low on the front forks in the center of the wheel was by far the best system. A sample of the options found to be less suitable in rough order of highest suitability: 1) equal weight in front and rear panniers, both at standard heights, and small handlebar bag; 2) weight carried low on both front and rear panniers, with small handlebar bag; and 3) large rear panniers with a large handlebar bag and no front carrier. Finally, it was noted that different bikes may show some variance from their test results.

Bicycle. For serious touring, get a *touring bike*. These steeds are built to carry a varied and heavy load over long distance. Frames are less stiff (absorbing shock better), wheelbases are longer (for a more comfortable and controllable ride), and gear-ratio ranges are wider to accommodate the variety of terrain traveled and increased total weight. The longer wheelbase also accommodates a longer chainstay (typically 17-18 inches) to allow sufficient heel clearance from the rear panniers. Low-end (for climbing) gear ratios are typically in the 0.75 to 0.95 range and high-end about 3.6 to 4.0, roughly 20-25 gear-inches and 94-104 gear-inches, respectively, for 26-inch tire bikes. (See BICYCLE TOURING [Daytime/Nighttime] for terminology.)

Dana Point, Orange County, California

Touring bikes always have frame-mounted, threaded fittings (braze-ons) to which you can fasten carrier and fender struts at the dropouts, carrier mounting fittings on the seat stays and front forks, and water bottle mounts (two minimum) on the down tube and/or seat tube. Some have additional braze-ons, for instance, at the underside of the down tube. To minimize breakdown over the miles, think about investing some extra cash into a model with side-pull brakes, freehub rear hubs with stronger axles, sealed bearing hubs, low-maintenance bottom-bracket bearings, and smoother, more accurate index shifters (as opposed to friction shifters).

Some use *mountain bikes* fitted with road tires for extended touring. The beauty of this option is that the bikes traverse potholes and climb over road debris with the minimum of disturbance or loss of stability. They put more rubber to the road, making them superior in wet weather. They are equipped with "gonzo" brakes, a decided advantage when you are forced to slow on a steep downhill with your gear-laden bicycle. Mountain bikes are more convenient for plying compact-dirt roads leading to some camping areas. The penalty is that you work harder, pushing the added weight along and working against the added road friction brought on by the additional tire surface on the road. Another issue is the difficulty of finding gear carriers which mount to bikes with pneumatic suspension. (Even with single suspension, this forces you to load up the rear wheel.) Only recently have a couple of manufacturers put such carriers on the market -- they are more expensive and the limited selection may not work for your bike model.

Most long-distance cyclists are all-weather bikers. Many mount light, plastic *fenders* to keep water and mud off themselves and their gear. Ensure that there is sufficient clearance between fender and wheel to allow the passage of small pebbles that may be picked up by the wheel. Trapped debris could cause wheel lockup and an exciting flight over the handlebars! An option to fenders is *mud guards*. A set of permanently-attached mounting brackets on each wheel allows you to snap the mud guards onto and off of the frame by hand. The least-robust, but lightest and most convenient alternative, is a small *fender section* that fits under the down tube and is attached with Velcro. The section prevents most front-wheel spray from reaching the biker. It is probably the single viable option for front-suspension mountain bikes used on the road.

Panniers and Racks. For long-distance cycling, don't leave home without them. Large-gauge, hollow-rod *racks* will fit most applications. Large-gauge, heavier solid-rod racks are best for very heavy loads on-road and a must for mountain biking. Two-bag, "low rider" models which fit over your front wheel are preferred to assemblies where each bag is attached to a separate front fork. They provide better balance because the panniers tend to ride lower on the bike.

Downtown Los Angeles, California

Extended-touring panniers usually are made for either front or rear rack use. (Interchangeable bags are limited in capacity, as driven by practical front-wheel use.) The most important pannier characteristics are ruggedness of construction, attachment stability, ease of attachment/detachment and capacity. The better bags will have a sturdy internal support frame and an abuse-handling exterior material such as Cordura. Bags having overflaps with sturdy cinch straps and cinch hardware provide dependable integrity against external elements and protection against accidental gear loss. Where zippers are used, they should be heavy-duty, wide-teethed models with snag-free movement.

Rack mounting mechanism(s) should provide snug fit, be easy to operate and hard to accidentally dislodge. A lock-down mechanism to secure the attachment to the rack is a must. The attachment to the lower rack structure, normally with a spring-loaded cord and attachment hook, should require that strong (but not so excessive as to bind the hand) tension be applied for mounting. The detachment process should require no more work than the simple attachment. Most bags have wide, heavily-sewn carry straps for hauling the load when it is off the bike.

Panniers normally come in pairs or as an integral unit with two large side pockets. Some of the integral units have a detachable fanny pack. Smaller bags may have about 1200-1500 cubic inch capacity, while larger models might double that volume. (All are volumes per bag pair or total integral unit.) The smaller bags are generally single compartment. The roomier models may have multiple interior compartments and a quick-access outer compartment or two.

Mountain bike panniers tend to have even more emphasis on rugged interior and exterior construction and strong lock-down mechanisms. Bag protection from the elements, from above and below, is enhanced, To keep gear from shifting inside of the pannier, the most protective models have an interior drawstring in addition to a sturdy flap lockdown or protected zipper. When you think about off-roadies riding through brush, over rocks, through streams and generally bumping about, these extra precautions make sense.

As watertight as your panniers (and rain cover) might seem to be, water will always find some insidious route into critical gear such as sleeping bags and insulating-layer clothing. This is even more the case for stream-crossing mountain bikers. It is important to doubly *protect this water-sensitive gear*. See the discussion of "Stuff Sacks" in the VEHICLE-ACCESSIBLE CAMPING section, as well as that under "Pack Liners" in the BACKPACKING activity for insights into protective methods.

Bungee Cords/Straps. Bring a couple for contingency use. The weight penalty is light and it is amazing the clever ways cords and straps can be used, particularly for stowing gear on the bicycle.

Clip-on/Clipless Pedals. Clipless pedals are a natural for long-distance touring because of their efficiency. The downside is that any non-repairable problems with the cleats could put you into a position of having to struggle into the next town for repair if you don't have "multi-purpose" pedals. (A strong case for a choosing a set of camp shoes with a gripping tread for contingency biking use.) From our observations on the road, mountain-bike riders on extended road tours tend to side with clip-ons.

Front and Rear Lights. If you always get to your destination by dusk, there is no need to read the next two gear item discussions. Motorists traveling on one- or two-lane roads at speeds in excess of 50 miles per hour are not typically on the lookout for cyclists. Pot holes, glass and soft shoulder are impossible to track, even with a full moon. Ever tried to cruise into a camping area and find your way around with some semblance of order? The message of all of this is: mount a good headlight and rear blinker on your bike, regardless of your nominal plans!

Reflective Gear/Tape. Yes! Yes! Yes! The "extra weight" may save your life.

Water Bottles/Cages. For extended tours, we have the capacity to store water in three quart-bottle cages and carry any additional water in the panniers. The amount of water carried is dependent upon the expected availability of water sources. Even though "a pint's a pound the world around," don't hedge on this most valuable commodity to save weight.

Bike Trailer. Instead of loading up with racks and panniers, some long-distance cyclists opt to tow a trailer. These have many of the child-trailer features; most attach to the seat post and a few have optional drum brakes that are activated when the handlebar brakes are applied. Unlike the child trailers, these are low to the ground and highly aerodynamic in shape. Better designs have a watertight mating surface between the entry panel and *cargo box* when the panel is tightened down, and are lockable. Some disassemble such that the entire frame can fit inside the cargo box itself. The advertised load capacity for one popular model is 50 pounds and cargo space is about 22 inches (length) x 14 inches (width) x 12 inches (depth).

Trailers can be a pain in town, since you must always compensate for the added-length contour on both turns and on the straight and narrow. However, they are a dream on the flat, open road and generally more stable and easier to handle on the uphill (work is still work, in any case) and downhill. We do not recommend hard braking stops on slick pavement with the trailers -- there have been a few "tail-wagging-the-dog" stories floating around!

Newly on the market is a *trailer with a frame only*. You store your gear in a waterproof duffel bag(s) and place it into the frame well, batten it down with straps or bungee cords, and you're off. The manufacturer claims that it attaches to mountain, cross and road bikes, tandems and even recumbents. It is touted as useful on- and off-road, and "... riders use it on trails." (We have certainly been on trails where it would be impossible not to have to detach and carry it for appreciable stretches.) The trailer is narrow profile, has a low center of gravity, is lightweight and aerodynamically clean. The advertised load capacity is 70 pounds and cargo space is about 25 inches (length) x 16 inches (width) x 18 inches (depth).

Personal Gear

Cycling Pants and Shorts (padded). Bring both for a long trip if there is any reasonable likelihood of encountering cool or cold weather during the day or early evening. Extra padding for crotch and sit-bone area is a blessing. Excellent options are a thick chamois pad or a chamois pad with a second layer of wicking material bonded to the underside for wicking away perspiration and providing an extra padding layer. There are also very fine multi-layer synthetic liners. Most meld cushion and wicking layers and some add a layer of tricot. This material is claimed to allow the liner to move with the body and not the outer fabric of the pants or shorts, further reducing the chance of irritation. One newer synthetic liner includes a layer of gel in the sandwich for the purpose of additional cushioning.

Cycling Jacket/Sweater & Parka. In moderately cold weather, the cycling jacket/sweater might also suffice as an insulating layer for camping. Parkas (down or synthetic batting) are, by design, meant to retain heat and are not highly breathable -- they are rarely warn under exertion. The bottom line is: bring both if you will be camping in freezing or below-freezing conditions.

Port of San Diego, California

Cycling Shoes. True cycling shoes in conjunction with clipless pedals are the preferred option for long days on the road.

Underwear. There is a school of thought that underwear should not be worn under cycling shorts on long trips, because it can bunch up and cause more than the normal chafing. If this does not accommodate your style, find thin underwear that fit snugly and have seams and elastic that will not cause additional irritation. Silk underwear works well only if you perspire lightly. Washable, lightweight wool or wool blends are effective if you are not allergic. Polypropylene shorts are another option, though they require special washing care to keep their surfaces from becoming abrasive.

Raingear. Since you may spend long periods toiling in rainy weather, opt for a quality highly water-resistent, breathable rainsuit.

Camp or Town Pants/Shorts & Shoes. Bring a versatile set of clothes that will provide camping comfort, yet fit the dress codes of eateries or other establishments along the route. Best bet for footwear are those versatile cross-trainers that are comfortable in camp or on the street, and can be used in a pinch to push the pedals.

Camping Gear

If it works for backpacking, it works for extended touring. An oversimplification, maybe, but it applies most of the time. Light-weighted, relatively non-bulky (including compressibles), easy-use gear is what you should carry.

A digression. As a cyclist, don't accept a "Camp Site Full" sign even if you don't have a reservation. Some campgrounds reserve a fixed number of sites for bicyclists, and the sign may not represent those sites. Most public campground personnel understand the plight of a cyclist rolling into camp with few other campsite options available. They may offer to squeeze you in, since the space you occupy is small. Alternately, they may direct you to more remote sites not accessible to automobiles.

Route 66 Near Cadiz Summit, California

Cooking Stove/Primer. If your extended-tour route takes you by recreation gear outlets or large shopping centers often enough, then any "backpacking" stove will do. Otherwise, bring a stove that uses fuel that you can find in the towns that you pass through. Multi-fuel stoves are best. Gasoline is always purchasable, with kerosene and white gas following in terms of availability. Liquefied fuel stove cartridges may be harder to find and bringing a sufficient cache of canisters may be too great a weight to carry.

Fuel usage varies with the amount of cooking, weather, stove type and other factors. However, an "average" camper with an "average" gasoline/kerosene/white gas stove can expect about two hours of use at peak flame and 12 hours at a simmer setting with 20 ounces of fuel. Our experience is that 20-40 ounces will cut it for about a week.

Daypack. It is hard for us to conceive of an all-day cycling effort with weight and sweat on our backs. Thus, we use a simple, compressible daypack only for storage of gear that we want to keep together and for hauling filled-up collapsible water bags and the like, while in camp. The daypack doubles for use in hiking explorations along the cycling route.

Safety

Weather Radio. A wallet-sized weather and news radio may help you select routes, decide when to "pack it in" in severe weather, or provide entertainment value when things are slow. A model with a quality tuner, earphone outlet and telescoping antenna will bring in a surprising number of long-wave AM and FM stations in most areas throughout the world. If you are willing to spring for a little extra cash, get a radio with a few short-wave channels. Weight is in the 16-ounce range for a typical model which runs on two "AA" batteries). Look for a radio that comes in its own sturdy, sealable pouch.

The "Wall," Solvang-Santa Maria Century, California

Accessories

Sewing Kit. The kit is for patching personal or camping gear as well as panniers. (Refer to the BACKPACKING section.) It is important to carry for any lengthy tour, but is a critical item if you will be out of touch with civilization for days on end.

Tool Kit

The gear described below is in addition to that described in the BICYCLE TOURING (Daytime/Nighttime) activity.

Tools:

Hub Grease/Hub Wrenches. Only for extended tours, bring a tube of hub lube and a set of wrenches to remove the hub assembly. (This is one of the many pre-ride items that should be checked before departing.) Neither is needed if you have sealed bearings.

Repair Gear:

Duct Tape. This stuff can be used for temporary tire repairs, tying down loose water bottle cages, temporary patching of torn personal or camp gear, holding down rackborne gear in a pinch, etc. The uses vary with the nature of the problem and are only limited by you imagination.

Bailing Wire. This item is particularly useful for patching up load-bearing gear on a bicycle. Potential uses are to replace missing hardware such as rack screws and bolts or for wiring up loose peripheral equipment.

Boot Material. This material may be a patch from a "retired" conventional tire which is placed over the damaged tire section and held in place with duct tape. You'll never forget the ride! Better yet, use a patch from a sew-up tire. In this instance, the (relatively thinner) patch is inserted between the damaged tire and tube.

Replacement Gear:

Spare Tire. If you manage to shred or otherwise damage a tire, a spare is the only robust repair option. Replace the spare at first opportunity.

Spare Shifting and Brake Cables. The spare shifting and brake cables should be long enough to reach the rear derailleur or brake. You can cut to fit if the problem is a front unit.

Spare Spokes. These are spares to fit front and rear wheels (1-2 spokes per wheel, with nipples).

Spare Nuts and Bolts. Tailored to your bike and based on your prior experiences (mixed in with current trip expectations), bring the spares that would most critically affect your trip if they break or work free.

Meals

Tourers have options to camp out, to stay in hotels/motels/homes along the way, or to mix the two options. For either option, if you dine out in town, look for those all-you-can-eat joints -- try to leave some food for the others! If your plans are to eat camp food, shop for dinner and breakfast at the last town or burg before reaching your campsite.

Secondary Activities

HIKING, swimming (WATERSPORTS) and both LAND and SEA FISHING are typical of activities which might be linked with overnight touring. If you have such plans refer to those activities for their unique additional needs.

Lake Mission Viejo, Orange County, California

BICYCLE TOURING
(Overnight)

Select items based on trip needs and worst-case weather conditions.

ITEM	DATE				
Bicycle Gear					
Auto Gear Rack					
Bicycle(s)					
Horn/Bell					
Rearview Mirror (bike/helmet)					
Rear Pannier Rack/Panniers					
Front Pannier Rack(s)/Panniers					
Handlebar Bag/Rack Trunk					
Bungee Cord(s)/Strap(s)					
Tire Pump					
Lock & Cable					
Clip-on/Clipless Pedals					
Front & Rear Lights#					
Reflectors#					
Reflective Gear/Tape#					
Water Bottles/Cages					
Timepiece/Odometer/*Altimeter*					
Bike Trailer					
Camping/Fire Permit					
Motel/Hotel Reservations					
Personal Gear					
Cycling Pants (padded)					
Cycling Shorts (padded)					
Cycling Jersey (long sleeve)					
Cycling Jersey (shirtsleeve)					
Cycling Jacket/Sweater*					
Parka (w/p stuff sack)*					
Windbreaker					
Underwear/Thermal U-Wear*					
Socks/*Foot Warmers* *					
Cycling Shoes					
Helmet					
Pullover Hat (fit under helmet)*					
Raingear					
Cycling Gloves (padded)					
Warm Gloves/Mittens*					
Bandanna/Sweatband					
Camp or Town Pants/Shorts					
Camp or Town Shoes					
Camping Gear					
Tent & Rainfly					
Stakes & Poles					
Seam Sealer					
Ground Cloth					
Tent Broom & Sponge					

BICYCLE TOURING
(Overnight)

ITEM	DATE				
Sleeping bag (w/p stuff sack)					
Sleeping Pad					
Head Netting					
Stove & Windbreak, Primer					
Fuel Bottle					
Fuel funnel/Strainer					
Waterproof Matches & Lighter					
Cooking Pot(s)/*Tea Pot*					
Skillet/Frypan					
Non-stick Cooking Lubricant					
Scouring Pad					
Pot Holder/*Pot Gripper*					
Plate and Cup					
Cooking Utensils					
Can & Bottle Openers					
Eating Utensils					
Paper Towels					
Biodegradable Dish Soap					
Spare Stuff Sacks					
Resealable Plastic Food Bags					
Candle Lantern					
Litter Bag					
Collapsible Water Bag					
Daypack (storage)					
Hygiene					
Towel & Wash Cloth					
Biodegradable Soap					
Biodegradable Shampoo					
Personal Toiletries/Ditty Bag					
Toilet Paper & *Towelettes*					
Toilet Trowel					
Sun Shower					
Clothespins					
Laundry Bag					
Safety					
First Aid Kit (see FIRST AID)					
Water Filter/Tablets					
Sunglasses & Lanyard					
Sunscreen					
Insect Repellent					
Lip Balm					
Whistle					
Fire Starter/Heat Tabs					
Emergency Blanket					
Map(s)					
Compass					
Altimeter/GPS Receiver					
Pocket Knife					

BICYCLE TOURING
(Overnight)

ITEM	DATE				
Flashlight#					
Extra Batteries & Bulb#					
Reading Glasses & Repair Kit					
Thermometer					
Phone change					
Portable Radio (weather)					
Communication Device					
Animal Repellent					
Pen & Notepad					
Accessories					
Nylon Cord					
Camera; Extra Film & Battery					
Camera Bag, Lens Cleaning Kit					
Brochures, Articles, Books					
Binoculars					
Sewing Kit (see "Tool Kit")					
Fanny Pack					
Swim Suit					
Sitting Pad					
Indoor & Outdoor Games					
Auto Tool Kit					
Spare Keys/Credit Card/$					
Tool Kit					
Tools					
Tire Levers (2-3)					
Allen Wrench Set					
Crescent Wrench					
Screwdrivers (Phillips & flat)					
Vice Grips					
Valve Stem Remover					
Socket Wrench Set					
Chain Rivet Tool					
Spoke Wrench					
Hub Wrenches/Hub Grease					
Repair Gear					
Patch Kit (+ talcum powder)					
Chain Lube & Cleaner/Oil Rag					
Duct Tape/Boot Material					
Bailing Wire					
Replacement Gear					
Spare Tube/Valve Caps					
Spare Tire/Tire Spokes					
Spare Shifting & Brake Cables					
Spare Nuts & Bolts					
Meals (see MEALS section)					

Italicized items are optional (niceties or special purpose). *items for cold weather #night-riding items

MOUNTAIN BIKING (Daytime)

See "INDEX" for checklist items not discussed below.

In the daytime MOUNTAIN BIKING activity, rain gear is specified as a contingency item. Plan your tour around rainy weather and allow plenty of margin. Mountain biking in mud can be a downer, as anyone knows who has watched the mud accumulate on tires or who has slipped and slided in the ooze. Besides, biking in these conditions can leave permanent runoff channels and scars on bike trails. Biking in the rain in true mountainous terrain can be terrifying and flat-out dangerous! If you are going to test Mother Nature in wet off-road conditions, we suggest that you confine your riding to well-compacted fireroads and logging roads.

We have met cyclists who ply the off-road territory at night by design. The Los Angeles Times newspaper featured a cohort from our employment who rides the local Puente Hills with a group of night riders. Riding fire roads is one thing, but trail riding at night requires well-developed cycling skills, a keen eye, and a large dose of patience. For our discussions, however, night mountain biking is included primarily for the contingency that you meet dusk before reaching a suitable outlet.

Safety Considerations: 1) review the **GENERAL CONSIDERATIONS** and TEN ESSENTIALS sections; 2) start your off-road activities on fire roads and the less-difficult, well-maintained trails. Hone your bike-handling, "graceful-exit," first-aid, and bike-repair skills on these routes and work up to more challenging terrain. Learn to get off and walk your bike if the trail sections appear to be potentially dangerous and above your skill level. (No disgrace here!); 3) keep your speed under control and your eyes vigilant for tricky terrain and for others sharing the route; 4) don't venture off the road or trails unless the area permits this practice and you know what you are doing; 5) keep your bike in safe running condition; 5) wear a helmet; 6) if you plan to bike under wet trail or road conditions, equip your bike with mud fenders. If severe weather threatens, get out! If heavy rain flows cause water crossings to appear dangerous, wait the storm out.; 7) if you want to night ride, go with a grizzled veteran to learn the ropes. Install top-of-the line lighting equipment. Refer to item 3) above, over and over and over!

In the checklist, items that are considered optional (niceties or special purpose) are *italicized*. Essential night-riding gear are noted with a pound sign(#). Items for cold-weather biking are noted with a asterisk(*).

<u>Bicycle Gear</u>

Bicycle. Mountain bikes have shock-absorbing, fat, knobby tires that grip the trail for steering control and good traction on slippery surfaces. They utilize heavy, rugged frames that are built to take the punishment of the trail. These bikes have flat handlebars that help you keep steering under control on rough surfaces and allow you to sit more upright than road bikes so that you can see what's ahead. They typically come with a much wider gear range than road bikes to facilitate steep hill climbing. Most mountain bikes have index shifters on the handlebars as opposed to the more common friction shifters located on road-bike down tubes. This feature allows you to focus on the trail surprises lying ahead while changing gears. Single-wheel and two-wheel shock-absorbing fork designs are available. The shock-absorber(s) cushions you from the bouncing and jarring of the wheels while cranking over rocks, ruts, roots, and even tree limbs on the trail.

• *Bicycle Structure* is a prime consideration and will have the most impact on cycling power, speed and endurance .... and price. Along with a suspension system, the structure will dictate your riding comfort. Key structure parameters to consider are frame material, frame size/type and overall body fit after adjustments to frame-attached components have been made ("fine tuning").

Frame Material. See the BICYCLE TOURING (Daytime/Nighttime) section.

Frame Size/Type. See the BICYCLE TOURING (Daytime/Nighttime) section.

Fine Tuning. See the BICYCLE TOURING (Daytime/Nighttime) section. If you know another bicyclist who has the model that holds your interest, ask him about its strong and weak features. Then, in your most polished demeanor, ask if you might borrow his bike for a short test ride in the local hills.

• *Suspension forks or not?* Mountain bikes in the recent past came without suspension systems. You can spring for the additional cost of a front suspension stem or a full-suspension (front and rear) system. There are numerous manufacturers of suspension bikes and many more who make retrofit kits for non-suspension bikes. There is a trade between the smoother, less jarring ride of suspension bikes and the associated modest compromise in bicycle handling and responsiveness. Safety and reduced hand fatigue favor getting at least the front suspension -- the handlebars are less likely to come out of your hands on a jolting bump and the shock absorption will certainly reduce the pounding on the hands and lower arms.

Upper Santa Ynez River, Santa Ynez Mountains, California   Courtesy of Sam Nunez

Currently, there are four major types of suspension forks on the market: 1) an air/oil type uses a combination of air pressure and oil, which is forced through valves on compression and decompression: 2) a type which uses a type of rubber called a "bumper" to absorb road shock; 3) a bumper in combination with coiled spring; and 4) a coiled spring model. Early high-quality suspension forks used springs only. Beware of newer, low-price imitations of this older design that are purely cosmetic re-creations. Push down on the handlebars; if there is little or no compression on the spring, move on to other models.

• *Shifting Mechanisms and Gearing* have their own cost impacts. Most mountain bikes have index shifters most often located on both sides of the handlebars. The best option is an under-bar mounting. This mount keeps your hand in a more stable position on the handlebar grips while you shift (with the thumbs).

Beyond the entry level, mountain cycling requires a wide gear range. "Granny gears" are a necessity when climbing steep grades, particularly if you are packing in overnight gear. Most mountain bikes have 21-24 gear combinations or speeds, usually with three chainwheel sprockets and 7-8 free-wheel cogs. Gear ratios relate the number of teeth on the chain-wheel to that on the free-wheel that you are engaging. Typical mountain bikes have lowest ratios (for hill climbing) on the order of 0.80-0.95 and highest ratios (for speed) of about 3.6-4.0. In the industry's terms, these translate into 21-25 gear-inches and 94-104 gear-inches, respectively, for 26-inch diameter rear wheels. The high end gearing is primarily for showing off as you leave the dirt and race to your prearranged post-ride meeting spot on pavement. (A natural for us city dwellers!) Other off-the-shelf gearing choices are available. Custom installment is another option, although it is important to ensure that derailleur capacity is consistent with the planned upgrade.

Lake Tahoe, California — Courtesy of Susan Cohen

More expensive mountain bikes will tend to have a wider gear-ratio range and components which provide smoother, more accurate shifting. Also, their components will tend to provide considerably more refurbishment- and repair-free miles.

- *Handlebars* come in many modest variations in style, although all are flat. Look for models with permanent bar ends, roughly six-inch metal bars that project forward from the handlebars. Located near the end of the handle bars, you tuck into an aerodynamic position to grip them. They are used when you power uphill or go all out on the flat. There are low-cost kits to add bar ends if they are not already installed.
- *Tire and tube* selection is another important consideration. For riding on tough, rocky terrain, mountain bike tires generally have thick, closely-space knobs for traction. There are equally-knobby trail grippers with more emphasis on cross-centerline channeling that excel in wet conditions. Some designs are back wheel only and are most useful when you need traction on steep uphills. Other designs have

reinforced sidewalls for added resistance to the cuts and bruises of the trail. Hybrid designs, with knobs placed to create a relatively smooth centerline, are a compromise tire for both trail and road biking. Most mountain bike tires require directional mounting, i.e., a given sidewall must always face a given fork. (Tires are marked to indicate direction of tire rotation when moving forward.) You lose most of the benefits of the tread design (e.g., traction, ability to "shed" mud in the rain) if you reverse-mount them.

Mesa Peak, Santa Monica Mountains, California

Roughly the same tube options for road bikes are available for mountain bikes, although there is an added emphasis on tube toughness. We prefer the heavier-weight, more hardy tubes and use a plastic liner between tube and tire. We have had one true tube puncture through the tread, a case where a nail was picked up in a knob and driven into the tire over many wheel rotations. All other punctures have been through the sidewall (a few) or have been a result of tire under-inflation and resultant "snake-bite" incisions (too many).

• *Brakes* for mountain biking are most often of cantilever design. Brake hardware is heftier and robust and equipped with heavier-duty, wider-contact-surface-area pads than road bikes. A heavier bicycle and requirements for frequent hard slowing or stopping on steep terrain drive the design.

• *Seats* are important to mountain biking, but probably less so in the sense of comfort, than for extended road touring. In the mountains, you tend to be on and off the seat and constantly adjusting position according to the terrain. What is needed is a reasonably comfortable seat which has sufficient padding to cushion road shock. Typical candidates are firm, but pliable, leather or gel-filled seat pads. A low cost upgrade option is a gel-filled pad that is tied down or otherwise secured atop the existing seat.

Almost all mountain-bike frames have a quick-release seat height adjustment which, when retightened, secures the seat post (as opposed to adjustments requiring tools). Since frequent seat adjustment is required to optimize the ride on all but the most benign trips, we consider this feature a necessity. The seat should have adjustable tilt, normally accomplished using a standard or Allen wrench. Some newer models have a forward-backward adjustment which allows the rider to vary biking posture "on the fly." New on the market is a custom post (called the Power Post) that allows fast, accurate index seat adjustment both laterally (fore and aft) and in tilt (up and down).

• If your mountain biking activities may include some wet-weather riding, think seriously about mounting some form of *fenders*. The best bet is mud guards for suspensionless bikes. For each suspension-supported wheel, substitute a fender section in place of a mud guard. (See the discussion in the BICYCLE TOURING (Overnight) section.) Wheel clearance should be at least two inches.

Rear Bike Rack. Because we haul a lot of gear for use in writing touring books (camera(s), tripod, altimeter, hand-held recording device, spare batteries, extra maps and other goodies), we need at least one pannier and a rack to hang it on. Thus, the rack has become a permanent fixture on both of our bikes. Racks aren't that much added weight, even if not utilized. With a pannier(s), a rack can serve many useful day-trip purposes, particularly on group outings. The best one is hauling in picnic supplies, cameras, binoculars or other fun things for the group. As is also true for gear placed in handlebar bags and rack trunks, ensure that impact-sensitive gear is well padded.

Handlebar Bag/Rack Trunk. On trips that take us through water, we put our gear that needs to be kept dry in one or the other of these types of storage devices, because they are high on the bike. Our preference is to keep the handlebar bag light so it doesn't affect steering. It is reserved for gear that we need frequent access to such as maps, reading glasses, snacks and a camera. The remaining gear goes into the rack trunk.

Fishbowls Area, Los Padres National Forest, California

Bungee Cords/Straps. These items are multi-purpose. We bring them whether or not we have an immediate use in mind. Either is excellent for compressing rack trunks to keep gear from shifting and bumping while navigating the bumpy world of the off-road. On cleanup details, we have used them to tie down trash bags filled with people litter.

For overnight use, they serve to tie down the bulky gear on the rack trunk such as a sleeping bag and sleeping pad. In a couple of instances, where collecting downed wood was legal, we have ferried tied-down, cut wood to our campsite for an evening fire.

Tire Pump. We have a tire pump that has been jarred off of its mounts so many times that we finally retired it. We just weren't sure how much abuse it could take before it pooped out on us at some critical juncture. The lesson we finally learned was that the pressure-fitted pump assemblies that work on-road have no place on the mountain "cobbles." The solutions: 1) buy a pump with a surefire mounting/lock-in assembly and, if necessary, back up the assembly with a Velcro strap; or 2) buy a mini-pump and stuff it into a pannier.

Red Rock Canyon, Nevada Courtesy of Sally Bond

Clip-ons. We have observed many bikers in clipless pedals on fireroads and a few on moderately-challenging trails. Ditto for clip-ons. This is fine if you are both big on confidence and know the route well. Our recommendation is to stick with the saw-tooth pedals that come with mountain bikes and drop the straps, unless you are on quality mountain roadways or using your mountain bike on-road. (Another option is to leave the straps on and use the other side of the pedal in risky terrain. The problem here is that the straps frequently drag on the trail surface; they can also get snagged in brush.) Road and trail hazards in the mountains frequently come up without much warning. When you take a tumble and can't uncouple from the bike, there are two things to consider: 1) "flying the bike" offers fewer safe options than "free flight"; and 2) the bike is not going to give, but your body will.

Front Light. For night travel, look seriously into the "higher-power front lights" discussed in the BICYCLE TOURING (Daytime/Nighttime) section. Most lights are handlebar mounted, although helmet-mounted models are available. The latter have the advantage of allowing you to focus light on terrain which is not directly in the path of the bicycle.

Permit. Some areas limit access through permits in the same fashion as for hikers and backpackers. Check first. Note that, in the U.S., mountain bikes are not permitted in Wilderness-designated locales.

Personal Gear

Cycling Shorts and Pants. The same features that are discussed for BICYCLE TOURING apply to MOUNTAIN BIKING. However, forget bibs and one-piece outfits, as they are far too constraining for mountain tours. *Pants* are appropriate for cold weather and overnighters, or for competition to cut down on wind resistance. They are a blessing on overrun trails with plentiful scrub and in high brush which may be tick-infested. One time, we "bulldozed" our way down an unmarked trail in the Verdugo Hills near Los Angeles in shorts. Between the brush whip, the tree-branch pokes, and the hauling of bikes down steep, caved-in trail sections, our legs got pretty cut up. (By the way, we found a trail closure sign at the lower trail entry!)

Below Sandstone Peak, Santa Monica Mountains, California

In the general circumstances, however, most savor the relative comfort and coolness of shorts (overheated, sweaty legs are a drag). Mountain biking shorts are designed for exceptional durability, featuring highly abrasion-resistant fabrics and sturdy construction to handle the additional rigors of trail riding (and falling). A fair fraction of the mountain biking shorts are loose fitting, in sharp contrast to most roadie models.

For trips in very rough terrain, there are some additional considerations. If you opt for *shorts*, thick wool knee socks or neoprene guards can be worn to protect the shins. If you are really pushing the envelope, consider wearing kneepads.

Socks. For serious mountain biking, get athletic or *special biking socks* with flat toe seams, extra cushioning on top for protection on the upstroke and added padding for heals. Some designs have dual layers to limit direct sock-foot rubbing and resultant blisters. Good wicking qualities are desirable. Polypropylene, polypropylene/wool blends, polyester and cotton/nylon blends are the most common materials used.

Cycling Shoes. A good pair of cross-training shoes or lightweight, low-top trail hiking shoes will get you started. However, more-serious mountain stomping calls for a shoe better tailored to the task. In moderate weather on ordinary terrain, wear low-cut, well-ventilated shoes designed for off-road riding. These shoes have thick, sturdy soles that protect the tender underside of your feet from the pressure of pedaling on sawtooth-edged pedals. Choose models with a solid, gripping tread and sturdy construction that will see you through trail biking, bike pushing, water-crossings and diversionary hikes. If your history indicates that your ankles have a fatal attraction to bike parts, think seriously about high tops. For colder weather and rides on rougher terrain, many use light-weight, high-topped hiking shoes.

Cycling Jersey. The choice of long-sleeve versus short-sleeve shirt is governed by the same considerations as for cycling shorts versus pants above. Consider substituting a wool long-sleeve hiking shirt for a jersey in cooler weather and wear a polypropylene mesh undershirt. With this option, you do sacrifice the pockets on the lower jersey back. This may mean a couple of extra stops to dig into your handlebar bag or rack trunk for maps or snacks -- additional opportunities to slow down and check out the scenery.

Cycling Gloves (padded). To protect hands from the effects of handlebar gripping and trail shock, relatively thick pads at the palms are needed. Foam padding is the norm, while gel-filled and gel-filled with neoprene gloves represent the upper comfort end. Avoid models with bulky seams on the palm. Gloves should have finger openings which fit snugly, but do not bind. Long finger lengths, which come up near the knuckles, provide added protection against scrapes. The gloves should have an effective gripping system for control on rough trails and fabric that provides good ventilation (nominally on the glove topside). Velcro straps are used to snug up the gloves at the wrist for most designs.

For cold weather biking, one option is wool or synthetic dot gloves which have little gripper dots on the palms and fingers. An alternative is to seek out gloves with insulating liners. Hand covers such as mittens, that compromise the grip on the bars or manual dexterity, are not recommended.

Tool Kit

Refer to the BICYCLE TOURING (Daytime) section for a description of toolkit items.

Secondary Activities

The most likely linkages to other activities are swimming (WATERSPORTS), HIKING and LAND FISHING. Refer to those activities for their unique gear needs.

MOUNTAIN BIKING
(Daytime)

Select items based on trip needs and weather conditions.

ITEM	DATE				
Bicycle Gear					
Auto Gear Rack					
Bicycle(s)					
Rear Bike Rack					
Handlebar Bag/Rack Trunk					
Bungee Cord(s)/Strap(s)					
Tire Pump					
Lock & Cable					
Clip-on/Clipless Pedals					
Water Bottles/Cages					
Timepiece/Odometer/*Altimeter*					
Front Light#					
Battery Pack#					
Permit					
Personal Gear					
Cycling Shorts/Pants (padded)					
Cycling Jersey					
Cycling Jacket/Sweater*					
Windbreaker					
Underwear/Thermal U-wear*					
Socks/Oversocks/*Footwarmer**					
Cycling Shoes					
Helmet					
Pullover Hat (fit under helmet)*					
*Over Booties (contingency)**					
Raingear (contingency)					
Cycling Gloves (padded)					
Bandanna/Sweatband					
Toilet Paper					
Toilet Trowel					
Safety					
First Aid Kit (see FIRST AID)					
Water Filter/Tablets					
Sunglasses & Lanyard					
Sunscreen					
Insect Repellent					
Lip Balm					
Whistle/Signal Mirror					
Waterproof Matches & Lighter					
Fire Starter/Heat Tabs					
Emergency Blanket					
Map(s)					
Compass					
GPS Receiver					

MOUNTAIN BIKING
(Daytime)

ITEM	DATE				
Pocket Knife					
Flashlight#					
Extra batteries & Bulb#					
Reading Glasses/*Repair Kit*					
Thermometer					
Phone Change					
Pen & Notepad					
Accessories					
Camera, Extra Film *& Battery*					
Camera Bag, Lens Cleaning Kit					
Binoculars					
Nylon Cord					
Daypack/Fanny Pack					
Swim Suit					
Trash Bag (small litter bag)					
Auto Tool Kit					
Spare Keys/Credit Card/$					
Tool Kit					
Tools:					
Tire Levers (2-3)					
Allen Wrench Set					
Crescent Wrench					
Screwdrivers (Phillips & flat)					
Vice Grips					
Valve Stem Remover					
Socket Wrench Set					
Chain Rivet Tool					
Spoke Wrench					
Repair Gear					
Patch kit (+ talcum powder)					
Chain Lube/Oil Rag					
Replacement Gear					
Spare Tube					
Valve Caps					
Snacks (see MEAL:S section)					
High Energy Bars					
Trail Mix/Granola					
Fresh Fruit/Dried Fruit					
Beef Jerky					
Nuts					
Electrolyte (for water bottle)					
Secondary Activities					

Italicized items are optional (niceties or special purpose). *items for cold weather #night-riding items

MOUNTAIN BIKING (Overnight)

(includes multi-day, extended trips)

See INDEX for checklist items not discussed below.

Few activities place more of an emphasis on keeping the gear load light than mountain biking. The checklist is filled with a large array of items that look like an overwhelming ensemble. If there is any doubt on a comfort item, the general rule is to leave it at home. Consider more austere versions of high-weight-impact items, e.g., consider a tube tent or breathable, water-repellent sleeping bag covers versus a tent. Take a bare-bones cooking set and learn to love freeze-dried food. With careful selection of the proper light-weighted gear and choosing only what is critical, our total gear weight per bike rarely exceeds 30-35 pounds for a several-day excursion in cool weather.

For group touring, mountain cyclists should share gear. Careful planning can result in a dramatic reduction in gear weight, whether it involves sharing tents, cooking gear, tools, the "master" first aid kit or binoculars. One caution, however, is that the sharing of some critical items (e.g., master first aid kit) places a stronger need for the group to stay in reasonable proximity during the ride.

Safety Considerations: 1) review the **GENERAL CONSIDERATIONS** and TEN ESSENTIALS sections; 2) review the "Safety Considerations" in the MOUNTAIN BIKING (Daytime) activity, as applicable; 3) for extended tours, install a front light in the event that you may be forced to ride after dusk; 4) for extended tours or, where weather may be a factor on shorter trips, equip your bike with mud fenders; 5) Bring a well-thought-through tool kit, repair and replacement gear; 6) load your bike to minimize steering and braking instability; and 6) bring extra food and stove fuel, should you be stuck at your campsite for an extended period because of weather.

In the checklist, items that are considered optional (niceties or special purpose) are *italicized*. Essential night-riding gear are noted with a pound sign(#). Items for cold-weather biking are noted with a asterisk(*).

Bicycle Gear

About *gear load distribution*. With our front-suspension bikes, we had learned to get along without any front-wheel loading. (Until recently, there were no carriers that could be mounted on the suspension forks of a mountain bike.) Our style is to distribute most of the load over the rear wheels and on our backs, with modest weight in a handlebar bag. We load the rear panniers with a light layer of cushioning items on the bottom and place the heaviest gear on this cushion and close to the bike frame. The tent bag and sleeping pad ride on the rack. The daypack or rucksack is loaded with light, cushiony items on the bottom and heaviest articles as near the biker's back as possible. If you plan to include front-wheel loads, keep the weight percentage low, since even a little weight hanging over the front wheels can dramatically affect steering. Keep your water-damageable gear high and separately bagged if you plan to ford creeks and streams.

To conduct a loading test at the trailhead, place the panniers directly over the hubs, then stand up and pedal. If the front end lifts, move the bags forward. Similarly, if the rear end skids on braking, move the panniers forward. If you have reached the limit where your heels rub your panniers when pedaling, redistribute heavier pannier forward or shift some weight to your back.

Front Light. For contingency purposes, we recommend equipping your bike with the "higher-power front lights" discussed in the BICYCLE TOURING (Daytime/ Nighttime) section.

Panniers. As watertight as your panniers (and rain cover) might seem to be, water will always find some insidious route into critical gear such as sleeping bags and insulating-layer clothing. This is even more the case for tours involving stream and river crossings. It is important to doubly *protect this water-sensitive gear*. Our standard mode is to pack this gear in a heavy plastic bag, compress the air out, seal with a twist tie, and curl the tie ends. Next, we tuck the bag into a stuff sack and tighten it down firmly. This is even more critical if the gear is going to be top-mounted and exposed to brush and rocks. See the discussion of "Stuff Sacks" in the VEHICLE-ACCESSIBLE CAMPING section, as well as that under "Pack Liners" in the BACKPACKING activity, for more insights into protective methods.

Personal Gear

Upper Santa Ynez River, Santa Ynez Mtns., California

Warm Gloves /Mittens. These items are for in-camp use in cold weather. The caveats noted in the MOUNTAIN BIKING (Daytime) section explain why they should not be used for biking.

Camp Pants /Shorts & Camp Shoes. Particularly if you've got "snuggywear" bike shorts or pants, you'll want to shift into something more comfortable. The clothing options discussed in the VEHICLE-ACCESSIBLE CAMPING section are applicable. Stay light by forgoing camp shoes and wearing your mountain biking shoes at day's end. If they are not sufficiently comfortable to do that, bring an old, worn-in pair of athletic shoes. (Also rethink your choice of biking shoes.)

Camping Gear

Tent and Rainfly/Tube Tent/Cover. In moderate weather, learn to enjoy sleeping under the stars. If atmospheric moisture is low, a ground cloth, sleeping bag and, maybe, mosquito netting should do it. Add a waterproof *sleeping bag cover* in higher-moisture conditions. The next step up is a lightweight (2-3 pound) polyethylene *tube tent* for mild weather. The tent folds up into a compact form about the size of a folded king-size bed sheet. It opens like a trash liner without the sewn-in bottom and has imbedded grommets to allow securing the tent to trees, logs, rocks and other natural hangers (similar to a tarpaulin). The ends of the tent can be secured somewhat to cut down on wind, but not sufficiently to provide dry shelter in driving rain. The tube tent does not breathe, so the more you close it up the more moisture you collect on the sidewalls and, eventually, the tent floor. If this won't cut it, then it's back to the higher-performance, higher-weight *tent* options discussed in the BACKPACKING section.

Verdugo Hills, Los Angeles County, California

Lake Tahoe, California Courtesy of Susan Cohen

Tool Kit

Refer to the BICYCLE TOURING (Daytime) and BICYCLE TOURING (Overnight) sections for a description of toolkit items.

Secondary Activities

HIKING, swimming (WATERSPORTS) and both LAND and SEA FISHING are typical of activities which might be linked with mountain bike touring. If you have such plans refer to those activities for their unique additional needs.

MOUNTAIN BIKING
(Overnight)

Select items based on trip needs and worst-case weather conditions.

ITEM	DATE				
Bicycle Gear					
Auto Gear Rack					
Bicycle(s)					
Rear Pannier Rack					
Rear Panniers					
Front Pannier Rack					
Front Panniers					
Handlebar Bag					
Bungee Cord(s)/Strap(s)					
Tire Pump					
Lock & Cable					
Clip-on Pedals					
Water Bottles/Cages					
Timepiece/Odometer/*Altimeter*					
Front Light#					
Battery Pack#					
Camping/Fire Permit					
Personal Gear					
Cycling Shorts/Pants (padded)					
Cycling Jersey (long/short slv.)					
Cycling Jacket/Sweater*					
Parka (w/p stuff sack)*					
Windbreaker					
Underwear/Thermal U-Wear*					
Warm Gloves/Mittens*					
Socks/*Foot Warmer**					
Cycling Shoes					
Over Botties (contingency)*					
Helmet					
Pullover Hat (fit under helmet)*					
Cycling Gloves (padded)					
Raingear (contingency)					
Head Netting					
Bandanna/Sweatband					
Camp Pants or Shorts					
Camp Shoes					
Swim Suit					
Camping Gear					
Tent, Rainfly/Tube Tent/Cover					
Stakes & Poles					
Seam Sealer					
Ground Cloth					
Tent Broom & Sponge					

MOUNTAIN BIKING
(Overnight)

ITEM	DATE				
Sleeping Bag (w/p stuff sack)					
Sleeping Pad					
Stove & Windbreak, Primer					
Fuel Bottle					
Fuel Funnel/Strainer					
Waterproof Matches & Lighter					
Cooking Pot					
Skillet/Frypan					
Non-stick Cooking Lubricant					
Scouring Pad					
Pan Holder/Gripper					
Cup *& Plate*					
Cooking Utensils					
Can Opener					
Eating Utensils					
Paper Towels					
Biodegradable Dish Soap					
Litter Bag					
Candle Lantern					
Spare Stuff Sacks					
Resealable Plastic Food Bags					
Collapsible Water Bag					
Daypack (Storage)					
Hygiene					
Towel *& Wash Cloth*					
Biodegradable Soap					
Biodegradable Shampoo					
Personal Toiletries/Ditty bag					
Toilet Paper & *Towelettes*					
Toilet Trowel					
Sun Shower					
Laundry Bag					
Safety					
First Aid Kit (see FIRST AID)					
Water Filter/Tablets					
Sunglasses & Lanyard					
Sunscreen					
Insect Repellent					
Lip Balm					
Whistle/Signal Mirror					
Fire Starter/Heat Tabs					
Emergency Blanket					
Map(s)					
Compass					
GPS Receiver					

MOUNTAIN BIKING
(Overnight)

ITEM	DATE				
Pocket knife					
Flashlight#					
Extra batteries & bulb#					
Reading Glasses & Repair Kit					
Thermometer					
Phone Change					
Communication Device					
Pen & Notepad					
Accessories					
Nylon Cord					
Camera, Extra Film & Battery					
Camera Bag, Lens Cleaning Kit					
Brochures, Articles, Books					
Binoculars					
Sewing Kit					
Fanny Pack					
Sitting Pad					
Auto Tool Kit					
Spare Keys/Credit Card/$					
Tool Kit					
Patch Kit (+ talcum powder)					
Tire Levers (2-3)					
Spare Tube					
Allen Wrench Set					
Crescent Wrench					
Screwdrivers (Phillips & flat)					
Vice Grips					
Valve Stem Remover					
Valve Caps					
Chain Lube/Oil Rag					
Socket Wrench Set					
Chain Rivet Tool					
Spoke Wrench					
Spare Tire					
Spare Gear & Brake Cables					
Spare Spokes					
Bicycle Grease					
Spare Nuts & Bolts					
Duct Tape					
Boot Material					
Bailing Wire					
Meals (see MEALS section)					

Italicized items are optional (niceties or special purpose). •items for cold weather #night-riding items

ALPINE SKIING/SNOWBOARDING (Daytime/Nighttime)

See INDEX for checklist Items not discussed below.

This activity description is heavily weighted towards skiing or snowboarding in commercial ski areas. Warming huts, a kick-back snack area and the ski patrol are assumed to be a ski run away. Further, it is assumed that nightfall will greet you with a warm chalet, motel or the like as opposed to bedding down in the snow. The discussion is still broad enough to account for seasonal weather variations, as well as skiing within or outside of the groomed areas, but within the ski-area boundaries. If you choose to snow camp during your skiing/snowboarding adventure, refer to the NORDIC SKIING activity for information on the "apres-ski roughing it" gear needed. If your plans include plying the non-groomed "outback," whether just outside the ropes or in the true backcountry, check out the NORDIC SKIING and GLACIER/WINTER CLIMBING activities. Study the safety information and gear descriptions, particularly as they apply to avalanche issues and overnight survival equipment.

Safety Considerations: 1) review the **GENERAL CONSIDERATIONS** and TEN ESSENTIALS sections, as applicable; 2) keep your gear in safe working order, with particular emphasis on bindings; 3) work out between trips to keep in, or improve, your physical shape; 4) practice your skiing/boarding (including falling) technique on the slopes in addition to having fun; 5) take lessons, no matter what your skill level; 6) pay attention to warning and information notices posted in the ski area; 7) stick to runs that are at your level. A common form for marking runs is: green circle for beginners, blue square for intermediate-level and black diamond for advanced/ expert skiers; 8) if you try a run above your level or an untried run, go with a partner with experience and proficiency at least at that level -- this deserves further emphasis if you are going off the groomed slopes ("tree skiing"); 9) ski/board under control and defensively. Learn and follow safe skiing practices and proper slope etiquette.; 10) if you are into doing tricks, start small and work up. Avoid crowded areas.; 11) don't play distracting games, such as "toss and catch," on the slopes; 12) remain with an injured skier or boarder and send someone else after the Ski Patrol; 13) stay off the slopes if you are tired. Rethink that "bomb run" that you have planned at the end of the day; and 14) don't ski or board outside the ropes unless it is legal and you are a proficient, suitably-equipped backcountry person.

In the checklist, items that are considered optional (niceties or special purpose, such as skiing outside the ropes) are *italicized*. Items noted with a pound sign(#) are needed for nighttime slope activities.

Skiing Gear

Auto Gear Rack. We remember a ski trip in college days with three people and all their gear for a week crammed into an old Volkswagen "Bug." Today, you see more sensible people (with maybe a tad more in their bank account than we had) with a roomier car equipped with a ski rack. With four in the car, or for longer ski vacations, consider the addition of a sealed gear storage unit on top -- there are many racks that have this combined capacity. Bottom line, particularly if you are a multi-sport enthusiast, is to purchase a sports utility rack and travel in comfort.

Skis. It seems that modern technology has brought a ski for every conceivable type of user. Each ski type has specific technical characteristics that enhance its performance for specific applications.

• The *ski core* is most often a choice of wood or foam for all levels of skiing. As ski construction gets more complex, core elements affect performance less and less. In general, the former offers a resilient, lively snap and is known for its durability. The latter offers a consistent flex and lighter weight.

• The *sidecut radius* is calculated by taking into account ski profile in terms of the ski's tip, waist and tail measurements. The more pronounced the ski's physical sidecut (i.e., the larger the difference between the waist width to the tip widths), the smaller the sidecut radius. The larger the sidecut radius, the longer the ski's turning radius, meaning the ski is at it's best carving long, smooth turns. Conversely, a ski with a smaller radius will have a shorter turning radius and will excel in short, quick turns.

The classic skis have had very little sidecut and, because they are relatively difficult to turn (particularly at low speed), forced learners to go through a progression of "skid skiing" steps to become efficient parallel skiers. The growth process was often measured in terms of ski seasons. With super-sidecut skis (also called "parabolic" skis by some), novices can start making turns on groomed slopes using a parallel stance in only a few days.

Mammoth Mountain, California Courtesy of Sam Nunez

• Optimal *ski length* is largely determined by your skiing style and ability. A long ski tends to be more stable at high speeds. A shorter ski usually makes it easier to initiate turns at slower speeds and is more maneuverable on varied terrain. Consult with the skiing specialist at your store if you are uncertain about the "proper" choice.

• To maximize enjoyment, select *types of skis* that match your style, ability and terrain preferences. Consult a qualified specialist at your outdoor recreation shop if you have doubts about your equipment needs -- an informed decision will improve your chances of having the most fun and minimize the likelihood of a visit to the "bone doctor." The first three types in the discussion below are for beginning- and intermediate-level skiers, while the remaining are "growth" options.

Entry Level Skis. Lowest on the cost ladder, these skis are the choice for newcomers to the sport. They are most forgiving in terms of keeping you upright when making beginner's moves. These models are typically short in length and characterized by a short turning radius. With these skis, you use ski poles.

Short Skis. This relatively new addition to skiing has you on reduced-length skis, frequently with no poles. Their key advantage is that they are highly maneuverable, at some compromise to downhill speed. There is far less variability in length selection, with some models having a "one size fits all" offering. Most are in the 150- to 180-centimeter length range, with width and sidecut selected for the skier's primary use. The wider models give you a better platform for powder, while narrower is preferred for cutting tight turns on packed slopes. Sidecut affects turning agility and downhill speed as described above.

The ultimate in short skis are designs such as Saloman's Snow Blade, measuring in the 90-centimeter length range. These skis are never used with poles. They offer a deep sidecut which, when combined with short length, make them extremely maneuverable. They are the skier's answer to the snowboard, and are most often used by the more skilled for performing exotic tricks.

Jackson Hole, Wyoming   Courtesy of Doug Holker

Sport Skis. These styles are designed for novices or skiers looking to get to the next level of performance with confidence and ease. They are slightly more expensive than entry level skis, but will take you more comfortably further up the skill ladder. Sport skis are typically longer than the entry-level models, with the attendant longer turning radius. They provide a stable ride and a good level of forgiveness -- meaning that technical mistakes made by the skier won't transfer readily to the ski.

All-Terrain Skis. These skis are built for a little bit of everything for more skillful skiers. They provide a dandy compromise for skiing on tame, groomed slopes as well as on rough surfaces, moguls and for jumps.

Performance Skis. These are a favorite of skiers with solid, all-mountain skills on a wide range of terrain and snow conditions. Performance skis give you many of the same advantages of the Race/Expert skis, but are a bit more forgiving to accommodate skier mistakes and variations in terrain. They generally feature medium speed and carving characteristics.

Off-Piste Skis. For out-of-bounds, beyond-the-ropes adventures, these skis are designed for all-condition use. Alpine skiers can expect a "tough-as-nails" ski for backcountry use on ungroomed snow, ice, unpacked chutes and every form of crud. Many are wood skis with rugged core construction and a medium turning radius.

Slalom Skis. These are traditionally-shaped skis designed for competitors and advanced skiers who tackle the entire mountain as if it were a race course. Slalom skis are stiffer in the tail to help you snap into your next turn. They offer great maneuverability in tight spots, on hardpack and on moguls. Their length (the longest of the skiing family) and core design give the unusual set of characteristics of high-speed stability and slalom course maneuverability.

Race/Expert Skis. The Oversized version is intended for expert skiers who enjoy carving at high speeds. They are similar to the Carve version, but are slightly longer, with narrower tips. They are characterized by a medium-to-long turn radius. The Race/Expert Carve version is also built for carving clean, crisp turns. They are slightly shorter than the Oversize version and feature a more accentuated sidecut, but still deliver race-level responsiveness, with a short-to-medium turning radius. The wide surface of their tips helps them to excel in deep powder and crud.

• There are an array of *ski bindings*. As a minimum, however, they share at least a minimum of two common performance features. They hold your boot firmly in place in normal skiing, and release your boot from the ski when the pressure on the bindings exceed a preset limit. Almost all are "step-in" bindings, consisting of two separate units, a heel-piece and a toe-piece. There are also "risers," step-ins that have both pieces constructed as a part of an integral unit.

The separate heel and toe designs are far and away the most common. Some of the most popular are described below.

Binding With Single-Pivot Toe Piece. This binding has a standard vertical heel release and a toe piece that works as a single pivot sideways release. It also incorporates a special compensation system to prevent any upward pressure of the boot on the toe-piece interfering with the sideways release mechanism.

Diagonal Heel-Release Binding. The heel unit of this binding releases diagonally as well as upwards. This is useful in forward twisting falls where the sideways release of the toe-piece may be prevented. The toe-piece itself operates on the double-pivot system -- which means that, if necessary, each "arm" of the unit is capable of releasing independently.

Turntable Heel Binding. The principle of the "turntable" system is that, in addition to the usual upward release, the whole heel unit rotates. As well as giving additional support to the heel of the boot at all sides, the heel-piece of this type of binding pivots on a point directly beneath the pivot point of the skier's heel. This aids the release of the toe-piece in twisting falls.

The riser system has many similar binding types. The main purpose of mounting both heel and toe pieces on a single structure is to raise the skier's boot further above the snow surface. Why, you ask? Advanced skiers on high-sidecut skis can edge out so far that the boot makes contact with the snow and literally lifts the ski off of the snow, resulting in loss of ski control.

Regardless of type, skiers of different weight and abilities need bindings that are designed and adjusted to release under different stress conditions. A lightweight beginner needs a binding that releases more easily than that of a heavy, expert skier. The release settings are based on the DIN (Deutshe Industrie Norman or German Industrial Standard) system, measuring from 1-10. Settings in the 3-7 range typically cover advanced beginners to low expert ratings. Most skis have a simple switch-like manual DIN adjustment, allowing simple change of settings even on the slopes.

Nowhere in the skiing activity is there a greater need for equipment care. It is critical that bindings be kept well-lubricated, serviced often, and that release settings reflect safe operation at your current performance level.

• *Ski brakes or safety straps* are required at the predominantly all alpine skiing facilities. If you have ever seen a loose ski rocketing down the slopes, one cry from above that simply says "SKI!" will have you moistening your shorts until you can spot it and try your best to get out of its path. Ski brakes are an integral part of the ski and require no connection to the skier. They employ a spring-loaded set of rubber-tipped "feet" for each ski which deploy when the skier "departs" from the binding. The feet act as a ski brake in much the same fashion as a person digging his heels into the snow on a downhill slide.

The old classic safety straps are stout leather or fabric strips that clip or tie to the upper rear tip of each binding and are secured around your ankles. Safety straps are rarely seen on the slopes today. Some ski areas no longer allow them, considering them less safe than brakes because (by design) the skis stay attached to the skier in a fall.

Carry Straps/Ski Bag. Skis ain't cheap! A set of rubber *carry straps* not only make it more convenient to haul your skis to and from the slopes, but they also minimize the rubbing of ski surfaces during transit. Many skis equipped with brakes can be "locked" together, forgoing the need for the extra rubber straps. In a pinch, the safety straps on skis so equipped can be tied around the skis -- this is the least robust option. Finally, there are special carriers equipped with both an integral cable and lock that are designed to discourage theft. When you hit the ski hut, simply place the skis in the holder, wrap the cable around some sturdy object, and lock the unit.

Additional protection in automobile transit to the ski area is offered by a *ski bag*, whether you are stuffing skis into a car interior, latching them down to an external rack, carrying them in a topside gear storage unit, or checking them into an airport terminal. For the latter, consider placing extra padding around the skis to minimize the trauma of the "delicate handling" normally associated with airports. (Believe it or not, multiple-ski cases with wheels, comparable to much of today's hand luggage, are now on the market.) If carried on a roof rack, the bag should be of rugged construction and waterproof.

Board bags are also available, with and without padding. Unlike most skis, they can be easily accommodated in a car trunk, car interior or gear storage unit.

Poles. Poles are strictly for use in the skiing and snowshoeing (as opposed to snowboarding) domain. *Pole shafts* are most often made of lightweight aluminum, although some fiberglass models can be found on the slopes. Many racers opt for lightweighted graphite or graphite-Kevlar models. Although most are of solid design, some manufacturers have at least one telescoping (adjustable-length) pole in their inventory. Their advantages are that they can be adjusted for use by more than one person, they store compactly, and they add to your control on long, steep traverses or side-stepping your way up a mountain.

North Star, California

Poles are commonly fitted with plastic *baskets*, most of which have at least one cut-out so that you can clip the poles together for carrying. Some models have grips that also clip together.

The *tips* of the poles vary in shape. You want a shape that will grip ice and snow, but will not skewer you in an inopportune fall. Most have either four very small pointed projections or a dish-shaped grip.

The most common *grip style* is the traditional design with a simple bicycle-handle-type grip. This style has an adjustable wrist strap attached to the pole which prevents you from losing your pole in a fall. Also popular is the molded or "breakaway" grip -- essentially a traditional grip, sans wrist strap, with a nearly full-wraparound guard over the fingers. The traditional style is most useful to beginning skiers (though used by all classes) because the pole tends to stay with the skier in a fall, reducing the recovery effort. The bad news is that in some falls, it is safer to have the poles separate from the skier. When selecting, try the grip styles with your ski gloves on.

The straight ski poles are used by virtually every skier, from beginners to experts. The bent poles are used by downhill racers, and are shaped to fit around the body to limit wind resistance. The on-site thumbrule method of *sizing* a pole is to push the basket into a flat snow surface -- with your hand on the grip, your forearm should be parallel to the ground. In the store, reverse the process. Place the pole upside down with your hand gripped just below the basket. Again, your forearm should be parallel to the ground.

Snow Board. Nearly non-existent on groomed slopes a few years ago, snowboarders are appearing on the slopes in increasing numbers. The driving force is the enhanced ability to maneuver and perform tricks, at any level of skiing ability, relative to skis.

• Like skis, the *board core* is most often a choice of wood or foam. The tradeoff between the two is very similar to that discussed for skis.

• The *sidecut radius* is calculated by taking into account board profile. The sidecut is the difference between the nose width and waist width. The smaller the radius, the sharper the turning radius; a longer sidecut radius initiates wider turns.

• *Effective edge* is the part of the board that is actually in contact with the snow. Longer running length means greater stability at high speeds and more edge-grip in turns; shorter length makes it easier to initiate turns, maneuver and spin.

• *Inserts* are small threaded cylinders implanted in the board to reinforce the area where screws attach the binding. The number of inserts and their pattern determine binding compatibility.

• Though not yet as specialized as for snow skis, there is an array of *board types* which can be matched to your style, ability and terrain preferences. Some are further matched to limited boarder weight classes and a few are made for the extremes of foot sizes. A (non-universal) sample of board types is provided below.

Entry-Level Boards. For those just starting out, these are the most economical choice. Most often these are freestyle models, versatile all-mountain boards for carving, cruising, catching air or doing tricks. For entry-level use, they typically have a nominal overall length, sidecut radius and relatively small effective edge.

Sport Boards. Once you've got the basics down, these boards are for tackling new tricks and more difficult terrain. As with their high-performance counterparts (below), these boards come in freestyle, freeriding or technical models. Freeriding use includes big powder, big air and steep slopes -- the board has a turned-up nose and tail for better float in fluffy powder. They are the "stretch" boards with lots of effective edge. Technical models are optimized for trick riding. They are short, have limited effective edge, and are generally symmetrical(i.e., have identical nose and tail dimensions and a centered-stance pattern).

High-Performance Boards. These are boards for black-diamond runs and skiing on all terrain, under any conditions.

Professional Boards. If you've seen a professional sports video, you'll know that these are for those performing the "impossible" tricks. Most often, they are specialized freestyle and freeride variants.

• *Board bindings* provide the linkage between boots and board. It's essential to choose the best match for your style of riding and skill level to ensure highest performance from your board. Note that the insert pattern on your board must be compatible with that on your binding. Bindings are installed on boards most frequently for left foot forward, although many boarders are more comfortable with the right foot forward or "goofy-foot" configuration.

Mammoth Mountain, California Courtesy of Sam Nunez

The two most basic types are *soft bindings* and *step-in bindings*. Both are used in combination with "soft" boots. The soft binding is generally a two-buckle system with several quality levels that depend on type of construction and materials. These bindings provide numerous adjustment options and offer excellent support for carving turns or doing tricks. Step-in bindings are equally versatile in design and use. Their appeal is in the boarder's ease and convenience of getting on and off the board. They will most often come at an increased expense.

At advanced levels, some boarders are more interested in speed than doing tricks. They require a form-fitting boot that is highly-responsive to foot movement. These racers most often choose *plate bindings* in conjunction with "hard" boots.

Ski Boots. Boots are as important to the enjoyment and safety aspects of skiing as are the skis and bindings. They critically affect ski control as well as protect your feet and ankles, The boot has an effective outer shell for rigidity and an interior liner for comfort and fit. With regard to *fit*, new ski boots should feel quite snug. With usage, your feet compress the boot interior liner and gradually loosen the fit. Unless you start with very snug boots, they may become loose enough to compromise your control. Each manufacturer's boots fit a little differently; the best way to find the one that is right for you is to try on a number of brands in your boot class. It's not uncommon to need some type of boot modification to get the best possible fit.

• The *shell index* measures boot stiffness. In general, the stiffer the boot, the greater its response and precision. These properties become more important as the level of performance sought increases. Below is a rough guide for discussion purposes.

Soft Shell. The shell is designed for comfort and a forgiving ride. The shell can be easily flexed, but not enough to allow the skier to easily fall out of a proper skiing stance.

Moderate Shell. Designed for performance skiing and comfort, this mid-level, forgiving shell allows for a greater range of motion for all types of terrain than the stiffer boots.

Stiff Shell. This shell is for high-performance skiing. It has many of the advantages of a race shell, but with a little give built in.

Very Stiff Shell. Designed for racing and other hard-core activities, this boot optimizes edge hold and turning precision.

• The *shell types* include Overlap and Mid-Entry designs. The former has the classic front entry and features a two-part overlapping shell. The latter has cuff entries in front and back, allowing for easy entry and exit. This also makes it easier to walk comfortably when not on skis. The mid-entry design is most commonly associated with entry-level boots.

• The *shell dynamics* feature includes Fixed-Shell and Variable-Shell designs. The fixed models are just that -- fixed. They cannot be adjusted for stiffness and stance. A variable shell can be adjusted for comfort and/or flex. A boot with "forward-flex adjustment," for instance, features a mechanism that allows you to change the boot's stiffness. "Forward-lean adjustment" lets you change the stance of the boot by increasing or decreasing the angle of the cuff relative to the front of the boot. As the boots are used at higher performance levels, the proportion of variable to fixed designs increases.

• To maximize your skiing enjoyment, choose a *class of boots* that match your skiing style, planned usage and technical ability. The boots should be compatible with your skis and bindings. If you have special foot needs, look into off-the-shelf or custom orthotics that can be fitted into your boot. A rough (non-universal) guide to boot classes is provided below.

Entry-Level Boots. Soft-flexing and forgiving, these boots are designed for newcomers looking for affordable (yet, still high-quality) equipment that will shorten the learning curve. They commonly employ a soft, fixed, mid-entry shell.

Casual Recreational Boots. This class is made for skiers with competent basic skills, especially those wanting to improve their carving technique and tackle more difficult terrain.

Serious Recreational Boots. These boots are equal parts forgiving and supportive. They are intended for experienced skiers who are comfortable on almost any terrain, but are more interested in finesse than power.

Aggressive Performance Boots. Built to be highly responsive, this class is built to handle quick turns, high speeds and bumpy slopes.

Racer/Expert/Hard-core Boots. These are the most responsive boots that you can buy, and are designed for extremely aggressive skiers who thrive on power and speed. They are the standard for those who participate in competitive or advanced recreational racing. Almost all have a very-stiff, variable, overlap shell.

Board Boots. "Soft" boots are somewhat like the old-fashioned alpine skiing models. Softness is a desirable feature for boarding (in sharp contrast to skiing) since flexibility of movement is at a premium for executing many board maneuvers. They use lace-up designs or lace-ups with ratchet, Velcro or power straps. Individual models are typically designed for soft straps or step-in bindings, but not both. The most common boot materials are natural or synthetic leather, waterproof polyurethane or nylon, or combinations of those materials. "Hard boots" are more similar to the current alpine skiing models, consisting of an outer plastic shell and an inner liner; they typically use a buckle-down system to secure the foot within the boot.

Selection of a boot should be based on your boarding style, planned usage and level of ability. A generic set of *boot classes* is discussed below.

All-Mountain Basic Boots. For those just starting out or looking for an extra-versatile, economical boot, this is probably the best choice. They are almost all lace-up boots meant for use with soft bindings.

Freestyle Boots. Designed for all-around use, the freestylers are meant for carving, cruising, catching air or doing tricks. In most cases, these boots are shorter and softer (i.e., more give) than freeride boots.

Freeride Boots. These boots are optimal for steep hills, big air and deep powder. Freeride boots are generally taller and stiffer than freestyle boots, and offer more support for riding at high speeds or making big air landings.

Racing Boots. These hard boots are the counterparts to the alpine skier's "Racer/Expert/Hardcore Boots," both in overall design and use.

Whistler Mountain, Canada Courtesy of Walt Bond

Boot Rack. A rack simplifies carrying your boots through all the stages of getting to the ski area. More important for flexible boots, it also prevents the sole from curling during storage. Most *rack* structures are constructed of rugged plastic or metal. You simply mount each boot on the rack and adjust a lock-down mechanism over the boot's toe lip. Particularly with more expensive boots, consider purchasing a padded boot bag.

A simple solution for transporting boots to and from the slopes is the *boot tote*. Most models have a simple gripping handle with a cord loop attached to its center. The loop is locked under one or more buckles of each boot (or, for lace-up models, the laces of one boot are passed through the loop and tied to the other boot's laces). A single-hand lift of the handle allows you to conveniently transport a set of securely attached boots. When not in use, you simply stow the device in a pocket.

Boot Glove. Cold feet can ruin a great ski outing. A recently introduced solution is a contoured piece of neoprene with Velcro straps that fits over ski boots without interfering with the bindings. Simply slip the glove over the boot and trim to fit. Manufacturer's tests claim that the same skier in minus 5-degree Fahrenheit (°F) weather will be in boots at the ambient temperature within a mile without the glove, and in 47°F boots once the gloves are added.

Ski/Board Wax. Most skiers and boarders sharpen edges and wax before heading to the slopes, or have the work done at the local ski shop. The classic mode is to use the average wax for the average conditions. The second is to call the ski area beforehand and guess ahead about the slope properties. Some forgo a full-scale wax job until they reach the slopes. (Still others forget to wax their skis on the first day of a new season and suffer the "hanging-on-the-slope" syndrome.) Whatever, the basic idea is to use the wax that helps the ski or board slide as fast as possible on the downhill!

All skiers might be well advised to take a little wax as a contingency, for themselves or fellow downhillers. For the more serious, this frequently translates into bringing an array of waxes that will, hopefully, cover the range of snow conditions to be encountered. The colder the snow, the harder the wax needed; the warmer the snow, the softer the wax. Though not a universal convention, typical wax types are made for cold snow, extremely cold snow, freezing snow, wet snow, and for "all conditions." Waxes are covered in greater detail in the NORDIC SKIING/SNOWSHOEING (Daytime) section.

Water Container/Bota Bag. Like any other outdoor activity, you will require some water while working the slopes. Rather than hit the ski hut or water outlet every time you get thirsty, the prevalent option is to carry water. The most common modes are to wear a fanny pack or carry a bota bag.

With a well-chosen *fanny pack*, you can carry your liquid refreshment as well as a mini-medical kit, sun block, spare goggle filters, a few snacks and the like. If you go with a *bota bag*, you might get by with storing all the side gear in your pockets. The bota is commonly a soft leather, stomach-shaped bag with a top stopper and attachment cord. You carry the bag by placing the cord around your neck. The method of use (during or after skiing) is to lift the bag slightly above mouth level, cock your head, aim the spout and enjoy the liquid.

Backcountry Gear. If you are a backcountry alpine skier, consider taking a *daypack* fitted with gear selected from the NORDIC SKIING (Daytime) section. Ensure that you understand the ski area rules with regard to outside-the-ropes skiing. Whether or not you ski in a commercial or natural (backcountry) area, make sure that you know how to recognize potential avalanche areas, understand how to safely route around them, and how to deal with avalanche victims should Mother Nature act up. The subject of avalanche rescue equipment and techniques is discussed in the GLACIER/WINTER CLIMBING section.

Personal Gear

Few outdoor activities have spawned the wide variety of clothing as has alpine skiing. Though there are a limited variety of basic styles, there are a myriad of variants in terms of accessory features, colors, patterns and the like. Whatever your stylish preferences, the fundamentals for staying warm and dry apply equally to skiing as for the other cold-weather activities discussed in this book. In addition, you want gear that is not restrictive to your skiing movement. For the outer clothing layer, you also want gear that will keep out the snow (particularly if you fall) and is made of anti-skid material. One proviso relative to some of the more remote activities in this book: If you become uncomfortable, there is always the warming hut, the ski lodge or perhaps a short trip to the car or elsewhere for a change of clothes.

As with other outdoor activities, the *layered clothing concept* applies. For upper and lower torso coverage, a typical outfit on a warm day might be lightweight, moisture-wicking longjohns, ski pants, a sweater and possibly a vest. On a very cold day, the outfit might be medium-to-heavy longjohns, wool or synthetic turtleneck/ pullover sweater combination, heavily-insulated ski pants and jacket ,and windproof outer shell. If your activities will require more than the normal downhill exertion (e.g., tree skiing or backcountry skiing), strongly consider a breathable, wind and waterproof shell.

Ski Pants/Knickers. We've seen skiers in jeans and a "T"-shirt, but wouldn't want to take their places after a couple of falls. The most popular, reasonable and versatile option is to get a *two-piece (pants/jacket) outfit* where the two pieces are of comparable quality in terms of warmth and durability. (Gee, maybe a matching outfit?!) The highest quality ski pants are two-layered designs with an outer, water-resistant, breathable layer and an interior thermal lining. Some have mesh ports on the interior to transport moisture. Common materials are nylon and nylon/polyester weaves.

One common style is the overall, with over-the-shoulder suspenders (frequently called bibs or bib overalls). They are generally equipped with cinches or adjustable belts at the waist. Some have a sewn-in section near the boot with elastic backed up by snaps -- consider this as an "interior gaiter." Others have a full-length side zipper that allows you to get in and out of your outfit with your boots on. Many have abrasion-resistant patches near the boot area to minimize potential ski and boot damage to the pants. Pockets are normally equipped with a zippered or Velcro-closed overflap to prevent snow entry.

Some skiers prefer the *stretch ski pants* commonly used by racers. They have elastic straps that go under the insteps together with integral shoulder straps. The key advantage of this style is their low wind resistance -- they are also very sheik. The major drawback is that you can only fit a pair of thermal underwear beneath and the combined outfit is not as highly wind-resistant as the two-layered styles discussed above. The preferred designs ride high above the waist, particularly in the back area.

Jackson Hole, Wyoming Courtesy of Doug Holker

If you are a Nordic skier, another option is to wear a modest variation of your *cross-country skiing outfit*. Since alpine skiing is generally less highly aerobic, you might want to go to a heavier thermal underwear for a given set of weather conditions. Also, since the Nordic experience has no real counterpart to riding a lift chair in cold, high wind, a hearty windbreaker is more of a necessity during the day when plying the slopes. A warning: Be prepared to answer questions from a few alpine skiers along the line of, "Is this the latest in the ski clothing line?"

If you are not highly style conscious, you may find that some of your BACKPACKING or WINTER/GLACIER CLIMBING GEAR will serve you well in downhill skiing. In leaner times, we have skied in our "*climbing wool*" (thermal underwear, Army surplus pants, "logger's shirt" covered by a sweater, with a down parka or parka and windbreaker acting as the shell layer).

Ski Jacket/Parka. The companion to the two-layer pants is a similarly constructed *jacket*. The most-functional styles extend down at least 8-10 inches below the waist and have a cinch strap or adjustable belt at the waist. The jackets frequently have an interior mesh liner and mesh interior breathing ports, snaps or Velcro closures, flap-covered exterior pockets, and a couple of mesh interior pockets. Some are pullovers, although most have frontal zippers (with protective overflaps) -- the former are warmer and less likely to admit snow, while the latter allow you to adjust the opening to suit the environment. Some models have underarm zippers which, for the zippered models, allow you to keep the front closed while still adjusting ventilation. It is essential that they have tight elastics and/or fasteners at the neck and wrists to keep the snow out and a high collar for neck warmth. A common extra is abrasion patches on the shoulders and sides. A less common design feature is "zip-out" sleeves, useful for warm days on the slopes.

Some jackets are equipped with an integral hood, a significant feature on cold windy days. The most useful designs have a behind-the-neck hood storage pocket, frequently secured with Velcro. The hood itself has a drawstring and/or fasteners to allow you to snug the hood against your face, as well as keep wind from entering near your neck area. When combined with a snug pullover hat or balaclava and goggles, this set will keep your discomfort to a minimum.

Though you will see many skiers with down *parkas*, there are a few cautions. When worn as a shell, the parka will absorb moisture after you take a couple of dunkings in wet snow or expose it to hours of falling wet white stuff. The parka is also less-well designed for falls, sliding, snagging tree branches and other skiing hazards. It is best to wear a cinchable windbreaker as the outer shell if you anticipate rough usage or wet slope conditions.

Ski Outfit. This is really a label for a one-piece skiing outfit, sometimes referred to as a "powder suit." They are made of the same materials as discussed above, but are warmer because there are no openings at the waist area. With a one-piece, it is very important to ensure that it is comfortable in all your "maximum stretch" positions. A few have a zippered mid-section that lets you remove the jacket on particularly warm days or when relaxing or lunching in the ski lodge.

Sweater/Turtleneck. There is tremendous versatility in combining turtlenecks with pullover sweaters. On warm days, a light turtleneck may suffice under your ski jacket. As the wind chill drops, there are options for the same turtleneck under a sweater or a heavier turtleneck under a high-bulk sweater. The same type of gear as discussed under "Sweater/Turtleneck" in the VEHICLE-ACCESSIBLE CAMPING activity are useful for skiing, although you may want to opt for sportier weaves and colors.

Turtleneck Dickey or Scarf. No matter how carefully you dress, there may be times when the wind finds its way down your neck. One solution is a *turtleneck dickey* (or "neck gaiter"). This single-piece stretch item is pulled over your head and placed around your neck. Common materials for this 4-6-inch length gaiter are wool blends and synthetics interwoven with elastics. Another option is a wide *scarf* with sufficient length to wrap around your neck twice -- one full wrap is actually used and the "tails" are tucked into the ski jacket.

Vest. A vest is ideal for warm to cool weather skiing because it provides warmth at the most critical area and is the least encumbering of the many types of outer layer gear. It is sometimes worn over one-piece suits on cold days. The most common insulating material is goose down, which is enclosed by a rugged nylon or nylon-blend shell. Other materials include synthetic pile. The most useful styles have wide openings in the armpit area, high collars and flap-covered zippers. Those with pure snap-down fronts are also popular, although they will admit more wind and snow.

Windbreaker. Many ski jackets will carry you through all reasonably-expected ski conditions except high winds. If you are planning on skiing in these conditions (most skiers wisely retire to the ski hut), the solution is to add a windbreaker, whose properties are described in the VEHICLE-ACCESSIBLE CAMPING activity.

Headgear. Adequate protection for head and hands is essential because these are the parts of the body from which most heat is lost. Never be tempted to ski without headgear, even if it means carrying it in your pocket, because mountain temperatures can change very rapidly. Many styles are available, varying from simple pullovers to ski masks to peaked hats with earflaps. As a minimum, they should cover your ears and forehead. Desirably, they will also cover the back of your neck. Once again, sounding like cranky old folks, stick with materials such as wool, polyester and fleece that will retain warmth when wet. Helmets are increasingly being worn by adults and are recommended by many resorts for small children.

Gloves/Mittens. One ski run without gloves, particularly if the wind-chill is nasty or if you tumble into the snow, will be the last time you leave them behind. One basic choice is between *gloves or mittens* -- mittens are warmer, but gloves allow more freedom of movement. A second choice has to do with materials; treated leather is classic, while newer fabrics such as heavy-duty, treated ripstop nylon are more common. Both types have some models with water-resistant/breathable nylon panels and either elastic or Velcro closures to cinch the mitt to the forearm.

Whatever the selection, purchase gloves or mittens that are well insulated, water repellent, have long, close-fitting cuffs, provide padded palms with a good gripping surface, and fit snugly (but not so tight as to stop circulation in your fingers). Most models have heavy elastics or zippers to snug the gloves around your hands, thus minimizing snow entry. Look for products that are equipped with a security cord (which prevents glove loss when taken off the hand), or sew on your own. If your hands are perpetually cold while skiing, note that some gloves and mittens come with built-in pockets for hand warmers (heat packs).

In extreme weather, thin silk or synthetic *liner gloves* are frequently worn under the outer set. Some ski gloves and mittens are sold with liners. Note that it may be a struggle to find a proper fitting liner for the gloves (less so with mittens) that you purchased separately. Snowboarders sometimes wear *wristguards* for protection during falls. If you plan to use wrist guards, wear them when you are fitting for gloves or mittens.

Mammoth Mountain, California Courtesy of Sam Nunez

Socks. It is important that your feet and socks fit into the boot snugly, enough to assure good foot contact with the boot, but not so tight that you prevent good blood circulation. If you are renting boots, bring several sizes and thicknesses of *outer-layer socks* to ensure a good fit. For acceptable cushioning, wicking ability and thermal insulation, a single ski sock will cut it under normal conditions. Socks made of natural fibers such as wool or synthetic insulators using hollow-core polyester fibers are ideal. They are frequently blended with acrylic and polypropylene to take advantage of the wicking properties of these materials. In addition, they frequently employ Spandex or other stretchable material to ensure a lump-free fit when your tootsies are inside the boots.

Thin *liner socks* of silk, polypropylene, polyester (or related blends) are worn under the insulating pair in cold weather or by people with cold-sensitive feet. They provide an extra insulating layer and also are very good at wicking moisture away from the feet. A regression: Some top-of-the-line boots have a separate insulating liner that may allow you to get by with only a liner sock, even in cold weather. Since these boots are intentionally sized to fit snugly, adding another layer may actually cause the loss of some circulation and defeat the liner's intended purpose.

Gaiters. As with other snow activities, these devices are designed to keep your lower pants dry and keep snow out of your boots. Unlike the gaiters described in the HIKING activity, however, they rarely have a tie-down which fits under the boot instep. They come in pure slipover or side-zippered designs. Padded versions of the standard gaiter provide both added insulation for warmth and a protective surface, should you tumble and run a ski edge also your leg.

Ski Goggles/Filters. Plastic, polarized, full-eye-covering sunglasses will see you through most ski conditions, but in heavier snowfalls and gusty conditions with blowing snow, ski goggles are needed. Key properties are wide field of view, comfortable fit (foam padding next to the face and a wide adjustable headstrap are preferred), proper ventilation and good anti-fogging capability. In the latter case, look for goggles with sealed double lenses or lenses coated with an anti-fog chemical. Additional measures available are to wipe the lenses with a chemically-treated cloth or fog-retarding paste. Finally, if you need prescription glasses for good vision, ensure that the goggles fit over them.

Goggles with interchangeable (various tint) lenses are most versatile, since they allow you to optimize to potentially fast-changing lighting conditions. Look for glasses or goggles with high-UV blocking properties and low light transmission. Lens properties and selection of tints for different lighting conditions are discussed further in the TEN ESSENTIALS section.

Fanny Pack or Day Pack. If you can tuck all your daytime goodies in your pockets, then these items are moot. Most commonly, skiers use a *fanny pack* to store water, snacks, extra sunglass or goggle filters, a mini-first-aid kit and personal items. If you are heading outside the ropes, note that you can squeeze the "Ten Essentials" into a medium-size fanny pack.

A *daypack* has more space, making it better suited to backcountry skiing. If you already have one, it may also save you the cost of a fanny pack for groomed-slope skiing. In either case, it may interfere more with normal skiing motions than a fanny pack, particularly if it is not tightly fitted. In addition, it will cut off air circulation to the underlying back region, resulting in the dreaded "sweaty back."

Safety

First Aid Kit. The ski patrol is "right around the corner" for all but outside-the-ropes and backcountry skiers It is still wise to carry a mini-kit to handle small boo-boos. This will minimize the chances of infection as well as allow you to continue skiing in relative comfort without having to seek out an aid stop. Consider bringing moleskin to prevent blisters or protect feet after a blister onset caused by boot rub. (See FIRST AID for kit details.)

Ski Area Map/Topo Map. Commercial ski areas provide *maps* that typically show ski lifts, ski runs (with difficulty symbol), first aid areas, ski huts and ski lodges, ski area limits and other useful information. Unless you know the area "in your sleep," stuff one in a pocket where it won't come out and refer to it whenever there is any doubt. Though more for use if you are going outside the ropes, bring a *topographic map* of the area if you are a playful adventurer. (Darnit, why not just bring those "Ten Essentials" that we keep harping about!?)

Just recently in Southern California, a snowboarder survived six days in the winter snows after venturing just a short distance outside the ski area bounds. He was found two miles from his ski area exit point, had no idea even at the outset of the general direction back to the ski area, and was heading in the opposite direction from the single main (open) highway. What a difference a topo map and a compass might have made! (A post-note: He subsequently passed away in the hospital.)

Accessories

Apres-Ski Boots. These boots are for comfort and safety. Nothing beats getting into a warm, snugly pair of boots after a long day on the slopes. They are also meant to keep you from slipping on ice and falling on your bottom as you wander away from the slopes and head for the Jacuzzi or into town. (One of the authors switched from treaded boots to street shoes in preparation for the drive home after a week of skiing. As luck would have it, he slipped on the ice while getting into his car, forced his finger into the door jam, and broke it -- honest!)

Boot types range from trim, lightweight styles suitable for casual wear to rugged, heavyweight styles designed for extreme sub-zero conditions. There are also less-functional, but more pleasing-to-the-eye boots for in-town cruising -- these are not covered below. Boots are characterized by a *comfort rating*, a rough measure of boot warmth that is more specifically determined by your individual metabolism, activity level and conditions encountered. The lightweight styles are for use in the near-sub-zero temperatures, while the heavy-duty models may be advertised for use down to -100°F. The boot insulation most often has a wicking inner layer and an outer layer or layers that absorbs foot moisture and traps warmth. The materials in each layer are many and varied -- too numerous to list -- with many excellent models in different price ranges available. Some have removable liners that permit you to add or subtract insulation depending on conditions of use.

The *boot uppers* come in many materials, including heavy-denier nylon, leather and combinations of fabric and leather. There are a lesser number of rubber uppers. Leather uppers are more rugged, but also tend to be heavier than their fabric counterparts. The better boots are equipped with a heavy, deep-set *tread pattern* to help you maintain traction on slippery surfaces. The most common patterns are lug and bar cleat. *Outsoles* are typically made of rubber, predominantly natural, thermal, molded or thermoplastic types.

Boot Dryer. In addition to storing your boots with the buckles latched, it is wise to dry them out before long-term storage. Further, you may want to dry your boots after each day's skiing. Take the inner boot out and let it dry at room temperature. Do not put boots near any form of direct heat (room heater, stove, etc.) or leave them outside.

There is an option to use a low-capacity *boot dryer*. It is shaped to fit into a boot and forces warmed air into the boot bottom using a small fan. Some have an exhaust port that you can place a glove over for simultaneous boot and glove warming. Some decadent skiers even use these dryers to warm their boots and gloves before hitting the slopes.

Spare Keys/Credit Card/$. Bring a batch of change (usually quarters) if you plan to use the ski lockers.

<u>Tool Kit</u>

Tools. Bring any tools required for adjustment of release settings for your particular bindings. If other mechanical problems occur on the slopes, visit the local ski shop for repairs.

Repair Gear. Consider bringing a sewing/patch kit for repair of your ski apparel. The kit might include safety pins, thread, sewing needles, yarn, buttons and patch material.

Replacement Gear. You may or may not take them on the slopes with you, but a spare pair of sunglasses/goggles, gloves/mittens and headgear may save you from having to spend precious Jacuzzi time out shopping for replacement gear.

<u>Secondary Activities</u>

You may couple your downhill skiing trip with HIKING, NORDIC SKIING /SNOWSHOEING, SNOWMOBILING or other winter-related activity. The gear needs associated with those efforts can be found in the appropriate activity description.

ALPINE SKIING/SNOWBOARDING
(Daytime/Nighttime)

Select gear items to fit your trip needs, worst-case weather conditions and level of luxury desired.

ITEM	DATE				
Skiing/Snowboarding Gear					
Auto Gear Rack /Locks					
Skis/Carry Straps/Ski Bag					
Ski Brakes or Safety Straps					
Poles					
Snowboard					
Ski/Board Boots					
Boot Rack & Boot Tote					
Boot Glove					
Ski/Board Wax					
Water Container/Bota bag					
Lift Ticket					
Personal Gear					
Ski Pants/Knickers					
Ski Jacket/Parka					
Thermal Underwear					
Turtleneck Sweater or T-shirt					
Pullover Sweater					
Turtleneck Dickey or Neck Scarf					
Vest					
Windbreaker					
Headgear					
Socks					
Gloves/Mittens					
Wrist Guard					
Ear Muffs					
Gaiters					
Bandanna/Sweatband					
Ski Goggles/Filters/Anti-fog Lqd.					
Fanny Pack or Day Pack					
Safety					
First Aid Kit (see FIRST AID)					
Sunglasses & Lanyard/Goggles					
Sunscreen					
Lip Balm					
Whistle					
Emergency Blanket					
Waterproof Matches & Lighter					
Fire Starter/Heat Tabs					
Ski Area Map/Topo Map					
Compass					

ALPINE SKIING/SNOWBOARDING
(Daytime/Nighttime)

ITEM	DATE				
Reading Glasses & *Repair Kit*					
Timepiece					
Thermometer					
Pocket Knife					
Flashlight#					
Extra Batteries & Bulb#					
Avalanche Beacon					
Phone Change					
Accessories					
Camera; Extra Film & Battery					
Camera Case & Lens Cleaner					
Monocular/Small Binoculars					
Sitting Pad					
Boot Dryer					
Apres-ski Boots					
Evening Clothes					
Swim Suit (Jacuzzi, hot springs)					
Towel					
Soap					
Shampoo					
Personal Toiletries/Ditty Bag					
Toilet Paper					
Indoor & Outdoor Games					
Auto Tire Chains & Anti-freeze					
Auto Tool Kit					
Spare Keys/Credit Card/$					
Tool Kit (skiing)					
Tools					
Repair Gear					
Replacement Gear					
Snacks (see MEALS section)					
High-Energy Bars					
Trail Mix/Granola					
Fresh Fruit/Dried Fruit					
Beef Jerky					
Nuts					
Electrolyte (for water container)					

Italicized items are optional (niceties or special purpose -- outside-the-ropes skiing). #night-skiing items

NORDIC SKIING/SNOWSHOEING (Daytime)

See INDEX for checklist Items not discussed below.

This activity description spans short daytripping runs on groomed trails to full-day adventures in the Mother Nature's backcountry. Compared to alpine and Nordic activities in groomed areas, backcountry skiing/snowshoeing requires significantly improved levels of physical conditioning, knowledge of the outdoors and survival skills.

Safety Considerations: 1) review the **GENERAL CONSIDERATIONS** and TEN ESSENTIALS sections; 2) review the GLACIER/WINTER CLIMBING (Daytime) activity safety and gear discussions; 3) study the trip beforehand, establishing a route and alternatives that are within your group's physical and technical capabilities; 4) master the reading of both weather and snow/ice (including potential avalanche) conditions; 5) work on physical conditioning and ski/snowshoe techniques between major trips; 6) practice rescue techniques with your group before attempting the next-level trip; 7) ensure that there is a group leader with experience in higher-difficulty tours than the one you are attempting; 8) develop plans for contacting rescue units in an emergency; 9) practice techniques needed to extricate an injured tourer from the backcountry area; 10) bring severe-weather contingency gear in the event that you are forced out overnight; and 11) turn back at the first indication of severe weather onset.

In the checklist, items that are considered optional (niceties or special purpose) are *italicized*. Items noted with a pound sign(#) are needed for nighttime travel, as a contingency.

<u>Skiing/Snowshoeing Gear</u>

For entry-level Nordic skiers, it makes sense to rent, borrow and find dual use for other equipment that you might already have, e.g., alpine ski poles, track skis (doubling for light touring use), etc. Nordic equipment is not high-tech relative to Alpine skiing, in otherwords, not as critical for achieving an exact fit and performance match in the entry phases.

Renting has the advantage that stores tend to emphasize gear that is popular (read that as rentable), thus up to date and easy to use. As described below, the best bet is probably to start with waxless touring or classic (track) skis with standard three-pin bindings. The touring skis are more versatile, perhaps not optimized for groomed-track skiing, but far better for mild exploring off the track. If your plan is to stick with groomed tracks, consider switching to Nordic classic bindings.

Entry-level snowshoers should consider the same renting/borrowing/improvising options discussed above for initial activities. Snowshoeing is the low-tech end of the (non-machine) snow-related activities, which is definitely one of its attractive features. Start with a waterproofed set of hiking boots strapped into recreational-level snowshoes.

The discussion below spans the gear designed for learning to that for focused, advanced applications. It assumes that your desire is to become a proficient, serious Nordic skier or snowshoer. If so, it makes sense, after a limited learning period to find where your interests lie, to spend the bucks to buy the gear that is optimized for your needs.

Nordic Skies and Bindings. Though hand-crafted, wooden skies are beautiful, they have been replaced by higher-performing, more-durable synthetic models. Like alpine skiing, it seems that modern technology has brought a ski for every conceivable type of user. Each ski type has specific technical characteristics that enhance its performance for specific applications.

• The *ski base* is most often a choice either extruded (solid) or sintered (porous) P-Tex. Although slightly more expensive, skis with a sintered base are more durable, hold wax better (both gripping and gliding waxes), turn more easily and offer a better glide. Some skis have graphite mixed into the base material to further improve glide.

• The *sidecut radius* is calculated by taking into account ski profile -- the ski's tip, waist and tail measurements. The larger the sidecut radius, the longer the ski's turning radius, meaning the ski is at it's best carving long, smooth turns and offers faster, smoother track performance. Conversely, a ski with a smaller radius will have a shorter turning radius and will excel for shorter, quicker turns.

• Ski *camber* is the bow in the ski. The "grip zone" (the middle third of the ski) is centered around the highest point in the camber, which is the stiffest flexing portion of the ski. This enables the ski's wax or traction pattern to grip the snow when you press down, and to spring back up when you ease up for gliding. Depending on primary usage, skis have a Nordic or flat (alpine) camber.

Huntington Lake, California Courtesy of Doug Holker

• A soft-*flexing* ski will grip better and turn more easily on soft snow and at slow speeds. A stiff flex is better suited for firm snow and fast speeds.

• Optimal *ski length* is largely determined by your skiing style and ability. Generally, a long ski is more stable at high speeds. A shorter ski usually makes it easier to initiate turns at slower speeds and is more maneuverable on varied terrain.

• Both *no-wax* and *waxed skis* are available. A textured pattern on the bottom of no-wax skis digs into the snow and grips, but reduces glide somewhat. Well-waxed skis provide better overall comparative performance in consistent temperatures, either above or below freezing. However, selecting the proper wax can be difficult right around the freezing point. If you live where temperatures are highly variable, no-wax skis are probably your best bet. But even "waxless" skis perform better with glide wax applied to tip and tail.

• To maximize enjoyment, select *types of skis* that match your style, ability and terrain preferences. Consult with a qualified specialist at your outdoor recreation shop if you have doubts about your equipment needs -- an informed decision will improve your chances of having the most fun and minimize the likelihood of a visit to the "bone doctor."

Touring Skis. An all-around touring ski is designed for traveling on both groomed tracks and striding over snow-covered back roads. They offer very good striding and turning performance. Touring skis are wider than pure track skis for increased flotation over soft, unpacked snow. Most are still light and skinny enough to be used on prepared tracks at ski areas. Their Nordic camber makes for easy striding and moderate sidecut offers turning ease, without excessive drag in the tracks. More experienced skiers sometimes opt for slightly heavier skis with metal edges, which provide better edge control on hills and hard or icy snow.

Classic/Skate Skis. Both ski types require the firm, groomed snow of a cross-country ski area. Classic (track) skis are designed for use with the age-old diagonal stride technique. To improve striding ease, they have minimal or no sidecut. All classic skis have a Nordic camber, while choice of flex is dependent on your intended use and ability level. The newer compact skis are sized one to two sizes shorter than regular skis, aimed particularly at making learning easier.

Skate skiing is a graceful technique that maximizes speed. Skate skis also have minimal or no sidecut, but are stiffer than the classic skis, and have more torsional rigidity and less flex. Their blunt tips are designed to not catch on snow. Skate skis have a different camber than the classic design and do not have a grip zone. The choice of flex depends on the same factors as for classic skis. These high-speed skis are sized 10-20 centimeters shorter than standard classic models.

Backcountry Skis. Made for both touring and turning, these skis are shorter, wider and stronger than all-around touring models. These metal-edged designs are the best choice for rolling terrain or rough snow conditions, and for cutting a few telemark turns down moderate slopes. The metal edges help you initiate and hold a turn, a critical feature on hard or icy snow. Typically, they are 5-10 centimeters shorter than the traditional length for touring skis. Backcountry skis have substantial sidecut compared to all-around touring skis, but less than telemark skis. They have either a Nordic or alpine camber, with flex chosen to suit the planned use and level of expertise.

For the ascent of steeper slopes, Backcountry and Telemark skis are fitted with *climbing skins*. They have a fur-like texture, with the fur lie oriented to provide resistance to backward ski slippage. The skins are removed prior to descent. The attachment hardware is the same as that for mountaineering skis, as described in the GLACIER/WINTER CLIMBING (Daytime) section. These skins should be wide enough to cover all but the metal edges of your skis.

Telemark Skis. These skis are made for downhill turning. Alpine-cambered and metal-edged, they excel for use on untracked mountain slopes and backcountry bowls. They are wider and shorter than other Nordic skis -- typically, you'll want a ski that's 10-20 centimeters shorter than the "to your outstretched wrist" height used for touring ski selection. Telemark designs have the most sidecut of any Nordic skis.

Like alpine skiing, the key considerations when purchasing *bindings* are intended usage, price and special features desired. The tradeoffs in these areas are provided below.

• With respect to usage, there are several *binding types*. Cross-country or 75 millimeter, three-pin bindings have been the standard for many years They are typically the least expensive option. More recently, specialized bindings that are optimized for the specific Nordic activity have been gaining popularity. These include the New Nordic Norm (NNN) system and Salomon Nordic System (SNS) options.

Touring Ski Bindings. The NNN system and SNS include both standard touring and backcountry options. They are easy to step in and out of and offer a forward-flex motion plus the torsional rigidity you need for turning. Most can be adjusted for forward flex.

Classic/Skate Ski Bindings. Unlike for other uses, few skiers use the three-pin system. Nordic classic and skate bindings are easy to enter and exit. They offer full forward flexibility for a natural foot movement plus the torsional rigidity for the more modest turning demands. Most are adjustable for forward flex.

Backcountry Ski Bindings. See "Touring Ski Bindings" above.

Telemark Ski Bindings. Heavy-duty three-pin and/or heel cable bindings are the norm for telemarking. There are releasable cable models available, including add-on cable options.

• There are *other considerations* when purchasing bindings. Whatever the option, the binding system selected must be compatible with the boot. The least expensive bindings require that you bend over and set the bindings to your boots, somewhat of a hassle if you are carrying weight on your back. A "step-in" feature, which allows you to engage or release the binding with the ski pole tip, is an option of particular usefulness on long tows with heavy packs. These step-in bindings come with a higher price tag.

Along with bindings, you can purchase heel-centering devices, where a small stub attached to the boot heel fits into a "V"-groove installed on the ski. These devices minimize side to side motion and improve the skier's efficiency. The "V"-grooves have a tendency to break with extreme or extended use and require periodic replacement. However, they will not inhibit the skiing motion if broken.

Sun Valley, Idaho — Courtesy of Doug Holker

Ski Poles. To find the correct length for touring, the top of the hand grip should reach the armpit for a person standing erect. Classic striding poles should reach the top of your shoulders, while skating poles should be sized to reach as high as your chin or even up to your nose. The shoulder-length criterion is a typical choice for backcountry or telemark skiing. However, adjustable-length poles are a better choice for backcountry use if you plan on doing much turning and nearly a necessity for telemarking, where you prefer to optimize length for uphill, downhill and traversing.

Even for day trips, we recommend the poles with conventional hand grips and strap, as opposed to the molded grips with no straps. The first time you lose your pole and it slips over even a small embankment, this will all make clear sense! Start with a cheap *bamboo-like* pole while training on packed tracks or light, non-packed snow.

(The pole will probably be decimated by the time you achieve a modest level of proficiency.) Another option is to use your alpine pole, provided that you don't mind subjecting it to a beating.

At a higher proficiency level, stronger poles (read that as nearly unbreakable) are highly recommended. *Metal* (lightweight aluminum alloy) or *fiberglass poles* are the most popular. For backcountry skiing, avoid the cross-country racing models (springy fiberglass or carbon filler with small, frequently asymmetric baskets). Telemark skiing calls for a strong, lightweight aluminum-alloy pole; also, since avalanche danger is a real concern, consider poles which knock down and screw together to form an avalanche probe.

Rock Creek, Sierra Nevada Mountains, California Courtesy of Doug Holker

Look for a large *basket* to handle the soft snow of off-track conditions or a small basket if you plan on doing lots of track skiing. For multiple conditions use, look for a pole with interchangeable baskets. Stick with the circlar shape for general use as opposed to some of the assymetric designs; the latter are designed for racing. Pole *tip designs* include one with a small cylindrical projection for snow penetration and others with a sharp "tooth" for leverage on ice. Most tips are either bent forward or cut with a forward, angled taper to better grip the snow while poling. They are mostly constructed of hardened steel or sintered carbide alloys. (See the GLACIER/WINTER CLIMBING (Daytime) activity for additional information on ski poles for backcountry use.)

Nordic Ski Boots/Boot Rack. In addition to price, key considerations for purchasing *ski boots* are intended use and boot fit. These considerations are treated below.

• *Boot use* and resultant sking style are integrally related to the ski and binding you choose. There are a variety of boot types from which to chose.

Touring Boot. Touring boots offer flexibility for striding, along with torsional rigidity for turning and stopping. These boots most often have more insulation than track or skating boots. As with most other uses, touring boots have synthetic, waterproof-leather or waxed-leather uppers, molded rubber or Vibram soles and lace-up closures.

Classic/Skate Boot. Classic boots should be flexible because their nominal counterpart bindings offer the torsional rigidity needed. Skating boots are stiffer and most are relatively high-cut.

Backcountry Boot. These boots offer the warmth and support needed for day-long and multi-day trips in the snow. Most are insulated. Torsional rigidity is essential for good ski control and thus easy turning, especially when wearing a heavy pack. As a result, backcountry boots are heavier, stiffer and cut higher than touring boots.

Telemark Boot. Telemarkers wear the heaviest, thickest and highest-cut of all Nordic boots. The boots need to have exceptional lateral support and rigidity, because telemarking requires excellent edge control. However, they are designed to provide the flexibility needed at the ball of the foot when in the telemark position. Traditionally, heavy leather boots have been the norm, but many newer models are made in all or part plastic and are starting to look more like alpine ski boots. Many have buckles in addition to the normal lace-ups.

• *Fit* is critically important for more-experienced skiers when selecting boots. Wear the usual two pairs of socks when trying them on: thin liners and thicker wool or synthetic outer socks. New ski boots should feel snug with no sharp pressure points, but not so tight as to cut off circulation. Snugness is essential since the boot is the means of transferring your body motion to the binding/ski. Each manufacturer's boots fit a little differently; the best way to find the one that is right for you is to try on a number of brands in your boot class.

A *boot rack* simplifies carrying your boots through all the stages of getting to the ski area. More important for flexible boots, it also prevents the sole from curling during storage. Most *rack* structures are constructed of rugged plastic or metal. You simply mount each boot on the rack and adjust a lock-down mechanism over the boot's toe lip. Particularly with more expensive boots, consider purchasing a padded boot bag.

Cork/Scrapper (ski wax tools). Layers of wax are smoothed using a waxing cork for polishing and old wax is removed with a scraper. A waxing cork and scraper or a combination cork/scraper are the minimum waxing tools.

Ski Wax. It's simple. Bring the wax that makes the ski grip securely going uphill and helps it slide faster on the downhill! This translates into bringing an array of waxes that will, hopefully, cover the range of snow conditions to be encountered. The colder the snow, the harder the wax needed; the warmer the snow, the softer the wax. The simplest approach, though non-optimum, is to use a *two-wax system*. Adequate grip for climbing is usually more important than downhill speed -- consider this when selecting a simple kit. When a variety of ski conditions is expected, more experienced skiers will bring an array of stick waxes for new snow conditions and blisters (sticky substances in a tube dispenser) for old snow.

Snowshoes. There are several general categories of *snowshoe types*. Recreational models are ideal for casual-to-moderate hiking and sport walking -- they are the least expensive. Backcountry/mountaineering snowshoes are designed for hiking and mountaineering. These types offer the best in aggressive traction and technical design. Racing snowshoes are made for competitive trail running and cross training, with an emphasis on low weight and durability.

Traditional *framing* is a straight-grained, strong-fibered, pliable wood. However, frame stiffness and light weighting have tilted most snowshoers to aluminum-tubing frames. A few manufacturers have recently come on the market with an apparently competitive "frameless" snowshoe, substituting a resin material construction for tubing.

Decking connects the frame with the binding and helps keep you "afloat" on the snow. Deckings may be of either laced or solid construction. Traditionalists prefer rawhide thong for decking although neoprene webbing is lighter, does not stretch when wet, is rodent-proof and is impervious to petroleum products (the latter two are storage considerations). Both, which are laced, have given way in popularity to high-tech composites such as Hypalon, the same tough material used in whitewater rafts. There are also competitive options featuring various durable polymer materials. Most advanced-composite bindings are of solid construction.

Bindings should hold the boot in place with no side-to-side or front-to-back slack, should hinge up and down about 45 degrees when the snowshoe is lifted well off the ground, and should be convenient to buckled or attach to the boot. The best, most efficient bindings feature some kind of stirrup into which the boot toe is placed directly over the crossbar. A strap or two around and behind the boots holds it in place.

Curved-up tips provide additional safety when heading downhill. Metal-plated *hinges* built into the crosspiece improve parallel tracking (i.e., minimize side-to-side shoe flip-flopping). Serrated metal edges (effectively *crampons*), preferably on both heel and toe on the bottoms of bindings, provide a built-in traction system for improved gripping on hardened or icy uphill surfaces.

Generally, short, broad shoes are easiest to maneuver and are preferred for woods and brushy trails. Longer, narrower shoes are most frequently chosen for open terrain. Floatation is how well you stay on top of the snow. It is determined by the decking, weight and size of the snowshoes, your weight and the snow conditions themselves. Stomping around on fluffy, dry or powdery snow requires a larger snow shoe than the same activity on wet, firm snow. There are tradeoffs -- larger snowshoes are heavier and less maneuverable than smaller ones. Your best bet is to get the smallest size that will support your weight for the average snow conditions in your area. Check an outfitter or catalogue for nominal recommendations. Better yet, rent shoes and test under conditions of normal usage before buying.

A side note provided by your Nordic skiing buddies to snowshoers: "Please stay out of the tracks laid out by us Nordic skiers. Yes, although the snowshoeing is easier for you, your imprints raise havok with the track!"

Snowshoe Poles/Ice Ax. Snowshoe, ski or trekking *poles* will offer you extra stability and balance when snowshoeing. Poles should be at a comfortable height that allows your elbows to be at a 90-degree angle when the poles are planted just to the outside of your snowshoes. Telescoping two- and three-section poles adjust to the needed height, can be set so one pole is longer than the other for traverses, and pack down to a small size in your rucksack or frame pack.

An *ice ax* is essential for mountaineering-level snowshoe trips on steep, icy snow. For this level of adventure you should be proficient in use of the ax for self-belay and self-arrest. (See the GLACIER/WINTER CLIMBING activity.)

Snowshoe Boots. No special boots are required. A snowshoer can wear any boots that have a history of providing comfort and warm/dry wear for other winter activities. One option is to use waterproofed *hiking boots* associated with BACKPACKING or GLACIER/WINTER CLIMBING and fit them to the snowshoes. A word of caution, however: A key element in the level of exertion is boot weight, thus you should lean to the lightest weight boot that is practical for your particular trip plans. If your style is for highly-exerting all-day or multi-day backcountry tours, you might want to consider buying a boot tailored solely for this activity.

There is a big payoff for minimizing the weight of bootwear. Some speculate that the future of close-in day touring might be in combining breathable, water-proof oversocks in combination with a heavy athletic shoe. (See the HIKING activity for a description of these shoes.) Time will tell!

Kneepads. This item is a fixture for some in the telemark skiing community. It's purpose is to protect the knees against tree stumps, rocks and other paraphernalia which may "jump out at you," particularly during a heady descent.

Crampons. You may want to bring *instep crampons* if your route will take you over short, exposed icy sections of terrain. Their use requires removal of the skis or snowshoes and attachment to your boots. (See the HIKING activity. Also, there is a more in-depth discussion of crampon characteristics in the GLACIER/WINTER CLIMBING section.)

Personal Gear

Nordic skiing and snowshoeing can be highly aerobic. You'll be producing a lot of sweat when you're moving, yet when the wind picks up or you stop for lunch, you can easily get chilled. There are many similarities to the HIKING and BACKPACKING activities at high altitude and the GLACIER/WINTER CLIMBING activity. Much of the personal gear description provided in those sections applies here. One difference: Choose the gear to ensure that it doesn't restrict the natural motion of your poles.

Jackson Hole, Wyoming Courtesy of Doug Holker

As for other outdoor activities, the *layered clothing concept* applies. For upper and lower torso coverage, a typical outfit on a very cold day might be moisture-wicking longjohns, wool or synthetic-pile knickers, wool or synthetic shirt/sweater combination, and a breathable, wind and waterproof shell. A jacket or parka comes on when you stop for lunch or take an extended breather. On a warmer day, many shift to lighter-weight long pants or shorts over longjohns, a heavy buttonable shirt or sweater, and a light windbreaker shell (using the same materials just mentioned).

Long Pants/Ski Pants/Knickers. Whatever you choose to wear, make sure that the fit is comfortable and allows the full freedom of leg movement. If your ski pants have too much loft, you may find that the inner leg area chaffs with each stride. This is not only inefficient, but the chaffing sound can become very irritating. Winter pants are discussed in the VEHICLE ACCESSIBLE CAMPING activity, ski pants in the ALPINE SKIING/SNOWBOARDING section, and knickers in the GLACIER/WINTER CLIMBING arena.

Down Parka/Vest/Jacket. The *parka* is for use on long rest stops in severe weather or for overnight camping. It will have you roasting if used while under exertion and will trap moisture. Many choose to wear a down or synthetic pile *vest* in cold, calm weather. Either keeps the torso warm, is less restrictive than a parka or jacket, and is easily stored when not needed.

In severe weather, many wear a *jacket* over their base insulating layer (shirt, sweater, etc.). Typical choices are warm, wicking heavy synthetic pile jackets or breathable water-resistant shells with a wicking insulating layer. Some have additional insulation in the frontal and shoulder areas. Whatever the choice, it is important to purchase a jacket with numerous adjustable closures which allow you to vary ventilation to account for both ambient conditions and level of exertion. Preferred models have zippered or buttoned closures in front and at the wrists, neck and underarms. Many of the water-resistant shells have a mesh breathing vent at the back that is covered by an overflap. Look for high necklines with snug closures that prevent heat loss and neck exposure. (Additional information about the down and synthetic pile options is provided in the VEHICLE-ACCESSIBLE CAMPING activity.)

Gaiters. Gaiters will keep the snow out of your boots. Maybe not so necessary for track skiing or light touring, it is a must for any telemark skiing or aggressive backcountry activities. (Refer to the HIKING activity for a detailed discussion.)

Safety

This activity is inherently in a snow-covered environment. Nearly all sources of natural fuel will be wet, which encourages bringing a conservative supply of the materials needed for starting fires (waterproof matches and lighter, fire starter/heat tabs, pocket knife) as a contingency.

Avalanche Beacon and Snow Shovel. For telemarking skiers who ply the untracked mountain slopes, these items should be part of the team package. (See the GLACIER/WINTER CLIMBING (Daytime) activity for a detailed description.)

Tool Kit

Tools. Bring any tools required for adjustment of release settings for your particular ski bindings. If experience with your bindings indicates that other tools are needed, bring them. A small set of pliers might prove useful for "jury-rigging" snowshoe repairs.

Repair Gear. For aggressive single-day Nordic skiing activities, consider bringing a plastic ski tip and duct tape to cover the contingency of tip breakage. A small coil of heavy wire could serve to temporarily shore up a damaged snowshoe. For aggressive single-day outings, both skiers and snowshoers should consider bringing a mini-sewing kit (assorted needles, thread and buttons, safety pins, and fabric).

Replacement Gear. Snowshoer's should consider carrying a spare set of bootlaces and tie-down strap. For aggressive single-day outings, both skiers and snowshoers might bring a spare set of sunglasses or goggles and a spare pole basket.

Secondary Activities

Related activities might include dunking in hot springs (if you are so lucky) or peak bagging. In the latter case, see the GLACIER/WINTER CLIMBING (Daytime) section for the additional unique gear needs.

Sun Valley, Idaho — Courtesy of Doug Holker

NORDIC SKIING/SNOWSHOEING
(Daytime)

Select gear items based on trip needs, worst-case weather conditions and degree of trip difficulty.

ITEM	DATE				
Skiing/Snowshoeing Gear					
Auto Gear Rack/Locks					
Skis/Skins/Carry Straps/Ski Bag					
Poles					
Ski Boots/Boot Rack					
Cork/Scrapper (ski wax tools)					
Ski /Board Wax					
Snowshoes					
Snowshoe Poles					
Ice Ax					
Snowshoe Boots					
Kneepads					
Crampons					
Water Bottles/Water					
Permit(s)					
Personal Gear					
Long Pants/Ski Pants/Knickers					
Underwear					
Thermal Underwear					
Long-sleeve Shirt					
Turtleneck Sweater					
Pullover Sweater					
Down Parka/Vest/Jacket					
Windbreaker					
Sox					
Gloves/Mittens					
Mitten Shells					
Pullover Hat & Brimmed Hat					
Raingear					
Gaiters					
Bandanna/Sweatband					
Turtleneck Dickey or Neck Scarf					
Goggles & Filters					
Daypack/Rucksack					
Fanny or Belt Pack					
Toilet Paper					
Toilet Trowel					
Safety					
First Aid Kit (see FIRST AID)					
Water Filter/Tablets					
Sunglasses & Lanyard					
Sunscreen					
Insect Repellent					
Lip Balm					
Whistle/Signal Mirror					

NORDIC SKIING/SNOWSHOEING
(Daytime)

ITEM	DATE				
Waterproof Matches & Lighter					
Fire Starter/Heat Tabs					
Extra Heat Tabs					
Emergency Blanket					
Map(s)					
Compass/ *Clinometer*					
Altimeter/GPS Receiver					
Timepiece					
Pocket Knife					
Flashlight#					
Extra Batteries & Bulb#					
Thermometer					
Reading Glasses & *Repair Kit*					
Nylon Cord					
Avalanche Beacon					
Snow Shovel					
Phone Change					
Communication Device					
Pen & Notepad					
Accessories					
Camera; Extra Film & Battery					
Camera Bag, Lens Cleaning Kit					
Brochures, Articles, Books					
Monocular/Small Binoculars					
Sitting Pad					
Sewing Kit					
Swim Suit (hot springs)					
Litter Bag					
Reusable Plastic Food Bags					
Auto Tire Chains & Anti-freeze					
Auto Tool Kit					
Spare Keys/Credit Card/$					
Tool Kit					
Tools					
Repair Gear					
Replacement Gear					
Snacks (see MEALS section)					
High Energy Bars					
Trail Mix/Granola					
Fresh Fruit/Dried Fruit					
Beef Jerky					
Nuts					
Electrolyte (for water bottle)					

Italicized items are optional (niceties or special purpose). #contingency night-skiing items

NORDIC SKIING/SNOWSHOEING (Overnight)

See INDEX for checklist Items not discussed below.

This activity description is devoted to multi-day backcountry adventures with your survival on your back. The scope may range from relatively flat-terrain tours to remote alpine adventures with significant elevation change, varied snow and ice conditions, and potential avalanche danger.

Rock Creek, Sierra Nevada Mountains, California Courtesy of Doug Holker

Safety Considerations: 1) review the **GENERAL CONSIDERATIONS** and TEN ESSENTIALS sections; 2) review the safety and gear discussions noted for NORDIC SKIING/SNOWSHOEING (Daytime) and GLACIER/WINTER CLIMBING activities, as applicable; and 3) bring a healthy contingency of food and stove fuel, as you may be stuck in your tent for significant periods in severe weather.

In the checklist, items that are considered optional (niceties or special purpose) are *italicized*. Items noted with a pound sign(#) are needed for nighttime travel, as a contingency.

Personal Gear

Framepack and Cover/Liner. Internal-frame packs are preferred over the external-frame models for both Nordic skiing and snowshoeing. Their redeeming features are lower center of gravity and more body-hugging design, which promote greater stability while allowing the necessary freedom of movement. An additional benefit is that internal-frame packs are less likely to snare in thickets. On a negative note, internal-frame packs offer little or no air ventilation to the back and are more expensive. Frame packs are discussed in detail in the BACKPACKING activity.

Tool Kit

The "Tool Kit" items discussed for the daytime activity become essential for remote, multi-day tours. The following are additional equipment.

Tools. Bring any tools required for adjustment/disassembly of camping items such as stove, water filter or tent. (See the BACKPACKING activity.)

Repair Gear. Repair gear for wearing apparel, pack and camping items are discussed in the BACKPACKING section.

Replacement Gear. Replacement gear for pack and camping items are discussed in the BACKPACKING section.

Secondary Activities

Related activities might include dunking in hot springs or peak bagging. In the latter case, see the GLACIER/WINTER CLIMBING (Daytime) or (Expedition) sections, as appropriate, for the additional unique gear needs.

Rock Creek, Sierra Nevada Mountains, California — Courtesy of Doug Holker

NORDIC SKIING/SNOWSHOEING
(Overnight)

Select gear items to fit your trip, worst-case weather and trip duration/remoteness.

ITEM	DATE				
Skiing/Snowshoeing Gear					
Auto Gear Rack/Locks					
Skis/Skins/Carry Straps/Ski Bag					
Poles					
Ski Boots/Boot Rack					
Cork/Scrapper (ski wax tools)					
Ski Wax					
Snowshoes					
Snowshoe Poles					
Ice Ax					
Snowshoe Boots					
Crampons					
Water Bottles/Water					
Collapsible Water Bag					
Permit(s)					
Personal Gear					
Long Pants/Ski Pants/Knickers					
Underwear					
Thermal Underwear					
Long-sleeve Shirt					
Turtleneck/Pullover Sweater					
Turtleneck Dickey or Neck Scarf					
Down Parka/Vest/Jacket					
Windbreaker					
Socks					
Gloves/Mittens					
Mitten Shells					
Pullover Hat & Brimmed Hat					
Raingear					
Gaiters					
Bandanna/Sweatband					
Goggles & Filters					
Backpack/Rucksack					
Frame Pack & Cover/Liner					
Camping Gear					
4-Season Tent					
Stakes & Poles					
Seam Sealer					
Ground Cloth					
Tent Broom & Sponge					

NORDIC SKIING/SNOWSHOEING
(Overnight)

ITEM	DATE				
4-Season Sleeping Bag					
Sleeping Pad					
Cooking Stove & Primer					
Fuel Bottle					
Fuel Funnel/Strainer					
Waterproof Matches & Lighter					
Cooking Pot					
Teapot (hot water)					
Non-stick Cooking Lubricant					
Scouring Pad					
Cup & *Plate*					
Eating Utensil(s)					
Candle Lantern					
Paper Towels					
Reusable Plastic Food Bags					
Litter Bag					
Spare Stuff Sacks					
Sitting Pad					
Hygiene					
Towel & *Washcloth*					
Biodegradable Soap					
Biodegradable Shampoo					
Personal Toiletries/Ditty Bag					
Toilet Paper & Towelettes					
Toilet Trowel					
Pee Bottle					
Laundry Bag					
Safety					
First Aid kit (see FIRST AID)					
Water Filter/Tablets					
Sunglasses & Lanyard					
Sunscreen					
Insect Repellent					
Lip Balm					
Whistle/Signal Mirror					
Fire Starter/Heat Tabs					
Extra Heat Tabs					
Emergency Blanket					
Map(s)					

NORDIC SKIING/SNOWSHOEING
(Overnight)

ITEM	DATE				
Compass/*Clinometer*					
Altimeter/GPS Receiver					
Timepiece					
Pocket Knife					
Flashlight#					
Extra Batteries & Bulb#					
Thermometer					
Reading Glasses & Repair Kit					
Nylon Cord					
Avalanche Beacon					
Snow Shovel					
Phone Change					
Communication Device					
Pen & Notepad					
Accessories					
Camera; Extra Film & Battery					
Camera Bag, Lens Cleaning Kit					
Brochures, Articles, Books					
Monocular/Small Binoculars					
Sewing Kit (see "Tool Kit")					
Swim Suit (hot springs)					
Litter Bag					
Indoor Games					
Auto Tire Chains & Anti-freeze					
Auto Tool Kit					
Spare Keys/Credit Card/$					
Tool Kit					
Tools					
Repair Gear					
Replacement Gear					
Meals (see MEALS section)					

Italicized items are optional (niceties or special purpose). #contingency night-skiing items

SNOWMOBILING (Daytime/Nighttime)

See INDEX for checklist Items not discussed below.

The snowmobiling activity described assumes a daytime venture, with the contingencies for a latter-than-planned night return or emergency overnight. Some snowmobilers travel at night on a regular basis, although the vast majority are highly-experienced riders with a previous knowledge of the territory. Some groups organize "hut-to-hut" trips, overnighters or multi-day tours with daytime travel and overnight stays at pre-established shelters. This typically requires the logistics of a "good Samaritan" to haul fuel and oil, and to drop it at shelters or at agreed-on drop-off points. Consider that the higher-powered models get 7-9 miles per gallon of gasoline, or less under hard pulling loads, and that tank capacities are roughly in the 10-11 gallon range.

As discussed below, snowmobiles have very limited storage space. Somewhat like activities where you carry all your gear on your back, there is a premium to taking low-bulk gear. Gear weight is not as critical, unless you carry much of it on your back. Regardless, significant additional weight will certainly affect snowmobile performance.

Safety Considerations: 1) review the **GENERAL CONSIDERATIONS** and TEN ESSENTIALS sections.; 2) take a course(s) in snowmobile use; 3) practice your snowmobile-handling skills on more benign terrain and work up; 4) master the reading of both weather and snow/ice (including potential avalanche and frozen-waterway) conditions; 5) practice towing and rescue (including avalanche and frigid-water) techniques with your group before attempting the trip; 6) learn basic snowmobile repair in the outdoors; 7) do not go alone. A group of at least three is the desirable minimum for remote travel; 8) practice techniques needed to extricate an injured snowmobiler from the tour area; 9) perform a full snowmobile inspection and tune-up at the beginning of each season; 10) study the trip beforehand, establishing a route and alternatives that are within your group's technical capabilities and within snowmobile mechanical capabilities; 11) ensure that there is a group leader with experience in higher-difficulty tours than the one you are attempting; 12) develop plans for contacting rescue units in an emergency; 13) perform a pre-tour snowmobile checkout and replace all under-performing, worn or suspect gear; 14) bring severe-weather gear in the event that you are forced out overnight; 15) wear a quality helmet and goggles; 16) turn back at the first indication of severe weather onset.

In the checklist, items that are considered optional (niceties or special purpose) are *italicized*. Items noted with a pound sign(#) are needed for nighttime or overnight travel, as a contingency.

Snowmobiling Gear

Auto Gear Rack. As with other activities, a storage unit will aid in providing more passenger space within the car.

Snowmobile Gear Trailer. Some snowmobilers have the luxury of starting from the doorstep. Where this is not the case, or where the trip start point is far from home, a snowmobile trailer is needed. Both side-by-side and in-line snowmobile placement trailers are on the market. The trailers may double for hauling all-terrain vehicles (ATV's) or other equipment in the off-season. Key properties are a strong, durable construction that can carry the weight; a sturdy, easily deployable ramp; positive-securing tie-downs; and a sturdy bed that can take the beating of driving the snowmobiles onto the platform, but which are constructed such that they allow convenient sliding of the machines off of the platform.

Snowmobile. The discussion of snowmobiles is intended to be introductory. When you reach the point of getting serious about purchasing a snowmobile, consult the experts at your local snowmobile or sporting goods shop. They will provide additional detail to help you narrow down which model is right for you.

In the discussion below, the term "high performance" refers to vehicles used for racing, back country climbing and/or remote touring. "Mid-range performance" indicates the lower-powered snowmobiles primarily for road and established-trail running. The term "entry level" is used to mean very-low horsepower models for novices, light family ventures and for children. (Note that all specifications and ranges of specifications in the discussion below are intended to be roughly representative. They are not intended to note hard boundaries between snowmobile classes.)

Targhee National Forest, Idaho Courtesy of Marvin Mackie

• The snowmobile's *general features* are described below for the engine, drive, suspension and braking systems and several overall characteristics.

Engine. Almost without exception, snowmobiles are equipped with two-cycle, valveless, gasoline-fed engines. Two cylinder, and to a lesser extent, three-cylinder engines are marketed at the upper performance end, the different models used for racing, aggressive hill-climbing or two-passenger backcountry touring. One cylinder models are found only in the entry-level machines.

The high-performance end features big-displacement, high-horsepower engines meant to provide both muscle and speed. At the true upper end are three-cylinder designs with roughly 1000-cubic centimeter (cc) displacement providing an estimated 160-180 horsepower (hp). More commonly, one sees 500- to 700-cc displacements, with associated ratings of 90-130 hp. Entry-level snowmobiles might be in roughly the 300-cc, 50-hp class for adults and 50-cc, 5-hp regime for children.

The classic snowmobiles have relied on air (fan-induction) cooling. Today, most lower-performance models have retained that design feature. However, most other models on the market now incorporate a liquid-cooled design. Though this feature increases the vehicle weight, it lowers the engine operating temperature. The result is that horsepower can be boosted by designing engines with closer tolerance, higher-compression combustion systems.

Oil-injection lubrication is the standard for about all machines, except in the lower end of the entry-level class. In the latter case, a fuel-oil mix is used. At each tankup, the rider is required to pour in a prescribed amount of oil commensurate with the amount of gasoline added.

Carburetion is provided by a relatively narrow set of basic designs, with two main exceptions. One key choice is between choked and primed designs. The former are hand-choked designs similar to earlier-era automobiles. The latter provide automatic choking, but with some penalties -- the mechanism is more complex, incorporates a primer diaphragm which requires periodic replacement, and can catch fire if the unit sets the mix too air-rich. A recent advance in the commercial snowmobile world is the addition of turbo-charged carburetion as an option. This hardware is designed to pull in sufficient air to meet the needs of the engine regardless of power setting or ambient air density. The main attraction over standard designs is that you do not lose horsepower at higher altitude.

Targhee National Forest, Idaho Courtesy of Marvin Mackie

The exhaust system on the high-performance and many mid-range performance machines incorporates a tuned exhaust pipe or pipes and muffler(s). Typically, a lower-cost snowmobile is limited to a tuned muffler. At the lowest end of the performance spectrum, integral tuned mufflers are common, as well as canisters for the children's vehicles.

Drive. Essentially all machines are belt-driven. A clutch is used to select between a neutral or drive setting. The clutch is set to automatically disengage and throttle returned to idle position if the driver is thrown off.

Skis/Ski Stance. Skis made of both plastic and steel are common, although plastic has the edge at the upper-performance end because of its weight advantage. Plastic is tough and more flexible, but is more likely to break when stressed to extremes. Snow has a tendency to stick to steel skis, particularly wet (typically Spring) snow. To counteract this, snowmobilers sometimes spray their skis with a substance not unlike alpine or Nordic ski wax.

Unlike the tradeoff between aluminum and steel for the frame, the weight differential between the two materials is not a significant fraction of the overall snowmobile weight. Ski stance represents the ski width at the post connector, which is at or near the ski's center. Wider skis offer better stability while narrower designs provide better maneuverability and side-hilling capability.

Front and Rear Suspension. The suspension system smoothes out the ride when going over rough terrain. This feature becomes more necessary as trips are extended in length. However, as a tradeoff, a stiffer suspension provides better hill-climbing ability and better performance in deep snow.

Front and Rear Travel. The travel of the skis and tracks expresses the vertical range of movement. It is measured by the difference in position (relative to the frame) in the sitting position to that under maximum compression. The travel feature allows the skis to maintain the proper blade depth relative to the snow surface for the smoothest, most controllable ride. The skis operate independently of each other. The greater the travel, the softer the ride; however at some point, excessive travel in either the skis or tracks compromises the snowmobile's ability to travel efficiently through softer snow.

Track Dimensions. A vast majority of snowmobiles have a 15-inch track width, although there are some variations on either side. The most common variations are width extensions, with a few out to 20 inches. The prime effect of track width extension is to enhance the surface area in contact with the snow to improve traction, particularly on powder snow.

Increased track length, which also extends the track surface area in contact with the snow, improves both traction and achievable speed. The longest tracks are generally found on hill-climbing and two-person machines. The longer tracks compromise some maneuverability, particularly in terms of instantaneous response and turning radius. They are also harder to manage on turns, particularly on the ever-popular side-hill climbs. While track lengths in the 50-inch range (circumference measurement) may be common to the entry-level models, 135 to 140-inch designs are becoming common for some trail and backcountry applications. One manufacturer has a 154-incher for two-person use on trail and in powder.

Tracks are equipped with cleats (or lugs) for traction, much as car tire treads are designed with lugs and normal street tires are fitted with snow chains. Deep cleats for powder running can be as long as two inches. As a general guideline, backcountry users and hill climbers tend to prefer 1- to 1-1/4-inch lugs while trail and frontcountry riders typically find that 0.75- to 0.85-inch cleats are a good choice. Deeper cleats are noisier and will cost some speed.

Throttle. Heated throttle and brake grips are fairly standard. Single-person throttle control is the norm, although a few two-passenger machines have a set for each rider. Almost all snowmobiles are equipped with a fail-safe feature that disengages the clutch and idles the engine in neutral when the throttle is released. This eliminates the chance of a snowmobile "chasing down" a thrown rider. (There is still the issue of a machine landing on a thrown rider -- these 500-pound class behemoths can do a lot of damage to a careless or unlucky rider in an awkward spill!)

Brakes. Self-adjusting hydraulic brakes are standard for high performance and most mid-range performance machines. Hydraulics are a necessity to slow and stop these heavy machines, which can operate at extremely high speeds (80 miles per hour top speed is not unusual and some machines can exceed 100). At the lower end of the performance spectrum, self-adjusting mechanical brakes are the norm.

Frame. A large majority of frames are constructed of aluminum. The motivation for use is to combine strength with lighter weight. Some mid-performance and most entry-level machines are constructed of steel, obviously a strong material, but a compromise in terms of weight. A newer and lighter option than aluminum is the use of titanium, a very strong material used in many of today's aircraft. As with every outdoor activity in this book, purchasing ever-more-lightweighted gear will have a heavy pocket-book impact.

Instrumentation. The standard instrumentation on the higher performance models is a fuel gauge, speedometer (with trip mileage meter), tachometer and engine temperature gauge. Mid-range performance models may forgo the tachometer as standard equipment, while entry-level vehicles may have only a fuel gauge.

Windshield. Both high- and low-profile windshields are available, though not necessarily an option with each manufacturer's model. The low-profile models minimize wind resistance and are primarily associated with racing or uses where riders place a high value on speed. The high-profile windshields provide superior head protection from the elements and low-hanging tree branches, among other things. The latter are most common to tourers at all levels, trail and road drivers and those just getting acquainted with the snowmobiling activity.

Headlight. Almost without exception, today's snowmobiles are equipped with headlights. In most designs, the lights activate automatically when the ignition is activated. Lower-performance family models are frequently equipped with an incandescent light, which is more than adequate for its design uses. Higher-performance models are almost universally equipped with halogen bulbs for greater brightness and atmospheric penetration. Single-setting bulbs are the norm, although certain uses cry out for the option of low- and high-beam operation. In response, some models are equipped with two-beam or even three-beam operation.

Targhee National Forest, Idaho Courtesy of Marvin Mackie

Optional Features/Special Modifications. Some higher-performance machines may be equipped with a reverse drive. After plowing into a snow bank, you might be able to pass up a tow -- hopefully, you can just put the engine into reverse and back it out! Another benefit is the greater ease of getting a snowmobile off of its trailer. Another option: The classic snowmobile designs have a mechanic (crank) starting mechanism. With the addition of an electric starter, you are just a button push away from starting on your adventure. Fear not, these models retain the mechanical backup! Addition of these optional features comes with a weight, complexity and cost penalty.

If you are into longer tours, you might want to consider adding a backrest to your snowmobile. They can be purchased pre-installed or retrofitted using manufacturer's kits; both options apply for some, but not all, models. (Of course, all optional equipment comes with the penalties of added weight and complexity.)

In addition to custom work on the engine and exhaust systems, snowmobilers are known to change or add modifications to the structure. (Note that many of these mods. have been the impetus for subsequent manufacturers' improvements.) Hill and mountain climbers sometimes fasten "L"-brackets to the running boards. Particularly for side-hill climbing, the brackets serve as a foot brace for leveraging during the high-angle maneuvers.

Jackson Hole, Wyoming Courtesy of Marvin Mackie

Fuel Capacity. Nearly all higher-performance snowmobiles have fuel capacities in the 10- to 11-gallon range, Mid-range performance machines have roughly half that tankage and the entry-level children's model may hold a gallon or less.

Overall Dimensions. The nominal higher performance and serious touring machines are of the order of 9-10 feet in length and about 3-1/2 feet in width. In contrast, the children's "runabout" versions are roughly 4-5-foot length with about a two-foot width.

Dry Weight. A lighter machine is easier to maneuver and handle. The smaller classes are frequently used by children, family tourers and drivers in a learning mode. The smallest weigh in at the 100-pound-plus regime. At the other extreme, even with the constant lightweighting of components such as frame, engine cowling, skis, etc., the more powerful machines are in the 500-pound-plus class. A few push the 600-pound mark and beyond.

Gear Storage Capacity. Snowmobiles have a limited capacity for gear storage. Most have a shoe-box size storage under the seat. Some owners add a small extension behind and below the seat level for (exposed) storage of a 2-1/2 gallon tank of gas or the equivalent bulk of other gear. (Note that this placement makes the snowmobile a little more difficult to manage.) Some add a "bag trunk," a commercial item that is fitted between the dashboard and the windshield. Another simple option is to carry gear in a daypack or light backpack.

• There are several *classes* of snowmobiles. They range from extreme-performance racing models to lower horsepower family "runabouts." For touring use, snowmobiles require higher performance as their use progresses from roads to trails to hills to mountains. The classes noted below are not universal; rather they are our attempt to put some order to the large number of snowmobile options.

High Performance Snowmobile. These brutes are built for maneuverability and speed. They are common to racing and high-performance nearcountry and some backcountry use. These machines are lightweighted to the maximum and have high horsepower engines with two or three cylinders; some models are supercharged. They lean to narrow ski stances, mid-range travel and stiff suspension systems. Racing and nearcountry models have nominal track lengths and short-length lugs, while longer tracks and mid-length lugs are more characteristic as their use swings more to the backcountry.

Mountain Snowmobile. These are the snowmobiles that are primed for hill- and mountain-climbing. Though the goal is the climb, the machines must be sufficiently versatile to handle the backcountry approach. They typically have high horsepower, 2-3 cylinder operation, and some have supercharging to maintain power at higher altitudes. Nominal ski stances are most common, though some lean to narrower designs -- a trade between a more stable approach vehicle and a more maneuverable one on the climbs. Long track lengths are selected for improved control on the approach and enhanced climbing power, while some choose nominal track lengths to take advantage of the improved maneuverability and shorter turning radius when side-hilling. Most select mid-size track cleats, mid-range travel and mid to stiff suspension systems.

Injured Snowmobiler Walt Bond, Whistler Mountain, Canada Courtesy of Stephanie Levine

Touring Snowmobile. These machines are designed to explore the backcountry at a more leisurely pace, while still having ample climbing power and achievable speeds to cover territory. Sub-classes might be: 1) those for backcountry sightseeing, including breaking trails and riding deep powder ("exploratory" touring); 2) those less optimized for powder, but built for more challenging terrain and with more emphasis on speed ("aggressive" touring); and 3) those for less aggressive travel, but still off-trail ("light" touring).

The exploratory machines might be mid- to upper-mid-horsepower models (probably upper-mid end for two-passenger models) with 2-3 cylinders. They typically have narrow stances, limited travel, and soft- to mid-range suspension systems. Long tracks with deep cleats are the norm.

Aggressive tourers are designed for a single passenger, but are in the upper-mid end in terms of horsepower, with 2-3 cylinders. Typical characteristics are nominal stances and travel, together with long tracks with short- to mid-length lugs. Light-touring vehicles might be a scaled-down version of the aggressive touring machine in terms of both horsepower and track length.

Trail Snowmobile. Primarily for use on established trails, this 1-2 passenger model is the "trainer" for adults (one-person) or a great way for a veteran to introduce a friend to the world of snowmobiling. It is at the lower-horsepower end, with wide stance, limited travel and relatively "mushy" suspension (it is not designed for the bruising rides of the higher performance machines). Short tracks with small cleats are the standard.

Family Snowmobile. The emphasis on these snowmobiles is fun, with safety. They are for general family use (1-2 passenger) or can act as a "starter kit" for the wary beginning adult. Some models are specifically geared for small children. This class of snowmobile is ideal for running on established roads and trails. All are low horsepower, small-sized, low-range vehicles with (intentionally) limited technical performance features.

• *Preventative Maintenance* is key to safety and enjoyment. Like any other machinery, particularly that where you are potentially "betting your hide" on its safe and uninterrupted operation, regular maintenance and upkeep is a given.

Test your snowmobile's operation before each trip. This includes electric, lighting, brake, fuel and starting systems. The tests should include controls (throttle and emergency brake), reflectors, handgrips, seats, shields and guards.

At the start of each winter season, perform a full tune-up covering ignition, carburetor, lubrication and the drive belt. Each of these items should be adjusted or replaced as necessary. In addition, the machine should be thoroughly checked in accordance with the operator's manual. Make all required adjustments and be sure to follow the company's safety recommendations.

Extra Fuel. Extra *fuel* is carried in a container (typical a 2-1/2 gallon size or smaller) on a built-in or retrofitted shelf located behind the seat. The extra fuel is carried aboard on the relatively light-challenging approach portion of the ride. The snowmobile tanks are topped off and bivouacked before attacking the challenging section(s) of the day's ride (i.e., the assumed ride's objective). On the return, the remaining fuel is poured into the snowmobile tank and the container resecured for the trip home. Spare oil is rarely carried on tour, since most snowmobiles will eat up at least 2-3 tanks of gas before the oil sump needs to be topped off.

Tow Rope. Unfortunately, snowmobiles get stuck in situations where the only viable solution is to tow them out. Short tows for non-repairable breakdowns are sometimes needed. (In some cases, the only option is to park the snowmobile in a safe and easily-spotted location, and return for repairs on another day.) Tow-out situations call for 50 feet of nylon rope of 1/4-inch or more thickness. When towing, ensure that the towed vehicle's drive belt has been removed.

Used Drive Belts. On potentially treacherous downhills, the snowmobile brakes alone may not provide the needed control. Some attach used drive belts to the skis to provide additional friction between the skis and snow surface.

Metal Insulated Bottle(s). Metal insulated bottles or canteens are common for carrying water or other liquids. The insulators are handy both for keeping hot liquids hot, as well as keeping other liquids from freezing. Metal containers are preferred because they don't have liners that can break when jostled by a hard landing or accidental drop onto the hard snowmobile surface. Both metal insulators and canteens will stand up to inadvertent placement near the hot exhaust pipes relative to the "classic plastic" bottles so often carried by other outdoor adventurers.

The bottle is frequently stored in the trunk bag, together with other items that rider's typically want to keep close at hand. Most likely, these are such items as maps, spare gloves and snacks.

Personal Gear

Though sometimes thought to be a "sweatless" activity, maneuvering a 400- to 600-pound snowmobile through the virgin backcountry can be exerting, as can extracting it from a snowbank or pushing a non-functioning machine off the trail or to a protected spot. In spite of this, many of today's "war-scarred" snowmobile veterans wear flannel shirts, cotton "T"-shirts and jeans underneath a snowmobile suit. However, given that it isn't a sweatless sport and given that the unexpected may happen (e.g., a required hike out or a forced overnighter), we feel we would be remiss not to make our usual pitch for moisture-wicking, and warm-when-wet clothing. (Here they go again! Pounding the pulpit against that "killer cotton!")

Targhee National Forest, Idaho Courtesy of Marvin Mackie

The *layered clothing concept* applies to snowmobiling as it does for many other cold-weather activities. The underwear and insulating layer gear discussed in the VEHICLE-ACCESSIBLE CAMPING and several of the winter-related activities apply here with limited exceptions (e.g., neck gaiters versus neck scarves), which are discussed separately. The shell layer has significant variants, because the wind-chill while riding in cold weather is unique and the potential to take a dunk in frigid water is enhanced relative to most other activities. This particularly applies to wind-chill protection for the torso, hands and head. A summary of the recommended layers is provided below.

Underwear or base layer - choose synthetic (treated polyester and polypropylene) or wool-blend long underwear. Wear the weight for the weather conditions and the level of activity exertion. Light- or medium-weight suits are preferred during active periods of an outing, while expedition-weight serves best on winter camping excursions or on long stretches of inactivity. Light-weight synthetic socks are a frequent choice as an underlayer. Soft polypropylene or light, wool glove liners, serve well as the base covering for the hands. They have very good wicking properties, maintain warmth when wet, and are nimble enough to limit the loss of manual dexterity when you handle gear or make repairs on your snowmobile.

Insulating layer - look for non-constricting pants, such as sweat pants, made of dense wool, synthetic pile or fleece which have a sturdy belt. A wool or heavy synthetic shirt, sometimes combined with a light fleece sweater (100-200 weight) under severe conditions, protects the torso. High-bulk wool or fleece socks, which fit comfortably in the boots (too tight a fit will inhibit circulation), are a popular overcover for the base-layer socks. A pair of high-top, insulated boots fits over the socks. (Gaiters are optional.) Insulating gloves include wool, water-resistant leather, and fleece in a variety of synthetics. A pullover cap or balaclava under the helmet prevents heat loss from the head.

Shell layer - a classic set includes snowmobile suit, water and windproof outer gloves or mittens, and helmet.

Snowmobile Suit. The shell layer for the torso and lower body is frequently a snowmobile suit. They come in one-piece and two-piece styles. The former is warmer, but more constricting to some body movements when maneuvering. The pants for the most common two-piece model extends above the waist and are held in place with suspenders. The suit should have a well-insulated interior liner and be both water resistant and highly wind resistant. Wind resistance is probably more critical for snowmobiling than any other activity, considering that riders are traveling at high speed in a cold ambient environment. One method to test for wind-resistance is to put the material against your lips and blow into it. Strong resistance to blowing with little or no air passage is a highly desirable sign.

Most suits have deep pockets on both upper and lower body areas with study overflaps that are cinched with Velcro or zippers. They also have cinches or other closures at the neck, wrists, ankles and, for the two-piece model, at the waist. Full-length chest and leg zippers make suit entry and exit simple, even when the snowmobiler is fully appareled. The top-of-the-line suits, in terms of ultimate wind resistance, have sewn-in interior flaps at the zippers. When zippered, the flaps seal off the suit. Such suits may be lined with flotation material in case your vehicle breaks through the ice over a waterway. Some suits have a flotation device which can be inflated with a few quick puffs.

Neck Gaiters. A loose scarf can be a hazard, given its potential to get caught up in the machinery. Rather, snowmobilers opt for over-the-head scarves or "neck gaiters" for neck protection. These polypropylene or fleece neck-warmers double and triple as hats, earmuffs, or even as a balaclava. Thin silk or polypropylene neck gaiters can provide the necessary warmth in less-severe weather. Silk balaclavas also serve in that capacity.

Snowmobile Boots. High-topped boots with tied or cinched closures at the top are the standard for snowmobiling. Many lean to rubber-bottomed boots with felt liners. The boots are normally worn under the snowmobile suit pants. It is not uncommon to carry an extra set of liners to replace those that may get wet.

Socks. Warm socks are a necessity for snowmobiling. The good news is that your boots are not making contact with the snow for long periods of time. The bad news is that your feet are not getting the work and resultant blood circulation, as with other more aerobic activities. In cool weather, a heavy pair of *hiking socks with a liner* might be good enough. Colder weather might call for *boot socks*., again with a liner or double liner. The pros and cons of these choices are discussed in the HIKING activity. Use of boot insoles/inserts or footwarmers are also viable options for this activity. Refer to the **INDEX** for further discussions of these items.

Gloves. Soft polypropylene or light, wool liners serve well as the base covering for the hands. They are typically gloves (rather than mittens) and should fit snugly. Insulating-layer gloves/mittens include wool, water-resistant leather, and fleece in a variety of synthetics. Waterproof shell-layer gloves or mittens should not fit tightly nor have a shell that gets stiff when cold. Shell-layer handwear should have rubber, leather or leather-like strips or dots on the palms for gripability.

Mittens are warmer than gloves because the fingers are in contact and warm each other. Insulated ski gloves are preferred by some and are fine if you find them comfortable. They, along with many other styles on the market, serve for both insulating and shell layers. Whatever you choose, always carry an extra set of shell-layer handwear in the event that the primary pair gets soaked or punctured. Other features of gloves and mittens for cold weather use are discussed in the GLACIER/ WINTER CLIMBING and ALPINE SKIING/SNOWSHOEING activities.

Helmet. Wear an approved helmet at all times. Some models have a projecting chin-area guard and an open slot for goggles, while others are open-faced with an adjustable bubble-type enclosure in front of the face. Most are Hydron-treated to prevent fogging and are developed of scratch-resistant materials. When the Hydron coating wears, there are anti-fogging pastes which can be used as a substitute. The preferred all-weather bubble tint is amber, which excels in providing contrast in low-light conditions. (This is a highly desirable feature when traveling over a highly-contoured "blanket of white" at high speed!) Pullover masks or balaclavas are commonly warn under the helmet for warmth.

Goggles. Goggles act as sun shields and protect the eyes against cold, blowing snow, as well as against tree branches and other such obstructions. They also protect against snow blindness, and protective lenses can prevent freezing of the eyeballs. Desirable goggle design properties are similar to those discussed in the GLACIER/WINTER CLIMBING activity. Amber, rose and gold tints enhance contrast and are preferred for low-light conditions. Green or gray/brown lenses are most commonly used for lower-speed sightseeing tours in well-sunlit conditions, as they tend to render colors most true. Additional information concerning desirable lens properties for use in snow is provided in the TEN ESSENTIALS section.

Targhee National Forest, Idaho — Courtesy of Marvin Mackie

Gaiters. If there is a reasonable chance of getting snow in your boots, consider wearing gaiters. If you plan on trudging through the snow at some time during your trip, whether to visit a scenic site or assist in snowmobile extraction, they might be worth a second thought. (See the HIKING activity for more information.)

Ear Plugs. Pipes are loud. Tuned pipes are very loud. Make a practice of wearing ear plugs when snowmobiling.

Daypack, Fanny or Belt Pack. Gear that can't be stored on the snowmobile can be carried on your back or waist. This gear is discussed in the HIKING activity.

Safety

Snowshoes. Snowshoes are a contingency item for the event that you suffer a non-repairable machine breakdown and are forced to hike. Although snowshoes are highly adaptable to boot/shoe size and style (see the NORDIC SKIING/SNOWSHOEING activity), ensure that the two are compatible before packing up.

Avalanche Beacon/Probe/Snow Shovel. The merits and uses of these items is discussed in the GLACIER/WINTER CLIMBING activity. In early 1998, an Olympics-level snowboarder was buried under an avalanche near Lake Tahoe while with a film crew -- none of this gear was brought along. By the time he was found, he had suffocated. Yet the most careless back-country travelers are typically snowmobilers. Of the 36 fatalities involving avalanches during the first half of the 1998 snow season, 16 were snowmobilers, nine were skiers, three were snowboarders and the rest were hikers and snowshoers.

Snowmobilers run into more trouble because they ride such heavy, powerful machines and travel longer distances into avalanche terrain. Most problems occur when "high-marking" (climbing as high up onto the slope as the machine will allow) and then executing a broad, sweeping turn before descending.

Because the probe and snow shovel can become lethal objects if not properly stowed, seek out telescoping probes and fold-up shovels which can be carried in the internal compartment. If the shovel cannot fit, create a homemade blade cover of rubber or sturdy fabric and secure the shovel to the snowmobile exterior.

Targhee National Forest, Idaho — Courtesy of Marvin Mackie

Camp Stove, Windbreak and Fuel. If a fire is required, you can use fuel and/or oil drained from your snowmobile to aid in igniting wet wood.

Waterproof Matches and Lighter. If your fire starting equipment is not available or not functioning, it is possible to start a fire using your snowmobile's ignition system. Remove a spark plug, reattach the plug wire to the plug, ground the plug against the snowmobile, crank the engine and a spark will be created. Use extreme caution to prevent an unmanageable fire.

Engine Manual. If you know your engine like the back of your hand, you may not need this. However, one experience of being stuck in the backcountry without engine power, particularly if it's a simple fix explained in the "When Things Go

Wrong" section of your manual, will convince you to bring it. You should also know how to evaluate and make simple repairs to such as faulty electrical connections and fuel delivery system hardware, as well as how to replace spark plugs.

Tool Kit

The tools, repair and replacement gear needed will vary according to your snowmobile. A few examples are provided below. Consult your operator's manual for specific needs.

Tools. Screwdrivers (conventional and Phillips-head), locking pliers, adjustable wrench, set of open-end wrenches, spark plug socket wrench, vice grips and any special tools that are unique to your machine are all candidates.

Repair Gear. Consider duct tape for temporary hose repairs and miscellaneous fixups and electrical tape for wiring problems.

Replacement Gear. This group might include spare spark plugs, plastic fuel hose (long enough to be used as a siphon), extra drive belt(s) and extra bolts (typically 1/4- and 3/8-inch).

Secondary Activities

Snowmobiling might be linked with such activities as SNOWSHOEING and LAND FISHING. If you plan on linking up such efforts, refer to those activity descriptions for their own unique gear needs.

Winter Spectator Courtesy of Sam Nunez

SNOWMOBILING
(Daytime/Nighttime)

Select gear items to fit your trip, considering worst-case weather conditions and trip difficulty/duration.

ITEM	DATE				
Snowmobiling Gear					
Snowmobile Trailer					
Snowmobile					
Extra Fuel,					
Tow Rope					
Used Drive Belts					
Metal Insulating Bottle(s)					
Snowmobile License					
Personal Gear					
Long Pants/Ski Pants/Knickers					
Underwear					
Thermal Underwear					
Long-sleeve Shirt					
Turtleneck/Pullover Sweater					
Snowmobile Suit					
Neck Gaiter					
Windbreaker					
Socks/Inserts/*Foot Warmers*					
Gloves/Mittens; *Hand Warmers*					
Mitten Shells					
Pullover Hat & *Brimmed Hat*					
Raingear					
Snowmobile Boots					
Gaiters					
Bandanna/Sweatband					
Helmet					
Goggles & Filters					
Ear Plugs					
Daypack					
Fanny or Belt Pack					
Wash Cloth					
Toilet Paper					
Toilet Trowel					
Safety					
First Aid Kit (see FIRST AID)					
Water Filter/Tablets					
Sunglasses & Lanyard					
Sunscreen					
Lip Balm					
Whistle/Signal Mirror					

SNOWMOBILING
(Daytime/Nighttime)

ITEM	DATE				
Waterproof Matches & Lighter					
Fire Starter/Heat Tabs					
Extra Heat Tabs					
Emergency Blanket					
Map(s)					
Compass/ *Clinometer*					
Altimeter/GPS Receiver					
Timepiece					
Thermometer					
Pocket Knife					
Flashlight#					
Extra Batteries & Bulb#					
Reading Glasses & *Repair Kit*					
Nylon Cord					
Avalanche Beacon					
Snow Shovel					
Flare Gun & Flares					
Hatchet					
Wood Saw					
Communication Device					
Engine Manual					
Pen & Notepad					
Phone Change					
Accessories					
Camera; Extra Film & Battery					
Camera Bag, Lens Cleaning Kit					
Monocular/Small Binoculars					
Swim Suit (hot springs)					
Litter Bag					
Reusable Plastic Food Bags					
Auto Tire Chains & Anti-freeze					
Auto Tool Kit					
Spare Keys/Credit Card/$					
Tool Kit					
Tools					
Repair Gear					
Replacement Gear					
Snacks (see MEALS section)					

Italicized items are optional (niceties or special purpose). #night-snowmobiling items

CANOEING (Daytime)

See INDEX for checklist items not discussed below.

The daytime canoeing activity is focused on all-weather canoeing in inland and protected coastal waters. Some discussion assumes that the day trip will involve on-land activity (e.g., inclusion of the "Boots/Socks" item). If your day trip is totally waterborne, tailor your gear accordingly. Relative to such activities as BACKPACKING or GLACIER/WINTER CLIMBING, there is less restriction on the amount of gear that you can bring. In terms of carrying gear for safety or comfort, err on the side of bringing it. Small weight additions will have a minor impact on achievable speed. Adding non-paddling passengers will have a readily noticeable effect. This simplistic viewpoint needs to be modified if your trip will involve significant portaging. In this case, there is a premium to keeping weight to a handleable minimum and packing gear to minimize the number of round-trip hauls needed to get you to your next let-in point.

Safety Considerations: 1) review the **GENERAL CONSIDERATIONS** and TEN ESSENTIALS sections; 2) develop swimming skills commensurate with the level of activity you are planning; 3) take lessons to learn about canoeing do's and don'ts and to enhance your skills; 4) practice your paddling technique and develop navigation skills on successively more demanding tours. This is particularly important if you are working up to whitewater canoeing and/or remote tours; 5) study the trip beforehand, establishing a route and alternatives that are within your group's physical and technical capabilities; 6) practice rescue (and, for whitewater, lining techniques) with your group before attempting the next-level paddle; 7) ensure that there is a group leader with experience in higher-difficulty canoeing than the trip you are planning; 8) learn basic first aid and develop plans for contacting rescue personnel in an emergency; 9) ensure that the boat(s) and gear are in proper working order and that contingency boat patching equipment is packed; 10) bring cold-weather contingency gear in the event that you are forced out overnight; and 11) wear a PFD, plus a hard hat if the trip warrants its use.

In the checklist, items that are considered optional (niceties or special purpose) are *italicized*. Items noted with an asterisk(*) are for cold weather. Pound sign(#) entries are contingency gear for nighttime travel.

Authors' note: The photos provided in this section by David Kiel represent the canoeing portion of a journey that started at the headwaters of the Colorado River and terminated in the Sea of Cortez (now called the Gulf of California). On that expedition, David and his former wife, Rebecca, backpacked along the river from Rocky Mountain National Park, through the Grand Canyon, to Lake Mead. They canoed back up into the Western Colorado River region, reversed direction, then proceeded down the lower portion of the river, through the seldom-traversed Delta region, to the sea.

Boat Gear

Boat Rack and Tie-downs. Most canoes can be secured to an auto using a *manual tie-down technique*. The process uses heavy padding and heavy tie-down line. Develop a process for your auto using rolling or taut-line hitches for the bumper or tow-hitch tie downs and binders across the fore and aft set of tie-down lines. Padding between the gunwale and the rack should be thick enough when compressed not to damage the gunwale when the auto travels over rough road and should not tear or break up easily in any weather. Though the cheapest and the old classic method, there are potential problems. Any boat movement may result in padding movement and potential auto surface scratching. Inadequate tie-down could see your canoe attempt a "lift-off," or, worse yet, achieve it!

One tie-down option is to use a soft synthetic line, such as Dacron or nylon, just to protect the finish of your boat. Better, though, is to use the synthetic and low-stretch webbing offered by rack manufacturers. Loop the webbing through the slots on both sides of the cradle, and cinch it down using a cam fastener.

Western Colorado River Courtesy of David Kiel

The most convenient, safest option is to invest in an *auto gear rack*. These sports utility racks, which come with all the fittings to hold the canoe securely in place, have been on the market for some time. There are fittings which cushion the gunwales and prevent side-to-side motion, overstraps to secure the canoe to the rack, and bow/stern tie-down straps to finish the job. All fittings are heavy duty and easy to use. Whether you can get two canoes mounted depends on the canoe widths, your car roof width, and the rack model.

Unfortunately, people steal canoes (and racks), making it prudent to invest in two sets of *locks*. One set of locks will hold the towers to your car and another (usually a cable lock) will hold the canoe(s) to the rack. Most commercial racks are designed to accept slip-in locks which fasten the rack to the car. The locks which secure the boat to the rack are commonly a separately-purchased item.

Canoe. Dependent on the kind of paddling planned, there is a canoe for every purpose. *Recreation canoes* are made for fun and relatively flat-water traveling. They serve exceptionally well for light trips, birding, photography or fishing. Their stable designs emphasize tracking and sure handling more than agility. They are designed with a mild rocker (i.e., limited curvature at both ends) and the most "squat" characteristics (widest at gunwale, smallest length, and least keel depth) which account for these characteristics. Typical carrying capacities are in the 400-900 pound range. Weight varies widely (30-80 pounds), although weight tends to be one of the least critical issues, assuming that significant canoe portaging is not planned. Recreation canoes are the shortest of the lot, measuring from about 13-16 feet. Many of the same materials used at the lower cost end of the more "sporty" canoes discussed below, are available. They include fiberglass, Royalex, CrossLink and Polylink hulls and aluminum, wood or vinyl gunwales. All are well-tested materials which trade off resiliency, strength, buoyancy, stiffness, insulation, weight and abrasion resistance. These canoes are lowest on the cost ladder.

Western Colorado River Courtesy of David Kiel

Versatile canoes are designed to handle everything from calm lakes to whitewater. They offer greater maneuverability and greater loading capacity per unit canoe weight than the recreational styles. Included in this category are "tripping" canoes which track well and paddle easily with heavy loads, making them ideal for extended ("overnight" in the parlance of this book) trips. These canoes have a mid-range rocker and a more streamlined shape than recreation canoes. Canoe weights are in the 40-80 pound range with corresponding carrying capacities between about 800-1300 pounds. For smooth water or running single, a 15-16 foot canoe might suffice. For added buoyancy and load-carrying capacity and more general outdoor use 17-18 foot models are the norm.

Longer models are more typically used for extended family-with-small-children excursions or lengthy expeditions. Relative to recreation canoes, there is added emphasis on stiffness, resiliency, strength and abrasion resistance. Light-weighting hull options include Kevlar and lightweight Royalex which reduce weight by about 15-25% relative to fiberglass and the standard Royalex, respectively. (It may not sound like much, but consider its impact when hauling one of these beauties one or two miles between lakes on slush!)

River Canoes are specifically designed for whitewater adventure, which translates into running rapids and negotiating Mother Nature's finest water obstacles. Maneuverability is it! These canoes are the streamlined upper end -- narrow beam, deep keel and a lot of rocker. Additional features are high abrasion and impact-resistant construction combined with high sides to deflect water. These canoes weigh 50-75 pounds, and provide corresponding capacities of 600-1100 pounds. Most-highly maneuverable, day-use models can be as short as 11-14 feet. Less maneuverable, but higher-buoyancy models include lengths out to 18 feet. Many of the models have Royalex or Kevlar hulls with vinyl or wood gunwales.

Since boats depend a great deal on *thwarts* for rigidity, there should be at least two thwarts on the shorter-length models and three foot the 17-foot and up category. (This is in addition to the *seats*.) They should be sturdy and firmly attached to the boat. This is particularly important for the middle thwart, which carries the canoes weight on portages. Also check for strong seat attachments. Seats support your body weight as you bounce through rapids. Though rescue operations should not rely on them for pulling a submerged boat free of the current, there are times when you have no choice. Ideally the seats are comfortable, have lightly-tapered edges and/or drilled holes to encourage runoff, and have no water-collecting pockets. Finally, the lower edge of the seat should be high enough to allow stowing your feet underneath in the kneeling position and easy extrication in the event of a capsize.

Painter attachments are another consideration. Ideally, lines should be placed at both stems at the waterline. An eyebolt or even a drill hole centered on the deck is an acceptable second choice. Considering their potential use for lining or lifting a sunken canoe, the attachments should be mechanically hardy.

Canoe color becomes an issue if you can reasonably expect to overturn and part from your canoe in your travels. Choose bright colors that tend not to blend with natural background. Yellow and red are popular. Green canoes that may fade into the scene of green water and trees and blue models that may meld with oceans or lakes are probably not the best of choices.

Western Colorado River — Courtesy of David Kiel

Some canoeists buy a canoe with a built-in *rowing seat* and (bronze) *centered oarlocks* or install a custom version. The claim is that one person rowing is as fast as two paddling. This option is more tailored to quiet-water boating and requires an acquired rowing technique (the arms overlap in mid-stroke for the standard canoe widths). It is most often installed on family-oriented canoes. The canoe can be used for single-person rowing, one rower and one paddler, or the seat can be used for a couple of small passengers with two paddlers. Rubber oar collars are needed to protect the oar's shaft when rowing.

Issues of *gear storage, tying down gear within the boat, gear placement and distribution* are most relevant for overnighters and expeditions. These issues are discussed in the next section.

Western Colorado River Courtesy of David Kiel

Painter. For lake and placid-stream canoeing, a short line of eight feet may suffice. This is about right for easy *docking* and tying canoes together for a community lunch or "town meeting." If you plan to tie up to fixed points for several hours or more at a time, ensure that you have sufficient line to allow for boat rise or fall with the tide. Want to guess how we felt on our first canoe trip when our "Simon Legree" tour guide had us haul our canoes well beyond the tide line and tie them down onto some heavy shoreline vegetation? Imagine our surprise next morning when we found our canoes dry, but riding above the tie point. (On this tour of the Topock Gorge area of the Colorado River, water was released out of the upstream dams at various intervals, causing the tidal rises -- this is normal practice.)

At the other extreme are the needs for manually guiding boats through rapids using bow and stern lines controlled from the water's edge. This technique, called "*lining*," is sometimes the only alternative where portage trails along the route are infrequent. Most experienced canoeists recommend at least 1/2-inch (1100-pound test) braided nylon. The thinner 5/8-inch (700-pound test) line may have enough strength, but is tough on the hands when hauling free a submerged canoe and is more likely to get tangled in your feet when you unexpectedly wind up bobbing down the rapids.

A coil of 25 feet is satisfactory for most lining and also safer in a spill than longer lengths. An option is to store a couple of extra 50-foot lengths, reserved for more difficult river sections, if you might possibly be pushing your paddling limits. This is a particularly good planning option for remote tours where a little conservatism rarely hurts.

Paddles. You'll be lifting and pulling your paddle through the water hundreds or even thousands of times on a trip. This places an emphasis on selecting a paddle for your optimal mix of performance, comfort and enjoyment. Select the lightest paddle that fits your needs, as even a slight reduction in weight can reduce fatigue over a long day of paddling. The standard *weight* range for most commercial lines is 18-24 ounces for adults and 12-16 ounces for young paddlers.

Lake Mead Courtesy of David Kiel

Most paddle *materials* are polyethylene/aluminum, wood and fiberglass. Blade widths and lengths for adults are in the 6-1/2 to 8-1/2 inch and 20-22 inch range, respectively. For the younger set, the comparable parameters are 5-1/2 to 7-1/2 inches and 14-16 inches. Polyethylene/aluminum paddles are least expensive and most common for entry-level canoeists and as a spare paddle. Typical construction is a polyethylene plastic blade attached to an aluminum shaft with a plastic T-grip. The aluminum shaft is usually quite stiff, and the blades flex a bit, which makes these paddles less comfortable to use for long periods of time. The aluminum shaft can also get cold, so most are covered with vinyl or foam where your lower hand grasps them.

Wood is preferred by many canoeists for its beautiful appearance and pleasant feel. Wood retains the warmth of your hands in cool weather. It helps transmit the feel of the water well, assisting you in achieving a smoother stroke. Wood does require some maintenance to repair dings and to keep the protective finish. It is also not as durable as its metal counterparts. Many manufacturers enhance the durability of wood paddles through tip guards -- pieces of composite plastic or fiberglass built into the tips. Some also overlay fiberglass or Kevlar on the blade surface.

Fiberglass is often used on the shaft and blades of more expensive paddles. It allows manufacturers to vary flexibility and performance to match intended end uses. Because of its durability, fiberglass is frequently the choice for whitewater canoeists. The weight of fiberglass paddles varies greatly, with the lightest models generally at the upper end of the price range.

Standard *paddle grips* are the palm and T-grip. The tear-drop or pear-shaped palm grips fit most comfortably into the palm of your hand. The grip provides good control and is least tiring to the hands over hours of travel. The T-grip gives the most control over the angle of the paddle blade, making it a good choice for whitewater. This grip is also easier to hang onto in rough conditions and easiest for small hands to grasp.

Shaft design includes both straight and bent options. Straight shafts are the traditional choice for a trip with a variety of paddling conditions. On rivers, almost all canoeists use them because they are most amenable to performing a wide variety of maneuvering strokes. Bent-shaft paddles are best used for flatwater paddling or cruising. These paddles feature a bend in the shaft that helps position it for maximum efficiency. The bend orients the paddle roughly vertical in the water at the strongest point of the stroke. It also helps the paddle enter and exit the water more smoothly. Most bent shafts have a 14-degree bend. Models with less bend are also available. The choice of bend angle is a tradeoff between stillwater paddling efficiency and the ability to perform a greater variety of maneuvering strokes.

Paddle lengths vary from about 50-66 inches for adults and 36-48 inches for youngsters, for straight-shaft designs. To estimate proper shaft length, sit in your canoe and measure the approximate vertical distance from your nose to the waterline. The overall paddle length is that shaft length plus the length of the blade for your model preference. If measuring in the store, kneel down and keep your bottom about six inches off the floor. Flip the candidate paddle and hold it vertically alongside, with the grip on the floor -- the blade should start about even with your nose. For bent-shaft paddles, deduct about two inches from the length determined above.

Lake Mead — Courtesy of David Kiel

Spare Paddle. For extended tours, even on quiet water, lash a spare paddle along an interior gunwale. Remote tours which include stretches of whitewater call for bringing one spare per paddler. In the event of paddle loss or damage, the normally lesser-expensive spare will serve to get you out or to a location where you can attempt to repair damage. Another option is to bring an equal-quality spare which is optimized for a different function (e.g., a palm-grip model in addition to a "T"-grip model).

Personal Flotation Device. First, a few *general statements about PFDs*. The one and only PFD to use is a wearable life jacket (as opposed to relying on a seat cushion or life ring). Beginners should think seriously about wearing them at all times. More experienced canoeists sometimes place the jacket within easy reach, say under the canoe seat, under benign water conditions. The jacket should provide positive buoyancy to shoulder level and allow reasonable paddling freedom below the armpits. It should allow enough bending freedom so as not to inhibit the paddling stroke and not rub against the body (particularly the neck) while paddling. Finally, the jacket should not ride up on you when you are struggling in the water (or when you are trying to maintain your dignity). Don't skimp on quality when you purchase this valuable piece of gear!

Portaging, Lower Colorado River — Courtesy of David Kiel

When you shop for a PFD, you'll see two sets of buoyancy numbers. One represents the minimum buoyancy supplied by the PFD, the other the weight of the person that PFD is designed to support. The Coast Guard uses *five categories to identify PFDs*. Type I PFDs are the big, bulky "offshore jackets" with a minimum of 22 pounds of buoyancy, They are designed to float most unconscious people face up. They are also the most bulky and probably the most uncomfortable to wear when actively paddling. Type II, the "near-shore buoyancy vest," is the traditional horse-collar life jacket with a minimum of 15-1/2 pounds of flotation. It can float an unconscious person face up, but not as high out of the water as the Type I. This PFD is not designed for comfort when paddling. Type IV, the square seat cushion or life ring, is not worn but rather thrown to a person in the water. Type V are special purpose devices, an open category which the Coast Guard regulates. An example is the hybrid, which combines about 7-1/2 pounds of foam flotation with inflatable cells that bring the total buoyancy up to 22 pounds when inflated (not practical for paddlers). Several companies have recently begun manufacturing Type V devices primarily for white water use.

This leaves us with the *Type III PFDs* which are the "flotation aid" vest-type devices worn by most paddlers. They are slimmer than the Types I and II and designed to accommodate both arm and neck freedom when paddling. They have a minimum of 15-1/2 pounds of buoyancy, but won't necessarily roll you face up in the water.

About *design*. Most Type III PFDs on display at your local canoeing/kayaking store are either waist length (called "shorties") or have a definite break in the flotation above and below the waist tie. That break allows the paddler the required bending freedom at the waist. For the kayaker, the tie also allows the paddler to fold out the cuff below the waist so that it doesn't interfere with the spray skirt. Shorties typically provide buoyancy in the 15-1/2-pound class, while the below-waist models are more likely to be in the 20-pound class. The latter are particularly popular with whitewater boaters and rafters.

Most current designs use a closed-cell foam (frequently polyvinyl chloride or PVC) cased in a rugged, waterproof shell (e.g., rip-stop nylon). The most popular are vertically compartmented, the claim being that this structure is more conducive to accommodating body motion when paddling. Most models have heavy front zippers and side-strap adjusters, while some are secured with lace-up ties and/or heavy snaps. Front pockets of mesh and zippered pockets with protective overflaps are beginning to appear on more PFDs. They are useful for storing small items to which you would like ready access. (With your PFD as the outer layer, it gets testy trying to dig out these small items from lower clothing layers.)

Avoid the "float coats" which are more common to boating than paddling activities. Though they are Type III devices, they allow little ventilation and will have you thinking about shedding them after an extended period of normal paddling.

When *fitting your PFD*, make sure that it has sufficient room to accommodate the clothing layers that you may wear in cooler/wetter weather. When not wearing this regalia, you can always use the side adjustment straps or lace-up ties to tighten down on the fit. Some designs have only shoulder straps, which allows the maximum freedom of paddling motion. Depending on your anatomy, the PFD may ride up once you are waterborne. Alternately, you may be tackling whitewater and the turbulence may be trying to remove your PFD, Solution to both problems: get a model with a pair of crotch straps that go from the back of the PFD, between the legs and secure to the front. You may not want to "strap in" while doing leisurely cruising, but they are there when you anticipate an upcoming water challenge.

Bailer. To remove water from the canoe, the classic item of choice is a *hand bailer*. Typically, a one-gallon plastic bleach bottle cut into a scoop form, with the handle retained, will suffice for quiet-water travel. For heavier-duty whitewater trips, bailers should be made of heavy plastic, and they can vary in capacity from one to three gallons. The three-gallon size is the best for rivers with large rapids, that require bailing large amounts of water. Beyond this size, the bucket gets hard to handle (water weighs about eight pounds per gallon) and difficult to use in tighter spaces.

If the bucket comes with metal handles, remove them and replace with more durable nylon cord. The bailer is tied through the handle and the other end of the 10-foot cord secured to a convenient post on the boat's interior such as the stern seat. Where smaller securing structures are available, some canoeists tie off the cord using an attached carabiner. (Rafters can use the raft's "D"-rings or equipment frame.) Though not as typical as for river rafting, bailers also have been known to serve for initiating water fights on recreational canoe tours.

Foot and Knee Braces. Most canoe interiors are made of the same materials as the exterior. Since the exterior is built to slide off of water obstructions, it is literally "slippery when wet." In tough rapids, where paddlers must be firmly braced in their canoe, the slip-and-slide problem can be solved by installing custom-fitted friction pads for the seat, knees and feet. The rubber from inner tubes works well. Simply cut the tubing to shape, apply contact cement and smooth into place.

Backrest. An option for back support and comfort is to use a "*canoe chair*." A sample model is a closed-cell foam, waterproof-nylon jacketed, 1-1/2 pound chair. The portable seat is simply placed on the thwart and strapped down. Both seat and backrest, which are connected by side straps, are cushioned. Seat tilt is adjusted with the side straps. There are also heavier models with stronger seat and/or strap construction. One example is a wooden fold-up chair with wicker seats and backrest. When unfolded, the seat is grooved to slip around one thwart and is held to the next thwart through the use of heavy friction pads. When decoupled from the boat, the seat serves as a low-boy camp chair.

Fenders. Fenders are useful for group excursions on quiet lakes and riverways. They keep canoes from banging against each other when you decide to have a group lunch or "town meeting" while afloat. They are also handy if you plan to tie up against a dock or other docked boats during your day tour.

Permit. Some waterways require day-use permits. If so, bring that valuable piece of paper with you and avoid any potential conflicts with the permitors. A turnaway can spoil an entire day!

Personal Gear

The type of apparel worn is dependent on the weather. In the discussion below, we offer general *examples of outfits* (not including the standards like sunglasses, sunscreen, etc.) that might serve your purpose in order from warm weather to successively cooler conditions.

Warm weather: shorts or swim suit, "T"-shirt, boating gloves, sun hat. (Add a windbreaker or paddling jacket for windy conditions.)

Cool weather: warm shorts or long pants, long-sleeve "T"-shirt, warm sweater, heavy windbreaker, boating or neoprene paddling gloves, sun hat or pullover hat. An option is to add lightweight thermal underwear as a base layer or substitute a "shortie" or full-length wetsuit for the lower and upper torso clothing.

Cold weather: thermal underwear, long pants, long-sleeved "T"-shirt and warm sweater under a paddling/spray outfit, athletic shoes or lightweight hiking shoes with warm socks or wetsuit booties, paddler's neoprene gloves, pullover hat under sun hat. An option is to substitute a full-length wet suit for the upper and lower torso clothing.

Boating Shorts. Short trips on hot days may simply call for wearing your swim suit. For longer, hot-weather ventures, wear baggy swim-suit bottoms or athletic shorts that do not bind when sitting and paddling.

Tidal Mudflats, Coast at Sea of Cortez — Courtesy of David Kiel

Long Pants. The old standard, wool or wool-blend trousers, remains popular with cold-weather canoeists. However, synthetics such as polyester pile are appearing more frequently. The favored options are regular trousers and sweat pants, the latter drawing favor because of their loose, comfortable style.

Undershirt/Long-Sleeve Shirt. This is a workable combination in cool or warm weather. Polyester or polypropylene *fishnet underwear tops* or solid, paneled tops are popular options. A full set (tops and bottoms) of heavier thermal underwear may be called for in colder weather. (Both are discussed in the VEHICLE ACCESSIBLE CAMPING activity.)

Quick-drying, warm-when-wet polyester or acrylic long-sleeve shirts worn over thermal underwear will provide the needed warmth in cool weather. Worn with fishnet underwear, they will also keep you comfortable and provide sunburn protection in warm weather. The shirt should not bind around the arms when paddling -- forget being style conscious and buy the shirt oversize and baggy. Consider heavy wool or polyester-pile shirts or sweaters (equipped with buttons or zippers for ventilation adjustment) worn over either type of underwear in cold weather.

Canoeing in hot weather is one circumstance that justifies breaking the "no-cotton rule." An example: While paddling the sometimes-stifling lower Colorado River (say, below the Hoover Dam) in summer, nothing beats a periodic dowse of water or dip in the river while wearing cotton. Now the water-retentive and resulting cooling properties of cotton work to your benefit. A light breeze blowing on your wet cotton shirt on a hot day provides a great attitude adjustment.

Paddling/Spray Outfits. Paddling jackets and spray outfits (jacket and pants), are designed to keep canoeists comfortable in the ocean-spray environment. They also should be considered as a canoeist option for some activities. These clothing items are discussed in the KAYAKING activity.

Boots/Socks. Boots are dictated both by on-land activities (camping, portaging) and waterborne effects. Lightweight shoes with flexible soles that will cushion and grip rocky stream bottoms (such as *athletic shoes* or *light-weight hiking shoes*) will probably suffice for short tours with little portaging. Invest in a new pair of athletic shoes if the current model is too comfortable and worn down -- they may not have the gripping surface needed nor take the punishment of high exertion activities. High-top models will protect against ankle scrapes and are less likely to be pulled off your feet in strong current. If you plan to wear these shoes with wet suit booties, you may need a size or two larger shoe than you normally wear.

Hiking boots are a better option if significant portaging is required. A high-top boot (8-10 inch) may be preferred if travel through bogs and mud holes is anticipated. Many of the desirable properties of hiking boots discussed in the HIKING activity apply. A quality trail hiking boot with proper construction and careful water-proofing to minimize water leakage into the boot is needed. Another option is the *shoepac*, a combination of rubber shoe and leather upper, especially useful in boggy country. On a negative note, the older models of these shoes are prone to encourage foot sweating, lack good arch support, and are inferior to lug-soled hiking boots for traction. More recent (and more expensive) models have moisture-wicking liners using materials such as Gore-Tex, which at least, improve the ability of the feet to "breathe."

In hot weather on casual recreation outings, many paddlers get by without wearing socks with their athletic shoes, or even switch over to sandals such as those discussed under "Camp Shoes/Land Shoes" in the VEHICLE-ACCESSIBLE CAMPING activity. Another option is a bootie with a cloth/neoprene top in combination with a tread sole, worn with or without socks. In cooler weather, consider the *athletic socks* discussed in the VEHICLE-ACCESSIBLE CAMPING activity. If you expect to get sprayed on or dunked, the wise choice is to go with the wicking, warm-when-wet type of athletic socks. Multiple layers will keep your feet warmer, provided the boots are not so tight as to restrict circulation. For cold water travel linked with on-shore activity, think seriously about neoprene *booties*, placed inside your shoes, to keep your feet warm.

Paddling Gloves. Unseasoned canoeists may want to consider gloves to prevent blisters. Some more-experienced paddlers wear them on extended trips to lighten the near-constant pressure on the palms. In moderate weather, a set of *boating gloves* should fill the bill. The gloves have a gripping material in the reinforced palm (typically leather), are cut off to expose the finger tips, have a nylon mesh backside, and are equipped with Velcro wrist closures.

In cold weather, the gloves of choice are *paddler's neoprene gloves*. The gloves are warm, waterproof and have a rough palm surface that is conducive to maintaining a firm paddle grip. Typically, the gloves have well-sealed seams and a Velcro closure at the wrists. Glove thickness choice is dependent on the water temperature in which they are to be used, similar to that as described for the wet suit and booties below. Note that there will be an increasing loss of manual dexterity as thicker gloves are used.

Wet Suit and Booties. Wet suits are more prevalent among kayakers plying cold, coastal waters. However, some canoeists do use them for inland waterway travel and, for the few that ply the region, in coastal areas. Their key function is to prevent hypothermia, should you capsize. Preference is for *high-waisted wet-suit trousers and comparable thickness tops* with plenty of armpit room or with the arms cut out all together. Because of their heat-retentive design, you may find yourself sweating during paddling exertion, even on very cold days. (In the extreme case, this could lead to dehydration.) One millimeter thickness is common for use in cool waters (60 degree Fahrenheit range) while 3-4 millimeter suits might be more reasonable in near-freezing water. Even the thinnest suit can be very restrictive for maneuvering in whitewater. Thus, the thickest suits are usually reserved for quieter water, where heroic moves are seldom required. (See the KAYAKING (Daytime) and WATERSPORTS activities for additional information.)

One popular choice for cold water footwear is *neoprene booties*. Together with a wetsuit and neoprene gloves, you have a warm, but somewhat restrictive clothing layer. (Throw in a mask and set of flippers, ...) The booties are not designed for extensive use on land. Used as a shoe, they will quickly wear. On sharp, rocky surfaces, they can easily puncture or tear.

Sea of Cortez Courtesy of David Kiel

Helmet. With open canoes, the paddler is separated from the vessel when it capsizes, unlike the situation for covered canoes and sit-in kayaks. As a result, most experienced open-boat canoeists forgo the helmet in all but spirited whitewater. However, if it makes you feel more secure with a helmet, wear it. Key helmet properties are solid construction, well-padded interior, snug but comfortable fit, protection for the upper head and temples, and a secure strap-down system. Most designs have air holes on the top and sides for ventilation. If there are plans for use in cold weather, ensure that you can slip a pullover hat under the helmet.

Knee Pads. For a simple change of paddling positions, when in rough water, or when attempting to reduce body profile in the wind, there are times when the canoeist may opt to paddle from the kneeling position. Long stints may raise havoc with the kneebones. *Pull-on pads* with plenty of flex, that aren't so tight as to cut off circulation on the backside of the knee, and which have a thick center pad at the kneebone, are one solution. Though materials vary, one of the most widely used designs has 1/8-inch thick neoprene covered with nylon at the knee.

Another option is to use mini-cell *foam pads*. There are channeled knee-cups for whitewater, as well as flat and contoured (angled) pads for touring and tripping. Temporary-placement designs have a low-skid bottom surface. There are also permanent-placement designs where the lower pad surface is bonded to the canoe floor. (See "Foot and Knee Braces," discussed above in this section)

Ankle and Wrist Guards. In addition to the bug-repelling measures discussed in the VEHICLE-ACCESSIBLE CAMPING section, some outdoorspeople use elastic bands or anklets to keep insects from entering at the trouser bottoms. Pants tucked into calf-length socks will do the job just as well, provided you are not in "black fly country." To prevent those pesky creatures from burrowing under the sock to the flesh, saturate the vulnerable borderline between pants and shoes with insect repellent. If your gloves do not have a strong elastic cuff below the wrist, elastic bands can also be used to prevent invasion from under glove openings. Some even opt for sewing on their own elasticized cuffs.

Safety

Map(s). The always-valuable USGS topographic maps and their limited worldwide counterparts (e.g., Canada, Europe) are a cornerstone for any trip. They should be the only map you need for day trips on well-traveled waterways. Bring a sufficient number of maps to cover the planned tour. If you are day-tripping in more remote settings, consider bringing the outlying area maps that might be needed should you have to hike out at some point in the trip. These peripheral maps might also help identify more-distant landmarks, a fun diversion on open lakes or when taking hiking side trips. If relevant, buy a *guide book* that discusses the tour and provides the necessary advance warnings of problematic stretches, route selection/decision data and interesting sites-to-see information.

There are additional needs for remote (usually overnight) tours on waterways that are little or seldom used. No question, bring the outlying topo maps. Guide books are probably not available. The topographic maps are great for general tour planning. However, it is difficult (sometimes impossible) to confidently estimate whether the drop between elevation contours is over an abrupt ledge or down a more gentle pitch. The USGS does publish *river-profile maps* for a small number of rivers. These charts, available only for rivers marked in blue on the state USGS indices, will indicate the precise nature of the gradient. Also consider purchasing aerial photography (see the HIKING activity), if it is available. Finally, make inquiries of other canoeists/ organizations or of local officials nearest the region to be traveled.

Map stays, which keep a map securely fastened in place, are sometimes used. This keeps the map constantly in view while navigating waterways. The map is opened and placed in a watertight sleeve. The sleeve corners are secured to the thwarts using attachment cords.

Accessories

Dry Pack. See the CANOEING (Overnight) section which follows.

Tool Kit

The tool kit should be tailored to your particular canoe. A few suggestions are provided below.

Tools. A pair of pliers is useful if you have to wire down a seat that comes unattached. An adjustable wrench serves to secure the replacement nuts and bolts used for thwart repair.

Repair gear. A roll of waterproof duct tape will handle minor leaks in a pinch. A roll of moderately-strong wire can be used to secure an unattached seat. Spare nuts and bolts can be used as a temporary replacement for securing thwarts whose rivets have come loose.

There are products such as Ding Stik, advertised as a durable epoxy for quick and permanent patching of small cracks and holes, which are designed to work on plastics, fiberglass and metal. For fiberglass boats, consider taking along extra fiberglass cloth, a can of resin with its small bottle of hardener and a brush. Familiarize yourself with the properties of the mixture and the general repair process before you leave.

Replacement gear. Bring an extra set of shoelaces or bootlaces, particularly if your trip involves land activities. (Don't forget the spare paddle mentioned above.)

End of Expedition at El Gulfo de Santa Clara, Mexico   Courtesy of David Kiel

Secondary Activities

Canoe trips can be linked with other activities, such as HIKING, WATERSPORTS and LAND FISHING. Refer to those sections for the associated unique gear needs.

CANOEING
(Daytime)

Select items based on trip needs and worst-case weather conditions.

ITEM	DATE				
Boat Gear					
Boat Rack & Tie Downs					
Canoe					
Painter/Lining Rope					
Paddles					
Spare Paddle					
Personal Flotation Device					
Bailer					
Foot & Knee Braces					
Backrest					
Fenders					
Water Jugs/Water Bottle(s)					
Dry Pack(s)					
Portable Ice Chest					
Ice & "Blue Ice"					
Permit					
Personal Gear					
Boating Shorts/Swim Suit					
Long Pants					
Mesh Undershirt					
Underwear					
Thermal Underwear*					
Long-Sleeve Shirt					
Paddling/Spray Outfit					
Windbreaker					
Boots or Athletic Shoes/Socks					
Paddling gloves (padded)					
*Wetsuit, Booties & Gloves**					
Helmet (whitewater)					
Knee Pads					
Brimmed Hat *& Pullover Hat**					
Head Net					
Ankle & Wrist Guards (insects)					
Bandanna/Sweat Band					
*Parka (w/p s/s)/Jacket**					
Toilet Paper					
Toilet Trowel					
Safety					
First Aid kit (see FIRST AID)					

CANOEING
(Daytime)

ITEM	DATE				
Water Filter/Tablets					
Sunglasses & Lanyard					
Sunscreen					
Insect Repellent					
Lip Balm					
Whistle					
Waterproof Matches & Lighter					
Fire Starter/Heat Tabs•					
Emergency Blanket•					
Map(s)					
Compass					
Altimeter/GPS Receiver					
Timepiece					
Thermometer					
Pocket Knife					
Waterproof Flashlight#					
Extra Batteries & Bulb#					
Reading Glasses & *Repair Kit*					
Nylon cord					
Phone Change					
Communication Device					
Pen & Notepad					
Accessories					
Camera; Extra Film & Battery					
Camera Bag, Lens Cleaning Kit					
Brochures, Articles, Books					
Binoculars					
Siting Pad (land use)					
Sewing kit					
Resealable Plastic Food Bags					
Litter Bag					
Daypack/Rucksack (storage)					
Frame Pack & Cover (storage)					
Auto Tool Kit					
Spare Keys/Credit Card/$					
Tool Kit					
Tools					
Repair Gear					
Replacement Gear					
Snacks (see MEALS section)					

Italicized items-optional/special purpose. •items for cold weather #nighttime travel contingency gear

CANOEING (Overnight)

See INDEX for checklist items not discussed below.

The overnight canoeing activity is focused on all-weather canoeing in inland and protected coastal waters. It could vary from an overnighter or a lengthy expedition. For stillwater travel not involving portaging, err on the side of bringing extra gear for comfort. Considerations of portaging, as well as canoe freeboard and maneuverability, may alter this free-wheeling attitude for longer trips on rougher water. The requirement to carry camping gear, additional water, food and clothing, as well as extra contingency items such as additional paddles and expanded medical and tool kit(s) may limit the allowance for amenities. As with many other outdoor activities, canoe loading can be reduced significantly by having your group share common items such as cooking gear, tent, water filter and master medical kit.

Safety Considerations: 1) review the **GENERAL CONSIDERATIONS** and TEN ESSENTIALS sections; 2) review the "Safety Considerations" in the CANOEING (Daytime/Nighttime) activity, as applicable; 3) develop plans for contacting rescue personnel in an emergency and practice techniques needed to extricate an injured paddler from the canoeing area; 4) ensure that a full set of contingency boat repair equipment is packed; and 5) bring foul-weather contingency gear, including extra food and stove fuel, in the event that the weather goes sour.

In the checklist, items that are considered optional (niceties or special purpose) are *italicized*. Items for cold-weather canoeing are noted with an asterisk(*). Pound sign(#) entries are contingency gear for nighttime travel.

Boat Gear

Canoe. The necessary buoyancy, tracking stability and load-carrying capacity for most overnight and multi-day outdoor use favors 17-18 foot length canoes. Longer models are more typically used for extended family-with-small-children excursions or lengthy expeditions.

Gear storage, tying down gear within the canoe, gear placement and distribution are especially important issues for overnight trips and expeditions. First, we can't overemphasize the need to pack items in large, but handleable units. When hauling the gear into the campsite, it is a nuisance to make numerous trips to bring in a large number of individual items. When portaging, this need to make a large number of gear-hauling round trips can bring havoc to your trip schedule and also make the trip a lot less fun. Frame packs and day pack/rucksacks are ideal because they are designed to store and carry gear. Large, heavy-duty duffel bags, including dry packs for waterproof gear storage are another option. Lashing this gear on separate carry or pack frames will accommodate easier off-loading and carrying in many cases.

Nominally, the gear is stored on either side of the center thwart (or between center thwarts for four-thwart canoes) and roughly weight-balanced in a side-to-side sense. For ease of storage and removal, a single line is recommended for tie-down. The most common method is to start with a quick-release tautline hitch on the forward thwart against the gunwale and weave the line to form an "X" over the gear between the forwardmost thwarts. The line is slipped under pack straps and through frames where possible and is double-looped around each thwart at each contact point. This ties down the gear in the forward well between thwarts. The same process is continued to tie down the gear in the aft well and the line secured at the end point with a second tautline hitch.

Dry Packs. Sleeping bags, down parkas/vests, clothes and food are a few things that come to mind that need protection from the elements. For short overnighters, one low-price option is to store this gear in double layers of 3-mil *trash bags*, which are tied off separately and then tucked into one of the large storage packs. Water is insidious for finding the single tortuous, minuscule route to attack the gear that you want to protect. The bags are also very easy to puncture. Inspect the bags before each repacking and bring along plenty of duct tape or your own favorite alternative to cover holes and tears.

Heavy-duty pressure- or zip-locked *freezer bags* are handy for storing some of the smaller items such as food. If you don't own a watertight camera, consider storing it in large-size, double or even triple layers of freezer bags. Our preference is the zip-locked version. You can test the seal of an air-filled bag by simply zipping it closed and squeezing on it. Now, when you press the air out of the bag and reseal it (in preparation for packing it into the larger storage pack), you can be confident of a tight seal.

Plastic boxes with snap-on lids, similar to those found in most home kitchens, are also an inexpensive method of waterproofing gear. These are exceptionally lightweight, and the lid is pressed down around the entire rim of the container to assure a perfectly watertight seal.

Quetico Provencial Park, Ontario,Canada　　　Courtesy of David Kiel

The preferred option for longer tours (particularly in remote areas) is to spend the bucks for waterproof storage gear made for this type of activity. (This is in addition to the cheaper storage devices noted.) For example, there are both light- and heavy-duty *waterproof stuff sacks*. Many designs use PVC, neoprene or Hypalon-reinforced nylon as the base material for the waterproof shell. The standard design uses a top flap that is folded over a couple of times (more if the sack is not fully loaded) and is tied down on both sides using heavy-duty clips or Velcro closures. Adjustment straps allow the clips to be placed in position to achieve a tight fit. The sacks come in widely-variant sizes, colors (including clear) and styles. Some of the larger sacks (e.g., three feet in length and 1-1/2 foot diameter) come with built-in carry straps for hand or back hauling.

The "waterproof" claims are probably justified for normal use and even for short periods floating on the water. There is less optimism about performance when the bags are immersed for more than a short time in stillwater or are accompanying your overturned canoe down a set of rapids. We suggest that you return to the good ole' trashbag as an inner liner if either scenario is a reasonably possibility.

There are other heavier, more-cumbersome gear containers, generally metal, that can truly stake the claim to being waterproof. Most have a generous seal on the base container and a pressured, lock-down sealing mechanism on the cover. The most popular types for river use is the *military surplus ammunition container*, typically available in various sizes. In addition to surplus boxes, several models of fiberglass and metal *waterproof boxes* are commercially available. Finally, wooden boxes are made specifically for waterborne activities. To ensure water tightness, the edges are fiberglassed or caulked and weather-stripping inserted around the box lid.

Quetico Provencial Park, Ontario,Canada Courtesy of David Kiel

Personal Gear

If space and/or weight is an issue, one method of load lightening is to take along as much dual-use (canoeing/camping) wearing apparel as is practical. Much of the apparel used for backpacking is amenable to use for both activities.

Tool Kit

The items listed below are in addition to those noted in the CANOEING (Daytime) activity.

Tools. Add the tools needed for adjustment or repair of camping gear as described in the BACKPACKING activity.

Repair Gear. Add a sewing kit for repair of wearing apparel, tent, sleeping bag, etc., as described in the BACKPACKING activity. Consider bringing spot- and seam-repair sealants for neoprene clothing items.

Replacement Gear. See the BACKPACKING activity for the additional replacement items needed for land-use.

Secondary Activities

See the CANOEING (Daytime) activity.

Quetico Provencial Park; Ontario,Canada Courtesy of David Kiel

Quetico Provencial Park; Ontario,Canada Courtesy of David Kiel

CANOEING
(Overnight)

Select items based on trip needs and worst-case weather conditions.

ITEM	DATE				
Boat Gear					
Boat Rack & Tie Downs/Locks					
Canoe					
Painter/Lining Rope					
Paddles					
Spare Paddle					
Personal Flotation Device					
Bailer					
Foot & Knee Braces					
Fender					
Backrest					
Water Jug/Water Bottle(s)					
Collapsible Water Bag					
Dry Packs					
Portable Ice Chest					
Ice & "Blue Ice"					
Permit					
Personal Gear					
Boating Shorts/Swim Suit					
Long Pants					
Mesh Undershirt					
Underwear					
Thermal Underwear*					
Long-Sleeve Shirt					
Paddling/Spray Outfit					
Windbreaker					
Boots or Athletic Shoes/Socks					
Paddling Gloves (padded)					
*Wetsuit, Booties & Gloves**					
Helmet (whitewater)					
Knee Pads					
Brimmed Hat & Pullover Hat*					
Head Net					
Ankle & Wrist Guards (insects)					
Bandanna/Sweat Band					
Camp/Land Shoes					
Parka (w/p s/s)/Jacket*					
Gloves *& Mittens**					
Toilet Paper					
Toilet Trowel					

CANOEING
(Overnight)

ITEM	DATE				
Camping Gear					
Tent & Rainfly					
Stakes & Poles					
Seam Sealer					
Ground Cloth					
Tent Broom & Sponge					
Sleeping Bag (w/p stuff sack)					
Sleeping Pad					
Sleep Area Netting					
Stove & Windbreak, Primer					
Fuel Bottle					
Fuel Funnel/Strainer					
Lantern/Fuel					
Waterproof Matches & Lighter					
Camp Grill/Hand-held Grill					
Cooking Pot					
Skillet/Frypan					
Teapot (hot water)					
Non-stick Cooking Lubricant					
Pot Holders/Pot Grippers					
Plate & Cup					
Cooking Utensils (spatula etc.)					
Dish Tub					
Scrubber & Sponge					
Dish Towel					
Can Opener					
Eating Utensils					
Biodegradable Dish Soap					
Paper Towels					
Spare Stuff Sacks					
Litter Bag					
Reusable Plastic Food Bags					
Sitting Pad (land use)					
Camp Chairs					
Hygiene					
Towel					
Wash Cloth					
Biodegradable Soap					
Biodegradable Shampoo					
Personal Toiletries/Ditty Bag					
Toilet Paper & *Towelettes*					
Toilet Trowel					
Sun Shower					
Laundry Bag					
Portable Toilet & Liners					

CANOEING
(Overnight)

ITEM	DATE				
Safety					
First Aid Kit (see FIRST AID)					
Water Filter/Tablets					
Sunglasses & Lanyard					
Sunscreen					
Insect Repellent					
Lip Balm					
Whistle					
Fire Starter/Heat Tabs*					
Emergency Blanket*					
Map(s) & Compass					
Altimeter/GPS Receiver					
Timepiece					
Thermometer					
Pocket Knife					
Waterproof Flashlight					
Extra Batteries & Bulb					
Reading Glasses & Repair Kit					
Nylon Cord					
Phone Change					
Weather Radio					
Communication Device					
Pen & Notepad					
Accessories					
Camera & Extra Film *& Battery*					
Camera Bag, *Lens Cleaning Kit*					
Brochures, Articles, Books					
Ax & Wood Saw					
Binoculars					
Sewing Kit					
Daypack/Rucksack (storage)					
Frame Pack & Cover (storage)					
Indoor Games					
Auto Tool Kit					
Spare Keys/Credit Card/$					
Tool Kit					
Tools					
Repair Gear					
Replacement Gear					
Meals (see MEALS section)					

Italicized items-optional/special purpose. *items for cold weather #nighttime travel contingency gear

KAYAKING (Daytime)

See INDEX for checklist items not discussed below.

The daytime kayaking activity is focused on all-weather kayaking in inland and protected coastal waters, as well as under fair-weather conditions in open ocean. For continuity of discussion, some gear choices that extend into the Overnight/ Expedition activities are also included. Some discussion assumes that the day trip will involve on-land activity (e.g., inclusion of the "Boots/Socks" item). If your day trip is totally waterborne, tailor your gear accordingly. Storage hatches or open storage space (normally fitted with flotation bags, as described later) are required, even for day trips, if you are going to carry a large number of the gear items discussed. Otherwise, you are restricted to whatever gear can be stuffed into the cockpit (without obstructing your movement) and tied down on the deck. (The latter is a very tenuous option since: 1) topside gear can markedly affect your boat's roll stability; and 2) you expose your gear to the elements and potential loss overboard.) Bottom line: Lack of quality storage space will severely limit the scope of activities that you can safely conduct.

Safety Considerations: 1) review the **GENERAL CONSIDERATIONS** and TEN ESSENTIALS sections; 2) develop swimming skills commensurate with the level of activity you are planning; 3) take lessons to learn about kayaking do's and don'ts and to enhance your skills; 4) master the reading of weather and its implications on both atmospheric conditions and water state. Check weather forecasts before departure and every several hours on open-ocean trips. Head for shore if a deteriorating weather pattern develops; 5) practice your paddling technique and develop navigation skills on successively more demanding tours. This is particularly important if you are working up to whitewater or open-ocean kayaking and/or remote tours; 6) study the trip beforehand, establishing a route and alternatives that are within your group's physical and technical capabilities; 7) don't go it alone -- find a reliable and capable partner(s); 8) for sit-in kayakers, practice roll techniques to the point of high confidence of successful execution. This is a matter of aggravation level (a failed roll puts you in the water and requires that your compadres assist you back into your boat) in warmer water and potentially a life-or-death issue under frigid conditions. Practice one-on-one and two-on-one-boat rescues with your group; 9) ensure that there is a group leader with experience in higher-difficulty kayaking than the trip you are planning; 10) learn basic first aid and develop plans for getting an overwhelmed/exhausted/injured kayaker to shore. Include kayak towing into your exercises; 11) certify that the boat(s) and gear are in proper working order and that contingency boat patching equipment is packed (and that you know how to use it); 12) bring cold-weather contingency gear in the event that you are forced out overnight; and 13) wear a PFD -- add a hard hat for sea entries/exits and whitewater kayaking. For ruddered boats, confirm that your rudder is securely stowed when entering the surf line.

In the checklist, items that are considered optional (niceties or special purpose) are *italicized*. Items noted with an asterisk(*) are for cold weather. Those noted with a pound sign(#) are gear items for planned or contingency kayaking at night.

Boat Gear

Boat Rack and Tie-downs. There are numerous, well-proven *kayak racks* for most vehicles. Some of the more popular models have two rack-mounted, cushioned saddles that wrap around the underside of the boat, one fore and one aft. An over-the-top strap that attaches to each saddle secures the kayak. There are also kayak stackers that mount two kayaks on edge. Each kayak lies on its own set of rack-bar pads. The kayaks rest against a fore and an aft stacker bar. The boat is held in by a set of around-the-bottom straps which are themselves secured to the stacker bar and rack.

Unfortunately, people steal kayaks (and racks), making it prudent to invest in two sets of *locks*. One set of locks will hold the towers to your car and another (usually a cable lock) will hold the boat(s) to the rack. Most commercial racks are designed to accept slip-in locks which fasten the rack to the car. The locks which secure the boat to the rack are usually a separately-purchased item.

An interesting option is short-distance kayak hauling with a (generally foldable) *boat cart*. This method eliminates the physical stress of having to lift the boat onto a car roof. In the Pacific Northwest, where kayaks are welcome aboard ferries (they fit nicely under low overheads), the boat cart is a natural. Basically, these are a pair of wheels, a small frame incorporating a simple cradle, and webbing to lash the kayak to the cradle. The cradle also serves to transport the boat directly to water's edge by hand. Some models come equipped with a long tongue that fastens to the seatpost of a bicycle (preferably a mountain bike) for use in close-to-home shuttles. Better to test the latter option before you try it on the city streets.

"Pond Kayaking," Stanwood, Washington Compliments of Don Stromberg

Though some choose *homemade tie-downs* for kayaks, we don't recommend this securing method for all kayaks. They work reasonably well for canoes, which rest upside down and have gunwales making contact with your car roof or homemade crossbars. Similarly, they work for relatively flat-decked sit-on kayaks. However, most kayaks don't have that broad, flat topside surface on which to rest. If you cinch down the lines holding your sit-in kayak to your homemade crossbars (we do not consider direct placement on the roof a smart option for any kayak), you can stress-crack the hull of a fiberglass boat or deform the hull of a plastic boat.

Kayak. Key properties to consider are kayak type, materials and construction, and options for outfitting. These properties are discussed below.

• *Types of kayaks* include touring, day touring, sit-on tops and whitewater. These are our "home-grown" categories, selected for convenience of discussion. Whatever your application, the kayak should have the displacement to keep you and your gear afloat, the narrowest hull that is consistent with your needs to balance moving ahead efficiently while maintaining stability, and the maneuverability to handle the all-around conditions for use.

Touring Kayak. Though used for daytime trips, ("sit-in" or enclosed cockpit) touring kayaks are more inclined to be loaded up for weekend trips or expeditions. They have ample cargo space and can be paddled efficiently when loaded. They sit low in the water to minimize the effects of the wind. Both solo- and tandem-paddler boats are on the market. Tourers are typically designed with the greatest beam at the midpoint of the hull. Single-paddler models are in the 55-70 pound weight class, 15-18 feet in length, and have beams in the 22-25 inch range. The hull shape includes a bottom designed to run straight and track well, a narrow bow that promotes smooth linear flow and a narrow stern to minimize drag. This results in bow profiles that tend to sport a relatively deep keel and keel profiles that most often are flat or have a mild rocker. Touring kayaks are typically hardshell (fiberglass or plastic) or rigid-frame-with-flexible-fabric-skin hull designs. (The latter is discussed in the KAYAKING [Overnight/ Expedition] section.

Day Touring Kayak. The day-touring category typically includes smaller kayaks, canoe/kayak hybrids and inflatables. Most *small kayaks* are designed for use by novices or light-recreation paddlers. They are mainly used in inland stillwater, sheltered coastal areas and, less frequently, under benign open-ocean conditions. They are budget friendly and easy to paddle, although they are below touring kayaks on the paddling-efficiency scale. Like their touring big brothers, they come in solo- and tandem-paddler models. Most small, single-paddler kayaks are light (30-45 pounds), have short lengths (9-13 feet) and broad beams (25-30 inches). Hull profiles are roughly similar to those for touring kayaks. The day-touring kayaks are typically made of plastic.

Now, a few words about *inflatable kayaks*. Like sit-on top kayaks, inflatables have gotten the rap by many as being good-weather recreation craft. Most inflatable boats do fall into this niche as far as paddler use. Now, with new materials, emerging technologies, and careful engineering, inflatable kayaks are coming into their own as safe and comfortable boats for every level of paddler. With their high buoyancy hulls, these kayaks are incredibly stable and among the easiest in which to learn basic handling techniques. However, the inflatables rank below hardshells in terms of paddling efficiency. They can also be paddled a fair distance while packing a heavy gear load. At the time of publishing, higher-quality inflatables have been used to circumnavigate many of the Hawaiian Islands and for 1000-mile voyages along the Alaskan coastline. They have also found their way into the whitewater world. Inflatables are built using such materials as polyvinyl chloride (PVC) and nitrile/natural rubber coatings over nylon.

Sit-on-Top Kayaks. This fast-growing category encompasses about every facet of kayaking. At one extreme are the stubby wave skis, shaped like platters, for plying the ocean surf. At the other end are 17-foot-and-up, narrow-beamed models used for open-ocean racing. Ease of use and freedom of movement of these boats has made them incredibly popular, particularly in warmer climates. Unlike the sit-ins, there is no need to Eskimo-roll or initiate complex procedures to reenter the boat after capsize. You simply get the boat upright and scramble back on board. Most designs have scuppers that allow the water to simply drain out of the cockpit. With modern protective clothing designed for paddlers, including wet suits and dry suits, the touring versions are becoming proven year-around craft even in the northern U.S.

Typically they are small inland or fair-weather, open-ocean day-trippers which also serve well as fishing, swimming and scuba-diving platforms. They are not as paddling efficient as the touring kayaks. Solo and tandem designs are available. Larger models have interior cargo holds that can support overnight ventures. Most sit-ons are light (40-70 pounds), have short lengths (10-14 feet) and broad beams (28-34 inches). The smaller boats have weight capacities in the 250-350 pound range, while those in the broad-beam, 13-14 foot length arena can handle up to about 450 pounds. Most current sit-on cockpits are completely open, however several manufactures have recently introduced a cruising version with a wrap-around spray deck similar to that used with the sit-ins. There are a few whitewater sit-ons with special outfitting such as foot straps/slip-in forms and knee braces so that you can roll back after a capsize. Most sit-ons are constructed of plastic.

Whitewater Kayaks. These specialized kayaks are built to run everything from Class II to Class V rivers. They are typically designed with the greatest beam located aft of the cockpit. Most are short (9-13 feet), have a shallow curved or "V" bottom to clear underwater obstructions and a highly-rockered keel profile for quick maneuvering. Typical widths are about 23-26 inches and weights are 35-50 pounds. Most are designed-limited for use by paddlers weighing no more than 200-250 pounds. Many are fitted with custom braces to allow the paddler to mold with the boat in treacherous water. Most whitewater kayaks are made of toughened polyethylene plastic.

Clair Engle Lake, California — Compliments of Walt Bond

Solo Versus Tandem Kayaks. The arguments favoring solo kayaks are that they offer solitude and control of your immediate destiny, as well as a greater gear load per person than two-person models. Unlike tandems, solo kayaks do not require a synchronization between paddlers, a knack that must be acquired through practice. They are easier to carry and can be loaded onto automobile racks with greater ease. On the other hand, tandems provide the chance to share the adventure in real time. Two paddlers of equal strength and skill will go faster and farther or will arrive at their destination less tired if paddling one double kayak rather than a pair of solos. A double is more stable than a single of equal design. It allows two paddlers of different skill levels to travel together -- no impatient, more-skilled paddler waiting for her cranky, you're-going-too-fast companion. Finally, tandems offer the chance to haul a tired or injured kayaker or bring along small children.

• *Kayak materials* are a key consideration in design. The overwhelming majority of today's modern kayaks are fabricated from one of four materials: fiberglass, polyethylene (plastic), wood or fabric. Traditional hardshells, boats where the skin provides the structural component that gives the boat strength and rigidity, are typically fiberglass and plastic. Wood is a less frequent option. Kayaks which obtain strength and rigidity using a skin formed around a rigid skeleton use fabric as that skin. Inflatables are built using such materials as polyvinyl chloride (PVC) and nitrile/natural rubber coatings over nylon.

Fiberglass Structure. Fiberglass kayaks may be made from traditional fiberglass or a sandwich of materials including Kevlar. The many types of resins poured over the fabric give fiberglass exceptional strength and rigidity relative to most other materials for a given weight boat. Most fiberglass kayaks have a layer of pigmented resin or gel coat on the outside of the hull and deck. This layer, in addition to carrying the bright colors of the boat, provides a wearing surface against the abrasion of landings, as well as shielding the resins and fabrics from the sun's piercing rays. The fiberglass boats tend to have finer ends bow and stern for streamlining than those made from other processes. They also create less water resistance when underway, provided the wearing surface is in good condition. However, buyer beware! The pricey fiberglass kayaks are for paddlers at the performance upper end. With aggressive use, the outer coating will become scratched and worn and must be resurfaced to maintain the kayaks low-drag characteristics. Most experts feel that entry- or intermediate-level kayakers, given equally priced fiberglass and plastic boats, will see little difference in paddling performance.

A fiberglass hull should be rigid. It shouldn't creak or flex underneath you, and it shouldn't develop patterns of hairline cracks nor have its tape peel away from seams, etc. When you shift your weight from the shore to the cockpit rim on entry, you shouldn't feel the deck slump in. When you slide your weight into the seat, you shouldn't feel the cockpit rim compress toward your hips.

Run your fingers along the seams or under the edge of the cockpit. A smooth finish is not a guarantee of overall high quality work, but it is a good sign. Stick your head into the cockpit and look out through the side of the hull. If the gel coat is of uniform resistance, the light coming through the hull will be uniform. If you see splotches of light and chunks of shadow glimmering through the gel coat, you should suspect an uneven gel coat or a hull of unexpectedly varying thickness. Look for bubbles, scabs or what looks like colorless rust -- they are all symptoms of flaws in the manufacturing process. Finally, take a look down the hull and deck. Don't expect a mirror-smooth finish, but you should have some concern if you are looking at a highly-wavy surface.

A few manufacturers can supply "take-apart" fiberglass kayaks. These are rigid-hulled boats that have been cut into three or four pieces. The sections can be bolted into a single, strong and waterproof hull -- and since the sections can nest somewhat, the take-apart hull is a bit easier to store or transport. They are nowhere near as collapsible as the take-apart, rigid-frame-with-flexible-fabric-skin hull designs discussed in the KAYAKING (Overnight/Expedition) section.

Polyethylene (Plastic) Structure. While today's fiberglass is still the most popular material for top-of-the-line cruising kayaks, polyethylene plastic products are improving year-by-year and may threaten that status in the future. Plastics dominate almost all other competitive areas. Its advantages include substantial cost savings, abrasion and impact resistance, and the ability to be molded into complex shapes. Plastic hulls are made using a variety of molding processes and variations of polyethylene. Four prominent types are linear, cross-linked, HTP and superlinear. HTP has the highest stiffness, characteristic of a more responsive and roomier boat (i.e., one which requires less internal bracing), followed by cross-linked and super linear types. Linear is least stiff. The same ranking holds relative to impact and abrasion resistance. Linear polyethylene is the least expensive. All materials are amenable to small, temporary patch repairs using commonly available kits. All except cross-linked surfaces are easy to permanently repair using simple welding and can be recycled by the manufacturer.

Plastic boat construction is not nearly the art of that for fiberglass -- as a result, there are fewer things to go awry. The cues as to plastic boat quality are that it have a thick wall (uniformity is rarely an issue) and that it not have any appreciable nicks or chinks in what should be a smooth hull.

Wood Structure Today, the most common wooden kayaks are built with thin strips of edge-glued wood -- cedar is the material of choice -- shaped over removable molds and covered with one or two layers of fiberglass. Hulls and decks are formed separately and coupled once the hull is off its mold. Wood boats tend to be very strong, very light and very expensive. The latter characteristic is because of both the scarcity of knot-free cedar and the labor-intensive process needed to build them. Wood kayaks are among the most aesthetically pleasing, frequently designed with inlays, painted decorations and a host of special flourishes.

Frame and Fabric Structure. This option is discussed in the KAYAKING (Overnight/ Expedition) section.

Inflatables. An inflatable kayak is a series of air-tight tubes engineered into a long and relatively narrow form, with a floor joining the tubes. Backrests, seats and footbraces may be added; spray decks, however, are an uncommon option. Some inflatables have the floor supported above the water level, and valves and slots in the floor allow water to drain out of the cockpit. Multiple air chambers offer more security than a single chamber, at the expense of weight for the additional walls and seams required. Most recreational users opt for the less expensive single-chamber design.

An inexpensive kayak may be built of unreinforced or unsupported PVC, plastic or rubber. The low initial cost is counterbalanced by a more fragile hull and normally a less paddling-efficient design. Most enthusiast-caliber inflatables are made with a base fabric topped with an air-tight and abrasion-resistant coating. Nylon has been the most common base material, with polyester catching up in popularity. Some manufacturers are now fitting inflatables with fabrics such as Kevlar into high-wear areas for lightweighting combined with durability. The key attributes of higher-quality fabrics are the tightness of weave and bursting or tear strength.

Strait of Juan de Fuca, Washington Pygmy Boats Incorporated

The most common coatings use bases of neoprene, Hypalon, PVC, urethane and ethyl propylene diene monomer. For a given coating type, a rule of thumb is that the greater the percentage of base material in the coating, the better the quality.

• *Outfitting of the kayak* is the next consideration. Beyond the selection of basic hull design and materials comes the issue of finding a model that is comfortable and properly equipped for your planned uses.

Seat(s). If your seat and back aren't comfortable, you'll be in for a long trip -- even on a short trip. A seat with a good support is a must because of the way you use your back when kayaking. Look for a kayak with a seat that comfortably fits your bottom and has adjustable back support. One option is a backband type of support that is adjusted by a line fed through a jam cleat on the side of the seat itself. Some adjustable seats have a curved back panel hinged at the bottom, with an adjusting mechanism that allows you to dial in the most comfortable seat angle.

Some opt to purchase a backrest which supplements or replaces the original equipment. A sample model is a closed-cell foam, waterproof-nylon-jacketed chair. The portable seat is placed in the cockpit and butted against the in-place backrest or simply replaces the current equipment. In the latter case, the back is attached to the stern wall of the cockpit using a water-impervious adhesive bond. Both seat and backrest, which are connected by side straps, are cushioned. Seat tilt is adjusted with the side straps.

Finally, there are a few sit-in boats sold without any form of back support system. The backless seats are designed to have a dry bag strapped behind the retrofitted seat, so one solution is to use the bag itself as part of the seat assembly. This less-than-optimum option means that you have to carefully pack a full dry bag each time that you decide to use your kayak.

Cockpit. The sit-on kayaks have an open cockpit. For sit-ins, the seat, in many ways, determines the size of the cockpit. Small cockpits mean small spray skirts (decks). A small spray deck may be set more tightly and is less likely to be blown off than a larger one. You are also less likely to lose a smaller, tighter spray cover when rolling your boat. For these reasons, narrower cockpits are preferred by most for launching off of exposed beaches and for transits in turbulent seas. Larger cockpits mean boarding and exiting are easier, and larger items may be stowed in the cockpit itself. These are considered primo advantages by most paddlers who are less inclined to test Mother Nature and who place a higher premium on trip comfort, including access to gear while underway.

Spray Skirt. The spray skirt (or deck) should fit snugly, but safely. Cockpit coaming should be at least 3/4-inch wide and have sufficient clearance to allow a person's fingers to pass between it and the deck. The spray cover should fit tightly around the cockpit coaming sufficient to remain in place if a wave wets you down, It should also have a secure and efficient release strap. Most spray skirts have an elastic fabric release strap sewn across the narrow point at the front of the skirt. To ensure that the strap is accessible (i.e., not inadvertently tucked under the skirt and coaming) in an emergency, some paddlers tie a drilled-through golf ball to the release strap.

Some paddlers prefer coated nylon spray decks because they dry easily, although they do require an elastic cord or (in most cases) suspenders to keep them up around the torso. Others prefer neoprene decks, which, since they are stretchy, fit snugly around the torso and still allow a full range of motion. The rap on neoprene skirts is that they seem always to be damp and can be too warm under even nominal paddling conditions. A word of warning: A few kayakers don't wear their skirts at all times. They may find that the skirts take longer to put in place than the few seconds between hearing a wake-making power boat and watching its wake roll up on the kayak!

Foot Pegs. Some foot peg (pedal) assemblies are built into the hull itself -- this is frequently the case for whitewater kayaks. This requires that you find the right fit before buying (and pray that you don't shrink too much with age). Most are adjustable, allowing you to vary the distance between the back support to the foot peg. Another alternative is an adjustable foot peg which doubles as the control pedal for the rudder system. More about rudders and skegs later.

Bulkheads and Hatches. When selecting a kayak, you can opt for sit-in models that have sealed bulkheads fore and aft, aft only, or no bulkheads at all. Sit-on kayaks have an inherent flotation chamber or chambers. With bulkheads, you get additional flotation at the expense of some added weight. Many boats equipped with sealed-off bulkheads have entry hatches, providing a place to store your gear. (Some day-trippers, particularly those who use kayaks mainly for workouts or short jaunts, go for the hatchless models.)

There are two common types of hatches. One is circular, much like a giant jar lid, which is effectively screwed onto or off of a mating deck fitting. The other type may be of any shape -- usually rectangular or trapezoidal -- and is held in place by clips or by over-the-top cinch straps. There is no perfect hatch. All hatch systems will leak, whether you roll your kayak or paddle through light spray. Remember to pack anything that you want to keep dry in a dry bag or other waterproof enclosure. If you are concerned about leakage and willing to forgo convenient access to the hatch interior while underway, consider adding a thin neoprene cover which fits under the hatch. (More is said about the most robust hatches in the KAYAKING (Overnight/Expedition) section.)

Flotation. If you don't have bulkheads, or if you have only a rear bulkhead, you'll need inflatable "flotation" bags secured in the end(s) of your boat. Rather than just stuffing them into position, they need to be secured, lest you watch your bags float away from your desks-awash kayak. Flotation bags may hold more than air. Several makers build bags that can be opened and filled with your gear, resealed, and then inflated.

Sit-in boats with "watertight" fore and aft bulkheads, folding kayaks with air sponsons (see the KAYAKING [Overnight/Expedition section]), and sit-on kayaks effectively have their own built-in floatation systems. A word of caution, however. Consider what the penalty might be if you develop even a modest leak on your journey. If your plans are to day paddle in off-shore coastal or quiet waters, you might come to a different conclusion than if the agenda has you doing long-distance, open-ocean paddling. Whatever category you belong to, bring the necessary contingency gear to handle such a problem.

Rudders and Skegs. While you use your weight and paddle to turn the kayak, rudders and skegs are intended to help maintain course. Rudders are variable-direction devices that allow you to compensate for wind and current to track a given course. Most kayaks designed for light touring, plastic sit-on kayaks, and all boats built for whitewater running are rudderless, while those designed for longer, all-weather treks are rudder equipped. (A qualifier: most double kayaks, for any use, generally require rudder control.) There are three basic types of rudders. One is either fixed to the boat or controlled in the up or down position with a cotter pin. (Since the latter is relatively inaccessible when you are waterborne, it is effectively a fixed rudder once you lock it in the down position.) Since it cannot be used when beaching or to prowl around in shallow water, the locking rudder has appeal only to a limited group of paddlers.

The other two types of rudders can be raised or lowered using the foot pegs in the cockpit. One design lets you retract the rudder out of the water into a flush well on the deck. With the rudder thus locked, your foot pegs are rock-solid and the rudder is protected -- even during transport. On the negative side, you need two lines (one to raise, one to lower), you must center the rudder before retracting, and you have a more complicated mechanism.

The second design merely lifts the blade out of the water and dangles it like a rooster tail in the air. These are mechanically simpler -- one line both lifts and drops the rudder -- and most can be moved and stowed inside the boat during transport. The disadvantage of this design is that you have no way of locking your foot pegs in position when the rudder is out of the water. As you apply paddling or leaning pressure to each pedal, the peg gives a little and the rudder waves in the air. This effect is disconcerting at first, but most users assert that it just takes a little getting used to.

Since both basic retractable designs are well proven, the key issue is the quality of the linkage between the rudder and foot pedals. It should be smooth operating, not likely to foul on anything, and able to be jury-rigged with simple equipment in the event of breakage.

A skeg is a fixed-direction, rudder-like blade that you can dig deeper into or remove from the water. It provides mechanically simple directional control in wind and sea. It does not, however, offer the fine tuning for course maintenance that a rudder provides.

If your journeys will take you in and out of the surf line, there are some necessary precautions, particularly for non-expert kayakers. Consider purchasing a rudderless kayak or at least one that has a secure "up"-position locking mechanism. Cases of kayakers flipping in the surf and getting impacted by rudders and skegs are well documented. Some resultant neck and head injuries have been fatal. Since the kayak itself can be lethal, ensure that you learn to paddle in the waves with a trained professional or surf veteran.

Santa Rosa Island — Compliments of Sally Bond

Deck Fittings. There should be sufficient deck fittings for the kayakers intended uses; this might include fittings for gear tie-down line(s), tow line, grab lines, etc. The most common fixtures are cleats (for securing lines) and padeyes (for controlled line channeling). Day-trippers who kayak in sheltered areas where help is always near can probably get by without any special fittings. (Bow and stern loops, effectively padeyes, are standard equipment for all kayak designs.)

Serious adventurers will have an array of fittings. An example: 1) cleats and padeyes behind the cockpit, on both port and starboard sides, used to set up for a paddle float or as a towline tieoff; 2) a jam cleat on either side at the rear corner of the cockpit for securing a paddle float line or tying off a sea anchor (drogue); 3) padeyes on the deck periphery for grab lines; and 4) and four padeyes arranged in a square pattern just forward of the cockpit. With shock cord run through the set on the perimeter, then in a criss-cross pattern, the unit serves to strap down a map and to temporarily hold down other objects.

The method of securing heavy-load-bearing fittings, whether retrofitted or "factory equipment," requires scrutiny. Your safety could rest on the robustness of these devices. Cleats and padeyes should not just be screwed into the deck. Each should be fastened down into a reinforcing pad built into the underside of the deck.

Add-on Sponsons. These devices are in effect a pair of fabric pontoons, about six inches in diameter and three feet long, that strap on either side of your kayak. Their purpose is to provide added stability and flotation beyond a kayak's basic design. Some use them for fishing -- folks who paddle narrow kayaks who delight in the additional stability. Others use them to provide an extra safety margin in rough weather or for taking less-experienced kayakers out into the open ocean.

Straps go underneath the boat from sponson to sponson. Straps passed over the deck fore and aft of the cockpit buckle from one sponson to the other. One method of use is to leave the sponsons deflated, with only a stern strap attached and the deflated sponsons tucked under rear bungee cords. With the second strap passed under the hull and then snapped into place, the two air chambers can be inflated in moments. Whether inflated or deflated, the sponsons will place noticeable, additional drag on the kayak

• Issues of *gear storage, tying down gear within the boat, gear placement and distribution* are most relevant for overnighters and expeditions. These issues are discussed in the next section.

Bow Line. A bow line is useful for tying up your kayak securely after landing or at a dock. Tie it to the bow loop and bring it back at least to the cockpit, latching into a secure attachment point.

Grab Line. These tightened-down lines are secured around the foredeck (and reardeck for some). They are useful for temporarily securing items onboard. Since boat surfaces are slippery when wet, they serve for general kayak handling by other boaters, and for some rescues, including self-rescue with a paddle float.

Tow Line. The tow line is an emergency device for towing disabled boats or fatigued, ill or injured kayakers. Its use is most often restricted to highly-proficient kayakers, since towing will often present more dangers than simply waiting it out or markedly slowing the travel pace. In-line towing is generally the most efficient, while alongside-towing may be needed if the towed party is having difficulty keeping his kayak stable.

The line is typically anchored behind the cockpit with either a jam cleat or a rope loop; the latter is nominally a custom fitting. The line is passed through a spliced eye or one made from plastic at the stern. It is fed forward to a terminal point behind the cockpit. This free or working end is secured to a cleat or custom-fitted "stuff box." Whichever system is used, it must be quickly deployable and cause no danger to the person towing. When deployed, the line is secured to the bow loop of the towed boat directly or to a carabiner which has been passed through the bow loop.

A floating towline of at least 20 meters and, preferably 40 meters length, is needed to cover the major family of towing options. Alongside-towing requires the least line. The longer towline is safer than a short one in rough water, particularly with a following sea.

Bow and Stern Toggles. These are plastic- or wooden-handled devices which are tied into small holes in the bow and stern. The circumference of the hole is sealed off with fill, which keeps water from entering the boat interior. (Some toggles are molded into the deck, a bad design because they are difficult to replace.) They are the most comfortable way to drag or carry a kayak and are also safest to use when towing a kayak to shore after a beyond-surf line capsize. Unlike simple rope loops, they will not twist around and potentially trap your fingers while you are in a rough surf.

Paddle with Drip Rings. The paddle is the simple device that you use to propel the craft. It is also one of the most critical gear items and deserves a thoughtful selection.

• *Paddle materials* are typically wood, fiberglass or polyethylene/aluminum. Wood is most elegant in looks, retains hand warmth and best transmits the feel of the water. It requires some upkeep to maintain appearance. Many wood paddles have an outer protective layer of material such as fiberglass or have a tip guard to protect the exterior surface. Woodies weigh in at the 2-1/2 to 3 pound range. Fiberglass requires little maintenance, is typically lightest weight (2-1/4 to 2-3/4 pounds), comes in a wide variety of different weights, shaft and blade flexes, and blade shapes. Polyethylene/aluminum paddles which have polyethylene blades with aluminum shafts, require almost no upkeep. They are the heaviest (3 to 3-1/2 pound range), but cost the least. New on the market are carbon-fiber paddles, which tip the scales in the 1-3/4 pound arena and lightweight your wallet accordingly.

Mats Mats Bay, Washington   Compliments of Pygmy Boats Incorporated

• *Paddle swing weight* characterizes how a paddle feels and how balanced it is. A paddle that has most of its weight in the shaft and has light blades will feel lighter than the equivalent-weight paddle with heavy blades and a light shaft. Ideally, blade and shaft weights should be balanced. To evaluate swing weight, select a group of similar weight paddles and move through your full paddling motion with each several times, then mentally compare. This aesthetic approach to paddle evaluation is no substitute for the real activity, but will help you narrow down your candidates.

• *Paddle size* is critically dependent upon the intended kayak activity and is also a matter of personal choice. Since you will be stroking the water hundreds or thousands of times on a single journey, paddle selection is right behind choosing the right kayak in order of importance.

Touring Kayak Paddles. Longer paddles are popular because they're suited to a mostly horizontal motion that's comfortable for extended paddling. An average size person should consider paddles 230-235 centimeters long. Tall people or those in wide boats, such as tandem kayaks, should look for 240-245 centimeters lengths. Size isn't so critical for light day touring -- many day tourers find that paddles in the 220-230 centimeter class are a good choice.

Whitewater Kayak Paddles. Shorter than touring paddles, whitewater paddles are used for quick strokes in tight spots, where your strokes will be more vertical. To estimate paddle size, lift one up and rest its center on your head (honest!), positioning your hands with elbows bent at roughly 90 degrees. The blades on the paddle that's the correct length will be 4-5 inches from the ends of your of your hands. An thumbrule estimate of a person's height to paddle size range: 5' 0" to 5' 4" - 197 to 200 centimeters; 5' 3" to 5' 8" - 200 to 201 centimeters; 5' 9" to 6' 1" - 202 to 204 centimeters; and 6' 2" to 6' 4" - 205 to 207 centimeters.

Sit-on-Top and Inflatable Kayak Paddles. Their greater width and high paddler placement requires slightly longer paddles than standard touring or whitewater kayaks mentioned above. If you'll be using your sit-on-top mainly in the surf, consider short touring paddles (around 220 centimeters) or whitewater paddles (around 206 centimeters). Because surf kayaking requires quick strokes and lots of bracing, these shorter paddles will be easier to use.

• *Blades* may be unfeathered or feathered, the latter meaning the blades are rotated relative to each other. While feather angles of 45 to 90 degrees. may be optimum for whitewater kayaking, smaller angles are easier on the wrist and are more typical for day kayaking and touring. Most whitewater paddles are right-hand controlled. Most touring paddles have take-apart shafts that allow for feathered or non-feathered configuration and choice of right- or left-hand control in the feathered mode.

Blades also come with other shape variations. A recent innovation is a blade shaped ever so slightly like a spoon. The claim is that these paddles grip the water more easily and create less cavitation. Another newer design has the bottom and top half of the blade shaped differently to provide the most mechanically advantageous energy transfer. Generally speaking, asymmetric cruising paddle blades will be quite a bit longer than they are wide.

• You can improve your grip on the paddle with a couple of simple add-ons. One is with the addition of *drip rings*. These simple devices are installed outside the position where each hand grips the shaft (i.e., between hand and blade). The rings prevent water from running down the shaft onto your arms on the lift side of the paddle stroke. The second is to use the same *tape* tennis players wrap around their racquet to improve gripping surface on the shaft.

Paddle Leash. The leash, which keeps the paddler from parting with his paddle, can be made using light shock cord. Wrist and paddle cuffs can be made by crimping cord sections together using precut pieces of stainless steel or by binding elastic sections together with twine.

Paddle Park. This clever device consists of a short cord with a loop at one end which slips over the paddle and a clip (a broom clip will do) at the other end to hold the paddle to the kayak. The park is a handy item when filming, fishing, eating or rescuing.

Breakdown Paddle. In the event of main paddle loss or breakage, a spare paddle or a friendly tow becomes a necessity. The most common mode is to store the spare (commonly, a paddle with a break-apart shaft) under taut elastics located on the rear deck.

Personal Flotation Device. The discussion of PFDs in the CANOEING (Daytime) section applies. Some additional considerations: 1) much kayak activity is ocean-oriented. Hedge on the flotation ability of your PFD if you envision paddling in rough sea conditions; 2) for sit-in kayaks, the PFD should allow unobstructed paddler motion within the confines of the cockpit; 3) consider models with small Velcro-sealed pockets for holding flares. (Together with a whistle safely tied to your PFD, you are now prepared for attracting rescue attention, if needed.)

Paddle Floats. Paddle floats or float bags are designed for unassisted kayak reentry in calm water for boaters unable to conduct an Eskimo Roll or underwater reentry and roll. It is a soft, strong, double-walled plastic bag that is inserted over the end of the paddle blade and inflated by mouth. Once inflated, it remains securely attached to the blade until the air is let out. Using the buoyant end of the paddle and the other end, which is secured to the kayak's deck elastics, the kayaker reenters the kayak. A *stirrup loop*, attached to the deck-secured paddle, is used by some as a step to assist in boat reentry. Some carry two float bags, generally using the second as a backup or, for a few, to allow a unique style of kayak reentry. Notes of caution: 1) like most other outdoor activities, emergencies happen. Think twice about going out alone; and 2) many crusty kayakers profess that self rescue with float bags takes a lot of practice to master. Don't bet your life on this option if you have not become proficient at it!

Oahu, Hawaiin Islands Compliments of Walt Bond

Pump/Bailing Container. The minimum gear to remove water from the bilges is a *large sponge*. Since sit-on kayaks have scuppers built-in to transport most water out of the cockpit, it is generally adequate for those boats. For sit-ins, full dependence on its use is most often restricted to day touring in quiet water. In any case, with the sit-in kayak, you have to remove your spray skirt to use this bailing technique.

A better sit-in option is a *portable hand pump*. The pump is stored under the elastic straps on deck. It is connected to a safety strap in case of a mishap. When needed, the kayaker slips the pump under the torso band of his spray skirt, places it low enough to immerse the lower suction tube into the bilges, and manually pumps the top handle. Note that the sight of a kayaker with a steady stream of water coming out from under his spray skirt can be startling to powerboaters out for a family cruise!

Sit-on kayakers might also think about carrying one portable hand pump with the group as a contingency. A pump with a lengthy suction tube might come in handy, should a faulty hatch seal or hull crack cause a problem-sized leak into sealed compartmentation.

Another sit-in option is to install a *manual bilge pump* or find a boat that has a built-in device. Most manufacturers place the pumping mechanism on the deck just aft of the cockpit. Also available are foot-operated pumps (e.g., Lendal model) which are attached to the footrest. These have a lower discharge volume than hand pumps, but their use does not interfere with the paddle stroke. Conservative expedition kayakers favor having both types of pumps on board. Consider getting extended-length suction hoses, as they can be used to help others empty out their kayaks if necessary.

Sponge. Keep a big, thirsty sponge tucked alongside your seat. You can mop up the last few dribbles of water with it, leaving you with a comfortably "dry" cockpit.

Body Braces. Braces are needed to allow the paddler leverage for maneuvering the kayak and critical for performing rolls. With good fortune, the original boat may be a perfect fit for at least the former function. If not, the braces can be retrofitted at key locations where high friction leverage is needed. For maneuvering, this probably means at least good friction contact at the feet and upper knees/thighs. For conducting rolls, add the requirements for high-leverage contact at the hips and back. One popular method is to glue custom-shaped pieces of closed-cell foam with contact cement at key locations.

Fenders. A couple of small fenders will keep your kayak exterior surface from getting beat up when at the dock. If you are with a social group, it is also a handy item when you tie up with other kayakers for a rest break, lunch, fishing or a strategy-planning session.

Drogue. A drogue or sea anchor is handy for keeping the bow headed into the wind without the effort of paddling. Applications are to maintain stability while fishing, eating, relieving yourself or even snoozing. More serious uses are to sit out a storm without undue drifting. A single-bucket design of canvas-like material and open at both ends is preferred by most over the harder-to-handle multi-string parachute-type drogue. The roughly 30-foot line passes through the bow toggle loop and the drogue line is fastened to the deck line. The trip line, attached at the rear of the drogue, is connected to a fitting or line within easy kayaker reach.

Chart Table. Rig a flat spot forward of the cockpit to strap down waterproofed maps and a compass. This is a convenience feature which precludes laying out the equipment at each navigation point. (See "Deck Fittings")

Personal Gear

As with other outdoor activities, the principal of wearing layered clothing applies. You add or subtract layers depending on weather conditions and your degree of exertion. There are unique differences, however. One is that you don't have the freedom to stop at any point, dig into your gear pack, and change into the optimal outfit. Changing gear in a kayak demands more advanced planning of what you might need during the day, making it accessible, and having the dexterity to make the change while floating about. (There are few trips where you would want to put in to shore every time you made a major gear change.)

In a sit-in kayak, your lower body is sheltered from the wind and waves. A good thing, because changing gear on your lower extremities is a bit of work. With sit-ons, both upper and lower body are exposed, but this is balanced by the greater freedom available to make a change. In both cases, the upper torso is exposed. In the discussion below, we offer general *examples of outfits* (not including the standards like sunglasses, sunscreen, etc.) that might serve your needs in the order from warm weather to successively cooler conditions.

Warm weather: shorts or swim suit, "T"-shirt, sandals, paddling gloves, sun hat

Cool weather: warm shorts, long-sleeve "T"-shirt, warm vest, sandals with socks, sailing gloves or pogies, sun hat. An option is to substitute a paddling jacket, dry-suit or wet-suit top for the upper torso clothing.

Cold weather: long pants under dry suit pants, long-sleeved "T"-shirt and warm sweater under dry suit top, sandals with sox or wet-suit booties, pogies or wet-suit gloves, pullover hat under sun hat. An option is to substitute a wet suit for the upper and lower torso clothing.

Shorts. A loose fitting *swim suit* may do the trick in hot weather. A quick-drying nylon suit with a mesh interior will serve well. Some use *padded Lycra shorts* which are similar to their bicycling kin. For cooler weather, the sequence for improved warmth might be *Lycra shorts with a neoprene bottom*, then *pure neoprene shorts*. For those not into neoprene, the *guide shorts* found in many river shops (heavier, quick-drying material with a mesh liner) may be a better choice.

Long Pants. Cold-weather kayakers sometimes pull a pair of full-length *cycling tights* over their shorts for leg warmth in cool weather. Others opt for the old *wool-trouser* standard that keeps popping up in activities throughout this book. There is a strong contingent that prefers quick-drying, *heavy synthetic-pile pants*, and leans heavily towards comfortable-fitting sweatpants. For severe weather, paddling and dry-suit pants are the most frequent outer-layer choice.

"T"-Shirt. Very hot weather kayaking is one of the few instances where *cotton* might be recommended. Wet it down and any breeze running through it will cool you. For warm weather, consider a *polypropylene* tee-shirt. Short sleeve models are adequate, unless your kayaking day may turn cool or you sunburn easily. If you are sensitive to the sun, there is *sunblock clothing* that filters UV radiation as well as SB 30 sunblock. (Most light clothing is inadequate at this UV blocking function.) Even with this clothing, it is wise to use a sunblock on any exposed or particularly sensitive skin surfaces.

Sandals/Socks. Footwise, *watersports sandals* work well in warm or moderate conditions. Your choice will depend on what's comfortable for you in a kayak, yet provides the needed hard soles for bracing against the foot pegs and protects your feet from sharp objects when you step ashore. (Also see the discussion of "Camp Shoes/Land Shoes" in the VEHICLE-ACCESSIBLE CAMPING activity.) In cooler weather, a popular option is to wear *sandals with breathable, waterproof socks over a light pair of wool socks*. The inner layer supplies warmth, while the outer layer provides foot moisture-wicking ability coupled with water repellency. For cold weather, consider a neoprene *wet-suit bootie with a rigid sole*.

Morro Bay, California — Compliments of Sally Bond

Vest/Sweater. A *synthetic pile fleece vest* over a polypropylene "T"-shirt will keep the upper torso comfortable in cool weather while paddling. The logical extension for cold-weather boating is to go with a *full-length synthetic pile or wool sweater*. Preferred are high-necked styles that can be unbuttoned or unzipped to accommodate level of paddling exertion or weather change.

Paddling Outfit. So, what keeps you dry when paddling through the cool ocean spray or wind-whipped lake water? The answer is a paddling jacket, the breathable, waterproof overgarment that lets your body breathe while you furiously dig into the water with your paddles. Though materials vary, a favorite is a polyurethane outer layer that sheds the spray while a lightweight polyester fleece on the interior provides insulation and wicks away your body moisture. Not meant to keep you dry in a dunking, the classic jacket has an overflap-protected front zipper that lets you adjust ventilation, A typical model might have Lycra/Spandex cuffs and (high) neck, and an elongated back panel for warmth as well as for prevention of water seepage down to your bottom. Zippered stretch-mesh pockets, as well as flap-protected, zippered or Velcroed solid-material pockets are among the options offered -- most are placed on the jacket exterior.

Many jacket makers offer a matching set of pants. The full set is desirable to have for a sit-in kayak and a must-have for sit-on-tops. This lower torso wear has the same Lycra/Spandex material for its waistband and ankle cuffs and a zippers at the ankle area. Most are featured with small storage pockets.

Wet Suit. A wet suit won't keep you dry, but it will keep you warm. In cool weather, the preference is for *one-millimeter*, high-waisted wet-suit trousers ("Farmer John" style) and comparable thickness tops with plenty of armpit room. There are also "shorties," the same suit but cut off at the knees. There is limited constriction of movement with this weight suit. When restricted to use under cool, but not cold, ambient conditions, some cut out the arms all together. In icy waters, *three-to-four millimeter* thicknesses, comparable to what divers wear when penetrating depths of a hundred feet or more, are needed. The thicker suit is sufficiently constrictive to compromise full performance of some paddle strokes.

There are other drawbacks to wet suits. One, you have to don them ahead of time. It takes a kayak-wise Houdini to put the full suit on once in the kayak. Two, they trap your body heat very well, and you'll toast under most conditions. Three, they also can become rank when worn for extended periods of time without being aired and sunned out. Some sportsmen make a habit of taking their wetsuits to the shower with them at each available opportunity. (See the CANOEING (Daytime) and WATERSPORTS activities for additional information.)

Dry Suit. Most United States coastal waters are relatively cold. Survival time of immersion at 60-degrees Fahrenheit (60°F) is seven hours, at 50°F survival is three hours and 40°F is one hour. "Life" only gets worse at lower water temperatures. Thus, unless you are in warm water or are an expert kayaker who insists that kayaking is a "dry sport," a dry suit or wet suit is a must for frigid-water kayaking trips. Dry suits are usually one-piece waterproof nylon shells with interior mesh liners and sealed seams. They are designed to repel water, but require underlayers of clothing to maintain body warmth in cold water. Most have tight-fitting neoprene bands at the neck, wrists, waist and ankles, are fitted with waterproof zippers, and are devoid of exposed openings which might admit water. Unike the paddling jackets, most styles on the market have no pockets (or only a limited set) on the exterior. (Refer to the WATERSPORTS section for more information.)

Gloves/Pogies. Gloves prevent blisters. Many experienced paddlers wear them on extended trips to lighten the near-constant pressure on the palms. In moderate weather, a set of *boating gloves* should fill the bill. The gloves are constructed of heavy-duty nylon, have a gripping material in the reinforced palm and Velcro wrist closures.

In cold weather, the gloves of choice are *paddler's neoprene gloves*. The gloves are warm, waterproof and have a rough palm surface that is conducive to maintaining a firm paddle grip. Typically, the gloves have well-sealed seams and a Velcro closure at the wrists. The optimum choice of glove thickness is dependent on the water temperature in which they will be used.

Another popular option, specifically designed for a kayak paddle, are *pogies*. They are a combination of bag and palmless mittens that wrap around the paddle shaft. Your hand fits into the wrist opening so you can grab the paddle shaft inside the bag -- while the external fabric keeps the cold wind and spray off your hands. Neoprene Smittens and the simpler muffins are two examples of this item.

Brimmed Hat/Pullover Hat. A big, *floppy-brimmed hat* is essential to keep the sun off of your face and neck. Purchase a model (or make your own) which has a lanyard that can be cinched under your neck -- this prevents loss when wind gusts attempt to put your hat to flight. For cooler conditions, consider the hood of a waterproof outer shell worn over a squashed-down floppy brim cover, a low-profile baseball cap or a large peaked *trucker's hat.* The large peak provides facial protection when paddling into the wind. A pullover *neoprene hat*, as well as a *heavy wool pullover hat or balaclava* worn under a waterproof shell, are excellent choices for cold ambient conditions.

Helmet. Crash helmets are a must for ocean surfing and whitewater activities They are also highly desirable for kayaking in rough sea conditions. Dependent upon activity and boat type (sit-in or sit-on), the helmet is intended to keep your head from banging directly into the ocean floor, river rocks or the boat itself. Properties of a good kayaking helmet are discussed in the CANOEING (Daytime) section.

Relief Bucket and Bottle. When you're out on the water, nature calls require a little innovation. Since you can't "hang out" on the stern like on a sailboat, there are few options. If you have scuppers in your cockpit, use them. If not, a common alternative is to bring a small, flat bucket (and bottle, if it is called for) for relieving yourself. A couple of tries and a little innovation and you'll be a veteran. (Standing up is considered bad form -- besides, you'll soon be in the water!)

Safety

First Aid Kit. Securely wedge this vital gear into the cockpit, attach a lanyard, and tie it to a firm hold. Otherwise, when needed, you or your companion(s) may not be in a position to quickly and safely dig into a boat hatch to access it.

Signal Mirror/Whistle/Air Horn. A *signal mirror* is useful under sunlit conditions for attracting the attention of aircraft, other oceancraft or landlubbers. Lightweight and taking up little space, it also can be used to confirm the terrible state of your hair or other exposed features. Probably the most useful is a version of the USAF signal mirror. It has a sighting hole to assist you in orienting the mirror to reflect light to the location of the desired recipient. The whistle and airhorn are useful signaling devices both day and night and, possibly most important, in foggy conditions. In fog, they can be used to signal paddler location or to provide a distress signal within the group. All normally come with lanyards or clips for attachment around your neck or to your outerwear (mirror and whistle) or to kayak hardware (air horn).

U.S. Coast Guard-approved *whistles* provide a required sound level at a "shrill" frequency. Some models allow you to blow at multiple (simultaneous or non-simultaneous) frequencies, which opens up the option for an improved between-kayaker signal system. Fewer still are designed for cold-weather use. They are made from materials which won't stick to your lips, have no moving parts and are designed very thin so as not to trap water.

The *airhorn* is the noisemaker of choice on more remote trips or for trips which cross shipping lanes. It provides warning to larger craft, which might otherwise leave a string of kayak litter behind. (One long blast and two short blasts are the international warning signal to indicate you are a craft which maneuvers with difficulty.) A lung-powered airhorn, which puts out a high volume of noise, is preferred over a gas-operated version because of its reliability. Fasten the airhorn to the deck elastics with a long cord. A dose of reality: Since powered craft may not even hear an airhorn, the smartest move is always to try and stay out of their way.

Flare Gun and Flares. Day-trippers tend toward *ground-level flares* (typically sold in a small three-pack that will fit into a PFD pocket). The flare cap is pulled off and the flare automatically ignites. A *flare gun* will propel flares to altitudes that provide significantly improved visibility relative to flares placed at ground level. This is a contingency item for most day trips, but a necessary gear item for overnight and more remote adventures. You should be schooled in its safe and proper use before relying on it in an emergency situation.

Use waterproof flare containers to keep flares operational under all conditions. One clever option is to use plumbers' plastic pipe. Paint the containers a fluorescent orange to make them easier to find, day or night, and make a note of flare expiration dates.

Radar Reflector. See the KAYAKING (Overnight/Expedition) section.

Compass. Day-trippers generally find that a *compass on lanyard* tucked around the neck will do the job admirably. Major transits or trips in unknown waters may steer you to favor a *deck-mounted dome compass* firmly attached a bit ahead of your cockpit. The compass is held off of the deck by a small stand or binnacle. The choice is mainly one of convenience, since you don't have to keep pulling your compass out of your shirt for each reading. Some deck-mounted models have a battery attachment to provide lighting (usually in dull red so as not to obstruct night vision). Some are permanently fixed while others have a stand that can be readily removed from the kayak.

Coastal and Sea Charts. The charts should cover the planned area with some excess to allow spotting distant landmarks or to "cover your backside" if you extend the trip or inadvertently stray. Learn how to read the charts (e.g., general symbology including daylight and nighttime buoyage marks, coastal features, abbreviations) and also to interpret the charts in terms of identifying safe landing and protected shelter sites and their approaches. Store the charts in waterproof containers which have easy, repeatable access, spray waterproofing on the charts, or buy a flat, waterproof sleeve that allows you to slip in an unfolded chart. The latter option works well with the "Chart Table" item discussed above. (See the SAILING activity for more information on charts.)

GPS Receiver. The Cadillac of locating devices is the Global Positioning System (GPS) receiver, a waterproof, hand-held computer navigator. It is a costly investment, but rewards the buyer with position information to about 20 feet with the push of a button and a quick look at the appropriate chart. Key example situations for use are: 1) to establish speed and make an estimated time of arrival (ETA); 2) to support pinpoint location when rescue assistance is needed; and 3) to establish position during long sea transits or extended periods of poor visibility or when coastal landmarks are non-distinct or ambiguous.

Lower Colorado River — Compliments of Sally Bond

Current/Tide Tables. The tables are needed, in addition to the coastal charts mentioned above, to establish periods of safe approach to and exit from coastal landmarks and landing sites. Together with the coastal charts, these tables are also useful for establishing optimal routing in terms of minimum exertion and safety.

Waterproof Flashlight, Night Sticks. Most boaters consider this a standard gear item for all but short excursions in protected waters. Sometimes, day trips spill over into evening or a mishap extends the trip past nightfall. A *waterproof flashlight* with a setting for blinking an SOS would be a very valuable item to have in these circumstances.

Some kayakers cruise in the evening and beyond by design. Flashlights are useful in these instances for letting other craft know where you are. Some of these "night riders" keep extremely bright *strobe rescue lights* pinned to their PFDs, to help locate them in case of an accident at night.

Some paddlers use *"night sticks,"* chemicals in a tube that, when activated, glow with a green or red light. Typical size for a 12-hour duration stick is about that of a dinner-table candle. When attached to the kayak hull, they can serve as makeshift running lights (red to port, green to starboard).

Weather Radio. A simple weather radio, tuned to the National Oceanic and Atmospheric Administration's (NOAA) permanent broadcast channels, should be an essential component if you venture beyond coastal waters or are making overnight trips in general. Check the weather before departure and at least morning and night of each day you're on a paddling trip. The Canadians offer a similar 24-hour radio weather forecasting service. Many other seafaring countries offer a similar or reduced-scale service in their native languages.

Bang Stick. See the KAYAKING (Overnight/Expedition) section.

Accessories

Dry Pack(s). Equipment carried both inside the cockpit and in hatched compartments should be inside waterproof containers. In the latter case, this serves as gear protection not only should a rock or other object put a hole in the kayak, but also to account for the ever-present, insidious water leakage into "watertight" compartments. Any watertight bag or container can be used provided it can be handled, as well as opened and closed repeatedly, without damage. Examples discussed in the CANOEING (Overnight) section are applicable, with a couple of caveats. One is that bags must be sufficiently narrow to fit through the kayak deck hatch(s). The second is that the "trash bag" option (consider for short-duration trips, only) is more tenuous because the thin bags must be stuffed through hatches that are frequently sharp-edged.

Tool Kit

The repair and replacement gear that you bring depends upon type of kayak, trip duration, type of intended boat use, and degree of access to populated areas. For single day trips, a general guideline list is provided below.

Tools. Sample items are pliers (for wiring down loose items), adjustable wrench and screwdriver (for tightening down or replacing loose nuts, bolts and screws), and scissors (for cutting repair patches). Note that scissors in your first aid kit can serve double duty,

Repair Gear. Waterproof duct tape (as a temporary fix for small leaks) is the simplest line of defense for hull repair. Also, there are products such as Ding Stik, advertised as a durable epoxy for quick and permanent patching of small cracks and holes. They are designed to work on plastics, fiberglass and metal surfaces.

Replacement Gear. Examples are spare nuts, bolts, screws, wire and bungee cords.

Secondary Activities

Kayak trips can be linked with other activities, such as HIKING, WATERSPORTS and both LAND and SEA FISHING. Refer to those sections for the associated unique gear needs.

KAYAKING
(Daytime)

Select items based on trip needs and worst-case weather conditions.

ITEM	DATE				
Boat Gear					
Boat Rack & Tie Downs/Locks					
Kayak/_Sponsons_					
Spray Skirt					
Bow Line/Grab Line/Tow Line					
Bow & Stern Toggles					
Paddle & Drip Rings					
Paddle Leash/Paddle Park					
Breakdown Paddle					
Personal Flotation Device					
Paddle Floats					
Pump/Bailing Container					
Sponge					
Body Braces					
Fenders					
Drogue					
Chart Table					
Water Jug/Water Bottle(s)					
Collapsible Water Bag					
Portable Ice Chest					
Ice & "Blue Ice"					
Permit(s)					
Personal Gear					
Shorts					
Long Pants*					
"T"-Shirt					
Sandals/Socks					
Vest/Sweater*					
Paddling Outfit					
Wet Suit*					
_Dry Suit_*					
Gloves/Pogies*					
Brimmed Hat/Pullover Hat*					
Helmet					
Bandanna/Sweatband					
Towel					
Change of Clothes (sightseeing)					
Hiking Shorts/Land Shoes					
Daypack					
Toilet Paper/_Toilet Trowel_					
Relief Bucket & Bottle					
Safety					
First Aid Kit (see FIRST AID)					

KAYAKING
(Daytime)

ITEM	DATE				
Water Filter/Tablets					
Sunglasses & Lanyard					
Sunscreen/Lip Balm					
Insect Repellent					
Signal Mirror/Whistle/*Airhorn*					
Radar Reflector					
Locator Beacon/VHF Radio^					
Waterproof Matches & Lighter					
Fire Starter/Heat Tabs*					
Emergency Blanket*					
Flare Gun & Flares					
Compass/Coastal & Sea Charts					
GPS Receiver					
Current/Tide Tables					
Timepiece					
Thermometer					
Pocket Knife					
W/P Flashlight, Night Sticks#					
Extra Batteries & Bulb#					
Reading Glasses & *Repair Kit*					
Nylon Cord					
Phone Change					
Weather Radio					
Bang Stick					
Pen & Notepad					
Accessories					
Camera; Extra film & Battery					
Camera Bag, Lens Cleaning Kit					
Brochures, Articles, Books,					
Binoculars					
Siting Pad (land use)					
Sewing Kit					
Dry Pack(s)					
Resealable Plastic Food Bags					
Litter Bag					
Auto Tool Kit					
Spare Keys/Credit Card/$					
Tool Kit					
Tools					
Repair Gear					
Replacement Gear					
Snacks (see MEALS section)					

Italicized items are optional (niceties or special purpose). *cold weather items #night-kayaking gear

KAYAKING (Overnight/Expedition)

See INDEX for checklist items not discussed below.

The overnight kayaking activity is focused on all-weather kayaking in both inland/protected coastal waters and on the open sea. Expedition kayaking implies making trips of days/weeks duration in remote and/or little-traveled locations. We believe that neither trip allows any hedges on gear for your or the group's safety. Safety-related equipment redundancy is a necessity. As an example, there should be at least two rescue packages with each kayaking party that include a spare paddle, stirrup loop, a portable bilge pump and a floating tow line. Like other group outdoor activities, many of the gear items discussed below can be shared amongst individual members (e.g., tent, cooking gear, water filter).

Gear packing and storage in the hatch compartments require some forethought. Gear items must fit through the hatch entry, requiring that you purchase duffels and dry bags of suitable diameter and weed out oversize equipment. The two-burner stove that you use for camping may have to give way to a backpacking stove, for example. No matter the number of hatches, the gear should be weight-distributed in roughly equal parts fore and aft and side to side. The equipment bags should be tightly stuffed together or tied together if there is a chance of their shifting in rough water. Place gear to which you might want most ready access nearest the hatches. When storing in (typically-hard-to-reach) open compartment space, a popular method is to tie each gear bag strap or loop to a single accessory cord. Tugging on the lead line brings out each bag in its pre-tied sequence.

Safety Considerations: 1) review the **GENERAL CONSIDERATIONS** and TEN ESSENTIALS sections; 2) review the "Safety Considerations" of the KAYAKING (Daytime) activity; 3) develop plans for contacting rescue units in an emergency; 4) practice techniques needed to extricate an injured paddler from the boating area; 3) err on the conservative side for bringing contingency gear, including food and stove fuel; and 4) bring contingency boat patching/repair equipment (and know how to use it).

In the checklist, items that are considered optional (niceties or special purpose) are *italicized*. Items noted with an asterisk(*) are for cold weather and those for night kayaking noted with a pound sign(#). Gear nominally reserved for expeditions is noted with a carrot mark(^).

<u>Boat Gear</u>

Kayak. Many of the kayaks discussed in the prior section can be used for overnighters and short tours. The extended-touring or expedition kayak is effectively the upper end of the kayak spectrum introduced in the prior section. They are larger, have significantly more cargo space and can be paddled efficiently when loaded with gear. These stable, comfortable boats are better at "tracking" (staying on course) and sit lower in the water to minimize wind effects. Touring kayaks are in the 60-80-pound weight range with typical widths of 21-24 inches and lengths of 15-17 feet and beyond.

Currently, most long-distance touring kayakers prefer hardshell kayaks. They favor *fiberglass hulls* over polyethylene because of its improved stiffness, better abrasion resistance and the improved leak-resistance of its bulkheads relative to plastic boats over time. In addition, customizing the plastic boats is generally limited to addition of deck fittings, together with basic bulkhead and hatch alterations (probably more than adequate options for all but the most demanding paddlers). On the debit side, fiberglass is not as shock resistant as polyethylene, requires more in the way of general hull upkeep, and is significantly more expensive.

The aerodynamic hull shaping and cockpit features previously discussed in the KAYAKING (Daytime) section are even more critical here. The exception is that a narrower *cockpit* is preferred, with the paddler supported in much the same way as the river paddler -- support at the feet, knees, thighs and seat. (The kayaker can compensate for lack of support by gluing custom-shaped pieces of closed-cell foam with contact cement.)

Brooks Peninsula, Vancouver Island, Canada Compliments of Kees Kolff

A revival of an old Eskimo concept for fiberglass boat enthusiasts is the *pod* (also called a cockpit liner or sea sock). Currently, pods are fitted as a separate item after boat purchase. The pod is a fiberglass capsule that seals off the space needed by the paddler from the rest of the hull. In the event of capsize, the pod takes in pints versus gallons of water and empties almost completely when the kayak is righted, then leaned over on its side. The self-contained unit has built-in thigh braces to permit rolling and the roll can be conducted without the use of a spray cover. The pod's rim is attached to the mating rim on the kayak, which is formed inside the deck opening. It inherently reinforces the center section of the kayak. Though some kayaks with pods have a large non- or lightly-bulkheaded design, most leading kayak designers agree that to make pods completely safe for all conditions of use requires fitting them with bulkheads. On the negative side, the cockpit can make one claustrophobic and it makes previously reachable space inaccessible.

The touring kayak has forward and aft *hatches* which must be wide enough to accept gear to be carried; some kayaks are fitted with a hatch fitted into the forward bulkhead for long items such as fishing rods. Robust hatches, which cannot be knocked off or displaced during deep-water rescues or when breaking seas crash across the deck, are a necessity for lengthy at-sea tours or expeditions. Hatches that are held in place by flimsy twin buttons, thin shock cord or snap clips may be acceptable for near-harbor kayaking, but questionable for surf entry/exit and boating in rough coastal chop. Screw-on hatches with neoprene inner covers are considered a limited cost, but robust, option. Frank Goodman's or the Henderson hatch are examples of designs favored by many touring experts.

Deck fittings for gear such as tie-down, towing and grab lines become more of a necessity for the longer, more-exposed kayak tours. Recessed deck fittings are preferred. They keep grab lines close to the deck. With no protrusions, there is less possibility of boat damage or personal injury during deep water rescues. Finally, there is less chance of snagging spray skirts, waterproof bags and the like with the recessed hardware.

The Ultimate Kayak. Though out of the general scope of this book, we would be remiss about discussing one additional kayak option. The few world-class kayakers with month-long journeys into uninhabited areas or ocean crossings in mind (or lesser-goal-motivated paddlers with big wallets) tend to take a very different tack. Frequently, they opt for the *rigid-frame-and-flexible-fabric-skin hull designs*. They are the direct descendants of the Inuit kayaks updated with modern components. In terms of combined dependability, efficiency and toughness, these are the best cruising kayaks ever built.

Bunsby Island, Vancouver Island, Canada   Compliments of Kees Kolff

The internal frame or skeleton is normally made from shaped wood or aluminum. The traditional skin fabric was cotton, although the trend is toward use of polyester cloth. The fabric is typically coated with Hypalon, a synthetic, rubber-like coating. A lesser number are coated with vinyl, which is lighter and less expensive than Hypalon, and a few hulls use nylon fabric with a urethane coating. These designs are heavier than their fiberglass counterparts and slightly less paddling efficient than the higher-quality hardshells. Most can be disassembled with a few clips and nuts and are transformable into a bag of struts and braces alongside a rolled-up skin.

Most fabric boats have sponsons along the outside edges of the hull, providing flotation as well as keeping the skin taut. Most hardshell boats contain their flotation in the tight ends of the bow and stern. As a result, many hardshells tend to rotate freely when swamped. With the well-distributed sponsons, the fabric-and-fabric kayaks are far more stable when swamped. Some tandem boats have individual cockpits for each paddler, while others have a large cockpit holding both with a two-hole spray skirt covering the cockpit.

Finally, a few words about the two predominant methods for holding the skin taut to the frame. Some kayaks have a snug-fitting skin snapped to the frame with the final skin tension achieved as the paddler inflates air bladders within the skin structure. These boats tend to have excellent flotation and stability. Other manufacturers go with a skin that must be pulled tight and hooked to the frame -- a slower, more difficult, but less expensive alternative. Assembly time can range from five minutes to half an hour, depending on model and manufacturer.

__Personal Gear__

Some of the personal gear used for kayaking serves a double purpose for camping on overnight trips. The two key questions are: 1) is the gear dry or can it be dried quickly to make it useful in camp (e.g., boating shorts, thermal underwear, long pants, sweater); and 2) do I want to use kayaking gear in a camping environment (e.g., paddling outfit)? With proper selection, most gear can serve dual use. Where the answers are in the negative, the solution is to bring additional gear. This is why you will see entries in the checklist that include items such as "Camping Shorts/Long Pants," "Long-Sleeve Shirt/Sweater," and "Raingear."

Camping Gear

Choice of camping gear is limited by kayak loading and storage space, as well as hatch size. Kayakers are somewhere between backpackers and canoeists relative to what can be carried on an extended trip. Some kayakers carry items that cannot fit into a hatch secured to the deck elastics in order to enhance carrying capacity. This will affect the roll-stability of the kayak, a most serious issue when in rough water or surfing into a beach. Also, as a kayaking instructor once expounded, however, "You can always strap it on topside, but it may just wind up being company for the fishies!"

Bunsby Island, Vancouver Island, Canada — Compliments of Pete Lauritzen

Safety

Radar Reflector. It is not generally wise to "play" around in shipping lanes, although trips such as those from the Southern California coast to the Channel Islands inherently cross busy shipping passages. A "corner reflector," which provides a large radar cross-section to ships or boats having radar as part of their navigation aids, can be bought or made by hand using 16 S.W.G. (Standard Wire Gauge) *aluminum or aluminum alloy circular discs and clips* to fasten the disks together. Discs should be at least eight inches in diameter and near perpendicular (at right angles) to each other. (If you don't have the tools to construct the sides within 1-2 degrees of each other, buy the reflector.) The assembly should be hung as high as possible and suspended vertically from three apexes such that the trough formed by the three enclosed sides would act as a rain catcher.

An easy, though much lower performing, alternative is to lightly form *aluminum kitchen foil* into a ball about nine inches in diameter and place in an open-mesh bag.

Suspend the bag from the end of a thin metal rod or secure it under the reardeck elastics.

Locator Beacon. Think about carrying an *Emergency Position Indicating Radio Beacon* (EPIRB). Pull the tab and this little transmitter begins to shriek out a distress signal. You have to register and license each EPIRB, but if you are paddling in remote waters, the paperwork may be worth it. Paddling closer to home, you might consider cellular telephones or *VHF marine radios*. Neither are cheap, but could be well worth the investment, depending on the level of challenge of your itinerary. (More is said about each device in the SAILING section.)

Bang Stick. This self-defense weapon is a useful precaution for a remote tour that may enter shark-infested waters. It is gear that is rarely brought along in U.S. waters, but is far more common in other (particularly) tropical seas. Operation of the bang stick requires releasing a safety pin and forcing the power head, containing a 12- or 20-gauge shotgun shell, against a firm surface. The device is made to fit over a spear without threading. The explosive effect with direct contact is to injure or kill, while the shock wave from a proximity blast may drive the shark off. Familiarize yourself thoroughly with the use of this weapon before attempting use. Ensure that the safety pin is secure and cannot be accidentally dislodged. Do not hold the device in line with any part of your body when activating. The bang stick must be completely submerged if the recoil is to be absorbed by water.

Kyuquot Sound, Vancouver Island, Canada — Compliments of Pete Lauritzen

Tool Kit

The items noted below are in addition to those discussed in the KAYAKING (Daytime) section.

Tools. Bring any special tools which might be needed to repair the rudder linkage. For expedition-level kayaking, some groups carry a waterproof torch for permanent minor or major hull repairs. Add the tools needed for adjustment or repair of camping gear as described in the BACKPACKING activity.

Repair Gear. For fiberglass boats, take along extra cloth, sandpaper, a can of resin with its small bottle of hardener and a brush. Familiarize yourself with the properties of the mixture and the general repair process before you leave. Similar patch-and-glue repair kits are on the market for PVC inflatables and plastic kayaks.

Add a sewing kit for repair of wearing apparel, tent, sleeping bag etc., as described in the BACKPACKING activity. There are also spot- and seam-repair sealants for neoprene clothing items.

Replacement Gear. Bring accessory cord to replace broken or lost bow or stern toggles. As a hedge, bring stainless-steel clips for joining shock-corded elastic. These items, which are crimped onto the cord sections with pliers, will serve to repair deck elastics. See the BACKPACKING activity for additional land-use replacement items.

Secondary Activities

Kayak trips can be linked with other activities, such as HIKING, WATERSPORTS and both LAND and SEA FISHING. Refer to those sections for the associated unique gear needs.

Bunsby Island, Vancouver Island, Canada — Compliments of Kees Kolff

KAYAKING
(Overnight/Expedition)

Select items based on trip needs and worst-case weather conditions.

ITEM	DATE				
Boat gear					
Boat Rack & Tie Downs/Locks					
Kayak					
Spray Skirt					
Bow Line/Grab Line/*Tow Line*					
Bow & Stern Toggles					
Paddle & Drip Rings					
Paddle Leash/Paddle Park					
Breakdown Paddle					
Personal Flotation Device					
Paddle Floats					
Pump/Bailing Container					
Sponge					
Body Braces					
Fenders					
Drogue					
Chart Table					
Water Jug/Water Bottle(s)					
Collapsible Water Bag					
Dry Pack(s)					
Permits					
Personal gear					
Swim Suit/Kayaking Shorts					
Long Pants*					
"T"-Shirts					
Sandals/Socks					
Vest/Sweater*					
Paddling Outfit					
Wet Suit*					
*Dry Suit**					
Gloves/Pogies*					
Brimmed Hat/Pullover Hat*					
Helmet					
Bandanna/Sweat Band					
Towel					
Camping Shorts/Long Pants					
Underwear					
Thermal Underwear*					
Long-Sleeve Shirt/Sweater*					
Parka (w/p s/s)/Jacket*					
Windbreaker					
Raingear					
Head Netting					
Gloves & Mittens					
Land Shoes/Camp Shoes					
Land Socks					

KAYAKING
(Overnight/Expedition)

ITEM	DATE				
Camping Gear					
Tube Tent/Sleeping Bag Cover					
Tent & Rainfly					
Stakes & Poles					
Ground Cloth					
Tent Broom & Sponge					
Sleeping Bag (w/p stuff sack)					
Sleeping Pad					
Stove & Windbreak/Primer					
Fuel Bottle					
Fuel Funnel/Strainer					
Waterproof Matches & Lighter					
Cooking Pot					
Skillet/Frypan					
Non-stick Cooking Lubricant					
Scouring Pad					
Cooking Utensils					
Can Opener					
Eating Utensils					
Plate & Cup					
Biodegradable Dish Soap					
Sponge					
Paper Towels					
Litter Bag					
Spare Stuff Sacks					
Lantern					
Resealable Plastic Food Bags					
Daypack (storage/hiking)					
Hygiene					
Towel					
Wash Cloth					
Biodegradable Soap					
Biodegradable Shampoo					
Personal Toiletries/Ditty Bag					
Toilet Paper & Towelettes					
Toilet Trowel					
Sun Shower					
Laundry Bag					
Relief Bucket & Bottle					
Safety					
First Aid Kit (see FIRST AID)					

KAYAKING
(Overnight/Expedition)

ITEM	DATE				
Water Filter/Tablets					
Sunglasses & Lanyard					
Sunscreen					
Lip Balm					
Insect Repellent					
Signal Mirror/Whistle/*Airborn*					
Flare Gun & Flares					
Radar Reflector(^)					
Locator Beacon/VHF Radio(^)					
Weather Radio					
Fire Starter/Heat Tabs*					
Emergency Blanket*					
Compass					
Coastal & Sea Charts					
Current/Tide Tables					
GPS Receiver (^)					
Timepiece					
Thermometer					
Pocket Knife					
W/P Flashlight, Night Sticks#					
Extra Batteries & Bulb#					
Reading Glasses & Repair Kit					
Nylon Cord					
Bang Stick					
Phone change					
Pen & Notepad					
Accessories					
Camera; Extra Film & Battery					
Camera bag, Lens Cleaning Kit					
Brochures, Articles, Books					
Binoculars					
Sitting Pad (land use)					
Sewing Kit (see **Tool Kit**)					
Indoor Games					
Auto Tool Kit					
Spare Keys/Credit Card/$					
Tool Kit					
Tools					
Repair Gear					
Replacement Gear					
Meals (see MEALS section)					

Italicized items are optional. *cold weather gear #night-kayaking items ^expeditionnary items

SAILING (Daytime/Overnight)

See INDEX for checklist items not discussed below.

This activity focuses on sporting craft under sail. This includes Class A (those less than 16 feet in length), Class I (16-26 feet) and Class II (26-40 feet) boats. The scope of the activity varies from daytime outings to "overnight" adventures. Overnight, in this section's context, means anything from a true overnighter to long-range, port-to-port sailing. There is no intent to cover needs for such high-powered endeavors as world-class racing, transoceanic ventures or the general upper end of sailing activities. Rather, the aim is to deal with the needs of sailors, ranging from learners to moderately-accomplished seafarers. Included in the discussion below is the assumption that the sailcraft may have an auxiliary motor. (However, the more detailed discussion of boat motors is provided in the POWERBOATING section.)

There is no intent to describe sailing in depth, rather to provide an introduction to the activity. Minimal attention is paid to equipment that is integral to the boat structure, other than Coast-Guard-mandated safety equipment. The emphasis is on gear that you may need to transport from home to the launch area and/or recheck before actually launching the boat; this includes replenishable boat items, portable safety equipment, repair gear, personal hygiene and clothing items, as well as accessory equipment that can make the boating experience more pleasurable. Obviously, many of the listed items can be ignored if your boat is already dockside, rather than brought in by trailer.

There is also a limited discussion of boat trailers that concentrates on their key features. For a more-detailed treatment in any area, or for information about subjects not treated here (e.g., launching by ramp or sling, Rules of the Road, boating technique, navigation, weather, etc.), we refer you to the Reference sources. If you plan on linking your boating with other activities (e.g., hiking, camping, watersports, fishing), refer to the relevant activity to identify the additional gear needed.

Safety Considerations: 1) review the **GENERAL CONSIDERATIONS** and TEN ESSENTIALS sections; 2) if you are skippering, you need to know the Rules of the Road -- this includes prudent seamanship when docking, undocking and anchoring. If you are crewing, you should be adept and safe in carrying out orders. If you are a passenger, you should understand how to stay out of harm's way and, generally, stay out of the way; 3) at least one passenger should know the basics of operating the boat and how to contact assistance in an emergency; 4) if you are the boat owner, it is your responsibility to outfit the craft with the necessary navigation, communication, weather, emergency, boat repair and other gear needed for safe boating and know how to use them; 5) perform a boat inspection each time before getting underway, including testing for engine-compartment fumes, ensuring watertight-status/closure of drains and sea-cocks, checking that safety equipment is aboard and operational; 6) learn to "read" the weather and sea state and develop a sense as to when to seek the safety of a protective shelter; 7) learn to use and wear a PFD whenever the situation even remotely calls for it; 8) ensure that you understand your boat's emergency procedures and your personal responsibilities; 9) develop swimming skills commensurate with the level of activity planned; 10) learn basic first aid; 11) bring cold- and wet-weather contingency gear if there is any doubt about its availability; 12) let friends and/or the harbormaster know your plans, including destination and estimated time of arrival (ETA) -- leave your call letters; 13) learn how to signal distress and interpret responses; and 14) consider bringing along a cell phone for near-shore sailing and plan to carry a single-sideband radio and EPIRB for remote touring and/or blue-water adventures.

In the checklist, items that are considered optional (niceties or special purpose) are *italicized*. Items noted with an asterisk(*) are for inclement weather, while those with a pound sign(#) are for gear needed at night. The cross symbol (†) is for gear generally not brought along for day ventures, but which are candidate items for overnight and multi-day trips. The plus symbol(+) indicates equipment associated with an auxiliary engine(s).

<u>Boat Gear</u>

Boat Trailer. *Larger boats*, typically with inboards, are rarely trailerable. However, the greater portion of powered craft and many sailcraft can be, and are, trailered to the launch site. The trailer should be compatible with your boat size and fully-loaded weight. It should leave no major area of the boat unsupported. Supports may be rollers, pads or a combination. Rollers are most convenient for launching, while pads provide the best, most broadly-distributed support.

St. Johns, Caribbean

The hitch size should be compatible with the load placed on it -- the hitch assembly generally has hitch/lock-ball combination with a safety chain attached to both ball assembly and trailer as a backup. Manual winches are acceptable for most *Class-I boats*, but an electric winch is essential for *larger Class I and most Class-II craft*. The winch post supports the winch and holds the bow of the boat firmly in place while trailering. In addition to this frontal support, a wide tie-down strip is needed which secures the corners of the stern to prevent sideways shifts.

Waterproof tail lights that double as brake lights and turn signals are necessary. Trailer brakes are recommended if the trailer weight is over 1500 pounds. Brakes may be hydraulic or electric, controlled by cables to the tow car and activated when you press the brake pedal. The trailers are two-wheelers with a tongue wheel for frontal trailer support when it is unhitched. The tongue wheel can be cranked up and stowed for trailering. A key note: Bring a spare trailer tire along when you head for your launch site.

The smallest or *Class-A boats*, less than 16 feet in length, can be carried on the roof of many automobiles. The methods for securing them are nearly identical to those as described in the CANOEING (Daytime) section, the exception being that the sailing craft do not have thwarts for tying into. To compensate for this, an increased number of ties in the sailboat's center section are used.

The trailers for these small boats are also less complex than those described above, being generally winchless and without a tongue wheel. The two most common types are the "A"-frame and "T"-frame models. The T-frame trailer has a strong center beam and is frequently adjustable to best accommodate different boat lengths. The A-frame type, while not usually adjustable, can be combined with a launching dolly so the boat can be moved on its dolly directly onto the trailer, thus avoiding any heavy lifting. The dolly is self stowing on the trailer and locks into position.

Sailboat. There are a multitude of sailboat options. The discussion below provides the key characteristics which differentiate sailboat types and their intended use.

• There is a fair diversity of basic *keel types*, starting with the division between monohulls (single-hulled vessels) and multihulls (catamarans and trimarans). There are a good many more monohulls and their key distinguishing feature is their deeper draft. Monohulls, the focus for the discussion below, can be divided into boats with a retractable centerboard or daggerboard and those with a fixed keel.

Small Centerboard Boats. The former are generally referred to as small centerboard boats, dinghies or centerboard dinghies. Their key advantage is that they can sail in shallow water and run ashore on beaches without damage. Both centerboards and daggerboards can be retracted flush with the hull, although the daggerboard is hoisted simply by pulling it directly upward into the fore-aft aligned trunking. In contrast, the upward pressure on a centerboard causes the unit to rotate about a pin until it is secure in a similarly-sized and oriented trunking. The advantage of a centerboard over a daggerboard is that it will kick up of its own accord if it touches bottom.

In a dinghy, the hull shape and broad beam play an important part in the stability of the craft. Hulls are nominally round-bottomed or hard-chined (built to simulate a rounded surface by joining the flat siding pieces together). Owing to a relatively broad beam, the average dinghy is, initially, fairly stable. However, after a certain point, stabilization decreases as the boat heels. The dinghy can capsize since its center of gravity is higher than that of a keelboat. Crew weight is used to keep the boat upright and this is an important difference between dinghies and small keelboats. Larger dinghies sometimes utilize a ballasted centerboard, which gives the boat improved roll stability at the expense of ease in centerboard manipulation.

Keelboats. In contrast to the centerboard boats, keelboats usually have a fixed ballast keel under the hull, which places the center of gravity well below the waterline. These boats are almost impervious to capsizing, short of hull punctures, water pouring through an open hatch when the boat is heeling in a strong wind, or other problematic situations where water can enter sealed spaces in an unbalancing fashion. In general, the more the boat heels, the greater are the forces that act to right the boat. These boats also have a self-bailing cockpit, using scuppers to redivert cockpit water back overboard. These are the "blue water" sailing craft.

The variety of keel profiles includes the conventional full (or long) keel, cut-away keel, fin and skeg racing keel, bulb and keel with spade rudder, fixed keel with centerboard, twin keels and others. Though the conventional full keel was the standard for cruising yachts for decades, the recent trend has been toward styles developed for racing yachts. These are the deep, narrow fin keels combined with either free-standing rudders or rudders attached to a narrow support or skeg.

The fixed keel with centerboard (keel centerboarders, typically 18-to 24-foot boats with a light centerboard) offers the ability to ply shallower waters. Another variable-draft option includes lifting keelboats, where the entire keel is hydraulically or mechanically raised and lowered. There are also twin-bilge-keelboats (and even triple keel) which are very popular in tidal waters. Their draft is less than single-keelers and the boat weight can be supported by the keels without damage, an advantage in a drying mooring. The disadvantage is that they do not sail as well as single-keel boats under most conditions.

• There are a number of *basic hull designs* in terms of the hull cross-sectional shape. Several of the more prominent designs are described below.

V-Section Hull. The V-section presents minimal wetted surface (i.e., that part of the hull and keel in contact with the water). Boats with this design often are combined with a long-keel and typically have narrow hulls. They heel more than most designs because the initial stability is relatively low.

U-Section Hull. An established shape with high stability, this hull design is often accompanied by a bulb keel (a slender upper keel with a bulbous lower section). It is considered one of the fastest shapes because it enables small and medium-sized yachts to plane (effectively, to ride more on the surface of the water). This design is not considered so suitable for larger (particularly, cruising) boats as it provides an uncomfortable ride in rough seas.

St. Thomas, Caribbean

• At the higher-performance end, there are a relatively limited number of boats that utilize more *exotic hull shapes*. A few examples are provided.

Semi-Circular-Section Hull. Seldom found in their true shape, these are often combined with the U-shape, for example. When mated with a fin keel, this overall design provides the minimum wetted surface and consequently, the least skin friction.

IOR Hull. The International Offshore Rule (IOR) design is one of the best hull sections, since it promotes both a small wetted surface combined with a large righting moment. At high speeds, the boats using this design are very seafarer-friendly. The construction of this hull-type is relatively complicated and expensive.

Double-Chine Hull. A variation of the IOR cross-section, the smoother-flowing IOR design is imitated using two chines, which makes the hull construction easier and, thus, less costly. The performance achieved is very similar to that for the IOR hull.

• Another variable in differentiating between boat types is the *rigging*. The key differentiation is the way in which mainsails and foresails are combined, and the number and arrangement of masts. The most common rigging types are generalized below.

Cat. The simplest single-masted rig is called a cat or uni-rig and consists of a mainsail alone. Boats with this rig are typically single-handlers such as dinghies and Class-A catamarans. They are a favorite for learners and both near-marina and small lake boaters.

Sloop. With the addition of a sail forward of the mainsail (called a foresail), the boat is rigged as a sloop. This configuration has more wind-catching sail area and allows more versatility in using the wind for sailing. The majority of sailing yachts and racing boats today are of this design.

Cutter. A cutter employs two foresails (a jib and a staysail) and offers an increased number of sail combinations. This rig is most common to sailors on smaller cruising boats, although some larger craft also use it.

Yawl. On large yachts, a rig with two masts is more practical, particularly for cruising. Although having a large sail area, the individual sails are smaller and, therefore. easier to handle. If the aft mast -- the mizzen mast -- is relatively small and stepped aft of the rudder post, it is classified as a yawl. This rig is relatively uncommon in modern boats.

Ketch. In the ketch rig, the mizzen mast is typically larger and is located forward of the rudder post. It is far more prevalent than the yawl rig. Though usually rigged with a single foresail, the employment of two foresails is not uncommon.

Schooner. If the aftermast is taller than the foremast, the boat is described as a schooner. The schooner rig, which can also have three masts (or more), is not a common sight in modern yachting. One of its major drawbacks is that the large mainsail is difficult to handle. Though the rig performs well off the wind, it is not very efficient to windward.

• Wood was the classic *boat-building material* in the past. Many well-maintained or restored craft with 40-year working lives or greater are not uncommon. A few medium- and large-size yachts are still built around the strength of steel, however it is heavy and subject to saltwater corrosion, particularly in warm, salty waters. Aluminum alloys are ideal boat-building materials, combining lightness and strength with relative freedom from saltwater corrosion. The catch is that it is still relatively expensive for all but the largest racing yachts and powerboats, since its welding involves special techniques. Some home-constructionists built boats using a ferro-cement poured into a steel-mesh skeleton, producing a quality (but again, heavy) hull when cement is skillfully applied. The latest technology produces very light and high-strength boats using such materials as foam and Kevlar sandwiches, end-grain balsa held by thin wooden skins inside and out, and carbon fiber.

However, fiberglass is the material of choice for most sailboat construction today. Its key virtues are flexibility, durability, low maintenance and reasonable cost. Fiberglass processes vary, with the rule of thumb being that less expensive processes tend to produce boats of less overall strength. Frequently, the hull and cockpit/deck sections are molded separately. The interior bulkheads, cabin access structure and deck support features are then bonded to the hull section. The basic hull and deck are reinforced throughout and specific high-stress areas are strengthened by separate techniques. Addition of floatation material is an integral part of the process. Many of the hull and deck construction processes, reinforcement and support are similar to those described in the POWERBOATING activity. Most often, the complete hull construction described above is accomplished prior to bonding of the hull to the deck/cockpit.

• There are *additional outfitting gear* that will make the boat more versatile, more convenient to use, more comfortable or provide some combination of these benefits. The practicality of using some gear is dependent on whether the boat is a sailcraft or powerboat, is underway or in port, as well as whether the specific boat design can accommodate the additional equipment.

Boarding Ladder. The boarding ladder may be an integral piece of boat equipment or a securely-latching portable add-on. It is sometimes helpful for dockside entry and exit, but is a must if you plan to engage in watersports activities. For powerboaters, it is also a standard safety item for getting overboard persons back on the boat.

For sailing, a ladder is rarely a permanent fixture, since it will interfere with crew movement on the deck. The retrieval of an overboard passenger is most often accomplished using good old "Norwegian steam," that is, to manually pull the person on board. On larger boats meant to sail in high sea, a (non-injured) waterlogged victim is required to swim to, and place his upper body inside of, a deployed sling in preparation for being winched aboard.

Anacapa Island, California Courtesy of Walt Bond

Stern Platform. Some larger sailcraft and powerboats with auxiliary jetdrive or inboard engines have an integral stern platform (also called swim steps) on the transom, near the waterline. The platform gives easy water access for watersports activities.

Canvas Covers. Few, if any, smaller sailboats can afford the luxury of having canvas covers for sun protection while underway. With sailing vessels, the problem is that the covers must not interfere with working the sails or reduce visibility -- a tall order. The same is true for many larger sailcraft, the exception for some boat designs being a small cover (or "dodger") near the cockpit area. This is a metal frame with canvas topping and, in some cases, a small vinyl windshield on the forward section to prevent any helmsman's visibility blockage. The dodger's purpose is to shield both the helmsman and cabin area companionway from direct spray.

In port or at anchor in warm-weather areas, some sailors pack a portable *canvas spray shield* which can be rigged over the boom with a couple of battens. The resultant construct serves as a topside shelter for sleeping in lieu of having a below-decks cabin. Another option is to lay out a similar rig with snap-on side curtains -- this increases the living space, regardless of weather.

For sun protection while underway, many powerboaters have a *Bimini* or navy top fitted by a boat dealer (some come with the feature factory-installed).

As a retrofit, this requires some additional mounting brackets that hold a tubular (generally) aluminum framework on which the cover is secured forward. The aft attachments are frequently the existing rear port and starboard cleats. If you want protection from the wind or spray, order a dodger or side curtains that have clear vinyl panels for visibility.

Convenient Gear Storage. Convenient, protected storage access on the *smaller day boats* is very limited. Ready access to such items as emergency gear, spare clothing, water and snacks is needed. Many day sailers are restricted to small built-in lockers and/or partially-exposed storage space, located so as not to interfere with the performance of normal sailing activities.

Powerboats typically have on-deck storage lockers built behind or under the seats or connected to the hull, although the latter will be at the expense of cockpit space. Water skis, paddles and fishing rods are frequently stored along the powerboat cockpit's interior sides in brackets. (Freedom of unobstructed movement around the cockpit is not such a critical issue, as it is for sailing.)

For larger day boats, there may be other usable spaces, such as a forward locker that houses the anchor and rode. The remaining solution is to store gear on deck in waterproof bags, using anything from plastic trash bags to the dry bags discussed in the CANOEING (Overnight) and KAYAKING (Daytime) activities. It is prudent to lash down this gear, regardless of sea state, and to place it in a non-interfering location.

For the *cruising class boats*, there are several additional options for stowage, counterbalanced by the fact that you will be carrying more gear aboard. These additional spaces are the cabin (including lockers below bunks and galley equipment), below the cabin floor, anchor/rode locker, lockers near the helm and even the bilges.

To *maximize cabin space usage*, repackage grocery items into zip-locking bags and waterproof plastic containers. Canvas duffel bags for personal gear store more easily than suitcases; if the bags don't have a lined pocket for wet clothing storage, use large plastic trashbags. Bed linen and blankets can be stored in a spare pillowcase during the day and sleeping bags returned to their stuff sacks. Small hammocks, sold in marine and sporting goods stores, can be bracket-mounted in the cabin interior and used to stow jackets, swim suits and other more frequently-used items.

Barbados, Caribbean

• A few words about *auxiliary engines for* sailboats. Most reasonably-sized sailing yachts rely on an inboard engine, while some use an inboard/outboard option.

Smaller yachts usually have an outboard(s) mounted on special brackets on the reinforced transom. The auxiliary engine(s) is normally used when leaving moorings or entering crowded anchorages where the use of sails is impractical or sometimes dangerous. (Some marina operators ban sailing within the confines of the general slip area.) Several types of engines, some of which may also be found on sailing craft, are discussed in the POWERBOATING section.

• The focus for *intended boat use* may range from pure daytime in-shore or lake fun sailing to racing to long-distance cruising. In many cases, the boat may support multiple uses, including support of other waterborne activities. The choice between the boat characteristics identified in the preceding discussion will be strongly influenced by the owner's intended uses. Some broad examples of popular choices, by primary intended use, are described below. (Transoceanic yachts have their own unique characteristics, which are beyond the scope of this book.)

Fun Boats. Built for short stints in protected in-shore areas, these small, simple and inexpensive craft run in sizes of about 7-13 feet and have a single, unstayed mast. Many can be carried on top of a car and all are easily trailerable. Numerous models are single sail, while some can be rigged as a cat or sloop. Most are constructed of fiberglass or plywood. They come in a variety of hull forms, with round, flat, or V-bottoms and range from the traditional dinghy to board boat (effectively a surf board with a sail). Practically all have built-in flotation and will remain afloat when capsized or upright and full of water. They are the best craft for the inexperienced to learn the fundamentals of sailing, as well as an excellent choice for pure recreation. They also serve as versatile yacht tenders. Fun boats and predominantly all day-sailing boats do not have self-bailing cockpits (in essence, the boat is an open, floating cockpit).

Day-Sailing Boats. The day sailer is a small sailboat under about 20 feet, safe and easy to handle, for daytime use by family or friends. All are trailerable. Predominantly all are sloop-rigged and have a centerboard, fin or twin-bilge keel. Many designs allow the use of high sail-area working rigs and some can accommodate use of spinnakers. Hulls are typically wood, plywood or fiberglass and hull forms include V- and U-bottoms, as well as semi-circular and double-chine designs. Nearly all have (or should have) built-in flotation and some are designed to be self-righting in the event of capsize. A fair fraction of these boats are designed to accommodate an outboard motor on the reinforced transom.

Key to day-sailer selection is whether it is for pure relaxation or will also be used for racing. If planned for the former, the boat should have good initial stability, ample beam and a moderate sail area. It should not require constant live-weight shifting to maintain balance or hiking out in hefty wind gusts to prevent capsize. This pleasure craft should have a large cockpit, preferably with seats, so that you can sit in, rather than on, the boat. If also intended for racing use, then a compromise on some of the pleasure features noted is required.

There are also a number of day-sailer cruisers with limited accommodations for weekend cruising or overnight trips. They have a small cabin, effectively a couple of tight berths, a head, and space for a small galley. With a small outboard clamped on the stern, you have a midget cruising auxiliary.

Racing Sailboats. True racing boats are highly engineered, high-performance craft with complex high-sail-area rigs. Very fast and exciting to race, the more competitive boats require expert handling and a crew that is agile, mentally alert and has quick reflexes. They are typically a lightweight, planing type of boat with few amenities. Some of the more competitive designs are equipped with a trapeze for heeling counterbalance in high wind.

Most have fiberglass hull construction although some use molded plywood. A variety of single-hull/centerboard or keel combinations mentioned earlier are used, however minimum wetted surface is where it's at and there is a willingness in design to compromise some stability. Some of the most spectacular racing boats are the double-hulled catamarans, which are among the most highly responsive to wind bursts and which sail well in very high winds, particularly on a reach.

The most common racing boats carry a crew of two to five, are sloop-rigged and many are factory-equipped with full spinnaker gear. Almost all have built-in flotation. There are also some designs that serve the dual purpose of day sailing and racing, a sub-class of which are also equipped with a cuddy cabin for overnight trip use.

Elk Lake, Oregon

Cruising Auxiliaries. These boats are most often characterized as having a generous beam, moderate sail area and enough freeboard and deck space to sail dry and a large enough cockpit for several people to relax in without interfering with sail handling or operation of the boat. Most are of fiberglass construction. At one extreme are the small Midget Ocean Racing Club (MORC) boats with comparatively simple rigs, that can be sailed by one person to larger, more-complex-rigged craft that require a crew.

The small cruising sailers, 24 feet and under, are the most common. They are mainly of shoal draft (3 to 3-1/2 feet) which encourage gunkholing, that is, exploring out-of-the-way coves, estuaries and inland waterways, seeking private moorings, etc. Boats with drafts in the 4- to 5-feet range are more likely to be constrained to sail within buoyed channels. Some are centerboarders, others have a keel and centerboard. Twin-bilge keels are also popular because they combine shoal draft with the characteristics of a true keel boat. They are generally sloop-rigged. Boats at the upper end of this class approach the trailering limit.

Larger cruising auxiliaries, better outfitted for off-shore and open-ocean sailing, have additional living space and headroom belowdeck. They may be single-hulled, catamarans or trimarans. Typical additions beyond the smaller size cruising auxiliaries are more berthing space, a more private head, a larger galley (often equipped with a refrigerator, as opposed to an icebox), more storage space, and possibly a shower. They tend to be sloop- or yawl-rigged and have deep and heavily-ballasted keels. Fin keels are most popular, although other options such as conventional long keels and fixed keels with centerboards are not uncommon.

Life Raft/Dinghy. Small sailcraft and powered runabouts may only have room for a small inflatable raft. Larger cruising auxiliaries and powered cruisers can, and frequently do, carry a dinghy. The *dinghies* are most frequently used for transport from a moorage to land. However, the most important reason to carry this additional craft is in the event that you have to abandon the host boat. Dinghies come in many designs, from oar-paddled, plywood skiffs to motorized, rigid-bottom inflatables to small, high-powered runabouts on the largest boats.

Because of the way that *inflatable life rafts* are now constructed, they are a lot safer than the old-fashioned lifeboats. Life rafts come in several types and sizes and vary primarily in their approach to ballast. The more expensive (and less likely to overturn) models employ ballasting material that encircles the bottom of the raft. Other designs rely on smaller ballast pockets, which simply hold water.

Most rafts today are stored in rigid containers that occupy little on-deck stowage space. They can be activated manually by pulling on a long, well-marked lanyard, once the container has been tossed over the side. Many rafts inflate automatically, the deployment sequence starting when the stored raft package has submerged to about six feet. It floats toward the surface, with the deck-securing lanyard severing as the raft fills and floats upward. Common designs for small in-shore boats are generally open, single-layer rafts. The best life rafts, more often reserved for long-distance bluewater sailing, have a double floor and a double tent or canopy to retain body heat and to protect occupants against the elements. They also have a grab line secured on the boat periphery and a cloth ladder for access to the boat from the water.

An emergency kit that is easily transferable to, or permanently stationed in, the life raft is essential. Its contents are described as a separate item below under "Emergency Kit."

Warp/Heaving/Lead Lines. The most suitable lines for mooring and towing use *(warps)* are made of nylon and polyethylene. They have great strength and high stretch properties. The mooring lines frequently double for towing. The line thicknesses are dependent on boat size, with eight-millimeter thickness (0.31-inch thickness or one-inch circumference) frequently used for boats under 15 feet and double that used for boats in the 30-foot length range.

Heaving lines are often made of polypropylene. This material's key properties are that it is light, of medium stretch and buoyant. Lengths of 35-50 feet and one-inch circumference are typical for use in throwing lines to dockside personnel, to another boat or to boaters who have gone overboard. These lines are also used for waterskiing.

Lead lines are used for manual measurement of the water depth. They are handy for estimating depth under keel in shallow water, but also serve to provide addition information to assist in determining position. The standard is a 10-fathom (60-foot) line, which is marked with either colored, printed plastic at every fathom or in the traditional fashion from sailing ship days (two fathoms, two strips of leather; three fathoms, three strips; five fathoms, a piece of white cotton rag; seven fathoms, a piece of red flannel rag; ten fathoms, a piece of leather with a hole in it). The latter is more messy to use and stow, but is readable at night just by feel (the classic argument is that it may be difficult to handle both the line and a flashlight in rough weather). The heavy lead weight at line's end may have a hollow; when the hollow is packed with grease or soap, it can be used to bring up bottom samples. The depth measurement, together with the sample (clay, mud, sand, pebbles, etc.) may assist in further localizing the boat's position.

Fenders. Fenders protect your boat's hull while tying up or moored to a pier. It is common practice to carry three small, but tough fenders, equipped with lanyards and fitted with holes at both ends so they can be hung vertically or horizontally. Cylindrical rubber and plastic fenders are available for small boat use; their higher initial cost may be justified by their longer life than canvas fenders.

Paddle or Oar. For smaller sailcraft, this item could become the single means of locomotion in the event of any disaster that compromises the ability to use the sails. It is just that, by design, for non-powered secondary craft on larger boats at all times. Paddles and oars are also useful for pushing off and provide some of the services of a boat hook. For smaller boats, they can be used as a makeshift rudders. Combined with a couple of "C"-clamps or other appropriate rigging, they can serve as a makeshift tiller. In the instance that the boat hull is pierced and taking in water, this item might serve the secondary use as a brace or jam for the gear used to plug the hole. See the POWERBOATING activity for uses with problematic outboard motors.

Boat Hook. This item is frequently used for leveraging on dockside and moorings, picking up mooring attachment hardware and snagging lines in the water. It also serves for retrieving gear that has fallen overboard. Drill a hole about an inch from the end and tie a six-inch loop of 1/4-inch nylon to serve as a handle.

Motor Oil, Coolant & Lubricants. Refer to the POWERBOATING activity.

Canvas Covers. In addition to the sail stowage covers, many boaters rig canvas for sun and wind protection when not underway. There are custom covers which can be conveniently rigged for specific boats and generic covers where the boat owner must use some ingenuity and, sometimes, boat retrofitting. These may be overhead panels or a combination of top and side units, where the latter are more for wind protection. For those boaters who want to watch the marina's comings and goings, side curtains with clear vinyl panels are substituted.

Pail or Bucket. When the bilge pumps are not operating at full capacity or fail or when, for any reason, water is entering the boat faster than makes you comfortable, it's time to hand bail. On smaller boats this calls for one- or two-gallon buckets, while on larger boats, the five-gallon size is probably most useful. Choose plastic buckets, since their metal counterparts will rust.

Deck Swab. After a period underway, your decks may get icky from a combination of water spray and passenger activities. Hauling fishermen, divers, water skiers or other sportsman is particularly likely to result in foul decks. Some of the residue can be ground into the decking. The solution: grab a swab and your trusty bailing bucket and give the deck a rinse. If you like punishment, substitute a large, thirsty sponge, get on your hands and knees and wipe away! The same gear will be useful when you wash and wipe down the decks after returning to dockside or placing your boat back on its trailer.

Sea Bags. Since suitcases and rigid bags are hard to stow, carry your personal clothing and gear in a soft-sided duffel bag. Your duffel should have a waterproof inner section for wet swim suits or clothes, as well as outside pockets for often-needed items such as sunglasses and suntan lotion. Look for models with both hand-carry and over-the-shoulder-carry straps.

Engine Ignition Key and Spare. Locking your keys in your automobile is one thing, but losing your only auxiliary engine ignition key (if there is one) while at one of your favorite remote anchorages could be a vacation disaster! Bring a spare set and tuck it away in a safe place. Unless you enjoy the challenge of searching the bottom for your dropped key, attach each ignition key to a floating keyring or other type of flotation hardware.

Water Jug or Bottle(s). Bring a supply of water, even if your plans are for a short sailing venture. Nothing dampens the fun of a trip like being thirsty. For overnight or longer sailing tours, even with potable water tanks, you may find yourself carefully rationing water. Fresh water is reserved for drinking and cooking. This means using sea water for personal hygiene, dish washing and even clothes washing in a pinch. Note that there are several brands of liquid soap that produce suds in saltwater. Also note that potable water in the Caribbean can cost as much as ten dollars a gallon when purchased dockside.

Float Plan. A float plan is the boating version of an aviation flight plan. Before you head off on a trip, give a copy to a friend or relative. In some cases, harbormasters at your port of exit will accept them. The U.S. Coast Guard discourages your filing with them in order to keep from getting inundated.

A full float plan has the following information:

1) Boat Owner Data - today's date, boat owner's name, address, phone number and an identification of next of kin
2) Boat Description - physical description of the boat, radio gear, call sign, lifeboat type, engine or auxiliary engine type, horsepower, number and fuel capacity
3) Passenger Identification - name, address, phone number and age of each person
4) Itinerary - departure date, time and location and estimated arrival and departure date and time at each additional destination
5) Overdue Notification Data - date and time to contact the Coast Guard or local authority and contacting information (generally a phone number)

When you return, contact your friend or relative holding the plan and ask them to discard it. Alternately, if you plan to change your itinerary (particularly if you plan to extend your trip), contact the plan holder and provide an update.

Registration Papers. All boats are required to display a registry number and boat name. If stopped by the U.S. Coast Guard or port authorities, you will be asked to show your boat registration papers. This will also be the case in most non-U.S. waters. Store them in their own waterproof pouch in a conveniently accessible place.

Passport. For any travel outside the U.S., it is a requirement for each member of the boat to have an up-to-date passport.

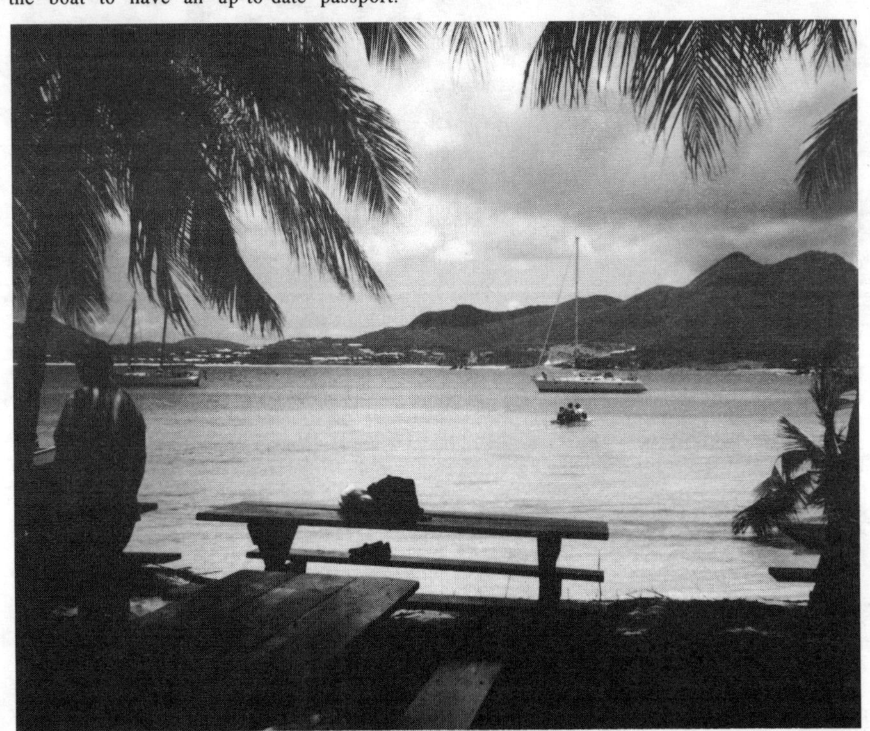

St. Martin (French Side), Caribbean

Personal Gear

As with other outdoor activities, the principal of wearing layered clothing applies. You add or subtract layers depending on weather conditions and your degree of exertion. Keep in mind that weather conditions can change rapidly, so ensure that your clothing gear is easily accessible. Also, while on deck on a sailing craft, your total body is exposed to the wind and spray. Given the same weather and sea state, this will be less of a factor if you are on a keelboat than if you are sailing a dinghy. In the discussion below, we offer general *examples of outfits* (not including the standards like sunglasses, sunscreen, etc.) that might serve your purpose in order from warm weather to successively cooler conditions.

Warm weather: shorts or swim suit, "T"-shirt, deck shoes, sailing gloves, sun hat

Cool weather: underwear, warm shorts or long pants, long-sleeve shirt or sweater, waterproof windbreaker or jacket, deck shoes with socks, sailing gloves, sun hat. An option is to substitute a wet-suit top for (all) the above-mentioned upper torso clothing or a paddling jacket or dry-suit top to replace the windbreaker/jacket.

Cold weather: thermal underwear bottoms, plus long pants if needed, under dry-suit pants, thermal underwear top and warm sweater under dry suit top, deck shoes with socks or wet-suit booties, wet-suit gloves, pullover hat under sun hat. An option is to substitute a wet suit for (all) the upper and lower torso clothing.

Swim Suit/Deck Shorts. Shorts material is not much of an issue, other than consideration of longevity -- a sturdier material and better construction will provide longer life. A few times of hiking out on the rail or accidentally snagging a cleat or other sharp deck fitting will convince you. Water spray and a periodic dowse of water may be a blessing in hot weather, particularly while wearing cotton shorts. Now the water-retentive and resulting cooling properties of that material work to your benefit. Where you are seeking quick-drying properties, look to options like nylon swim suits with mesh liners.

Short-length shorts or swim suits may become a problem if you are packing out. In this case, you do want enough length such that your legs are not rubbing directly against the rail. The shorts should be loose fitting to allow full freedom of movement and to minimize cinching around the pelvic region. Look for designs that have a reinforced seat.

Long Pants. If the problem is merely chill factor, you can easily get by with the same trousers that you use for camping or lounging around after a day of watersports. In moderate weather with some spray, you'll want a material that retains warmth when wet and dries quickly. For sheer comfort, many prefer heavy synthetic-pile pants -- comfortable-fitting sweatpants are a frequent choice. If it is wet, and particularly if it is wet and cold, they can be worn under foul-weather gear.

Shirt/Sweater. Very hot weather sailing is one of the few instances where a *cotton* top actually might be recommended. Wet it down and any breeze running through it will cool you. For warm weather, consider a *polypropylene* "T"-shirt. Short sleeve models are adequate, unless your sailing day may turn cool or you sunburn easily. If you are sensitive to the sun, there is *sunblock clothing* that filters UV radiation as well as SB 30 sunblock. (Most light clothing is inadequate at this UV blocking function.)

The frequent choice for cold-weather boating is to go with a *full-length synthetic pile or wool sweater*. Preferred are high-necked styles that can be unbuttoned or unzipped to accommodate your level of sailing-activity exertion or weather change. They can be worn as an outer layer, under a windbreaker or under foul-weather gear depending on boating conditions.

Headgear. As with many other outdoor activities, headwear plays an important role. In mild weather, a wide-brimmed canvas hat or mesh-topped, *long-peaked (trucker's-style) hat* serves the purpose of protecting both your eyes and the top of your head from the sun. In cold weather, a hat that is highly efficient at retaining body heat is needed. Tight-fitting synthetic or wool *pullover headgear* (sufficient to cover the ears or entire face -- like a balaclava) is sometimes worn under a water-shedding hat in extreme cold. One overhat option is a *sou'wester*. These are the full-circumference brimmed hats that appear in many classic sea paintings. Today's version typically is a two-layer design with a PVC exterior, nylon interior and a mesh liner in the crown. Whatever the style of hat you wear, ensure that it is equipped with a chin-strap or is attached to a piece of light line that connects securely to a buttonhole or other part of your outerwear.

Gloves. A pair of half-fingered boating or nautical gloves, or a full-fingered set in colder weather, are useful for line handling and other deck chores. Leather palms and fabric backs provide added protection for line handling and other deck duties. Velcro straps, available on many designs, allow the gloves to be snugged or quickly retightened to the wrist. The backside of the glove most often has a hearty mesh weave to allow the hands to "breathe." They should be tight fitting to prevent any baggy or loose material getting caught in winches or blocks.

Deck Shoes. Skid-resistant *deck shoes*, those rubber-bottomed footwear with deep wavy slits in the sole, are your best bet. If you are crewing, with the decks frequently awash, they are a must. Deck shoes come with canvas and leather uppers. Leather is more expensive, is slower drying, and tends to retain foot odor longer, although many top-flight sailboaters still prefer them for their superior rigidity. For more benign conditions, rubber-soled land shoes without heels, but with solid tread are acceptable. However they are more prone to leave you on your backside if the decks get slick.

Bring an extra pair in case the original set gets waterlogged. Added notes: Make sure that your sole materials will not mar the deck. Also, as a courtesy when boarding, clear out rocks, pebbles or any other substance from your shoes that might cause damage. You may get a rude "earful" and probably won't be invited back if your shoes leave permanent scars.

Underwear/Thermal Underwear. Cotton underwear are comfortable in warm weather, but polyester and polypropylene materials are preferred in any other conditions. The suggested choice for thermal underwear is polyester, of the proper weight for your planned level of exertion. Refer to the VEHICLE-ACCESSIBLE CAMPING activity for a more detailed discussion.

Foul-Weather Suit. Dinghy sailors generally can count on getting wet regardless of the weather or sea state. This is a given if the crew is sitting or standing out. In very cold weather, most prefer waterproof *drysuits* as the shell layer. The materials and most peripheral features are not significantly different than those described in the KAYAKING and WATERSPORTS activities. Higher-quality trousers, specifically for sailing, are often equipped with patched seat and knees to absorb the harsh wear. Frequently, either a "shortie" or full length set of longjohns act as the underwear layer and, if needed, synthetic fiber-pile overgarments are the insulating layer.

In milder cold weather, the preference swings to *wet suits*. There are single-piece and two-piece models, with above-hip and "Farmer John" two-piece styles. In all cases, there are full-length suits and "shorties," the latter with partial exposure of the legs. Preferences vary, but most competitive dinghy sailors lean to the "shortie," one-piece styles. (See the KAYAKING activity for additional information.) Many sailboaters wear a very loose-fitting swim suit shell or shorts over their wet suits to protect the neoprene from the battering it would otherwise take from deck fittings.

Keelboat sailors are provided with an even wider set of options than dinghy sailors. While also using a three-layered system concept, the keelboater's shell need not be as resistant to water leakage, because there is increased opportunity to add or delete layers while underway. In other than very high seas, keelboaters forgo the drysuit and replace it with a *breathable-fabric foul-weather shell*.

Another keelboater option in foul weather is the modern-day version of the classic yellow *"slicker."* This is a two-piece outfit with both jacket and trousers having a two-layer exterior. The surface layer is commonly 100% PVC (treated with a polyurethane sealant) and is combined with an interior nylon layer. Since the surface is waterproof (i.e., non-breathable), it has a group of widely-separated, internal mesh breathing ports and a large mesh liner under a shoulder-level cover flap. The jackets typically have an attached, draw-string hood and come in both pullover and zippered designs. The latter models are equipped with flaps that snap or Velcro-attach to close off the zipper from direct exposure. The pants are most often of high-waisted design. Both are typically equipped with overflap-protected pockets.

Foul-Weather Boots. Boots will be necessary when water is washing the decks. They require highly-grippable tread and should be waterproof. As with other wet outdoor activities, consider breathable boots if your pocketbook can afford it. This footwear has material that allows foot perspiration to escape, but effectively seals out the larger water molecules external to the shoe. The nominal boot has a standard top-lacing design, however side-lacing models are available. The advantage: When you sit-out or stand-out, the laces do not dig into the top of your feet.

Underway Living Gear

What gear you bring will be governed by such considerations as trip type and duration, boat size and layout, number of passengers, galley size and completeness, and planned menu (plus all the other things we forgot to mention that you will curse us for later).

Stove/Fuel. For cooking while underway, most deep-water sailing and power craft are equipped with built-in stoves on gimbals to counteract the effects of boat motion. In contrast, shorter-range boats are built with hard-mounted units, the assumption being that skippers will seek protected shelter in rough weather or forgo cooking altogether for the assumed short trip duration.

Mexican Coast, Pacific Ocean   Courtesy of Walt Bond

Alcohol and propane are standard fuels for boating, alcohol for its universal availability and propane because of its high energy output and ease of use. A concern with alcohol and other volatile liquid fuels is that, if spilled, they could find their way into the bilges and create a potential fire or explosion hazard. Similarly, high-pressure propane piping systems (pipes, connections, gauges and valves) must be checked periodically for leaks. Propane is highly explosive and heavier than air and will accumulate at the lowest accessible point, whether it be the cabin deck or the bilges. One spark, including hitting the engine ignition key, can have potentially disastrous results. (The safest boat designs have the tank stored in a locker outside the cabin, completely isolated from the cabin, as well as an overboard drain.)

A newer development is compressed natural gas (CNG) which is called SAFGAS in the U.S. and Australia, where there are abundant supplies of natural gas. It is not readily available in most other sailing areas. It has the efficiency of propane, and it is lighter than air, meaning that the normal airflow in well-ventilated spaces will keep it from accumulating. Beware that, in poorly ventilated areas, the gas that could be trapped in cabin corners or behind lockers is still lethal.

Additional cautions: Never try to fill a liquid fuel stove while underway. Never use a portable stove while underway.

Cookware/Dinnerware. The two schools of thought on cookware suggest either stainless steel or Teflon-coated *pots and pans*, The former will last longer, while the latter are easier to use and to clean. For everything else in the galley -- *cooking and eating utensils*, even the can opener -- should be stainless steel. High-carbon steel rusts.

For *dinnerware*, some boaters use yachting ware, that is, plastic plates and cups with non-skid rubber rings on the bottom. They are easy to handle, usually stack conveniently in nests and can handle shipboard abuse. They are also light, which can actually be a drawback in heavy sea when they are nearly empty of contents. Another school of thought is to use old potteryware. With a tube of silicon, you can run a ring of compound around the plate or cup, let it dry, and enjoy the usage of a relatively non-slip dinnerware set. However, a separate set of non-rubberized or non-siliconed pottery cookware is needed if you use a microwave.

Table Mats/Tablecloth. To minimize movement of your tableware while underway, consider using table mats or a tablecloth with rough undersides. Another option is to use a damp towel or towels.

Hygiene

Towels. Bring a healthy supply of cloth towels for watersports activities, for general hygiene, and for use as table mats when underway -- don't hedge on your supply of this item.

Safety

A condensed summary of the "Coast Guard-Mandated, Minimum Required Safety Equipment" is provided in the table below. The word "Minimum" should be clearly noted. Many other items are important to ensure safe boating as evidenced by the large number of "Safety" gear items listed in both the SAILING and POWERBOATING activity checklists.

Emergency Kit. Emergency equipment should be readily accessible. On cruising boats, many put together a "grab bag" which contains such items as the first aid kit, flares, water and other emergency essentials. The bag is stored near the helm.

The kit for remote, deep-water sailors, who may have to survive at sea for days before rescue, sets the upper limit. The liferaft is fitted with: sea anchor, paddles, knife, bellows, signaling equipment (mirror, torch, several flare types, whistle, dye marker), baler, sponges, raft repair kit, rescue quoit (ring) and line, drinking water, emergency ration tins and openers, sunburn cream waterproof survival leaflet, and first-aid kit. (See the FIRST AID section for more detail on the first aid kit contents.) Additionally recommended are a solar still, radar reflector and basic fishing gear.

Water Filter/Tablets. These are contingency items, available should you run short of water or your potable water tanks become contaminated, or where you are unsure of the quality of a land source of water.

PFDs and Throwlines. See the "Coast Guard-Mandated, Minimum Required Safety Equipment" table for PFD gear needed. Most commonly Type II and III PFDs are used, with designs that are comfortable to wear, easy to put on and that afford protection from bruising when you "interface" with deck and sail gear. You may want to carry a throwline, particularly if you are not carrying a Type IV PFD for overboard crew members. The line will provide a solid means of preventing the in-water person from drifting and, in the best of situations, allow you to haul them in without committing a swimmer to provide assistance.

Coast Guard-Mandated, Minimum Required Safety Equipment

(Condensed Summary)

	Equipment	Class A (<16 feet length boat)	Class I (16 to <26 feet)	Class II (26 to <40 feet)
All Vessels	PFD	One Type I, II or III (wearable) or Type IV (throwable) PFD for each person on board	One Type I, II or III PFD for each person on board and one Type IV PFD for each boat	
	Navigation Lights	Sailboat Under Sail: A white stern light visible at six points abaft the beam on both port and starboard sides (135 degrees total) at a distance of two miles, plus red (port) and green (starboard) bow (side) lights, visible from the bow to two points abaft the beam (112.5 degrees) at a distance of one mile. The white stern light must be placed higher than the side lights. Sailboat Under Auxiliary Power or Powerboats: Same as above except for 32-point (360 degree) white stern light		Sailboat Under Sail: Same. Sailboat Under Auxiliary Power or Powerboats: add white bow light(s) with same total coverage (225 degrees) as side lights
All Power Craft	Horn or Whistle	- (not required)	One hand, mouth or power-operated horn or whistle, audible at least one mile	One power-operated horn or whistle, audible at least one mile for a two-second duration
	Bell	-	-	One ship's bell, when struck, produces a clear, bell-like tone of full-round characteristics
	Portable Fire Extinguisher Only	At least one type B-I approved portable fire extinguisher		At least two type B-I approved portable fire extinguishers OR at least one B-II type
	When Fixed Fire-Extinguisher System is Installed in Machinery Space(s)	- (no portable units required)	- (no portable units required)	At least one type B-I approved portable fire extinguisher
	(definition of Types B-I and B-II fire extinguisher)	Type B-I approved hand-portable fire extinguishers contain: Foam, 1-1/4 up to 2-1/2 gallons; Freon, 2-1/2 pounds; Carbon Dioxide, 4 up to 15 pounds; or Dry Chemical, 2 up to 10 pounds Type B-II approved hand-portable fire extinguishers contain: Foam, 2-1/2 gallons; Carbon Dioxide, 15 pounds; or Dry Chemical, 10 to 20 pounds		
	Backfire Flame Control	One approved backfire flame arrestor on the carburetor of each gasoline engine		
	Ventilation	At least two unobstructed ventilator ducts fitted with cowls or their equivalent for every engine and fuel tank compartment on gas-powered boats.		

Harness and Lifeline. For offshore keelboats, a *harness and lifeline* for everyone on board is standard. On the racing circuit, to get the boat to heel in the desired orientation, the crew frequently gets to act as "rail meat." They sit out on the rail to counteract the wind's tendency to heel the boat over when reaching. Performing this function requires similar gear.

The harness and lifeline should be worn if there is the slightest doubt regarding safety. The harnesses enable crewmen to work on deck in rough weather with both hands free. Also, a person going overboard has a 100% chance of being recovered; the odds drop for someone left behind in the wake and for whom the boat has to return.

The typical harness fits over the upper torso much like a PFD and is designed with wide armholes and shoulder straps. The harness is snugged up over the PFD using adjustment straps. Frequently, the harness is padded. To use, you put on the harness and attach the other end of the connecting line to a strong padeye or deck stay or clip into another line which has been secured to those fittings.

There are also *combined PFD and harness* designs. The lifejacket in this combined model is worn deflated and then inflated automatically or by mouth if needed. The garment incorporates back and crotch straps to prevent it from riding up when in the water. The lifeline can be detached from the harness so the harness can also be used as a lifejacket alone.

For standing out, a maneuver typically confined to racing catamarans, a *trapeze* is used. A typical trapeze system suspends a crew member(s) on wires running from the upper mast fittings on both sides of the boat. There is a comfortable handgrip attached to the lower end of the wire and the trapeze ring (made of plastic or stainless steel) is below that. A piece of shock cord pulls the trapeze wire back into a non-interfering stored position after use.

Horn or Whistle. See the "Coast Guard-Mandated, Minimum Required Safety Equipment" table.

Bell. See the "Coast Guard-Mandated, Minimum Required Safety Equipment" table.

Power Megaphone. Be the only "kid on the block" who can talk to neighboring sailors while underway. Few follow through with this option, and some find this communication mode irritating. Prime use is most often by powerboaters engaged in group watersports activities for communication between boats and between a boat and its in-water personnel.

Signal Flags. Flags beat the pants off of communicating through hand signals! The problem is that they are only useful to the those who can interpret them, which is a very small number of boaters. If your cadre is adept at reading signal flags and some of the group lack radios, this is an elegant solution. Otherwise, consider them for their entertainment value.

Flares, Water Dye, Smoke Maker. There are numerous ways to attract attention in distress situations. All are visible from the air, while flares and smoke makers (or smoke flares) are also visible to other boaters and people on land. Water dye has a relatively long life (tens of minutes to hours, depending on water state) compared to flares and smoke makers, the latter generally measured in minutes of visibility.

Handheld flares are ignited by scraping against a rough surface, or they might be designed to ignite when exposed to air. They should be gripped by the handle and held over the side of the boat so that burning matter falls harmlessly overboard. This requires that smoke flares be held over the water on the downwind corner of the boat.

Flares should be stored in a cool, dry, readily-accessible locker and their condition checked periodically. They should be replaced at or before their expiration date. Flares bought for waterborne use are generally in waterproof packaging, while those for land use are not. If you buy the latter, seal them in a plastic zip-locking bag or other positive-sealing container.

Flare Gun. Flare pistols have the advantage of putting flares at altitude, in order to enhance their visibility range. They can use varied "ammunition," including aerial flares, orange smoke flares, parachute flares, distress flags and signal lights.

Learn how to operate these pistols before using, as they can become dangerous weapons otherwise. To make the point, aerial flare guns must be registered in some states as fire arms.

Radar Reflector. Particularly for use in limited visibility conditions, large commercial vessels carry radar equipment. If your sailing boat is to stand any chance of being picked up on a large vessel's radar screen at a safe range, a radar reflector is needed. It should be mounted high on the boat, unobscured by sails or other boat equipment -- the mast head, backstay or on a flag halyard near the spreaders are typical locations. It should be no smaller in diameter than 60 centimeters (about two feet).

Fire Extinguisher. See the "Coast Guard-Mandated, Minimum Required Safety Equipment" table.

Sunglasses and Lanyard. Beyond those functions described in the VEHICLE-ACCESSIBLE CAMPING activity, low-UV transmission, polarized glasses serve additional purposes. Sailing into the sun provides added problems for the trimmer -- sunglasses are essential to allow the trimmer to watch the luff of the sail at all times. Fishermen staring at the water all day will have a clearer, lower-glare look at what her future catch is doing when it is surfaced.

Flashlight. For general night use, it is always smart to bring along a flashlight, even if your plans are only for a daytime adventure. Uses include reading charts, making repairs, picking out dock or water object features, distress signaling or as a makeshift collision warning device. In the latter case, assuming you are running without lights or they are not working, it is shown to an oncoming craft in time to prevent collision. (Shining the light on the sail area, or superstructure of a powerboat, is less confusing than shining the light at the oncoming craft.) A high-brightness (two, and preferably 3-4 "D" batteries) waterproof light with an armored shell is preferable. (See the TEN ESSENTIALS section for more detail.)

Lantern. The lantern is an adjunct to, not a replacement for, a flashlight. It provides more light but less portability -- certainly a neat item for planned overnight and multi-day trips. A typical model might have a water resistant (preferably waterproof) plastic shell and something like two long-life six-volt batteries. Rowing (Class A) boats, whether under oars or sail, can use this at night to illuminate the boat and/or sails to prevent a collision.

Spotlight. If the boat is so equipped, the waterproof, focused-beam spotlight(s) is commonly *hard-mounted* to the structure of the boat. They are powered off the boat's generator and are sufficiently high-powered to serve as a trusty aid in identifying navigation aids, including reading numbers on buoys, and spotting water obstructions at night. The light(s) is either adjusted directly by hand or through a mechanical linkage if not within hand reach. *Portable models*, either battery-powered or plug-in, are also available. This is a handy piece of gear to have for the contingency of night boating not was not in your original plans.

Compass. A compass is useful even if you don't plan any long-distance navigation. In new territory or at night, for example, where you don't recognize many landmarks or see few, it assists you in setting a base course. In open water, it is essential. The compass is nominally hard-mounted near the helm, although there are also (less accurate) portables that can be easily mounted and unmounted, particularly where there is a concern for theft. Small boat sailors with limited assets are still advised to bring even a hand compass for contingencies.

The classic equipment is the *magnetic compass*. It's positive features are that it is time-tested, relatively robust and its limitations are well understood. The key limitation is that the boat structure and some electronic equipment disturb the local magnetic field. Thus, the compass has to be calibrated for a variety of boat headings and a deviation table developed to get the needed compass accuracy (the variation of magnetic north from true north is well-documented worldwide and is not an issue). Some higher-quality models have adjustment screws around the compass base which allow you (or, better yet, a professional) to physically compensate your compass for deviation. Many conditions can cause this compensation to degrade, thus it must be checked periodically and recalibrated.

Skippers of larger boats (i.e., with deeper pockets) may spring for a *flux-gate compass*. It is electronic and not subject to the deviation error. It is also more accurate and more responsive. The sensor can be mounted separately from the readout, thus it is easily isolated from electronics, electrical wiring and other potentially disruptive sources.

Aruba, Caribbean

Coastal and Sea Charts/Light List. Bring an up-to-date set of charts for every area that you plan to visit, with some overlapping coverage if you are the spontaneous type. This applies whether you are sailing a familiar lake or harbor or in unfamiliar waters.

The charts that you may use are dependent upon your trip plans. A primary source of charts for U.S. waters is the National Oceanographic Service (NOS). Some of the types of charts provided by NOS are noted below.

Sailing charts have the broadest area coverage. The scaling of the largest chart has one inch on the chart representing 600,000 inches (about 8.2 nautical miles) on the earth's surface (1:600,000 scale). These are used to fix a mariner's position as she approaches the coast from open ocean or for sailing between distant coastal points.

General charts have scales of 1:150,000 to 1:600,000. They are a standard for coastal navigation outside of outlying reefs and shoals, generally within sight of land or navigational aids.

Coast charts are for inshore navigation, entering bays and harbors of considerable width, and sailing large inland waterways. Typical scales are from 1:50,000 to 1:150,000.

Harbor charts use scales of 1:50,000 and larger. They are for navigating harbors, anchorage areas and smaller waterways.

Small craft charts are for specialized use in inland waters or are special editions of conventional charts, showing data on facilities, tide predictions, weather broadcast channels or frequencies, etc. They have scales of 1:80,000 and larger.

Magnetic Deviation Tables. Refer to the "Compass" item above under the magnetic compass discussion. If the deviation is highly varied with boat heading, a calibration at every 15-degree change may be needed.

Parallel Rulers/Dividers. The most basic gear needed is a set of parallel rules, dividers, sharp pencil and gum eraser. A protractor can be substituted for, or used together with, the parallel rulers. Add a pelorus for direct or relative bearings; an option for taking coarse relative bearings is to mark the lines on deck (or some other ship-body-fixed suitable surface) at 4-point (45-degree) intervals.

Waterproof Chart/Table Covers. The best of all worlds is having a chart table near the helm that is protected from the elements. Having a large flat, well-lit and dry table to work on simplifies the navigation task. The opposite extreme might have you doing navigation out of an exposed cockpit. For this instance, consider mounting the chart on a portable flatboard with a hard plastic surface placed over the map and held down with stays. In the worst case, you may find yourself plotting courses with a waterproof grease pencil directly on the plastic cover.

For short trips on very space-limited boats, another option is to use a waterproofing spray directly on the chart. In this instance, the chart will most likely be hand-held and used for landmark and navigation-aid recognition rather than for course plotting. In all cases, set aside locker space for map storage to provide accessibility, dry storage and to prevent loss.

VHF Radio/Cellular Phone. Big boats that venture far out into the ocean require long-distance communication devices, typically single-sideband marine radios. These come with a high price tag. For the class of boats discussed here, a line-of-sight limited Very High Frequency (VHF) radio is the norm. For the cruisers, they are normally structure-mounted and utilize a deck-mounted antenna. For smaller boats, a portable or hand-held VHF device is the next best bet, followed by the now-popular *cellular phone* designed for land use. The latter two are only for near-shore use and the cellular phone only for use near populated areas. The hand-held VHF also makes a good auxiliary radio for larger boats. Bring a spare set of batteries for these models.

Like Swiss Army knives, the *VHF radios* come in basic through exotic models. The basic features needed are: 1) adequate transmitting power, typically twenty-five watts for structure-mounted models, and about six watts for portables with fresh batteries; 2) high selectivity or ability to select and listen to given frequency (channel), while filtering out other sources of noise, including near-frequency transmissions (expressed in negative numbers of decibels); 3) high sensitivity or ability to pick up a weak signal and make it stand out against the normal background static (expressed as the number of microvolts required to produce a given level of signal strength) -- this is less important than selectivity; 4) easy-to-use operating characteristics, particularly in an emergency (e.g., separate one-button push to get Channel 16, the hailing and distress frequency); 5) sufficient channels to allow selectivity in high usage areas and ability to receive several weather channels; and 6) solid physical construction (consistent with operation in a high-moisture environment) with a high reliability record.

EPIRB. Emergency Position Indicating Radio Beacons (EPIRBs) are intended, once activated, to transmit maritime distress signals. The signals can be picked up by aircraft in the area, governmental rescue agencies, nearby boats or to other ground-based rescuers, via satellite. Historically, the receipt of a maritime distress signal will set off a full-scale search-and-rescue within 24 hours (most often much sooner) of first receipt. Any pleasure craft that travels offshore, beyond the range of its VHF radio, should be equipped with a class-A or class-B EPIRB, although it is not currently bound by law to do so.

The *class-A types* are usually bracket-mounted to a vessel's exterior. They float free if the vessel sinks and activate automatically. They are required by law for many commercial boats. *Class-B units* are less expensive and probably make more sense for recreational boats. They don't have deign-in flotation, although owners often equip them with separate flotation collars. They can be activated either manually or automatically. Both transmit a distinctive signal that can be picked up on two aircraft frequencies. The signal can alert aircraft as far away as 200 miles. Selected satellites, which are monitored by several nations of the world, also receive and pass on these signals.

Class-C EPIRBs are intended for use by boats in coastal or inland areas that don't have VHF radios and are the least expensive. Class-C types transmit an emergency signal on VHF channel 16, hopefully to be picked up by another boater or ground-monitoring station within close proximity.

Another EPIRB is the "*mini-B*," a lower-cost, lower-power version of the Class-B which can be attached to a boater's PFD. Currently considered as too expensive for recreational use, the recently-developed *Type 406* signals satellites exclusively. It transmits a serial number specifically identifying the vessel under distress by means of a descriptive card mailed in at the time of purchase.

Engine Manual. See the POWERBOATING activity.

Pen and Notepad. Consider bringing waterproof paper and an appropriate marker.

St. Johns, Caribbean

Accessories

Brochure/Articles/Books. Few activities are more amenable to bringing along reference and pure reading material. Potential local destinations for the smaller Class-I boats are many, while those for the larger Class-II cruisers are nearly endless, provided you can forgo transoceanic adventures and have a willingness for port-to-port hopping. Travel books and brochures, boating guides that identify great docking/mooring/anchoring sites, guide books for watersports and land activities, the latest bestseller -- all will help you plan and modify your trip or, in the slow times, keep you entertained.

Binoculars/Telescope. Binoculars are multi purpose. They are helpful for picking out buoys and landmarks; checking the status of nearby boats, swimmers or divers; for spotting fish; and for general sightseeing. The most commonly used are nominal magnification, wide-field (e.g., 7x50-format) glasses. High-magnification, narrow-field glasses or telescopes have little wide-area search capability and are incompatible with holding a subject while on a moderately-rocking boat. They are unparalleled, however, for nature studies of relatively fixed objects while in calm water or on land.

Daypack. Though the preference is for sea bags, consider bringing your soft-shelled daypack as added baggage on longer tours or as your sole storage unit on day trips. The deep well storage, plethora of pockets and the ability to carry the bag on your back are all positive, relevant features for this activity. True, this may get you a friendly rebuff or two, but it may also save you the cost of an extra sea bag.

Spare Auto Keys/Credit Card/$. Unlike for many other activities, these items become absolute necessities for trips of any duration.

Tool Kit

Perhaps nowhere else in this book are there more options for selecting the tools and gear needed to handle equipment loss, reduced equipment performance, breakdown or other emergency situations. We have listed some of the more common items below. A tailored list should be based on your sailing craft, trip type and duration (racing sailors interested in speed, and probably more knowledgeable about jury-rigging repairs, will take the absolute minimal amount of gear), and acceptable margin of safety above minimum needs. Tool-kit items solely for the auxiliary engine are discussed in the POWERBOATING section.

Very commonly, boaters store many of their tools in a tightly-sealed plastic *tool box*. Metal tools should be sprayed with anti-rust lubricant before being stored. Water-impervious items might be stored together in a sea bag. All should be stowed securely in a readily accessible space.

Tools. Bring the deck gear/rigging hardware tools that are consistent with your boat. Examples are hammer(s), files, chisels, pliers/vice grips, wrenches, screwdrivers, rotary drill with drill bits and other attachments, wire clippers/ srippers, mallet and awl, For long-distance, foul-weather sailors, the kit should include the tools needed to cut the standing rigging in case the boat is dismasted. Should this occur, it will be necessary to clear all the rigging away from the boat before starting the auxiliary engine to avoid it fouling the propeller. Tools needed include a heavy-duty wirecutter and hacksaw with spare blades. Some add swaging tools and iron swage for constructing jury-rigged sailing rigs.

Repair Gear. Gear needs might include a sail repair kit, with both sail materials and mending tape, electrical tape, sandpaper, hull patch kit and personal sewing kit,

Replacement Gear. The "fixer-upper" and spares items brought could include seacock plugs, tapered softwood plug used in the event of hull puncture, spare hose and hose clamps, extra navigation light bulbs and spare tiller or spare tiller assembly. The latter might be a one-inch outer diameter galvanized iron pipe, threaded and capped at the end and equipped at the other end with a fitting to engage the head to the rudder. A more austere version could be a paddle or oar used with "C"-clamps).

Snacks/Meals

For day cruising, bring along some snacks to keep your energy level up as well as to keep your stomach from rumbling. If you have the time and the territory supports a nice mooring or beaching spot, consider a picnic on land as part of your daytime travel. The possibilities for meals on overnighters are as varied as you want to make them, within the limits of your galley gear. (See the MEALS section for a detailed discussion of snack and meal options.)

Secondary Activities

Examples of the prevalent activities that can be linked to sailboating are CAMPING (and picnicking), HIKING, BICYCLE TOURING, MOUNTAIN BIKING, WATERSPORTS and both LAND and SEA FISHING. To determine unique gear needs associated with a linked activity, refer to the relevant activity section.

SAILING
(Daytime/Overnight)

Select items based on trip needs, considering type of boat, trip type/duration and weather conditions.

ITEM	DATE				
Boat Gear					
Boat Trailer/Tie-Downs/Locks					
Sailboat					
Boarding Ladder					
Lifeboat/*Dingby*					
Mooring Line/Towing Line					
Heaving/Lead Lines					
Fenders					
Paddle or Oar					
Boat Hook					
Motor Oil, Coolant, Lubricants+					
Canvas Covers					
Pail or Bucket					
Deck Swab					
Sea Bags (storage)					
Engine Ignition Key & Spare+					
Water Jug or Bottle(s)					
Float Plan					
Registration Papers					
Passport					
Personal Gear					
Swim Suit					
Deck Shorts					
Long Pants					
Shirt/Sweater					
Underwear					
Thermal Underwear*					
Jacket*					
Headgear (sun & cold weather*)					
Gloves					
Deck Shoes					
Foul Weather Boots*					
Windbreaker					
Foul Weather Suit*					
Bandanna/Sweatband					
Land Shoes					
Underway Living Gear					
Stove/Fuel†					
Fuel Funnel/Strainer†					

SAILING
(Daytime/Overnight)

ITEM	DATE				
Coffee Pot					
Skillet/Frypan†					
Cooking Pots†					
Non-stick Cooking Lubricant†					
Pot Holders/Grippers†					
Dishware (plates, bowls etc.)†					
Paper Plates					
Cups (plastic, paper)					
Cooking Utensils (spatula etc.)†					
Can & Bottle Openers					
Eating Utensils					
Sponge & Scrubber†					
Dish Tub/Dish Towel†					
Paper Towels/Napkins					
Biodegradable Dish Soap†					
Water Jugs/Bottles					
Portable Ice Chests					
Ice and "Blue Ice"					
Insulating Bottle					
Table Mats/*Tablecloth*					
Sleeping Bags/Blankets/Sheets†					
Sleeping Pads†					
Pillows†					
Hammock					
Hygiene					
Towels					
Wash Cloth					
Personal Toiletries/Ditty Bag†					
Toilet Paper & *Towelettes*					
Toilet Trowel					
Sun Shower					
Laundry Bag†					
Portable Toilet & Liners					
Safety					
First Aid Kit (see FIRST AID)					
Water Filter/Tablets					
PFDs & Throwlines					
Harness & Lifeline					
Horn or Whistle (portable)					

SAILING
(Daytime/Overnight)

ITEM	DATE				
Bell (portable)					
Power Megaphone					
Signal Flags					
Flares, Water Dye, Smoke Maker					
Flare Gun					
Radar Reflector (portable)					
Fire Extinguisher(s) (portable)					
Sunglasses & Lanyard					
Heavy-duty Sunscreen					
Seasick Remedy					
Lip Balm					
Insect Repellent					
Waterproof Matches & Lighter					
Fire Starter/Heat Tabs					
Emergency Blanket					
Flashlight(s)#					
Spare Batteries & Bulb#					
Lantern#					
Spare Batteries & Bulb#					
Spot Light (portable)#					
Hand Timepiece#					
Thermometer					
Pocket Knife					
Compass (portable & hand)					
Coastal & Sea Charts/Light List					
Current & Tide Tables					
Parallel Rules/Dividers					
Waterproof Chart/Table Cover					
GPS Receiver					
VHF Radio (portbl.)/Cell Phone					
EPIRB					
Engine Manual(s)+					
Reading Glasses & Repair Kit					
Shark Repellent					
Phone Change					
Pen and Notepad					
Accessories					
Camera & Extra Film & Battery					
Camera Bag/Lens Cleaning Kit					
Brochures, Articles, Books					
Binoculars/*Telescope)*					
Sewing Kit (personal gear)					
Trash Bag(s)					
Resealable Plastic Food Bags					
Spare Stuff Sacks					
Daypack (storage)					

SAILING
(Daytime/Overnight)

ITEM	DATE				
Indoor & Outdoor Games					
Auto Tool Kit					
Spare Auto Keys/Credit Card/$					
Tool Kit					
Tools:					
Hammer(s)					
Files/Chisels					
Pliers/Vice Grips					
Wrenches					
Screwdriver(s)					
Rotary Drill(s)/Drill Bits					
Spare Wire, Clippers/Strippers					
Mallet & Awl					
Heavy-Duty Wirecutter					
Hacksaw & Spare Blades					
Swaging Tools/Swage					
Engine Wrenches+					
Repair Gear:					
Sail Repair Kit					
Electrical tape					
Sandpaper					
Hull Patch Kit					
Personal Sewing Kit					
Water-Displacing Lubricants+					
Replacement Gear:					
Spare Seacock Plugs/Hull Plugs					
Spare Hose(s), Hose Clamps					
Extra Navigation Light Bulbs					
Spare Tiller					
Spare Cable+					
Spare Drive Belt(s)+					
Extra Spark Plugs & Plug Wires+					
Spare Injectors+					
Distributor Cap & Rotor+					
Spare Hose(s), Hose Clamps+					
Spare Fuel & Oil Filters					
Spare Electronic Ignition					
Spare Propeller+					
Spare Pins (shear, cotter, etc.)+					
Snacks/Meals (see MEALS)					

Italicized items-optional •cold/foul weather items #night use items †overnight trips +auxiliary engine

POWERBOATING (Daytime/Overnight)

See INDEX for checklist items not discussed below.

This activity focuses on small-medium sporting craft under power. This includes Class A (those less than 16 feet in length), Class I (16-26 feet) and Class II (26-40 feet) boats. The boats discussed are gasoline-powered. As the boats approach larger class, some burn diesel fuel -- almost all big boats are diesels. The scope of the activity varies from daytime outings to "overnight" adventures. Overnight, in our context, means anything from a true overnighter to short-range, port-to-port boating.

There is no intent to describe powerboating in depth, but rather to provide an introduction to the sport. Minimal attention is paid to equipment that is integral to the boat structure, other than the "Coast Guard-Mandated Minimum Required Safety Equipment" described in the SAILING activity. The emphasis is on that gear that you may need to transport from home to the launch area and/or recheck before actually launching the boat; this includes replenishable boat items, portable safety equipment, repair gear, personal hygiene and clothing items, as well as accessory equipment that can make the boating experience more pleasurable. Obviously, many of the listed items can be ignored if your boat is already dockside, rather than brought in by trailer.

For a more-detailed treatment in any area, or for information about subjects not treated here (launching by ramp or sling, Rules of the Road, boating technique, navigation, weather, etc.), we refer you to the referenced sources. If you plan on linking your boating with other activities (e.g., hiking, camping, watersports, fishing), refer to the relevant activity to identify the additional gear needed.

Safety Considerations: Refer to the SAILING activity.

In the checklist, items that are considered optional (niceties or special purpose) are *italicized*. Items noted with an asterisk(*) are for inclement weather, while those with a pound sign(#) are for gear needed at night. The cross symbol (†) is for gear generally not brought along for day ventures, but which are candidate items for overnight and multi-day trips. The plus symbol(+) indicates equipment associated with the boat's engine(s).

<u>**Boat Gear**</u>

Powerboat. A full description of powerboat options is a book in itself. The discussion below provides the key characteristics which differentiate powerboat types and their intended use.

• The number of *hull designs* is highly varied, given today's use of fiberglass to create complex shapes optimized for specific uses. Skiffs and rowboats most often retain the classic flat-bottomed contour hull designs, while most other craft have anything but this basic shape. The most common are discussed below:

> Deep-V Hull. The keel profile, the silhouette when looking at the boat head-on, is essentially wedge-shaped from bow to stern. Small horizontal strips below the waterline, called strakes, serve to lift the hull out of the water at cruising speed, as well as to push spray out to the sides. The deep-V hull is the smoothest riding in choppy conditions since it softens the pounding from waves. This design is commonly used by offshore powerboat racers. The key drawback of these designs is they tend to roll excessively at low speeds or when at rest in choppy water.
>
> Modified Deep-V Hull. Most modern powerboats utilize this shape, a combination of some of the best features of others. Like the deep-V, it is highly wedge-shaped forward, but flattens out near the stern to a flatter V-shape. At cruising speed, the deep-V forward helps to cushion the ride and push the spray aside. The flatter area near the stern provides greater roll stability at low speeds and, in smooth water, helps increase speed by allowing the hull to ride on top of the water.

Tri-Hull. There are many shapes of tri-hulls, also called cathedral hulls. The basic design consists of three V-shaped hulls placed side-by-side. This shape provides a highly stable platform. The boats are speedy in smooth water, but have the drawback that they pound in rough water and create significant water spray.

Lower Colorado River Compliments of Sally Bond

• There are many basic *powerboat layouts*. The layout design is strongly dictated by intended use. A grouping of some general types that span the small-to-medium powerboat spectrum are highlighted below.

Runabout. These boats are the most popular, the standard for fun in the sun. They are daytime-use craft, serving for about every boat-related sport activity. Protected by a windshield and featuring a covered deck forward, it usually has seats which can be folded flat into sunning pads. Folding tops with clear side panels add all-weather protection, however this is generally a fair-weather craft.

Bowrider. An off-shoot of the runabout, the bowrider has an open area forward of the windshield with bench seating. Reached through a folding, walk-through windshield, the area adds room during low-speed operation and provides more fisherman space than a runabout. The open area is highly exposed and seldom occupied during high-speed running. For spray protection in the cockpit, a snap-on tonneau cover is often supplied or available on order.

Center Console. Though also used for day-cruising and waterskiing, this design has the fisherman in mind. The steering console is surrounded by a walkaround cockpit and the boats frequently sport an easily-detached windshield. These features allow a fisherman to work a fish with full movement around a relatively obstruction-free cockpit. This type of boat generally has scuppers to drain away cockpit moisture caused by spray, rain or choppy water. It usually comes with built-in bait and holding tanks, as well as integral fishing-rod-holding fixtures.

Cuddy Cabin. Though smaller than a cruiser, this layout includes a small enclosed forward cabin, frequently containing two dove-tailed bunks with a portable toilet between them. Classically, the steering console is amidships, with a cabin-entry door between the console and an adjacent passenger seat. The design allows two passengers to overnight in reasonable comfort.

Cruiser. As the cabin grows, the cockpit room diminishes; as a result, the steering console is forced further aft. The cruiser design emphasis is enhanced cabin space. In addition to a set of bunks, there may be a dinette that folds into a berth, the toilet may be in an enclosed compartment for privacy and the kitchen (galley) may have a sink with fresh water, an icebox and a stove

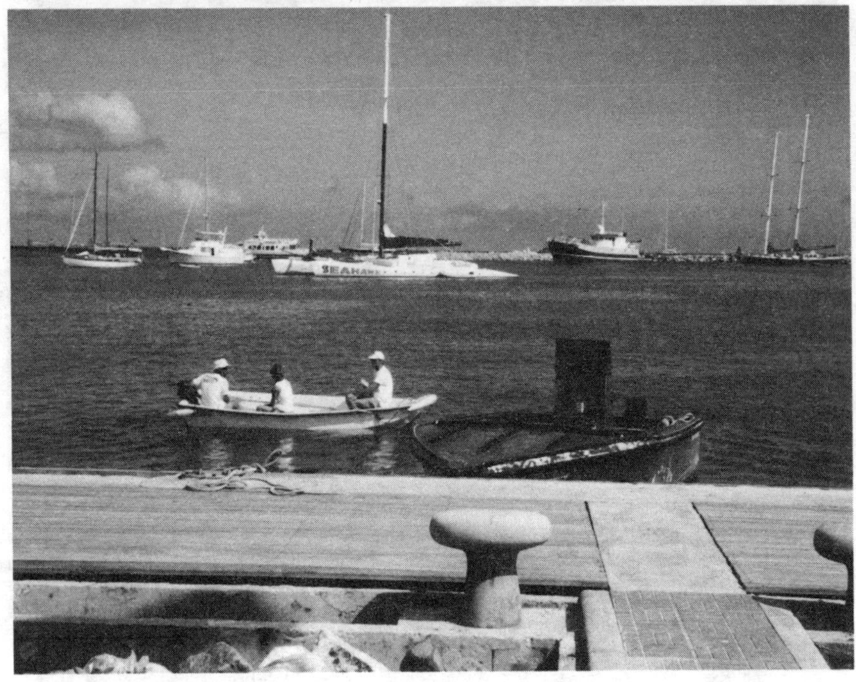

St. Martin (French Side), Caribbean

• Fiberglass is the material of choice for most powerboat *construction*. It's key virtues are flexibility, durability and low maintenance. Fiberglass construction methods vary, with the general rule being that less expensive processes tend to produce boats of less overall strength. The basic hull and deck are reinforced throughout and specific high-stress areas are strengthened by separate techniques.

Construction Methods. The method used will determine the strength and resilience of the hull and deck. The *chopper-gun* method uses a machine which spreads random fibers and resin into a mold, or form, that gives the hull its shape. It is an inexpensive method best used on small powerboats where strength and impact resistance are not critical. The *hand-layup* technique is the process of laminating a hull from fabric and resin, by hand. It is stronger than the chopper-gun method but also more expensive. It's use is commonly for high-speed and off-shore powerboats. The *solid-fiberglass* approach is to build a hull from layers of resin and fabric, without other reinforcing materials. It is the most common construction method for small powerboats.

Reinforcement. Adding to the hull and deck strength and adding thickness for penetration-resistance are reinforcement cores. The core is sandwiched between added layers of fiberglass. *Balsa coring* is light and strong, but subject to rot if not completely sealed off with fiberglass. Foam coring is impervious to rot but is less resistant to impact and crushing from hard blows. Although expensive, it adds insulation as well as strength. *Plywood* is often used to reinforce decks, but must be protected from water seepage and rot. Less expensive than foam or balsa, it is also heavier.

Support. *Closed-cell foam* is used on many boats to provide flotation, add strength and provide insulation against sound and moisture. In many designs, it fills all inaccessible areas of the boat. Beams that run fore and aft along the bottom of the hull, called *stringers*, serve to support the cockpit floor and are used as engine mounts. These may be solid wood beams encased in fiberglass or fiberglass sections filled with foam. Boats with outboards require an enhanced-strength *transom*. The most common process is to use extra-thick marine plywood sealed in fiberglass for this surface. Sterndrive boats may have either wood or thick fiberglass transoms. Most inboards, which place little strain on the transom, use standard-thickness fiberglass.

• Amongst *engine configuration choices* are outboards, sterndrives, jetdrives and inboards. Most are single engine configurations. Larger boats are sometimes equipped with twin engines to improve maneuverability in tight spaces and to provide redundancy in the event of an engine breakdown. Also, some outboard owners mount two different engine classes, using the big outboard for long runs and a smaller "kicker" that can be used for trolling and emergencies.

Outboard Motor. Less expensive than other engines, outboards provide the best power-to-weight ratio. They are available up to several hundred horsepower in V-8 configurations. The stern-mounted configuration maximizes the usable cockpit space for passengers or storage. Most outboards are two-cycle engines that require a gasoline/oil mix. The outboard tilts up to protect the propeller, a handy feature in shallow water. The engine can also be locked into a given tilt configuration to trim the boat for speed or balance.

Sterndrive. Also called an inboard/outboard or I/O, this option combines an inboard engine with a drive system similar to an outboard's. Like the outboard, the drive will kick up in shallow water or when hitting a shallow object and can be trimmed up or down to balance the boat. The engine is usually installed under a solid cover which takes up cockpit space, but this top is often covered with foam cushions and use as a sunning deck.

Jetdrive. Rather than use a propeller, this engine provides propulsion with expelled water. An inboard engine is connected to a high-pressure jet pump that propels the boat with a focused stream of water, much like a firehose. Steering is accomplished by turning the direction of the jet nozzle. Reverse is achieved by using internal gates and alternate channels to redirect water backwards and under the boat hull.

Inboard Motor. These are rarely found on small trailerable powerboats, but are very common to larger off-shore and racing powerboats as well as many larger-size cruisers. The typical inboard is a four-cycle engine. Most of the assembly is internally-mounted, with propeller shaft, shaft mounting bracket or enclosure, propeller and rudder being the externally-exposed elements. Unlike the other three designs, the drive mechanism is hard-mounted and exposed and, therefore, subject to likely damage when hitting an underwater obstacle or striking bottom.

• There is *additional outfitting gear* that will make the boat more versatile, more convenient to use, more comfortable or provide some combination of these benefits. These items are discussed in the SAILING activity under the "Sailboat" heading.

• The focus for *intended boat use* may range from pure cruising or supporting other waterborne activities. In many cases, the boat may support multiple uses. The choice between the boat characteristics identified in the preceding discussion will be strongly influenced by the owner's intended uses. Some general examples of popular choices, by primary intended use, are described below. (Racing boats have their own unique characteristics, which are beyond the scope of this book.)

Day Cruising. Runabout or bowrider layouts with deep-V or modified deep-V hulls and outboard engines are most typical for this use. Chopper gun and solid fiberglass overall construction are prevalent (true also for all but the "Weekend Cruising" option below) and the transom holding the motor is generally extra-thick marine plywood sealed in fiberglass.

Weekend Cruising. Cuddy cabin or cruiser layouts are best suited for weekenders. Most users choose deep-V or modified deep-V hulls and either outboard, sterndrive or, at the upper end in boat size, inboard engines. Construction methods similar to that for day cruisers is often used, although many opt for the strength of hand-layup construction, particularly for larger cruisers and any size where the user demands additional reliability and toughness. Runabout or bowrider layouts, when combined with on-shore camping, also can serve weekend duty.

Detroit Lake, Oregon

Diving. All boat layouts accommodate diving, however an abundance of cockpit room is a boon to divers and their cumbersome equipment. All hulls are used, although many favor the stability of tri-hulls, as do waterskiers and fishermen. Engine type is not highly important, because most activities are performed while the boat is anchored or operated at low speed to maintain steerageway.

Waterskiing. This activity places some of the most varied set of demands with respect to selecting the right boat and outfitting gear. All types of engines are used, depending on the load, speed desired and safety considerations. With regard to the latter, many prefer the jetdrive, since it eliminates the danger of propellers to skiers.

Low-speed *towing of saucers and kneeboards* requires as little as a 5-1/2 horsepower (hp) motor, with about 10 hp needed to provide all the necessary momentum for "trick" saucering or boarding. The average, well-performing *ski boat* is a 14-footer with wide beam (60-70 inches), equipped with 25-40 hp motor. This is the minimum to pull one skier with two people on board, a driver and an observer. The wide beam is for safety in cornering and stability against the pull of a strong skier cutting sharply to side of the boat.

For greater hauling versatility, a 15-17 foot boat with 50-100 hp will pull 2-3 skiers with more passengers on board, Also popular in this size range are the inboard/outboard types, which some users find have less of a wake problem than the more powerful outboards. Inboard boats also perform well for skiing and are preferred by some. These may be 15-18 feet in length with a 90-210 hp motor or combination. However, these craft have a larger maneuvering area (larger turning radius, lesser responsiveness) than an outboard combination of comparable total horsepower.

For most inboards, the standard *propeller* will serve well for towing skiers. For most outboards, lower-pitch propellers specially designed for towing skiers are available, although these should not be used at full throttle when towing. The rationale is to avoid overspeeding the engine with possible permanent motor damage.

There are various philosophies about use of *windshields* when towing skiers. Some remove them since they become covered with spray and reduce visibility. Plan to get a little wetter if you follow this plan. An additional aid used by boat drivers to add another set of eyes in tracking the skier(s) is a rear-view mirror.

The *attachment of the tow line* on a boat is most important for outboards; the rope must be hitched to clear the motor on swings and turns (the top of the motor casing is usually the highest point on the stern). There are a number of tow bars and brackets on the market. Whatever the choice, the rope should be attached fairly high so it doesn't foul the propeller when; 1) dropped by a downed skier; and 2) doesn't drag in water for trick skiing when slack develops in the line. Beware of using the two lifting handles commonly found on the transom -- in most cases, they are too low and possibly too weak. Don't use mooring cleats, as they are too low.

For *inboards*, the best arrangement is a pylon or post, bolted to the beams of the boat, set somewhere on the centerline between the middle of the boat and the transom. It should be at least three feet high. With this type of hitch, care should be taken to remove any stern fittings, cleats or other fixtures which could snag the line. Refer to the WATERSPORTS activity for information about waterskier tow lines themselves.

Fishing. For dedicated fishermen, the center layout is highly popular and outboards are the norm. Some go with high-powered engines to allow getting to widely-dispersed "fishing holes," while others settle for lower-powered models, where the emphasis is on trolling and a general slow-it-down pace. Outboards can be a distinct handicap when used with a downrigger, which is traditionally mounted at the stern. Another problem is that it's easier to tangle a fishing line on an outboard. This has tilted some to jetdrives and sterndrives.

Warp/Anchor Lines. The best line for dock use and rode is nylon, which is also handy for towing. For powerboats, the most frequently used nylon is the hard-laid, three-strand variety at least 5/8 inch thick. Nylon as anchor rode makes sense for powerboats because all-chain rode, when stored in a rope locker on the bow of almost any boat, will adversely affect performance. Boats that are designed to plane at speed do not like a lot of extra weight in the bow.

Although the rode may be nylon, ensure that 20-30 feet of chain is used to connect it to the ring at the top of the anchor stock. (Use a shackle to do this, then use an adjustable wrench to tighten the bolt hard. Wire it in place, or use plastic twist ties.) Once the anchor is deployed, the weight of the chain causes a more horizontal tension on the anchor, better ensuring it will not break loose. Also, the chain will not chafe on the bottom and sever, as line may sometimes do.

Paddle or Oar. For smaller boats or for powered secondary craft on larger boats, this item could become the single means of locomotion in a breakdown. Paddles and oars are also useful for pushing off and providing some of the services of a boat hook. Many outboards have a quick-release fitting for the steering system that allows you to remove the frozen steering system and steer the boat by turning the engine by hand. Because there's a powerful torque involved, the paddle or oar can be lashed along the side of the outboard to act as a tiller.

Paddles and waterskis can be used as makeshift rudders in the event of rudder failure (smaller boats only). With the engine at idle speed, you can drag the paddle on one side of the boat to make it turn in that direction. If this doesn't work, try putting the engine in neutral, swinging the boat to the proper heading, and reengaging the engine. In the instance that the boat hull is pierced and taking in water, a paddle or oar might serve the secondary use as a brace or jam for the gear used to plug the hole. (No. Martha, we are not trying to stimulate the paddle and oar business!)

Motor Oil, Coolant & Lubricants. Even if you follow a strict maintenance and upkeep schedule and check the boat religiously before departure, it is just good practice to bring along some spare engine oil and the lubricants needed for shift and throttle cables and steering systems, as well as grease for equipment such as water pumps. If needed, bring spare engine coolant. What and how much to bring is dependent on the particulars of your boat. Also bring a small bottle of distilled water for your battery for longer tours.

Sitka, Alaska

Personal Gear

The powerboating activity is not as physically exerting as sailing. In addition, there is less of a need to be exposed on deck when underway. As a result, personal clothing needs are less stringent. The layered clothing concept still applies, however there is less emphasis on paying the cost for waterproof, breathable outerwear. Rather, apparel that is simply waterproof will generally suffice for this activity. In the discussion below, we offer general *examples of outfits* (not including the standards like sunglasses, sunscreen, etc.) that might serve your purpose in order from warm weather to successively cooler conditions.

Warm weather: shorts or swim suit, "T"-shirt, deck shoes, sailing gloves, sun hat

Cool weather: underwear, warm shorts or long pants, long-sleeve shirt or sweater, waterproof windbreaker or jacket, deck shoes with socks, sailing gloves, sun hat

Cold weather: thermal underwear bottoms plus long pants, thermal underwear top and warm sweater, deck shoes with socks, pullover hat under sun hat. In high spray or wet conditions, consider an inexpensive plastic rain suit for limited on-deck activity. For enhanced protection, consider the "slicker" or breathable-fabric foul-weather shell and foul-weather boots discussed in the SAILING activity. The breathable shell may be an overkill in terms of cost, unless you plan to use it for other outdoor activities as well.

Deck Shoes. The footwear options described in the SAILING activity also apply to POWERBOATING. One proviso: If your boat uses diesel, get a pair of rubber boots to wear for engine-room maintenance. Wear socks with the boots, otherwise you may be facing an aroma that rivals that of "salty" leather and then some.

Safety

A condensed summary of the "Coast Guard-Mandated, Minimum Required Safety Equipment" is provided in the table in the SAILING activity. The word "Minimum" should be clearly noted. Many other items are important to ensuring safe boating as evidenced by the large number of "Safety" gear items listed in both the SAILING and POWERBOATING activity checklists.

Engine Manual. If you know your engine like the back of your hand, you may not need this. However, one experience of bobbing around without engine power, particularly if it's a simple fix explained in the "When Things Go Wrong" section of your manual, will convince you to bring it. You should also know how to evaluate and make simple repairs to such as faulty battery connections, the master switch, circuit breakers and wiring, as well as to replace spark plugs/spark plug wires and engine belts. Finally, you should be proficient at checking and clearing such items as the cooling water intake(s) and fuel filter(s).

Tool Kit

As with the SAILING activity, there are many options for selecting the tools and gear needed to handle equipment loss, reduced equipment performance, breakdown or other emergency situations. We have listed some of the more common items below. A tailored list should be based on your powered craft, trip type and duration, as well as your acceptable margin of safety above minimum needs.

Very commonly, boaters store many of their tools in a tightly-sealed plastic *tool box*. Metal tools should be sprayed with anti-rust lubricant before being stored. Water-impervious items might be stored together in a sea bag. All should be stowed securely in a readily accessible space.

Tools. Typical of the tools which might be carried are hammers, files/chisels, pliers and/or vice grips, a full set of engine wrenches (fixed, adjustable, Allen, spark-plug), screwdrivers, rotary drill with drill bits and other attachments, and wire clippers/strippers with spare wire.

Repair Gear. Among the repair items are electrical tape, sandpaper, hull patch kit and personal sewing kit

Replacement Gear. A sample of spares which might be carried include seacock plugs, tapered softwood plugs used in the event of hull puncture, spare hose and hose clamps (for both engine and hull fittings), spare control system cabling, drive belts, spark plugs and plug wires, distributor cap and rotor (latter four for gasoline engines), injector(s) (diesel engines), water-displacing lubricants (to keep moisture out of critical electrical parts), fuel filter and oil filters. Specifically for outboard motors, consider adding a spare electronic ignition, propeller, shear pins, split pins and cotter pins.

Secondary Activities

Refer to the SAILING activity.

POWERBOATING
(Daytime/Overnight)

Select items based on trip needs, considering type of boat, trip type/duration and weather conditions.

ITEM	DATE				
Boat Gear					
Boat Trailer/Tie-Downs/Locks					
Powerboat					
Lifeboat/*Dingby*					
Mooring Line/Towing Line					
Heaving/Lead Lines					
Fenders					
Boarding Ladder					
Paddle or Oar					
Boat Hook					
Motor Oil, Coolant, Lubricants+					
Canvas Covers/Spray Curtains					
Pail or Bucket					
Deck Swab					
Sea Bags (storage)					
Engine Ignition Keys & Spare+					
Float Plan					
Registration Papers					
Passport					
Personal Gear					
Swim Suit					
Deck Shorts					
Long Pants					
Shirt/Sweater					
Underwear					
Thermal Underwear*					
Jacket*					
Headgear (sun & cold weather*)					
Gloves					
Deck Shoes					
Foul Weather Boots*					
Windbreaker					
Foul Weather Suit*					
Bandanna/Sweatband					
Land Shoes					
Underway Living Gear					
Stove/Fuel†					
Fuel Funnel/Strainer†					
Coffee Pot					
Skillet/Frypan†					

POWERBOATING
(Daytime/Overnight)

ITEM	DATE				
Cooking Pots†					
Non-stick Cooking Lubricant†					
Pot Holders/Grippers†					
Dishware (plates, bowls etc.)†					
Paper Plates					
Cups (plastic, paper)					
Cooking Utensils (spatula etc.)†					
Can & Bottle Openers					
Eating Utensils					
Sponge & Scrubber†					
Dish Tub/Dish Towel†					
Paper Towels/Napkins					
Biodegradable Dish Soap†					
Water Jugs/Bottles					
Portable Ice Chests					
Ice and "Blue Ice"					
Insulating Bottle					
Table Mats/*Tablecloth*					
Sleeping Bags/Blankets/Sheets†					
Sleeping Pads†					
Pillows†					
Hammock					
Hygiene					
Towels					
Wash Cloth					
Personal Toiletries/Ditty Bag					
Toilet Paper & *Towelettes*					
Toilet Trowel					
Sun Shower					
Laundry Bag#					
Portable Toilet & Liners					
Safety					
First Aid Kit (see FIRST AID)					
Water Filter/Tablets					
PFDs & Throwlines					
Horn or Whistle (portable)					
Bell (portable)					
Power Megaphone					
Signal Flags					
Flares, Water Dye, Smoke Maker					
Flare Gun					
Fire Extinguisher(s) (portable)					

POWERBOATING
(Daytime/Overnight)

ITEM	DATE				
Sunglasses & Lanyard					
Heavy-duty Sunscreen					
Seasick Remedy					
Lip Balm					
Insect Repellent					
Waterproof Matches & Lighter					
Fire Starter/Heat Tabs					
Emergency Blanket					
Flashlight(s)#					
Spare Batteries & Bulb#					
Lantern#					
Spare Batteries & Bulb#					
Spot Light (portable)#					
Hand Timepiece#					
Thermometer					
Pocket Knife					
Compass (portable & hand)					
Coastal & Sea Charts/Light List					
Current & Tide Tables					
Parallel Rules/Dividers					
Waterproof Chart/Table Cover					
GPS Receiver					
VHF Radio (portbl.)/Cell Phone					
EPIRB					
Engine Manual(s)+					
Reading Glasses & Repair Kit					
Shark Repellent					
Phone Change					
Pen and Notepad					
Accessories					
Camera & Extra Film & Battery					
Camera Bag/Lens Cleaning Kit					
Brochures, Articles, Books					
Binoculars/*Telescope*					
Sewing Kit (personal)					
Trash Bag(s)					
Resealable Plastic Food Bags					
Spare Stuff Sacks					
Daypack (storage)					
Indoor & Outdoor Games					
Auto Tool Kit					
Spare Auto Keys/Credit Card/$					

POWERBOATING
(Daytime/Overnight)

ITEM	DATE				
Tool Kit					
Hammer(s)					
Files/Chisels					
Pliers/Vice Grips					
Wrenches					
Screwdriver(s)					
Rotary Drill(s)/Drill Bits					
Spare Wire, Clippers/Strippers					
Electrical tape					
Sandpaper					
Hull Patch Kit					
Personal Sewing Kit					
Seacock Plugs/Hull Plugs					
Spare Hose(s), Hose Clamps					
Extra Navigation Light Bulbs					
Spare Cable+					
Spare Drive Belt(s)+					
Extra Spark Plugs & Plug Wires+					
Spare Injectors+					
Distributor Cap & Rotor+					
Water-Displacing Lubricants+					
Spare Hose(s), Hose Clamps+					
Spare Fuel & Oil Filters+					
Spare Electronic Ignition+					
Spare Propeller+					
Spare Pins (shear, cotter, etc.)+					
Snacks/Meals (see MEALS)					

Italicized items-optional equipment *cold/foul weather items #night use items †overnight trips +engine

WATERSPORTS (Daytime)

See INDEX for checklist items not discussed below.

WATERSPORTS include activities such as swimming, snorkeling, scuba diving, water skiing, boardsurfing, windsurfing, rafting and jet skiing. Each is treated as a single-day activity. Water-skiing deals only with gear needed for the skier and that in the boat which supports the skier. (Boating-specific needs are treated in the POWERBOATING activity.) The single nighttime adventure treated is scuba diving. For multi-day camping adventures, refer to the additional equipment needs specified in the VEHICLE ACCESSIBLE CAMPING activity. If you are hiking, biking or boating into the site, check out the added gear needs as listed in the relevant activity.

Some gear unit properties in this section are defined in international metric units. This particularly applies to windsurfing boards, most of which are made in Europe. To convert, use the following: 1 millimeter = 0.0394 inch; 1 meter = 39.4 inches or 3.28 feet; 1 gram = 0.0352 ounces; 1 kilogram = 2.20 pounds; 1 square meter = 10.8 square feet; 1 liter = 1.06 quarts = 0.265 gallon.

Safety Considerations: 1) review the **GENERAL CONSIDERATIONS** and TEN ESSENTIALS sections; 2) learn to use and wear a PFD or BCD whenever the activity demands it; 3) develop swimming skills commensurate with the level of activity planned; 4) for all water activities, never go it alone; 5) take courses and practice the skills needed to engage in the relevant watersport; 6) obtain a scuba diving certification before venturing out "on your own"; 7) maintain gear, including powered craft, in safe operating condition; 8) for activities requiring gear assembly on site, perform a thorough pre-use inspection; 9) ensure that you understand and follow safe powered-craft operating and water-skiing procedures; 10) for water skiers, boardsurfers, windsurfers and jet skiers, learn how to bail out safely into the water when you lose it; 11) learn the notification and emergency signals associated with your watersport; 12) develop skills to read weather and water conditions and learn when to retreat to safety; 13) particularly for diving, plan your activity with consideration for water current, clarity, temperature and potentially dangerous underwater obstacles; 14) master the identification of potentially hazardous water creatures; 15) have in place and be able to execute an emergency situation plan; 16) learn basic first aid; and 17) bring foul-weather contingency gear, not only for comfort, but also safety.

In the checklist, items that are considered optional (niceties or special purpose) are *italicized*. Items noted with an asterisk(*) are for cold weather. Those noted with a pound sign(#) are gear items for night ventures.

Water Sports Gear

Gear Trailer/Auto Gear Rack. As with any other activity, a properly-equipped gear storage rack serves to increase passenger room, and related comfort, inside the vehicle. It is close to a necessity for hauling surfboards and windsurfing gear. If you have a large-internal-capacity sport utility vehicle (SUV) and only a couple of passengers, however, you may be able to get by without a rack. If you are hauling jet skis or a boat, you'll need a suitable trailer that is easy to load and unload from a water ramp. (Boat trailers are discussed in the SAILING section.)

When using an *auto gear rack* for surfboards and windsurfing equipment, the lowest cost and secure method for tie-down is to use wide webbing straps that lock on sprung teeth. The bars on the rack should have some form of padding before putting on the board (try rubber insulation tubes over the rack crossbars), with the windsurfer boom and mast placed on top. Feed the webbing through the front rack mounts and over the top of the gear, tightening down securely, but ensuring that the tie-down buckles do not physically contact the board. Get sufficient webbing to ensure there is a double set of strands over the top of the equipment. Next, perform the same procedure using the rear rack mounts. Look into models that have gear locks if you value your equipment highly.

Getting surfboards and windsurfing equipment from the car to the beach may call for additional equipment, provided you don't want to hand-carry the gear to the let-in point. The simplest is a *shoulder strap* equipped with slings that fit over the board. Simple two-wheel *trolleys* are sometimes used. You securely lash your gear to a crosspiece on what looks like a military bed headboard, then grab the other end of the sports gear and start walking. The wheels should be wide and of large enough diameter to cope with soft sand. More complex trolleys are also available. (Of course, you could always buy waterfront property, as have two of our major contributors, and forgo this hauling equipment!)

• Swimming

Pure recreational swimming, as a self-contained activity, requires a swim suit (most often), a set of goggles (if you want them) and a goal, whether it be to just enjoy playing around or to propel yourself to some objective. Swimming ability is also a fundamental part of the safety requirements of all other watersports activities. As an example, a person interested in skin and scuba diving should be able to: 1) tread water, feet only, for three minutes; 2) swim 300 yards without fins; 3) stay afloat 15 minutes without accessories; 4) swim underwater 15 yards without fins, without a pushoff; and 5) tow an inert swimmer 40 yards without fins.

• Skin and Scuba Diving

Mask. Face masks for snorkeling and scuba diving are designed to fulfill a specific need, which is to provide a constant layer of air between your eyes and transparent lens. They are designed to cover the eyes and nose. Inclusion of the nose permits pressure equalization of contained air with that of the ambient water. (Eye goggles can be used for near-surface swimming, but they demand that you come up for air and lose the constant underwater viewing pleasure offered by snorkel and scuba gear.)

The basic keys to selecting a mask are its comfort, efficiency for your intended uses and durability. For the first two keys, issues are size, shape, wearing comfort and positive seal. Size and shape are important, but not the most critical issue. The standard is a low-volume mask that is easily cleared in a single breath. High-volume masks offer side ports for enhanced peripheral vision, but may require two breaths to clear. There's nothing unsafe about the two-breath process, however some people are uncomfortable with water on their face for that long a period. Mask shapes vary from single lens, round and wraparound shapes to dual-lens designs (separate lens over each eye). Each type finds its own advocacy group, however certain features are a necessity regardless of style -- these are described below.

Comfort of fit and positive seal are the most critical properties. To check *mask fit*, place it over your face without donning the head strap. The skirt edge should contact your face completely. Inhale slightly with the mask in place -- the desired seal is obtained if the mask remains in place until you exhale. When worn, the strap should not put uncomfortable pressure on any part of your head. Old-style metal buckles are least expensive, but are harder to use. Higher-quality hard-rubber or silicon strap buckles can be adjusted without taking the mask off and are spring-loaded, making them effortless to use.

Base mask materials are most often rubber or silicone. With a proper fit, both will provide a quality seal. Rubber costs less than silicone, but rots far more quickly. The best designs have a shatterproof or tempered glass lens (plastic scratches easily and has a greater tendency to fog) which is buried in a rubber or silicone channel. The single-lens model is sometimes equipped with a tightenable metal band, and all good single- or dual-lens designs have an adjustable, head-fitting, well-anchored head strap. Some have a purge valve in the nose area, a convenience for clearing the mask, but also an addition to the "things to check" list. Others have nose-pinch pockets in the skirt, which allow you to close off your nostrils for clearing your ears.

There are many *fog-preventative measures* for the mask. The simplest is to periodically expose your inner mask to the ambient environment -- this could be a total rinseout at the surface or allowing a light water seepage into the mask when underwater. External preventatives used include saliva, seaweed, tobacco, raw potato or one of the commercial preparations.

A few major "don't do's": *Mask/snorkel combinations*, those with an integrated mask and snorkel, are considered hazardous. Concerns with them are that they require an unnatural breathing routine, may put excessive suction on your face sufficient to cause tissue damage, and allow a chance of dangerous carbon-dioxide buildup in the mask or tube. Also avoid use of *non-equalizing goggles* unless you are confining your effort to near-surface activities. They prevent equalization of the eye sockets and cause eye squeeze. The caution about *earplugs* is: "never use them!" They prevent pressure equalization of the outer ear and cause outer-ear squeeze. In a more severe instance, it is possible that earplugs may drive through the eardrum and destroy the auditory bones in the middle ear.

Newer on the horizon is *Snuba*, an easy-to-master cross between snorkeling and scuba diving. This option uses a standard snorkel mask and employs a (typically) 20-foot airline connected to an air tank that floats on a raft. With snuba gear, you are able to stay submersed well below the surface or near-surface depths typical of snorkeling, without having to take the more complex qualifying process associated with scuba diving. Depth is limited and you must contend with the hose while maneuvering.

St. Martin (French Side), Caribbean

Noseclip. Some scuba divers find that a noseclip is helpful for equalizing pressure in the ears and sinuses. A properly adjusted noseclip is comfortable and doesn't interfere with pressurizing the separate face mask or with expelling water. It can be valuable for keeping the nose dry if the face mask is flooded or lost. (In any case, all serious divers should be able to remove, replace and purge the face mask underwater without a noseclip.)

Snorkel. The diver's equipment is a *physically-separated mask and. snorkel set.* The snorkel is classically made of neoprene, plastic or rubber in a "J" or "S" shape. A properly-sized unit should be about 3/4-inch in diameter and about 12-14 inches long (measured above mouth level). Too small a bore may have you feeling like you are sucking through a straw, while a too large a snorkel tube will be more difficult to clear when you surface. Both should be made without sharp angles, sharp surfaces or internal reduced-bore sections that restrict airflow and create turbulence during breathing.

Some devices are fitted with an automatic shutoff or float valve to prevent water entry into the tube during full submergence. This reduces the amount of water that you have to clear when surfacing. Others have purging valves located below the mouthpiece. When you surface, the water in the snorkel above the outside water level drains through the purge. Both are convenience features that add to complexity, thus increasing the number of things that need to be checked regularly. The snorkel is held in the mouth by a molded rubber mouthpiece, which should fit easily and evenly, and has a thick rubber band or strap to hold it in place alongside the mask. The mouthpiece is fitted with bite-down "knobs" or a full oval bite-down surface.

Fins. The three basic fin types are body-surfing fins, full-foot fins and fins with heel straps. The body-surfing models are too small and too flexible to generate the propulsion needed for diving. Full-foot fins are worn like shoes. Your entire foot goes into the fin and there is no retaining device other than the resistance of the contacted rubber surface. With heel-strap fins, only the front two-thirds of your foot goes into the fin and a heel strap holds your foot in place. Heel-strap fins require booties to be worn to ensure a proper fit. Since booties insulate against the cold, these are the preferred style fins for cold-water divers.

If you are a weak swimmer, due to lack of experience or weak legs, look into fins which have a vent on the blade. They are designed to let water pass through the vent when kicking in one direction and to seal when kicking in the other. The design requires less leg strength to move the fins, but at some loss of propulsion efficiency.

Though both rubber and plastic fins are on the market, the former are generally preferred because plastic is less flexible and may crack or break under conditions of high stress. There are some variations in blade surface area, outline, curvature and degree of stiffening. Since blade size is usually proportional to foot size, only a limited degree of personal preference in blade size is possible.

Most fins are available in graduated sizes to fit small through large feet (usually two shoe sizes are accommodated by one fin size). Sizing fins should account for whether you dive barefooted (heel-strap fins) or wear neoprene booties, socks or the like (heel-strap fins). Modest fit adjustments are sometimes accomplished by lightly sandpapering inner surfaces (fit is too tight) or using waterproof adhesive tape (fit is too loose).

Weight Belt. Used by divers to provide negative buoyancy, this item should be of sturdy construction, flexible and wide enough to be comfortable when worn next to your body or outside an exposure suit. For safety purposes, it is equipped with a buckle that permits positive release with one hand. The wire buckle is favored by many scuba divers because it is different from those used on other scuba gear items. This allows the diver to find and release the belt by sense of touch, a valuable feature in situations where the belt must be dumped quickly.

Belt-size (girth) adjustment methods vary with buckle design. Such adjustment is necessary, not only to fit the individual, but also to provide additional length when protective clothing is worn. A plethora of pockets is desirable for varied weights placement -- an even distribution of weight is desirable for diver stability. Weights should be so constructed that they can be readily added or removed from the belt. They are normally uncoated lead (the cheapest) or plastic-coated weights.

Buoyancy Compensator. Formally known as a buoyancy control device (BCD), this gizmo serves the dual function of buoyancy compensator and personal flotation device (PFD), and is used by both skin and scuba divers. For scuba diving, the design should have an inflation system which is fed by the diver's regulator and a backup which operates independent of the diver's air supply. For both types of divers, the compensator should provide sufficient buoyancy when fully inflated to provide positive surface buoyancy with the wearer having flotation in the "face-up" position.

Many have a convenient set of zippered or Velcro-secured pockets in front, just below chest level, for storage of small gear items, including flares.

These apparel come in several different formats. The *standard BCD* is the classic "horsecollar" vest which circles the head and chest. This is the most popular style and is available with the widest range of features, including separate air cylinders for filling the vest. The *back-mounted BCD* has an inflatable bladder that circles the tank and does not attach directly to the body. Because of its slim, "out of the way" profile, it is widely used by cave divers. It is controversial among many ocean divers because it lacks a backup inflation system and will not support a surfaced diver in the face-up position. Concerns with the back-mounted models led to development of a *vest or jacket BCD*. Designed like a suit vest, it combines many of the best features of the first two designs, i.e., non-interfering design, primary/backup system inflation options, and positive, face-up surface buoyancy. The *skin-diving vest* is a lower-profile version of the standard BCD with less buoyancy volume. This format provides the needed flotation for a skin-diver, since he is unencumbered by the heavy scuba gear. It is inflated by mouth or by use of a CO_2 cartridge.

St. Johns, Caribbean

Base Float. A *base float* provides a place for gear and out-of-water fish storage, a platform for a diver's flag, a resting station and, in an emergency, as a rescue device. It should be brightly colored on it's above-the-water surface. It may be an inner tube, inflated raft or boat, modified surfboard. or other improvisation. Suitable racks or holding devices are frequently added to the float -- one standard is an inner tube or life ring with a net attached in its center well. If random diving coverage of a large area is anticipated, and if conditions permit, a towline attached to the float and diver can keep the station in close proximity.

The *diver's flag* is meant to advertise that diving is in progress in the area. The flag is red with a diagonal white strip from upper staff to lower outside corner. Most boaters, who the flag is primarily meant to warn, are familiar with the flag and give it wide berth.

Scuba Equipment. An open-circuit scuba system is one where air is breathed from a tank and exhausted to the surrounding water, as opposed to being recycled within a closed system. The latter (closed-circuit) scuba use requires special training and maintenance and is beyond the scope of this book. Open-circuit scuba systems are classically made up of the following basic components: scuba (air) tank(s), tank valves, demand regulator, and associated equipment including breathing and exhaust tubes, mouthpiece and mask. There are many types and manufacturers of these items on the market, many of which have proved useful for a varied class of divers. No one manufacturer or model, however, is ideal for all divers. Each diver will have individual requirements and preferences and should consult a diving instructor or other equally-qualified divers before making a final selection.

• *Scuba tanks* are available in a number of sizes and are generally made of steel, the historic standard, and aluminum alloy, the more recent (and lighter) addition. They are equally durable if kept free of damage and maintained in a clean and dry state inside. Steel tanks should be galvanized outside to protect against rust -- other protective surfaces will suffice, provided that scratches on the coating do not result in loss of rust inhibition. Tanks commonly in use in sport diving vary in capacity from about 18 to 80 cubic feet (cu ft) and a working pressure of 1800 to 3000 pounds per square inch (psi). The upper extremes are both more characteristic of the aluminum alloy tanks. The "seventy-one" or 71.2 cu ft steel tank, one of the most popular designs, weighs about 28 pounds empty, 35 pounds when filled, is about two-feet long and eight inches in diameter, and has a working pressure of about 2475 psi.

Peripheral tank gear is needed to carry the tank(s) and facilitate their use. The key components supporting those functions are the backpack and tank boot, respectively.

Backpack. A pack is used to strap the air tank(s) in a comfortable position on the diver's back. It consists of a main body and a tank-retaining band, which is attached to the main body. The pack is made in a variety of styles and can be worn in or out of the water. Two adjustable straps on the main body fit over the shoulder and one other around the waist. The waist strap and at least one shoulder strap should have a quick-release buckle for fast removal of the pack. A retaining band designed for ease in changing tanks locks the tank to the pack body. All parts should be made of corrosion-resistant material.

Tank Boot. Many divers use a boot to protect the tank bottom and to allow the tank to be stood up in an upright position. The unperforated, cup-like type, because it retains water, is less desirable than the open boot. Both types should be removed and rinsed after use to prevent corrosion from moisture held against the tank, whatever the tank material.

• *Tank valves* control the flow of air from the compressed-air tank to the diver's breathing regulator. They are designed to be screwed directly into the threaded neck of the tank, where they remain until removed for tank inspection or replacement. The most common types are an on-off valve ("K" valve) and another that signals when the air reserve has dropped to a specified pressure ("J" valve).

"K" Valve. When turned to the on, or open, position, air flows to the demand regulator until the internal tank pressure equals water pressure or the air supply is exhausted. Because this design lacks a signaling device to warn of low pressure, it is not recommended for use below 25 feet. This is about the depth that an emergency ascent is neither dangerous in terms of a diver relying on her inherent lung's air capacity nor suffering from decompressive effects.

"J" Valve. The "J" valve contains a spring-operated reserve mechanism that automatically shuts off the flow of air when the internal tank pressure falls to 300 psi. When the diver experiences difficulty in taking air from the mouthpiece, he or she is warned that the reserve is running low. The next action is to manually pull down the lever on the "J" valve to again release air and then begin the ascent.

Both types of tank valves contain a *burst disk* or *blowout plug* that releases tank pressure harmlessly in the event of overfilling or pressure build up due to overheating. Valves without this feature are illegal. Some valves have a small safety hole drilled through the threaded part that screws into the tank neck. This is an additional safety feature that allows air in the tank to escape slowly and easily before the valve is fully removed. Unscrewing the valve from a pressurized tank is extremely dangerous and should only be done by a professional.

Tank valves use a high-pressure black *"O" ring* as a seal between tank neck and valve, as well as between valve and regulator attachment. Without an "O" ring between the latter set, because of loss or damage, the valve is useless. For this reason, it is advisable to carry a spare "O" ring in case one needs to change the regulator attachment.

Buck Island, U.S. Virgin Islands, Caribbean

• *Demand regulators* come in single- and two-stage models. With the single stage type, tank pressure is reduced to ambient water pressure in a one-step operation. Although simpler than the two-stage design (in terms of the number of working parts) and being both easier to maintain and less expensive, it is harder to breathe through and is therefore more tiring for the diver. For this reason, most experienced divers recommend the two-stage design for sport diving.

Double-Hose, Two-Stage Regulator. In this design, both the first and second stages are contained in one housing and attached to the valve of the air tank. In the first stage, high-pressure air from the tank flows through a spring-operated valve into an intermediate air chamber at about 120 psi above the ambient water pressure. In the second stage, ambient water pressure acts directly against a flexible rubber diaphragm. The diaphragm is stationary until the diver takes a breath, at which time the diaphragm activates, forcing a mechanism to open a spring-operated valve in the first stage. Air then flows from the tank to the diver through a semi-rigid, flexible air hose running from the regulator to the right side of the diver's mouthpiece.

When the diver stops inhaling, the equalized pressure on both sides of the diaphragm causes the valve to close off the airflow. As the diver exhales, air from the lungs is forced from the left side of the mouthpiece into a similar hose, to the regulator, and exhausted into the surrounding water.

This regulator is commonly used in specialized activities such as salvage, commercial underwater photography and cold-water diving, but seldom for recreational diving. It does have advantages over the single-hose type: exhaust bubbles from the diver's mouthpiece are vented at the regulator behind the diver's back, thus allowing uninterrupted vision through the mask. In addition, this design is less likely to freeze up in special, cold water diving, an activity reserved for the well-practiced veteran.

Single-Hose, Two-Stage Regulator. With this regulator, the first stage is also located at the tank valve. In contrast, the second stage is built into the diver's mouthpiece. Air is carried from the first stage to the second stage by a single hose and exhaled air is exhausted through the lower part of the regulator. The first stage incorporates a diaphragm similar to that for the two-hose design or uses a piston valve. For both types, high-pressure air from the tank is sent to an intermediate air chamber, through the high-pressure hose, to the second stage at about 120 psi above ambient pressure.

In the second stage, air in the single hose is reduced to ambient pressure at the level of the diver's mouth. There, a second air chamber is separated from the surrounding water by a flexible diaphragm. As the diver inhales, a partial vacuum is created inside the chamber, allowing ambient water pressure to force the diaphragm inward. This activates a movable lever that opens an inlet valve connected to the high-pressure hose. As the diver stops inhaling, air pressure from the hose forces the diaphragm outward and the inlet valve is closed when air pressure inside the chamber balances with the ambient water pressure. It is this variable-depth balancing action of the second-stage regulator that allows the diver to breathe naturally.

The flow of air through the second stage can also be controlled manually by pressing inward on the *purge button* attached to the outside of the diaphragm. This action also opens the intake valve and allows air to enter the second-stage air chamber.

Exhaled air is released through the lower part of the regulator. As the diver breathes out, the increased pressure in the chamber opens a non-return exhaust valve and the used air is exhausted into the water. The regulator is then ready for the next cycle.

Octopus Regulator. An invaluable addition to the single-hose regulator is a second hose and mouthpiece that can be connected to the lower port on the first stage. Called an "octopus," it serves as a backup in case of failure of the primary mouthpiece, and can be used to supply air to a buddy diver in an emergency. Its inclusion as a standard part of the diver's equipment is highly recommended.

Depth Gauge. Depth, time at depth and elapsed dive time are the essential factors that a diver must monitor. Three gauge types are most prevalent. The *capillary gauge* is built around a small-diameter plastic tube which is open to the water on one end. It is mounted on or in the perimeter of a calibrated dial. As depth increases, the water forced into the tube reduces the trapped air volume. It is reasonably sensitive, relatively inexpensive and accurate to about 33 feet of depth.

The *Bourdon tube* works on the principle that ambient pressure is transmitted into a curved metal tube that tends to straighten as pressure increases. A change of tube curvature drives a gear system through a linkage, causing movement of a gauge indicator needle. This gauge must be protected against loss of seal and thoroughly rinsed after use to prevent obstruction of water entry ports. More expensive than capillary gauges, these devices are accurate to about 200 feet of depth, the maximum recommended for scuba use by even the most proficient divers with the top-of-the-line gear and expert buddy/support crew. (Dives beyond a depth of 130 feet are considered impractical for sport diving because of the limited air supply and the need for decompression -- even these depths should only be plied by expert divers.)

Liquid- or gas-filled gauges are most expensive and accurate at all practical depths. They rely on pressure variance upon an outer surface of the body of the gauge which is designed to be flexible. Such movement of the flexible area is then transmitted to the internal mechanism which, in turn, activates the indicator on the calibrated dial face. Although sealed against water, this gauge should be rinsed in fresh water after use, kept free of dirt and crystallized materials, and treated as a delicate instrument.

Timepiece. Though useful in other water activities, a timepiece is critical for scuba diving. It is used to keep track of elapsed dive time, for controlling the rate of descent and ascent and timing your underwater operations. One accepted standard for serious divers lists the need to have a *wrist-mounted watch* that is waterproof and pressure resistant to at least 220 feet or eight atmospheres. A desirable feature is that it be non-magnetic. The dial should be easy to read, have a visible sweep-second hand and adjustable bezel (stem) to indicate elapsed time. Other needed features are a non-corrosive case and a wrist band that is large enough to fit over the wrist of a wet suit.

Another option is get a bottom *time/surface interval gauge.* It automatically keeps track of your dive durations and the how long you spend out of the water between dives. Both wrist-mounted and console-mounted gauges are available.

Submersible Pressure Gauge. The *underwater pressure gauge* is attached to the tank valve or high-pressure part of the air regulator. It has a gauge which registers the exact pressure within the tank. A high-pressure hose 2-3 feet long, connecting gauge to tank, allows you to attach it to a tank strap or buoyancy compensator where it is readily accessible underwater.

Some divers buy a *gauge console* that puts all the gauges at the end of the submersible pressure gauge hose. Nominally, you buy the console fully equipped although custom designs are not uncommon. The latter allow you to select amongst brands and carry your preferred gear, gauge by gauge.

Dive Computer. Dive computers combine all the gauge functions into one unit. They provide standard information such as dive elapsed time, current depth and tank pressure. More impressive, simply look at your computer and it tells you how long you can stay at any given depth. During the dive, the computer tells you how much time you have remaining; it will automatically adjust this time if your depth changes. Some models will calculate how much longer your air will last based on your current consumption rate. There are numerous other available features, depending on intended use (particularly if you are a deep-water diver who must follow a safe decompression profile when ascending).

St. Johns, Caribbean

Key properties to consider: What readouts does the computer provide? What is the limit on computer storage capacity with regard to number of dives? Among other considerations are the computer's method of activation and characteristics of the power system. Typical on/off mechanisms are manual switches, water-immersion mechanisms and scuba tank/pressure-activated devices, each with their positive and negative features. The main power system considerations: What is the battery life span and are the batteries replaceable without returning the computer to the manufacturer. Can you change the battery without losing information stored in the computer? Is there a low battery warning or indicator? Consult an expert at your local dive shop for more information and tradeoffs dealing with these devices.

Knife/Prying Tool. It is a general precaution in scuba diving and more advanced skin diving to carry a *knife* sheathed in a scabbard on a suitable belt. Encounters with kelp, grass, derelict lines and the nightmare of monofilament fishing line (yeah, from those guys in the LAND FISHING and SEA FISHING activities) require a good blade to prevent or undo tangling. It is firmly attached in an accessible location on the diver's person, usually the leg. To prevent accidental loss when not in use, the knife is secured to the belt with a detachable lanyard. Many divers attach the lanyard around the wrist when using the tool.

The well-designed knife should have a reasonably sharp, serrated or sawlike edge, strong blade, a hole or ring in the handle for attaching a lanyard, and an easy-to-grip handle. Two satisfactory types of knives are the standard diver's knife and the Army combat sheath knife, which are available at dive shops and sporting goods shops/Army-Navy surplus stores respectively.

An alternative to the knife is a prying tool that has many of the same features of the knife, but a stronger blade and a chisel-shaped versus pointed end. It provides the same safety functions as the knife, but is better suited for prying and digging.

Life Lines. One variant is commonly referred to as a *buddy line*. Nominally 6-10 feet long, each team member secures one end of the line to himself, with one line per pairing. This rig is for use in poor visibility conditions or at night, with the purpose of keeping team members in close proximity. In addition, the rig provides a means of communication between divers through a system of tugs that all members have agreed on before the dive. These tugs might be informational instructions or emergency signals.

The *float line* is a line long enough to reach from the desired depth to the surface. One end is secured to a float and the other to the diver's body (not his equipment). The line may be marked with knots to indicate depth and associated decompression stops. When the diver surfaces, he is assured of being in close proximity to a potential life-saving piece of floating equipment. At the very least, he finds a nice rest stop and place to store his catch or gear found to be unnecessary. When attached to a boat, this becomes known as a *surface line*. Either line can be used to signal topside partners of intentions or an emergency.

• Water Skiing

Ski Boat. Ski boat characteristics are discussed in the POWERBOATING section under "Water Skiing" as the key *"intended boat use."*

Water Skis. The two basic types of water skis are *combination* (or combo) and *slalom skis*. Combos are two nearly identical skis designed to be easy to ski in, and are the natural choice for entry-level skiers. They are relatively easy to get up on and stable. Some intermediate and almost all advanced skiers prefer the single slalom ski, which has the advantages of being faster and more maneuverable. The slalom ski has two foot bindings on the one ski. The rear binding generally has no heel support, so the foot can slide in and out easily.

• *Ski length* is a tradeoff of skier weight and boat horsepower. Both higher skier weight and lower engine horsepower drive water skiers to increased length to obtain increased buoyancy. Longer (and broader) skis are better for the rough water often found on large lakes or near-shore ocean water. Shorter (and thinner) skis will turn sharper and work better on small, calm lakes and rivers. Specifics of ski selection for different classes follows the definition and description of ski characteristics below.

Though it varies with the boat type, ski design and water conditions, the following minimum-horsepower (hp) thumbrules are provided for boats with outboard motors: For the longest ski (about 72 inches), roughly a 10 -to 15-hp motor is needed to tow a 100- to 125-pound (lb) person at moderate (20-30 miles per hour or mph) speeds and greater than 40 hp for a 200 -to 250-lb person. At the other extreme, for children and small adults weighing 75-100-lbs on 48-inch skis, at least 40 hp is needed, while 20-30 hp is adequate for the same weight group using 54-inch skis. In actual practice, the most popular weight/ski-length combinations currently used are: under 140 lb/64 inches; 140-175 lb/66 inches; and over 175 lb/67-68 inches.

• *Ski bindings* are designed to keep you on your skis as well as act as the means of transmitting power from your legs to the ski or skis. The binding should fit snugly, yet release readily when you fall or want out of your skis. Most combos, have adjustable bindings (generally, a fixed toe piece and adjustable heel binding on each ski), so that you can alter the fit as you learn more about what is optimum for you. This feature also allows multi-person use of the skis. Further, purchase a set that has a rear toe binding on one ski so that when you are proficient enough, you can use it as a starter slalom ski. The bindings on more expensive skis are made of higher quality rubber and offer more support than the lower cost models. Ensure that the bindings have holes for your fingers so you can grasp them to assist in getting your foot inside.

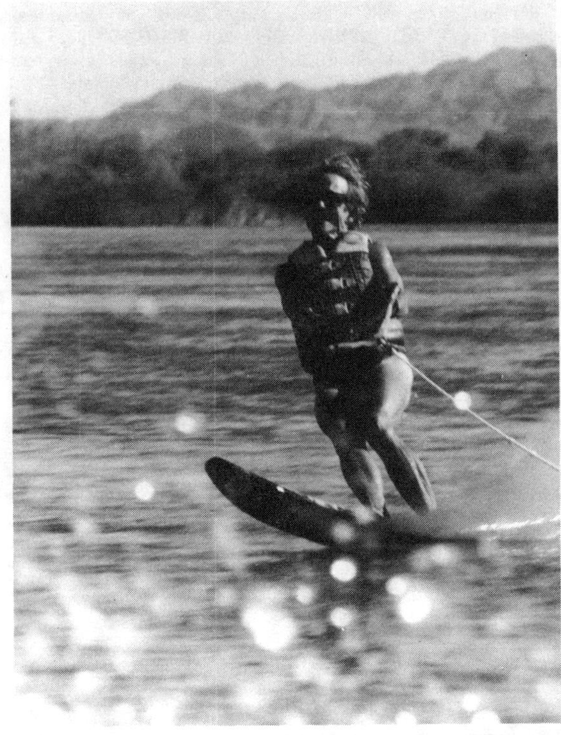

Lower Colorado River Compliments of Walt Bond

The better slalom skis have foam or softening pads inside to cushion the feet and are made of heavy rubber for strong foot and ankle support. These bindings are usually adjustable; either the toe piece stays fixed while the heel piece slides forward or vice versa. Sometimes they are mounted directly on the ski rather than on a plate. These types are characteristic of lower end beginner slalom skis and are even found on a few intermediate models. Plate mounting provides a sturdier ski.

The binding may or may not come with ankle wraps, which offer the ankle additional support through use of a long rubber piece that crisscrosses around the ankle and is adjusted with a Velcro-type closure. High-performance bindings that the advanced and competitive skiers use have double-high wraps -- strips of heavy rubber that go around the ankle in two directions. In addition to the standard open-toe rear binding, the higher-performance designs offer the option of a double-high wrap, which provides improved support. If your style is to keep the rear foot free when doing deep-water starts, you'll have to stick with the open-toe design.

• With regard to *materials*, most skis are made of fiberglass with some kind of interior strengthening fiber such as graphite, Kevlar or ceramic composite. The amount and type of fibers used and their placement affect the stiffness of the ski. Less-expensive, less-durable skis are made from the reaction-injection molded (RIM) process, while the higher-priced designs are built using the compression molding method. The former is somewhat more of an assembly-line process, while the latter involves each ski being individually constructed by a skilled craftsman.

There are a varied combinations of *ski shapes* which are selected based on the skiers intended use and level of proficiency. The shape selected will affect general ease of use, ultimate speed, turning agility and acceleration, and stability.

Bottom Design. This is the shape of the ski bottom as viewed front-on or rear-on. Flat bottoms are least expensive. Narrow channels are more stable and track better, while wide channels or rails provide better lift with good stability. Wide concave designs sit deeper, allow changing edges with less effect, but feel less stable on the water. Shallow concaves cause the ski to ride higher in the water, making for easier turns.

Perimeter Shape. This is the overall silhouette as viewed from directly above or below the prone ski. A wide front allows easier deep-water starts and hard turns while standing on the nose. A narrower front drops into the water more easily during the turn, but will throw a skier forward off the ski if his weight is too far forward. Wide midsections allow easier turning, but make it harder for the ski to hold an edge. Wide tails improve stability, making them better for beginners, while narrower tails provide more responsive turning performance.

Bevels. The shape of the ski edge, best viewed front-on or rear-on, is the bevel. A sharp bevel (e.g., a vertical edge that gives way to a sharply-angled edge) provides lift for the ski, keeping the ski fast and limiting spray. A rounded bevel (a completely rounded edge) allows the ski to roll from edge to edge with less resistance, making linked turns easier. The larger the bevel (the larger the angle between the vertical and angled edges), the slower the ski will be due to drag, but also the more stable. The smaller the bevel, the higher the ski will ride.

Rocker Shape. When viewed side-on, the rocker is effectively the curvature of the ski base. The toes (tips) of skis are universally curved upward to avoid digging into waves. Continuous fore-to-aft rocker makes it easier to turn when the skier's weight is on the tail; a flat section in the overall rocker makes the ski more stable and works well for a skier who rides forward. Tail rocker slows a ski down, but enables a skier to turn more easily. Conversely, less tail rocker allows more turning acceleration, though the ski is harder to turn.

Flex. Effectively the ski stiffness, soft skis turn more easily, but provide less acceleration on turns. Soft flex allows a skier to move around more on the ski without falling; stiff flex gets the skier through the wakes faster allowing more set up time for the next turn.

Fin Shapes. Most combos and predominantly all slalom skis have a tail fin. The fins assist in tracking a course and provide a measure of roll stability. A flat leading edge holds the tip of the ski up, while a rounded front edge pushes the tip down. A cutoff back edge allows skis to pivot more quickly.

• A *summary of desirable ski characteristics by class* is provided below, based on the detailed discussions above. The summary is a nominal guideline only. Your specific needs are best fleshed out by talking with the experts at your local waterskiing or watersports shop.

Beginning-Intermediate Skier. A good entry-level set of combination skis might have: adjustable bindings; one ski with an added rear toe binding; RIM construction (compression-molded manufacture if you are very serious and willing to spend the money); flat, concave or narrow-tunneled bottom design; wide perimeter shape; flat edges or large bevel; mild rocker; soft flex; and shallow fin.

Advanced Intermediate Skier. After graduation from combos, slalom skis might have: adjustable or fixed bindings; RIM or compression-molded construction; concave or tunneled bottom design or a combination of the two; narrower nose than that for combos, with a medium taper from body to tail; sharp bevel; enhanced rocker; mid-range flex; and deeper fin.

Advanced Skier. Performance-seeking slalom skiers might have: adjustable or fixed, high-wrap or double-high wrap bindings; compression-molded construction; wide concave or tunneled bottom design or a combination of the two; narrower nose than that for intermediate-advanced skis, with a narrow taper from body to tail; rounded, sharp or combination bevels; significant rocker; mid-range flex; and deepest fin, possibly with attached wings.

• *Saucers* offers many of the thrills of water skiing, but at lower speed (about 10-12 mph) and with the advantage of being able to perform more stunts than are possible on water skis. Horsepower requirements for the pulling boat are modest compared to water skiing. The saucer is a circular piece of marine plywood, approximately 40 inches in diameter and 1/4-inch to 1/2-inch thick. It is usually brightly painted for style, but the surface coat also serves as a protective coat.

• Perhaps even more popular recently are *kneeboards*. This is the kneeling version of water skiing, also known to many as "knee skiing." It is the easiest form of water skiing, doesn't require a lot of the strength or skill of actual water skiing and, like saucering, is performed at low speeds (between about 18-22 mph for simple planing, where the upper speed range is needed for heavier boarders). The board is a more aerodynamic version of a bodysurfing board with a "cockpit," having padding for the knees and feet and a restraining strap which passes above and over the knees.

Board Types. There are two basic designs for kneeboards. The flat-bottom "slalom" kneeboards have less drag, which makes it easier to switch from rail to rail (the side edges) across wakes and when turning. Convex-bottom "trick" kneeboards have a pronounced rocker which gives them lift off the wake. They have a softer flex than the stiff slalom board, so when you hit a wake, they flex and give you lift. The convex bottom prevents you from catching the rails, just the opposite of the slalom boards.

Board Construction. The majority of boards have a polyurethane shell and are foam filled, although some expensive, custom boards have a foam core like surfboards and sailboards. The latest version is a compression-molded board made like a slalom ski.

Board Features. Most kneeboards have grooves or channels on the sides for better tracking. Some come with fins, others without, and some have retractable fins. Fins are good for slalom use, but they won't allow the board to spin for tricks. Most beginners find it easier to learn on a board with fins.

The lower cost boards merely have flat pads in the cockpit bottom; the more comfortable models have a wall of foam around the edge of the cockpit and hollowed-out foam wells for the knees. Some models have a center foam strip between the legs to keep them from banging together. Another improvement is the addition of ankle roll pads, which provide both additional comfort and board control.

The restraining strap is a seat-belt-like contraption which holds the kneeboarder in, but also releases under the pressure of a wipeout. A two-inch width with a strip of Velcro for hold-down is typical. Trick knee skiers commonly use a three-inch strap, which allows more control, leverage and support for maneuvers. These straps may have an extra neoprene pad to go across the thighs and a double-Velcro closure to keep the strap from releasing during heavy-leverage tricks.

• Finally, there are *trick skis*, typically slalom skis that are much shorter than the standard types, only 36-44 inches in length, and nominally 8-10 inches wider. They generally have no bottom fins and are made of the same high-tech materials as the classic slalom skis. These skis are in the domain of advanced skiers who concentrate more on "hot dogging" than racing competition.

Towline. A 75-feet length line is optimal for most skiing and saucer riding, with 70 feet of line and a five-foot handle bridle. A shorter line will pull the skier too close to boat's spray and back wake, while a longer line could drag in the water. Towlines that are one continuous length of rope, with no loops for adjustments, are known as *jump lines*. Those that have multiple loops at specific line lengths are *slalom lines*; they can be progressively shortened for slalom competition.

Since the line can be used to bring the towed person closer to the boat and, thus, more into its wake, the slalom line is also the choice for hauling saucerers, kneeboarders and tuberiders. Typically, taking 28 feet off the standard 75-foot slalom line (the third loop, which is usually yellow), is a good length for kneeboarding behind an inboard. If you'll be kneeboarding behind an outboard, which will have a bridle on its transom, try 32 feet off (green, or fourth loop), which will give you a little shorter line to make up for where the rope attaches to the boat.

Lake Tahoe, California — Compliments of Susan Cohen

With regard to *materials*, the least expensive, but most stretchy and most short-life towrope is the eight-strand monofilament line. Twelve-strand polypropylene ropes, on the other hand, are specially designed for skiing. They can take a stronger pull without breaking, are less stretchy, are far more sun resistant, and they float. There is also a specialty rope designed for trick skiing and barefoot skiing, which is made of Kevlar. This very expensive line is made for dead pull (no stretch), well beyond the needs of all but expert waterskiers.

Tow-line *handles* can be purchased as a part of the tow line or bought separately and attached. Most often, they are designed to float. Although double handles are still available, the single handle is safer and easier to use, as there is less chance of becoming tangled. If you intend to do one-handed slalom turns, the single handle is a must. They are most often made of aluminum tubing that is filled with wood to prevent bending; the tubing is covered with a soft grip material, typically smooth rubber. Most handles come in round, rectangular or oval shapes. You should choose whatever feels best to your hand, or if sharing, select the best compromise design.

For information on boat-fixed skier tow hitches, refer to the POWERBOATING activity.

Personal Flotation Device. Water skiers must, by law, wear PFDs in most locales. Most skiers wear a Type III personal flotation device (PFD). (See the CANOEING (Daytime) activity for Type descriptions.) The Type III is generally selected because it will keep your head above water without paddling and is not so bulky as to restrict the normal skiing motions (other than the horse-collar vest, which should be avoided).

The PFD should have extra-large armholes for movement and fit snugly when cinched. It should close by use of external buckles (buckles next to the body can cause real discomfort in a fall), a zipper or both. Length sufficient to reach your waist is acceptable, however models that reach down to your hip bones are preferred.

The cheapest models are shiny, soft-vinyl jackets, which break down relatively quickly in sunlight and have the annoying habit of sticking to your skin. A few skiers go with neoprene vests, which are long-lasting and more body fitting, plus they tend to retain warmth better. However, the bulk of the community uses nylon-covered PFDs, generally in the mid-pricing range and most often having more flotation than comparably-sized neoprene designs.

• Boardsurfing

Perhaps the wildest and fastest of the non-powered watersports, speeds up to 40 mph can be reached as the board follows the crest of a 20-foot wave. As with any other activity, there are numerous equipment styles and designs which can be tailored for the surfer's use and capability level.

• Several different types of *surfboard materials* are used. Modern boards made of balsa wood and weigh about 25 pounds. In addition to shaped balsa boards, others are made from balsa and plywood, filled with foam plastic for additional buoyancy. Top of the line are fiberglass boards. Finally, some surfboards are made of marine plywood or masonite hulks containing an air chamber for buoyancy.

• There are numerous *types of boards* in use. Though a few use a square-sterned board, the Malibu board, with its pointed tip and sharply-rounded stern, is the popular favorite. This board is about 2-1/4 feet in width and is somewhat shorter than older boards, averaging less than six feet in length. Its proponents say that it is easier to carry, less tiring to paddle and takes off more rapidly in a wave. A few of the board designs and associated use are described below. Most have a fiberglass top and bottom, a 7-1/2-ounce deck patch of isothalic resin, and a 1/8"-balsawood or 1/16"-redwood centerstringer.

Single-Fin Designs. The shape is made for the beach break, designed for quick turns and use on smaller (under six feet or so), fast waves. It is most frequently used by surfers who like to turn a lot and drive hard across and through the wave with a quick rhythm. Average dimensions (width and thickness vary with length) are 5' 10" x 21-1/2" x 4". This board has a rounded bottom, a Malibu top-surface profile and a 10"-depth fin, .

Short Deck-Shaped Designs. This shorter board is made for easy paddling and fast response under varying surf conditions. Average dimensions are 5' 5" x 22" x 3-1/2". The board has a flat bottom, a nearly-square stern with either pointed or round nose, and three guidance system boxes in conjunction with two 6" fins or a single 10" fin.

Twin-Fin Designs. This medium-length board is best suited for use on larger, heavier waves. It is fast and the twin fins help draw the turns out for maximum acceleration. It is designed for the surfer who wants to develop a fast-running, smooth rhythmic style. Average dimensions are 5' 8" x 22" x 4". The board has a rounded bottom, a diamond- or square-shaped tail with a pointed nose, and two or three guidance system boxes in conjunction with twin 6" fins

• Boards should be stored in a shady place, and the cork in the nose of the board, which is put in for an air hole, should be removed when the board is not in use.

Otherwise, air inside the board will expand, then contract when the board is put in cooler water. A few of these expansion-contraction cycles may actually cause the board to crack.

Maui, Hawaii

Some watersports enthusiasts combine skin diving with the use of a surfboard, which serves as transportation to the site and acts as a base float. Surfboards also have been fitted with a short-masted sail with a long rudder controlled by the feet or with a tiller or cross-member. Keel or centerboards provide stability. These are effectively surfboards rigged for sailing.

Few, if any wear PFDs -- they are actually a potential hazard. When a surfer is plunged into the trough of a wave (or "pearl dives"), his or her best bet to avoid the potentially-lethal wayward board is to stay under long enough for the wave to pass and the board to surface.

• Windsurfing

Board. Key properties to consider are board type, materials and construction. When choosing a board, match those characteristics which are best suited to your skill level and intended use.

• *Types of boards* include basic flatboard, all-round funboard, open class roundboard, the true funboard, and the sinker. The first two are entry level/ intermediate boards, while the latter are specialized boards for advanced sailers. All designs have a lift in the nose profile ("rocker") which prevents the board from diving into waves. The degree of curvature is least for the basic flatboard and tends to increase as the design is more attuned to challenging or riding waves.

Flatboard. This is the design that started it all. It is the best to start on, and one of the most popular for all-around use. Flat-bottomed, stable and forgiving, almost every manufacturer has a board in this class. Common dimensions are 3.8 meters (m) in length, 19 kilograms (kg) in weight with a sail in the 5- to 6.5-square meter (sq m) range. It typically has a snubby nose and square tail, with a large, fixed dagger.

All-around Funboard. This type has displaced the basic flatboard as the most popular type you will see today. Sizes are much the same, but both nose and tail are tapered. This board also comes with all the trimmings of footstraps, small retracting dagger and a variable-position mast track versus a fixed mast anchoring foot. The trimmings are not of much use for the learner, but make control of the board easier as you improve skills and sail in stronger winds.

Funboard. The true funboard is designed to be used in high winds and must be planed (skimmed across the water, as opposed to sailing through it) at all times. Lengths in the 2.9 m-range are most common, with some out to 3.2 m. Small size, combined with small daggerboard, give the funboard the right mix of speed and maneuverability while being relatively easy to sail.

Open Class Roundboard. These are specialized, advanced-design four-plus m racing boards, most often used in Open Class Division II triangle racing events. They are tricky to sail owing to their rounded bottom shape (which makes the craft relatively unstable), and tricky to manufacture down to minimum weight due to their high volume. Some are hollow with a foam sandwich skin, while others are custom-made from foam block.

Sinker. The extreme surfboard for real experts, the sinker is in the 2.6 m length range and is very light (about eight kg), providing minimal buoyancy. Waterstarts (a complex maneuver, requiring that you start sailing when lying in the water, with the sailing rig on top of you to the windward of the board) and power gybes (gybing by forcing the rig against the wind to turn the board) are mandatory maneuvers for those using this board. It has 1-3 skegs, no daggerboard, and a mast foot which is located forward. Typically, it is a shaped foam block covered in fiberglass or something like Kevlar.

There are also *tandem boards*. They typically have a large single daggerboard and a big fin at the tail. They have mastfoot positions for two sailers. but also usually have a central position so the board can be sailed with one rig single-handedly. Many are funboards, with extended length and heavier weight compared to the solo versions.

St. Martin (French Side), Caribbean

• *Board materials* are many and varied, particularly with the large number of custom designs that ply the waters. The discussion below treats the most commonly used materials for both board and board components.

Board. Made from plastic, there should be no bumps, hollows or cracks and the join along the sides should appear perfect. There should be a good non-slip finish on deck, but be wary of hard angles -- odd-shaped decks tend to be cosmetic rather than functional. The hull should be completely foam filled. Check that there is enough buoyancy to carry your weight -- at least 1.3 liters for every pound of your weight (e.g., 195 liters for a 150-pound person).

Fin. The fin is plastic, frequently Lexan polycarbonate or stronger glass-filled polycarbonate.

Daggerboard. Nominally plastic, you will find alloy or laminated plywood daggerboards on race boards -- they are lighter and stiffer, but the ply ones require careful looking after. For ease of use, consider daggerboards which retract into the hull.

Fin Boxes, Dagger Board Cases, Mast Footwells and Tracks. These elements are either integral with the molding of the board, or separate plastic units bonded into position. Often one specialist manufacturer supplies a common unit for several different boards, so they are interchangeable.

Universal Joint. Classically, this is a rubber coupling (also called the "UJ" or "power joint") that links the rig to the board.

Rig. Boards and rigs (sails plus rigging) are usually sold together, however most boards and rigs are interchangeable. Choose which sail and rigging suits your weight and physical capabilities best when starting to windsurf, then add more rigs to your inventory as you improve your technique.

St. Thomas, Caribbean

Quality of cloth and cut of the *sail* vary. There are all sorts of sail materials from basic polyester fiber sailcloth (e.g., Dacron and Terylene) to more exotic plastic-film laminants (Mylar, Melinex, etc.) with superior weight and stretch characteristics. The latter are more expensive and appear to be less durable.

A lower-end design for learners in light winds is the basic triangle. Designs for strong winds have at least one full-length batten supporting the head and some for more extreme weather have several full-length battens spaced across the sail face (or luff). These heavy-duty designs most often have enhanced reinforcement at all three corners of the sail. A large window for good sailing vision is considered a bonus to some and a necessity by others, particularly wave riders and racing sailers who frequently find themselves sailing in a tight pack.

The following are general guidelines for sail size selection: An average beginner wants a sail that is easy to handle, say 3.0 sq m for children and 4.8 sq m for a relatively-small adult; 5.6 sq m for someone of average size and strength; and a full 6.5 sq m for a strong, agile six-footer -- this assumes sailing in light wind. For experienced sailers in medium-to-strong wind use (Force 4 on the Beaufort Scale or 11-16 knots), a reasonable sail area might be 5.8 sq m, dropping to 5.2 sq m as the wind level increases. For very-high winds (Force 6 or 22-27 knots, or more), 4.1 sq m would be about right, and in extremely-high wind, consider dropping down to 3.0 sq m.

Typically, *masts* are made of fiberglass in a process similar to constructing fishing poles. If it breaks in the surf, it can often be repaired on shore. Tapered alloy extrusions are used for racing because they weigh less and are more responsive. However, they are less robust than fiberglass and must be repaired in a properly-equipped repair shop.

Standard *wishbone* design calls for a rubber-sleeved alloy with plastic end fittings. The less flex in the wishbone (or boom), the better. For stronger winds, a short boom length with a fairly high clew (the outer corner of the sail which is attached to the end of the wishbone) is preferable. It makes the rig easier to pull out of the water, and it is likely to make the center of effort more stable and easier to control. A boom length of around 2.1 m is about normal for a 5.8 sq m sail, while smaller sails can have much shorter booms which are best suited to short boards under 3.0 m.

Harness. The harness allows you to put your back into windsurfing rather than beating those tired arms to death. Before you use a harness, you should be a proficient sailer in strong winds -- the rationale is that you should be able to sail out of a stressing situation if your harness or harness lines break. Try using the harness on dry land first, practicing the hook-in, hook-out techniques until you feel proficient in its use.

The harness should give maximum support to your rib-cage, which is compressed during use, and your back from shoulders to waist. It should be a tight, but comfortable fit with foam padding along the frontal straps and across the back. The harness lines should be pre-stretched Terylene of around 5 millimeter (mm) diameter. The length should be that which is comfortable to you, but not longer than 130 mm. Although you can make your own harness lines cut to length, it is probably safer and more reliable to buy specially-made lines which have webbing and Velcro attachments at each end.

It is recommended that the harness have a quick release buckle. Some commercial models also have a plastic buckle for making adjustments to line length. Another harness feature is a backpack or pocket for carrying a spare harness and other small useful items. For the safety conscious, the harness should have some buoyancy, though few are designed to float you above water, face upwards.

Personal Flotation Device. Ideally, a windsurfer could wear a life jacket or Personal Flotation Device (PFD) which is designed to provide positive surface buoyancy with the wearer having flotation in the "face-up" position. These are Type I or II PFDs as described in the CANOEING (Daytime) activity. However, Type I and II PFDs are too bulky for windsurfing and many feel the Type III designs are still too constrictive. One solution for more benign activities is to wear a simple, unobtrusive *buoyancy aid* which makes staying afloat easier, but is not self-supporting. A safer option is to get a CO2/orally-inflated *Type V PFD* that can be combined with a harness and won't constrict movement or get in the way. This, in essence, is the scuba diver's buoyancy compensator without the tank feed inlet.

Storage Bags. You can get *bags for your board, rig and daggerboard.* A bag is useful if the board is fragile, or if you just don't want it to fade in the sun. A bag for your rig is very useful, preferably a sausage-shaped model that can enclose a rolled-up sail plus mastfoot and the battens. The bag should be rainproof and have an easy access (e.g., with Velcro closures) exterior pocket or two. A board bag for the daggerboard is only needed if it is very fragile -- if so, get a padded bag.

Many also carry a *personal bag*. One good option is a yachtsman's soft carry-all, the best of which has separate sections for wet clothing, as well as pockets for tools, tape, repair gear, etc. Those with a netted section on the exterior for wet gear are among the most practical.

• Rafting

This section is geared to self-guided rafting with entry-level rafts or floating equipment on relatively quiet rivers and lakes. A discussion of professionally-guided whitewater ventures, where the outfitter provides the rafting equipment, is included. In both cases, the number of gear items supplied by each participant are modest. The limited number of rafting items in the gear list reflects that.

Juneau, Alaska

Even with this in mind, however, we have provided a detailed discussion of higher-technology rafts used in whitewater ventures. The purpose is to introduce self-guided rafters to the raft-specific equipment that they may want to purchase at a later date. In addition, for those considering professionally-guided rafting, this knowledge may assist in selecting an outfitter for your next trip(s).

There are many types of professionally-guided rafting offered by outfitters. Both single and multi-day tours are available on almost every scenic river in the U.S. and in many areas throughout the world. Some tours have you acting as a crew member, paddling under the guidance of your tour guide. On others, you travel as an observing passenger, with a primary duty of observing and photographing Mother Nature.

Some trips are in remote areas, while others have a gear truck awaiting each day at your let-out point. Some take beginners, while others demand a more advanced level of proficiency. You may be provided with camping gear or asked to bring your own. In almost all cases, you supply your base-layer personal wear, hygiene stuff, and miscellaneous accessories for your own comfort. The outfitter may supply the foul-weather/river running gear (and probably will supply other safety-related equipment) or expect you to provide some of it. Some meal options: they cook, you sit; they cook, you clean; or you are responsible for your own meal preparation. Invariably, they provide the rafting gear.

For these guided ventures it is important to get an outfitter-recommended gear list that reflects anticipated conditions, including weather. Further, you should clearly understand what they are and are not providing. (Occasionally, outfitters provide lists which require some interpretation.) Finally (but probably least significant), if you want to bring special gear, check that they can accommodate it or if they recommend against it -- at worst, it will sit in your car trunk during your rafting tour.

If you do decide to pursue a self-guided, multi-day tour, refer to the CANOEING activity (both Daytime and Overnight sections) for additional outfitting information. If you are planning on self-guided rapids-running, refer to the CANOEING (Daytime) or KAYAKING (Daytime) activities, the latter as it deals with whitewater kayaks.

Raft/Kayak/Inner Tube. If your plans are for ***self-guided, quiet-water rafting***, consider the joys of a simple float trip on a small rubber *raft*, high-buoyancy rubber or plastic *float tube* (that looks like an overgrown air mattress), an *inner tube*, or other suitable floating device. The inner-tube family ranges from plain ole' tubes to fancy commercial models with a seat, netting and gear-storage pockets. At a higher experience level, consider more well-equipped, multi-person rafts or even a lower-end *inflatable kayak.*

Make sure to have a buddy ready to transport you back from the agreed-on let-out point. On even some of the less-remote rivers, the route back to the start point is significantly longer than that measured as the fish swims. If it is practical and legal and you can arrange it, another option is to have a boat tow you back to the start point.

• When selecting a raft for ***self-guided, whitewater rafting***, the key considerations are intended use (coupled with your level of expertise) and the size of your wallet. Specific selection criteria include dimensions, design and materials/ manufacturing techniques.

Dimensions. The length and width of the raft chosen depend on the needed capacities for persons and gear, as well as maneuverability and stability desired. As a generalization: If overnight/multi-day gear is carried and a rowing frame is used, a nominal six-man raft (about 12 feet by 6 feet) will carry two persons; a seven-man raft (13 feet by 6-1/2 feet) will handle three rafters; a 10-man raft (15 feet by 7-1/2 feet) will accommodate a group of four; and a 14-man raft (17 feet by 8 feet) will serve five or six persons. If the raft is paddled instead of rowed, the capacity increases by one person in the six- to seven-man raft and by two persons in the 10- to 14-man raft.

(A digression: For most daytime use, a raft frame is not needed, [More is said later about raft frames.] Where raft crews are limited to several people, smaller rafts than those characterized above, can be used. These are basically scaled-down versions with most of the same design and materials/manufacturing considerations as those described below.)

Maneuvering of larger rafts requires more effort and, thus, physical strength. Since they are slower to respond, their use also requires greater anticipation and forethought to maneuver through rapids. However, larger rafts are generally more stable, a valuable asset in big-volume rivers or those with larger rapids.

Design. The size and shape of buoyancy tubes, the number of air chambers and the number and the presence of cross tubes (like thwarts on a canoe) affect the raft's handling characteristics and also contribute to its safety. The 12- to 14-foot rafts have tubes about 16-19 inches in diameter, while the 15- to 17-foot models employ tubes between 18-21 inches. Larger buoyancy tubes, and the resultant increased raft surface area in the water, make the raft less responsive to an oar or paddle stroke. They also place paddlers further from the water, requiring a greater stretch to make a stroke. The main advantage of the larger tube is its ability to prevent excessive amounts of water from coming into the raft, which would otherwise become sluggish and difficult to control. Some paddle rafts with smaller tubes use an inflatable spray shield which surrounds the raft perimeter to buy back some of the advantage of the larger tubes.

The raft may have a raised bow and stern buoyancy tube feature, which allows the raft to glide more easily after a stroke and also aids in deflecting water. The uplift is generally about eight or nine inches off the water, although it may be as pronounced as 11-12 inches on some models.

Multiple air chambers have become standard on most whitewater rafts. While some have two main chambers, most rafts in the 12-16 foot range use four primary chambers, with supplemental chambers in the cross tubes. These multiple air chambers serve as a safety feature in the event that there is a puncture while underway. They also aid in the stability of a raft because the chambers reduce the shifting of air which occurs as the raft flexes through the waves of rapids.

Cross tubes aid flotation as well as provide lateral stability to the raft. They also provide a place for passengers to sit, especially in vigorous rapids where passengers need to move closer into the raft's center to avoid falling out. The penalty of cross tubes is the amount of space they occupy, thus reducing gear capacity.

Large valves, such as military high-volume valves, are preferred since they allow both quicker inflation and deflation. Both integral valves (where the valve does not separate from the core) and two-piece valves have well-proven histories in the whitewater. The valve core should be well attached to the raft and neither it or the valve should leak. Recessing of valves is another desirable option, as it prevents gear from pushing up against the valve and causing a leak.

Rafts are equipped with "D"-rings for attachment of storage frames and as a source of other gear tie-downs, Among the best rings are those made of welded stainless steel, while less-expensive rings are cadmium-plated or galvanized steel. The rings should be mounted mid-way down the outer side of the tube and not on the top. This preferred placement allows the pull to remain at a right angle to the flat side of the "D"-ring, thus preventing the ring from tearing away from the hold-down patch that secures it to the raft.

South Fork, American River, California Unknown Commercial Photographer

Materials/Manufacturing Techniques. Some of the most commonly used base fabrics are nylon, Dacron polyester and DuPont Kevlar. These are listed in ascending order of strength by weight, relative difficulty in cutting and assembly, and also reflect the general order of price. Kevlar, which is stronger by weight than steel, also produces the most rigid boat -- the additive and detractive value of this rigidity is subject to considerable debate among experienced rafters. Over-fabric coatings most frequently used are neoprene, Hypalon, polyvinyl chloride (PVC) and polyurethane. For a detailed discussion of the positive and negative features of these materials (and, more likely, material mixes), consult the Referenced sources.

The vast majority of inflatable boats are made by cutting panels from coated fabric and then gluing them together. The principal methods of seam construction include the lap seam and butt seam. The lap seam is one in which one part of the material is laid over the top of the other approximately 3/4 inch. The butt seam is constructed whereby the two cut edges are brought together and taped inside and out to ensure air tightness. The lap seam provides greater strength; however butt seams are fine if at least a three-inch tape is used and correct vulcanizing and gluing processes are followed. One should check the quality of the seam tape, ensuring that the seam tape has adhered to the raft without any gaps and that there are no air bubbles anywhere in the tape. A more in-depth discussion on raft construction is provided in the References cited.

• ***Professionally-guided, white-water rafting*** outfitters use a variety of rafts and other craft. Most *rafts* are paddle rafts (paddled by all participants), oar rafts with aluminum rowing frames (controlled by professional guides), or paddle/oar rafts (those paddled and controlled by both guests and guides). Highly maneuverable and stable *inflatable kayaks* (paddled by one or two guests) are also becoming increasingly available for river rafting customers, particularly during low water levels.

The most commonly used rafts hold four to six persons, Next in popularity are the eight-to-twelve passenger models. In the Western U.S., large motorized rafts are used on some of the high-volume rivers in Arizona, Utah and British Columbia. These rafts are rugged and highly flexible.

In addition to rafts and inflatable kayaks, a few outfitters use wooden *dories* (similar to that used by John Wesley Powell in his historic 1869 journeys on the Colorado and Green Rivers). In the Western U.S., their use is most common to Idaho's Salmon and Snake Rivers, Idaho's and Oregon's Owyhee River and the Grand Canyon of the Colorado River. Another wooden craft used is the *McKenzie whitewater drift boats*, popularized by Oregon steelhead fishing outfitters. Their use is mostly on several Oregon and Idaho rivers.

Raft Frame. A raft frame's primary function is to enable gear to be secured above the floor of the raft. Light, simple frames are generally the best. They do the job well, are inexpensive, and easy to transport and store. Moreover, if wooden frames are assembled with carriage bolts, or if metal frames slip together, these frames may be broken down for easy transportation to and from the river. A floorboard is often suspended from the frame by means of chains encased in a plastic hose. The floorboard provides additional space for gear to be stowed above the raft's floor. A rule of thumb is that the floorboard should not extend more than halfway down from the top of the buoyancy tubes -- lower placements may result in a rock ripping the raft floor when jammed against the floorboard.

The frame selected should not hamper access to the valves of the raft, and easy bailing should be possible. Most importantly, the frame should be sufficiently sturdy to handle the severe punishment of heavy rapids. The specific frame chosen will depend upon such factors as amount of gear, use of oars versus paddles, wear of the frame on the raft, position of the passengers, bailing methods, and type of trips planned.

Wood frames (typically pine or fur) are cheaper than metal and relatively easy to construct. Metal frames are most often made of small-diameter steel tubing or larger-diameter aluminum tubing. They are typically stronger than wood frames. Aluminum is lighter than steel, although generally more expensive because of the cost of the heliarc welding process. Steel frames will rust if the coating (frequently epoxy) is damaged or worn through. The hard metal frames are frequently coated with padding such as foam rubber -- this is to prevent possible injury should a rafter be thrown against the frame during an upset of the raft.

Paddles/Oars. For rafting, proper fit, durability and cost are the prime factors in selecting paddles and oars. The materials used for, and construction of, raft paddles is similar to that discussed in the CANOEING (Daytime) activity. Overall paddle design, including handle options, are also similar. Sizing and fitting, however, are different issues.

Paddle length depends on several factors. In addition to personal preference, these factors include the size of the raft's tubes, height of the paddler, and often, the position of the paddler in the raft. The normal range includes lengths of 4-1/2 to 6 feet, with 5 and 5-1/2 feet most common. Rafts with smaller tubes (16-18 inches) will necessitate smaller lengths, while 20-inch and larger tubes will probably require five-foot paddles. With regard to height (knee to top of head), the paddle should not be so short as to force the paddler to lean out of the raft to make a stroke, nor should it be so long that the stroke is executed with one arm above the head. A paddler in the bow straddling the tubes has only a short distance to reach and thus may want a shorter paddle. The rafter in the middle of the stern, however, needs a longer paddle to steer and make draw strokes to turn the raft.

Oars designed for river work feature long blades, normally spanning one third the length of the entire oar. Most of the materials options for oars are similar to that for paddles, although there are a higher percentage of oars that use two different materials for the shaft and blade.

The length of oars used for rafting will vary according to raft length; generally, oar length is approximately two-thirds the length of the raft. Heavier loads and larger rapids will necessitate longer oars, while low-volume and rocky rivers require shorter oars to aid maneuverability in tight river stretches. The distance between oarlocks will also affect the length of the oar. The oarlocks should be correctly positioned on the oar shaft to obtain the most effective fulcrum point for easy rowing. In addition, when the oars are lifted out of the water during a stroke, the oar handles should remain several inches apart to avoid pinching the hands.

If your decision is to go with oars, you will have to select the type of oarlocks, oarlock stand, connecting hardware and location of the equipment in the raft. For a detailed discussion of these issues, consult the Referenced sources.

• Jet Skiing

Jet Ski. More generally called personal water vehicles (PWVs), jet skis (a Kawasaki-owned trademark) are primarily used for all-around frolicking in the water. Alternately, they are sometimes carried as an adjunct for larger boats for boat-to-shore transportation and some higher-powered, lower-geared models are used to tow water skiers. Jet skis are treated as boats by the Coast Guard -- each vehicle must be registered and the registration number must be affixed to the craft.

• Though individual construction and design characteristics may vary, there are several *general features* which are common to all PWVs.

Hull Design/Construction. Most hulls are constructed of fiberglass or fiberglass blends. They are partially or near fully padded on the top surfaces with which the rider(s) may make contact. Keel shapes depend on usage, with semi-"V" and deep-"V" hulls found on most PWVs and specialized designs such as hyperbolic hulls found on special-purpose models. The hulls are fitted with streamlined sponsons below the waterline which are filled with low-density materials such as closed-cell foam to provide flotation. Sponson design is custom-fitted to the craft's intended use; the properties of this design will affect the speed and controllability of turns.

In some cases, hulls are equipped with integral splash deflectors to minimize spray into the cockpit. Some designs have a small boarding platform for more convenient reentry into the cockpit after a bailout. Another feature of some models is a rear-face grip handle, which provides a leverage point for easy boat reentry. Some models are designed to allow the rear grip handle to double as a skier towline attachment point.

Garrison Reservoir, North Dakota Compliments of Doug Holker

Cockpit. Some PWVs have an open cockpit and the operator either stands or kneels when operating the craft. Effectively, the open cockpit is a shallow well fitted with scuppers for water drainoff. More commonly, however, the cockpit is a raised, cushioned seat which places the operator directly behind the control column. There are slots or a running board (with a raised outer edge, it becomes a splash deflector) for foot placement.

Depending on the model, the seat is designed to carry one, two (most common) or three people. The seat is heavily padded, although some designs add a modest suspension internal to the seat. At the expense of added weight and complexity, the suspension smoothes the ride, definitely a comfort feature when enduring the jarring caused by passing through boat wakes or traveling on choppy water.

An integrated glove box, commonly mounted near to or on the lower part of the control column, is featured on many models Its use is for storing small items that require easy accessibility (gloves, goggles, sun glasses, etc.). Some of the larger jet skis feature a watertight storage area under the seat or front hood for tucking away larger articles, such as a windbreaker, water bottles and snacks. The latter is also the common location for a fire extinguisher. Other storage options for some makes are custom-fit, waterproof handlebar bags and rear-side stowed saddlebags.

Propulsion. Jet skis are generally powered by a two-stroke, twin-cylinder or triple-cylinder gasoline engine working through a jet drive. The drive is composed of an intake, driveshaft, impeller (a small internal propeller), and steering nozzle, all contained at the stern in a pump housing within the hull. Water is drawn through the intake into the pump housing. When it reaches the impeller, the water is pressurized and forced out of the steering nozzle, which directs the jet ski. Nozzle direction is controlled by the direction of the rider-controlled handlebar which sits atop the control column near the front of the jet ski.

Some PWVs are equipped with a variable electric trim feature. With it, you can adjust the attitude of the craft for the number of riders, heavy or lightweight loads, or for choppy or smooth water. Setting the proper nozzle angle results in best craft performance for the given ride conditions. If installed, most designs with automatic trim control have a manual-override feature.

Cultus Lake, Oregon

Control Column. The jet ski speed and direction is controlled using the handle bars at the top of the control column. On sit-down models, the column is an integral part of the hull design. For stand-up and kneel-down models, the control column is levered out from the front end of the hull. Handlebar orientation and height is fixed for both sit-down, stand-up and kneel-down designs for virtually all PWV makes. There are variations in handlebar height, length and tilt, however the non-adjustable nature of the column and handlebars make it important to test that the configuration fits your particular physical stature and intended use. Jet ski selection may be complicated by this lack of adjustability if several people intend to share in it's use.

Most commonly, the "start" and "stop" button(s), and throttle are located on the handlebars regardless of whether the jet ski is a sit-down, standup or kneel-down design. When so equipped, the trim control switch is typically also mounted on the bars. Choke, shifter and other controllers (if the craft is so equipped) are normally located either on or near the control column.

In addition, many boats are equipped with a readout console. Depending on the model, this may consist of a fuel/oil gauge set, a malfunction indicator, RPM gauge, speedometer, trip mileage indicator or some limited subset of the group. Many newer models replace the analog gauge set with a non-glare digital readout device that displays "oversize" readout characters. The are most often mounted forward of the control column, placed behind a spray mounting that doubles as a driver's spray shield.

For safety purposes, Most PWVs are furnished with a "start"-button-mounted tether cord that is attached to the operator's PFD. Once you fall, the tether is pulled and automatically shuts off the engine. All craft feature a "forward" setting, while a few boats are also equipped with "reverse." The latter feature is highly useful when maneuvering or exploring in tight places. It is required if you are towing skiers. (An aside: When towing water skiers, most states in the U.S. require a driver to be accompanied by a passenger who acts as a spotter for the skier. Most often, they further specify that the towing vehicle be a three-seat craft with a reverse-drive capability.)

• There are numerous *types of jet skis* in use. We have provided a "home-brewed" set of classes below, if only to provide an overall feel for the differences in intended use. The design ranges noted are approximate.

Runabout. This is a general pleasurecraft and the most popular style. Typically a 1-2 person craft with a seated cockpit, a lower-powered runabout in the 60- 90 horsepower (hp) range might suit beginners and intermediates, while beefier, 90-130 hp models typically appeal to more experienced jet skiers. Weights typically range from 400 to 500 lb. The standards for length and width are in the 100-110 inch and 40-45 inch ranges respectively. Both runabouts and the "family/touring" models discussed below tend to have semi-"V" or deep-"V" keel shapes and 10-to 15-gallon gas tanks. Most models have twin-cylinders, although a few triple-cycle models are made at the upper end of the power spectrum.

Family/Touring. This is a beefier, longer version of the runabout, with seating for 2-3 people and a wider hull for stability. Day touring, family or group riding and exploring are the most common use for these craft. Dry weights typically range from 500-650 lb. Typical lengths and widths are in the 115--125 inch and 40-50 inch ranges respectively. At the lower end, these craft may have 80-90 hp engines. To maintain speed while carrying three riders or two riders and a water skier, some seek heftier power plants out in the 110-hp range. Both dual-cylinder and triple-cylinder engines are common to this class.

Many are fitted with splash guards and most models are equipped with a storage area. It is not uncommon to have a "reverse" engine setting on these craft. These models are typically the most well-endowed with indicator gauges.

High-Performance/Competition. These upper-end horsepower-to-weight-ratio machines are meant for stunting, whether it be in quiet water, boat wakes or racing the ocean surf. They are also the standard for competition racing. They have an open, one-person cockpit and special hull shapes, including unique sponsons. This enhances capability to make controllable turns at high speeds. Almost all have a two-stroke, twin-cycle engine.

Though not at the upper end as far as horsepower (90-110 hp is typical), they have dry weights in the 300- 400 lb class. The low weight is achieved with a smaller size hull, lightweight cockpit, smaller fuel tank (4-8 gallon capacities), austere gauge set, and the absence of such goodies as a reverse setting on the engine. Typical lengths and widths are in the 85-105 inch and 25-35 inch ranges respectively. The narrow hull results in some sacrifice in the craft's general stability.

Jet Ski Goggles/Sunglasses. At high speed, water spray can be bothersome to the eyes. Some wear safety goggles or sunglasses (non-glass, shatter-resistant) for eye protection. If either is used, they should be secured with a tight head strap to prevent loss. Padded goggles are probably the best bet, since they will minimize "skid marks" after a face-first encounter with the water. Clear goggle lenses are the norm. Most that use sunglasses go with a highly polarizing set of lenses tinted to preserve observation of water features. Sunglasses and selection of tints for different lighting conditions are discussed further in the **Ten Essentials** section.

Lower Colorado River Compliments of Walt Bond

Jet Ski Fuel, Oil. Even with their 4-14 gallon gas tanks and 3-5 quart oil reservoirs, bring some gasoline and lubricating oil reserves or ensure they are available on- or near-site. This is particularly true for full-day or multi-day outings where a significant amount of jet skiing is planned.

Jet Ski Fire Extinguisher. Many jet skis come equipped with a small fire extinguisher, while others are retrofitted. Their purpose is to quickly extinguish a blaze without having to put electrically-conducting liquids such as lake or sea water on the engine. The extinguisher should be firmly attached to the watercraft's body and placed in a location where it can neither interfere with the jet skiing activity nor protrude sufficiently to impede your bailing out when it is called for. (Most factory-equipped extinguishers are located under an easily-accessible cowling and are bracketed or clamped in place.)

Air Pump. For general watersports activities, it is hard to imagine that an air pump would not find good use, whether for pumping up a raft, a float, beachball or volleyball. A discussion of air pumps is found in the VEHICLE-ACCESSIBLE CAMPING activity.

Specifically for ***rafting***, high-volume (300-400 cubic inches) pumps are desirable for inflation. Some also have features for rapid and thorough deflation. Electric pumps provide the easiest method of inflation, operating off of commercial electric current, an automobile cigarette lighter, or an automobile battery. A good mechanical alternative is a large barrel pump of the military style, nominally 18-20 inches high and six inches in diameter. These pumps usually have two foot pedals for stability while pumping, and many models have two hoses, thus allowing inflation of two raft chambers simultaneously.

Some of the more lengthy and/or remote trips may necessitate your bringing the high-volume pump. If so, look for a pump with a good operational track record and a simple design (as few parts as possible) for reasons of reliability and ease of assembly/disassembly. The pump should have a minimum number of metal and die-cast parts; metal corrodes and die-cast parts are frequently irreplaceable, unlike other parts that can be easily obtained at hardware stores or from the pump manufacturer. Finally, make sure that the pump is immersible -- most pumps with metal fittings within the pump will corrode and rust when wet.

Regardless of whitewater trip duration and what other pumping gear might be carried, a small-volume hand pump is a standard contingency item. It is normally used for topping off the raft before the day's run, but also may be used to refill a mildly-leaking or repaired chamber, the latter in the absence or non-workability of the high-volume pump. Typically 12 inches long and three inches in diameter, they are compact and easy to store. The pumps usually contain fittings that either screw or fit closely into the valve of a raft for the high-pressure inflation required.

Personal Gear

The type of apparel worn is dependent on the weather. In the discussion below, we offer general *examples of outfits* (not including the standards like sunglasses, sunscreen, etc.) that might serve your purpose in order from warm weather to successively cooler conditions. (The asterisk(*) indicates optional items.)

Scuba diving - warm (swim suit, "T"-shirt*); cool (wet suit, booties, skull cap, gloves); cold (dry suit, booties, skull cap, gloves)

Water skiing - warm (swim suit, "T"-shirt*, windbreaker*); cool (wet suit, skull cap, gloves); cold (wait for Spring)

Boardsurfing - warm (swim suit, "T"-shirt*); cool (wet suit, booties, skull cap, gloves); cold (wait for Spring)

Windsurfing - (athletic shoes*, swim suit, "T"-shirt, windbreaker*); cool (wet suit, booties in athletic shoes, skull cap, gloves); cold (dry suit, booties, skull cap, gloves or wait for Spring)

Rafting - see CANOEING (Daytime) activity

Jet skiing - (swim suit, "T"-shirt, windbreaker*); cool (wet suit, booties, skull cap, gloves); cold (wait for Spring)

Since the WATERSPORTS activity includes several "sub-activities," we have used a special font to indicate which sub-activity the gear item applies to. In the discussion below, the sub-activities called out are those involving ***divers, waterskiers, boardsurfers, windsurfers, rafters and jet skiers***.

Wet Suit. Whatever the watersports activity, seek a close, comfortable fit sufficient to minimize significant, continual water leakage into the suit. Afterall, the design's value is based on the body heating only a trapped thin film of water between body and suit. The suits are either single- or double-lined. The double lined suits are hard-wearing on both sides; the single-lined version is warmer, but more prone to damage. Various thicknesses are available, and the one chosen should be a matter of personal body-temperature comfort and local air/water conditions where it is used. One-millimeter thickness is common for use in cool waters (60 degree Fahrenheit range) while 3-4 millimeter suits might be more reasonable in near-freezing water or for diving to deep depths.

Wet suit components include short- or long-legged pants; vest-style, short-sleeved or long-sleeved jacket with or without hood; a combination of the two ("Farmer John's" and "step-throughs"); and boots, mittens and gloves. The Farmer John style is preferred by many because the two layers of neoprene over the chest provide additional warmth over that critical area. Step-throughs consist of a single piece jacket and short-legged pants, topped by full-length Farmer John pants. This combination provides double layering over both groin and chest areas. (See the CANOEING (Daytime) and KAYAKING (Daytime) activities for additional information on wetsuits.)

Wetsuits fitted with kneepads are favored by many in watersports activities, particularly ***divers, boardsurfers and rafters***. These pads slow down the wearing process that might otherwise become evident after a few dives around rocks or a couple of days on a surfboard. Likewise, some buy suits with elbow pads for the same reason. However, they make the arms of the suit stiffer, resulting in some limitation of movement that many divers, particularly, find bothersome.

For ***water skiing*** "shortie" designs are most popular. They have sleeves to just above the elbow and legs to just above the knees. Many suits are variable thickness, with the most popular style being two-millimeter thickness for the body and one millimeter for thc sleeves, the latter to allow maximum arm flexibility. Similar variable thickness designs are available for the Farmer John-style wetsuit. Since the key flex points for skiers are the knees and buttocks, some designs add high-performance material, such as Bion (a stretchy, breathable material developed for medical uses) at these points to enhance freedom of movement. Shortie designs are also the preference for ***jet skiing and rafting*** in chilly water, since they allow the freedom of movement needed for those ventures.

Some special considerations for ***windsurfers***: The wet suit sleeves should not constrict the muscles of the forearms, which could otherwise lead to cramping. They should be made of soft neoprene or loose waterproofed nylon. With this style, it is important that the water drains out from the sleeves when you fall in, otherwise swimming becomes very difficult.

Lake Tahoe, California Compliments of Susan Cohen

Dry Suit. The dry suit design is intended to literally keep the person in the water in a dry interior. Being watertight also means that it does not breathe and, therefore, will have you in a "steam room" in all but very cold conditions. The one-piece designs are essentially *waterproof-nylon baggy suits*. They feature watertight rubber seals at the neck, wrists, ankles and at the heavy-duty, watertight zipper (step-in) section. Since they lack the insulating qualities of neoprene, they are generally worn over thermal underwear for diving and with a variety of layered apparel, if needed, for the on-water activities. The air space created by the suit and skin by the underwear adds considerable buoyancy which, for the ***diver***, must be offset by the addition of weights. Tearing or leaking of the suit will destroy the protection against cold. In addition, this could have the effect of making a diver heavier underwater through loss of buoyancy. (Note; use of any drysuit in ***diving*** requires special training -- they are not for beginners.)

Manufacturers also make single-piece *dry suits of material similar to that for wet suits*, but with the addition of special watertight stitching and the watertight closures mentioned above. This design, like the wetsuit, has little room for even the sheerest of insulating clothing. This design offers greater freedom of mobility than the baggy nylon models, and is less likely to tear. As a result, this dry suit option is often preferred by cold-water ***divers*** (and a few super-hearty ***windsurfers***). The *neoprene variable-volume dry suit* permits the addition of air into the suit, from a ***diver's*** scuba tank, to counter the pressure-driven buoyancy decrease encountered on the descent. (See the KAYAKING (Daytime) activity for additional general information about dry suits.)

Lower Colorado River Compliments of Walt Bond

Headgear. Particularly for cold-water ***divers*** and ***surfers***, the head is best protected using a neoprene pullover *skullcap* -- the cranium is one of the greatest areas of heat loss on the human body. It is a useful add-on for any activity where a wet suit is needed.

Other watersport activities may call for a different headpiece, e.g., a floppy-brimmed hat for ***rafting*** or ***beach-rafting***. Discussions of various headpieces are scattered throughout the book and can be found by referring to the **INDEX**.

Beach/Deck Shoes. Beach sand can get very hot and near-shore rocks can be very hard to walk upon or can damage your feet. For activities that involve shore-based operations or frequent transition from shore to water (e.g., ***swimming, surfing*** or ***rafting***), consider beach shoes. These footwear have a thick rubber sole and elastic, mesh uppers. Although these shoes can also be used for ***jet skiing***, a better bet is to wear the deck shoes described in the SAILING activity. This is particularly true for stand-up skiing in an open-cockpit craft.

Booties. ***Divers*** wear booties under their heel-strap swim fins for warmth and/or foot protection. Both *firm or soft-soled neoprene booties* are used. The booties prevent chafing by the fin itself, sand or other rough surfaces. The better the sole, the greater the protection, particularly on the foot's underside. This consideration is particularly important if you are diving in shallow water or near coral. There are also special *coral shoes* on the market which have soles sufficiently tough to resist tearing and shredding even on sharp coral.

Some booties have zippers, a feature that comes with added cost. If you are involved with an activity that requires adding or removing booties with some frequency (i.e., a boat owner requires it), then this feature may be for you. The zippered models don't provide the warmth of integral booties and the zippers themselves can become jammed by sand, a particularly negative feature for divers launching from the beach.

For ***windsurfers***, bare feet, a plain athletic shoe or a neoprene bootie tucked into an oversized athletic shoe are candidates, the choice depending on the ambient temperature and board surface material. (The tucked bootie concept is also used by ***rafters***.) There are also specialized windsurfing shoes and above-ankle boots with treadless, soft-rubber bottoms. These neoprene-topped models are specifically designed for gripping wet, slippery board surfaces.

Gloves. For ***divers***, both fingered and mitten-type gloves are used. Both will reduce the sense of touch and hand efficiency, which may be very important or critical in certain situations -- this tends to favor use of the fingered models. Their most frequent use is keeping hands warm in cold water. Neoprene-based gloves are common, normally designed with ribbing on the backside to accommodate hand flexing, with straps to secure them above the wrists. Their length should be sufficient for the straps to tighten at least an inch above the end of the bodysuit sleeve. They come in both zippered and non-zippered styles. The same considerations that applied to zippers on booties apply to zippers on gloves.

In warm water, divers frequently go without gloves unless hand protection is needed against the likes of sharp rocks, stinging corals, shells, sea urchins or fish spines. Though dive shops sell these special purpose gloves, many get by with a sturdy pair of snug-fitting work gloves. If gloves are used, it is advisable to practice the various diving skills requiring use of hands under benign conditions before departing for challenging underwater adventures.

A good pair of ***waterskiing gloves*** can lengthen your ride time and provide protection against blisters, especially if you don't ski regularly. The most commonly used are nylon and soft leather styles, both in exposed- and covered-fingertip designs. The soft leather gloves have the feel of a chamois-like material; they should be fairly snug when you try them on in the store because they will stretch in the water. They may even feel a bit small the first time you use them, but they'll stretch. Some skiers wear an inner-outer glove set -- a thin under-pair and a thicker, well-padded pair over them. This is similar to wearing a set of socks when hiking, for the purpose of blister prevention. Finally, some gloves have built-in metal grips that assist in keeping your fingers bent over the ski handle.

In warm weather, most experienced ***windsurfers*** go without gloves. However, if you are a learner, you may want to have a pair in store should your hands get sore. In colder weather the standard is neoprene, normally shaped in the contour of a fist clenched over a wishbone. In both cases, seek fingerless models with a ventilated backside and a heavily-reinforced palm.

Jet skiers sometimes wear gloves for longer hauls to prevent hand soreness, for warmth, and/or to maintain throttle grip in water spray. Although specialized jet ski gloves are available, a set of boating gloves will serve much the same purpose. (Refer to the SAILING activity.) A set similar to the paddler's neoprene gloves described in the CANOEING (Daytime) activity will suffice for cold water jet skiing.

The latter two options also apply for ***rafting***. Additionally, rafters with oars frequently wind adhesive tape around the handles to reduce chafing. Plastic sleeves that slip over the handles of the oars to provide a more comfortable grip are also available.

Helmet. Plastic or fiberglass helmets are worn on by ***rafters*** on most Class IV-V rivers to prevent injuries from rocks or flailing paddles. The use of helmets on any river is a decision of the outfitter and, if provided, must be worn, at least, during whitewater stretches. Surprisingly, some outfitters feel that helmets are unnecessary. If you desire the added safety of a helmet, you can make this a priority when selecting an outfitter, or you can bring your own.

Hardhats are sometimes worn by children and frequently worn by ***jet skiers*** in race events. The primary purpose in the latter conditions is to protect the head after a bailout from other boats in what frequently is a close-packed environment.

St. Johns, Caribbean

Safety

Flares. There are small packs of flares specially designed for watersports activities. ***Divers*** can carry them in a wetsuit pocket or secured to scuba gear. If ***windsurfing*** in rough water and/or outside sheltered areas, carrying flares is a sensible precaution. You can carry them strapped to your leg, in a harness pack, in the pockets of your protective clothing (if worn), or in a sail pocket -- the three latter options obviously are dependent on gear design, but make a case for accessible pockets. ***Rafters*** and ***jet skiers*** planning remote activities can place them in a dry bag or storage compartment respectively.

Compass. For ***scuba diving***, there is an *underwater magnetic compass* which is housed in a waterproof and pressure-resistant case that is generally worn on the wrist. It is valuable when navigating, both on the surface and underwater, particularly in conditions of reduced visibility. Acceptable underwater compasses are sold at dive shops and sporting goods stores. You may also be able to purchase a naval-type wrist compass at an Army-Navy surplus store.

The wrist strap should be large enough to fit over a wet suit. All markings should be easily readable and should include a "lubber line" that can be aligned with the longitudinal axis of the body for reference to actual direction of forward progress. Some models also have a movable face that can be rotated to mark a specific course.

There are larger compasses that are designed to fit into a gauge console. In addition to having the features mentioned above, they also have a larger face plate than the wrist-mounted models, making them easier to read.

Underwater Light. For ***scuba diving***, a flashlight can be useful in dark or murky water, although its effectiveness falls off as the amount of suspended sediment increases. (Any underwater activity that demands the use of a light requires that you be a highly-proficient diver and a careful and thorough dive planner or team member.) *Small-power lights* are relatively portable and are generally reserved for contingency nighttime or murky water use, for peering into dark places in daytime, or for nighttime use in clear water at limited depth. High-power lights are more cumbersome and are normally reserved for advanced pursuits such as deeper-water night diving, wreck diving or cave diving.

Accessories

Underwater Camera. Photography underwater requires either a camera specifically designed to operate efficiently underwater or one in a waterproof, pressure-resistant external case. The most simple of the former are the non-focusing, "pin-hole," *throwaway cameras* that operate in a wet environment, on-surface or near surface. The least complex example of the latter option is effectively a *flexible plastic bag* with about a six-inch hard-plastic window. Controls for pin-hole and even 35-millimeter cameras are manipulated through the plastic bag. Use of this option is limited to about 15-20 feet depth. Higher quality (and significantly more expensive) options are discussed below.

There are a fair number of *tailored underwater cameras*, which a good diving shop (and a few camera stores) can demonstrate for you. There are many moderately-priced 35-millimeter cameras for use to 15-20 feet depth. They function exactly like any land camera, but have a waterproof body. For higher quality, more versatile and deeper depth photography, there are outfits like the Nikonos System, which can be fitted with (or alternately, is limited to) several different lens and strobes. Once loaded with film, you can take the camera to the water, jump in, and start taking pictures. It is considerably less bulky than the underwater housing options discussed below. This particular system is limited to a rangefinder, that is, you do not view through the picture-taking optics when selecting subject format. What you see through the rangefinder may not be exactly what is captured on film.

Underwater housings are available for most popular still and motion-picture cameras in metal (usually cast aluminum) or plastic (typically Plexiglas). Metal housing is usually suggested for divers planning deep work, or those whose equipment will take much abuse. The plastic housing allows viewing at all settings on the camera, and more controls can be set in a plastic housing than a metal one. Generally, plastic housings are tested for depths down to 60 feet and metal to about 150 feet. The housings can be built for positive, negative or neutral buoyancy at a buyer-specified rough reference depth.

With housings, you have an almost unlimited selection of lenses to choose from, limited only by what your camera will accept. A drawback of the housed system is its bulk -- it definitely takes two hands to operate. Another consideration is that, for comparable quality, you will pay more for the housed system (camera plus housing) than for most tailored underwater cameras.

Spear/Spear Gun. Before making the investment in spearing equipment, first check the legality of its use in your intended diving areas. Once purchased, learn how to safely and properly use the gear. *Pole spears*, whether of the hand or rubber-sling thrust type, are designed for impalement of fish (not your diving buddy's ankle) at little more than arm-thrust range. The impalement head may be a lance, barbed lance, trident or other shape. *Spear guns*, whether powered by elastic sling, CO2 cartridge or explosive cartridge, are designed to propel a shaft at penetrating force. Effective underwater range varies with design and is rarely more than several times the effective length of the shaft. Heads may be similar to that for pole spears or, alternately, have power heads which fire a cartridge on impact and shoot the barbed spear head through the prey.

Tool Kit (* below indicates that gear is brought to the let-in site, but not carried during the performance of the activity)

Tools.

Scuba diving* - screwdriver, pliers, specialized tools
Water skiing* - pliers, knife
Boardsurfing* - scraping knife
Windsurfing* - screwdriver, adjustable wrench, scraping knife
Rafting (self-guided) - channel lock pliers, scissors
Jet skiing* - screwdriver, engine-specific wrenches including spark plug wrench, specialized tools

Repair Gear.
Scuba diving* - wet suit or dry suit patch kit
Water skiing* - wet suit or dry suit patch kit
Boardsurfing* - ding repair kit, wet suit patch kit
Windsurfing* - wet suit or dry suit patch kit, waterproof insulating tape, light hull repair kit
Rafting (self-guided) - wet suit or dry suit patch kit, raft patch kit (including patch material, adhesive, solvent/ thinner, glue brush, buffer tool/sandpaper, and rolling tool, upholstery needles, nylon or waxed thread, duct tape, epoxy glue, silicone rubber sealant), bailing wire
Jet skiing* - wet suit or dry suit patch kit, duct tape, light hull repair kit

Replacement Gear.
Scuba diving* - "O" ring(s), spare tank(s)
Water skiing* - spare skis, towline
Boardsurfing* - spare leash, alternate boards
Windsurfing - spare harness line and clip, alternate sails, spare rigging
Rafting - oar or paddle, assorted nuts and bolts, air valves, "D"-rings, radiator hose clips
Jet skiing* - spark plugs, spare hose and hose clamps

Secondary Activities

WATERSPORTS can be linked with activities such as CAMPING, HIKING, SAILING, POWERBOATING and both LAND and SEA FISHING. If you plan such a linkage, refer to the applicable activity to determine its additional unique gear needs.

Copper Canyon, Lower Colorado River — Compliments of Walt Bond

WATERSPORTS
(Daytime)

Select items based on trip plans, worst-case weather conditions and level of luxury desired.

ITEM	DATE				
Water Sport Gear					
Trailer/Auto Gear Rack/Locks					
Mask					
Noseclip					
Snorkel/*Anti-Fog Preparation*					
Fins					
Weight Belt					
Buoyancy Compensator (BCD)					
Base Float					
Scuba Tank(s)/Regulator					
Tank Boot/Backpack					
Depth Gauge					
Timepiece/Alarm					
Submersible Pressure Gauge					
Dive Computer					
Knife/Prying Tool					
Life Lines					
Windsurf Board					
Windsurf Rig					
Windsurf Harness					
Personal Flotation Device					
Water Skis					
Towline					
Surfboard/Leash/Wax					
Raft/Kayak/Inner Tube					
Raft Frame					
Painter/Lining Rope					
Paddles/Oars & Spares					
Bailer					
Jet Ski					
Jet Ski Goggles					
Jet Ski Fuel, Oil					
Air Pump					
Water Jugs/Water Bottles					
Dry Packs					
Storage Bags					
Use Permit(s)					
Personal Gear					
Swim Suit					
"T"-Shirt					
Beach Towel					
Bandanna/Sweatband					
Wet Suit Jacket/Pants*					
Dry Suit*					
Headgear (sun/insulation*)					
Beach/Deck/Athletic Shoes					
Booties (protect feet/warmth*)					

WATERSPORTS
(Daytime)

ITEM	DATE				
Gloves/Mittens*					
Windbreaker/Paddling Jacket					
Warm Shorts/Long Pants					
Underwear					
Thermal Underwear*					
Sweater*					
Lightweight Hiking Boots					
Socks					
Helmet					
Land Shoes					
Land Sweater /Pants (warmth)					
Eveningwear					
Hygiene					
Towel					
Wash Cloth					
Biodegradable Soap					
Biodegradable Shampoo					
Personal Toiletries/Ditty Bag					
Toilet Paper					
Toilet Trowel					
Sun Shower					
Safety					
First Aid Kit (see FIRST AID)					
Water Filter/Tablets					
Sunglasses & Lanyard					
Sunscreen					
Lip Balm					
Insect Repellent					
Whistle					
Flares					
Waterproof Matches & Lighter					
Fire Starter/Heat Tabs					
Emergency Blanket					
Map(s)/Chart(s)					
Compass					
Pocket Knife					
Flashlight#/Underwater Light					
Extra Batteries & Bulb#					
Thermometer					
Reading Glasses & *Repair Kit*					
Phone Change					
Pen & Notepad					

WATERSPORTS
(Daytime)

ITEM	DATE				
Accessories					
Portable Ice Chest(s)					
Ice & "Blue Ice"					
Insulated Bottle					
Collapsible Water Bag					
Nylon Cord					
Brochures, Articles, Books					
Binoculars					
Trash Bag(s)					
Camp/Beach Chairs					
Portable Radio					
Sun Canopy/Mesh Screen					
Camera/Underwater Camera					
Extra Film & Battery					
Camera Bag/Lens Cleaning Kit					
Spear/Spear Gun					
*Portable Heater**					
Reusable Plastic Food Bags					
Stuff Sacks					
Daypack/Fanny Pack					
Indoor & Outdoor Games					
Auto Tool Kit					
Spare Keys/Credit Card/$					
Tool Kit					
Tools					
Repair Gear					
Replacement Gear					
Snacks (see MEALS section)					
High Energy Bars					
Trail Mix/Granola					
Fresh Fruit/Dried Fruit					
Beef Jerky					
Nuts					
Sandwiches					
Barbecue Items					
Chips & Dips					
Cookies/Candy					
Electrolyte (for water bottle)					

Italicized items are optional (niceties or special purpose). *cold weather items #nighttime activity gear

LAND FISHING (Daytime)

See INDEX for checklist items not discussed below.

The LAND FISHING activity is treated as a daytime venture, although it could be linked with overnight camping or sleeping aboard sail or powerboats to become a multi-day activity. In addition, the approach to the fishing site could be via hiking, bicycling, skiing/snowshoeing, snowmobiling, canoeing, kayaking or other means. Consult the activity descriptions associated with those individual entry methods for additional gear needs. As used here, LAND FISHING includes freshwater (stream, lake or ice) or inshore saltwater angling. Fishing can be conducted waterside, in-water (with "bare body," waders, float tubes or kick boats), or on-board (e.g., kayak, canoe, fishing boat).

In the discussion below, no attempt is made to optimize the tackle needed to catch the large variety of fish in the multitude of geographical regions under the highly-varied local site conditions. Only passing references are made with regard to fishing line, floats, strike indicators, hooks, bait, lures and flies. Consult the **REFERENCES** section in the back of the book and the numerous publications that treat specific fishing issues that are nearest and dearest to your heart.

Safety Considerations: 1) review the **GENERAL CONSIDERATIONS** and TEN ESSENTIALS sections; 2) when boating, learn to use and wear a PFD wherever called for by common sense -- if in doubt, wear it; 3) when fishing in running water, wear the necessary flotation aids and know how to activate and use them; 4) develop swimming skills commensurate with the level of activity planned; 5) ensure you can get out of waders if the situation demands; 6) develop a safe casting technique; 7) learn basic first aid; 8) bring cold- and wet-weather contingency gear if there is any doubt about the weather; 9) wear a hat, not only for protection from sun or cold, but also to protect yourself against wayward casters; and 10) if ice fishing, adhere to safe practices on the ice (see the discussion on safe ice thickness below) and learn proper rescue techniques.

A few words about *safe ice thickness*: The American Pulpwood Association's "Ice Thickness Table" suggests the following permissible loads based on "standard ice" (clear, blue hard ice above a pond or lake) thickness: two inches - one person on foot; three inches - group in single file; 7-1/2 inches - one car (two tons); eight inches - light truck (2-1/2 tons); 10 inches - truck (3-1/2 tons); and 12 inches - heavy truck (7-8 tons). There are two further qualifiers: 1) ice over the running water of a river and slush ice are roughly 20% and 50% weaker, respectively, than standard ice; and 2) some veterans will not fish on any ice less than five inches thick or drive a light truck on ice less than 15 inches thick.

In the checklist, items that are considered optional (niceties or special purpose) are *italicized*. Items noted with an asterisk(*) are for inclement weather and those with an ampersand(@) are specific to ice fishing.

Fishing Gear

Auto Gear Rack. As with other activities, a quality gear rack serves well for fishing. With rods secured on a your rack, there is more passenger room in your vehicle. More important, consider just the things that can happen to rods on the way to your fishing site -- the potential nasty effects of car doors and windows, the human body, rods resting against a car which fall, etc. -- invest in a rack! Better yet, purchase a roof-mounted storage unit which can hold your fishing gear inside and completely unexposed. (See the "Auto Gear Rack" item description in the VEHICLE-ACCESSIBLE CAMPING ACTIVITY.) Only if you are towing a boat which has space to secure your gear against both damage, weather and theft should you not consider this option.

Fishing Rod(s). As in any other outdoor activity, there is a wide selection of gear options, whether it be in terms of intended gear use or level of user expertise.

There are tradeoffs in terms of cost, materials, styles, perceived performance, versatility for multi-fishing-arena use, peripheral gear compatibility, and available accessories -- to name a few.

• In terms of *rod materials*, bamboo has all but disappeared. Its successor, fiberglass, is revered by a limited group that like its relatively greater "give" (relative to more modern rods) which produces a more sensitive feel for setting hooks. Fiberglass also survives in heavy-duty saltwater rods. High-stiffness graphite now dominates the scene for almost all rod types. This is not pure graphite, which is considered too brittle by most rod-makers, but a high percentage of graphite mixed with other material, such as fiberglass. Over the last several years, boron has been making a move to become an alternative to graphite. Contrary to graphite fans, proponents feel that boron equals and even surpasses graphite in terms of sensitivity and durability.

Lower Colorado River — Compliments of June Hardy

• There are several generic *rod design and performance features* to consider when evaluating rods. Obviously, the plan is to select those features that suit your specific fishing needs.

Rod "Action." The flexibility of a rod's shaft (or "blank"), i.e., the manner in which it bends and how rapidly it straightens, determines its "action." In rods with "fast" action, only the top one-third flexes, while the entire shaft bends for a "slow" action rod. A rod having "progressive" action has a tip that bends more than the middle section which, in turn, bends more than the butt end.

As a general rule, stiff rods have faster action, which allows casts of greater distances and makes maneuvering the lure easier. A stiff fly rod tend to produce tighter line loops between the back- and fore-cast. More flexible rods with slower action are preferable for more delicate presentations.

Rods used for plastic-worm- and jig-fishing tend to have firm tips for greater sensitivity and ease in setting the hook. Live bait, however, calls for a rod with relatively slow action, since too strong a "snap" will rip worms and other fleshy creatures off the hook. Bottom-fishing requires a relatively strong rod because bait is more likely to get caught on objects on the bottom.

Reel Seat. The reel seat is the assembly to which the reel is attached to the rod. One configuration, a classic that is seldom seen today, has a set of sliding rings. The lower ring (nearest the butt) is slipped over the reel's rear protruding plate, while the upper ring is positioned over the front reel plate. This allows some degree of adjustment of the reel's position on the grip. Another choice is a fixed butt cap with one sliding ring. Somewhat more popular are the uplock designs (where the seat fits into a slot at the grip's top end) and the downlock (the seat fits into the rod's butt end); in both cases, a sliding ring or screw holds the other end of the reel in place.

Fishermen who subject their gear to rough use and big fish and are concerned with having the reel ripped off the rod (surf-casting fishermen, for example) may choose to use backup tape over the reel-seat assembly. Alternately, they may simply tape the reel directly to the cork base. The proven mode is to use the most durable packing tape available. Once taped on, the rig is left in place for the season.

Regardless of configuration, reel seats made out of machined metal are more precisely and durably made than stamped-out models. Nickel-silver is favored for its self-lubricating quality, with aluminum a very acceptable alternative.

Line Guides. Guides, through which the line passes along the length of the rod, come in single-foot and two-foot styles. The former is wrapped onto the blank by its sole projection. The latter's twin projections may make it twice as secure, but some anglers feel that the dual wrapping adversely affects the rod's action. The most durable, top-of-the-line guides are constructed of silicon carbide. Aluminum oxide guides are more prevalent and also less expensive.

Handle. Cork is the traditional material for rod handles and is still favored by a large number of anglers ranging from novices to tournament fishermen. However, many baitcasting fishermen (with the exception of those using pistol-grip handles) prefer an EVA foam composition. Foam is touted by its' advocates as being more durable and offering better gripping features when wet.

• Given the generic rod features above, it's time to talk about the *general classes of fishing rods*. The categories focus on the types of fishing that one might pursue as opposed to the general rod characterization provided above.

Baitcasting Rods. Choosing the "right" length and weight of a baitcasting (or "conventional") rod depends in large part on the weight of the particular class of lures you intend to use. Manufacturers have grouped rods into several categories: at the extremes are 6 to 6-1/2-foot length, "extra-light" rods, used for casting lures in the 1/8- to 1/4-ounce range and 4-1/2- to 7-1/2-foot "heavy" rods for 3/4- to 1-1/4-ounce lures. Rods that fall into the "medium" group (4-1/2- to 6-feet for .5/8- to 3/4-ounce lures) are considered the best for all-around, general-purpose use. There is significant overlap within the categories because proper length depends on the type of conditions you must cope with and the kind of presentation you're aiming for. A short rod delivers a lure in a relatively flat trajectory, an essential need if you're fishing in a heavily-wooded area. Conversely, and foliage permitting, longer rods tend to cast bait in a high arc.

Relatively short "pistol-grip" handles have a hook projection for the baitcaster's index finger. The one-handed style is popular for baitcasting and is usually found on short (5-6 foot) rods where, according to its fans, pistol-grips permit snappier and more accurate casts.

"Flippin" (underhand or slingshot casting) rods and "pitchin" (overhand or sidearm casting) rods have many similar characteristics. Both have a flexible tip and the lower 80% of their blanks are stiff. This property allows for tossing bait a long distance ("pitchin") or to penetrate heavy weed cover ("flippin"). Classically, the pitchin rods have been the shorter of the two. However, there is now a tendency to use the same rod for both techniques, with a compromise length of 7-1/2 feet.

The "trigger-stick" handles are most often found on "flippin" and "pitchin" rods. They offer index-finger support, but unlike their "pistol grip" counterpart, the handle itself is longer. The extra length accommodates a two-handed casting grip.

Spinning Rods. One of the advantages of spinning tackle is its ability to present lighter bait than baitcasting gear. This feature is primarily a result of the properties of the reel, which is discussed below. Accordingly, line thickness becomes relevant, as does lure weight in selecting the "right" weight of a spinning rod. Rods are divided into several categories: at the extremes are "ultra-light" rods, used for line diameters of 0.005 to 0,008 millimeters and lures in the

1/16- to 5/16-ounce range and "extra-heavy" rods for line diameters of 0.015 to 0,024 millimeters for 3/4- to 1-1/4-ounce lures. Most freshwater rods range from 5-1/2 to 7 feet in length. The upper end of that spectrum is most effective for longer casts and for catching larger fish. There are also two-handed-cast spinning rods for salmon and steelhead fishing in the 7-8 foot range.

Saltwater fishing from boats calls for spinning rods of about 6-10 feet for bait weights of 3/4 to 2 ounces. At the extremes, "super-light" surf-casting spinning rods are 8-10 feet for casting lures weighing between 3/4 ounce to 1 ounce and "heavy "rods of 16 feet-plus for lures in the 3-1/2 ounce-plus arena.

Unlike line coming out straight from a bait-casting reel, line cast from a spinning reel comes off in spirals. The (nominally single-foot) guides on spinning rods diminish in size with progression from the reel to the tip-top. They effectively compress the spiral to the point that the line is nearly flat when it leaves the rod. Ceramic guides are best at dissipating heat caused by line friction.

Spinning rods use three types of mechanisms to hold the reel: 1) sliding rings slip onto the reel handle to hold the reel in place by tension against the handle (rarely found on higher-quality gear); 2) a fixed reel seat screws the reel in place -- there is greater security, but the metal corners can chafe your fingers; and 3) a sliding reel seat combines the first two devices and has the added advantages of great comfort and security.

Ashley Lake, Sierra Nevadas, CA   Compliments of Doug Holker

Most, but not all, spinning rods are designed for light-tackle casting. Many boat rods and surf-casting rods are big brawny members of the family. They are designed for long-distance casting for larger fish than their lighter cousins.

Fly Rods. For baitcasting and spinning rods, the weight of the bait provides the force that carries the line during a cast. That's why such rods are described in terms of optimal bait weight. In flycasting, the line moves because of its own weight and the propelling force of the cast. Accordingly, the rods are described in terms of weight of the line they are intended to hold. (Fly line weight is based on a standard computed in grains (not ounces) based on the line's first 30 feet. For example, a 1-weight corresponds to 60 grains, while 6-weight is 160 grains.) A list of the broad line-weight classifications: 1-weight through 3-weight is used for small trout and panfish sought with delicate presentations of tiny light flies on small, slow-moving streams; 4-weight through 6-weight is more common for larger trout and walleye; 7-weight through 8-weight is designed for relatively larger streams and lakes for bass fishing (and its heavier flies); 9-weight through 11-weight is typical for salmon and steelhead fishing, where long casts on fast-running streams are needed in fast streams. These weights are also appropriate for bonefish and small tarpon on typically windy saltwater flats; 12-weight through 15-weight is used for playing and landing such substantial deep-sea quarry as sailfish, tarpon or tuna.

As for action, a stiffer ("faster") rod will cast a line further, while a more supple ("slower") design will toss the fly in a more lazy lob, a desirable characteristic for more delicate presentations. The vast majority of casts made for trout (bass and panfish, too) are 25 feet or under, well within the parameters of a medium-action rod. However, casts of from 40 to 70 feet are routine when coping with wind and longer distances across saltwater flats or salmon and steelhead rivers. For the latter situations, a faster rod is called for.

With regard to length, an 8-to 9-foot rod is common to many trout fishermen. A shorter rod makes sense for fishing in small streams with heavy overgrowth. A 9-foot length is appropriate for salmon and steelhead fishing. A small amount of weight will make a big difference in terms of comfort over a day of casting. All else being equal, most anglers select the lighter rod.

The rule of thumb is one guide for each foot of rod plus one extra for the tip-top. Some anglers prefer models with an enlarged butt guide (nearest the handle) relative to the other guides. Both one-foot and two-foot guides are popular.

Fly rod handles, which are traditionally made of cork, come in a variety of shapes. The "cigar" is the most popular, although its tapered shape offers relatively little support to the angler's thumb. The bulge at the top of the "half-wells" style of handle and the twin-bridges of the "full-wells" offer far greater support, making them preferable for heavier tackle and bigger fish. Heavier rods have a "fighting butt," a knob at the handle end, that can be pressed against a fisherman's stomach. These designs offer better leverage for fighting salmon. steelhead and saltwater species.

Saltwater Rods. Subtlety of casting is not much of a factor when surf fishing. Therefore, rods made of fiberglass and graphite heavily-doped with composites are found as frequently as those predominantly of graphite. Surf-casting rods are built for ultra-long casting, up to 200 feet or more. The four categories of (typically spinning) surf-fishing rods: 1) "superlights" are 8-10 feet long and cast bait in the 3/4- to 1-ounce class; 2) "light" rods are 11 to 12-1/2 feet for 1 to 2-3/4 ounce bait; 3) "mediums" and "semi-heavies" are 13-15 feet for 2-1/4 to 3-1/2 ounce bait; and 4) "heavies" are 16 feet plus for 3-1/2 ounce bait and larger.

There are also fly fishermen who ply the surf, typically using 9-11 weight line for bonefish and small tarpon, especially on saltwater flats where ocean winds are an ever-present factor. These anglers lean toward rods with full-well rod grips and fighting butts.

Pack/Telescoping Rods. Some situations call for rods that can be carried in a limited space and through "gear-unfriendly" terrain. These rods are characteristically used by hikers, backpackers and general backcountry tourers. Also, some avid anglers carry them in the trunk of their car, using them at any available opportunity. They may be baitcasting, spinning, fly or saltwater rods. For "pack" rods, two variants are most common.

Multi-piece pack models are basically the standard length device when the three to six individual sections are combined. They are joined together by ferrules. The open cylindrical end of one section fits over the solid end of the next. They may be baitcasting, spinning, fly or saltwater rods. A quality multi-section rod is just as durable as the classic one- or two-piece styles and have little or no objectionable action.

Integral or single-piece pack rods are, most often, the light, small, packaged rod-and-reel sets that you see at both fishing stores and major shopping outlets. They are not prized so much for their technical qualities as they are for their size, weight, cost and usefulness in catching "meals." They are the "poor man's version" of a baitcasting rod. A typical model is 4-5 feet in deployed length and is constructed of a graphite composite.

Also designed for ease of transportation, *telescoping rods* slide into themselves like the shafts of some umbrellas. Commonly used for fresh-water fishing in more inaccessible areas, they are found less frequently as saltwater angling tools. They are typically slower than multi-piece pack rods.

Ice Fishing Rods. These rods have their own unique characteristics. (In this arena, rods and reels will be discussed together.) The sport is very different in nature than water fishing. There are two primary techniques used in ice fishing.

Jigging Technique. Jigging, alternately lifting and lowering the lure-weighted line, calls for a short, stiff rod from 2-3 feet in length. Although available commercially, many jigging rods are homemade. A common method is to use the tip section of a broken spinning or fly rod mounted onto a cork or foam handle. Some jigging rods use no reel. Rather, line is looped around two hooks mounted above the handle and unwrapped or rewrapped as needed. Many others use a rudimentary reel which is simply an attached line spool with little or no drag adjustment. Recently, small spinning reels are becoming more prevalent.

Tip-Up Technique. The other technique is to use a tip-up, an apparatus that signals (usually by tripping a flag) that a fish is on the line. The technique does not require a rod. A reel is mounted on the end of the tip-up or else it is suspended underwater. The advantage to the former style is that you don't have to lift the entire tip-up out of the water before setting the hook and retrieving a fish. On the other hand, wet line on an underwater reel doesn't freeze to the spool as it's apt to do if exposed to cold air and wind.

• There are many tradeoffs in *rod selection*, starting with its intended purpose(s) as described above. Secondly, there is the issue of what your pocket book can handle. Once you have homed in on the class of rods that fits your needs, there is an issue of assessing rod compatibility with your style.

Cost Tradeoff. Better materials and careful craftsmanship will cost more than cheaper materials and average-quality workmanship. A rod made of premium graphite, a defect-free cork handle, and solid hand-machined fittings will handle better, last longer, and look better than one that comes off the assembly line. Usually, there are several levels of quality from which to make a selection. At the lower end are packaged "starter" kits that include rod and reel. They generally cost less but tend to be the manufacturer's "bottom of the line." Truly cheaply-made tackle lack the action and sensitivity that classically lead to a novice's immediate enjoyment and quick progress.

Assessment of Rod Quality. The initial check is for straightness, evaluated by sighting down the length and rotating the rod. Assess that the guides are aligned, securely wrapped, and sealed off with an even coat of varnish. If the handle is made of cork, test that it is solid, snug and free of defects (cracks, pits and gouges). Confirm that the seat is snug and secure. Test the rod's feel when performing a casting motion. (Particularly for the latter check, the most reliable test is to fully rig the outfit and try it outdoors. If this is impractical, options are to rent a similar outfit or borrow from an acquaintance.)

Rod Cases. Storing and transporting a rod in a hard protective case greatly reduces the chance of its being stepped on, snapped or otherwise damaged. Rod cases are a must for multi-piece rods used for hiking and backpacking, both to prevent damage or loss. (There is a rod tip probably still lying in the thick brush of our improvised trail at Mineral King in the Sequoia National Forest.) If your rod didn't come with a case, you can buy one at most tackle shops or mail-order outlets. A homemade option is to get PVC pipe (nominally used for plumbing) of the required diameter, cut it to the needed length and fit with rubber plugs.

Rod Carrier. Carrying even one strung rod, especially when broken down into its component sections, is likely to produce a tangled line. There are many carrying devices that prevent this. A typical design might have two rubber clamps which hold the sections together and secures the line in the process. Similarly, there are commercially available designs that hold multiple rods.

Holeb Pond, Maine Compliments of Doug Holker

Reel(s). There is at least one reel type that accompanies the rods discussed above. Many of the same types of tradeoffs discussed for rods apply to the accompanying reels, i.e., cost, materials, styles, perceived performance, versatility for multi-fishing-arena use, peripheral gear compatibility, available accessories -- to name a few.

• In terms of *reel materials*, the highest quality reels are made from bar stock metal that is honed to highly-precise specifications. Another method is to cast metal parts out of molds, a somewhat less-expensive process. Other reels are molded from plastic or graphite, or mass-produced from stamped metal. One benefit of the lower end of the craftsmanship ladder is that mass-produced reels tend to handle abuse (abrasions, bangs and other traumas that occur with normal use) better than their handmade ultra-precision brethren. (This is somewhat analogous to the comparison of a mass-produced commuter car with a high-performance sports car.) Brass and steel are extremely durable, as is man-made graphite. Though hyped as a space-age material, plastic remains at the fragile end of the spectrum.

• Two generic *reel design and performance features* that are important to reel selection are discussed below. The specific needs in the two feature areas will vary with the type of fishing planned and angler level of expertise.

Reel Drag. Drag is essential to any discussion of reels. It is simply resistance, which translates into the amount of tension that a line (including a leader, if any) can take before it breaks. To prevent such breakage, reels contain drag mechanisms that automatically disengage the reel spool and, thus, release line when a certain pressure is reached.

Reel Gear Ratio. The gear ratio of a reel indicates the number of revolutions it takes to rewind a certain length of line. If a 1:1 ratio reel picks up five inches of line each revolution of the winder, then a 3:1 ratio model of equivalent circumference will retrieve 15 inches with the same winding motion. Ratios of 4:1 are near the top of the line.

• Given the general reel features above, this leads to a discussion of the *general classes of fishing reels*. The categories below focus on the types of fishing that one might pursue in much the same fashion as already discussed for rods.

Baitcasting Reels. What distinguishes these "conventional" reels from those used in other types of fishing is the revolving spool from which the weight of the bait pulls the line. Because of the line tangle that can result when the spool spins faster than the line can be released, many reels contain "magnetic brake" mechanisms. These devices limit the speed at which the spool revolves during a cast; the brake can be adjusted to reflect the weight of the plug or whatever other bait the reel is being asked to cast.

To prevent uneven line distribution on the spool during the rewind, many reels have a level-winder device. This is an elongated loop that slides back and forth across the spool to ensure that the line lays even and flat.

Particularly for the hard-fighting fish in saltwater angling, baitcasting reels are set up with either of two kinds of braking systems. The "star-drag" system consists of a series of discs that increase or decrease pressure against the spool's drum. It's a durable system that is operated by one or two star-shaped wheels mounted between the reel casing and the winder. The "lever-drag" system contains a single lever that exerts pressure against the reel drum. Many fishermen consider reels with this system more sensitive than their star drag counterparts. Most drag systems are manually adjusted for the desirable performance both before casting and often while a fish is being played or landed. Adjustable drags, as contrasted with their manual counterparts, automatically downshift to a lower gear that is more effective in fighting big fish. Some surf-casting reels have two-speed retrieval systems for even more precise control.

Ball bearings have become standard components of both freshwater and saltwater reels for both conventional and spinning outfits. They reduce friction for smoother rewinding under tension and at greater speeds.

Spinning Reels. Several key features gave rise to spinning reels as a desirable alternative to conventional assemblies. The absence of a rotary spool meant the virtual elimination of backlash, particularly a problem with earlier baitcasting reels. Moreover, with no rotating spool that needed a relatively heavy bait to activate it, spinning permitted the use of lightweight bait, 1/4 ounce or less Finally, fewer moving parts meant that spinning reels were easier, and therefore less expensive to manufacture.

The most popular type of line-retrieval mechanism is a *bail*, a metal hoop across the spool's face. One end is on the pickup bracket, the other on the rotating cup. The bail is opened manually by a flick of the angler's finger, then closes when the winder is cranked; the line moves along the bail until it reaches the roller, then proceeds onto the spool. A system found on older reels is the *automatic pickup arm*. It consists of a single curved arm that swings out of the way during the cast. As soon as the winder handle is turned, the arm strikes a cam and swings back to pick up the line. Finally, the simplest (and least likely to fail) mechanism is the *manual pickup*, simply a rotor on a revolving cup. The angler's forefinger slips the line over the roller. Few accomplished anglers still use this design, since placement accuracy is compromised.

With the spinning reels, drag is adjusted by tightening or loosening the nut found either at the front of the spool or the rear of the reel. The anti-reverse lock is a ratchet mechanism that prevents a reel from letting line unwind, except as allowed by the drag mechanism. Most spin-fishermen keep it on at all times in conjunction with a properly set drag. It's a particularly useful feature for such single-handed operations as netting a fish.

Whatever features you select, the choice of spinning reel should be based on line weight and line capacity. The following categories describe the range: "Ultra-light" for up to 8-pound test; "light" for 8-15 pound test; "medium" for 15-30 pound test; and "heavy" for 30-pound test and above.

Aruba, Caribbean

Spin-Casting Reels. A spin-casting reel is a spinning reel with a closed face. The enclosure is usually a rounded hood with a small hole in its face through which line passes. The fisherman's thumb on a release button or knob on the back end of the reel controls the line during the cast; the moment pressure on the line relaxes, no further line is released. With regard to line retrieval, a pin winds around inside the hood to settle the line on the cup. Some reels have more than one pin, which makes for a faster rewind.

Friction and line capacity are the two main considerations of spin-casting reels. With regard to friction, monofilament is the line of choice since braided line creates too much resistance. The hood makes line capacity somewhat restrictive relative to spinning reels, although this is not an issue for most "close-in" applications. Also, changing line with a spin-caster is far less convenient.

Spin-casting tackle is both easier to learn with and use than a spinning rod and reel. A misgiving is that you don't have the same accuracy of line control, since the release button is an all-or-nothing mechanism. However, a little bit of practice is all it takes to gauge the amount of time the button should be held down to achieve a respectable cast. This is not to say that spin-casting reels are for novices only. There are models used by experienced anglers that may include features such as 4:1 ratio retrieval, star-drag systems and power handles for better grip.

Fly Reels. Fly reels are categorized primarily according to the range of line weights that they are intended to hold. Reels designed for the lightest weights, 1 through 5, are necessarily smaller than those 9-15 weights meant for salmon, steelhead, and especially deep-sea fishing.

The reel weight becomes crucial to establish optimum balance. A reel that is too heavy means that the rod itself will feel too light, and that will interfere with line control while you cast. A reel that is too light, however, makes a rod feel too heavy, especially at its tip. This too creates casting problems. In the best of all worlds, a rod and reel will have their center of balance just in front of the grip.

Many fly reels adjust for drag by means of a single triangular *pawl* held by a spring against a geared wheel. Since pawls can slip and spring coils can lose their tension, a more precise mechanism is a *padded disc* that applies pressure against the spool. The least adjustable resistance control comes from the *click ratchet*, activated by an all-or-nothing switch. For reels designed with an exposed rim, resistance can also be applied manually by letting the flat of your hand rub against the wheel's rim ("rim palming").

A big fish can yank line so hard and fast that the reel's spool will rotate in excess of 5000 revolutions per minute, a potential problem if the reel handle makes contact with the knuckles. *Anti-reverse reels* eliminate this danger; the spool rotates as the line goes out, but the reel knob does not.

A system of internal springs and gears characterize the *"automatic" fly reel*. A flip of the lever (usually with your little finger) and the mechanism springs into action, pulling the slack on the line back onto the reel spool. Many anglers, especially who release lots of line fishing for salmon and steelhead, swear by automatics. Others, who prefer greater human control, cite that reduced drag control and reduced line capacity with no backing do not justify its benefits.

More widely accepted examples of mechanical advantage are *multiplier reels*. Their gear systems (typically a 3:1 ratio) offer fast line retrieval. This is a very useful asset when trying to land any of the larger and hard-fighting freshwater and saltwater fish.

• As with rods, there are many tradeoffs in *reel selection*, starting with its intended use(s). Secondly, there is the issue of what your pocket book can handle. Once you have homed in on the class of reels that fits your needs, there is the issue of assessing reel compatibility with your style.

Cost Tradeoff. Better materials and careful craftsmanship will cost more than cheaper materials and average-quality workmanship. Reels equipped with some of the special performance features mentioned will dent your wallet more than the more-basic styles. Ask yourself whether a precision-machined reel is compatible with your intended use; if there is a history of "reel abuse" in your past, strongly consider stepping down to a high quality, but more robust model. Typically, there are several levels of quality from which to make a selection. At the lower end are packaged "starter" kits that include rod and reel, as discussed for the "rod" gear item above.

Assessment of Rod Quality. The initial check involves a look-and-feel for reel imperfections. Check for loose, wobbling parts as you wind the reel, especially the spool and spool release (and any spare spools that you're also considering buying). Test the drag system, listening for unusual noises as you rotate the spool. Make sure the spool is large enough to accommodate your line capacity needs. Spools in the range of 50-100 feet of line should cut it for light fishing, 150 feet is probably adequate for any species of shallow water fish, while reels with capacities up to 400 feet might be needed in blue-water fishing for billfish, tuna, wahoo and large mackerel. For all major tackle items, and particularly for reels, confirm that defects occurring during the warranty period will be corrected or your gear exchanged.

Reel Bags. Leather or cloth reel bags are designed for the storage and transportation of reels. Padded versions of these bags are the most secure. Plastic zip-locking food bags make a handy, but riskier substitute. If your tackle box size permits, and the reel is properly packed, this is another excellent way to protect these valuable mechanisms.

Tackle Box Items. Stored inside your tackle box or tote bag may be items such as spare spools and reels, fishing line, leaders, floats, sinkers, spinners, swivels, snaps, hooks, lures, flies and angler's tools -- to name a few. Other than the brief discussions of items noted on the checklist, we have not attempted to treat the myriad of tackle-box goodies. For discussion of tackle-box gear, gear tradeoffs and optimal equipment selection to suit your trip needs, consult the **REFERENCE** section of this book, your local tackle shop, and/or the myriad of fishing publications on the market.

Upper Bow River, Banff, Canada   Compliments of Jim Cradduck

Tackle Box. Some consider this the angler's equivalent to a hiker's backpack. Every item thought to be essential is packed into the box and is checked and cross-checked before heading out on a fishing tour. In the fishing arena, however, weight and space availability will drive you to markedly different conclusions, depending on whether you are hiking into an alpine lake or fishing from a cabin cruiser. The solution may be to have several tackle boxes of different sizes or to skinny down to small tote bags if called for by the trip characteristics.

• There are many *styles of fishing gear carriers*, some of which are listed below. All styles will normally have compartmented trays or drawers.

Trunk Style. The trunk is the closest to the classic home toolbox. Simplest models have a single tray which lifts out, exposing the lower storage area. Higher-tech models have several tiers of unfolding stackable trays.

Flat Box Style. Think of an artist's briefcase with a snap or set of snaps in place of a zipper. You unsnap it and the transparent, box-like center section is exposed. This is the storage area with numerous, varying size compartments, each with its own transparent lid.

Drawer Box Style. This is a fisherman's chest of drawers. In essence it is a box with several slide-out drawers, generally with a top section that is exposed through a swing-back lid.

Hip Roof Style. This design has two facing tiers of up to three drawers that unfold away from each other when the box is opened. Additional items can be stored in the bottom compartment.

Hanging Racks Style. This is a deep box with parallel, vertical racks that can be removed individually. Items such as plugs and spoons can be hung from the racks to prevent tangling and permit rapid drying. Most of these boxes have compartments for bulkier spare spinnerbait, buzzbait blades and skirts.

Tackle Totes. Some choose to carry fishing tackle in a tote bag. Usually constructed of sturdy fabric, the most versatile of bags have outside compartments and internal pockets and pouches.

• There are several *key qualities* to look for when purchasing a tackle box. In terms of key questions: Does it provide the needed capacity, both overall and for the bulkier items that you intend to carry? Does it have sturdy overall construction, including handles and latches? (With regard to materials, most boxes are currently made of rugged, lightweight and rustproof plastic.) Is it configured to conveniently serve your intended uses? Is it "plastic worm-proof?"

Special Storage Containers. When packing your tackle box, small bags, boxes and other containers may help you better group/organize the tackle box's contents. Soft plastic worms, grubs and bait are made of materials that can eat through certain plastics. If your tackle box isn't designated as "plastic worm-proof," you'll need separate vinyl binders, bags or boxes for those items.

Creel. As opposed to laying caught fish on the ground or the boat floor, the creel serves as a temporary holding place. Many line their creel with wetted grass or leaves to preserve the catch's moisture. The traditional creel is effectively a wicker basket with a securable top lid. Most often, it has a shoulder strap for ease of hauling the catch out of the fishing site. Another option is to bring a canvas or linen "Arctic cooler" that retains moisture and coolness after being immersed in a stream or lake.

Bait/Bait Container. Live bait is a popular fish lure. Typical live bait for fresh-water fishing includes worms ("nightcrawlers," bloodworms, sandworms), baitfish ("minnows," which includes many types of small fish), leeches, crickets and grasshoppers, crawfish and frogs, to name a few. Under the "preserved" live bait category are pork rind, salmon eggs, maggots mealworms and many others -- they are pre-packaged. Examples of popular favorites among saltwater anglers are bunkers, snappers, tinker mackerel, mullet, herring and eels.

Live bait requires care to ensure that they are just that -- live -- when used, and thus the role for bait containers. They may vary from simple water containers maintained in a general temperature range to insulated, mulch-filled cartons that are periodically watered or iced to maintain the required environment. Check with your local bait shop for details on transporting your live bait.

Landing Net/Dehooker/Stringers. The *net* is used to retrieve fish that have been reeled in to near proximity; it's use minimizes losing the catch. Purchase a landing net that will handle the type of fish you're after. A large-hooped, large-handled net is designed for such as northern pike and muskellunge, while a smaller version is acceptable for trout.

Particularly for larger fish, consider using a *de-hooker*. The simplest version has a long. narrow plastic rod with a slot at its end. The slot allows you to track the fishing line down the fish's gullet to the hook. A higher-tech version is plier-like in function, but has a pistol shape and includes an extremely long, narrow barrel with tiny powerful "jaws" at the end.

Once caught, the fish are hooked into *stringers*. These are small lines that, when the free end is weighted down or tied to a heavy object, allow temporary fish storage in the water. They also make fish handling more convenient and are a must when you are standing in front of a camera with your catch.

Gaff. Typical ice holes are about three-feet wide, which doesn't give ice fishermen much room to net a fish when near the surface. That's why using a gaff is the customary way to prevent fish from escaping. It is also used as an assist, for varied types of angling, for hauling in a "lively" catch to minimize the chance of losing the fish in the end game.

Waders. For anglers who ply chilly streams, lakes, rivers and coastal surf, waders are a must. Size-wise, the two classic types are *hip waders* ("hippers") and *chest waders*. The former is for working in water that is no higher than pelvis-deep, the latter for deeper immersion.

Each type has two style offerings. One is the *boot-foot wader*, which has an integral upper and boot; the second is the *stocking-foot wader*, which includes an upper wader and separate wading shoe or boot. The key advantage of the integral model is convenience, since you don't have to spend time lacing and unlacing the boots. On the debit side, the boot-foot designs offer less ankle and heel support. This may not be an issue on smooth, relatively level surfaces (e.g., the sandy-bottom surfaces of coastlines), but could be a problem when coping with uncertain footing of a rocky-bottomed mountain trout stream, a rushing salmon river or a rocky surf. Also, the stocking-foot wader allows the versatility of matching the wading shoe or boot to the fishing environment -- a light wading shoe for cool-weather shore-line angling and a heavy, well-insulated, lug-soled boot for fishing in a fast-running frigid stream.

There are many *wader materials* from which to select. The classic rubber wader has been generally supplanted by lighter-weight nylon and other synthetics, the most tear-resistant of the many options. Synthetic fabric waders come in both single-layer and multi-layer designs. Single layer would be an excellent choice if one were looking for a lightweight, cooler outfit for summertime. Multi-layer designs, using waterproof and abrasion- and crack-resistant fabrics, keep the wearer warm as well as dry.

More recently, and at added expense, stretch fabrics like neoprene have revolutionized waders. The body-hugging fabric reduces water entry into the wader and is an excellent body-heat trapper. Their use by frigid-water kayakers and scuba divers should attest to those properties. (They are so efficient that anglers with chest waders may find themselves rolling their waders down to the level that the water depth permits.) Finally, near the top of the cost line, there are the breathable fabrics like Gore-Tex, which allow the body perspiration to escape, but prevent outside water droplets from entering, When properly cinched to prohibit direct water entry (through sleeves, neck, ankles and waist), and when worn with the proper underlayering in frigid water, there are no more comfortable fabrics than these. (The same characteristics make these fabrics excellent inclement-weather gear, as noted in several other activities treated in this book.)

Sizing of waders is important for all-round comfort, to prevent chafing, and to allow unimpeded casting motion. Particularly for boot-foot waders, try them on before purchasing or find a mail-order house that has a very liberal returns policy. Some anglers feel that the expense of having their waders custom-made is money well spent.

There are several *special features* that add to wader functionality. One is built-in knee pads (which also add to wader durability). Another is hand-warmer front pockets, which are useful in cold weather.

There are certain *safety-related wader items* to consider. Any chest wader that isn't form-fitting requires a wading belt. The belt straps around the wearer's chest to keep water out in the event of a dunking. Keep in mind that anglers have drowned in water-filled waders. The belt should have a quick-release buckle, should you have to get out of your waders in a hurry and swim for your life.

Waders should be equipped with a pair of suspenders to keep them high up on your body. Snaps are easier to attach and remove, but less secure than buckled or buttoned options. There are also inflatable suspenders which are activated by wearer initiation or immersion. The activation source is commonly a CO_2 cartridge.

A regression: For *stocking-foot wader boots*, many use the rugged outdoor designs like the "Bean Boots" found under the "Fishing/Hiking Boots" gear item described in this section. However, their is a strong case for comparing them with *wading shoes* before making a decision (or you could purchase both). Wading shoes are typically made of synthetic leather uppers and felt soles. These soles are common for rocky stream bottoms; in contrast, the same soles with attached metal studs are frequently used for muddy bottom surfaces. (For both boots and wading shoes, strap-on cleats can also be used to significantly improve traction.) The highest quality models come with a padded collar at the back, a sturdy tongue, solid eyelets (or quick and convenient Velcro bindings) and a thick and sturdy sole.

John Day Park, Columbia River, Oregon   Compliments of June Hardy

Wader Pack. An easy way to transport waders is with a wader pack. Its mesh side or top surfaces expedite drying. Some are equipped with a carpet pad, which you can use to stand on when changing in and out of shoes (beats standing on pine needles or pebbles with bare feet).

Fishing Gear Carrier/Fishing Vest. Methods of toting fishing gear on the body range from the old-time basics to use of sophisticated carriers.

• There are many ways to haul a limited amount of fishing gear when a tackle box is out of the question. Classic methods are tucking gear in pants and shirt pockets or using small carry or gear bags worn over the shoulders. Newer-model *gear bags* worn around the waist are regaining popularity. Other choices include the *chest fly box* and the *fishing belt*, usually equipped with one large main compartment and several smaller ones.

• A favorite among anglers, particularly fly-fishermen, is a *fishing vest*. There are many properties to consider before purchasing. The discussion below is weighted toward, but not restricted to, fly-fishing.

Vest Design. The vests have various sized pockets on the outside and inside and, for some models, even on the back. Pocket closure methods include rustproof metal or plastic zippers and Velcro-secured flaps -- some outfits have no flaps or fasteners at all. Most novices (and many experts) need no more than 10-12 pockets, while some expert pack-rats might opt for models with 30 or more.

A typical mix might be one or two expandable pockets for fly boxes, a couple of others for floatants and desiccants, others for leaders and tippet material, and the rest for strike indicators, leader sink-gunk, sunglasses and fishing license.

Items carried on the vest itself (held by retractable wire "zingers') might include a line cutter and hook-removing hemostat, to name two, as well as a landing net hanging down the back. Other exterior features might include D-rings for attaching such items as a wading staff; a fleece patch for drying flies; Velcro rod-holding tabs; buckle straps for carrying traveling rods in their tubes; and hand-warmer pockets in the front.

The best designed vests have deep armholes that permit unrestricted casting. Because a fully-loaded vest will carry several pounds of gear, a bias-cut, non-binding collar will distribute pressure evenly against the wearer's neck.

Vest Material. Cotton or cotton blends are the most common materials, while synthetics such as Supplex offer greater durability. Many fishermen favor vests of mesh or with mesh segments for their improved ventilation and lighter weight. The penalty for this option is that objects tend to become snagged in mesh more easily than with solid cloth.

Vest Length/Size. Vests come in both below-the waist and above-the-waist ("shortie") models. The lengthier version has more room for pockets. However, if you are going to wade in deeper water, you may want to sacrifice storage space for one of the shorties. When considering size, opt for a roomier vest; this allows room to wear bulkier undergarments in cold weather. In warmer weather, the roomy vest allows better air circulation for cooling. Another argument for buying "oversize" is that some vests, such as those made of cotton, will shrink after a number of dunkings and dryings.

Vest Color. Since a bright-colored vest will alert fish to the wearer's presence, solid and amber hues like tan, olive green, gray or camouflage are most popular and most commonly stocked. Green or tan is appropriate for anglers who fish where there is a lot of background foliage. By the same token, gray or slate blue will reduce the visual effect of standing out against an open sky.

Variations in Vest Design. Since just about every angler welcomes pockets, there are variants to the fly-fishermen vest design. Those designed for baitcasting and spinning fans who spend a fair amount of time in boats often include flotation safety features. These might be either built-in "life preserver" foam or an apparatus for inflation. The latter can be either the automatic inflating variety (activated by CO_2 cartridges) or the manually inflating type where the wearer blows into a valve. Some automatics have the manual mode as a backup.

Wading Staff. When working your way around flowing water or over shoreline rocks, a wading staff will help you maintain your stability. Frequently this tool is simply a downed piece of wood that you have de-limbed and sized for your use. Alternately, it might be your "walking stick" described in the HIKING activity or an old ski pole with the basket removed. Another, more expensive option, is an (generally) aluminum telescoping pole that can be compressed into an easily-storable unit.

Support Belt. Elastic support belts have been borrowed from designs for heavy construction workers and others who place long-duration stress on their lower backs. It's purpose is to reduce back strain for anglers who spend hours casting from along a shore or fishing from a boat. Many users prefer the style with built-in suspenders that keep the belt in place while the wearer is casting or playing a fish. Other models feature an adjustable belt that threads through the trouser loops, which serves the same purpose. Fishing-inspired support belts are beginning to look more and more like vests, with models that include built-in pouches and D-rings.

Fish Handling Gloves. A frequently-carried gear item is a pair of gloves for handling fish. Anything from garden gloves to the hand-warming articles have been used. There are also gloves designed specifically for this use. One clever option is called "The Udder Hand," which has latex rubber fingers and thumb to give a good grip on slippery fish. The glove also provides protection against hooks and fish teeth. When not in use, it adheres to your belt by a Velcro holder.

Float Tube/Kickboat. A *float tube* is a one-person, buoyant, chair-like apparatus for lake, pond, slow-moving water or light (protected-area) inshore fishing. The float tube originated in inland waters, but has been adopted by some of the harbor, bay and inlet saltwater fishing community. The wader-clad angler sits in the chair, suspended by the flotation equipment, and propels the craft using flippers on his feet. Today's float tubes may be round, open-ended or V-shaped. Most are extremely stable, provide ample back support, and allow for long outings on the water.

The most basic models consist of a rubber truck inner tube that is covered with a nylon shell. A seat in the center of the float tube that is attached to the shell supports the angler's weight. The backrest is nominally a smaller inner tube inflated in a zippered pocket on the top of the shell back. Recently, more tubes have taken on a square-shaped design; the shell is made so that much more of the inner tube is at the boat's rear. Such additional rear buoyancy allows the angler to float in a more upright fashion, reduces wave splash over the back, and facilitates mobility.

The float tubes may be "bare-bones" models or equipped with a variety of extra features. Potential extras include multi-layer seam stitching, extra-heavy zippers, side accessory pockets, Velcro rod holders, adjustable seat, fleece flypatches, backpack straps for holding additional gear and even an anchor.

For inland anglers on relatively quiet water, the choices are to fit flippers over either boot-foot or stocking-foot waders. Convenient and less-costly products designed to fit over a wading boot and cinched tight with laces are popular for inland fisherman on quiet water. In contrast, there is a strong sentiment toward diving fins and a boot-foot wader for inlanders in flowing water and almost all saltwater fishermen. The reason: The latter option provides a more reliable source of power for countering a running stream or flowing river water, as well as the swells and surge of saltwater. Besides, the cumbersome boots or wading boots can wear the legs down over an extended period.

Jalama Beach, California

Freshwater anglers in moving water and most saltwater fishermen feel that *kickboats*, an outgrowth of the float tube concept, are still the preferred choice. These boats entail a pair of banana-like pontoons separated by a fisherman-supporting frame. They ride higher in the water than float tubes and slice through the water like the twin hulls of a catamaran. Kickboats seat the angler higher above the water surface, creating less drag than a standard float tube as well as allowing exertion of more kicking power and freedom of movement. Some come equipped with the added features discussed above for float tubes. Some models are, or can be, equipped with oars for additional mobility.

A regression: In deep water, bring along a PFD in the event that your floating fishing platform fails or you otherwise have to "abandon ship." Some prefer to lash their PFD to the back of the float tube or kickboat, while the folks who give the "how-I-lived-to-be-100-years-old" interviews most likely wear them at all times.

Ice Auger/Ice Chisel. The most popular tool for cutting a hole in the ice is an auger drill powered by hand or a gas motor. An alternative is a spud, a long-handled chisel for chipping ice away.

Ice Removal Tool. A slotted spoon is one option for removing layers of ice that inevitably re-form over open holes. Or you can use a plastic cover, some models of which have a built-in tip-up. Another choice is something known as an Anti-Freeze Device, a cover with a thin plastic straw-like tube through which line can be fed even if the hole freezes up.

Tip-Up. Use of a tip-up for ice fishing is described in the "Tip-Up Technique" paragraph above. The most elementary tip-ups are made of two crossing sticks. More sophisticated systems have a sturdier structure and even such features as flashing lights for bite notification and wind-powered mechanisms that jig the bait below.

Rod Holder. Fishermen of all types have used rod holders when taking a break or when the fishing is slow. Land-based anglers frequently use implements of the surrounding terrain, e.g., rocks, logs, sand. A variety of commercial holders for land-based use is also available.

An ice fishermen has many similar options. Instead of holding the jigging rod all the time, it can be propped and held in place using the miscellaneous gear typically brought in. Another option is a commercial rod-holder with fluorescent orange handle; when fish bite, it will catch your attention day or night. (We apologize for yet another pun!) There are even rods with handles designed to keep the rod at a proper angle over the hole, as well as keeping the reel above snow and ice.

Portable Ice Shelter. A common method of brunting the effects of weather is to use an *ice-fishing shack*. Towed into position when the lake ice is capable of supporting it, it may be left in place for weeks or moved more frequently. (In the latter case, the foundation may include skis or a sled.) Shacks are customarily made of wood and are built in both single- and multiple-fisherman sizes.

Outfitting the shack is a matter of preference, particularly influenced by the levels of luxury and functionality desired. They are typically heated with a wood-burning or butane gas stove or a gas or electric heater, and are designed to provide proper ventilation. Shelves and/or cabinets provide space for tackle, extra clothing and other trip goodies. Furnishings may include hot plates or more sophisticated cooking facilities and even a portable television.

Less permanent and more austere, but wholly functional, are *windscreens* of canvas stretched between durable metal frames. Somewhat between these and wooden shacks are the *polyester tents and shelters* sold by many tackle shops and in catalogues. Features include Velcro window flaps, sturdy plastic floors (some with pre-cut, rip-stop sewn holes), cushioned seats and equipment storage pockets. Or. if the ice is thick enough to support vehicles, some choose to fish from their four-wheel drive sport utility vehicles or trucks.

Electronic Bottom-Finder. Some boats are equipped with bottom-finding electronic gear, frequently to aid in navigating shallow land or sea waters. There is a secondary boater use and primary ice fishermen use for this gear. The purpose is to find the line length necessary to reach bottom-feeding fish. The gear is highly efficient in terms of response time relative to the gear discussed below, though it does come with a price tag.

The old classic is to lower a sinker line, then mark the point where the slack line indicates that the sinker has reached the bottom. An alternative is to attach hooks at various points along the line; where bites occur is where the fish are.

Insulated Bottle. A nice hot cup of coffee, tea or chocolate on a cool fishing morning will pleasantly warm your "innards." An icy refill might serve to cool you down as the afternoon heats up.

Taku River, Juneau, Alaska

Personal Gear

Hiking/Fishing Shorts. Short pants are appropriate for fishing the Southern California shoreline, the flats along the Florida Keys, or other warm places. Quick-drying and cotton-soft Supplex has become the material of choice for shorts and for warmer-weather long- and short-sleeve shirts. However, since this material tends to trap perspiration, some garments are treated in a process known as Intera, which dramatically improves the clothing's wicking properties. Another dual-use option is the "Hiking/Camping Shorts" item discussed in the VEHICLE-ACCESSIBLE CAMPING activity.

Long Hiking/Fishing Pants. If hiking to the fishing site, consider purchasing a set of long-pants that are suitable for both. Our lean is to get a good, comfortable set of all-weather hiking pants described in the VEHICLE-ACCESSIBLE CAMPING activity. Another option is to wear quick-drying, *synthetic-pile pants* (clothing weight dependent on weather conditions), particularly comfortable-fitting sweatpants. In spite of our well-meaning advice, many (if not most) day-fishermen wear *plain ole' jeans*. Some manufacturers sell models, such as the cotton Wrangler Angler, with special pockets for such gear as pliers and knives and having Velcro flaps to secure the rear pockets.

For those days that you can't decide between long pants and shorts, you might try *"zip-off" pants*. With zippers that run around the trouser legs at mid-thigh, you simply unzip to convert long pant to shorts.

Underwear. Although many fishermen wear cotton, our preference remains with the polyester and polypropylene underwear described in the VEHICLE-ACCESSIBLE CAMPING activity.

Thermal Underwear. In cold weather conditions, it is not uncommon for shoreline fishermen to wear thermal underwear under clothing or in-water anglers to wear them under waders. The underwear weight depends on the level of exertion the activity requires, lighter for the higher effort levels and heavier as the activity becomes more inert. The best case for heavy- or expedition-weight longjohns rests with ice fishermen, where the conditions are guaranteed to be cold and the activity level minimal. The detailed characteristics of thermal underwear are discussed in the VEHICLE-ACCESSIBLE CAMPING activity.

Long-Sleeve Shirt. Shirts are for both for warmth and protection from the sun. For cold extremes, consider shirt/sweater or sweater/turtleneck combinations such as those discussed for "Long-Sleeve Shirt" and "Sweater/Turtleneck" items in the VEHICLE-ACCESSIBLE CAMPING activity. For sun protection, long-sleeve shirts, such as the Supplex types discussed, protect the full arms and are a traditional choice.

Choose shirts that are generously roomy, especially around the armpits. Go with shirts with collars that can be turned up to protect against wind or the sun's rays. Some anglers favor button-down collars which won't flap in the breeze, but can still be turned up when needed. Button-tabs on some models secure the sleeves when you roll them up. Look for styles with a myriad of pockets (even if you wear a vest, you'll never have too many). An added benefit is a model with an attached D-ring or two for attaching additional items.

Jacket. For cold, but not severe conditions, a comfortable and functional jacket will keep you comfortable. Err to the side of oversize around the sides, back and armpits to ensure freedom of casting and working the line. A comfortable jacket that is used for camping will work. Stepping up in class leads to the nylon and nylon-acrylic wind- and water-resistant jackets. Among the preferred styles are those with built-in sweatshirt linings and hoods. At the top of the line are models like the bomber-style jacket made of Airex flotation foam. Favored by fly-fishermen, but also used for other types of land fishing, are fleece pullovers made of non-absorbent, quick-drying, and breathable materials such as Polartec. (Refer to the VEHICLE-ACCESSIBLE CAMPING activity for more information about synthetic pile outerwear.)

Parka/Body Shell. A heavy shell layer is most critical in extreme cold/wind-chill environments such as when ice fishing. Because of its water-absorptive properties and unwieldy weight when wet, heavy shells are is restricted to land (versus in-water) use. A cocoon of a high-loft, quilted and hooded jumpsuit is standard apparel when the wind chill reaches the brutal stage. Some anglers let their snowmobile suits double in this capacity. For less severe conditions, anglers frequently opt for the less-fortified options discussed for the "Heavy Jacket/Parka" gear item discussed in the VEHICLE-ACCESSIBLE CAMPING activity.

Socks. Polypropylene and silk both wick moisture away from the skin, which makes either fabric an excellent choice as a liner sock. Outer socks of wool, acrylic or wool/acrylic are both functional and popular, as they provide warmth even when wet.

Another interesting option, particularly suited for activities in wet, or wet/cold conditions is a *waterproof, breathable over sock.* Considerably more expensive than the standard outdoor activity socks, these little dandies fit over your liner or outer sock and are of roughly equivalent height. They keep your feet dry and comfortable while stomping around the fishing site. When your boot interior is soaked, your feet are still dry, yet these over-socks will steadily wick the moisture out of the boot. See the VEHICLE-ACCESSIBLE CAMPING and HIKING sections for an in-depth discussion of socks.

Hiking/Fishing Boots. For fishing from a flat shoreline or boat, many get by with the comfort of a sturdy set of *athletic shoes*. (If the fishing is a part of an overarching boating activity, consult the relevant activity.) If access to a fishing site requires hiking in and plans are to fish from shore, the *hiking boots* described in the HIKING activity will generally suffice.

When plying rugged shorelines, a set of boots with waterproof bottoms and leather or rugged (say 100 denier) nylon are more appropriate. They are referred to by many as "*Bean boots*" after the style's innovator. A steel shank built into the boot makes them more durable. Molded heels and soft rubber or gum soles increase their comfort while still providing a good gripping surface. (They still do not offer the traction of lug-soled boots, however.) A desirable feature is the newer boots is breathable liners that wick moisture away from the feet. Some models come with insulating booties, which can be removed when insulation is not required.

An option for boot-clad fishermen, a particular favorite of those using stocking-foot waders, is to wear *overbooties* of neoprene or other synthetic materials. The bootie or oversock top folds gaiter-like over the boot-top to keep gravel and debris out of the boot.

When ice fishing, waterproof and insulated boots are essential. The Bean boots mentioned above are one option, although there are many hardier models with heavier interior insulation. They include the rugged, heavyweight styles designed for extreme sub-zero conditions mentioned in the "Apres-Ski Boots" item in the ALPINE SKIING/SNOWBOARDING activity. Some anglers routinely attach cleats to the soles of their boots to enhance safe maneuvering on the ice.

Grass Lake, Sierra Nevada Mtns., California Compliments of Jim Cradduck

Gloves/Mittens. In cold weather, choice of hand-warming gloves vary with the temperature and angler's preferences. Some prefer fingerless gloves, which reach to just below the knuckle level, because they allow greater digital dexterity. Others prefer full gloves or mittens as described in the VEHICLE-ACCESSIBLE CAMPING activity. If your rod handle is not made of highly-grippable material, seek out gloves or mittens with gripper dots or other surfaces on the palms. Under severe conditions, neoprene cold-weather gloves are a popular choice. They are far more water resistant than other classic materials and have extremely high heat-retentive properties. If necessary, thin polypropylene liners can be worn under these gloves.

Brimmed Hat/Pullover Hat. Hats serve to retain valuable body heat during cold weather, help prevent sunburn when the sun shines and protects against wayward flying fishhooks. For many anglers, they also serve as a storage spot for flies, bare hooks and other paraphernalia.

Choices include floppy brimmed hats, baseball caps, long-billed trucker's hats, western hats, "foreign legion" hats with a neck shade -- the list is long. There are also specialty models, such as a canvas number that is treated with closed-cell polyethylene in its crown. The hat remains afloat under most conditions. This leads to a digression: Our lean is to hats that provide all the features previously mentioned plus have a cinching cord that fits below the chin. This feature is very helpful on a windy day that may send your top-piece down a fast-running stream.

In severe weather, consider a warm, insulating *pull-over* cap of wool, polyester or pile to fit under your fishing hat. They generally cover the head and ears. A *balaclava* or wool stocking hat with limited facial exposure covers both head and neck.

Raingear. Much has been said about raingear in the VEHICLE-ACCESSIBLE CAMPING activity. An additional option that is more unique to fishing is the *wading jacket*. Most commonly used for fly-fishing, these jackets are waterproof (not just water resistant) and are equipped with large chest pockets. Some models feature a hood and drawstring waist to keep out the elements. The waterproof feature means that the jacket does not breathe -- a feature that is compatible with this generally light-exertion activity. Many jackets are light enough to be folded and carried in a fishing vest's pouch pocket.

Safety

Sunglasses and Lanyard. Sunglasses serve to protect your eyes from both the elements and errant fishing hooks. Desirable properties of sunglasses for a variety of activities are provided in the TEN ESSENTIALS section. A summary for fishing: Seek brown glasses to reduce glare on bright days, amber for improving vision on cloudy days or under dim light, and gray to enhance true colors. Best bet is to get "special purpose" glasses for high UV light reduction and highly-polarized lens for reducing reflected light off the water. Take a long look at frames with side shields, brow bars and nose shields if you plan to spend long periods near the water in bright sun.

Among the sunglasses specifically made for fishing are bifocals with magnifiers for close-up threading work on the lower half of each lens. An outgrowth is spring-hinge glasses that allow the separate magnifying lenses to pop up out of the field of vision when not in use. Whatever the glasses you choose, attach a strap or lanyard to them to prevent loss to "Davey Jones" when you are actively hiking, casting or bringing in a catch.

Whistle. Whatever your wearing apparel, take a whistle along to alert others should you need to signal for help. The whistle should be firmly attached to an outer garment (vest, shirt, jacket) such that it is on your clothing exterior and easily accessible.

Timepiece. In addition to all the safety and general use considerations discussed in the VEHICLE-ACCESSIBLE CAMPING activity, bring a water-resistant timepiece with an alarm or a separate alarm clock if you are fishing out of a campsite or boat. This device will wake you up in the early hours when the fish may be biting at their best.

Accessories

Sitting Pad/Portable Chair. Whatever your fishing locale, nothing beats having a comfortable place to sit during or after long angling periods. If practical for your trip, consider some of the options found under "Camp Chairs" for the VEHICLE-ACCESSIBLE CAMPING activity and under "Sitting Pad" in the BACKPACKING activity. Note that there are folding chairs on the market with built-in storage compartments -- a fisherman never has too much storage space!

Brochures, Articles, Books. Consider bringing a fishing guide, particularly if it provides hints about the local fishing area such as angling locations, best times of day to fish, successful baits and lures, etc.

Tool Kit

Tools. Bring a fingernail clipper or one that's specially designed for fishing line (many of the latter come equipped with a tiny needle for cleaning hook eyes). Carry it on a lanyard or elastic "zinger" around your neck. For super-strength line, you'll need a very sharp knife or other heavy-duty clipper. Wire-clipping pliers are very useful for sizing wire leaders and can also serve as a crimping tool. In the worst-case scenario, they can assist in the removal of imbedded fish hooks.

A hook file is handy for sharpening dull hooks. Carborundum files, specially designed for this purpose, are available at tackle shops and through catalogues. Other options are carborundum or steel fingernail files, auto ignition-point files and, for tiny hooks, the striking surface of a new matchbook cover.

Many knots are used for such purposes as tying leader to line. The nail knot is one sturdy option, for example; it is also an intricate knot to tie. There is a needle-like device which makes tying this knot (and others) a breeze. Many feel that super-strength line does not hold knots well and/or that the manufacturer's-recommended knots are difficult to construct. When using super-strength line, consider bringing along some super glue to secure the ends of your preferred knots.

To be sure that a leader needs a new tippet or that their ends are of compatible thickness, you might invest in a leader/tippet gauge that measures such diameters. It's small enough to be carried in a vest pocket or attached to outerwear by a lanyard or retractable "zinger."

Monofilament line, particularly the extra-heavy type used for leaders, comes coiled and has a "memory." One method of straightening out the line is with a leader straightener. A device composed of two pieces of leather, rubber or a synthetic fabric, through which the leader is rubbed, will decoil the monofiliment.

If you are going to eat your fish on site, bring a sharp cutting knife. For species that must be scaled, carry a serrated scaling knife. If the fish is to be sliced into fillets, you will need a very sharp, thin knife for that purpose.

Finally, bring any specialty tools needed for adjustment and repair of tackle. If you are hauling your gear to the site on foot, limit tools to those which are most likely to be used and which are readily packable.

Repair Gear. If you are the cautious type, bring along wader patch gear. Typically, this is a bicycle-type patch kit for rubber, industrial self-adhesive tape for nylon and a cement patch kit for neoprene. Also bring the appropriate patch kit if you are using a float tube or kickboat.

Replacement Gear. In the course of any angler's day, gear such as leaders, lures and line can be damaged or lost. Bring along the spares or alternates that you feel will be most appropriate. These are the items most likely to be compromised and that might have the greatest negative impact on your angling pleasure if not available.

Secondary Activities

Examples of the prevalent activities that can be linked to LAND FISHING are CAMPING (and picnicking), HIKING, BICYCLE TOURING, MOUNTAIN BIKING and WATERSPORTS. To determine unique gear needs associated with a linked activity, refer to the relevant activity section.

LAND FISHING
(Daytime)

Select items based on trip plans, fishing style and worst-case weather conditions.

ITEM	DATE				
Fishing Gear					
Auto Gear Rack/Locks					
Fishing Rod(s)/Rod Case(s)					
Rod Carrier					
Reel(s)/Reel Bag(s)					
Tackle Box Items					
Tackle Box					
Special Storage Containers					
Creel/Catch Storage Container					
Bait/Bait Container					
Landing Net/De-hook./Stringers					
Gaff					
Waders/Wader Pack					
Fishing Gear Carrier/Vest					
Wading Staff					
Support Belt					
Fish Handling Gloves					
Float Tube/Kickboat					
Personal Flotation Device					
Ice Auger/Ice Chisel@					
Ice Removal Tool@					
Tip-Up@					
Rod Holder@					
Portable Ice Shelter@					
Electronic Bottom-finder					
Water Bottles/Water Jug					
Collapsible Water Bag					
Insulated Bottle*					
Fishing License/Permits					
Personal Gear					
Hiking/Fishing Shorts					
Long Hiking/Fishing Pants					
Underwear					
Thermal Underwear*					
Long-Sleeve Shirt					
Jacket					
Parka/Body Shell*					
Turtleneck Dickey/Neck Scarf*					
Windbreaker					
Socks					
Hiking/Fishing Boots					
Gloves/Mittens*					
Brimmed Hat/Pullover Hat*					
Head Netting					
Raingear					

LAND FISHING
(Daytime)

ITEM	DATE				
*Gaiters**					
Bandanna/Sweat Band					
Swim Suit					
Toilet Paper & *Towelettes*					
Toilet Trowel					
Safety					
First Aid Kit (see FIRST AID)					
Water Filter/Tablets					
Sunglasses & Lanyard					
Sunscreen					
Insect Repellent					
Lip Balm					
Whistle/*Signal Mirror*					
Waterproof Matches & Lighter					
Fire Starter/Heat Tabs					
Emergency Blanket					
Map(s)					
Compass					
Altimeter/GPS Receiver					
Timepiece					
Thermometer					
Pocket Knife					
Flashlight#					
Extra Batteries & Bulb#					
Reading Glasses & Repair Kit					
Nylon Cord					
Phone Change					
Communication Device					
Pen & Notepad					
Accessories					
Camera; Extra Film & Battery					
Camera Bag, Lens Cleaning Kit					
Brochures, Articles, Books					
Monocular/Small Binoculars					
Sitting Pad/Portable Chair					
Litter Bag					

LAND FISHING
(Daytime)

ITEM	DATE				
Reusable Plastic Food Bags					
Spare Stuff Sacks					
Daypack/Rucksack/Fanny Pk.					
Gear Bag					
Portable Ice Chest					
Ice & "Blue Ice"					
Auto Tire Chains & Anti-freeze					
Auto Tool Kit					
Spare Keys/Credit Card/$					
Tool Kit					
Tools:					
Wire Clippers/Pliers					
Hook File					
Knot Tying/Securing Gear					
Leader/Tippet Gauge					
Leader Straightener					
Filleting Knife					
Tackle Adjustment/Repair Tools					
Repair Gear:					
Wader Patch Kit					
Float Tube/Kickboat Patch Kit					
Replacement Gear:					
Spare Leaders					
Spare Lures					
Spare Line					
Snacks (see MEALS section)					
High Energy Bars					
Trail Mix/Granola					
Fresh Fruit/Dried Fruit					
Beef Jerky					
Nuts					
Electrolyte (for water bottle)					

Italicized items-optional   *items for cold weather/snow   #contingency nighttime travel   @ice fishing

SEA FISHING (Daytime/Overnight)

See INDEX for checklist items not discussed below.

The SEA FISHING activity is treated as either a daytime or multi-day adventure. SEA FISHING assumes off-shore or blue-water fishing where your base of operations is a sail or powerboat and that you are going after bigger fish than those in the LAND FISHING activity. It further assumes you are on a chartered or friend's boat and, therefore, are not concerned with the needs of outfitting the boat. Considerations for outfitting a boat and further detail on more-robust personal gear than discussed below are covered in the SAILING and POWERBOATING activities.

Find out ahead of time what equipment your hosts will provide and seek recommendations on what you should bring. This includes tackle, clothing, bedding, safety items, tools, etc. Tackle checklists provided by charters are a good starting point, but many skippers will admit that their lists are an overkill. The reason is that no operator wants to be confronted by a passenger who, when faced with an unusual fishing situation, demands: "Why didn't you tell me?" Nearly all charter boats supply trolling gear, so you probably don't need to bring the heavier tackle. Some have on-board tackle which can be rented (e.g., rods and reels) and many more have a limited supply of smaller, "what's hot" items (e.g., lures, hooks, sinkers, line, leaders).

In the discussion below, no attempt is made to optimize the tackle needed to catch the large variety of fish in the multitude of geographical regions under the highly-varied local site conditions. Consult the **REFERENCES** section in the back of this book and the numerous publications that treat the specific fishing issues that are nearest and dearest to your heart.

Safety Considerations: 1) review the **GENERAL CONSIDERATIONS** and TEN ESSENTIALS sections; 2) learn to use and wear a PFD whenever recommended by your host or if you have the slightest concerns; 3) ensure you understand your boat's emergency procedures and your personal responsibilities; 4) develop swimming skills commensurate with the level of activity you are planning; 5) develop a safe casting technique; 6) learn basic first aid; 7) bring cold- and wet-weather contingency gear if there is any doubt about its availability; and 8) wear a hat, not only for protection from sun or cold, but also to protect yourself against wayward casters.

In the checklist, items that are considered optional (niceties or special purpose) are *italicized*. Items noted with an asterisk(*) are for inclement weather.

Fishing Gear

The amount of gear you bring will depend on trip duration, type and variety of fishing planned, and amount of on-board space available. Overnighters on a friend's smallcraft will lead you to one end of the spectrum, while ten-day, long-range charter tours will point you to the other. The former option will most likely lead you to make a series of educated guesses in order to "skinny down" to what appears to be the optimal gear. The latter option may see you making several trips up the gangway in order to get all your "cover-all-bases" gear on board.

Much of the terminology has been covered in the LAND FISHING activity. Also refer to that section for additional detail on gear that is common to both land-based and sea-based fishing.

Fishing Rod(s)/Reel(s). Subtlety of presentation is not a factor when casting or trolling from a boat at sea. As a result, fiberglass and composite rods are found as frequently as those made of graphite. Rods are designated according to their strength, specifically the amount of force needed to bend a rod 90 degrees. Several *classifications* have been assigned by the International Game Fish Association (IGFA) for trolling rods. The range spans from "ultralight" (6-, 12-, and 20-pound), "medium" (50-pound) to "ultra-heavy" (130-pound) and "without limit" (130 to 180-pound).

For world record-keeping purposes, the IFGA sets specifications on allowed number of sections (two, either separable), minimum rod length (40 inches), number of guides (five plus the tip-top) and other parameters. Rods used for fishing from anchored boats ("bottom fishing") usually measure 10 feet or less. The IFGA classifies these rods into 12-, 20-, and 30-pound categories.

The *monster boat rods* used for bluewater fishing are designated according to their line class. or the test strength of line that is designed to be used on them. Big-game rods, such as those used for tuna, range in length from 5-1/2 feet to 6 feet and take line between 50 and 130 pounds. These larger or big-game saltwater rods have roller (also called pulley) guides, as opposed to the standard, simple ring guides. This feature is used to compensate for the large amount of friction generated when playing a large, fighting species.

Rods attached to downrigger trolling tackle measure about eight feet and take 8-20 pound line. The downrigger is either a manual or electric battery-operated device, attached to the boat, that maintains the bait at a given depth. Most often the fishing rod sits in a rod holder built into the downrigger body. The fishing rod's line is snapped to a weight at the end of the downrigger's cable. When a fish strikes, the line is released from the weight, and the downrigger's cable is rewound to remove it from any position of interference with the rod line.

Homer, Alaska Compliments of Bob Hardy

Several types of lighter *casting tackle* are seen in saltwater fishing from boats. Baitcasting rods with star-drag or lever-drag reel systems are a popular option. Spinning rods between 6-10 feet that can cast lures between 3/4 ounce to 2 ounces are common. For playing and landing such substantial deep-sea quarry as sailfish, tarpon and tuna, there are 12-weight- through 15-weight-classification flyrods. These rods are most often equipped with high-multiplier reels. For most bluewater species the reels used hold 300-400 feet or more of line (and, if a fly reel, line plus backing).

On long-range trips, it is common to take *multiple angling outfits*. The most common mode is to bring rod/reel combinations that span the game weight class that you expect to encounter. For several-day trips in the Baja California area, anglers may take 20-, 30-, 40-, and 50-pound outfits and rely on the boats trolling gear for larger fish. In the case of the classic "seven- to ten-dayers," they may add 60-pound and 80-pound setups or larger.

Bungee Cord. Elastic cord may come in handy for securing rods and tackle boxes during rough weather. Cord with the classic end hooks are very versatile and will secure to about anything.

Tackle Box Items. Stored inside your tackle box(es) may be items such as spare spools and reels, fishing line, leaders, floats, sinkers, spinners, swivels, snaps, hooks, lures, flies and angler's tools -- to name a few. Other than the brief discussions of items noted on the checklist, we have not attempted to treat the myriad of tackle-box goodies. For discussion of tackle-box gear, gear tradeoffs and optimal equipment selection to suit your trip needs, consult the **REFERENCE** section of this book, your local tackle shop, and/or the myriad of fishing publications on the market.

Tackle Box. For short tours on boats with limited space, you may want to limit yourself to a small tackle box or tote bag, much like the land fisherman who has to lug his or her gear to the fishing site. Most long-range boats have sufficient room to allow anglers to bring on a suitcase-size tackle box and more.

Rod Belt/Rod Harness. For short bluewater tours, or if you lift anchor near waters where some larger fish are common, consider bringing a small or medium-size rod belt and possibly a harness. If you are on a week to ten-day, long-range tour or near waters where the really big game fish abound, bring a substantial pad and harness.

Prince of Wales Island, Alaska Compliments of Stevie Cradduck

One recommendation for the "big guys" is a quality aluminum or plastic rod belt as opposed to a leather model; they won't flex when using heavy gear on big fish. Small pads are preferable for wahoo and smaller tuna since the need to keep up with a fish along the rail means you want a pad that is situated close to your waist. Conversely, with 60- and 80-pound gear, you need a lower pad so you can reach higher on the rod and apply more pressure with less effort. Most seasoned veterans feel the pad should be gimbaled, and many support a gimbaled outfit for all rods from 30 pounds and up. The gimbaling keeps the rod from twisting while playing the fish. As for harnesses, kidney-belt models are adequate, but bucket-style or sit-down harnesses are preferred.

Hand Tape. Not infrequently, sea anglers get line cuts. Wearing gloves can reduce the dexterity needed to cast or to play a fish. A sports tape such as Flexx-Wrap might be the useful intermediate if line handling is a problem.

Catch Storage Container. Provided the boat does not have a refrigerated storage area, one option (for day trips) is to bring along an insulated, portable, ice-filled chest. Another is to bring a canvas or linen "Arctic cooler" that retains moisture and coolness after being immersed in the ocean. Long-range boats typically have a refrigerated hold(s). A few outfitters are prepared to clean and flash-freeze your catch on-board.

Weight Scale. A quality handscale serves as a foolproof means for setting line drag. Its secondary use might be to settle the classic angler arguments about fish weight.

Fish Cleaning Gear. Much of the same gear discussed in the LAND FISHING activity is needed for cleaning sea species. You may want to size up if your catch is anticipated to be larger than the classic freshwater varieties.

Personal Gear

The wearing apparel discussed assumes that you are a passenger, rather than an active crew member. As noted in the SAILING and POWERBOATING activities, there are specific properties of crewing gear that account for the dangers of handling line and deck gear or operating machinery.

Bring clothes that are loose and comfortable, allowing total freedom of casting. In hot, dry-weather conditions (aside from the spray you might get in your face), wearing clothes that don't retain your body heat when wet is one of those circumstances that justifies breaking the "no-cotton rule." Now the water-retentive and resulting cooling properties of cotton work to your benefit. A light breeze blowing on your wet cotton shirt on a hot day provides a great attitude adjustment.

For any other conditions, we remain advocates of the underwear, shirt and pants materials (polypropylene, polyester pile, wool, wool blends, etc.) discussed in such waterborne activities as CANOEING, SAILING and POWERBOATING. They will keep you comfortable as an outer layer in warm to cool weather and as an insulating layer under a shell in cold to severe weather.

In the discussion below, we offer *examples of outfits* that might serve your purpose in order from warm weather to successively cooler and wetter conditions.

Warm weather: shorts and underwear or swim suit, tee-shirt, deck shoes or rubber-soled, non-skid sandals, sun hat. If the gear gets wet, who cares?

Cool Weather: long pants and underwear, long-sleeve shirt, jacket, windbreaker (if needed), deck shoes or sandals with socks, fishing gloves, sun hat. In wet conditions, substitute foul-weather boots, remove the windbreaker, and add a foul-weather suit.

Cold weather: longjohns, long pants, long-sleeved shirt and warm sweater, windbreaker (if needed), foul-weather boots and insulating socks, fishing gloves/mittens, pullover hat under sun hat. In wet weather, substitute foul-weather boots, remove the windbreaker, and add a foul-weather suit.

Jacket/Parka. Refer to the "Heavy Jacket/Parka" gear item in the VEHICLE-ACCESSIBLE CAMPING activity for a discussion of these items. A qualifier: The down parkas described lose their insulating properties when wet and are useless when soaked. If brought aboard, they are meant to be worn under a well-protected waterproof shell or for land use when you set ashore.

Foul-Weather Suit. Between this gear and underlayering, the purpose of foul-weather gear is to keep you warm and dry. Find out what your charter-boat crew or boat owner wears and you probably have an excellent input as to your particular trip needs. There are many variations of foul-weather gear brought on board. The selection depends on the weather (temperature, sea state) in which you expect to fish, the level of exertion expected (fighting big fish can bring out a lot of perspiration), the degree of exposure of your fishing "perch" (smaller boats, with less freeboard, will be wetter), and the trip duration (more variations in weather can be expected on longer tours) -- among other considerations.

Many viable options are discussed in detail under "Raingear" in the VEHICLE ACCESSIBLE CAMPING activity. However, since ponchos and cagoules can get caught up in the wind, the non-breathable and breathable two-piece rain suits discussed there are probably better choices. The description of a well-constructed rainsuit in that activity has many applications to sea fishing. One difference: Rain will fall from overhead or a limited vertical angles, while waves and sea spray can come at you from a wide variety of angles. Consider this thought when you make any of the choices from this group.

Prince of Wales Island, Alaska Compliments of Stevie Cradduck

The venerable two-piece, rubberized-fabric rain suit or "slicker." is another option. It has a high-waisted, generally suspender-held set of pants with cinches at the ankles. It is accompanied by a long-length top with cinch bands at the hood, neck, wrist, and waist. Though heavier than the other options, this distinctly sea-going gear has certainly proved its worth over the years. If you canoe or kayak and own a paddling outfit, consider bringing that "made-for-the sea" option if conditions warrant. (See the KAYAKING activity under "Drysuit.")

Deck Shoes. Skid-resistant *deck shoes*, those rubber-bottomed footwear with deep wavy slits in the sole, are your best bet. (See the SAILING activity.) Rubber-soled land shoes without heels, but with solid tread are next best. As a courtesy when boarding, clear out rocks, pebbles or any other substance from your shoes that might damage decks.

Foul Weather Boots. If slogging around in you wet deck shoes doesn't cut it, try foul-weather boots. These can be waterproofed high-tops, preferably with a sewn-in tongue below the shoe ties/straps. Canoeists and land fishermen sometimes let their "Bean Boots" double for this use. Rubber rain boots, under waterproof rainsuit bottoms, are adequate under most conditions. Whatever you choose, ensure that they have low-skid or non-skid rubber soles.

Gloves/Mittens. In cold weather, choice of hand-warming gloves vary with the temperature and angler's preferences. Some prefer fingerless gloves, which reach to just below the knuckle level, because they allow greater digital dexterity. Others prefer full gloves or mittens as described in the VEHICLE-ACCESSIBLE CAMPING activity. If your rod handle is not made of highly-grippable material, purchase gloves or mittens with gripper dots or other surfaces on the palms.

<u>Underway Living Gear</u>

The short item list presented assumes that your host provides you with sheltered cabin space or that the weather is amenable to sleeping on-deck. If you will be bedding down in partially-exposed or open space under any other conditions, add to this list in accordance with the worst weather that you might expect.

Sleeping Bag and Blankets. Candidate sleeping bags for sea trips are included in the options described in the VEHICLE-ACCESSIBLE CAMPING activity. For cabin use, a lighter-weight bag in conjunction with blankets allows convenient temperature control at the least price. This combination also works for sleeping in partially-exposed spaces, provided you are protected from wind and sea spray.

Sleeping Pad. Unless your boat is equipped with padded bunks, it is nearly certain that you will be sleeping on an uncomfortable surface. Many options for sleeping pads have been discussed in the VEHICLE-ACCESSIBLE CAMPING activity. If needed, consider selection of the options that provide a maximal amount of padding and good enough insulation to keep you snugly. For this activity, there is less of a premium on weight and bulk relative to those that require carrying all gear on your back.

Prince of Wales Island, Alaska Compliments of Stevie Cradduck

Hammock. Depending on the boat layout, use of this comfortable option depends on the nature and amount of rigging and other usable appendages. (See the VEHICLE-ACCESSIBLE CAMPING activity for more detail on hammock characteristics.)

Mosquito Netting. This item is not so much for the open sea, but for those periods when near coastal shores or docked. Bring a small-mesh net of sufficient area to hang over your bunk and run down its sides.

Safety

Timepiece. Depending on your host, you may or may not have the luxury of a wake-up call. So that you don't miss that hot, pre-dawn bite, bring a timepiece with an alarm. If your timepiece is not so equipped, add a good old-fashioned alarm clock.

Accessories

Sitting Pad/Deck Chair. A long period of standing at the rail can be very tiring to the back. Periodic sit-down breaks on a comfortable pad may help alleviate the strain. If there is a reasonable chance of some periods of calm seas, consider bringing a light fold-up chair to ease your aching bones.

Tool Kit

Tools. Most of the tools needed are included within the LAND FISHING activity discussion. A qualifier: The heavier-duty tackle commonly associated with sea fishing may require more-robust tools. An example: Monofiliment (or fluorocarbon, for a few) leader material is a necessity for trolling lures and bait leaders for marlin or larger tuna. Many veterans use a monofilament swagging tool (wire-crimping pliers are different) for securing the leader with sleeves, in contrast to relying on knots. Particularly for long-range trips, bring along any specialty tools needed for adjustment or repair of your tackle.

Repair Gear. Bring a sewing kit for mending your personal wear. The kit might include safety pins, thread, sewing needles, yarn, string, buttons and patch material. Checking ahead about your host's repair inventory may alter the amount of gear that you bring aboard. If a critical piece of repair gear will not be available on board, strongly consider bringing it.

Replacement Gear. In the course of any angler's trip, tackle can be damaged or lost. Bring along the spares or alternates that you feel will be most appropriate or confirm that your host has these items on board. These are the gear items most likely to be compromised and that might have greatest negative impact on your angling pleasure if not available.

Secondary Activities

Examples of the prevalent activities that can be linked to SEA FISHING are CAMPING (and picnicking), HIKING, WATERSPORTS and LAND FISHING. To determine unique gear needs associated with a linked activity, refer to the relevant activity section.

SEA FISHING
(Daytime/Overnight)

Select items based on trip plans, fishing style, on-board gear available & worst-case weather conditions.

ITEM	DATE				
Fishing Gear					
Auto Gear Rack/Locks					
Fishing Rod(s)/Rod Cases(s)					
Rod Carrier					
Bungee Cord					
Reel(s)/Reel Bag(s)					
Tackle Box Items					
Tackle Box					
Special Storage Containers					
Rod Belt					
Rod Harness					
Hand Tape					
Catch Storage Container					
Bait/Bait Container					
Landing Net					
Gaff					
Fishing Vest					
Weight Scale					
Fish Handling Gloves					
Fish Cleaning Gear					
Water Bottles/ *Water Jug*					
Insulated Bottle					
Fishing License/Permits					
Passport					
Personal Gear					
Shorts					
Long Pants					
Underwear					
Thermal Underwear*					
Long-sleeve Shirt					
Jacket					
Parka*					
Windbreaker					
Foul-Weather Suit*					
Socks					
Deck Shoes/Foul-Wthr. Boots*					
Gloves/Mittens*					
Brimmed Hat *& Pullover Hat**					
Bandanna/Sweat Band					
Swim Suit					

SEA FISHING
(Daytime/Overnight)

ITEM	DATE				
Underway Living Gear					
Sleeping Bag *& Blanket*					
Sleeping Pad					
Pillow					
Hammock					
Mosquito Netting					
Hygiene					
Towel & Wash Cloth					
Biodegradable Soap					
Biodegradable Shampoo					
Personal Toiletries/Ditty Bag					
Toilet Paper					
Laundry Bag					
Safety					
First Aid Kit (see FIRST AID)					
Water Filter/Tablets					
Sunglasses & Lanyard					
Sunscreen					
Insect Repellent					
Lip Balm					
Personal Flotation Device					
Whistle/*Signal Mirror*					
Waterproof Matches & Lighter					
*Fire Starter/Heat Tabs**					
*Emergency Blanket**					
Compass					
Timepiece					
Thermometer					
Pocket Knife					
Flashlight#					
Extra Batteries & Bulb#					
Reading Glasses & Repair Kit					
Phone Change					
Pen & Notepad					

SEA FISHING
(Daytime/Overnight)

ITEM	DATE				
Accessories					
Camera; Extra Film & Battery					
Camera Bag, Lens Cleaning kit					
Brochures, Articles, Books					
Binoculars					
Sitting Pad/Deck Chair					
Reusable Plastic Food Bags					
Litter Bag					
Daypack/Rucksack (storage)					
Fanny Pack					
Indoor Games					
Portable Ice Chest(s)					
Ice & "Blue Ice"					
Auto Tool Kit					
Spare Keys/Credit Card/$					
Tool Kit					
Tools:					
Wire Clippers/Pliers					
Hook File					
Knot Tying/Securing Gear					
Leader/Tippet Gauge					
Leader Straightener					
Filleting Knife					
Tackle Adjustment/Repair Tools					
Monofilament Swagging Tool					
Repair Gear:					
Sewing Kit					
Replacement Gear:					
Spare Leaders					
Spare Lures					
Spare Line					
Snacks (see MEALS section)					
High Energy Bars					
Trail Mix/Granola					
Fresh Fruit/Dried Fruit					
Beef Jerky					
Sandwiches					
Chips & Dips					
Electrolyte (for water bottle)					

Italicized items-optional   *items for inclement weather   # contingency nighttime gear

FIRST AID

General Discussion

About the Checklists. The first-aid kit checklist is set up uniquely relative to those in other sections. Each column in the checklist is associated with one (or more, if gear needs are identical) activity and the gear items are listed in the rows. In this section, the list is used according to the activity planned and the kit is assembled as an integral unit. Once this self-contained kit is assembled and stored in the applicable automobile, backpack, pannier, boat, or other applicable location, the "First Aid Kit" item in the appropriate activity checklist is marked off.

An "x" in a given intersection of the checklist indicates our estimate that the gear is essential and an "o" that the gear may be useful for the activity listed in the column heading. A blank space at a given intersection says that we do not consider the gear necessary or, in some cases, relevant. These suggestions are based on a generic "Daytime" trip where it is assumed that professional medical aid is an hour or less away and an "Overnight" (one-week) tour where medical help will not be immediately accessible. This list is intended as a general guide. It should be reviewed and tailored to your particular trip needs.

In the column headings, abbreviations are used to represent individual activities. The following abbreviations are used: VAC - VEHICLE-ACCESSIBLE CAMPING; Hkg - HIKING; Bkpk - BACKPACKING; GW/d - GLACIER/WINTER CLIMBING (Daytime); GW/e - GLACIER/WINTER CLIMBING (Expedition); RkCl - ROCK CLIMBING; BkT/d - BICYCLE TOURING (Daytime/Nighttime); BkT/o - BICYCLE TOURING (Overnight); MtBk/d - MOUNTAIN BIKING (Daytime); MtBk/o - MOUNTAIN BIKING (Overnight); ASkSn - ALPINE SKIING/SNOWBOARDING; NSS/d - NORDIC SKIING/SNOWSHOEING (Daytime); NSS/o - NORDIC SKIING/SNOWSHOEING (Overnight); Snomo - SNOWMOBILING; CKR/d - CANOEING, KAYAKING, self-guided RAFTING (Daytime); CKR/o - CANOEING, KAYAKING, self-guided RAFTING (Overnight); SlPB - SAILING, POWERBOATING (Daytime /Overnight); ScSn - WATER SPORTS (Skin, Scuba Diving); WBWJ - WATER SPORTS (Watersking, Boardsurfing, Windsurfing, Jet Skiing); IFish - Inland Fishing; SFish - Sea Fishing (Daytime/Overnight).

About the First Aid Kit, In General. If you are traveling with an outfitter, he will normally supply first aid equipment. If not, you can purchase your kit outright, buy and modify a commercial kit or build your kit from the ground-floor. Purchased kits are highly compact, with packaging optimized to fit the maximum number of items in a given space. There are many excellent general-use and specialized kits on the market. You can tailor those kits by removing unneeded items and substituting your own, with some compromise in space-optimization. Many prefer to buy individual kit items and the kit container itself. In this fashion, you can optimize the kit and, in many instances, reduce its cost.

The kit items should be kept clean, dry, and in good condition at all times and preferably kept together as a group. A compact and sturdy waterproof and rustproof container is necessary for waterborne activities and desirable for others. Where this type of container is impractical to carry, consider placing the kit into single or double-wrapped, large-size Zip-Lock bags. In addition, store the kit contents themselves in waterproof wrappings or containers. Before each trip, check the first aid kit to make sure all items used on the previous trip have been replaced, and that all medications are fresh and/or within their expiration dates.

For activities such as VEHICLE-ACCESSIBLE CAMPING, SAILING, POWERBOATING and most WATERSPORTS, the group might rely on a central kit. This is inherently the case for activities such as CANOEING and RAFTING, where participants share the same craft. This may also be true for light general outdoor activities where all participating individuals are held to maintain a tight group. For more aggressive activities, each member should have a basic first-aid kit, with some individuals selected to carry agreed-on "group" items. High-end activities such as GLACIER/

WINTER CLIMBING typically call for individual team members to carry fully-stocked kits for the event of unplanned separation.

For all activities, each participant should carry any medication needed for individual medical problems. Parties going on long trips or to regions remote from medical aid may wish to extend the kit's contents. The majority of these additions require a doctor's prescription and special instruction concerning their use and potentially hazardous side effects.

To keep your carry-weight down, put careful consideration into you medical needs and leave unnecessary items behind. (Keep in mind that this process does require a conservative outlook in terms of allowing for contingencies.). Repackaging gear, particularly medications, will also allow you to reduce weight. The key is to estimate what you need, then repackage these items into baggies, small tubes and small plastic bottles, as applicable. (The tubes have a threaded section near "mid-waist" that allows you to pack pastes and ointments with ease. Once packed, you close it off by screwing the two sections together. To use, you simply remove the cap and squeeze, as with any other standard tube applicator.)

Keep medications separated and label all repackaged items. One popular method of storage is to put small baggies of individual items inside a larger plastic enclosure. For simple over-the-counter items like aspirin, you can use baggies that have a built-in writing strip and simply scribble down the bag contents. For more complex medications, include a small note within each individual baggie, noting medication type, expiration date, dosage and key warning information. (A tried and true method is to type out this information on a large sheet of paper, then cut the paper into relevant parts or "labels." Next, place transparent tape over each label and store the label in its individual baggie.)

Discussion of Kit Contents. Following the discussion of each item in the text below, the suggested quantity and type of item to be included for the generic one-week trip mentioned earlier, is noted in parentheses. This is for a non-centralized activity, where each member carries a full medical kit. For centralized activities, some items may be shared by the group. Once again, these suggestions should be tempered to suit the characteristics of your specific trip in terms of trip type, duration and potential dangers, as well as the nature of your individual constitution.

First Aid Manual

Outdoorsmen should know when and how to safely use every piece of equipment in their first aid kits. This is best accomplished by studying a good first aid manual and practicing the use of equipment. Bring along a condensed, lightweight version of the manual if you are weight-limited. For waterborne activities, the preferred manual is printed on some sort of waterproof paper. Examples of full and condensed general first-aid books are provided as the first two entries in the Reference list. Note that there are also many excellent books that are focused on the first aid needs of specific activities. The latter three entries are provided as examples.

Equipment

Cotton Swabs. Swabs are one of the best initial cleansing elements and antiseptic applicants for small cuts and abrasions, particularly when the injury is near sensitive areas such as the eyes. (repackaged set of twelve)

Scissors. A good-quality pocket knife with sharp-bladed scissors will get you through tape-cutting and gauze-cutting chores. If not available, look for a small, lightweight set of foldable scissors. A qualifier: If your first-aid requires cutting items that are snug to the body (e.g., tape, wetsuit), a blunt-tipped set of scissors is preferred. On remote expeditions, consider a set of EMT shears for cutting through metal, leather or heavy clothing. (one, three-inch foldable)

Razor Blade. The primary purpose is to shave hairy spots before taping. Though a cheap plastic razor will work for this application, a razor blade is more versatile for other (unplanned) uses. (one, single-edge)

Safety Pins. These gizmos may be useful for holding bandages in place or "jury-rigging" complex slings. They also may double to temporarily mend torn clothing or replace missing buttons or other closures. (three, different sizes)

Needles. These are hard point needles (e.g., sewing) to remove small imbedded objects such as splinters and to break blisters. If you have poor eyesight, add a small plastic magnifying glass. (two, small and medium sizes)

Tweezers. This multi-purpose tool serves to assist in removal of slivers or other foreign objects from the skin. It is a must for gently nudging imbedded ticks out of your skin. (one, home-use size)

Oral Thermometer. Nominally for checking the condition of ill compatriots on outdoor trips, this may become a life-saving device in selecting treatment for potential victims of hypothermia or heat exhaustion/heat stroke. Note that there is also a plastic-strip thermometer that is placed directly on the patient's forehead -- the patient's temperature range is registered by color. It cannot be read as accurately, but does have the advantages of being lighter and less prone to breakage. (one, enclosed in antiseptic container, measuring from 90 degrees to 106 degrees Fahrenheit)

Snake Bite Kit. Unless you know how to use it, particularly how to make the proper incisions near the fang marks, this can be more dangerous than helpful. No kit will remove even half of the injected venom, thus some outdoorsmen totally subscribe to use of tourniquet, immobilizing the patient, and getting professional help. (one, with usage instructions)

Pen Light. Evaluation of optical response for head or spinal injuries requires a focused, limited area light source. (one, pen-sized)

Tourniquet. Used to slow blood loss from a limb wound or to slow blood flow in the area above (that is, toward the heart) a snakebite, a separate device can be carried or it can be jury-rigged from available equipment. (jury-rig: one rolled-up strip of cloth of sufficient size to fit around the circumference of the limb, together with a tighten-down lever such as a 4- to 5-inch length, 1/4-inch or larger diameter tree branch)

Splints. We've known folks that carry newspaper, just for the purpose of creating makeshift splints. Other free spirits have expressed that, if an accident occurred, they would be at a location that had the natural goods that could be fashioned into splints. Forget that noise! The older standard is a wire mesh splint, which could be cut and shaped to fit the injury. Newer on the market are lightweight, inflatable vinyl air splints. (one wire mesh; or three vinyl, various sizes for different limbs)

Latex Gloves. This disposable item serves to minimize infection of the wound by the medical attendant as well as provide protection of the attendant against disease. (two pairs)

Resealable Plastic Bags. These bags can serve as an ice pack, can be used for irrigating wounds or, in the extreme for amputation care. (two, pint and quart sizes)

Bio-Hazard Waste Bag. To prevent the spread of infection, used throw-away instruments, bandages, dressings and other items used to treat wounds should be stored in a sealed waste bag. (one, quart-size)

Eye Dressing Kit. A representative kit might include special eyedrops for eye injuries, eye patch and eye ointments to prevent infection.

Dental Repair Kit. To handle dental emergencies on long, remote land trips or extended sea tours, buy or build a self-contained dental aid kit. In a good commercial kit, its contents include supplies, tools and instructions to take care of toothaches, broken crowns or bridges, fillings that have fallen out and irritating braces. Among the kit components are temporary filing material, temporary cement, denture repair liquid and thinner, toothache drops, tweezers and gauze.

Bandage and Dressing Materials

Band-Aids. These classic aids are for small punctures and cuts. (12, one inch x three inch)

Gauze Pads. These pads or flats are applied directly over the wound after it has been cleansed and anointed. They protect the wound from outside elements, while allowing the wounded area to breathe. (six, various sizes out to four inches x four inches)

Gauze Roller Bandage. Also called roller gauze, this wrapping is used to hold gauze flats and other dressings in place. (one roll, two inches x five yards)

Adhesive Compress. Where it is difficult to fashion a nominal bandage which is held in place by tape, a compress which has an adhesive surface is frequently used. (one box, one, two and four-inch sizes)

Battle Dressing. For large, bleeding wounds, a heavy, highly-absorbent dressing is needed. This may be a standard medical dressing, although some substitute a sanitary napkin. (one, four inches x two inches)

Triangular Bandages. Key use of this bandage is for supporting an injured arm and protecting dressings from contamination. They can also be used to form cravat bandages for holding splints in place. (one, 40 inch square)

Ace Bandage. This classic wrap is particularly helpful in supporting trick or sprained joints, particularly ankles, knees and wrists. Optimum sizes are two-inch width for hand and wrist, three-inch width for ankle, elbow and arm, four-inch width for knee, thigh or leg. If you have a precondition, bring the bandage that supports your needs in addition to a general first aid bandage. The classic bandage is secured using metal butterfly closures, although Velcro closures are more convenient. (one, three inches x 15 feet)

Moleskin. This product is used to cover "hot spots" on the feet to prevent blisters. Where blisters have already formed, a center portion of the moleskin/molefoam patch can be cut out and the patch centered over the blister. This keeps the pressure off of the blister. There are also special-purpose products available at drug stores for handling pre-existing problem sources such as callouses and bunions. (1/2 package moleskin)

Butterfly Closures. These are effectively butterfly Band-Aids for closing lacerations prior to bandaging the wound. (six, various sizes)

Adhesive Tape. Uses vary from holding dressings in place to securing the end of roller bandages. Though non-waterproof tape is most frequently used, the waterproof variety may be a better choice for activities around water. In a pinch, this tape can also be used to wrap sprained joints. (two rolls, 1/2-inch and one inch x 15-feet)

Sports Tape. This narrow adhesive tape is used on hands to prevent blisters, rope burns and cuts. It is particularly useful for paddling and rock-climbing activities and any activity that requires significant rope or line handling. (one roll such as Flexx-Wrap, 1/2-inch x 20 feet,)

Ointments/Topicals

Soap/Cleaning Cloth. Hot-water soaping is still one of the best methods for the initial cleaning of flesh wounds, particularly mild, wide-area scrapes. A popular alternative is Tincture of Zepherin. (one bar of anti-bacterial soap or one ounce of Tincture of Zepherin in a plastic bottle, clean 8-inch x 8-inch cloth in sealed package)

Antiseptic Towelettes. Also an initial cleansing element, these towelettes can double as a personal hygiene aid for activities where there is limited or no opportunity to bathe. This can not only keep you from getting rashes and sores, but may help keep your tent partners from rebelling! (twelve, individually sealed)

Antiseptic Medication. Antibiotic ointments are commonly used for minor cuts, abrasions and burns. Other frequently used medications are iodine or mercurochrome. (one ounce-tube of ointment)

Tincture of Benzoin. Application of benzoin makes tape adhere more firmly to, and toughens, the skin. Though useful on most parts of the body, it is frequently preapplied to the feet before applying moleskin, whether the moleskin is used alone or with a hold-down tape. (one-ounce plastic bottle)

Burn Ointment/Spray. For minor burns, standard commercial, store-shelf products or generics like aloe vera gel will suffice. For severe burns, non-stick dressings are highly preferred. They are available over the counter. Note that aloe vera gel is sometimes also used for frostbitten limbs.

Pain-Relief Medication. This item comes in pre-treated swabs, spray-on and in liquid forms. Its primary purpose is to reduce the initial pain of stings and insect bites. (four swabs)

Itch Relief Medication. Generally confined to sprays and liquids, this is the longer-term partner of the pain-relief medication above. Some of the most versatile assist in pain relief and provide relief from itching from stings, insect bites, allergic itches, minor skin irritations and rashes from poison ivy, oak and sumac. The historic choice is liquid calamine lotion, although several newer sprays have an edge in the area of pain-relief. (one-ounce, plastic spray container)

Eye Drops. This used-as-packaged item is useful for relieving eye-irritation, burning and redness through general eye irrigation. (1/4 ounce, plastic squeeze bottle)

Baking Soda. Baking soda, mixed with water, is a classic paste used to reduce the irritation of bites, stings or points of general skin irritation. Some use it in place of toothpaste for brushing teeth. (1/4 to 1/2 ounce, depending on number of uses planned)

Instant Cold Pack. When ice is not available and a cold source is needed to reduce swelling, numb an injury site or to cool down an overheated outdoorsman, a small chemically-activated cold pack is useful. These 1-2 ounce, one-time-use packs provide a reliable cold source for about 15-30 minutes. (one or two)

Heating Balm. The same balms and gels used to provide warmth for everyday muscle aches are also useful in the outdoors. Our preference is for greaseless products. (one ounce, repacked into a plastic squeeze tube)

Ammonia Inhalant. Used to revive an unconscious person, ammonia or "smelling" salts are sealed into small packages. For use, the package is torn open and the open seam is placed under the patient's nose. (two)

Internal Medication

Headache/Fever/Pain. For headaches, mild fever, mild pain and for reducing swelling, carry aspirin or aspirin-substitutes that work for you at home. Note that some of the substitutes have a limited shelf life. Also include any medication used for special, predictable conditions such as menstrual cramping. (six tablets, more if at high altitude or if your history suggests a greater stock)

Dehydration. Taken with plenty of water, salt tablets serve to support rehydration of individuals who are perspiring excessively and/or cramping. An adjunct to this method is to supply fluid electrolytes. (24 tablets; 6-12 ounces of powdered electrolyte for general trip use plus contingencies)

Stomach Upset. Antacids are the most commonly used item for indigestion, heartburn and gas. (six tablets)

Constipation. If your tendency is to get uncomfortable and irritable in the first couple of days of every new outdoor adventure, it may be due to a case of "blockus extremus." If this is your history, bring along the type and amount of laxative that works for you.

Diarrhea. Medications come in tablet, liquid and solid-bar forms. (two bar segments, chocolate; or four separate treatments of your own special favorite)

Cough. Undisturbed sleep is a great healer, particularly for your tired body after a hard day's activities. To quell fits of coughing, bring along cough medicine or throat lozenges. (one ounce medicine in plastic bottle or six lozenges)

Sinus Congestion. Decongestants provide relief from sinus headache, nasal congestion and sinus pressure. They most commonly come in nasal sprays or tablets. (six tablets)

Dental Pain. For relief of minor pain from toothache, bridge or denture irritation, oil of cloves is one of the standards. (1/4 ounce, stored in a plastic bottle)

Seasickness. The simplest and sometimes effective remedies are to eat crackers, watch the horizon, avoid coffee or inhaling odors of fried food and diesel fuel. Medications available exist in pill or intravenous form; a typical medication is

Dramamine. It can be taken before going aboard or, for less-affected persons, before a storm. Another prescription-drug option is scopolamine, which is absorbed through bandage-like patches that are usually stuck behind the ear.

There are also products such as Sea-Band, a set of small elastic bands with small buttons inside them that put pressure on one of the classic acupuncture points inside the wrist. The latter method involves no drugs and no potentially associated drowsiness. (These items are too dependent upon the individual's constitution to estimate needs. The key is to determine tolerance to motion on short trips, then to bring supplies accordingly.)

Ingested Poison. Ipecac syrup and activated charcoal are two over-the-counter medicines to combat the effects of ingested poisons. If outside contact is available, use only as directed by a medical authority. If not, ensure that you understand the conditions for its use, dosage, frequency of application, potential side effects, etc. before departing on your tour. (one. two-ounce plastic bottle)

Prescription Medication

The two broad categories of prescription medication for outdoor use are personal-need medications and contingency medications, the latter for lengthy, remote tours where professional medical help may not be available for days or longer. For this type of medication, it is critical that you get special instruction concerning their use and potentially hazardous side effects.

Personal Need. This medication could vary from that to combat strong allergy or seasickness reaction (see the "Seasickness" entry above) to that for a heart condition. (tailor the medication carried to your individual needs for the planned trip)

Contingency. One of the most common examples in this category is strong pain medication, which might include such as codeine-based or morphine-based drugs. Others are broad-spectrum antibiotics and other high-power infection-fighting drugs, anti-inflammatory medication, treatments for severe cases of colds, headache, diarrhea, constipation, colds, etc. (tailor the medication carried to your individual/ group needs for the planned trip)

FIRST AID

Tailor for your activity based on trip type & duration, potential dangers, & your individual constitution

Item	Activity						
	VAC	Hkg	BkPk	GW/d[1]	GW/e[1]	RkCl[2]	BkT/d
First Aid Manual	x	x	x	x	x	x	x
Equipment							
Cotton Swabs	x	x	x	x	x	x	x
Scissors	x	x	x	x	x	x	x
Razor Blade	x	x	x	x	x	x	x
Safety Pins	x	x	x	x	x	x	x
Needles	x	x	x	x	x	x	x
Tweezers	x	x	x	x	x	x	x
Oral Thermometer	x	o	x	x	x		
Snakebite Kit	o	x	x			o	
Pen Light	o		o		o		
Tourniquet	o	x	x	x	x	o	
Splints		o	x	x	x	o	
Latex Gloves	x	x	x	x	x		
Resealable Plstc. Bags	o	o	x	x	x		
Bio-Hazard Waste Bag	x	x	x	x	x		
Eye Dressing Kit	o		o		o		
Dental Repair Kit	o		o		o		
Bandages/Dressings							
Band-Aids	x	x	x	x	x	x	x
Gauze Pads	x	x	x	x	x	x	x
Gauze Roller Bandage	x	x	x	x	x	x	
Adhesive Compress	x	o	x	o	x	o	
Triangular Bandages	x	o	x	x	x	o	
Battle Dressing	x	o	x	x	x	x	
Ace Bandage	x	x	x	x	x	x	o
Moleskin	o	x	x	x	x	o	
Butterfly Closures	x	x	x	x	x	x	
Adhesive Tape	x	x	x	x	x	x	x
Sports Tape						o	
Ointments/Topicals							
Soap/Cleaning Cloth	x		x		x		
Antiseptic Towelettes	x	x	x	x	x	x	x
Antiseptic Meds.	x	x	x	x	x	x	o

FIRST AID

Item	Activity						
	VAC	Hkg	BkPk	GW/d[1]	GW/e[1]	RkCl[2]	BkT/d
Tincture of Benzoin	o		x		x		
Burn Ointment/Spray	x		o		o		
Pain-Relief Meds.	x	x	x	o	o	o	
Itch Relief Meds.	x	x	x	o	o	o	
Eye Drops	x	x	x	x	x	x	o
Baking Soda	x		x		o		
Instant-Cold Pack	o	x	x			x	o
Heating Balm	x		x	o	x	o	
Ammonia Inhalant	x	o	x	x	x	x	
Internal Medication							
Headache/Fever/Pain	x	x	x	x	x	x	x
Dehydration (salt tab	x	x	x	x	x	x	x
Stomach Upset	x	o	x	o	x		
Constipation	x		x		x		
Diarrhea	x		x		x		
Cough	x		x		x		
Sinus Congestion	x	o	x	o	x		
Dental Pain	x		o		o		
Seasickness							
Ingested Poison	o		o		o		
Prescription Meds.							
Personal Need	x	x	x	x	x	x	x
Contingency			o		o		

1assumes snow approach to climb 2gear carried by climber; see "Hkg" column for other items

FIRST AID

Tailor for your activity based on trip type & duration, potential dangers, & your individual constitution

Item	Activity						
	BkT/o[3]	MtBk/d	MtBk/o	ASkSn[4]	NSS/d	NSS/o	Snomo
First Aid Manual	x	x	x	x	x	x	x
Equipment							
Cotton Swabs	x	x	x		x	x	x
Scissors	x	x	x		x	x	x
Razor Blade	x	x	x		x	x	x
Safety Pins	x	x	x	o	x	x	x
Needles	x	x	x		x	x	x
Tweezers	x	x	x		x	x	x
Oral Thermometer	x	o	x		o	x	x
Snakebite Kit	o	o	x				
Pen Light	o		o			o	o
Tourniquet	x	x	x		o	x	x
Splints	x	o	x		o	x	x
Latex Gloves	x	x	x		x	x	x
Resealable Plstc. Bags	x	o	o	o	x	x	x
Bio-Hazard Waste Bag	x	x	x		x	x	x
Eye Dressing Kit			o			o	o
Dental Repair Kit			o			o	
Bandages/Dressings							
Band-Aids	x	x	x	o	x	x	x
Gauze Pads	x	x	x		x	x	x
Gauze Roller Bandage	x	x	x		x	x	x
Adhesive Compress	x	o	x		o	x	x
Triangular Bandages	x	x	x		o	x	x
Battle Dressing	x	x	x		o	x	x
Ace Bandage	x	x	x		x	x	x
Moleskin	x	o	x	x	x	x	
Butterfly Closures	x	x	x		x	x	x
Adhesive Tape	x	x	x		x	x	x
Sports Tape			o			o	
Ointments/Topicals							
Soap/Cleaning Cloth	x		x			x	x
Antiseptic Towelettes	x	x	x	o	x	x	x
Antiseptic Meds.	x	x	x		x	x	x

FIRST AID

Item	Activity						
	BkT/o[3]	MtBk/d	MtBk/o	ASkSn[4]	NSS/d	NSS/o	Snomo
Tincture of Benzoin	x		x				o
Burn Ointment/Spray	o		o			o	x
Pain-Relief Meds.	x	x	x		o	o	o
Itch Relief Meds.	x	x	x		o	o	o
Eye Drops	x	x	x	o	o	o	o
Baking Soda	o		o		o	o	o
Instant-Cold Pack	x	x	x				
Heating Balm	x		x		o	x	o
Ammonia Inhalant	x	o	x		o	x	x
Internal Medication							
Headache/Fever/Pain	x	x	x	x	x	x	x
Dehydration	x	x	x		x	x	
Stomach Upset	x	o	x		o	x	o
Constipation	x		x		x		
Diarrhea	x		x		x		
Cough	x		x			x	o
Sinus Congestion	x	o	x		o	x	o
Dental Pain	o		o			o	
Seasickness	o		o			o	
Ingested Poison							
Prescription Meds.							
Personal Need	x	x	x	x	x	x	x
Contingency	o		o			o	

[3]Assumes overnight camping [4]Assumes skiing inside the ropes

FIRST AID

Tailor for your activity based on trip type & duration, potential dangers, & your individual constitution

Item	Activity						
	CKR/d	CKR/o	SlPB	ScSn[5]	WBWJ[5]	LFish[6]	SFish[7]
First Aid Manual	x	x	x	x	x	x	x
Equipment							
Cotton Swabs	x	x	x	x	x	x	
Scissors	x	x	x	x	x	x	
Razor Blade	x	x	x	x	x	x	
Safety Pins	x	x	x	x	x	x	o
Needles	x	x	x	x	x	x	
Tweezers	x	x	x	x	x	x	
Oral Thermometer	o	x	x	x	x	o	
Snakebite Kit	o	x				o	
Pen Light		o	x	o	o		
Tourniquet	x	x	x	x	x	x	
Splints	o	x					
Latex Gloves	o	x	x	x	x	o	
Resealable Plstc. Bags	o	x	x	x	x	x	
Bio-Hazard Waste Bag	x	x	x	x	x	x	
Eye Dressing Kit		o	x	o	o		
Dental Repair Kit		o	x				
Bandages/Dressings							
Band-Aids	x	x	x	x	x	x	o
Gauze Pads	x	x	x	x	x	x	
Gauze Roller Bandage	x	x	x	x	x	x	
Adhesive Compress	x	x	x	x	x	o	
Triangular Bandages	x	x	x	x	x	o	
Battle Dressing	x	x	x	x	x	o	
Ace Bandage	x	x	x	x	x	x	
Moleskin	o	o	o			o	
Butterfly Closures	x	x	x	x	x	x	
Adhesive Tape	x	x	x	x	x	x	
Sports Tape	o	o	x	x			
Ointments/Topicals							
Soap/Cleaning Cloth	x	x	x	x	x		
Antiseptic Towelettes	x	x	x	x	x	x	o
Antiseptic Meds.	x	x	x	x	x	x	

FIRST AID

Item	Activity						
	CKR/d	CKR/o	SlPB	ScSn[5]	WBWJ[5]	LFish[6]	SFish[7]
Tincture of Benzoin	x	x	x	x	x	x	
Burn Ointment/Spray		o	x		x (J)		
Pain-Relief Meds.	x	x	x	x	x	x	
Itch Relief Meds.	o	x	x	x	x	x	
Eye Drops	o	x	x	x	x	x	o
Baking Soda	o	o	x	x	x		
Instant-Cold Pack	x	x	x	x	x	x	
Heating Balm	o	x	x	x	x		
Ammonia Inhalant	x	x	x	x	x	o	
Internal Medication							
Headache/Fever/Pain	x	x	x	x	x	x	o
Dehydration	x	x	x	x	x	x	
Stomach Upset	x	x	x	x	x	x	o
Constipation	o	o	x				
Diarrhea	o	x	x				
Cough	o	x	x				
Sinus Congestion	x	x	x				
Dental Pain	o	o	x				
Seasickness			x	x	o		x
Ingested Poison	o	o	x				
Prescription Meds.							
Personal Need	x	x	x	x	x	x	x
Contingency		o					

[5]Kit stored on land, boat or float [6]Assumes hike-in to fishing site [7]Charter boat provides first-aid kit

MEALS

A Little Homespun Philosophy

The discussion below is a brief introduction to the world of eating in the outdoors. We refer you to the limited Reference set provided for more information. There are also many additional sources at book stores and recreational outlets that are activity-specific.

The Power of Imagination. OK, so now that we've talked about all that outdoorsy stuff, it's time to get to the "feeding the face" part! In outdoor activities you are only limited by your culinary imagination, whether you drive your food in or pack it in on your back. Some examples: While weekend winter climbing in the San Bernardino Mountains, a group of us students watched our Sierra Club Basic Mountaineering Training Course (BMTC) advisors eat a gorgeous salad that was mixed/tossed inside a large baggy plus settle in to barbecued steaks. Two friends taught us how to make "Super Chicken," cooked in foil over a camping fire at a drive-to camp site beneath Mount San Jacinto -- it has since become a favorite for our backyard barbecues. Don and Walt shared one of the best (pre-prepared) lasagnas ever made while backpacking deep into the East Fork of Los Angeles County's San Gabriel River.

The possibilities for meal selection and preparation are enormous! Examples are: canned, frozen, powdered, freeze-dried or fresh food; pre-prepared food (including leftovers from home); cooking in a pan or over (or directly in) a campfire or in boiling pouches; eating uncooked munchies, etc. The ways to get food to the site are also varied. From our experience, we would suggest that you can drive your meals in, boat them in, paddle them in, carry them in, use a courier (or SAG wagon for bicyclists), rely on the postal service or stored cache, or forage. For some activities, you can also eat at a diner or restaurant or snack directly off what you buy at markets. There is also an option to combine these methods. Finally, there is the option to beg and borrow. However, more about all these options later.

Outdoors and the Sensitized Taste Buds. In our outdoor recreation activities, food that might be seen as common fare at home becomes a gourmet delight outdoors. You would never catch us salivating over beans and franks, canned stews or freeze-dried soups at home, but once in the outdoors, Mother Nature brings out the best in all of our appetites and taste buds. A qualifier, particularly for weight-limited activities: Don't forget to vary the menu, plus bring along some spices -- even on those adventures where meals primarily become a means to restore your energy, your attitude is buoyed tremendously by the thought of the next great meal. As before, more about this subject later.

Eating in Style, Depending on the Activity

The options for types of meals varies with the activity and, more so for the pack-in trips, the activity duration. The key issues are the weight and volume of food and cooking gear that you can reasonably haul, whether you have the facilities to bring items that require climate control (e.g., refrigeration of fresh or frozen food), and whether or not you have specialized dietary needs or tastes. In the latter case, there are many food products that advertise such as low-sugar, low-fat, low-sodium, low-cholesterol, vegetarian (meatless), organic (no pesticides used in growing), all-natural (no artificial additives or preservatives), made-by-elves -- you name it, it's out there.

Snacks for Daytime Activities. Many potential snacks for daytime ventures are noted in the checklist. This might vary from a baggie full of vegetables or a pocketful of fruit to high-energy snacks. The latter are the norm for high-exertion activities, where the mode is to snack continuously while on the move.

In addition to the store-bought varieties, many outdoorsmen make there own. Typical ingredients (take your choices) are nuts, dried fruits (particularly raisins, apples, pears), chocolate chips or hard candies, and coconut strips. Beware of such "stimulants" as dried prunes and apricots in large quantities, however. Don's multiple "searches for bushes" on a San Bernardino Mountains hike, which was mainly above treeline, is still one of the great jokes among some of his hiking companions.

Vehicle-Accessible Campers Have Nearly Unlimited Options. First, we'll glaze over Recreational Vehicle (RV) campers and cabin-cruiser sailors. Assuming that the participants have access to built-in stoves and ovens, a refrigerator (and, often, a freezer), and generous storage space, this is almost akin to eating at home. Vehicle-accessible campers (those who drive in or boat into a camp site) have only slightly fewer options.

Meal Selection. There is nothing on the checklist that you can't bring. The amount of food that you transport is probably limited only by the capacity of your ice chests, the availability of ice, and the space available to haul the sum total of your camping gear. Place a thermometer in you ice chest(s) -- perishable food items should be kept below about 45 degrees Fahrenheight. We have hauled in full watermelons, large cuts of meat to be roasted on a spit above the campfire and bagged, pre-cooked meals to feed a dozen campers.

For variety, consider both the options where you cook for the group and where individual campers cook their own food (e.g., hot dogs, marshmallows, shish kabobs). In addition to making meals on a stove, try cooking over a campfire. Another option is to place items such as corn-in-husks and meat-vegetable-basting-sauce combinations, wrapped in aluminum foil, directly in the campfire. The smoky taste added by campfire cooking is awesome.

Packaging and Organization. It is most common to bring food-related items in their original packaging. This is true whether it involves bringing cereal in it's original box, a bottle of catsup, jars of spices, or containers of pre-mixed liquids (as opposed to powders that require the addition of water). We would suggest limiting the amount of glass-packaged items as a general rule, in order to minimize the likelihood of breakage in transit or in actual use.

A good practice is to bring as many items as possible in tightly sealed containers to prevent spillage and to discourage camp critters from sharing your food. Bring rubber bands, clamps, twist-ties or other items to seal off bagged foods such as bread and chips from ants or other insects. Also consider bringing a hefty supply of shopping bags or the like to make the chore of hauling food items to and from the campsite easier. Restow all critter-attracting items (and any potentially dangerous cooking-related implements) in your vehicle before heading off for hiking, biking, fishing or other activities or retiring for the night.

Some campers organize their food by groups, For example, they place all grain items together, all canned goods together, all drinking items together. Others organize as much as possible by meal, where a preponderance of items for each meal are stored together. We tend to pack like boxboys in a supper market, where we only worry about putting heavy items on the bottom of the bag and lighter and fragile items near the top. Our food gear is just as disorganized when we depart as when we entered the campsite -- however, we feel there is always plenty of time while camping to sort out needed items as we go.

Canoeists, Kayakers and Rafters Have A Lot of Options Too. Though not unrestricted, participants in these activities are far less weight- and volume-limited than those where gear is carried in on the back. Kayakers have the additional restriction that all gear must fit through the hatches of the stowage compartments.

Meal Selection. For this and all activities below, however, the key considerations for selection are nutrition, weight, ease of preparation and taste. Nutrition may require that day's meals and snacks provide 3000-4000 calories. Add 500-1000 calories for the most highly-strenuous activities. The meals should contain foods from each of the four basic food groups. Carry a lot of complex carbohydrates and don't skimp on proteins or fat. If the weather is cool or cold, it's even more important that you take in some fat grams, as they'll keep you warm. If it's really cold, you'll sleep much warmer if the last meal of the day is calorie-rich and laced with fat grams.

Meals should be accompanied by a healthy liquid intake, particularly water. Strenuous activity causes increased perspiration and the associated loss of salt, requiring the additional salting of food to replace that which is lost and/or supplementing the meal with liquid electrolytes.

On trips lasting only a couple of days, it is not as critical to reduce weight and bulk as much as it is on extended trips. Such items as fresh meats, fruits and vegetables can be stored in ice chests for 2-3 days, with special care taken to detect spoilage. On trips of a few days, this fresh food can be supplemented with canned items, or canned goods can be used almost exclusively. Some paddlers splurge and bring a small Dutch oven for baking such items as casseroles, pizza, meat pies, breads, coffee cake and fudge brownies.

On lengthier tours, the menu may include a great first night feast, but dehydrated and freeze-dried foods will come to more and more dominate your meal planning as the trip length increases. A general rule of thumb is two pounds of freeze-dried food per day. Bring more if your body requires it to maintain performance or if you plan a highly-strenuous activity such as running difficult rapids in cold water. Regardless of trip duration or difficulty, don't forget the contingency food supply discussed in the **Ten Essentials** section.

A Few Words About Dehydrated and Freeze-Dried Foods. These foods are ultra-lightweight and compact, can be stored for months without refrigeration, and, if unopened, will not spoil. Many are pre-cooked and ready to serve after boiling water is added (referred to as "easy-prep"), while others may require a minimal amount of mixing and cooking.

Dehydrated foods are processed by moving through ovens that extract 80 to 95 percent of the food's moisture, shrinking it, and significantly reducing its weight. In some cases color and nutritional value are compromised; additives are provided to restore the losses in most of these instances. Many dehydrated foods are readily available in grocery stores (e.g., soups, fruits, vegetables, milk) and are less expensive than their freeze-dried counterparts. Freeze-dried foods are frozen in vacuum chambers at temperatures as low as minus 50 degrees Fahrenheit. The solid ice in the food is changed directly into a gas vapor that is wicked away in the chamber, leaving the food literally freeze-dried. This process preserves the original color, nutritional value and shape of the food, leaving it in a porous state for quick rehydration. They are available in most outdoor recreation stores and through catalogues. Breakfast fare, soups, stews, vegetables and fruits, an absolute multitude of main dinner courses, sauces and pastes, and many desserts are available in this form.

We recommend trying out these lightweight delights on short trips before heading out for an extended adventure. Some have been very pleasing, others great disappointments. We had a now-defunct manufacturer's pancakes and syrup breakfast on our first trans-Sierra Nevada backpack trip and had trouble finishing it. We begrudgingly ate it all because we knew we'd need the carbohydrates later. Be aware that there are basic add-boiling-water fares as well as more exotic dishes that require timely preparation and mixing of ingredients. If your activity calls for total simplicity, stick to the former. Take a wide variety of meals so that you don't get bored with the menu.

One of the "lifesavers" to achieve additional variety in dehydrated and freeze-dried foods are condiments, particularly spices. Popular varieties include salt, pepper, sugar, tarragon, garlic, cumin, beef flavor base and chicken-seasoned-stock base, dill seed, anise seed and apple pie spice. Additional flavor-enhancers include onion (flakes or juice), vegetable flakes, bell pepper flakes and meat tenderizer. Several sauces and spreads noted in the "Spices/Sauces/Spreads" entry of the checklist may also serve to put your taste buds at attention.

About Packaging and Organizing. For all overnight outdoor adventures, but particularly for those where you carry your gear on your back, packaging and organization of food is key. Remove all unnecessary cardboard and paper wrappers to eliminate as much weight and bulk as possible. Flour, sugar, coffee/tea, drink mixes and other appropriate food items can be placed in plastic bags to reduce space as contents are consumed -- this packaging also protects the contents from ocean or river water as well as rain. Crushable items (especially fresh eggs) should be packed in rigid plastic or lightweight aluminum containers. Freeze-dried food, as a standard, is packaged in lightweight, watertight containers and can be stored as is.

Many condiments can be bought in small, presealed containers similar to the packets that you get from diners or airlines. These include salt, pepper, cream, sugar, catsup, mustard, relish, mayonnaise, jelly etc, which can also be bagged in plastic. Also consider the use of plastic squeeze tubes for honey, jam, peanut butter, margarine and other items not available in the presealed containers mentioned above. To eliminate confusion, the food should be packed in an orderly manner. Sort the food either according to the meal (all breakfast items, lunch items, and dinner items separate) or by the day, and mark the containers accordingly.

Pack-in Living is More Austere. We admit to a weekend backpacking trip that included a totally decadent menu. We carried the heaviest loads of our backpacking lives. Further, we are ashamed (kinda) to say that it included several bottles of champagne, out-of-this world confections, pre-cooked lunches and dinners supreme -- it was the only way we could convince a friend to join us. (Yes, we hauled the junk out.)

However, that is the total exception for extended backpacking, glacier/winter climbing, bicycle touring, mountain biking and Nordic skiing tours. Yes, we have taken in an extravagant first night meal, by backpack, on skis and on bicycles. A mild first-day agenda plus a superb first-night meal has put us in a frame of mind that says we can tackle anything! However, from there it's generally back to the basics, lightweight dehydrated and freeze-dried meals. (The single way around this dilemma for backpackers is to hire a professional trail outfitter who will carry in the bulk of your gear on pack animals. This option is discussed in the BACKPACKING activity.)

In these activities, many outdoorsmen prefer to stick to a minimal cooking agenda. It typically involves a heavier load than the pure dehydrated and freeze-dried diet, but requires far less preparation time. Typical foods carried are dry cereals (and dried instant milk), dried fruit, trail mixes, jerky, "dry" deli-meats such as salami and pepperoni, crackers, high-energy bars, puddings and the like. Cooking may be limited to hot soups, coffee or tea, with scattered freeze-dried meals thrown in.

Other Options for Having a Meal on the Table. There are additional means for making food available beyond those mentioned above. Some examples are discussed below.

Relying on Couriers. Most commonly used by long-distance bicycle tourers, this method requires a good-hearted friend to meet you at pre-arranged locations. For on-road touring, this sometimes includes the courier (he and his vehicle are referred to as a "SAG wagon") making a periodic highway sweep to ensure that you haven't broken down or tumbled into a ditch. The SAG wagon nominally carries your food, clothing, bike repair gear and other essentials. We have known backpackers and mountain bikers that have used a less robust service that meets them at a prearranged outlet point within a given time window.

Using the Postal Service. This is an option primarily used by backpackers on tours that may last weeks or months. The method is to mail packages of non-perishable materials to post offices near the hiking route (with a clearly noted "hold" and estimated pickup date), scattered such that the backpacker can get from post office to post office with a margin of safety relative to food supplies. The penalty for this method of operation is that you most often have to leave the nominal route to get to the post office. This frequently entails an elevation loss that you must make up in returning to the original route.

Relying on Stored Caches. This is an option only for the skilled outdoorsman -- use of this method is particularly fraught with danger in situations where your life may depend on cache retrieval. The idea is to place non-perishable food stores (and sometimes, water) at strategic locations along the planned route. This requires careful packaging and storage sufficient to keep critters from raiding the cache. It also requires a sufficiently well-hidden placement to keep two-footed creatures from finding it, yet it must be in an unambiguous, accessible location for retrieval. A side note: Experience says that the safest bet is to place your own caches. There are numerous stories of ambiguous communication between cache setter and retriever having resulted in a non-retrieved cache. The outcomes have varied from severe inconvenience to the retriever to resultant death.

Foraging. Few outdoorsmen rely principally on foraging (we include plant and berry hunting as well as fishing) when they head outdoors for any lengthy period. Even then, they are only the very experienced and they always have contingency options available should the food source not pan out. However, many do supplement their menu with what can be found outdoors. This is particularly true where the standard fare of freeze-dried food can be swapped for freshly-caught fish.

Using the Credit Card. For variety, many outdoor people mix up their meals in camp with a periodic foray into "civilization." This is particularly true for vehicle-accessible campers, but also exercised by bicycle touring folk and others. The food fare sought varies with the group, but there is one notable favorite for touring cyclists. That choice is the "all-you-can-eat" establishments that lie along the bike route.

Begging and Borrowing. Periodically, it all goes wrong in the outback and you find yourself without sufficient food. We are proud of the fact that this has never happened to us. (Yes, we have run low on or been without our favorite snacks, moleskin, repair tools, replacement parts, camera film and quite a few other things.) The clear option is to seek out your outdoor brethren and ask for a little help. We met a couple who were a day and a half from their let-out point on the John Muir Trail and were basically without food. This was the result of losing an argument with a bear about who owned their food stores. Like the packers they had met in the morning, we gave them enough from our supply to make an austere evening meal. None of us doubted that they would get similar offerings the next day.

Alcohol and the Outdoors. Drinking alcohol is a matter of personal preference, as is the decision to carry alcohol for outdoor activities. For us, a nice bottle of wine at the camping table and a sip of brandy before retiring to our tent is a standard when car camping. We have frequently toted a small brandy flask into remote backpacking sites and, less frequently, on winter climbing trips. Alcohol consumption is enjoyed by some after a day on the ski slopes or after a watersports outing.

However, a few cautions: Don't drink while actively engaged in any potentially dangerous activity treated in this book. Drinking affects your judgment and motor skills, whether it involves chopping wood in camp, climbing rocks, or driving a jet ski. Alcohol use is not a good means to warm up your body; its long-term effect is just the opposite and it is dehydrating. Finally, few outdoor recreationalists enjoy being near a loud, out-of-control group in the outdoors -- have the courtesy to moderate your drinking.

The Dirty Details of Menu Planning

When deciding what food items to bring for an extended trip, we literally base it on a rough-cut, meal-by-meal breakdown. We figure what is unique to each meal and what are the common food items, then figure how much of each item to bring. An example of the worksheet we use for this basic breakout is shown below.

The list provides for a one week trip and can be copied to allow planning for longer stints. It provides space for identifying the specific main course items that will make up three meals a day. If there are specific condiments or other unique items that are associated with a given meal, we enter them within the same space as the main course items. It also has a "Miscellaneous" column for identifying general items that might be used for several meals or peripheral items that are in addition to the main courses. Examples are some condiments and daytime snacks, respectively. The list might also be used to identify the designated chef and dishwasher for each meal. (We're not really quite this organized, but it makes us really sound like we know what we are doing!)

MEAL PLANNER

Day	Breakfast	Lunch	Dinner	Miscellaneous
# 1				
# 2				
# 3				
# 4				
# 5				
# 6				
# 7				

MEALS

Select items based on activity type, weather conditions, trip duration and personal preferences.

ITEM	DATE				
Entrees					
Eggs, bacon/sausage					
Soups (dehydrated, canned)					
Stews (dehydrated, canned)					
Canned hash, chili, Spam					
Canned tuna, salmon, sardines					
Canned baked beans, macaroni					
Canned roast beef, ham					
Fresh or frozen meats					
- poultry					
- fish					
- beef					
Deli meats					
Beans					
Cheese					
Pre-prepared dishes					
Freeze-dried meals					
Fruits & vegetables					
Fruit: (fresh, frozen, canned)					
- mixed fruit					
- apples, oranges, grapes, etc.					
- melons					
Freeze-dried fruits					
Vegetables: (fresh, frozen, can)					
- mixed vegetables					
- carrots, celery, potatoes, etc.					
- lettuce, cabbage					
Freeze-dried vegetables					
Bread & Grain Items					
Cereals, breakfast rolls					
Biscuit & pancake mixes					
Bread, rolls, biscuits, buns					
Crackers					
Chips					
Flour, meal, rice					

MEALS

ITEM	DATE				
Spices/Sauces/Spreads					
Sugar, salt, pepper					
Other spices					
Margarine or butter					
Salad dressing(s)					
Syrup					
Basting/barbecue sauce					
Meat tenderizer					
Dips (premade, packaged)					
Spreads					
Mayonnaise, mustard, catsup					
Pickles, olives, peppers					
Peanut butter, jam, jelly					
Dessert Items					
Cookies					
Marshmallows					
Candy					
Puddings, gelatin desserts					
Pre-prepared dishes					
Freeze-dried desserts					
Cooking Aids					
Cooking oil, grease					
Pan sprays					
Drinks					
Milk (liquid, powdered)					
Fruit juices (frozen, canned)					
Coffee, cocoa, tea, cream					
Soft drinks					
Canned, powdered electrolytes*					
Alcoholic beverages, mixes					
Snacks*					
High energy bars					
Trail mix/granola					
Fresh fruit/dried fruit					
Beef jerky					
Nuts					

*Dual-purpose use in-camp and for out-of-camp activity

LIST of PRIORITY GEAR

General Discussion

Purpose and Scope of the Section. This section provides our one-page rough cut checklist identifying where you might initially invest your hard-earned cash on outdoor recreation equipment. The focus is on gear that provides immediate and broad-based activity use. We recognize that you cannot optimize any one piece of gear (e.g., sunglasses, compass, boots/shoes) for all activities, however the items listed are generally important for all the activities where they are noted as relevant. It is up to you to identify your preferred activities and select the best compromise version of the item or determine that more than one variant of that item is needed.

The list does tend to lean to walking, hiking and camping efforts since they are so common (as primary or secondary venues) to most activities in this book. Other than this "bias," you will find very little mention of the primary cost items for individual activities, such as technical climbing gear, bicycles, boats, snowmobiles, fishing rods and reels, etc. Selection of these items is totally dependent on your activity(s) of focus and tend to have a lesser range of use than those noted in the checklist.

About the Checklists. An "x" in a given intersection of the checklist indicates our estimate (or rating) that the item is essential and an "o" that the gear may be useful for the activity listed in the column heading. A blank space at a given intersection says that we do not consider the gear necessary or, in some cases, relevant. The intersection ratings are consistent with the scope of each individual activity as described at the beginning of each section. Note, for example, that ALPINE SKIING/ SNOWBOARDING is treated as a daytime/evening activity confined to within the ski area boundaries, SEA FISHING assumes that you are on a chartered vessel, etc. Also, the ratings provided reflect an allowance for inclement, but not extreme, weather. This list is intended to serve as a general guide. It should be reviewed and tailored to your particular activity needs.

As with the "First Aid" section, abbreviations are used in the column headings to represent individual activities. The following abbreviations are used: VAC - VEHICLE-ACCESSIBLE CAMPING; Hkg - HIKING; Bkpk - BACKPACKING; GW/d - GLACIER/WINTER CLIMBING (Daytime); GW/e - GLACIER/WINTER CLIMBING (Expedition); RkCl - ROCK CLIMBING; BkT/d - BICYCLE TOURING (Daytime/Nighttime); BkT/o - BICYCLE TOURING (Overnight); MtBk/d - MOUNTAIN BIKING (Daytime); MtBk/o - MOUNTAIN BIKING (Overnight); ASkSn - ALPINE SKIING/SNOWBOARDING; NSS/d - NORDIC SKIING/SNOWSHOEING (Daytime); NSS/o - NORDIC SKIING/SNOWSHOEING (Overnight); Snomo - SNOWMOBILING; CKR/d - CANOEING, KAYAKING, self-guided RAFTING (Daytime); CKR/o - CANOEING, KAYAKING, self-guided RAFTING (Overnight); SlPB - SAILING, POWERBOATING (Daytime/Overnight); ScSn - WATER SPORTS (Skin, Scuba Diving); WBWJ - WATER SPORTS (Watersking, Boardsurfing, Windsurfing, Jet Skiing); IFish - Inland Fishing; SFish - Sea Fishing (Daytime/Overnight).

Priority Gear Items

In the discussion below, brief qualifiers to the item name are provided. For each item, a reference (or references) to keywords in the **INDEX** is provided in parentheses The purpose of the keyword identification is to steer you to the best locations in the book for getting more information, specifically item usage and a rationale for its need.

Auto Tool Kit. This includes all the gear needed to get your auto to the inlet site. (*see* "auto tires and anti-freeze" and "automobile tool kit")

Maps/Charts. Included are all reference materials for navigating your route, as well as finding and identifying landmarks. (*see* "charts," "guide books" and "maps")

Compass. This may be a basic hand-held or special-purpose model. The compass may be augmented by other location-finding equipment (*see* "altimeter," "compass" and "GPS receiver")

OUTDOOR RECREATION CHECKLISTS

Flashlight. Flashlights range from compact, low power land-use models to high-intensity, waterproof underwater lamps. They may be augmented by other light sources, depending on the activity. (*see* "flashlight," "front lights," "headlamp," "lantern," "rear lights," "strobe rescue light" and "wands")

Extra Food and Water. These are contingency items beyond the planned needs. Food in airtight, watertight containers is preferred. Spare water supplies include the need to have drinkable water in suitable containers. (*see* "extra food," "food storage/protection," "extra water," the MEALS section, "water containers," "water filter/tablets" and "water purifier")

Extra Clothing. Included are clothing to cover contingencies of being forced out overnight and/or being subjected to unexpectedly severe weather. (*see* "extra clothing," "layering of clothes'" and discussions of individual clothing items below)

Sunglasses. This could be an inexpensive set of UV blockers, special purpose glasses or goggles. (*see* "sunglasses")

Pocket Knife. Variations of the "Swiss Army Knife" as well as special-use knives are included. (*see* "knife/prying tool" and "pocket knife")

Waterproof Matches. A throw-away butane lighter is included as a backup. (*see* "waterproof matches")

Fire Starter. Depending on the activity, there are several methods to start a warming fire in the outdoors. (*see* "fire starter")

First Aid Kit. Purchase a commercial off-the-shelf kit, modify that kit or build your own from scratch. (*see* "first aid kit" and FIRST AID section)

Timepiece. For many activities, your everyday city watch may suffice. A step up is the purchase of impact- and water-resistant models. There are also specialized designs for such efforts as glacier/winter climbing and snorkeling/scuba diving. (*see* "timepiece")

Emergency Signaling Equipment. These items can vary from a simple notepad for leaving messages, a whistle for alerting nearby outdoorsmen of your location or signaling a problem, to high-tech coded beacons to signal distress via space satellite transceivers. (*see* "airhorn," "avalanche beacon," "bell, "CB transmitter/receiver, "cellular phone," "EPIRB, "flare gun and flares," "flashlight," "marine radio," "night stick," "pen and notepad," "signal flags", "signal mirror," "strobe rescue light," "walkie-talkie," "waterproof flashlight" and "whistle")

Protective Ointments. Protection from both the sun and insects may dictate how well you enjoy your venture. Neglect in these areas could also affect your well-being. (*see* "insect repellent," "lip balm" and "sunscreen)

Boots/Shoes. Footwear for the variety of activities can vary from walking shoes to mountaineering boots to fishing waders.(*see* "booties," "boots" and "shoes")

Socks. Included are socks for in-shoe comfort and warmth, as well as the addition of inserts to enhance those properties. (*see* "socks")

Underwear. For hot-weather activities near water, cotton underwear may suffice. However, for most outdoor ventures, underwear which wick away moisture from the body and dry quickly are the standard. (*see* "T-shirt" and "underwear")

Shorts/Long Pants. Cargo shorts are great for camping in moderate weather while heavy, warm-when-wet pants or knickers serve the needs of winter wanderers. (*see* "long pants" and "shorts")

Swim Suit. Comfortable, quick-drying swimwear is the standard for watersports people as well as those hand-powering a boat on the water in moderate weather. (*see* "swim suit")

Shirt/Sweater. There are many combinations of shirts and sweaters to provide warmth in a variety of weather conditions. (*see* "long-sleeve shirt," "sweater" and "turtleneck")

Windbreaker. This gear is for knocking down the cooling effects of wind, coming in both standard and water-resistant designs. (*see* "windbreaker")

Jacket. The land-use version of this item may vary from a goose-down parka to a synthetic-pile, jacket, depending on the need for insulate-when-wet attributes. Spray and paddling jackets are more common to on-water efforts. There are also many auxiliary items that might share in providing warmth to the neck and trunk. (*see* "jacket," "neck gaiter," "scarf," and "vest")

Hat/Helmet. Headgear serves to protect from the sun, provide warmth and prevent heat loss, provide physical head protection, or some combination of these attributes. They may be augmented by other gear to enhance these attributes. (*see* "bandanna/sweatband," ear muffs," "hat" and "helmet")

Gloves. This article serves to provide warmth, protect the hands or some combination function. The category includes mittens. (*see* "gloves")

Raingear/Foul Weather Gear. Primarily for rain and waterspray protection, this gear also serves as a warming layer. Styles vary dramatically, particularly for land-based activities. The top of the line models are waterproof/breathable suits. (*see* "foul-weather suit" and "raingear")

Thermal Underwear. A key warming underlayer for many activities, these articles come in several different weights and a variety of useful material blends. (*see* "thermal underwear")

Wet Suit. A necessity for many on-water and in-water ventures in cold weather, these suits come in varying styles, cuts and thicknesses. For extremely-cold water applications, experienced adventurers adopt dry suits. (*see* "dry suit" and "wet suit")

Personal Flotation Device (PFD). This is the item known in days of old as a life preserver. Specifications for PFD types are provided in the CANOEING activity. (*see* "personal floatation device")

General Purpose Cord. Having a spare coil of cord can solve many unforeseen problems, particularly in camp. (*see* "nylon cord")

Storage/Hauling Gear. Prior to departure, you'll need to package some of your gear, whether for protection against the elements, for grouping similar items, or to facilitate hauling. Regardless of the activity, you need the means to haul your gear, whether it be around the countryside, to a boat or to the local beach. (*see* "carry straps/ski bag," "catch storage container," "daypack/rucksack," "dry pack," "food storage/protection," "frame pack," "handlebar bag/rack trunk," "haul bag," "laundry bag," "panniers," "resealable plastic food bags," "sea bags," "storage bags," "tackle box," "trash bags," "underseat bag" and "windsurfer storage bags") (*see also* the "Auto Gear Rack" item discussed below)

Toiletries/Ditty Bag. This is a separate storage container for personal toiletries, ranging from a pressure-locked plastic bag to a roomier home-use kit. (*see* "personal toiletries/ditty bag")

Camera. The first of two non-critical items on the list. However, the joy of performing any outdoor activity is enhanced when you have a permanent record. (*see* "camera and camera supplies")

Binoculars. Though a non-critical article for most activities (the possible exceptions are SAILING and POWERBOATING), magnifying lens allow you to better view wildlife and the surrounding natural terrain. (*see* "binoculars")

Tent/Pad. Tents range from one-person "bivy" sacks to multiple-person backpacking styles to family camping models. An option in some cases is to use a tarpaulin for cover. Tent pads or ground cloths serve to both protect the tent floor from abrasion and to prevent water leakage into the tent bottom. (*see* "ground cloth," "tarpaulin" and "tent")

Sleeping Bag/Pad. There are numerous styles, materials and comfort ratings for bags. The classic down bags are lightest in weight and least bulky for a given comfort rating. Unlike some of the newer synthetic bags, however, they lose most of their insulating properties when wet. Of the many pads available, the most useful provide a soft sleeping surface, thermal insulation from the ground and bag abrasion protection. (*see* "sleeping bag" "sleeping pad")

Dinnerware. This is the gear with which you feed your face, including plates. bowls, cups and eating utensils. (*see* "cookware/dinnerware")

Cookware. This article includes skillets, pots, pans, coffee pots, strainers and any other gear used to actually prepare the meal. (*see* "biodegradable detergent," "camp grill," "coffee pot," "cookware/dinnerware," "dish washing" and "non-stick cooking lubricant")

Stove. Campers regularly haul heavy multi-burner stoves to the site while those lugging all gear on their backs generally stick with compact, lightweight single-burners. Many mobile-home campers and some boaters have the luxury of built-in cooking units.(*see* "stove")

Equipment Repair Kit. Every activity requires tools, repair gear and replacement items to see it through with confidence. Almost any outdoorsperson can cite a trip where he or she wished that the means to repair equipment was available. (*see* "tool kit")

Sewing/Patching Kit. In addition to your base equipment, sometimes the ability to repair clothing becomes important for peace of mind or, in some instances, essential to your safety. (*see* "sewing/patching gear")

Weather Radio. Particularly for multi-day ventures in remote areas or for any efforts where your safety is strongly affected by weather conditions, a compact weather radio can be a lifesaver. If you plan to be outside weather-report reception areas, strongly consider learning how to become adept at estimating upcoming weather conditions by eyeball. (*see* "weather radio")

Thermometer. A thermometer may help you estimate the snow and ice conditions relevant to your intended route. Short-term changes in temperature may be a guide to upcoming changes in weather. Positive thinkers can use it for storytelling purposes after a trip has been completed. Whiners may use it as a tool to confirm how tough the trip is. (*see* "thermometer")

Air Pump. Simple air pumps are a blessing for inflating watersports equipment and a necessity for bringing life to bicycle tires in a "pinch" (inside joke). Heftier versions are demanded for inflating large rafts. (*see* "air pump" and "pump")

Ice Chest. One of the items that brings home to the outdoors is a portable ice chest. Unfortunately, they are difficult to tote on a backpack, therefore they are reserved for outdoor activities where weight and bulk are not vital issues. (*see* "portable ice chest")

Lantern. Like the ice chest, few will cart in this item on their backs, the exception being candle-powered mini-lanterns or small, broad area lights strung to illuminate a limited area. The full-blown luxury is reserved for those activities where weight and bulk are not at a premium. (*see* "lantern")

Auto Gear Rack. Once installed and with the proper add-on fittings, this article allows you to carry anything from a gear storage container to a couple of kayaks. (*see* "auto gear rack")

LIST of PRIORITY GEAR

Item	Activity						
	VAC	Hkg	BkPk	GW/d	GW/e	RkCl[1]	BkT/d[2]
Auto Tool Kit	x	x	x	x	x	x	x
Ten Essentials							
Maps/Charts	o	x	x	x	x	x	o
Compass	o	x	x	x	x	x	o
Flashlight	x	x	x	x	x	x	x
Extra Food & Water	x	x	x	x	x	x	x
Extra Clothing	x	x	x	x	x	x	x
Sunglasses	x	x	x	x	x	x	x
Pocket Knife	x	x	x	x	x	x	x
Waterproof Matches	x	x	x	x	x	x	o
Fire Starter	x	x	x	x	x	x	o
First Aid Kit	x	x	x	x	x	x	x
Day/Overnight							
Timepiece	x	x	x	x	x	x	x
Emergency Signaling	x	x	x	x	x	x	o
Protective Ointments	x	x	x	x	x	x	x
Boots/Shoes	x	x	x	x	x	x	x
Socks	x	x	x	x	x	x	x
Underwear	x	x	x	x	x	x	x
Shorts/Long Pants	x	x	x	x	x	x	x
Swim Suit	o	o	o			o	
Shirt/Sweater	x	x	x	x	x	x	x
Windbreaker	x	x	x	x	x	x	x
Jacket/Parka	x	o	x	x	x	o	o
Hat/Helmet	x	x	x	x	x	x	x
Gloves	x	x	x	x	x	x	x
Rain/Foul-Wthr. Gear	x	x	x	o	o	o	x
Thermal Underwear	o	o	x	x	x	o	o
Wet Suit							
PFD	o						
General Purpose Cord	x	x	x	x	x	x	o
Storage/Hauling Gear	x	x	x	x	x	x	o
Toiletries//Ditty Bag	x	o	x	o	x	o	
Camera	o	o	o	o	o	o	o
Binoculars	o	o	o	o	o	o	o
Overnight							
Tent/Pad	x		x		x		
Sleeping Bag/Pad	x		x		x		
Dinnerware	x		x		x		
Cookware	x		x		x		
Stove	x		x		x		
Equipment Repair Kit	x	o	x	x	x	o	x
Sewing/Patching Kit	x		x	o	x		
Key Additional Gear							
Weather Radio	o		o	o	x	o	
Thermometer	x	o		x	x	o	
Air Pump	x						x
Ice Chest	x						
Lantern	x		o		o		
Auto Gear Rack	o	o	o	o	o	o	o

[1]only selected gear carried on actual climb [2]bike tour not in remote area

LIST of PRIORITY GEAR

Item	Activity						
	BkT/o[3]	MtBk/d	MtBk/o	ASkSn[4]	NSS/d	NSS/o	Snomo
Auto Tool Kit	x	x	x	x	x	x	x
Ten Essentials							
Maps/Charts	x	x	x	x	x	x	x
Compass	x	x	x	o	x	x	x
Flashlight	x	x	x	o	x	x	x
Extra Food & Water	x	x	x	x	x	x	x
Extra Clothing	x	x	x	x	x	x	x
Sunglasses	x	x	x	x	x	x	x
Pocket Knife	x	x	x	o	x	x	x
Waterproof Matches	x	x	x		x	x	x
Fire Starter	x	x	x		x	x	x
First Aid Kit	x	x	x	o	x	x	x
Day/Overnight							
Timepiece	x	x	x	x	x	x	x
Emergency Signaling	x	x	x	o	x	x	x
Protective Ointments	x	x	x	x	x	x	x
Boots/Shoes	x	x	x	x	x	x	x
Socks	x	x	x	x	x	x	x
Underwear	x	x	x	x	x	x	x
Shorts/Long Pants	x	x	x	x	x	x	x
Swim Suit	o	o	o	o			
Shirt/Sweater	x	x	x	x	x	x	x
Windbreaker	x	x	x	x	x	x	x
Jacket	x	o	x	x	x	x	x
Hat/Helmet	x	x	x	x	x	x	x
Gloves	x	x	x	x	x	x	x
Rain/Foul-Wthr. Gear	x	x	x			o	
Thermal Underwear	x	o	x	x	x	x	x
Wet Suit							
PFD							o
General Purpose Cord	x	x	x		x	x	x
Storage/Hauling Gear	x	o	x	o	x	x	x
Toiletries//Ditty Bag	x	o	x		o	x	o
Camera	o	o	o	o	o	o	o
Binoculars	o	o	o	o	o	o	o
Overnight							
Tent/Pad	x		x			x	
Sleeping Bag/Pad	x		x			x	
Dinnerware	x		x			x	
Cookware	x		x			x	
Stove	x		x			x	
Equipment Repair Kit	x	x	x	o	x	x	x
Sewing/Patching Kit	x		x		o	x	o
Key Additional Gear							
Weather Radio	o	o	x		o	x	x
Thermometer	o	o	x		x	x	x
Air Pump	x	x	x				
Ice Chest							
Lantern							
Auto Gear Rack	o	x	x	o	o	o	o

[3]Assumes overnight camping [4]Assumes skiing inside ropes

LIST of PRIORITY GEAR

Item	Activity						
	CKR/d[5]	CKR/o[5]	SlPB	ScSn[6]	WBWJ[6]	LFish[7]	SFish[8]
Auto Tool Kit	x	x	x	x	x	x	x
Ten Essentials							
Maps/Charts	x	x	x	o	o	x	o
Compass	x	x	x	o		x	
Flashlight	x	x	x	o		x	o
Extra Food & Water	x	x	x	x	x	x	o
Extra Clothing	x	x	x	x	x	x	x
Sunglasses	x	x	x	x	x	x	x
Pocket Knife	x	x	x	x	(x)	x	x
Waterproof Matches	x	x	x		(o)	x	
Fire Starter	x	x	x		(o)	x	
First Aid Kit	x	x	x	x	x	x	o
Day/Overnight							
Timepiece	x	x	x	x	x	x	o
Emergency Signaling	x	x	x	x	(x)	x	
Protective Ointments	x	x	x	x	x	x	x
Boots/Shoes	x	x	x	x	x	x	x
Socks	x	x	x	o	o	x	x
Underwear	o	x	x	o	o	x	x
Shorts/Long Pants	o	x	x		(o)	x	x
Swim Suit	x	x	x	x	x	o	o
Shirt/Sweater	x	x	x	x		x	x
Windbreaker	x	x	x	x	(o)	x	x
Jacket		x	x			o	x
Hat/Helmet	x	x	x	o	o	x	x
Gloves	o	x	x	o	o	x	o
Rain/Foul-Wthr. Gear	o	x	x			x	x
Thermal Underwear	o	x	o			o	o
Wet Suit	x	x	x	x	(x)		
PFD	x	x	x	o		o	
General Purpose Cord	x	x	x	o		o	
Storage/Hauling Gear	x	x	x	x	x	x	x
Toiletries//Ditty Bag	o	x	x			o	x
Camera	o	o	o	o	o	o	o
Binoculars	o	o	o	o	o	o	o
Overnight							
Tent/Pad		x					
Sleeping Bag/Pad		x	o				o
Dinnerware		x	x				
Cookware		x	x				
Stove		x	x				
Equipment Repair Kit	x	x	x	o	o (x)	x	o
Sewing/Patching Kit		x	x		o		
Key Additional Gear							
Weather Radio	o	x	x				
Thermometer		o	x	o			
Air Pump	x	x	o	o		o	
Ice Chest	o	x	x		o	o	o
Lantern	o	x	x				
Auto Gear Rack	x	x	o	o	o	o	o

[5]Self-guided tour [6]Some gear stowed on land, boat or float; parenthesized entries primarily for jet skiing
[7]Assumes hike-in to fishing site [8]Charter boat provides most of non-personal items

REFERENCES

Provided here is a small sample list of references. There are many excellent books with emphasis in other areas for each activity which we have not included. The references below were selected because all have excellent introductory- and intermediate-level activity information. Some are standards in their activity area.. Most hit heavy on equipment aspects of activity, are personal favorites of the authors and/or provide excellent references to other sources. We suggest that you also look for specification sheets on many gear items that are put out by many outdoor recreation outlets such as Recreation Equipment Incorporated (REI). We have heavily exerpted from the sources noted in this section. -- all contain a great deal more depth beyond that provided in this introductory guide.

In the list below, we have indicated an International Series Book Number (ISBN) and Library of Congress Catalogue Card Number (LCCN) where available The parethesized information at the end of each entry is a thumbnail synopsis of that book's contents.

Minimizing Environmental Impact

National Outdoor Leadership School (NOLS), *Leave No Trace: Outdoor Skills and Ethics,* 1996. Information and materials: Telephone 1-800-332-4100; Web site; <http://www.Int..org>. (series of individual volumes covering varied outdoor activities, regions and climes)

Ten Essentials

1. Climbing Committee of the Mountaineers, The Mountaineers, *Mountaineering The Freedom of the Hills,* Fifth Edition, 1992, ISBN 0-89886-201-9, LCCN 91-26342. (Ten Essentials description and rationale)

2. Seidman, David, Ragged Mountain Press, *The Essential Wilderness Navigator,* 1995, ISBN 0-07-056323-3, LCCN 95-30840. (basic to advanced land navigation)

3. Elbert S. Maloney, Herst Marine Books, *Chapman Piloting, Seamanship and Small Boat Handling,* 62nd Edition, 1996, ISBN 0-688-14892-1. (basic to piloting and waterway navigation)

Vehicle-Accessible Camping

1. Michael Rutter, Globe Pequot Press, *Camping Made Easy,* First Edition, 1997, ISBN 0-7627-0043-2. (thorough camping equipment and general "how-to" camping guide)

2. Bern Kreissman, Bear Klaw Press, *The Complete Winter Sports Safety Manual,* First Edition, 1997, ISBN 0-9627489-6-X, LCCN 96-086484. (winter driving, automobile tool kit, safety and clothing information on multiple outdoor winter activities)

Hiking/Backpacking

1. Colin Fletcher, Alfred A. Knoph Publications, *The Complete Walker,* Third Edition, 1996, ISBN 0-394-72264-7, LCCN 83-48870. (classic hiking backpacking text for all levels, with numerous anecdotes)

2. Harvey Manning, Vintage Books, *Backpacking, One Step at a Time,* Fourth Edition, 1986, ISBN 0-394-72939-0, LCCN 84-40537. (beginner-intermediate guide, trip preparation through execution for adults and children; thorough equipment discussion - some modern equipment not included)

3. Dave Canci, Wilderness Press, *Desert Hiking,* Third Edition, 1993, ISBN 0--89997-168-7, LCCN 93-21334. (beginner-advanced guide to day hiking/backpacking, with emphasis on desert trips)

Glacier/Winter Climbing

1. Climbing Committee of the Mountaineers, The Mountaineers, *Mountaineering The Freedom of the Hills,* Fifth Edition, 1992, ISBN 0-89886-201-9, LCCN 91-26342. (classic mountaineering text; general outdoor gear with focus on mountaineering and rock climbing equipment and use)

2. John Moynier, ICS Books, *The Basic Essentials of Mountaineering,* First Edition, 1991, ISBN 0-934802-65-3, LCCN 90-26009. (top-level introduction to mountaineering)

Rock Climbing

1. Climbing Committee of the Mountaineers, The Mountaineers, *Mountaineering The Freedom of the Hills,* Fifth Edition, 1992, ISBN 0-89886-201-9, LCCN 91-26342. (see above)

2. Ron Hildebrand, W. W. Norton and Company, *Rock Climbing: A Trailside Guide,* First Edition, 1997, ISBN 0-393-31653-X, LCCN 96-52821. (equipment and climbing techniques for beginner through advanced level)

3. Layne Gerrard, Ten Speed Press, *Rock Gear: Everybody's Guide to Rock Climbing Equipment,* First Edition, 1990, ISBN 0-89815-366-2, LCCN 90-30835. (training and rock-climbing gear use and tradeoffs, numerous equipment photos and drawings)

REFERENCES

Bicycle Touring

1. Eugene A. Sloane, Fireside Publications, *Sloane's Complete Book of Bicycling*, Fifth Edition, 1995, ISBN 0-671-87075-0, LCCN 94-46788. (equipment, repair and use of touring, mountain and hybrid bicycles)
2. Richard A. Lovett, Ragged Mountain Press, *The Essential Touring Cyclist*, First Edition, 1994, ISBN 0-07-038849-0, LCCN 94-5926. (bike selection, equipment and use, biking techniques, camping essentials)

Mountain Biking

1. Eugene A. Sloane, Fireside Publications, *Sloane's Complete Book of Bicycling*, Fifth Edition, 1995, ISBN 0-671-87075-0, LCCN 94-46788. (see above)
2. Dennis Coello, Lyons and Burford Publishers, *The Complete Mountain Biker*, 1989, ISBN 1-55821-021-0, LCCN 89-7961. (bicycle selection, accessories, repair and mountain biking technique)

Alpine Skiing/Snowboarding

1. Carol Poster, ICS Books Inc., *The Basic Essentials of Alpine Skiing*, 1993, ISBN 0-0934802408. (equipment and use at all levels; conditioning regimen)
2. Jeff Bennett, *The Complete Snowboarder*, 1994, McGraw Hill Companies, 1994, ISBN 0-070051429. (equipment and use at all levels; techniques and tricks)

Nordic Skiing/Snowshoeing

1. Lurie Gullion, *Nordic Skiing: Steps to Success*, Human Kinetics, 1993, ISBN 0-873223942. (equipment and technique development for day and overnight skiing)
2. Sally Edwards and Melissa McKenzie, *Snowshoeing*, Human Kinetics, 1995, ISBN 0-873227670. (equipment and use, daytime and extended trips)

Snowmobiling

1. Washington State Parks and Recreation Commission, Outdoor Empire Publishing Inc. *Snowmobile Safety and You*, 1994. (write to Washington State Parks and Recreation Commission, 7150 Clearwater Lane, Olympia Washington 98504-2662). (safety guide including snowmobile use and related safety equipment)
2. Manufacturers' snowmobile specification sheets, brochures and maintenance manuals and snowmobiling magazines.

Canoeing

1. James D. West and John Rugge, Vintage Books, *The Complete Wilderness Paddler*, 1983, ISBN 0-394-71153-X, LCCN 82-40021. (all-level canoeing; trip planning and execution -- some equipment outdated)
2. I. Herbert Gordon, Globe Pequot Press, *The Complete Book of Canoeing*, Second Edition, 1997, ISBN 0-7627-0052-1, LCCN 96-31520. (modern equipment, canoeing techniques)

Kayaking

1. Dennis Stuhaug, Globe Pequot Press, *Kayaking Made Easy*, 1995, ISBN 1-56440-638-5, LCCN 95-3725. (introductory/intermediate kayaking, technique and equipment))
2. Derek C Hutchinson., Globe Pequot Press, *Guide to Expedition Kayaking*, Third Edition, 1995, ISBN 1-56440-721-7, LCCN 95-15108. (expedition kayaking, technique and equipment)

Sailing

1. Jim Murrant, Sheridan House, *The Boating Bible: An Essential Handbook for Every Sailor*, 1991, ISBN 0-924486-13-9, LCCN 90-29128. (thorough sailing reference with detailed gear and procedural checklists)
2. Elbert S. Maloney, Herst Marine Books, *Chapman Piloting, Seamanship and Small Boat Handling*, 62nd Edition, 1996, ISBN 0-688-14892-1. (classic boating reference, recommended by U.S. Power Squadrons and U.S. Coast Guard Auxiliary; later editions in print)

Powerboating

1. Christopher Caswell, Hearst Marine Books, *The Illustrated Book of Basic Boating*, 1990, ISBN 0-688-08931-3, LCCN 89-81523. (introductory powerboating, boat types, outfitting and use)
2. Bob Armstrong, International Marine Publishing Company, *Getting Started in Power Boating*, 1990, ISBN 0-877-42-267-2, LCCN 90-305514. (introductory powerboating, boat types, outfitting and use)
3. Elbert S. Maloney, Herst Marine Books, *Chapman Piloting, Seamanship and Small Boat Handling*, 62nd Edition, 1996, ISBN 0-688-14892-1.

OUTDOOR RECREATION CHECKLISTS

Water Sports

1. Bernard E. Empleton, Council for National Cooperation in Aquatics, Association Press, *The New Science of Skin and Scuba Diving*, Fifth Revised Edition, 1980, ISBN 0-695-81346-3, LCCN 79-24964. (complete, all-level basic manual; -- some equipment outdated)
2. Paul Mc Callum, Betterway Publications, *Scuba Diving Handbook*, 1991, ISBN 1-55870-180-X, LCCN 90-21714. (salt and freshwater diving guide, equipment outfitting, underwater photography)
3. Ben Favret and David Benzel, Human Kinetics, *Complete Guide to Waterskiing*, 1997, ISBN 0-88011-522-X, LCCN 96-40091. (outfitting for waterskier, skiing techniques)
4. Camille Duvall, A Fireside Book, *Instructional Guide to Waterskiing*, 1992, ISBN 0-671-74640-5, LCCN 92-3657. (beginning to advanced waterskiing, equipment, boat and driver needs)
5. Doug Werner, Tracks Publishing, *Surfer's Startup: A Beginner's Guide to Surfing*, 1993, ISBN 0-934793-47-6, LCCN 92-41284. (limited equipment discussion, surfing techniques)
6. Jeremy Evans, Facts on File Publications, *The Complete Guide to Windsurfing*, "New Edition-Completely Revised," 1992 (est.), ISBN 0-8160-1527-9. (all-level windsurfing, technique and equipment)
7. Jimmie Johnson, Stackpole Books, *Whitewater Rafting Manual.* 1995, ISBN 0-8117-3098-0, LCCN 94-16347. (outfitting for whitewater rafting, rafting techniques)
8. Cecil Kuhne, World Publications Inc., *River Rafting*, First Edition, 1979, ISBN 0-89037-154-7-0, LCCN 78-04389. (whitewater raft and equipment descriptions, general outdoor experience, rafting techniques; some technology out of date)
9. Bob Italia, Action Sports Library, *Jet Skiing*, First Edition, 1991, ISBN 1-56239-075-9, LCCN 91-073022. (brief introduction to jet skis and jet skiing)
10. Manufacturers' jet skiing specification sheets, brochures and maintenance manuals and jet skiing magazines.

Inland Fishing

1. Steven D. Price, Harper Perennial, *The Ultimate Fishing Guide*, First Edition, 1996, ISBN 0-06-273290-0, LCCN 95-19028. (thorough fresh- and saltwater-equipment guide, organizations and events directory)
2. Frank C. Golad (editor), DK Publishing, *The Dorling Kindersley Encyclopedia of Fishing*, 1994, ISBN 1-56458-492-5, LCCN 95-28861. (introductory guide to fresh and saltwater fishing, including fishing techniques and equipment)
3. Mike Toth, Alpha Books, *The Complete Idiot's Guide to Fishing Basics*, First Edition, 1997, ISBN 0-02-861598-0, LCCN 97-070268. (introductory guide to fresh and saltwater fishing, including fishing techniques and equipment, trip planning and fish cleaning/cooking)

Sea Fishing

1. Steven D. Price, Harper Perennial, *The Ultimate Fishing Guide*, First Edition, 1996, ISBN 0-06-273290-0, LCCN 95-19028. (see above)
2. Mike Toth, Alpha Books, *The Complete Idiot's Guide to Fishing Basics*, First Edition, 1997, ISBN 0-02-861598-0, LCCN 97-070268. (see above)

First Aid (most sources above provide limited activity-related first aid information)

1. National Safety Council and Alton L. Thygerson, Jones and Bartlett Publishers, *National Safety Council First Aid Pocket Guide*, 1996, ISBN 0-86720-843-0, LCCN 94-21045. (condensed general first-aid guide)
2. Tod Schimelpfenig and Lida Lindsey, The National Outdoor Leadership School/Stackpole Books, *NOLS Wilderness First Aid*, Second Edition, 1992, ISBN 0-811730840. (equipment and procedures for emergencies on land)
3. James A. Wilkerson, The Mountaineers, *Medicine for Mountaineering and Other Outdoor Activities*, Fourth Edition, 1993, ISBN 0-0898863317. (equipment and procedures for emergencies on land)
4. Neil Hollander and Harald Mertes, Hearst Marine Books, *The Yachtsman's Emergency Handbook:The Complete Survival Manual*, Revised Edition, 1986, ISBN 0-688066100. (equipment and procedures for emergencies underway)

Meals (most sources above provide limited activity-related meal information)

1. Carole Latimer, Wilderness Press, *Wilderness Quisine*, First Edition, 1991, ISBN 0-89997-114-8, LCCN 91-9288. (outdoor cooking - packing, menu and meal preparation, sample menus, recipes)
2. Harriett Barker, Contemporary Books, *The One-Burner Gourmet*, Revised Edition, 1986, ISBN 0-8092-5883-8. (outdoor cooking - packing, cooking stoves, tons of recipes)
3. John C. Payne, Sheridan House, *The Great Cruising Cookbook:An International Galley Guide*, 1996, ISBN 0-924486929. (cooking when underway - simple to exotic recipes, worldwide)

INDEX

The index provides page locations of descriptive text for the gear items noted. The location of gear items within the checklists themselves is not included. Note also that few individual items described in the FIRST AID and MEALS sections are referenced in the index. Refer directly to those sections for information in the relevant subject area.

In many instances, the items are used for multiple activities. The most complete description of these items is most often found in the first activity where it is used, with subsequent page references concentrating on item features which are unique to other activities which follow. Despite our attempted grand organization, we would still recommend that you peruse the item-of-interest description in all referenced pages. As an example, stoves for long-distance cycling tours are discussed in BICYCLE TOURING (Overnight) as they apply to that activity. However, the bulk of the information on compact lightweight stoves is found in the first activity where it is used, which is BACKPACKING.

For more ease of use, we have replicated the page ranges from the **Table of Contents** below.

OUTDOOR RECREATION CHECKLISTS

OUTDOOR RECREATION CHECKLISTS

____

ITEM	DATE				

ITEM	DATE				

OUTDOOR RECREATION CHECKLISTS

____

ITEM	DATE				

Reward for Helping Us Update Our Books

Corrections and updates will make these better books and are gratefully appreciated. Publisher will reply to all such letters or e-mail. We are particularly interested in updates to our latest book, *Outdoor Recreation Check Lists*. Where information is used in future updates, submitter will be acknowledged in subsequent printing and given a free copy of the current or subsequent printing (as specified by submitter). Mail comments to B-D Enterprises, 122 Mirabeau Ave., San Pedro, CA. 90732-3117; bnyduk@aol.com is our address for electronic mail (e-mail).

Books by Don and Sharron Brundige:

Bicycle Rides: Los Angeles and Orange Counties (Out of Print)
Bicycle Rides: San Fernando Valley and Ventura County (Out of Print)

R-1. *Bicycle Rides: Orange County (Revised 8/93)*
ISBN 0-9619151-2-9, Library of Congress Catalogue Card No. (LCN) 88-071407

R-2. *Bicycle Rides: Los Angeles County (Revised 8/91)*
ISBN 0-9619151-3-7, LCN 88-071407

R-3. *Bicycle Rides: Inland Empire (Revised 4/93)*
ISBN 0-9619151-4-5, LCN 88-071407

R-4. *Bicycle Rides: San Diego and Imperial Counties (6/92)*
ISBN 0-9619151-5-3, LCN 90-093234

R-5. *Bicycle Rides: Santa Barbara & Ventura Counties (8/94)*
ISBN 0-9619151-6-1, LCN 88-071407

R-6. *Mountain Biking L.A. County (Southern Section) (10/96)*
ISBN 0-9619151-7-X, LCN 88-071407

N-1. *Outdoor Recreation Check Lists (11/98)*
ISBN 0-9619151-9-6, LCN 88-071407

How to Find Copies of Our Books

Books R-1 through R-6 above are regional (Southern California) works. They are available at leading bicycle shops, regional recreation outlets, and both regional and national (chain) bookstores. They are also handled by major Internet booksellers.

Book N-1 is a national-level work which also applies for use outside the United States' borders. It is available at recreation equipment outlets, some specialty (fishing, diving, etc.) shops, book stores and on the Internet.

We prefer that you order through the above-mentioned sources, since they are established, networked businesses -- every order encourages them to either increase inventory and/or enhance their advertising of our books. However, if you have difficulty finding our books in your locale, we can steer you to businesses that carry our books or ship direct. Whichever you prefer, contact us at at our postal or e-mail addresses:

B-D Enterprises
122 Mirabeau Ave.
San Pedro, CA. 90732

or

bnyduk@aol.com

SEE YOU

IN

THE

OUTDOORS!